Modern Jewish History

Commodore Levy: A Novel of Early America in the Age of Sail, by Irving Litvag

The Jewish Women Prisoners of Ravensbrück: Who Were They?, by Judith Buber Agassi

"Non-Germans" under the Third Reich: The Nazi Judicial and Administrative System in Germany and Occupied Eastern Europe, with Special Regard to Occupied Poland, 1939–1945, by Diemut Majer

The Tailors of Tomaszow: A Memoir of Polish Jews, by Rena Margulies Chernoff and Allan Chernoff

Transcending Darkness: A Girl's Journey Out of the Holocaust, by Estelle Glaser Laughlin

Unwanted Legacies: Sharing the Burden of Post-Genocide Generations, by Gottfried Wagner and Abraham J. Peck

PILLAR OF FIRE

A. JAMES RUDIN

PILLAR OF FIRE

A BIOGRAPHY OF RABBI STEPHEN S. WISE

This book is typeset in Minion. The paper used in this book meets the minimum requirements of ANSI/NISO Z39.48-1992 (R1997). ∞

Designed by Jouve North America
Cover photograph/illustration by permission granted by the Stephen Wise Free Synagogue Archives

Library of Congress Cataloging-in-Publication Data
Rudin, A. James (Arnold James), 1934– author.
    Pillar of fire : a biography of Stephen S. Wise / A. James Rudin.
        pages cm. — (Modern Jewish history)
    Includes bibliographical references and index.
    ISBN 978-0-89672-910-0 (paperback) — ISBN 978-0-89672-911-7 (e-book)
1. Wise, Stephen S. (Stephen Samuel), 1874–1949.   2. Rabbis—United States—Biography.   3. Zionists—United States—Biography.   4. Jews—United States—Politics and government.   I. Title.
    BM755.W53R83   2015
    296.8æ341092—dc23
    [B]

                                                                    2015028641

15 16 17 18 19 20 21 22 23 / 9 8 7 6 5 4 3 2 1

Texas Tech University Press
Box 41037
Lubbock, Texas 79409-1037 USA
800.832.4042
ttup@ttu.edu
www.ttupress.org

Wise portrait by noted photographer Philippe Halsman, 1940.
Permission granted by the Philippe Halsman Archive.

To Marcia:

My muse, my inspiration, and my heroine. Her love, support, and patience made this book a reality and allowed Stephen Wise to become part of our family.

Contents

Illustrations

Acknowledgments

I could not have written this biography without the guidance and cooperation of many people and institutions.

I salute the staffs of the Sanibel Island, Florida, Public Library and the New York Society Library in New York City. Both libraries provided exceptional writing areas and extraordinary research facilities. The History Department of the University of Illinois in Champaign-Urbana encouraged my graduate studies of the Balfour Declaration and the 1919 Paris Peace Conference.

I am indebted to Dr. Abraham Peck, the former executive director of the Center for Catholic-Jewish Studies (CCJS), a collaborative project of Saint Leo University (SLU) and the American Jewish Committee (AJC). Abe is a superb historian who offered excellent advice and enthusiastic support.

Robert Mandel, the former director of Texas Tech University Press, and Richard Curtis, my literary agent, were key partners in this project. I thank Robert's successor, Courtney Burkholder, along with Joanna Conrad, Amanda Werts, Rachel Murdy, Jada Rankin, John Brock, and the entire TTUP staff for their excellent direction and strong encouragement. Special thanks to Bob Land, a superb copy editor. I am indebted to Arthur Berger, Judith Cohen, and Edna Friedberg of the United States Holocaust Memorial Museum for their research and assistance.

My thanks go to Dr. Gary Zola and Kevin Proffitt of the American Jewish Archives, Charlotte Bonelli of the American Jewish Committee Archives, Dr. Carl Steeg of the Stephen Wise Free Synagogue Archives, and Anne Levant Prahl of the Oregon Jewish Museum, along with the staffs of the American Jewish Historical Society Archives, the New York Public Library, and the Franklin D. Roosevelt Presidential Library and Museum.

Anyone writing about Stephen Wise must figuratively stand on the shoulders of the gifted scholar Melvin I. Urofsky, the author of the splendid *A Voice That Spoke for Justice: The Life and Times of Stephen S. Wise*. Mel and his wife,

Susan, are Sanibel Island neighbors and good friends. I am indebted to him for his insightful editorial suggestions and recommendations.

My rabbinic colleagues Cyrus Arfa, Floyd Herman, Ammiel Hirsch, Richard Sarason, and Ronald Sobel made significant contributions to this book. I am also grateful to Robert Rifkind and Harold Tanner, two former AJC national presidents, who aided in my research, as well as Robert and Liz Rosenman. John Guerra of Florida Gulf Coast University provided me the opportunity to offer classes on Woodrow Wilson, Franklin Roosevelt, and Harry Truman.

The American Jewish Committee has long been my professional home, an honor I never take for granted. Since 1991 the Religion News Service has distributed my newspaper columns, and I thank the RNS staff and management for that opportunity. It was my privilege to be a founder of the Center for Catholic-Jewish Studies located on the SLU campus in Florida, where I serve as a Visiting Professor of Religion and Judaica. However, the views and opinions expressed in this book are my own, and do not necessarily reflect those of the AJC, RNS, SLU, or CCJS.

Finally, my love goes out to our daughters, Rabbi Eve and Jennifer, and our granddaughter, Emma Mollie.

Introduction

I was a freshly minted twenty-year-old college graduate in September 1955 when I began my five years of rabbinical studies at 40 West 68th Street, the Manhattan home of the newly merged Hebrew Union College–Jewish Institute of Religion and an edifice that played a central role in the life and career of Stephen Samuel Wise. That autumn was an exciting time to be in New York City (but isn't that always the case?).

The buildings of the nearby Lincoln Center for the Performing Arts were then being constructed, and that fall the perennial also-rans, the Brooklyn Dodgers, defeated the lordly New York Yankees in the World Series in seven games. During the same school year, the legendary musical, *My Fair Lady*, opened on Broadway on March 15, 1956.

I experienced a vivid "remembrance of things past" inside 40 West 68th Street. Even though Rabbi Stephen Wise had died six years earlier, his spirit permeated the school where he was still reverently called "Dr. Wise." That was because many faculty members he had selected were still teaching in 1955.

In addition, there was "Dr. Wise's" long wooden worktable in his official office. It was alleged that a Roman Catholic cardinal once owned the large piece of furniture. The sculptor Robert Berks had fashioned a large head of "Dr. Wise" that occupied a prominent place in the lobby of the school.

The building also included a small synagogue/chapel on the top floor of the five-story building where the famed rabbi regaled his adoring students with weekly reports of his many political activities and where Stephen Wise offered loving but perceptive critiques of student sermons.

The building housed the auditorium where Mrs. Stephen Wise's funeral took place in December 1947, and in April 1949, 40 West 68th Street was where Dr. Wise's body laid in repose until it was moved to his own funeral service in Carnegie Hall.

During my years of rabbinic studies, I felt a connection to Stephen Wise not only because he created the Jewish Institute of Religion in 1922 but also because he successfully battled to establish the principle of a free and open pulpit for clergy—one not controlled or dominated by boards of trustees or powerful lay leaders.

Wise was an inspiration for Jewish and Christian clergy committed to social justice, and civil and human rights. Indeed, he was in my thoughts in February 1964 when I participated in an African American voting rights drive in Hattiesburg, Mississippi. Because he pioneered in building mutual respect and understanding between Jews and Christians, Wise was an important model when I served as the American Jewish Committee's interreligious affairs director.

But perhaps his greatest influence upon me and countless other rabbis was his lifelong commitment to Zionism, the Jewish national liberation movement. His untiring and often controversial leadership in this area helped transform Reform/liberal Jews into strong supporters of modern Israel, men and women dedicated to its security and survival.

Although I never met him in person, I owe Dr. Wise a great deal, and this biography is my way of repaying that debt. Readers will note that throughout the book I often refer to him by his first name. That is because biographers "live" with their subject for years. After devoting so much time and emotion to him, he became my posthumous rabbinical colleague. Some may call it an act of chutzpah on my part. I call it an act of affection, friendship, and esteem for "Stephen."

PILLAR OF FIRE

Chapter 1

The Hungarian Baron's Infant Grandson Comes to America

Because the mists of legend have enveloped Stephen Samuel Wise (1874–1949), it is conventional wisdom today to perceive him as a patrician, a charismatic "rabbinic prince" who was destined and trained from birth to be an extraordinary leader of the Jewish people and of numerous social and political causes in the United States and throughout the world.

So great was his reputation that during his long and controversial career, Stephen Wise received letters from all parts of the globe with only two words written on the envelope: "Rabbi USA." But the US Postal Service was never in doubt about the intended larger-than-life recipient of such skimpily addressed mail: there was only one "Rabbi USA."

No other rabbi before or since Wise has dominated the American and the international scene with such passion and power. During the tumultuous 1930s and 1940s, his admirers as well as his opponents—there was no shortage of either group—acknowledged him as the premier leader of the Jewish community in the United States and a major figure in American politics.

Wise, a powerful orator with a commanding baritone voice, burnished his public mystique with a personal mantra. In 1939 he wrote,

> I am an American Jew. I have been a Jew for four thousand years. I have been an American for sixty-four years. . . . I am of the American nation, and an American citizen; and there is no conflict.[1]

However, Wise was not born in the United States, but rather in Budapest, Hungary, on March 17, 1874. His parents were Rabbi Aaron Weisz (1844–1896) and Sabine Fischer de Farkashazy (1838–1917), and when he was seventeen months old, his parents and their four children—Ida and Wilma, daughters from Sabine's first marriage, and sons Otto and Stephen from her marriage to Aaron—immigrated to the United States.[2] They sailed on the S.S. *Gellert* from

Hamburg, Germany during the summer of 1875 and arrived in New York City on August 11 of that year.[3]

During Stephen's long career, ended by cancer in New York City's Lenox Hill Hospital on April 19, 1949, Wise rarely spoke of his birthplace, but he often noted that his birthday coincided with St. Patrick's Day, a fact that endeared him to many Irish Americans.[4]

He was a member of a wealthy and prominent family. In 1874 Hungary and its capital city of Budapest were part of the Austro-Hungarian Empire that the Roman Catholic emperor, Franz Joseph I (1830–1916), ruled from the Hofburg, an ornate royal palace in Vienna. But unlike millions of other Jews living in Central and Eastern Europe during the 19th century, the Weiszes were neither financially poor nor was Yiddish their mother tongue, the language of millions of European Jews; instead, the family was fluent in German and Hungarian and at home in both cultures. Stephen and his family were not among the indigent and impoverished shtetl (village or small-town) Jews who arrived in large numbers as immigrants to America during the late nineteenth and early twentieth centuries and are portrayed in the popular musical and film *Fiddler on the Roof.*[5]

Stephen's father came from a long line of distinguished rabbis—six generations—that began in Moravia, now a region of the Czech Republic. The family's original name was Weissfeld (German for "Whitefield"). However, over time that surname melded into the Hungarian "Weisz," and Stephen's paternal grandfather, Yosef Tzvi in Hebrew, was known as Rabbi Joseph Hirsch Weisz (1800–1881).

Some historians have erroneously claimed Weisz was "a distinguished chief rabbi of Hungary."[6] But the reality is that he became the chief rabbi of Erlau, Hungary, in 1840 and served in that position until his death.[7] "Weiss" is an incorrect spelling of the family name that in Hungary was "Weisz." Erlau, the German and Yiddish name for the town known as Eger in Hungarian, is about 110 miles northeast of Budapest.

It was a longtime center of Orthodox Judaism with its emphasis on strict ritual observance, segregation of the sexes in worship services, liturgy and spiritual education, intensive Bible and Talmudic studies for males, distinctive dress for men and women, and often a physical, spiritual, and cultural separation from the neighboring non-Jewish population.

Rabbi Weisz was a fierce foe of the new Reform Jewish movement that began with Israel Jacobson's (1768–1828) liberal religious school in Seesen, Germany, in 1810. Jacobson, a layman, is considered the "father" of Reform Judaism.[8]

Weisz also opposed the progressive or "Neolog" expression of Judaism that emerged in Budapest in 1868. The Neolog movement, while less radical than

Reform, represented the attempt of upwardly mobile Hungarian Jews to combine traditional Judaism with the "advances" and "advantages" of modernity.[9]

Joseph Hirsch Weisz's four decades as Erlau's chief rabbi were filled with controversy, conflict, and contention. Many religiously "enlightened" Hungarian Jews of the period attempted to end the privileged status that Orthodox Judaism held in the country. In fact, the reformers gained control of the Hungarian Jewish community for a period of time, but Orthodox rabbis like Weisz and others fought back within the civil court system. After twelve years of legal battles, they regained their favored position, but only with the help of the Roman Catholic hierarchy and the imperial authorities in Vienna, including the emperor himself.[10]

The religious reformers as well as the ultra-Orthodox Hasidic community of Hungary disliked Stephen's grandfather. In the eyes of the first group, Joseph Weisz was the quintessential "establishment" Orthodox rabbi who was supported by the Habsburg monarchy. The second group condemned Weisz because he was an adversary of the mystical, antirational Hasidic religious movement that began a hundred years earlier in what is now Ukraine under the leadership of Rabbi Israel ben Eliezer (1698–1760), better known as the Baal Shem Tov, the "Master of the Good Name." As a result, Rabbi Weisz, an unpopular leader, was attacked from both ends of the Jewish religious spectrum.

Years later as a rabbi in the United States, Stephen Wise rejected many of his grandfather's religious beliefs and practices. In fact, Stephen became a leader of "liberal Judaism" (Stephen's term for Reform), a movement that broke with Joseph Weisz's Orthodoxy. Reform permitted men and women to sit together during synagogue religious services that often featured an organ, a choir that included Christian singers, and the recitation of many prayers in English or other vernacular languages used by Jews. Reform leaders like Wise were no longer bound to halacha (Jewish religious law and tradition) that mandated strict Sabbath and holiday observances, kosher dietary laws, and a host of other religious requirements.

While affirming Orthodox Judaism, Rabbi Joseph Weisz was also an ardent Hungarian nationalist and patriot who supported Lajos Kossuth's (1802–1894) unsuccessful 1848 revolution against the Vienna-based rulers who had controlled Hungary as a province since 1668. Other Hungarian Jews, including members of the Weisz family, joined the "Revolution of Liberty."[11] In 1849 Kossuth served as governor-president of a revolutionary Hungarian government for only eighty-eight days before the Habsburgs, aided by their tsarist Russian allies, used military force to snuff out the short-lived independence movement. Kossuth to this day remains an enduring symbol of Hungarian national independence and freedom.[12] Following the collapse of the Kossuth revolution, Vienna imposed heavy retaliatory taxes on the Hungarian rebels, including the Jewish community, as punishment for the failed revolt. As part of that crackdown, Austrian authorities tried Chief Rabbi Weisz of Erlau on the charge of sedition, but he was eventually acquitted. During that tumultuous period, the rabbi was forced to hide from his imperial pursuers and, thanks to the local Roman Catholic archbishop, Bela Bartakovics (1792–1873), he found safe refuge in an Erlau monastery.[13]

The saga of Joseph Hirsch Weisz's political fervor remained a compelling model for Stephen, his rabbinic grandson. Because members of his family had fought with Kossuth, Wise liked to say the spirit of liberty and freedom was in his genes.

One reason for Stephen's defection from his grandfather's traditional Judaism may have been the religious training and general education of his father. Born in Erlau to Joseph Hirsch and Rachel Theresa, Aaron Weisz followed his family's rabbinic vocation, but he also attended two German universities—Leipzig and Halle—earning a Ph.D. degree from the latter institution in 1867. His thesis focused on angels and demons within the Jewish religious tradition. A devotee of "psycho history" might infer that Aaron's doctoral dissertation was a reflection of his father's many personal spiritual battles in Erlau, but that is only speculation.[14]

When Joseph Weisz died in 1881, his widow, Stephen's paternal grandmother, left Hungary a year later and moved to Jerusalem where she lived until her death in 1892. Rachel Theresa Weisz wrote,

> I must go to the Holy Land. I go not to live there but to die there. There I wish to pray; and there to die, to be laid to rest amid the sacred dust of Jerusalem; to be buried on the slope [the Mount of Olives cemetery] facing the Holy of Holies.[15]

Aaron Weisz received his rabbinic training and ordination at Rabbi Azriel Hildesheimer's seminary in the city of Eisenstadt, now a part of Austria. In 1844, the year of Aaron's birth, Hildesheimer (1820–1899) was awarded a doctorate from Halle, a rare academic achievement at the time for an Orthodox rabbi. He wrote several important books in the German language, and his seminary was a major center of the Jewish religious movement that became known as "modern Orthodoxy": a movement that attempted to maintain traditional Judaism while encountering the contemporary secular world. Hildesheimer embraced German culture and emphasized that Judaism was compatible with modern religious scholarship, technology, and science.[16]

After completing his university and seminary education, Aaron Weisz returned to Erlau, and as the chief rabbi's son, he supervised the Jewish community's schools. He also participated in a significant intellectual under-taking: the revision of Johannes Buxtorf's (1564–1629) classic 1607 work: *Lexicon Hebraicum et Chaldaicum cum Brevi Lexicon Rabbinico Philosophico* (A Glossary of Hebrew and Chaldaic Lexicon with Rabbinic Philosophy).[17] Even though Aaron was a leader of the Erlau Orthodox "establishment," the young rabbi was placed under a religious ban by the local Hasidic leadership for his alleged progressive views.

There is no dispute that Aaron married well. But there are two conflicting accounts about that event. The "official" story that has entered into most Stephen Wise biographical material is that Sabine Fischer, Wise's mother, was a widow. She was previously married to Ignac Totvarosi Fischer, with whom she had two children, Ida and Wilma.[18]

At age thirty-two, she was six years older than Aaron when they married in 1870. Two years later Otto Irving (1872–1919) was born, followed in 1874 by the arrival of Stephen Samuel, the couple's second child.

However, another version is that Sabine was not a widow, but rather, as a married woman, she fell in love with Aaron. Sabine's father, Moritz Fischer (1800–1900), a wealthy Hungarian magnate, attempted to dissuade his strong-willed daughter from seeking a divorce in order to marry the young Weisz, but like many other fathers in similar situations, all efforts to block his daughter's romance and marriage plans were unsuccessful. However, the wily Fischer ex-tracted a huge concession from his new son-on-law: Aaron would leave the active rabbinate and work in his father-in-law's porcelain business headquar-tered in Budapest.[19]

Moritz Fischer's own story is one of talent, skill, and ambition. In 1839, a year after Sabine's birth, he became the head of the Herend porcelain factory in Hungary that had been founded thirteen years earlier. Under Fischer's lead-ership, Herend became internationally known and competed against the bet-ter-known French Sevres and German Meissen ceramic brands.

In 1851 Queen Victoria of Great Britain (1819–1901) purchased one of Fischer's decorative porcelain lines with colorful flowers and butterflies that became world famous as the Queen's favorite. Coffee pots, sugar bowls, creamers, cups, saucers, and other tableware with that pattern are still avail-able today for purchase in the Herend inventory. In 1853 Fischer's company won an award at the New York Exhibition of Industrial Arts. His international commercial and artistic success earned him a large measure of social prestige, and in recognition of his achievements, Franz Joseph first made Fischer an imperial knight, and later in 1869 he elevated him to the rank of baron, a high honor for a Jew in the empire.[20]

But as the Industrial Revolution intensified in the mid-1870s, Herend's employees attempted to organize a trade union that would provide better pay and improved working conditions. Baron Fischer opposed all such efforts. How-ever, Aaron Weisz supported the porcelain workers in their campaign, an act that enraged his father-in-law. In a burst of familial fury that remains star-tling nearly a century and a half later, Fischer provided his "labor-loving" rab-binic son-in-law, his wife (the baron's daughter), and their children one-way tickets to travel from Budapest to New York City. It is perhaps no surprise that during Stephen Wise's rabbinic career in the United States, he was an ardent public supporter of unions and the economic rights of laboring men and women.

A year before Aaron Weisz and his family left Hungary, he first traveled alone to the United States and worked as a bricklayer in New York City as well as serving as the rabbi of Congregation Beth Elohim, a Brooklyn synagogue. Aaron returned to Budapest and in 1875 moved his entire family to America. It remains unclear whether Aaron was "pushed" out of the city by his father-in-law or whether he "jumped" at the opportunity to move to America, where he would be far away (4,371 miles to be exact) from both his rabbinic father and industrialist father-in-law.[21]

In many ways Aaron Weisz was the human bridge between his father's Orthodox religious beliefs and those of his son, who became the world's best-known Reform rabbi. As part of that evolution, when Aaron, his wife, and children arrived in New York City, the thirty-one-year-old rabbi, perhaps following the suggestion of a US immigration official, changed the family surname from the Hungarian "Weisz"—pronounced "vice"—to the more neu-tral "Wise."[22]

Stephen always regretted that he never met any of his four grandparents, especially his two powerful and domineering grandfathers. None of his grandparents ever visited the United States, and Aaron and Sabine Wise never took their children back to Hungary once they arrived in New York City in 1875.

Although Stephen Wise always asserted he was "of the American nation," it is necessary to focus on when and where he was born to gain a full under-standing of his life and career. Although Stephen left the Austro-Hungarian Empire as an infant, the cultural, religious, social, and political aspects of the empire helped shape Wise's worldview and the role of the Jewish people and Judaism on the global stage.

In the 1870s when Aaron and Sabine Weisz moved to Budapest from Erlau, the Hungarian capital had nearly 70,000 Jews—about 19 percent of the city's total population. But the Jewish roots in what is now Hungary go back more than sixteen hundred years. In 2008, archaeologists working in Halbturn, Austria, an area known in Hungarian as Feltorony, unearthed a third-century gold scroll containing an inscription with the central Jewish affirmation of faith, *Shema Yisrael* / Hear O Israel (Deuteronomy 6:4), indicating an early Jewish presence in the region.[23]

Like many other Jewish communities in Europe, Budapest's Jews encountered a series of anti-Jewish policies and persecutions emanating from Christian religious leaders as well as Hungarian political leaders. It was not until Emperor Joseph II's (1741–1790) ruling in 1783 that Jews were permitted to live in Buda and Pest, the twin communities that make up the Hungarian capital. But by the mid-1800s the Budapest Jewish community was prosperous and secure enough to establish a network of schools, synagogues, orphanages, hospitals, clinics, cemeteries, and homes for the aged.[24]

The first Budapest synagogue was established in 1787, and by 1859 the growing Jewish community erected the impressive Dohanay Street Synagogue, the largest Jewish house of worship in Europe. Built in the Moorish style of architecture, the twin-towered building survived the German occupation of Hungary during World War II, and it still serves as a visible and viable tribute to the earlier generations of Budapest Jews.[25]

In 1877 a modern rabbinical seminary linked to the Neolog movement was established in the city, and the Congress of Hungarian Jewry was organized ten years earlier. A key mandate of the congress was to settle disputes among the often-contentious elements within the diverse Jewish community, one that was also active in Hungarian national politics.[26]

Following the formal creation of the Austro-Hungarian Empire in 1867, and after previous decades of initial gains of Jewish emancipation that were followed by a series of setbacks, the newly empowered Hungarian government finally granted equal rights to its growing Jewish population. However, it was only in 1895, twenty years after the Weisz family left Budapest, that Judaism was recognized as one of the "official" religions in Hungary.[27]

Franz Joseph's empire was a combustible collection of restive peoples, and a major center of such restlessness was Hungary. Although militarily defeated in the late 1840s, rebellious Hungarian nationalists continued to threaten and challenge the fragile stability of an Empire that at its zenith in the years before World War I numbered fifty million people representing numerous ethnic, national, and religious groups. The emperor's realm included significant areas of eleven modern European nations: Austria, Croatia, the Czech Republic, Hungary, Italy, Montenegro, Poland, Serbia, Slovakia, Slovenia, and Ukraine.

The imperial capital city, Vienna, provided a dynamic "cohesiveness . . . where intellectuals of different kinds shared ideas and values with each other and still mingled with a business and professional elite proud of its general education and artistic culture."[28]

During the early 1870s Aaron and Sabine Wise lived in Budapest, about

1150 miles from Vienna, and were part of the cultural and intellectual "cohesiveness" that radiated from the imperial city to other parts of the Austro-Hungarian Empire.

Franz Joseph began his long reign as Austrian emperor at age eighteen in 1848, and he ruled for sixty-eight years until his death in 1916. He remains a legendary historical figure in European and Jewish history, with his elegant military uniforms, regal bearing, and muttonchops sideburns. But Franz Joseph was bedeviled by a dysfunctional royal family made infamous by the murder-suicide of his adulterous son, Crown Prince Rudolf (1858–1889), and his teenage mistress, Mary Vetsera (1871–1889), at the Mayerling Royal Hunting Lodge, and the kaiser's own loveless forty-five-year marriage to Elisabeth of Bavaria (1854–1898) that ended in 1898 when an Italian anarchist in Geneva stabbed the empress to death.[29]

Thirteen years earlier, in 1885, Franz Joseph began a three-decade-long love affair with Katharina Schratt (1853–1940), a prominent Viennese actress, which ended only with his death.[30] But the most significant of Franz Joseph's familial traumas was the June 1914 assassination in Sarajevo of Archduke Franz Ferdinand (1863–1914), the emperor's nephew and heir-apparent, at the hands of Serbian nationalists, an event that triggered World War I.[31]

But through it all, the stoic Franz Joseph persevered, arising each morning at 3:30 a.m. during his lengthy reign to rule an unwieldy, often turbulent kingdom. The Austrian kaiser, a devout Roman Catholic, was the royal human cement that held fifty million diverse people together in an empire of 240,000 square miles: an area slightly smaller in size than Texas, but with twice the Lone Star State's current population. Today, nearly a century after its destruction following World War I, the Austro-Hungarian Empire into which Stephen Wise was born is frequently portrayed in popular culture with such compositions and operettas as *Ein Waltzertraum* (A Waltz Dream) and "The Chocolate Soldier" by the Viennese Jewish composer Oscar Straus (1870–1954). The latter frothy work is based on George Bernard Shaw's "Arms and the Man," and is an opera bouffe often paired with "The Student Prince," an operetta written by the Hungarian-born Jewish composer Sigmund Romberg (1887–1951) and set in the pre–World War I German Empire.

Straus and Romberg were just two of the many Jewish composers, musicians, singers, physicians, authors, industrialists, lawyers, artists, rabbis, and journalists who gained prominence during Franz Joseph's long reign, including Sigmund Freud (1856–1939), the pioneer in psychoanalysis and physician-turned-writer Arthur Schnitzler (1862–1931), who wrote the often-produced play *La Ronde*. Tina Blau (1845–1916) was a talented Jewish artist born in Vienna, but because of her gender her paintings were little noticed until recently.

Gustav Mahler (1860–1911), a native of Moravia, achieved fame in Europe and the United States as a world-class composer and symphony orchestra conductor.[32] Another famous composer born in the Empire was Arnold Schoenberg (1874–1951). Joseph Pulitzer (1847–1911), the publisher of the *New York World* and the *St. Louis Post-Dispatch*, was born in Hungary.

Theodor Herzl (1860–1904), the founder of the modern Zionist movement, was born in a Budapest house located next door to the Dohanay Street Synagogue. He later gained prominence as a Viennese journalist and essayist before he began his public campaign to create a Jewish state.[33]

Years later in 1898, Herzl was to have a decisive life-changing impact upon twenty-four-year-old Rabbi Stephen Wise when the two Budapest-born Jews met for the first time during the Second Zionist Congress in Basel, Switzerland.[34]

When Stephen was born in 1874, Jews were among Franz Joseph's most loyal subjects, including those living within Hungary. The empire's Jews numbered 250,000, or about 5 percent of the monarchy's total population. For them, the long-serving and long-suffering emperor represented a regal source of stability and security in an increasingly hostile Europe.

Part of that animus stemmed from religious anti-Judaism that was based upon a widely held Christian belief that Jews had "rejected" Jesus of Nazareth as the long-awaited Messiah, were responsible for his death by crucifixion at the hands of the Romans around the year 30 CE, and as a result, Jews were eternally punished by God for their "spiritual blindness and error." The negative beliefs frequently evolved into the odious "Christ killer" charge that many Christians hurled at Jews for centuries.

But in 1879 the global Jewish community confronted a new form of hostility. In that year Wilhelm Marr (1819–1904), a little-known German Lutheran left-wing political activist, first introduced the term "anti-Semitism." He became disillusioned following his involvement in the failed 1848 revolution in Germany, and toward the end of his life he deserted progressive causes and became a bitter reactionary figure who endorsed human slavery, especially as it applied to blacks. Most of all, Marr hated Jews, believing they were bent on achieving global domination at the expense of Gentiles.

In 1879 Marr wrote *Der Sieg des Judenthums uber das Germanenthum von nicht confessionellen Standpunkt* (The Victory of Jewry over Germandom, Considered from a Nonreligious Point of View). Marr's phrase "anti-Semitism" still remains a code word for hatred of Jews and Judaism. It was designed to be a euphemism clothed in a veneer of academic respectability. Instead of the traditional religious "anti-Jewish" language, Marr's term provided a convenient cover to express age-old bigotry and prejudice. It was a new label for old, poisoned wine.[35]

The anti-Semitic Karl Lueger (1844–1910), elected Vienna's mayor in 1895, did not allow Jews to serve in his administration, and he derisively called the Hungarian capital "Judapest" because of its large Jewish population. Franz Joseph detested him and for two years refused to validate the anti-Semite's electoral victory. But the emperor was compelled to relent, and Lueger remained Vienna's *Burgermeister* until his death.[36]

In 2012, more than a hundred years later, the city of Vienna changed the name of a street honoring the anti-Semitic mayor—Dr. Karl Lueger Ring—and renamed it *Universitätsring*, or University Circle.[37]

Despite the presence of both religious anti-Judaism and secular anti-Semitism, many Jews became an integral part of the empire's cultural life. But the constant threat of bigotry and prejudice often created a bittersweet sense of Weltschmerz or world-weariness that is best expressed in the maxim, "In Berlin things are serious, but not hopeless, while in Vienna things are hopeless, but not serious." But things were quite "serious" in both capitals in the years leading up to World War I.

That four-year conflict destroyed not only the Catholic-led Austro-Hungarian Empire, but also the Protestant German, Orthodox Christian Russian, and Muslim Ottoman Empires as well.[38] In the years after the collapse of Franz Joseph's monarchy, many Jews of the Austro-Hungarian Empire insisted "their" emperor was more benign vis-à-vis Jews and Judaism than the brutal Russian tsars in St. Petersburg or the arrogant German kaisers in Berlin.[39]

In fact, aside from the ruling Austrian elites, the various Jewish communities, scattered throughout the Empire, always remained a source of support for Franz Joseph.[40]

Even though Stephen was less than two years old when Aaron Weisz's family left Budapest for New York City in 1875, there is little doubt that Wise, a voracious reader, was aware of the religious pluralism within the Budapest and Erlau Jewish communities that existed at his birth as well as the political diversity of the Austro-Hungarian Empire.

Rabbi Stephen Wise was a master builder of a large number of religious, social welfare, educational, and political institutions in both New York City and the United States, a city and a nation that in some ways were democratic versions of the multiethnic, multireligious, multinational Austro-Hungarian Empire.

The mélange of languages, nationalities, religions, and ethnic groups that Stephen Wise was born into and left as an infant was etched into his overall worldview—a view that demanded the creation of a secure and independent state for the always threatened Jewish people and the attainment of full civil, economic, cultural, and human rights for all peoples everywhere.

When the newly named Wise family left Budapest behind and arrived in New York City in 1875, Aaron did not return to Congregation Beth Elohim but instead became the spiritual leader of Baith Israel / House of Israel, another Brooklyn congregation. The two synagogues were professional stepping-stones that afforded Aaron the opportunity to master the English language and adapt to the political and religious realities of post–Civil War America.

Baith Israel, founded in 1856, and Beth Elohim, established in 1862, represented a progressive form of Judaism somewhat akin to today's Conservative movement. Both congregations conducted worship services in German and Hebrew, and shortly before the arrival of Aaron Wise as their rabbi, Baith Israel members voted by a two-to-one margin to install wooden pews in their building—an action that allowed for mixed seating of women and men similar to Christian houses of worship.

Aaron's new congregation also opted for a teenage "Confirmation" religious service to be held on the spring harvest holiday of Shavuot (Weeks), when, according to Jewish teaching, the Torah (the biblical books of Genesis, Exodus, Leviticus, Numbers, and Deuteronomy), including the Ten Commandments, was given by God to Moses on Mount Sinai following the exodus from Egypt. Although Aaron's first two congregations, Baith Israel and Beth Elohim, represented sharp departures from Orthodox Judaism, it was Stephen who completed the final break with his rabbinic grandfather's Orthodox Judaism.

Aaron's acculturation process in America was a rapid one, and in 1876 he became the rabbi of the prestigious Congregation Rodeph Sholom in Manhattan. Founded as an Orthodox synagogue by German-speaking Jews in 1842, the congregation's first edifice was on Clinton Street near Houston Street. The second building was erected further uptown at Lexington Avenue and East 63rd Street, and in 1930, the congregation moved to its current location on West 83rd Street on New York City's Upper West Side. By 1876 Rodeph Sholom had shifted from its Orthodox origins to a more progressive form of Judaism.

Aaron Wise was an energetic innovator during his twenty years at Rodeph Sholom. He wrote a religious school handbook and compiled a siddur or prayer book that was used by his congregation. Rabbi Wise was the editor of two Jewish newspapers—the *Jewish Herald* of New York City and the *Boston Hebrew Observer*. Thanks to Aaron, Rodeph Sholom provided social welfare services for the community, a program Stephen adopted when he established the "Free Synagogue" in the early 1900s. In 1886 the young rabbi from Hungary was also one of the founders of the Jewish Theological Seminary, the flagship seminary of what was to emerge as Conservative Judaism.[41]

Unlike the financially poor European Jews who came to New York City and other American urban centers during that period, Aaron Wise, with a wife and four growing children, was able to purchase a house on Manhattan's

East 5th Street for his family, a rare occurrence for an immigrant. In 1887, the upwardly mobile Wise family moved to a new home on East 30th Street that was within walking distance of Rodeph Sholom and the City College of New York, which was established in 1847 as an institution dedicated to educating the children of immigrants and the poor.

City College was an experiment in higher education because admission was based on a student's academic skill and talent, not on one's family wealth, religion, or status in society. "By the time [in 1913 when president John] Finley left City College, the people of New York had become accustomed to regarding the [College's] Great Hall as one of the important places of assembly."[42]

The historic changes that took place in the United States during Stephen's lifetime were profound and permanent in nature. When the Wises arrived in New York City, American Jews numbered about 280,000. When Stephen died in 1949, the Jewish population in the United States had grown to more than five million, the largest Jewish community in the world after the devastation of the Holocaust. During the same period, the American population grew from about 50 million to more than 150 million people.

In 1875 the United States was recovering from the trauma of the Civil War, and the nation was on the cusp of the Industrial Revolution that was fueled by millions of new immigrants, mainly from Europe. New York City experienced explosive growth during the last two decades of the nineteenth century; its population soared from 940,000 in 1880 to 3.4 million in 1900. In the same period, the city's Jewish population increased to 598,000, representing about a third of the total national Jewish population of 1,777,000. The figures reflect the extraordinary number of immigrants from many lands who remained in New York City.

Despite the Jewish population growth in the United States in the late nineteenth and early twentieth centuries, the older Jewish communities in America from Austria and Germany provided almost all of the leaders—economic, rabbinic, scholarly, literary, political, social, and cultural—of the burgeoning American Jewish community. While many people today express nostalgia about *Der Alter Heim*, the Yiddish term for "The Old Country and Home," it is often overlooked that by 1900, New York City's Jewish population of 598,000[43] had already exceeded the number of Jews residing in Berlin, Budapest, Bucharest, Lodz, London, Odessa, Vienna, or Warsaw.[44]

In 1874 the United States was a rural agrarian nation. But seventy-five years later when Stephen Wise died, America was an industrialized country, the world's strongest economic and military power following World War II, and the home of the world's largest Jewish community.

Stephen Wise, the seventh generation of rabbis in his family, required two large expanding stages—Jewish and American—to fulfill his lifelong ambition of becoming a great leader. But first he had to complete his rabbinic and university studies, and like much of Stephen's personal history, his education was as W. R. Gilbert and Arthur Sullivan wrote in their beloved 1878 operetta *HMS Pinafore*: "Things are seldom what they seem." Even today there is confusion and questioning about Stephen's rabbinic training and ordination as well as his Ph.D. thesis at Columbia University.

Chapter 2

Columbia, Vienna, and Oxford: The Education of a Thoroughly Modern Rabbi

Providing the best possible education for a child is an important decision for all parents. This was true once Rabbi Aaron Wise and his wife, Sabine, arrived in the United States and soon recognized that young Stephen was a precocious youngster eager to learn about all things Jewish and American.

It is difficult today to view Stephen Wise other than as a self-confident and talented global leader blessed with a commanding persona and a charismatic presence. However, as a boy he felt a distinct sense of inferiority when compared to Otto, his elder brother, who later became a prominent attorney. Young Stephen believed his brother—older by two years—"outshone me in every way."[1]

An astute Aaron perceived that his younger son was a self-doubter and not sure-footed about his abilities and skills. As an adult, a grateful Stephen wrote that his father "sensed and pondered over my need of something to help me overcome a feeling of inferiority which, if left unchecked, was bound to have a disabling effect upon my personality." Aaron conveyed a basic message to his younger son: "When you feel life is too much for you, remember to say: 'Always do what you are afraid to do.'"[2]

But *Challenging Years*, the hastily written autobiography that a cancer-stricken Stephen Wise composed in 1948 during the last year of his life, does not begin with the expected mention of his birth or an appreciation of parents and grandparents—the usual formula of many autobiographies. Instead, Wise opens his life story as a six-year-old living in New York City who was involved in the 1880 US presidential election that pitted two Civil War generals against one another: Winfield Scott Hancock (1824–1886), a Democrat, and James A. Garfield (1831–1881), a Republican.

In fact, the very first sentences of Wise's autobiography describe his campaign participation: "My interest in political affairs began at a rather early age. . . . I carried a torch in Hancock parades." When he learned his candidate had lost the election, "I came into the house weeping."[3] Whether this is an accurate account of a youthful political junkie does not matter. What it does reveal is that Stephen Wise wanted readers to know that his intense interest in "political affairs" originated early in life.

Faced with a bright but insecure son, Aaron and Sabine had to make critical choices about his schooling. One approach was to enroll the inquisitive Stephen in a New York City *cheder*, a traditional Orthodox Jewish system of religious education that originated in Eastern Europe near the end of the eighteenth century. *Cheder* is the Hebrew noun for "room," and it became a popular term to describe the venue where a group of young boys—Orthodox families usually educated their daughters at home—studied with a *melamed* or teacher who was frequently untrained in basic pedagogy skills.[4]

Because Aaron Wise earned a Ph.D. degree from a nineteenth-century German university and because Sabine Fischer Wise came from a wealthy prominent baronial family in Budapest, it is no surprise that they eschewed sending Stephen to a *cheder*. Instead, his early formal Jewish studies took place at the religious school of Rodeph Sholom, his father's Manhattan congregation.

In *Challenging Years*, Stephen Wise recounts many family dinners where his rabbinic father told Sabine and the children "the tale of what had been endured by the unhappy [Jewish] exiles who were then landing at Castle Garden." The latter was the New York City point of entry beginning in 1855 for many European immigrants before the more famous Ellis Island gateway was opened in 1892.[5]

Aaron described the brutal anti-Jewish policies the Russian tsar Alexander III (1845–1894) put in place following the 1881 St. Petersburg assassination of his father, the "moderate" Alexander II (1818–1881), who was killed by members of the revolutionary movement *Narodnaya Volya* (People's Will). As part of his revenge, Alexander III instigated a systematic persecution of Jews within his empire that began with the implementation of the infamous 1881 "May Laws" that restricted where Jews could reside and the harsh legislation that also banned Jews from many trades, occupations, and professions.[6]

Between the years 1881 and 1924, the year when the US Congress enacted a strict quota system on the number of immigrants who could enter the United States from Eastern and Southern Europe, more than two and a half million Jews, mainly from tsarist Russia, came to the so-called Golden Medina, the Yiddish expression meaning the "Golden Country."[7]

Although the Wise family was not part of the post-1881 wave of immigration, in later years Eastern European Yiddish-speaking Jews became major supporters of Stephen Wise and his many causes, especially Zionism and American trade unionism.

Aaron's parental influence was a vital factor in Stephen's youthful decision to become a rabbi, the seventh generation in the Weissfeld/Weisz/Wise chain of Jewish teachers and leaders. Once Stephen announced his intentions, Aaron realized that his son required more than the limited religious education offered by Rodeph Sholom.

Stephen's father arranged for Stephen to study privately with Rabbi Alexander Kohut (1842–1894), a world-class scholar and faculty member of the newly established Jewish Theological Seminary of America. Like the Wise family, Kohut was also born in Hungary, and just as Aaron had done a decade earlier, he came to the United States in 1885 to lead a progressive New York City congregation. In Kohut's case it was Ahavath Chesed (Central Synagogue), as well as acquiring a faculty position teaching Talmud at JTS.[8]

Joining Stephen in Kohut's small tutorial class were two other youngsters who later became outstanding Jewish scholars: Alexander's son, George A. Kohut (1874–1933), and Joseph H. Hertz (1872–1946). The latter served as the United Kingdom's chief rabbi for thirty-three years beginning in 1913 until his death. Hertz also compiled a major English language commentary on the Torah that is still widely used.

For his general studies, Stephen attended New York City's Public School 15 located a block from his East 5th Street home, an area now called the East Village. P.S. 15, at 333 East 4th Street, is one of the city's oldest schools.[9] Today it bears the name of Roberto Clemente (1934–1972), in memory of the Pittsburgh Pirates baseball All-Star who died in a plane crash off the coast of his native Puerto Rico while on a relief mission following a disastrous earthquake on the island.[10]

In the 1880s students generally attended NYC public schools for only six years; a seventh year was added if the youngster sought admission to a college or university. Then as now, a primary task of the city's schools was to teach the English language and the fundamental "American historical narrative" to children of newcomers to the United States.

As a child of immigrants from Hungary, Stephen excelled in his elementary school studies, and one teacher, Nathaniel Biers, transmitted to his eager pupil a knowledge and appreciation of the classic canon of English literature.[11] Young Wise's early training at P.S. 15 held him in good stead during his public career when he employed the English language in a masterful way in his sermons and other public speeches.

His authoritative voice and stirring choice of words made Wise into one of America's greatest orators. He was often compared to the three-time Democratic presidential nominee William Jennings Bryan (1860–1925) for rhetorical brilliance and power.[12]

Seven years after their father's death in 1949, Stephen's two children, James (1901–1983) and Justine (1903–1987), wrote about his literary passion:

> But it was in the field of English letters that first won and always held Stephen
> Wise's affection as a student. The very fact that English was not his mother

tongue—German being the first language of his home—determined him to master it. He pored over the writings of the British poets and prose stylists. Shakespeare and Milton, Matthew Arnold and Wordsworth were as familiar to him as Isaiah and Amos and Hillel.[13]

When Stephen Wise was thirteen years old, several important events took place in his life. He became a Bar Mitzvah, his family moved uptown from East 5th Street to East 30th Street, a block from his father's congregation, and he began his subfreshman public school year of study before entering the City College of New York.

Stephen's intellectual curiosity, his already formidable command of the English language, and his blossoming oratorical skills were on full display during his three years at CCNY. He won academic awards for Latin and Greek studies and became a member the college's debating club. But Wise did not complete his undergraduate studies at CCNY. Instead, he transferred to the more prestigious Columbia University for his final year, where he received his bachelor's degree in 1892.[14]

The usual reason given for the move to Columbia is that the future rabbi needed to pursue advanced Jewish studies with Richard James Horatio Gottheil (1862–1936), professor of rabbinical literature and the Semitic languages. Gottheil was the son of Rabbi Gustav Gottheil (1827–1903) who, at the time of Stephen's Columbia enrollment, was the spiritual leader of Temple Emanu-El, a large Reform congregation in New York City—a synagogue that fifteen years later was to play a decisive, career-changing role in Stephen Wise's life.

Attending Columbia during his senior year made it easier to study with Gottheil, but perhaps another reason for changing schools may have been Aaron's belief that a Columbia University degree was more impressive than one from CCNY.

Because Richard Gottheil had an important and lasting influence upon young Wise, it is important to devote some attention to the often-reclusive Columbia Semitics professor. Richard was born in Manchester, England, and the name "Horatio"—uncommon for a Jew—indicates his parents' esteem for Lord Horatio Nelson (1758–1805), the British naval hero who defeated Napoleon's fleet in the battle of Trafalgar in 1805, but lost his life during the battle. Although Stephen and Richard were both rabbis' sons, Gottheil did not follow in his father's profession. Richard received a Ph.D. degree from the University of Leipzig at age twenty-four, and he mastered several Middle Eastern languages including Hebrew and Arabic.[15]

Stephen wrote his senior college thesis under the tutelage of Gottheil. The subject was the Roman Empire's destruction of the Holy Temple in Jerusalem in the year 70. While it was a catastrophe for Jews that is still commemorated

each year with fasting and special prayers of lamentation, the Romans celebrated their victory by casting metal coins containing the Latin words, *Judaea
Capta* (Judah has been taken or captured). During the rest of Stephen Wise's
life—fifty-seven years—he worked to reverse the results of that defeat by re-
storing Jewish sovereignty in Zion, the land of Israel.

Stephen was eighteen years old when he received his bachelor's degree
from Columbia University, and it was time to commence his rabbinical studies that would culminate with the traditional ordination ceremony of *s'micha*,
when rabbis place their hands upon qualified students and confer the title of
"rabbi," an act symbolizing the unbroken line of Jewish teachers that began
many centuries ago. Following his graduation, an ambitious Stephen Wise
had two major goals that emulated his father's academic achievements in
Europe: rabbinical ordination and a Ph.D. university degree.

By 1892 Aaron Wise had broken with the Orthodox Judaism of his own fa-
ther, who had died eleven years earlier. Aaron represented the emerging
Conservative stream of Judaism in America that was similar to movements in
Europe that attempted to blend and balance traditional Judaism with the
modern contemporary world. For that reason it would have been natural for
Stephen to pursue his studies at the Jewish Theological Seminary in New York
City, the Conservative rabbinical school his father helped establish in 1886.
That may have seemed the obvious route for the Columbia University gradu-
ate, but it did not happen.

As a brilliant teenager, Stephen had received extensive private tutoring
from Kohut and Gottheil. Because of that heady experience, it is likely that
Stephen, perhaps with his father's approval, perceived himself a "special" student of Judaism who did not need to follow the usual seminary path to ordination. In addition, by 1892 he had moved closer to Reform Judaism and away
from the emerging Conservative Judaism of JTS.

Facial hair was a visible sign of the generational shifts in the Wise family
from Orthodoxy to Conservative to Reform. Joseph Hirsch Weisz had a full
beard and moustache that remains a traditional sign of many Orthodox men.
Aaron's cheeks were shaved, but he retained a trimmed beard that was much
shorter than his father's, while Stephen was clean-shaven—no beard and no
moustache.

Although Stephen did not enroll at JTS, he explored the possibility of
studying at the Hebrew Union College (HUC), the Reform seminary founded
in 1875 in Cincinnati, Ohio, by Rabbi Isaac Mayer Wise (1819–1900). The
Bohemian-born rabbi—no relation to Stephen's family—arrived in America
in 1846 and soon became the organizational leader of the expanding Reform
Jewish movement in the United States.

For the rest of his life Rabbi Wise sought to develop and organize an

"American Judaism" that would be liberal or Reform in ideology and practice. He believed that such a unified community was needed in the religiously open and pluralistic United States, a nation that provided Jews with the opportunity to practice their religion in a new environment that was relatively free of the bitter anti-Judaism and anti-Semitism of the Old World. But Isaac Mayer Wise's grand conception of a unified American Judaism never became a reality because the huge number of post-1881 Jewish immigrants to the United States were Orthodox in their religious practices, disinterested in Reform Judaism, or committed to a group of various political movements that had little room for an acculturated form of traditional religion.

Isaac Mayer Wise's dashed hopes for a singular American Judaism still remain in the names he assigned to the three organizations he established. In 1889 he founded the Central Conference of American Rabbis (CCAR), the Reform rabbis' professional association, and earlier in 1873 he formed the Union of American Hebrew Congregations (UAHC), the central body of Reform congregations. As noted above, he established the Hebrew Union College (HUC) in 1875.[16]

Key words in all three institutions are "American," "Central," and "Union."

In 2003 the UAHC changed its name to the Union for Reform Judaism (URJ). However, the CCAR and HUC have retained their original names. As we shall see in later chapters, Stephen Wise had a long series of confrontational and contentious relationships with all three Reform Jewish institutions. The fundamental issue was the anti-Zionism that emerged among many Reform rabbis and laypeople following the creation of the modern Zionist movement in 1897. [17]

In the 1890s HUC was the educational and spiritual center of German Jewish leadership in America. The school emphasized a universalistic definition of Judaism, "ethical monotheism," that was buttressed by the ideas of the European Enlightenment and philosophical rationalism. At the same time, the Reform seminary minimized or abandoned many of the ethnic, ritual, and liturgical aspects of Judaism. Most HUC faculty members of that era, including the school's president, abhorred anything and anyone that advocated the belief in a Jewish "return" to the biblical land of Israel.

In 1879 Isaac Mayer Wise wrote,

The colonization of Palestine appears to us a romantic idea inspired by religious visions without foundation in reality. The idea of Jews returning to Palestine is not part of our creed.[18]

Nearly forty years earlier, a similar sentiment was expressed at the 1841 dedication service of Temple Beth Elohim, a Reform congregation in Charleston,

South Carolina. Rabbi Gustav Poznanski (1809–1879) declared, "This country is our Palestine, this city our Jerusalem, this house of God our Temple."[19]

The views of Poznanski and Isaac M. Wise were not limited to Reform rabbis. Writing years before the advent of the modern Zionist movement, Rabbi Samson Raphael Hirsch (1808–1888) of Germany, one of the leading Orthodox rabbis of the nineteenth century, was committed to a spiritual "reunion" in the land of Israel, something he believed required the help of both God and the Messiah. Until that moment, Jews must content themselves with only "wishing and hoping" for Zion reborn:

> We mourn over the sin which brought about that downfall (the Jewish Diaspora following the Roman destruction of the Jewish Holy Temple in 70 CE). . . . We take to heart the harshness which we have encountered in our years of wandering as the chastisement of a father, imposed on us for our improvement, and we mourn the lack of observance of the Torah which that ruin has brought about. Not in order to shine as a nation among nations do we raise our prayers and hopes for a reunion in our land, but in order to find a soil for the better fulfillment of our spiritual vocation in that reunion and in that land which was promised, and given, and again promised for our observance of the Torah. But this very vocation obliges us, until G-d shall call us back to the Holy Land, to live and to work as patriots wherever He has placed us, to collect all the physical, material and spiritual forces and all that is noble in Israel to further the weal of the nations which have given us shelter. It obliges us, further, to allow our longing for the far-off land to express itself only in mourning, in wishing and hoping; and only through the honest fulfillment of all Jewish duties to await the realization of this hope. But it forbids us to strive for the reunion or possession of the land by any but spiritual means.[20]

When Theodor Herzl convened the First Zionist Congress in Basel, Switzerland, in 1897, the Hebrew Union College president denounced Herzl's efforts as a "momentary inebriation of morbid minds, and a prostitution of Israel's holy cause to a madman's dance of unsound politicians."[21] Two years later, the eighty-year-old Wise turned sarcastic:

> [Herzl] . . . came out with the grand scheme of establishing an independent Jewish State . . . made a heathen noise the world over, added shame to blasphemy, folly to falsehood . . . and bringing forth a mouse, and what a mouse! . . . We can never identify with ourselves with Zionism.[22]

Five years before the birth of the modern Zionist movement, the Reform seminary in Cincinnati was not a good fit for Stephen Wise, who by 1892 was a rabbinical candidate already taken with the idea of a Jewish "return to Zion." Young Wise also believed that religion had a major role to play in the rough-and-tumble world of politics, economics, labor, and culture.

In an attempt to bridge the gap between his personal beliefs and those of the HUC leadership, Stephen suggested the possibility of an independent rabbinical studies program for himself in New York City. Aaron supported his son's off-campus plan, believing that if Stephen did not enroll at the nearby JTS, he did not want his gifted son to study away from home at the distant—both geographically and religiously—HUC in Cincinnati.

Although Isaac Mayer Wise opposed the proposal for independent study and wanted young Stephen to move to Cincinnati for his seminary training, he reluctantly agreed: "But as your father seems to think otherwise and your taste runs in the same direction, I submit."[23]

Two weeks later, the HUC faculty began to design curricula for the student who was reluctant to leave New York City for Ohio. But Stephen never involved himself with the courses that were created for him. Instead, a year later in 1893, he received his *s'micha* not in Cincinnati nor in New York City, but in Vienna.

The year 1892 also brought sadness to the Wise family in New York City. Rabbi Joseph Hirsch Weisz's widow, Rachel Theresa, died that year. News of her death reached Aaron and Stephen Wise shortly before they were scheduled to sail from New York to visit her in Jerusalem. It was not until 1913, twenty-one years later, before Stephen made his first visit to Palestine, then under Ottoman Turkish control, where he was able to visit his grandmother's grave on the Mount of Olives, the oldest Jewish cemetery in the world.[24]

The summer of 1892 was important for Stephen in a more positive way because he encountered another scholar in addition to Gottheil who impacted upon his life and career: the Scottish American philosopher Thomas Davidson (1845–1896). Davidson was born in Scotland and studied several classical languages, including Greek. He graduated with honors from Aberdeen University and came to the United States in 1867 where he taught at various schools in St. Louis, Missouri, and elsewhere. He also became an expert on the teachings of the Catholic saint Thomas Aquinas (1225–1274). Even though Davidson was not a Catholic, the pope invited him to Rome to advise Vatican scholars on Aquinas, a singular honor in an era of fierce Catholic-Protestant rivalry and antagonism.

By 1882, with his wanderings over, the thirty-seven-year-old Davidson purchased some rural property in New York State's Adirondack Mountains and established Glenmore, a "summer school for the cultural sciences" that attracted many visitors, especially young people in search of human values, meaning in life, and a set of personal ethics. A Glenmore summer included nature hikes in the nearby Keene Valley, discussions, lectures, and in-depth conversations.

Davidson offered his followers and listeners a democratic view of philosophy and religion; he taught that each person has the potential to achieve full self-development and the ability to create a personality that can aid others to gain a practical ethical and philosophic idealism. Although Davidson was a Christian from Scotland, he also taught at the Jewish-sponsored Educational Alliance in New York City. The alliance was an institution that offered new immigrants, mostly from Eastern Europe, a series of lectures and instruction on a wide range of subjects, including Davidson's system of belief he called "Apierotheism," an eclectic mixture of religious pluralism mixed with a dash of pantheism and a healthy dose of ethics and morality.[25]

Davidson's élan and high spirits permeated these various schools of thought. If he were alive today, the print and electronic media would label him a Scottish "guru" or an intellectual Pied Piper whose appealing ideas and personality attracted many young people to Glenmore, including Stephen Wise.[26]

In some ways, it was another "special" educational event in Wise's life because in the 1890s it was unusual, indeed out of the ordinary, for a young Jewish man or woman to spend a summer away from home at a rural mountain retreat center led by a Christian philosopher. It seems clear that Stephen's progressive parents approved such a choice.

Even a cursory examination of Davidson's views reveals a close affinity to what is termed the Social Gospel that was emerging among some American Protestant leaders of the time, including Walter Rauschenbusch (1861–1918) and Josiah Strong (1847–1916). It is the belief that religion, in all its forms, must address the perceived ills and illnesses of the general society and not be limited to the usual diet of liturgy, sermons, and hymns. Clergy of all faiths need to be at the forefront in addressing critical issues, and must not remain silent in the face of perceived societal injustices.

Stephen later wrote that Davidson's teachings stressed that no "idols or fetishes" are to be "worshipped." Rather, "it is knowledge and wisdom" that need to be used for the "weal of others." Davidson also told the eighteen-year-old rabbinical candidate, "Judaism like all living things changes as it grows; that while the letter killeth, the spirit keepeth it alive. You will devise a twentieth-century Judaism fitted to meet the needs of the present day."[27]

More than a hundred years later, it is difficult to separate some of the beliefs and teachings of Thomas Davidson from those of Stephen Wise. But there is no mistaking that the 1892 Glenmore summer experience had a permanent impact upon the young Columbia University graduate because it validated his commitment to an evolving liberal Judaism that emphasized rabbinic activism in the American as well as the global arenas.[28]

During the autumn of 1892 Stephen, who was fluent in German, traveled to Austria to study with another remarkable teacher, Adolf Jellinek (1821–1893), a leading Viennese rabbi and one of the great liberal preachers of Europe.[29]

Jellinek, like Isaac Mayer Wise, was also born in Moravia, but he remained on the continent his entire life. He served congregations in both Germany and Austria, and in 1865 Jellinek became the rabbi of the prestigious Seitenstettengasse synagogue in Vienna and remained in that position until he died. Built in 1825, it was one of the first synagogues to be erected in Vienna and escaped Nazi German destruction during World War II. It remains in use today.[30]

Jellinek was a devotee of the rationalist approach to religion and was part of the intellectual movement called *Wissenschaft des Judentums* (Scientific Study of Judaism). Because of his remarkable oratory and literary skills, Jellinek was a staunch defender of Jews and Judaism in an increasingly anti-Semitic Vienna, but his influence reached far beyond the imperial capital. More than two hundred of Jellinek's popular German language sermons, a skillful combination of Jewish and contemporary sources, were published. It is evident why Adolf Jellinek always remained a model that Stephen Wise followed in his own career.[31]

But Jellinek's position about a Jewish return to the Holy Land differed from Stephen's views that were first shaped by Aaron Wise and the Gottheils. Jellinek, who died several years before Herzl, a fellow Viennese Jew, published *The Jewish State*, offering a more nuanced position than either Isaac Mayer Wise or Samson Raphael Hirsch.

Jellinek supported the Jewish community then residing in the land of Israel (Palestine), but he affirmed that Jews elsewhere were citizens of the nations in which they lived. He warned that "a small [Jewish] state like Serbia or Romania outside Europe would most likely become the plaything of one Great Power against another, and whose future would be very uncertain." Jellinek added that talk of a physical "return" to the land of the Bible undermined the precarious position of Jews in Western countries and that "almost all Jews in Europe" would vote against the scheme if they were given the opportunity. He stated,

> The Jews have no national characteristics as such. . . . Thanks to their universalism, they accept and adapt the characteristics of the nations in whose midst they have been born and educated. . . . Have they [the Jews] engaged their spiritual energies on behalf of emancipation in order to give up their achievements . . . in order to declare themselves homeless aliens, and vagabonds, with staff in hand, to seek out a problematic homeland? We are at home in Europe

and feel ourselves to be children of the lands in which we were born, raised, and educated, whose languages we speak and whose cultures constitute our intellectual substance.

We are Germans, Frenchmen, Englishmen, Hungarians, Italians, etc. with every fiber of our being. We long ago ceased to be genuine full-blooded Semites in the sense of a Hebrew nationality that has long since been lost. . . . In the rehabilitation of Palestine, the land hallowed by memories and hopes, we behold the promise of renewed life for many of our brethren. We affirm the obligation of all Jewry to aid in its up building as a Jewish homeland by endeavoring to make it not only a haven of refuge for the oppressed but also a center of Jewish culture and spiritual life.[32]

Stephen was able to study and learn from Jellinek shortly before the famous rabbi died. Jellinek recognized Stephen's potential and in a private ceremony in 1893 he ordained the young student from New York City and imbued Wise with the imperative to deal with modern society's problems as well as stressing the ancient Jewish teaching found in the Babylonian Talmud (chapter 39a) section dealing with "Oaths": *Kol Yisrael arevim zeh bazeh* (All Israel [the Jewish people] is inner connected, responsible to one another).[33]

When he returned to the United States after his months of study in Vienna, Stephen Wise was an ordained rabbi who had eschewed formal and lengthy seminary studies at either JTS or HUC. He had completed one half of his academic goal: rabbinical ordination, but a long path yet remained before he would become "Dr. Wise."

Acquiring a Ph.D. degree at Columbia University under the tutelage of Professor Richard Gottheil demanded much of Stephen's time and energy. His earlier tutor, Alexander Kohut, suggested a possible thesis subject for the ambitious rabbi: a book of ethics written by the eleventh-century Spanish Jewish philosopher and poet, Solomon Ibn Gabirol (1021–1058).

Wise followed Kohut's advice and gave his thesis the lengthy title of *The Improvement of The Moral Qualities: An Ethical Treatise of the Eleventh Century by Solomon Ibn Gabirol, Printed from a Unique Arabic Manuscript, Together with a Translation, and an Essay on the Place of Gabirol in the History of the Development of Jewish Ethics.*

Plato (424 BCE–348 BCE), the ancient Greek philosopher, was most influential in Ibn Gabirol's writings and beliefs. Even though Ibn Gabirol lived less than forty years, he was a prolific author and composed many secular and religious poems in Hebrew. Indeed, he is considered the major religious poet of Spanish Jewry's Golden Age that ended in the tragic Royal Edict of Jewish Expulsion from Spain in 1492. In addition to his poetry, Ibn Gabirol also immersed himself in complex philosophic explorations about form, matter, the human senses, the intellect, rationality, the quest for immorality, and the importance of every person engaging in individual introspection as a means of self-fulfillment.

Ibn Gabirol wrote mainly in the Arabic language. The title of his most famous philosophical work was translated into Hebrew as *Mekor Hayim*, but it is better known by its Latin title *Fons Vitae* (Living Fountain). In it Ibn Gabirol staked out a clear Neoplatonic position that, surprisingly for an educated and committed Jew, is devoid of any specific Jewish content: there are no references to the Bible, Talmud, or Midrash, and Plato is the only philosopher named in the work.

Because the Latin *Fons Vitae* became better known than the Hebrew *Mekor Hayim*, many medieval thinkers mistakenly believed for centuries that "Avicebron," the name given to the author of the work, was either a Christian or a Muslim. It was not until 1846 that a German Jewish scholar, Solomon Munk (1803–1867), established that "Avicebron," was, in fact, Solomon Ibn Gabirol. "Avicebron" is a Latin corruption of his Hebrew name.[34]

A thousand years before Ibn Gabirol, there was another Jewish Neoplatonist, Philo of Alexandria (20 BCE–45 CE). Although he had little impact upon his fellow Jews, Philo was an intellectual link between ancient Greek and early Christian thought. Ibn Gabirol influenced major Christian theologians including Duns Scotus (1265–1308), Albertus Magnus (1206?–1280), and Thomas Aquinas. However Ibn Gabirol's philosophy also attracted limited interest among later Jewish philosophers; his greatest influence upon Jews and Judaism is his religious poetry that became part of synagogue liturgy. Israel Zangwill, a prominent English Jewish author, admired Ibn Gabirol:

> For he was not only a great poet but also a great philosopher. His vision was broad and his penetration keen. He saw further than the ordinary poet and felt deeper than the ordinary philosopher. He even cultivated science in his effort to grapple with the riddle of existence.[35]

In addition to *Fons Vitae / Mekor Hayim*, Ibn Gabirol composed an Arabic language book of ethics whose Hebrew translation is *Tikkun Middot HaNefesh* (The Improvement of the Moral Qualities). That text was the basis of Stephen Wise's doctoral thesis. Such an arcane topic was problematic for several reasons. Ibn Gabirol wrote his "manual on ethics" in Arabic, a language less familiar to Wise than Hebrew or even Latin. Although Stephen took several Columbia University courses in Arabic, his dissertation is primarily an English translation of Ibn Gabirol's writings as they appeared in several faulty and/or inadequate Hebrew texts. The philosophical work was complex enough in its original language; adding two languages to the academic mix made Wise's task even more difficult.

It has been said that reading any translation is akin to "kissing through a handkerchief"—that is, it may be close, but it is not the real thing. For Wise there were two thick "handkerchiefs" in his thesis work. He first had to locate and read the difficult original Arabic text, and then it was necessary to study the several Hebrew translations or mistranslations—one dating back to the twelfth century—and finally Wise had to render Ibn Gabirol's often-dense Neoplatonic thoughts into understandable English.

Because he was unable to obtain or view a printed text of the Arabic text in the United States, Wise was forced to travel during the summer of 1895 to Oxford University's Bodleian Library in Britain to examine photographic copies of Ibn Gabirol's original version. In several communications with Gottheil, Stephen complained how demanding it was to understand, much less translate the obscure, sometimes-opaque philosophic ideas and themes written in Arabic.

At Oxford Wise was able to consult with Professor Adolf Neubauer (1831–1907), a leading Jewish scholar of the time whose field of expertise was the medieval period. But as Stephen wrote to Gottheil, the Oxford professor's eyesight was failing and Stephen had to grapple with the convoluted Arabic text alone:

> I am compelled to realize how much beyond my strength this task is. Much of the text is simple, but there are many obscure passages. . . . Occasionally I have gone to Neubauer for help, but his eye failing renders him almost useless. . . . And so I grind and grind away, patiently endeavoring to cast some light upon passages whose darkness is nothing less than Egyptian.[36]

It is the familiar cri de coeur of many students in quest of the Ph.D. degree—a process requiring scholastic drudgery in libraries, a lengthy study of a complex subject of narrow interest, and the sobering knowledge that fulfilling the requirements for a university doctorate demands an extraordinary commitment of both finite time and psychic energy. But Stephen's mission to Oxford was ultimately successful. Wise wrote to Gottheil,

> The translation is finished, subject of course to a revision at your hand. The [Arabic] text is all in type and all the proofs have been revised by me. . . . I shall endeavor to give a clear account of the principles of Ibn Gabirol's "Ethics." . . . This latter task will be hard because he had none, i.e. . . . no one has thus far been able to carry his ethical principles to any definite authority.[37]

In addition to listing the linguistic and other problems faced by Wise, there is the more important question of why he chose such a demanding topic. One answer may be found by comparing Ibn Gabirol's major theological and philosophical focus and Wise's personal beliefs.

Ibn Gabirol did not base his ethics upon traditional religious sources. Although he affirmed the existence of the God of Israel, the eleventh-century thinker cited no Jewish texts to support his ideas about the need for human ethical behavior. Instead, his intellectual foundation is psychological and philosophical in nature, one that urges inner human strength and self-discipline. However, Ibn Gabirol believed that if one is able to achieve an ethical life as he defined it, then that is a sign of the divine will that exists within each person.

Wise, in his thesis, called such a definition "ingenious" because it makes ethics "independent of religious law," a striking statement by a rabbi since Jewish ethics are based upon the divine commandments of an omnipresent Creator. Stephen saluted Ibn Gabirol's distinction between an "animal soul" and a "rational soul." Wise noted,

> [Ibn Gabirol] believes in the superior endowments of some souls, and refers to them frequently. It appears, moreover, that this mystic doctrine makes a sharp distinction between the purely animal and the higher, or intellectual, qualities of man; the former manifest themselves and work through the senses, and the latter, the inward senses, are divine endowments, which manifest themselves in the control they exercise over the animal impulses. The principal agent in the exercise of this control is reason intelligence. This intelligence is the mediator between the divine and the animal in man, and any human being who makes his intelligence master over his natural inclinations may enjoy the bliss to which Gabirol points.[38]

There is perhaps another reason Stephen was attracted to the writings of Ibn Gabirol. It is not too much of a stretch to link the eleventh-century Spanish Jew with Wise's nineteenth-century mentor, Scottish thinker Thomas Davidson. Both men stressed the perfectibility of human existence and the imperative, based upon a divine principle, to fulfill oneself through self-development and a robust intellectual effort.

Wise was not a religious mystic nor was he devoted to what is today called "systematic theology." That is perhaps why Ibn Gabirol's "godless" philosophy appealed to him. In a long public career that was filled with thousands of synagogue and church sermons and other public orations, Stephen did not speak much about experiencing God. But in a 1916 private letter to his wife, Stephen wrote,

I went to the Quaker meeting house, oldest in America. . . . Quaintness and simplicity itself . . . No reading, no sermon, no services, no singing—the only word spoken being that of an old lady who arose to thank me. The spirit moved me in truth—and I spoke as you, Carrissima [an affectionate term for Louise] would have liked on the eternal simplicities and verities of religion. There is such a thing as inspiration. God gave it to me yesterday *for a little while*. If but I could trust Him and myself a little more.[39]

After years of intensive study, transatlantic travel, many hours grappling with obscure Arabic philosophic phrases and concepts, and working in three separate languages, Stephen Wise completed his thesis and submitted it for approval. In its final form, Stephen wrote a twenty-eight-page introduction, provided an English translation of seventy-six pages, and added two appendices, and a reproduction of Ibn Gabirol's original Arabic text. For his efforts, Wise was awarded his long-desired doctoral degree, and in 1902 the thesis was printed in a Columbia University journal.

But after completing his Ph.D. requirements, a controversy commenced with critics questioning whether Stephen Wise, albeit a brilliant orator and gifted rabbi, had been the sole author of the Ibn Gabirol thesis. He was somewhat vulnerable to such charges because Stephen never claimed to be a scholar and lamented he had not chosen to be a university or seminary professor.

Critics, perhaps jealous of Stephen's growing fame and status, attacked the dissertation and doubted Wise's scholarship and authorship. They charged that much of the thesis was the work of Rabbi Henry Zvi Gersoni (1844–1897), a talented writer, and one of Stephen's teachers. Much of the criticism focused on the unscholarly mistakes that Wise had made when he translated Ibn Gabirol into English from various Hebrew versions, including one by Gersoni. As noted above, Stephen was aware of such linguistic and philosophical obstacles. However, after studying the controversy and criticism in detail, Wise biographer Melvin I. Urofsky concludes, "It would appear, then, that Stephen Wise did do the work himself. . . . At worst, he stands guilty of poor scholarship, but not of fraud."[40]

Critics also questioned Jellinek's private rabbinical ordination of Stephen since Wise did not attend either the Jewish Theological Seminary or the Hebrew Union College. Similar questions were also raised about the authenticity and quality of the rabbinic education of Isaac Mayer Wise.[41]

Another controversy erupted years later and centered on Wise's contribution to the Jewish Publication Society's 1917 English language version of the Bible—the Pentateuch or Torah, the Prophets, and the Writings—that was used in many Jewish communities throughout the world until it was replaced with a new JPS version a half-century later.

Wise is given credit for the translation of the Book of Judges, but again critics have questioned whether he actually did the work. Urofsky concludes that Stephen "did not do the translation of Judges, but none of the other luminaries did their parts either." A single scholar, the editor in chief of the JPS project, Max L. Margolis (1866–1932), was the author of the entire translation, except for Kaufmann Kohler's (1843–1926) English version of the book of Psalms. Margolis had earned a Columbia Ph.D. degree a few years before Wise and was on the university's faculty when Stephen was a doctoral candidate.

Urofsky notes that "not one of the invited contributors followed through on their commitments, but their names (including Stephen Wise) were nevertheless listed, both as a courtesy to them and to avoid embarrassment to the [Jewish Publication] Society, which had publicized that fact that so many noted scholars would be participating in this great undertaking."[42]

The years between his rabbinic s'micha in Vienna and earning a doctorate in New York City were filled with several momentous professional and personal events that decisively influenced the life of Stephen Samuel Wise.

Chapter 3

An "American Jewish Prince" Meets the "King of the Jews"

When Wise returned from his studies with Adolf Jellinek in Vienna, an exceptional rabbinical position awaited him at a prominent New York City congregation. He became the assistant rabbi of B'nai Jeshurun—the Hebrew means "Children of the Upright or Righteous"—then located on Madison Avenue between East 64th and East 65th Streets in Manhattan. Henry S. Jacobs (1827–1893), the congregation's senior rabbi and a close friend of Aaron Wise, was pleased to have his colleague's son on his staff.

B'nai Jeshurun was founded in 1825 and is one of America's oldest synagogues. Its first members were German-speaking Jews who broke away from the Orthodox Spanish-Portuguese congregation Shearith Israel, "The Remnant of Israel," the oldest Jewish congregation in the United States, which was established in 1654 in the Dutch colony of New Amsterdam.

Like many other historic Manhattan houses of worship, both Jewish and Christian, as the city's population moved farther north or uptown, and away from the lower end of the island, B'nai Jeshurun moved to be closer to its members. As a result, it has had five different locations. An early home, on the site of the famous Macy's Department store on West 34th Street and Sixth Avenue, was in use until the Madison Avenue edifice was completed in 1885. The congregation's final move took place in 1917 with the construction of its current building on West 88th Street, now a New York City Historical Landmark.[1]

During its long history, B'nai Jeshurun has been both a Reform and a Conservative synagogue, and is today an independent self-defined "passionate" congregation that has received international attention because of its popular avant-garde religious services that attract hundreds of people each week.

However, in the late nineteenth century B'nai Jeshurun was a staid Conservative synagogue guided by Jacobs, a respected leader of the "uptown" Jewish community. In 1887 he joined with Aaron Wise and Gustav Gottheil to protest the refusal of Dr. John Nagle, the director of the New York City Bureau of Vital Statistics, to recognize weddings performed by rabbis. Such ceremonies were, of course, "legal" under religious law, but the three prominent rabbis successfully demanded that civil authorities formally record Jewish weddings.[2]

Evidence that Jacobs was an "establishment rabbi" in Manhattan is confirmed in an 1886 *New York Times* story. The paper's anonymous reporter gushed over some "fashionable weddings" that had taken place in the city, including one conducted by Jacobs.[3]

In 1934 Stephen spoke with warmth about being Jacobs's "youthful mouthpiece" when he started his career at B'nai Jeshurun upon his return from Vienna in April 1893.[4] But that relationship did not last long because Wise's rabbinic mentor died a few months after Stephen arrived at the Madison Avenue congregation. In a rare action, after Jacobs's death, the congregation elected the well-spoken twenty-year-old Wise as its senior rabbi. While it was a signal honor for someone whose ordination was barely a year old, he had the difficult task of following a beloved rabbi who had served B'nai Jeshurun the previous nineteen years.

However, young Stephen impressed synagogue leaders with his already superb oratorical skills, and being the son of the esteemed Rabbi Aaron Wise solidified his selection as the spiritual leader of the congregation. Stephen served B'nai Jeshurun for seven years until 1900.

During that time Wise sharpened his sermonic talents, inaugurated many new programs within the congregation, including the establishment of a women's auxiliary society, as well as providing a myriad of social services for synagogue members. Wise invited Jewish scholars to speak at B'nai Jeshurun, and he encouraged younger members to increase their participation in congregational activities and religious services.

Stephen's studies at Columbia and Oxford Universities were challenging because during his seven years of thesis work, Wise also occupied an important high-profile congregational position in New York City that demanded time and attention. There were wedding ceremonies to perform, funeral services that required visitations to the bereaved family and long rides to cemeteries, preparing young boys for Bar Mitzvah services, writing Sabbath and holiday sermons, providing time for pastoral counseling, engaging in community outreach to the fast-growing New York City Jewish population, and building positive relations with the Christian clergy. In fact, interreligious activity soon became a hallmark of Stephen's rabbinate. But the energetic Wise was able to do both tasks: leading a large and prestigious Manhattan congregation and completing his Columbia University doctoral studies.

Two unrelated events occurred during his first years as B'nai Jeshurun's senior rabbi that signaled Stephen Wise's emergence as a bold activist rabbi. In 1894 the wealthy John Jacob Astor IV (1864–1912) planned to build a large townhouse residence at East 65th Street and Fifth Avenue, a block away from B'nai Jeshurun. Astor also submitted plans to erect a stable for his private carriages and horses on a lot adjacent to the synagogue building.

Wise and his lay leadership opposed Astor's second plan, charging that a stable would create annoying human and animal noises and unpleasant equine odors that would waft into the synagogue edifice. A dozen neighbors joined Wise and the congregation in protesting Astor's plans, and the millionaire mogul was forced to abandon his efforts. Years later Astor drowned in 1912 when he was a passenger on the ill-fated maiden voyage of the *Titanic*.[5]

In a bit of historical irony, Astor's mansion was on the same site where years later in 1929 Temple Emanu-El, the nation's flagship Reform synagogue, erected its "cathedral-like" building: the largest Jewish house of worship in the world.

A second more serious event for Wise occurred in early 1895 when Brooklyn streetcar workers led by the Knights of Labor trade union went on strike demanding better working conditions, a ten-hour workday, and a daily wage of $2.25. The trolley company owners rejected the workers' demands and used their influence to mobilize the National Guard to quell the labor unrest.[6]

The strikers fought two National Guard brigades in the streets from January 14 until February 28. During that time, the then independent city of Brooklyn—it officially became part of the city of New York in 1898—was placed under martial law for the first time in history. The brigades fired upon the strikers, and two trolley workers were killed. The strike collapsed after six brutal weeks that featured bitter winter weather, armed attacks, and weak union leadership. The Brooklyn trolley strike plays an important role in Theodore Dreiser's (1871–1945) novel *Sister Carrie*:

> Idleness, however, and the sight of the company, backed by the police, triumphing, angered the men. They saw that each day more cars were going on, each day more the company officials were making declarations that the effective opposition of the strikers was broken. This put desperate thoughts in the minds of the men. Peaceful methods meant, they saw, that the companies would soon run all their cars and those who had complained would be forgotten. There was nothing so helpful to the companies as peaceful methods.
>
> All at once they blazed forth, and for a week there was storm and stress. Cars were assailed, men attacked, policemen struggled with, tracks torn up, and shots fired, until at last street fights and mob movements became frequent, and the city was invested with militia.[7]

B'nai Jeshurun's young rabbi supported the workers in their efforts to gain better working conditions and increased wages, an action that drew the ire of a prominent synagogue member who owned stock in the Brooklyn streetcar company. But Wise did not back down in face of the opposition within his congregation:

> I spoke on the evil of shooting down strikers who sought nothing more than the right to live decently and humanly. . . . After the service . . . the treasurer of the synagogue, a member of a banking and investment firm, approached me and asked: "What do you know about conditions in that street car strike in Brooklyn?" . . . I answered, . . . "They are grievously overworked and underpaid." He grumbled and muttered inarticulately and I seized on a moment's pause to say: "I shall continue to speak for the workers whenever I come to feel that they have a real grievance and a just cause."[8]

Both events, the proposed Astor stable and the streetcar strike, illustrate that the twenty-one-year-old Wise was not afraid to oppose the ultra-rich Astor, a pillar of the American financial community. Nor did he fear supporting striking streetcar workers even if it offended leading members of his synagogue. Taken together, Stephen Wise's early confrontations on public issues was a preview of what was to come in later years when he often battled with formidable opponents and supported a host of social justice issues.

B'nai Jeshurun's youthful senior rabbi soon established a daily work routine: he walked from the Wise family home at 119 East 65th Street to his Madison Avenue synagogue attired in a fashionable, well-tailored, dark "Prince Albert" suit. He spent weekday mornings in his office preparing sermons and other public speeches, coordinating the congregation's calendar of activities, dictating letters (he remained an active letter writer all his life), meeting with members of his flock, and often participating in outside community luncheons and programs. That was Stephen's primary "day job" as a rabbi even as he pursued his Columbia University doctoral studies.[9]

Stephen succeeded in following his father's dual academic path of gaining rabbinical ordination and earning a doctorate from a prominent university. But Aaron Wise did not live to see his son receive the Columbia Ph.D. degree. In a tragic parental loss that haunted Stephen the rest of his life, Aaron died of a heart attack on March 30, 1896, the second day of the festival of Passover. He was fifty-two years old and had served Congregation Rodeph Sholom for twenty-one years.

The *New York Times* coverage of his death described in detail how a suddenly ailing Aaron was forced to leave his congregation's holiday worship services at Lexington Avenue and East 63rd Street. The elder rabbi Wise walked the few blocks to his home on East 65th Street, where he rested and soon felt somewhat better. He then walked back to his synagogue, and once again

Aaron felt weak and uncomfortable. He retraced his steps to his home, where he collapsed and died.[10]

Rabbi Aaron Wise's funeral at Rodeph Sholom attracted a large number of rabbis from the New York City area. The service was led by two of the city's most prominent Reform rabbis, Gustav Gottheil of Temple Emanu-El and Kaufman Kohler of Temple Beth-El.[11] Four years later Gottheil and Kohler co-officiated at a much happier religious ceremony: the wedding of Stephen Wise and his bride, Louise Waterman (1874–1947). In 1903 Kohler, a towering intellectual and spiritual figure in the early years of Reform Judaism, was elected president of the Hebrew Union College in Cincinnati, succeeding Isaac Mayer Wise.

To no one's surprise, the leaders of Aaron's grieving congregation were interested in luring Stephen away from B'nai Jeshurun so he could "return home" as the rabbi of Rodeph Sholom. It was an opportunity to follow his father's rabbinic path, but the twenty-two-year-old rabbi overcame the temptation and wrote his reasons for not even accepting an invitation to be a guest speaker at Rodeph Sholom eight months after Aaron's death. Wise refused and wrote to Benjamin Blumenthal, the congregation's president:

> My earliest religious instruction I gained while a pupil in your school. . . . Rodeph Sholom has been my dearly beloved father's home for the larger part of my life. . . . It might appear to some that I was a candidate for the vacant position [if he were to accept the invitation to deliver a sermon] and for such a position I must refrain from affording the slightest basis.[12]

For the rest of his life, Stephen Wise always remembered the family conversations when his father described in vivid detail the centuries-old yearning and need for a physical return of the Jewish people to the land of Israel. He described Aaron Wise as an "ardent Zionist" even though he died in 1896, a year before Herzl convened the First Zionist Congress that marked the start of the modern movement. Stephen also recalled his childhood years when he collected money that he donated to the visitors from Ottoman-ruled Palestine who came to the Wise home in New York City to solicit funds for Jewish charities in the "Holy Land."

As noted earlier, following her rabbinic husband's death in 1881, Rachel Theresa Weisz, Stephen's paternal grandmother, moved from Erlau, Hungary, to live out her final years in Jerusalem. The reality of his grandmother leaving her home to reside in the Holy City had a profound impact upon Wise even though he never met her.

If Aaron and Rachel Theresa provided Stephen with the emotional fervor and the family history required to initiate a lifelong Zionist commitment,

Gustav and Richard Gottheil transmitted the academic, historical, and intellectual foundations for the movement that was to remain Stephen's lodestar his entire life.[13]

Although Richard chose the academic life as a Columbia University professor instead of the synagogue pulpit, he did inherit and share his father's strong belief in the Jewish return to Zion, the land of Israel, where as a distinct and independent people Jews would live their lives as a national entity and not solely as a religious community. The Gottheils were both strong Zionists in the years, even decades before Theodor Herzl, the charismatic founder of the modern Zionist movement, published his history-changing book, *Der Judenstaat* (*The Jewish State*) in 1896.

At the First Zionist Congress in 1897, Herzl emerged on the world stage armed with a bold statement of purpose: "Zionism seeks to secure for the Jewish people a publicly recognized, legally secured home in Palestine."[14]

Herzl electrified the "yearning masses"—the words of the Jewish poet Emma Lazarus (1849-1885) that are emblazoned on the Statue of Liberty pedestal in New York City's harbor—of persecuted Yiddish-speaking Jews in Eastern Europe. However, the Hungarian-born Viennese journalist's dramatic call combined with the fact that he was establishing a serious political movement to achieve his goal alarmed many Jewish leaders in the West, including the United States. But Israel Abrahams (1858–1925), a prominent English Jewish scholar, saw something else in Herzl's call for a Jewish state:

I hear that there is going to be a new outburst of Jewish Nationalism—based on the [anti-Semitic] Vienna incidents. This is at present a secret, but we have had an exciting visit from a leading man of letters of Austria [Theodor Herzl] and the thing is likely to be promulgated soon. I have little sympathy with it and yet when I remember what happened when Ezra took back the Exiles and how the world's religion was then fixed for centuries, who knows but that the Religion of the Future may be formulated once more in Zion?[15]

Inspired by Herzl's leadership, Richard Gottheil established the Federation of American Zionists (FAZ) in 1897 and became its first president, but the movement attracted few followers in the United States. However, Gottheil made a shrewd choice for the nascent organization's secretary: twenty-three-year-old Stephen Wise. The rabbi held that position for more than fifteen years and used it as a springboard to speak throughout America on his favorite subject. The position also enhanced his rising national reputation as a Jewish leader.

A year later, Gottheil founded Zeta Beta Tau (ZBT), a well-known Jewish college fraternity. ZBT first began as a student Zionist organization and the three letters, albeit in Greek, referred to the Hebrew prophet's words: *Tzion Bemishpat Tipadeh* (Zion shall be redeemed in justice).[16]

The Gottheils, pere et fils, were attacked for their views from two influential but significantly different elements within the Jewish community. Many Reform Jews, including some leading rabbis, were fearful that talk of a physical return to a "Jewish homeland" would raise the ancient canard of dual allegiance. They believed such a charge had the capacity to undermine and call into public question whether Jews were or could ever be loyal citizens of the United States, Britain, Canada, France, Germany, or any other country.[17]

The new Zionist movement created by Herzl was problematic for Reform Jews who were eager to integrate or assimilate into the general American culture and society. They argued that the Zionist movement in the United States, even if it attracted only a few followers—the actual situation in the years before World War I—threatened the security and status of the small, insecure American Jewish community.

In 1885, eleven years before Herzl burst upon the world stage with his call for a Jewish state, eighteen prominent Reform rabbis, headed by Isaac Mayer Wise and Kaufmann Kohler, met in Pittsburgh, Pennsylvania, and adopted a series of resolutions in an effort to define their progressive faith. Their efforts became known as the "Pittsburgh Platform," and it remained a key foundational statement for the Reform movement for a half-century until it was revised in 1937, forty years after the rise of modern Zionism and on the eve of World War II and the Holocaust. One of the planks in the platform included the following resolution:

> We consider ourselves no longer a nation, but a religious community, we, therefore, expect neither a return to Palestine . . . nor a sacrificial worship under the sons of Aaron, nor the restoration of any of the laws concerning a Jewish state.[18]

At the other end of the religious spectrum, Orthodox leaders also criticized Zionism because its efforts for a physical restoration of the Jewish people to their biblical homeland did not require God's divine intervention nor did the Zionist enterprise require the leadership of the longed-for and promised Messiah. For Orthodox Jews, Zionism may have been a Jewish movement in name and membership, but it was a program without God, an undertaking that lacked a religious foundation, and it did not follow halacha, the sacred body of Jewish religious laws of the Bible, and the Talmud. Halacha is the Hebrew term for "the way to travel or go."

Richard Gottheil has been called the "reluctant father of American Zionism" because of his quiet temperament and abhorrence of intraorganizational strife. However, Stephen Wise was neither quiet nor was he a person who avoided personal or professional clashes with rabbinic colleagues or other perceived adversaries. Richard, twelve years Stephen's senior, may have been a brilliant exponent of Zionism, but Wise was the inspirational warrior for the cause that was always seeking converts.

A life-changing moment for Wise occurred in 1898 while he was still working on his doctorate and serving as B'nai Jeshurun's rabbi: Gottheil selected him to be an American representative at the Second Zionist Congress in Basel. An excited Stephen sailed for Europe in August 1898 with his Columbia professor to attend the congress sessions as part of the three-person American delegation. It was there that Wise first met Herzl, and it was a life-changing event that transformed the young rabbi; its impact remained undiminished for the rest of Stephen's life.

In his autobiography, Wise described that encounter:

> I journeyed to Basle merely as a delegate to a conference. I returned home a lifetime servant of the cause in the name and for the sake of which the Congress was assembled. I caught the first glimpse of my people as a people, gathered from many lands, one and undivided, not in creed but in their human faith.
>
> This faith was that the tragic dispersal of Israel must end, that the miraculous survival of the Jewish people did not forever guarantee survival in an increasingly hostile world, and that the ancient home of Palestine could and must be rebuilt.
>
> We were united by the faith that despite partial dispersion in many parts of the world, the survival of the Jewish people and the revival of its creative genius could only come to pass in the land of ancient glory, which needed to be awakened from its centuries-old and enfeebling slumber.[19]

Those words, written in 1948 just months after the creation of the modern state of Israel, represent a cogent summation of Stephen Wise's lifelong commitment to Zionism. His participation in the Zionist congress was his first encounter with Jews who were unlike himself and his family. Until then, Stephen had known mostly Jews from Western and Central Europe. In Basel he met representatives of the millions of Yiddish-speaking Jews living in Eastern Europe under wretched political, economic, and social conditions, many of them feeling the sting of Tsar Alexander III's post-1881 "May Laws."[20]

Wise would later write,

> I have always regretted and have been not a little ashamed that I barely knew or even touched the life of . . . the eastern European Jews. . . . My contacts with these as a child and youth were few and limited, though I came to know their children in connection with the work of the Hebrew Free School

Association and the Educational Alliance. . . . My personal relationships with
Jews had been largely limited . . . to the middle-class ghetto of New York.[21]

At the congress, Wise heard Herzl attack rabbinic opponents of Zionism:

Until now we have refused out of brotherly consideration to bring this contrast
to the fore. We can no longer stand by while agitation against Zion is carried
out on the Jewish religious communities. It is an impossible, contradictory situation, and we must put an end to it. Wherever the leaders of the communities
are not with us, there must begin a fight for elections. Men who have the standing and the capacity to occupy these honorable posts, and who are at one with
us and our views, must be elected to the leadership, and inducted into our centers in the name of our national idea. The authority of the religious community, the means which it commands, and the persons who constitute it, must
not be directed against the aspirations of the people. . . . Our next objective is
therefore the conquest of the communities.[22]

Those words became Stephen Wise's marching orders: his lifelong goal was
the Zionist "conquest of the communities." Within a month of his return to
the United States from the congress, he expressed gratitude to one of his first
"conquests," Thomas Davidson:

Let me thank you for your sympathetic lines concerning the great Zionist
cause, which is so dear to the hearts of all of us. . . . Nothing but good can
[come] to the Jewish people of all lands. . . . Concerning this, however, and
kindred Zionist affairs, I hope to have an opportunity to chat with you in the
future.[23]

The 1898 Zionist congress transformed Wise in another significant way:

I was a Jew by faith up to the day of the Congress in Basle and little more. At
Basle I became a Jew in every sense of that term. Judaism ceased to be a type of
religious worship. The Jewish people became my own.[24]

It is also striking that from the outset of his Zionist odyssey, Stephen was
always committed to the land of Israel (Palestine). But by 1902 Herzl recognized that the Turkish sultan opposed the idea of a sovereign Jewish state in
the Ottoman Empire's province of Palestine.
    As a result, a despairing Herzl, suffering chronic serious heart problems,
investigated the idea of locating a "Jewish state" in some other part of the
world, including the British government's proposal of the East African Guas

Ngishu plateau near Nairobi in Kenya, an area then under London's control. It was a trial balloon floated by Joseph Chamberlain (1836–1914), Britain's colonial secretary. Such an idea—a Jewish state in Africa—appeared to resonate with Herzl because of several events of the 1880s and 1890s: the Russian tsar's anti-Jewish policies, the anti-Semitic Dreyfus affair in France, and Karl Lueger's election as Vienna's mayor. The ill Zionist leader was desperate to secure a safe haven, any place, for the endangered Jewish people.

Herzl and several of his key associates expressed pleasure that a major world power accepted the concept of a Jewish state, although there is evidence that he always saw the East Africa plan as only a tactical diplomatic move; Herzl's ultimate goal remained the land of Israel.

But none of this mattered because the Guas Ngishu proposal was rejected at the Sixth Zionist Congress in 1903. Gottheil and twenty-five-year-old Martin Buber (1878–1965), who later became a world-famous philosopher, were among the delegates who voted "no."[25] When a new colonial secretary succeeded Chamberlain a year later, the London government scrapped the earlier proposal. Following Herzl's death in July 1904 at age forty-four, neither the Zionist movement nor Stephen Wise ever contemplated any other location for Jewish independence. It was always the biblical homeland and nowhere else.[26]

Despite agreement on that central issue, modern Zionism was never a unified movement. Herzl and Wise represented what is called "political Zionism" and its central focus on the creation of an independent "Judenstaat," a state for the Jewish people. Louis Lipsky (1876–1963), an American Zionist leader who worked with Wise for many years, noted that Stephen "was never able to rid himself of the overwhelming influence of Theodor Herzl and the prejudices of that early [Zionist] period."[27]

There were many expressions of Zionism, including political, religious, labor socialist, Marxist, and cultural. The various Zionist streams had articulate theoreticians, gifted leaders, and committed followers. But like many other national liberation movements, there never was "one" agreed-upon expression of Zionism. As a result, Zionist history is filled acrimonious intramovement fights and disputes.

Wise always remained a convinced political Zionist and was critical of other forms of the movement. He attacked the concept of "cultural or spiritual Zionism" expressed by the East European writer Ahad ha-Am, "One of the People," the nom de plume for Asher Ginsberg (1856–1927). The centerpiece of the latter's thinking was the creation of a spiritual and cultural center of the Jewish people that included the rebirth of Hebrew as a living language and the recrudescence of new literature, drama, music, philosophy, religious thought, and poetry all springing forth from the land of Israel. Because Ahad ha-Am

opposed political Zionism and its demand for a state, he became Herzl's foremost Zionist adversary.

Wise's reaction to Ahad Ha-Am's was withering. Lipsky wrote,

> He regarded the spiritual Zionism of Ahad Ha-Am as a form of opiate for the
> Jewish masses, which would keep them in the bondage of a culture that never
> would lead to political rebirth.[28]

Nor was Wise committed to a utopian, Tolstoy-like "labor Zionism" that
was celebrated by Aaron David Gordon (1856–1922), who expressed exulta-
tion when he witnessed the Jewish people striking its "roots deep into the life-
giving substances and to stretch out in . . . the sunlight of our homeland. . . .
[It] is the force attracting all the scattered cells of the people to unite into one
living national organism."[29]

Wise was not an advocate of Ber Bordochov's (1881–1917) Marxist ratio-
nale and foundation for Zionism—one that called for a "proletariat Zionism"
and defined Jewish nationalism as "among the progressive elements of oppressed nations."[30]

Wise also rejected the "religious Zionism" of the influential Abraham Isaac
Kook (1865–1935), a chief rabbi of the land of Israel. Kook taught that Zionism
was part of the ultimate unfolding redemption of the Jewish people, an event
that would hasten the arrival of the Messiah on earth.[31]

Wise was aware of all these streams of Zionism, but he always remained a
faithful disciple of Herzl. Wise commanded respect, if not agreement, for his
"pure" political Zionism that was devoid of subtle nuances and various doctrinal positions.

In years before 1914 and the outbreak of World War I, years of growing
manifestations of anti-Semitism in Europe, Zionism had to compete with several other Jewish movements that all vied for prominence, dominance, and of
course, membership. Some Jews supported socialism while others emphasized
Orthodox Judaism; others pressed for a Yiddish speaking antireligious secular
culture. Still other people opted for autonomous areas of Jewish nationalism
outside of the land of Israel. But it was Zionism, even with its many competing
forms, that emerged as the dominant national liberation movement of the
Jewish people.

Following his return from the 1898 Basel congress and his meeting with
Herzl, Wise set out to conquer the communities by attracting reticent rabbis
to Zionism. In 1899 he began a correspondence with Rabbi Max Heller (1860–
1929) of Temple Sinai in New Orleans, Louisiana. At the time Heller was the
best-known and most influential Jewish religious leader in the American
South. He was born in Prague and came to Chicago when he was seventeen.

Heller soon embarked on a rabbinic career and was ordained by Isaac Mayer Wise in 1884 as a member of HUC's second class of rabbinical students. Heller later taught Jewish studies at Tulane University and was elected the president of the Central Conference of American Rabbis in 1910. He was a dominant figure in the American rabbinate and someone who merited Stephen Wise's attention. In 1899 he wrote to the New Orleans rabbi,

> Let me thank you at the outset for your kindness in sending me your fine sermon on Zionism. I wish that all our opponents were as reverent and respectful and as earnest as you are. . . . I wish to Heaven you could be with us [in the Zionist movement], as I know you would like to be, and I some how feel that we yet shall have your valued co-operation and support. I think that failure is impossible, but even if failure were certain, and certain failure in a just and glorious cause is better than passive indifference and the cowardly lethargy of millions of the world's Jewry today.[32]

In time, Heller, the quintessential southern Reform rabbi, did, in fact, become Wise's ally in the Zionist movement and within the Reform rabbinate. Heller was Wise's first rabbinic "conquest." But in 1900 Stephen was about to make two other conquests: one personal and the other professional.

Chapter 4

Stephen Gains a New Job and a Bride

After the Second Zionist Congress ended, an inspired but restless Stephen Wise returned to his more mundane work as the spiritual leader of a prominent New York City synagogue, and he also resumed his quest for a Columbia University doctorate. Both activities were a letdown after the heady days in Basel when Stephen met Herzl and other Zionist leaders. But less than five months after the conclusion of the congress, Stephen's life was permanently changed; it was no longer mundane or routine.

In January 1899 a B'nai Jeshurun member died, and Louise Waterman, a twenty-five-year-old cousin of the deceased was the grieving family's designated representative chosen to inform the rabbi of the loss. She walked the three short blocks from her East 68th Street home to the Wise residence on East 65th Street where Stephen lived with Sabine, his widowed mother. As Louise began discussing the funeral plans, Wise was attracted to the young, intelligent woman, and it did not take long before he began an active courtship.

Louise grew up in a quintessential German Jewish family of that era. The Wassermans were from Bavaria, and Sigmund (1819–1899), one of three talented brothers, arrived in the United States and first settled in New Haven, Connecticut, during the 1840s. Like many other immigrants, the family's European-sounding last name was Anglicized and became "Waterman."[1]

Sigmund was a Renaissance man: he wrote poetry and was a professor of German literature at Yale, the first Jew to teach at that university. In 1848 he graduated from Yale's Medical School, also the first Jew to do so. After moving to New York City, Sigmund served as a police surgeon for thirty years, and he became a urology instructor at the City College of New York's Medical School. Sigmund also established a Jewish home for the aged, where he served as its medical director.[2]

In time, Sigmund's two brothers, Leopold (1821?–1854) and Julius (1825–1897), left Germany and also settled in New Haven. The former soon became an affluent businessman, but his life ended in 1854 during a transatlantic voyage to Europe when his ship, the *Albany Atlas*, collided with another vessel and sank near Newfoundland.

During his years in New Haven, Leopold was a leader in the Jewish and general communities of the city.[3] He was the first president of Congregation Mishkan Israel, Connecticut's oldest synagogue, which was founded in 1840. Contemporaries described him as "a most excellent young man . . . [with] a devotedly affectionate family."[4]

In 1847 Julius Waterman moved to New York City and began a successful business with his brother-in-law: their company manufactured women's corsets and hoop skirts. Louise, his third child and second daughter, was born in 1874 when Julius was forty-nine years old. Her older siblings were Leopold, named in memory of her deceased uncle, and Jennie.

Julius's wife, Justine Mayer, was also German-born, and the Waterman couple represented a high form of *Bildung*, a German term for education and culture. Louise's New York City childhood home was filled with books and music, and the young girl became fluent in several languages, including German and French. Her mother transmitted and personified a quest for beauty, truth, and the need for a purposeful life.

Louise was educated at the Comstock School in Manhattan, a fashionable finishing school of the time. Edith Carow (1861–1948), the wife of President Theodore Roosevelt, also attended Comstock, as did other daughters of the Gilded Age's elite families. At the school, Louise excelled in music and art in addition to an academic curriculum that did not include courses in science or mathematics—subjects that were considered off limits or too difficult for females. Years later Louise painted a portrait of Stephen Wise that today hangs in the Library of the Hebrew Union College–Jewish Institute of Religion in New York City.[5]

Louise was knowledgeable about the writings of many authors, including Charles Darwin, Herbert Spencer, and Thomas Huxley. Her personal library contained works by James Russell Lowell, Matthew Arnold, and Guy de Maupassant. Stephen had found his intellectual soul mate.

In that long-ago era when she first met her future husband, Louise Waterman at age twenty-five was already considered an "old maid," and Leo and Jennie, her older siblings, expressed concern about their young sister's delay in marrying. But Louise was no stay-at-home spinster waiting for the proper suitor to call. As an educated and sophisticated woman, Louise attended a myriad of musical recitals, dramas, and other cultural and social events in New York City.[6]

Louise was attracted to the philosophical lectures of Felix Adler (1851–1933), the founder and leader of the New York City Ethical Culture Society; in fact, she became a faithful devotee of Adler's humanist teachings. Although

Young Louise Waterman, c. 1877. Permission granted by the Stephen Wise Free Synagogue
Archives.

Julius and Justine Waterman had years earlier joined Temple Emanu-El, even
the ultraliberal version of Judaism offered at that Reform synagogue did not
meet Louise's spiritual and emotional needs or those of her parents.

Because of her involvement with the Ethical Culture Society, Louise offered art instruction to youngsters in settlement houses and she worked with
other society members to improve the wretched living conditions in the New

York City's tenement slums. In addition to her Ethical Culture involvement, Louise also attended an Episcopal church's Sunday school classes.[7]

Julius Waterman was a longtime widower when he died in 1897 at age seventy-two. Although Louise became an orphan in her early twenties, she was financially secure in an affluent and protective family that called upon Felix Adler and not Emanu-El's rabbi to conduct Julius's funeral at the Waterman home.[8]

Devoting some attention to Adler is important for several reasons. He shaped many of Louise's lifelong values, ideas about general society, and commitment to humane liberal causes. Although a quarter century older than Stephen Wise, Felix's teaching, preaching, and assertive advocacy on a series of public issues offered examples for the young rabbi to follow. Both Felix and Stephen were sons and grandsons of European rabbis, both received undergraduate degrees from Columbia University, both earned Ph.D. degrees, and the two men each became renowned religious leaders.

Felix was the founder of the Ethical Culture Society, and Stephen was a public champion of Zionism, a prominent advocate of Reform Judaism, and the founder of the Free Synagogue movement. Adler never became a Zionist, even though his brother-in-law was US Supreme Court justice Louis Dembitz Brandeis (1856–1941), who played a leading role in the American Zionist movement and in the life of Stephen Wise.

While Felix and Stephen traveled on different religious pathways, neither Wise nor his wife ever broke off their friendship with the rabbi's son who rejected Judaism and separated himself from the Jewish people. In an interesting historical coincidence, both the Ethical Culture headquarters building and the Stephen Wise Free Synagogue are today located only four blocks apart near Central Park on Manhattan's Upper West Side.

Felix was the son of Samuel Adler (1809–1891), a prominent Reform rabbi who served New York City's Temple Emanu-El between 1857 and his retirement in 1874. Felix was born in Germany and arrived in the United States with his family at the age of six when his father became Emanu-El's rabbi. After graduating from Columbia University in 1870, he returned to Germany for rabbinical studies at the Berlin *Hochschule fur die Wissenschaft des Judentums* (Academy for the Scientific Study of Judaism) while also pursuing graduate work in Semitics at the University of Heidelberg, where he received his Ph.D. degree summa cum laude in 1873.

But Felix soon discovered he did not believe in the traditional God of Israel who gave the Torah to Moses at Mount Sinai. Indeed, he rejected any concept of the divine and instead became a champion of Immanuel Kant's (1724–1804) moral philosophy and Ralph Waldo Emerson's (1803–1882) transcendentalism. Felix's strong humanist rationalism, devoid of a God concept, convinced him he could not continue his rabbinical studies.

However, following his return from Germany to the United States, Temple
Emanu-El's leaders asked Felix to deliver a guest sermon, a request that was
probably arranged by his father with the hope his son would succeed him as
the congregation's rabbi. Felix accepted the invitation and chose the alluring
title, "The Future of Judaism." In that address on October 11, 1873 (the first
and only time he spoke at Emanu-El), twenty-two-year-old Felix presented a
neo-Kantian humanistic view of religion, but he never once mentioned the
name of God. Congregational members were shocked, and young Adler was
never invited back to speak at the world-famous congregation.

But Samuel Adler's friends were able to fund a Cornell University teaching
position for their rabbi's religiously rebellious son. Felix taught Hebrew literature and "Oriental" (an arcane name for the Middle East) Studies in Ithaca,
New York, for three years, but in 1876, his atheism was considered too radical,
even dangerous for his students. Cornell officials no longer accepted the
Emanu-El financial grant, and young Adler was compelled to leave the uni-
versity. A year later, in February 1877 Felix established the Ethical Culture
Society that was founded on his humanistic approach to religion and society.
In 1902 Adler became a professor of political and social ethics at Columbia
University, a position he held until his death.[9]

Adler stressed the rights of women, the poor, labor, and children and the society was active in providing free kindergartens and nursing services. It pressed
for the improvement of housing in New York City. In 1928 the society created
the Fieldston School, which has remained a prestigious NYC private school.

Adler's Ethical Culture Society did not discard the external form of a conventional house of worship. At the society (congregation), Felix inaugurated
Sunday assemblies (services) where as rector or senior leader (clergyperson) he
delivered messages (sermons) that featured his nontheistic concepts of moral
philosophy and religion that stressed "deed before creed." In time, Felix attracted a membership that included Jews like the Watermans who were either
unable or unwilling to accept the religious beliefs of their ancestral faith.

The New York City society was primarily a humanistic extension of German
Reform Judaism and the societies established in other American cities that
were humanistic extensions of liberal German Protestantism.

A prime example of Felix Adler's break with the religious beliefs of his father came in 1885 following the publication of the Pittsburgh Platform, a set of
radical principles that was endorsed by nearly twenty leading Reform rabbis of
the time—all colleagues of Rabbi Samuel Adler. Felix had little trouble with
the platform's statement that rejected a Jewish return to Zion.

However, Adler was critical of the rest of the platform despite its wholesale
jettisoning of traditional Judaism. As an example, the Reform rabbis meeting
in Pittsburgh stressed the centrality of God and the Bible in Jewish life, but not

the Talmud. The platform rejected the kosher dietary laws, specific Jewish dress, and many rituals, and it saluted—indeed, embraced—modernity and rationalism. It also repudiated the Jewish belief in the resurrection of the body and affirmed the "modern discoveries of scientific research."[10]

Felix Adler offered an acerbic response to the Pittsburgh Platform:

> Why did the gentlemen not go all the way [as they had done in leaving the Jewish people and Judaism] and declare themselves to be Unitarians? They were right in that they began to sever the ties with the past, but they did not go far enough. Join me.[11]

It is understandable that Adler's split from the Jewish religion drew criticism from rabbis who labeled the Ethical Culture leader a traitor who merited only opprobrium. Kohler criticized Adler for eliminating a religious foundation for ethical behavior. Adler denigrated traditional religion as a form of human poetry, but Kohler disagreed:

> The rock of human conscience is not firm enough to build society upon it, unless it is, as religion shows it to be, founded upon a divine will re-echoed in the heart of man.[12]

But despite the attacks from many Reform rabbis, Stephen Wise was not one of Felix's detractors. In an 1899 letter to Louise, her future husband wrote,

> I was privileged to spend half an hour with [your] Professor Adler yesterday. How great a man! Why did we ever lose him? Such power, such strength, and withal such simplicity.[13]

When she first met Stephen Wise, it appeared that the brilliant and talented Louise Waterman was following Felix Adler's call by severing the ties that linked her to Jews and Judaism. But as we shall see, once she married the man who became "Rabbi USA," Louise developed into the "First Lady" of American Judaism, and in the 1930s and 1940s she was often called the "Jewish Eleanor Roosevelt" because of her charitable activities and leadership of many philanthropic organizations.

Although Louise and Stephen married less than two years after they first met, it was a difficult and sometimes long-distance courtship. Louise's siblings, Leo and Jennie, expressed doubts about Stephen's suitability as a husband for their young sister. Wise's roots were Hungarian and not Bavarian German like the Watermans. In addition, he was a rabbi, not a profession likely to provide economic security for their sister, and perhaps worst of all, Stephen Wise was an avowed Zionist, an unpopular movement that threatened, even undermined, the status of upper-class German American Jews like Leopold and Jennie.[14]

Thirty years earlier, the irate Baron Fischer in Budapest had sent his daughter Sabine on a long trip to escape and "forget" the handsome Aaron Wise; so, too, Louise was forced to spend the summer of 1899 far away from New York City. She went on an extended European "vacation," thousands of miles from Stephen Wise, the charismatic young rabbi. Just as such extreme measures failed to smother or end the romance between Sabine and Aaron, so a European tour failed to dissuade Louise and Stephen.

Before Louise departed New York City for her summer travels in Europe, Stephen gave her a decorative piece of jewelry in the shape of a six-pointed Star of David. The gold medallion contained the four Hebrew letters for "Zion." Many years later, Justine Wise Polier, the daughter of Louise and Stephen, recounted that her mother, in an act of defiance, wore the jewelry at social and cultural events despite her family's objections.[15] Stephen was delighted that Louise wore "the little pin" in public:

> You can never know what that meant to me. From the outset, you deeply sympathized with the aims and purposes of Zionism; aye, even before we met, you confessed you oft wondered at the "suffering of our people—if we could only help them." The little pin you have worn, subjecting yourself to a thousand questions and taunts and sneers, and worse for my sake, for the sake of what was dear and sacred to us both.[16]

Louise's rabbinic suitor was a master of the English language, and in an age of limited telephone and telegram service and no e-mail, texting, or other technological means of direct communication, Stephen wrote a huge number of love letters to Louise that are filled with numerous literary and historical references. Reading them today more than a century after they were first composed at the turn of the twentieth century, one is struck by the respect, diffidence, courtesy, but also by the unmistakable passion and tenderness in Stephen's words to his future bride.

A few years after the death of their parents, James Waterman Wise and Justine Wise Polier published much of Wise's personal correspondence written between 1899 and his death in 1949. Included in the volume are sixty-two printed pages of letters that Stephen wrote to Louise during the twenty-two-month courtship period before the couple was married.

In the volume's first entry, a diffident Stephen wrote,

> I find that I shall be busy giving (or hearing) a lecture every evening next week. May I, therefore, come in late in the afternoon? I shall not name a day, and, if I fail to find you in, will try again the following day. I may even IF I MAY, come

in to see you "at work" in your studio in the morning—I believe that artists are fondest of the morning light—and promise not to detain you for more than ten or fifteen minutes.[17]

A year later Stephen wonders about the durability of their love for one another:

I know, Louise, it may and has been said that prudence and wisdom should not be permitted to intrude into the world of enchantment and ideals. Still, inasmuch as we are considering the most sacred thing in life, it behooves us to ponder well,—I, for my part reverently and gratefully. I have asked myself ten thousand times, will I always love and adore you as at this time?[18]

There was, however, a reason for the extraordinary number of letters that Stephen sent to Louise. Between January 1899 when the couple first met and their wedding day on November 14, 1900, Louise and Stephen were sometimes separated from one another for weeks and even months at a time. This was true during the summer of 1899 when her two worried siblings dispatched Louise to Europe in a futile effort to end their sister's romance with the rabbi.

During the same summer, Stephen traveled throughout the United States in his emerging role as America's leading public proponent of Zionism. He was eager to answer Herzl's call to "conquer the communities" for the movement. In his flow of letters to Louise, it is clear that Stephen enjoyed the adulation and praise he received from his applauding and adoring audiences.

Stephen was on the road explaining and extolling Herzlian Zionism to appreciative listeners in California, New Jersey, Minnesota, Montana, Washington State, and Oregon. Wise was well received everywhere he spoke, but in Portland, Oregon, leaders of Reform Congregation Beth Israel were especially impressed by the dynamic young rabbi.

Founded in 1858, it was the city's establishment synagogue, and in the mid-1880s Beth Israel's prosperous members constructed a large edifice at SW 12th and Main Streets in Portland. The structure, the second in Beth Israel's history, was a Moorish-style building with two tall towers that became a familiar part of the city's skyline. The house of worship was similar in appearance to the Central Synagogue sanctuary in New York City and the Dohanay Street congregation in Budapest.[19]

The Portland synagogue was a huge building, with seating for 750 people, massive side windows, and a ceiling height of fifty-two feet; it was the largest religious space in the city. A feature of the sanctuary was a large rose window in honor of Portland, the City of Roses. A fire set by an arsonist destroyed the Beth Israel building in 1923, and a new synagogue building that is still in use was dedicated five years later.[20]

In a unanimous vote on July 30, 1899, that was followed by an official letter to Stephen, the congregation offered him a five-year contract. His salary would be $5,000 a year (the equivalent today of about $135,000) and Wise would be free to participate in his many extracongregational public activities, including the support of Zionism and progressive political causes. In addition, the contract also stipulated a two-month summer vacation for the rabbi.

Beth Israel's invitation to Wise was fulsome in both praise and anticipation:

> We have known of you for some years as a gentleman of highest standing . . . as well as a man of well-known piety, of learning and of eloquence. . . . With God's blessing, we feel sure, that during the five years of your ministration among us, [Beth Israel] will make such advances as will easily make it the leading congregation on this western coast.[21]

Stephen received the letter while he was in San Francisco with his mother visiting his brother Otto, a leading attorney in that city. On August 2 Stephen replied to the Portland congregation indicating that before he could make any decision he needed to consult with family and friends as well as informing the leaders of his New York City congregation of the invitation to serve in Oregon.

But in a separate private letter to Solomon Hirsch, the Portland congregational president, written on the same day, Wise was quite clear and most positive:

> If God spares me, I am fully and finally resolved to make my future home in Portland. I have considered the matter in its every bearing and now the feeling is become mine that in undertaking to labor among the Jewish residents of Portland, I shall be doing that to which the hand of God points as my nearest and holiest duty.[22]

The German-born Hirsch (1839–1902), a former US ambassador to Turkey and a former president of the Oregon State Senate, was eager to hire Wise, but he understood the diplomatic steps required before Stephen could leave B'nai Jeshurun in New York City and move three thousand miles to assume a new rabbinic position.

Like many other aspects of Stephen Wise's life, questions remain about this period. In this case, why did he leave New York City with its large and growing Jewish population, a city that was becoming the financial and cultural center of America, and a city where he had family roots and personal memories? Why indeed, the move to far away Oregon?

Several letters of the period—to Louise Waterman, Richard Gottheil, and

Theodor Herzl—help explain Wise's dramatic and unexpected move from New York City to the Pacific Northwest. He wrote to Louise,

> Friends within and without the congregation at home have written and wired urging me to withhold my acceptance which I shall do until after my return to New York. . . . A great field of labor and opportunity awaits me in the North West. A number of cities within 500 miles of Portland have their Jewish communities, but no minister and nothing of religious teaching and striving. These I shall try to build up. It will be hard work, but I welcome it.[23]

A month after receiving the Beth Israel invitation, Wise wrote to Gottheil and offered an insight into why he was interested in Portland:

> If I do good hard conscientious work in Oregon, I shall not be wholly forgotten [in New York City]. . . . [Portland] is a good place and certainly more extensive and promising than the limited sphere in which I am now permitted to work . . . and I mean to study, because even though I cannot be a scholar, I wish to indulge my scholarly taste and read widely and deeply in Jewish and kindred lore. . . . The truth is I am absolutely resolved to leave New York and go to Portland.[24]

On November 28, 1899, Wise explained his transcontinental move to Herzl:

> I am to take up my residence at Portland, Oregon, which is on the Pacific Coast some 3,000 miles away, so you can see for yourself that I am beginning to travel eastward [toward Jerusalem], though in a roundabout fashion.
>
> One of the reasons which induced me to accept the very kind and flattering call . . . was the hope, as occasioned by my experience in the West, that I may be enabled to be of great service to our cause [Zionism] in the western part of our land. I really and truly believe that I shall be able to win many men for the movement, and also to gain much material help for the cause in the West.[25]

Although his family and friends warned about "burying himself so far from the center of Jewish life . . . He felt that he needed to know more of the United States than New York City if he was to serve his country and his people in the fullest sense."[26]

Even at age twenty-five Stephen Wise already perceived himself as a special kind of rabbi who was not content to simply be one of many well-known rabbis in a city that contained a major Jewish seminary (JTS), several prominent Reform and Conservative synagogues, and a growing number of Jewish scholars, many of them arriving from Eastern Europe. As a Manhattan rabbi,

Stephen saw himself as a big fish, but he recognized he was working in a giant Jewish pond.

In Oregon he would be an even bigger fish, but operating in a very small pond. There he would function as a frontier American rabbi who he would make certain would not be "wholly forgotten" back in New York City. By 1899 Wise's self-promotional skill with the press and the general public was already well honed, and during his six years in Portland he worked to strengthen his national reputation.

In New York City he had several professional and personal safety nets, but Wise wanted to be on his own as a rabbi in Portland. In Oregon he would not be known as Aaron's son or Richard Gottheil's student or the poor rabbi who had married into the wealthy Waterman family. But in Portland he would be flying solo as a rabbi and a new husband, and beginning in 1901 as a father.

But before he could move to the West Coast, he had to announce his plans to the leadership of his New York City congregation. On October 3, 1899—two months after he was offered the Portland position—Stephen wrote to the president and board of trustees of B'nai Jeshurun. The letter notified the congregation of his intention to move during the summer of 1900. Wise's formal language is similar in tone and substance to letters written by many other rabbis to conclude a congregational relationship:

> I had been honored with a unanimous call as rabbi of the Congregation Beth Israel, of Portland, Oregon [and] I would reserve my decision until October 1, inasmuch as I could not accept any call before I had conferred with my present congregation . . . I have given to this weighty and solemn subject my searching and prayerful deliberation, and have been led to the conclusion that it is my duty to accept the call . . . and enter upon the enlarged field of ministerial work which awaits me . . . [on] September 1, 1900. I trust that the good-will and kindness which you have shown to me . . . may be continued in the future.[27]

But a private letter written during the transition between Manhattan and Portland reveals that the relationship between Wise and his congregation had become strained after seven years. A letter to Louise described the frustration and tedium that sometimes arises between rabbis and their congregations:

> I have tried to be of some service to my people in the East [B'nai Jeshurun], and have not been afraid to work. It is probably my own fault but I have not reached and touched and kindled the hearts of the people, as the servant of the Lord must needs do, if he is to help them and uplift their lives. I wish to begin work all over again, in a new (religiously) untilled and unexplored land, and I am persuaded that with God's help and blessing, I shall be able to further the cause of Israel and spread the gospel of Zion.[28]

While Stephen Wise was eager to make the professional move to Portland, he needed the personal approval of his bride. He was somewhat concerned about her response to a marriage proposal that was linked to a transcontinental move. But the New York City–born and bred Louise Waterman consented to both requests: starting her marriage to Stephen by beginning a new phase of life as a rabbi's wife in Portland, Oregon, far away from the familiar Upper East Side of Manhattan, the Comstock School, the Ethical Culture Society, and her brother and sister.

Perhaps in a last-ditch effort to discredit Stephen's courtship efforts, Leo and Jennie Waterman requested Felix Adler to learn more about their sister's persistent suitor. Adler, like Stephen, had also attended a summer educational retreat at Thomas Davidson's Glenmore estate. Responding to Adler's request about Wise, the Scottish philosopher gave Stephen an extraordinary "report card" that Felix passed on to the Waterman family:

> The fact is, I am so fond of Stephen Wise personally, that I cannot, perhaps, be trusted to judge him impartially. I have known him for the past six years or seven years, and my respect and affection for him have grown all that time. He is loyal in his personal relations, and socially attractive. I cannot think of him doing a mean thing. When roused, he is an eloquent and powerful speaker, with a delightful sense of humor.
>
> His is still young—only twenty-seven, I think—and may have some of the faults of the young and inexperienced, delight in the sense of power and perhaps desire for popularity, though the last is not especially prominent.
>
> He is distinctly a stirring man, original and forcible, with great schemes in his mind. I always leave him with the sense that I have been facing a brisk, bracing wind.[29]

In July 1900 Louise and Stephen became engaged and set November 14 as their wedding day. For a jubilant Stephen, it was a new century, a new bride, a new rabbinic position in a new city, and soon a new doctorate degree.

By the time Wise had accepted the Portland position, he was a strong proponent of Reform Judaism and had moved away from the more traditional liturgy and rituals that were an integral part of B'nai Jeshurun. In 1900, perhaps as a parting shot, Wise wrote a letter to the New York City congregation's board asking to make some changes in public worship, a letter Stephen told Louise "was ignored" by the board:

> Some slight changes should be introduced in the Ritual now followed in our Synagogue . . . with your consent. . . . In my humble judgment [a rare expression for Wise], . . . a number of Prayers be printed . . . to be read in common by the Rabbi and Congregation. The worshippers merely listen now while the

minister recites the English Prayers. . . . I trust you will understand that any
intention of amending or curtailing the Hebrew portion of the Service is very
far removed from my mind. The traditional Prayers in the Hebrew tongue are
too sacred by reason of their content as well as their historical associations . . .
to be lightly altered or abbreviated.[30]

The letter is an insight in Wise's thinking about public worship. In
Portland he abandoned the traditional worship service and moved to a full
public expression of what he termed "Liberal Judaism." In New York City, a
defined form of public Judaism bound him, but once in the "untilled and unexplored land" of Oregon, Wise was free to cut loose from any connection
with Conservative Judaism's liturgy and ritual.

However, in his final days with B'nai Jeshurun, he kept his frustration in
check and delivered a moving farewell to the members of his congregation, a
speech that brought tears to the eyes of Thomas Davidson when he read
the text:

[Your address] contains sentences that Jeremiah might have been proud of.
You are of the stuff that he was made of, and your life will be immortal. . . .
New York will be poorer for your absence. . . . We shall follow your career with
the deepest interest. . . . You will not forget that Judaism, like all living things,
changes as it grows. . . . You will diffuse a twentieth-century Judaism, fitted to
meet the needs of the present day. . . . "Truth and righteousness" will be your
motto.[31]

It was the last communication Stephen received from Davidson. The
Glenmore retreat leader died on September 14, 1900, about ten days before his
prize pupil delivered his first High Holiday sermon in Portland. Wise was depressed when he heard of Davidson's death and wrote Louise,

I cried like a baby. I revered him. . . . He has been an influence for good in
many lives beside my own. . . . His death makes me think. Oh, the marvel and
mystery of it all. . . . I cannot bring myself to believe he is perished and gone
forever. . . . He was Heaven's own soldier, he wielded the sword of the Spirit.[32]

When Louise became engaged to Stephen, she agreed to move with him to
Portland. However, she insisted that he undertake his new duties in the Pacific
Northwest without her for a few months. Louise was concerned that Wise
needed time to adjust to his new responsibilities as a congregational leader before beginning his role as a husband. Stephen agreed, and he left for Portland
by train in time to officiate at the Jewish High Holiday services of Rosh

Hashanah (the New Year) that began in 1900 at sunset on September 23 and Yom Kippur (the Day of Atonement) that commenced on the evening of October 2.

Stephen's life almost ended on his long train ride from Manhattan to Portland. In Duluth, Minnesota, he experienced severe pain in the area of his stomach and appendix, but a determined Wise pressed on with his journey to Minneapolis, where he delivered an hourlong address on Zionism to an admiring audience. However, the pain became too extreme to ignore, and a physician who boarded Wise's train after departing Minnesota urged him to have the appendix removed at the Missoula, Montana, State Hospital.

Wise paid the three-dollar fee for the medical visit and consultation, and then journeyed eighteen more hours on the train until Stephen reached Helena, where a Dr. Tracy, after examining his rabbinic patient, "declared that an operation was not immediately necessary." Wise in a letter reassured his fiancée that he was "myself again." Dr. Tracy "thinks I am of good sound constitution, somewhat worn out (he doesn't know of incessant preaching, Ph.D. work, Zionism and—you.)"[33]

The Helena physician's diagnosis was correct: no surgery was required, and Stephen hinted at one probable cause of his discomfort and pain: overwork. It also seems possible Stephen Wise suffered a severe anxiety or panic attack once he was on the train heading west to take on new professional responsibilities in a frontier city far from the familiar surroundings of Manhattan and once he realized he would soon be married: two major changes for anyone in a very brief period of time.

By the time he reached Portland, Stephen Wise had regained his health and was warmly received by the leadership and members of Congregation Beth Israel. He was about to embark on a six-year sojourn in Portland that would earn him the unofficial and affectionate title of "Jewish bishop of Oregon," a label that Stephen loved even though it was religiously inaccurate.

Chapter 5

Westward Ho to Oregon!

After a yearlong flurry of private and public letters, a series of community announcements, various newspaper articles, and a mysterious perhaps psychosomatic illness that caused him extreme pain on the train ride between New York City and Oregon, twenty-six-year-old Stephen Wise arrived in Portland in the late summer of 1900. He was ready and fit to serve as Congregation Beth Israel's ninth rabbi as well as Theodor Herzl's Zionist advocate in America's Northwest.

Portland's US Census population in 1900 was 90,426, including about 2,000 Jewish residents. Ten years later its population had more than doubled to 207,214, and it was the third-largest city in the region, trailing only San Francisco and Denver. When Wise began his work at Congregation Beth Israel, the congregation numbered between eighty and ninety families, but under his leadership the congregation grew to over two hundred families.[1]

Like many other cities in the western United States, Jews were among the early settlers in Portland; some arrived during the 1849 Gold Rush era when Portland's business community engaged in extensive trade with the booming California economy. The city, founded in 1844, was blessed with an excellent transportation location on the Willamette River just a dozen miles from its outflow into the Columbia River that leads to the Pacific Ocean a hundred miles away.

Oregon gained statehood in 1859, and Portland's economic prosperity increased with the construction of deepwater docks and the 1883 arrival of the Great Northern transcontinental railroad that ran westward through Montana and Minnesota (the same rail line Stephen Wise traveled on from New York City). When Wise moved to Portland in 1900, fishing, canneries, lumber manufacturing, and train transportation were among the leading industries in the fast-growing Oregon city.

Among Portland's early residents were Caroline and Philip Selling, the first Jewish couple to be married in San Francisco. They moved to Portland in the midst of the Civil War with their ten-year-old son, Ben (1852–1931). The youngster grew up to become a prominent business leader and philanthropist in the city and the president of the Oregon State Senate. For a brief period, Selling served as acting governor when the elected chief executive became ill and could not perform his duties. The Selling Building in Portland, built in 1910, was designated a national historic landmark in 1991.

By 1915 Portland's Meier and Frank was the fourth-largest department store in the nation. It is noteworthy that five Jews have served as Portland's mayor, beginning with Bernard Goldsmith (1831–1901) in 1869. In recent years Vera Katz, whose family fled Nazi Germany, was mayor from 1992 until 2005.

Overt anti-Semitism existed in early Portland despite the fact that Central European Jews were among the city's first residents and were leaders in politics, commerce, and culture. In 1867 a club was founded as a "gentlemen's" association where the city's male leaders could eat and drink in a convivial private setting. Many political and business deals were struck within the club that excluded Jews for over a century and women as members for 123 years. It was called the Arlington Club. "Just how that christening occurred is a matter of longstanding speculation. Perhaps it was derived from old English nomenclature in which Arlington signified the 'finest' or 'highest.' "[2]

Responding to the anti-Semitic Arlington Club policy, in 1878, Portland's Jews established a similar facility: the Concordia Club. In New York City, because Jews were banned from the prestigious Union Club, they established the Harmonie Club in 1852. The German spelling has remained in its name. The Standard Club was created in 1861 to serve Chicago's Jewish "elites" who were banned from joining the older Christian-only clubs in the city.

In the New York City of 1900, Stephen's friends and family may have visualized Portland as a small Wild West village, a remote outpost of frontier America that did not merit or deserve the abilities of a brilliant young rabbi. Such a description was inaccurate except for the adjective "wild." At the beginning of the twentieth century, Portland was filled with brothels, gambling parlors, public drunkenness, political corruption, and many children and women working under horrible conditions in fish canneries, lumber mills, and other industrial locales.

But Stephen Wise soon discovered that Portland, unlike New York City, was a young city with little more than fifty years of community history. It was the ideal place for a charismatic rabbi to offer his congregation a strong dose of Reform Judaism, a fierce dedication to Zionism, and an assertive social justice agenda. Wise, eager for a fresh start as a congregational rabbi, requested that he work without a written contract. He wrote to Solomon Hirsch, the synagogue president,

I, for my part, feel assured that you will never ask anything, which is not just and reasonable, nor will I ever insist on anything, which is not just and reasonable, nor will I ever insist on anything which you cannot cheerfully concede to me. Our mutual relations are to be of too high and holy a nature to be brought within the stipulation of a contract. Unless we can work together in a spirit of mutual confidence and helpfulness, it will be impossible for us to promote the spiritual interests of the Congregation.[3]

But the synagogue leaders were concerned that Wise, perhaps unable to resist the strong pull of family, fiancée, and friends in New York City, would not honor his commitment to move to distant Portland. An oral agreement with their new rabbi would not suffice for the Beth Israel leaders, and they wrote to Wise indicating their opposition to a no-written-contract arrangement. Their letter offered both a carrot and a stick:

Our people look forward to your coming with more than ordinary interest and will certainly cooperate with you in every move looking toward the advancement of Judaism in this Northwest Country. While we are very desirous of meeting your views in every possible way, we fear circumstances prevent us from relieving either you or the congregation from signing the formal contract. . . . It has been the custom . . . to have a contract with the officiating rabbi. . . . While we have not consulted any lawyer, yet as practical men of affairs, the Trustees felt they give no subscriber [the people paying Wise's salary] a chance of refusing his payment through a legal quibble.[4]

Wise understood the situation, and in December 1899 he signed a one-page document that provided for a generous contract at twice the salary of Beth Israel's departing rabbi, Jacob Bloch (1846–1916). Most rabbis, then and now, would be happy with Wise's arrangements: an adequate salary, a two-month vacation each year, freedom to travel and accept outside speaking engagements (for Stephen that meant a continuation of his Zionist activities), and attendance at all synagogue board meetings dealing with liturgy, ritual, and education.

Unlike the more staid B'nai Jeshurun congregation in Manhattan, Beth Israel's members, many of them political, commercial, and cultural leaders of Portland, were open to Wise's radical views on religion and the social order. It helped that Solomon Hirsch and Ben Selling were among his chief supporters. Hirsch died in 1902, but by that time Wise had already established himself as an outspoken rabbi who believed that religion had a major role to play in shaping the values of the general society.

His rabbinic installation service on Friday evening, September 7, 1900, was well attended: "Everybody in town seemed to be at the Temple. All the

Christian clergymen and the foremost people of all creeds. It was an inspiring assemblage."[5]

Rabbi Bloch, who had served Beth Israel since 1884, delivered the installation service's opening prayer. In a letter to Louise, Stephen noted, "Dr. Bloch, who throughout has been acting with infinitely better grace than I expected, offered up a touching invocation."[6] While we have no record of Bloch's feelings that night, it must have been a sad, if not bitter moment for him. At age fifty-four, he was being replaced by a New York City wunderkind who was twenty-eight years younger. In addition, Beth Israel's leaders had soured on Bloch's rabbinic style, which they found to be "somewhat contentious."[7]

In a letter to his fiancée in New York City, a haughty and overconfident Wise was "quite certain that after a time it will be possible for me to induce the congregation to engage Dr. Bloch as my reader and assistant."[8] But it rarely works out that way in congregations, and Beth Israel was no exception. Bloch soon moved from Portland to become rabbi of Congregation Emanu-El in Spokane, Washington.

The West Coast's most prominent rabbi of the time, Rabbi Jacob Voorsanger (1852–1908) of San Francisco, delivered the installation address or "charge" for Wise. Like many of his Reform rabbinic colleagues of that era, the Dutch-born Voorsanger was a foe of the new Zionist movement. He called Herzl's ideas "perverted doctrines."[9]

But debating with an older rabbi about Zionism was not Wise's concern the night he assumed spiritual leadership of the Portland congregation.

In his inaugural sermon in Portland, Wise made clear what he wanted, or better, what he demanded as Beth Israel's rabbi:

> I name but one condition. I ask it as my right. You will and must allow it. You would not respect me if I should waive it for a single hour. This pulpit must be free! THIS PULPIT MUST BE FREE! Be my good angels and help me bear my burden. Our acts as angels are—I ask your lives, your works, your conduct, your character.[10]

When Stephen Wise uttered the strong words "This pulpit must be free!", "The congregation almost rose to its feet—I could feel it. . . . The people . . . liked the tone of my 'declaration of independence.' . . . The things had to be said—and I said them."[11]

Today, more than a century after Stephen's fiery sermon, the principle of a free pulpit is commonplace within most Jewish and Christian houses of worship. But it was always so in 1900 when many synagogues and churches required sermons and other clergy pronouncements to be vetted and approved by congregational officers or boards of trustees. Rabbis and ministers in many congregations were forbidden to speak out on contemporary political, economic, cultural, or social issues; rather, they were limited to liturgy, rituals, rites of passage, Bible readings, and public prayer. It was a system designed to control the clergy and to shield powerful members of a synagogue or church from public embarrassment or criticism because of their economic wealth or political status.

But any type of pulpit silence or prior approval of sermons was not a part of Stephen Wise's rabbinic DNA. He made certain his public speeches were never censored, and he insisted on total freedom to address a myriad of issues, whether as a rabbi in New York City or in Portland. Stephen, the son and grandson of forceful rabbis, and the spiritual child of Thomas Davidson and Adolf Jellinek, never consented to pulpit restraints or restrictions. However, Wise wanted to make that position clear in his first public speech in Portland, and he did.

Following his triumphal installation in early September, attendance at worship services increased before the onset of the Jewish High Holidays. The religious school enrollment soon showed a 66 percent increase.[12] In the run-up to Rosh Hashanah and Yom Kippur, Wise met and greeted hundreds of people during his first weeks in Portland:

> The reception was magnificent, 300 people or more—I was so tired after it was all over, and my poor arm from handshaking. . . . Some said, "Dr. Wise can say almost everything, for his people are hypnotized." The very hunger and yearning and receptivity of the people has quickened my sense of responsibility. What an opportunity for every form of service. I simply must rise to it.[13]

Wise was cured of the physical and psychological pain he had suffered only a few weeks earlier on the train ride to Portland. He was also liberated from being the rabbi of a large urban congregation—B'nai Jeshurun—that had historic, well-established, often-restrictive norms, standards, and practices that predated his arrival. Because his predecessor had lost favor with the congregation, Wise had a free hand in Portland. In Oregon, Stephen provided a preview of what was to come later when he returned to New York City in 1906 and established the Free Synagogue—an institution that always remained an extension and a creation of himself until his death in 1949.

But Stephen Wise had another important duty and responsibility in the autumn of 1900: his marriage to Louise Waterman. Following her request, Wise first traveled to Portland alone and devoted his extraordinary energy to establishing himself as the city's Jewish leader. But less than three months after arriving in Oregon, Stephen returned to Manhattan for his November 14 wedding date. A few days before the big event, Wise hastened to Tiffany's, the famous jewelry store, to purchase two gold wedding rings.

He had the numbers "30:12" inscribed on the inside of his bride's ring, a reference to Psalm 30:12: "Thou didst turn for me my mourning into dancing; Thou didst loose my sackcloth, and gird me with gladness." While the Psalmist is referring to God, Stephen perceived Louise as the one who helped him overcome the loss of his father four years earlier, and the same biblical sentiment could be applied to Louise, whose parents had died by the time she married. Sixty-two-year-old Sabine Fischer Wise was the only living parent of either the bride or the groom.[14]

The wedding ceremony, led by Rabbis Gustav Gottheil and Kaufmann Kohler, took place at the Upper East Side Waterman home in Manhattan, and the couple soon boarded a train for the ride westward to Portland. Unlike his earlier journey, on that trip Stephen did not suffer any physical illness or pain.

At the wedding, Kohler warned the new Mrs. Wise about her husband's zeal for Zionism; the Reform leader termed it a *meshugass*, Hebrew and Yiddish for "craziness or foolishness."[15]

Stephen and Louise Wise always considered the half dozen years in Portland—1900–1906—as the happiest time in their lives. Stephen accepted numerous invitations to speak, usually on Zionism, to various audiences throughout the Northwest as well as in Alaska.

Although Stephen had completed his formal Ph.D. work in July 1900, a month prior to his move to Portland, it was two years before Richard Gottheil published Wise's study of Ibn Gabirol in an issue of the Columbia University Press. In those years, publication of a thesis was an academic requirement for doctoral students. To achieve that final goal, Wise was forced to divert attention away from his new congregational duties in order to review not only his English language translation and essay but also the Hebrew and Arabic texts.

However, Stephen's primary task in Portland was to revive a lethargic and financially struggling synagogue. To maintain its fiscal stability, Beth Israel, like many other congregations of the time, sold sanctuary seats to its members as a means of raising needed funds. Similar to an opera house or a symphony hall, front-row seating fetched the highest prices. In the case of a synagogue, greater status was accorded to those who sat closest to the Holy Ark that contained the sacred Torah scrolls. Laypeople paid for this honor or privilege, but Wise ended such sanctuary sales; instead, he advocated free seating, and to the surprise of the wary Beth Israel board of trustees, more money was raised by voluntary contributions than by the old feudal system.

Because the growing Portland population numbered many single workingmen, including Jews, Wise established an associate membership class for unmarried males. Thanks to Stephen's assertive leadership, Beth Israel's debt was soon erased, and by 1903 the congregation had achieved a surplus.

Once in Portland, Wise abandoned all traditional prayer books, including the one he used during his tenure at B'nai Jeshurun, a siddur the congregation had published in 1889.[16] He introduced Beth Israel members to the Union Prayer Book (UPB) that was published in 1895 by the Central Conference of American Rabbis. The volume was intended to replace the various siddurim or Jewish prayer books then in use by Reform congregations.

The 1895 UPB remained a liturgical standard until revised editions were published in 1918 and 1940. The late nineteenth-century prayer book included Sabbath and holiday services, personal meditations, children's services, and selections from Jewish ethical teachings. It removed all references to a personal Messiah, a Jewish return to Zion, and the land of Israel, and it shortened the length of Sabbath and holiday services.[17]

The 1895 UPB was a radical departure from earlier prayer books and minimized congregational participation. The Reform prayer book included a large amount of English language liturgical material, retaining only the essential Hebrew prayers while utilizing stilted King James Bible English. The old UPB used the term "minister" rather than "rabbi" or "reader" to denote the leader of the service.

Wise's form of Reform Judaism minimized the use of many traditional rituals and focused instead on the teachings of the Hebrew prophets, including Isaiah, Jeremiah, and Micah. Stephen's son offered a description of his father's vocation:

His calling is the ministry, the Rabbinate as it is termed among Jews; a calling which he understands and interprets as one very close in spirit to that of the ancient prophetic fellowship of Israel. The Minister's function he does not conceive to be primarily either that of pastor or educator or interpreter of the law. . . . Most of all it is the prophet's function as a truth-speaker that appeals to Wise.[18]

Stephen Wise did not wear a tallith (prayer shawl) during religious services. Nor did he don a head covering either inside or outside the synagogue. Most photos of a youthful Stephen show him in a formal dark suit complete with a high white collar, somewhat similar to a clerical collar worn by many Christian priests and pastors. While Stephen did not advocate or maintain the kosher (Hebrew for "proper") dietary laws of Judaism, he did express concern to Louise about the menu of their wedding reception:

If you have a buffet at the reception—no oysters, no ham, no lobster or shrimp salad! [all forbidden food items] You need not have "Uneedo Matzos" [Wise's collective term for kosher food] etc., but something reasonably Jewish in their gastronomic affiliations. . . . I suppose I shall have to write to Jennie [Louise's sister and a co-host with her brother Leo for the Wise-Waterman wedding].[19]

Once Stephen's synagogue base was spiritually and financially secure, he moved into the rough-and-tumble of Portland's civic life. He soon pursued a public campaign opposing child labor excesses in Oregon, political corruption, prostitution, and gambling. Wise immersed himself in the civic life not only of Portland but the entire state of Oregon. His social action agenda, influenced by the Christian Social Gospel movement, was both welcomed and opposed by many of Portland's power elites, some of whom were members of his congregation.

Rabbi Stephen Wise was a potent combination of several extraordinary attributes: a commanding physical presence, a powerful speaking voice, a boundless supply of energy, an eloquent writing style, and an unwavering commitment to Zionism and the cause of social justice.

A primary focus of Wise's agenda was on the widespread prostitution and gambling in Portland. Wise joined members of Portland's Christian clergy in opposing an attempt to legalize both the "houses of ill repute" and gambling. In a letter to Gottheil describing his actions, Wise's used the term "Puritan," an odd self-description for a rabbi:

> I must have my farewell shot at those who are weeping and wailing because we Puritans dare to restrict (not abolish) the evils of gambling and prostitution. I mean to present the moral aspects of the whole problem—that's what I'm here for. . . . I feel the call to speak. I should despise myself as a coward if I remain silent.[20]

Stephen's sermons on civic virtue attracted large crowds to Beth Israel's services. In one sermon, Wise thundered, "There will always be scarlet women; that is just as long as there are scarlet men. . . . This cannot be; this must not be."[21]

Wise's influence on Portland was both public and powerful because

> as [a] rabbi in a relatively small city . . . I came in closer touch with the things out of which grew the lawless power of civic corruption. It was the union of gambling and liquor interests plus organized prostitution, which, in collusion with city officials and above all with the police department, poisoned and corroded the life of the city.[22]

A 1902 handbill in Portland advertising one of Wise's many lectures in the region captures the enthusiasm and excitement he generated just two years after arriving in Portland. Stephen was one of the lecturers in the Oregon Lecture Bureau, and translated into today's prices, the fifty-cent ticket equals about $6.50:

"The Gifts of Israel to the World"—A Great Lecture by Rabbi Stephen S. Wise . . . A Brilliant Orator. Considered one of the ablest speakers in the Pacific Northwest—This will be an unusual opportunity to hear a great speaker on an important subject—At the Methodist Episcopal Church, Wednesday Evening, May 6th . . . Admission 50c Children 25c.[23]

Just as Stephen was criticized during the Brooklyn trainmen's strike when he was B'nai Jeshurun's rabbi, similar complaints erupted in Portland as a result of Wise's vigorous attacks on a host of targets. Indeed, the leader of the illicit gambling interests in the Rose City met with Beth Israel president Solomon Hirsch and demanded that Wise end his public antigambling campaign. Hirsch, a skilled diplomat, replied that he would not attempt to suppress his rabbi. However, the former US minister to the Ottoman Empire is supposed to have replied, "I cannot and would not try to, but perhaps you can. Why not go and see him [Wise] and do what you can with him?" Hirsch's suggestion was never followed.[24]

However, Wise's public opposition to entrenched gambling interests resulted in a bizarre scene that could have appeared in one of the popular *Godfather* films. While relaxing in the steam heat of a Turkish bath, Stephen heard a voice in a nearby cubicle speaking about "Dr. Wise":

I could not help hear rather than overhear the raucous remark, "If I ever get near that son of a bitch I'll shoot holes through him." In view of the circumstances that I lay on a slab in a booth adjoining that from which these pleasant oaths had come, I did not linger unduly in the bath. I dressed and hastened to my home to congratulate my wife on the fact that the would be assassin carried no gun with him when he might conceivably have recognized me.[25]

Wise's commitment to social justice continued unabated during his Portland years. Just two years after assuming his rabbinic duties, Wise became the first vice president of the Oregon Conference of Charities and Corrections. The organization was part of a national federation of state groups that concentrated on the poor, prisons, orphanages, child adoptions, the status of American Indians, and other societal issues.

Wise was a guest speaker at the November 1905 meeting of the New York State Conference on Charities and Corrections held in Manhattan. In his plenary address, Stephen affirmed the need for an interreligious effort to alleviate human suffering:

[We need] the regulation of the public and the supervision of the private charities. . . . The deepest morality lies in the lessening of human sorrow, in the

abatement of human misery. The hand of divine fellowship extends to everyone who may be moved to participate in the serving and saving of man.[26]

In 1903 Oregon governor George Chamberlain (1854–1928), a Democrat,
appointed Wise to the State Child Labor Commission, where he served until
1906 when Stephen returned to New York City. Harry Lane (1855–1917), a
physician and a dedicated progressive, was elected Portland's mayor in 1905.
Lane asked Wise to join his cabinet, but Stephen refused the invitation, believing a rabbi's role is to "awake and guide and lead to the end that civic life be
clean and incorrupt."[27]

But the political bug did bite Wise in Oregon:

> I was mildly tempted to seek public office for the first time in the United States
> Senate when it was felt by some of the Democratic party bosses that the state of
> Oregon was ready to revolt against the longtime Republican dominance.[28]

Wise's refusal to seek elective public office may have been influenced by the
example of Nathan the prophet and his encounter with King David. Both men
lived around 1000 BCE in Jerusalem. In the biblical account (2 Samuel 2–17),
Nathan is angry that his monarch has broken God's law by committing adul-
tery with Bathsheba and arranging for the death of Uriah, her husband. Once
Uriah was killed, David married the pregnant and newly widowed Bathsheba.

Nathan confronted the king and told him a parable about a wealthy man
who maintained a large flock of sheep. However, that was not sufficient, and he
took a poor neighbor's precious sheep for his own. David was either unable or
unwilling to grasp the connection between the actions of the rich sheep owner
and his own immoral behavior. In fact, he became angry and asked Nathan
for the identity of the greedy man so he could mete out royal punishment
upon the wrongdoer. Nathan's answer to David's question has resounded
through the centuries whenever prophetic men and women speak truth to
power: "You are that man!"

Only then did David recognize his own sin (2 Samuel 12:7). Nathan assured
the king he would not die for his immorality, but the baby, conceived in sin,
would not live. The infant contracted a disease and died. However, David and
Bathsheba had another child, Solomon, who succeeded his father as the king of
Israel and constructed the Holy Temple in Jerusalem, an honor that was denied
to the adulterous David. The Israelite king's action was an early version of what
Voltaire (1694–1778) described in his 1762 comedy *Le Droit du Seignuer*: the
right of a lord to exercise sexual control and power over his subjects.

Wise understood that the role of clergy was to "to awake and guide and
lead to the end that civic life be clean and incorrupt."[29] But Stephen also
acknowledged,

To me neither religion nor politics was remote or sequestered from life. Religion is a vision or ideal of life. Politics is a method, or "modus vivendi." To say that the minster should not go into politics is to imply that ideal and reality are twain and alien. Politics is what it is because religion keeps out of it.

I am persuaded that the minister can get into politics without partisanship, without compromise. . . . One of the dangers of all of us is that we are willing to fight for justice for ourselves along forgetting that justice will be for all or none.[30]

For Wise the choice was clear: he would not leave the rabbinate to seek an elective public office. Another prominent Reform rabbi, Edgar F. Magnin (1890–1984) faced a somewhat similar choice: whether to abandon his prestigious rabbinic position at the Wilshire Boulevard Temple, the oldest synagogue in Los Angeles, and become a film actor at the famous Metro-Goldwyn-Mayer studios. The MGM chief, Louis B. Mayer (1884–1957), and a member of the temple, believed Magnin, the grandson of the California department store magnate Isaac Magnin, had the potential for a lucrative career in the film industry as an actor, producer, or screenwriter.

Magnin refused the offer and told Mayer, "I love you . . . but I'm going to be a rabbi for life. I'm not going to work for you for two weeks."[31] Magnin was correct: he officiated at Mayer's funeral in 1957 and served his Los Angeles congregation for sixty-nine years until his own death in 1984.

In 1904 US senator John Hipple Mitchell of Oregon (1835–1905) and US representative Julius Kahn of California (1861–1924), both Republicans, introduced a bill in Congress to restrict Chinese and Japanese immigration to America. The fact that Kahn was Jewish did not in any way deter Wise from attacking the proposed legislation. He believed it would

> deal with every Chinese as if he were a coolie or a criminal . . . I felt it my duty to take into the pulpit for consideration every problem of public life that involved a moral question.[32]

In 1905 Wise was a prominent speaker in Oregon during the centennial celebration of the historic Lewis and Clark Expedition. Stephen was fearful of American imperialism and expansionism following the nation's quick and easy military victory over Spain in 1898. Wise sounded a theme he was to come back to many times in his career. His flowery, cascading words were pure Stephen Wise, a blending of traditional American values yoked to progressive ideals:

> Ours is become a nation too great to offend the least, too mighty to be unjust to the weakest, too lofty to be ungenerous to the poorest and lowest . . . The

Young Rabbi Wise in Oregon, c. 1905. Permission granted by the Stephen Wise Free Synagogue Archives.

standards in a democracy are to be based not on money but manhood, not dissent but assent, not acquisition but aspiration, not color but character. Caste and Class cannot be suffered to endure in a democracy which must needs fall as these triumph, for by the class goes mass, high caste implies low caste, and caste spells outcaste. The American democracy is a democracy of brotherhood and brotherliness.[33]

Stephen's work in the American Northwest as a champion of progressive causes and Zionism did not go unnoticed.

From [Portland] spread the report of a rabbi patterned after the ancient prophets of Israel. Wise became known, not only in Portland, but throughout the country, as an eloquent preacher who used his talents with which he was richly endowed for the benefit of his fellow man.[34]

Even after Wise moved from Portland to New York City, his views on social justice still attracted attention on America's Pacific coast. In 1910 he

"Everywhere I turned, directors of foundling homes and other parents lectured me about how wrong it would be to adopt an unwanted child, born to a poor and uneducated mother. And everywhere I went the poor children clung to me, begging me to take them home, calling me 'Mama.' "

Louise Waterman Wise, 1916

Louise with her children Justine and James

Louise Waterman Wise with children, James and Justine, in a 1916 article on child adoption. Permission granted by the Stephen Wise Free Synagogue Archives.

publicly attacked civic corruption in New York City, and the entire text of his speech was printed in a San Francisco newspaper.[35]

Wise's work schedule was demanding. He was the rabbi of a growing congregation that required not only officiating at Sabbath and holiday services but also the pastoral duties of any clergyperson: visiting the ill, officiating at rites of passage that for a rabbi included ritual circumcisions and student Confirmation ceremonies, as well as weddings and funerals. Stephen's sermons were lengthy and demanded extensive preparation time. The birth of his two children and his role and responsibilities as a husband brought Wise great joy, but they also required the expenditure of time and energy.

Even as Stephen offered previews of his future work as the rabbi of New York City's Free Synagogue, so, too, Louise's interest in nursing and children was also a foretaste of her work when in 1916 she established the Louise Waterman Wise Adoption Agency in Manhattan that continued until 2010 when it became part of the Spence-Chapin Children's Agency.[36]

Louise's activities as a newly married rabbi's wife may have surprised members of her family in New York City. Far away from the protective hot-house environment of her German Jewish family, Louise became an activist in her own right while also supporting her husband's many causes and issues. Louise transferred what she had done in New York City as part of the Ethical Culture social welfare program she had learned from Felix Adler.

In Oregon, she raised funds for the first Visiting Nurse Association in Portland. But first she had to convince the city's poor women about the impor-tance of personal hygiene and pre- and postnatal care of their children. In ad-dition, she had to overcome the resistance of the city's "well-to-do citizens" who believed there were "not enough poor . . . to justify the work."

Louise wrote,

> The cry of pain does not reach their ears. . . . Let them read in the young wom-an's face, aged and wrinkled before her time . . . bowed and bent by the weight of care and illness . . . the anguish that might have been averted had they [Portland's gentry] but opened their eyes to see . . . their hearts to feel . . . stretched forth their hands to help.[37]

These were not the words or actions of a pampered, indifferent daughter of wealth who was unaware of systemic poverty in society, lack of adequate med-ical treatment for poor women, and the urgent need to address such issues. Yet she still had things to learn about being a rabbi's spouse:

> She was prepared neither by background nor temperament. . . . She had no deep Jewish inheritance or training. Once in fact, she nearly caused a minor catastrophe. Stephen had invited two very Orthodox rabbis for dinner and suggested that Louise should serve them fish. Just before they arrived she in-formed her husband that she had ordered scallops—a non-kosher seafood. Fortunately the last-minute information came in time so that Stephen was able to revise the menu![38]

Stephen Wise's service on the state Conference on Charities and Corrections, the Child Labor Commission, and his active participation in Oregon society in general was a major part of his personal and professional agenda. He was a young man in a hurry to advance his career as a nationally prominent rabbi, Zionist leader, and civic reformer as well as being a loving husband, father, brother, and son. In September 1903, three years after moving to Portland, the strong and seemingly emotionally secure Stephen Wise suffered a major collapse—an event that many people once termed a "nervous breakdown."

He took an extended leave from his duties and commitments in Oregon and spent much of the winter of 1903–1904 recuperating—not in New York City, but at the luxurious Traymore Hotel in Atlantic City, New Jersey. The hotel boasted 450 rooms, each with five separate faucets; two for hot and cold city water, two more for hot and cold ocean water, and a final spigot for ice water. The large, well-known hotel, located at Illinois Avenue and the Boardwalk, was razed in 1972.

A fatigued Wise wrote to a friend that even a brief walk on Atlantic City's famous Boardwalk was a tiring experience. His family and friends were worried that the twenty-nine-year-old rabbi had reached the end of his meteoric career, a casualty of too much work and pressure. But Stephen Wise recovered, and resumed his myriad of activities.

By 1906 Wise had enough self-confidence to denounce the prominent Rabbi Voorsanger, the man who had "installed" him six years earlier as Beth Israel's rabbi. Following the April 1906 earthquake that devastated San Francisco, the two rabbis clashed over a celebrated criminal case of the time, and it revealed Stephen's fearlessness in criticizing both a well-known rabbi and a powerful Jewish political boss.

Attorney Abraham Ruef (1864–1936) was sentenced to San Quentin Prison for bribery and extortion. But Ruef claimed he was a victim of anti-Semitism, an American version of Alfred Dreyfus, the innocent French Jewish army officer whose humiliation and condemnation in Paris in the 1890s had troubled Theodor Herzl and helped spur him to publish his *Judenstaat* book. Voorsanger sided with Ruef, while Wise was critical of him and his claim of anti-Jewish prejudice. The San Francisco rabbi declared, "Stephen Wise is a brilliant and eloquent young man, but not of a well-balanced frame of mind."[39] In 1908 Voorsanger lashed out at another target: the anarchist Emma Goldman (1869–1940). He accused her of "moral insanity."[40] Despite their differences, when Voorsanger died, Stephen wired condolences to the deceased rabbi's family.[41]

The Ruef case continued to demand Wise's attention as late as 1915 when the disgraced San Francisco political leader again charged anti-Semites were using his case and incarceration in San Quentin Prison to tar all Jews with the brush of collective guilt. Stephen would have none of that and wrote,

Israel [Wise's term for the Jewish people] is not responsible for Ruef's crimes any more than the Roman or Protestant Church is responsible for the crimes of its communicants. . . . But . . . Israel is unutterably pained by this blot upon its record of good citizenship in America.[42]

Stephen Wise's half dozen years in Portland were filled with significant achievements and growing fame. In addition, the Wises' two children were born in Portland—James in 1901 and Justine in 1903. In many ways Stephen's rabbinical and community service experience outside New York City provided him with a fuller picture and understanding of a United States that in the early years of the twentieth century was emerging as a major power within the international community. Wise's Portland experience earned him an authenticity whenever he addressed the major issues America faced during his lifetime.

Stephen Wise—in appearance, dress, speech, education, and geography—could never be described or dismissed with the pejorative term, "New York Jew." Wise's knowledge of America was not limited to large urban centers like New York City, Boston, Philadelphia, or Chicago. Thanks to his tenure in Portland, Stephen was able to validate and enhance his claim of being "an American all my life."

When he returned to New York City in 1906, Manhattan became his home for the rest of life. After serving in Portland for six years, a mature Stephen Wise was on his way to becoming a famous rabbi, a powerful force in the American political arena, and a Zionist leader. Aiding him in reaching that goal were a sonorous voice, a personal magnetism, an extraordinary intelligence, a remarkable physical presence, and a dominant mien.

When Wise moved to Portland, geography prevented his active participation in the embryonic Federation of American Zionists (FAZ) that was led by Richard Gottheil. By 1904, relations between the US-based FAZ and the European leaders of the Zionist movement had become estranged. Wise was upset that the people around Herzl had little interest in the American outpost of the Jewish national movement. Although he held an official position on the World Zionist Organization's important Greater Actions Committee (GAC), Wise felt snubbed by his European colleagues. An angry Stephen wrote Gottheil that he planned to resign from the GAC:

> I cannot and will not work with men who refuse to place me in their fullest confidence. That Herzl and his colleagues fail to take counsel with the only American member of the Greater Actions Committee [Wise] . . . constitutes an indignity to which no gentleman can submit with honor. . . . I am as much a member of the Greater Actions Committee as Herzl or any man. It was and is his duty to deal with me, with us, frankly and honestly—I am not a Russian underling nor yet a Turkish landowner who must be kept in the dark as to the real purpose of things.[43]

In only six years Stephen had evolved from being Herzl's starry-eyed aco-
lyte in 1898 to perceiving himself as a co-equal with Herzl as a member of the
powerful GAC. When finished with his rehabilitation in Atlantic City,
Stephen traveled to Vienna, where he met Herzl only a few months before the
latter's death at age forty-four on July 3, 1904. It was there in the Austrian capital that Stephen had his second and final personal meeting with the founder of
modern Zionism.[44]

Herzl attempted to ease Stephen's concerns, and he assured Wise that, although the FAZ led by Gottheil had not been efficient and well organized, the
young American rabbi from Portland remained a full member of the GAC.
Wise told Herzl, "My residence in Oregon 3000 miles from New York pre-
cludes the possibility of any real participation in the [American Zionist] management. I have made that mistake long enough. I shall not do it all over
again." As Wise was preparing to return to the United States, he and Herzl,
both Budapest-born Jews and separated by only fourteen years in age, strolled
in one of Vienna's municipal parks.

"Veiss [Herzl's German pronunciation of 'Wise'], how old are you?"

"I am just thirty years," Stephen answered.

Herzl then placed his arm on Wise's shoulders and said, "Veiss, you are a
young man; I am an old man. I shall not live to see the Jewish State, but you
Veiss, are a young man. You will live to see the Jewish State."[45]

Herzl was wrong in describing himself as an "old man," but in 1904 he was
suffering some severe and debilitating heart problems and he died a few
months after his conversation with Wise. But his prediction was correct about
Stephen Wise living long enough to see the Jewish State. Forty-four years after
the two men had their last walk in the Viennese park, Israel declared its national independence on May 14, 1948. A cancer-ridden Wise died eleven
months later.[46]

Although Wise met Theodor Herzl only twice, he was one of the four
iconic figures, all from outside Stephen's immediate family, who played key
roles in Wise's life and were inextricably linked to his career: the other three
were US Supreme Court Justice Louis D. Brandeis (1856–1941) and American
presidents Woodrow Wilson (1856–1924) and Franklin Delano Roosevelt
(1882–1945). Wise's historic encounters with that august trio lay ahead as he
returned to New York City.

Chapter 6

The Battle of Temple Emanu-El

It is clear that after serving as Beth Israel's rabbi for five years, Stephen Wise wanted a change from the limited confines of Portland, a community thousands of miles away from New York City, the center of both American and Jewish life. But because he was older and more experienced than he was in 1900, Wise did not want to "come home" to New York City and resume his previous professional life in an ordinary synagogue.

His father had been dead for almost ten years, and Stephen was longer perceived as "Aaron's son." While Wise had experienced fame, success, and adulation in Portland, he was ready to strike out on his own by playing a major role on the American Jewish community's biggest stage: New York City.

That was the situation in late 1905 when Stephen Wise and the leaders of Manhattan's Temple Emanu-El began a choreographed and still controversial public minuet that focused on the possibility, whether real or not, that the gifted young rabbi would become the spiritual leader of the "cathedral" congregation of Reform Judaism. Emanu-El was the prestigious religious home of many prominent and affluent Jewish families in New York City. It was spiritually, culturally, politically, geographically, economically, and socially far removed from the Lower East Side of Manhattan, the crowded neighborhood where hundreds of thousands of recent Jewish immigrants from Eastern Europe lived in overcrowded housing conditions whose greatest enemies were financial poverty and physical disease.

Wise appeared to be a perfect fit for the congregation; his academic doctorate was from Columbia University, his rabbinic ordination from Vienna, and he was married to a member of a prominent German Jewish family. Stephen was handsome and a superb orator, his brand of liberal Judaism meshed with the Reform beliefs and practices of many Emanu-El leaders, and his vigor and energy were sure to attract younger Jews to the most famous synagogue in America.

Congregation Emanu-El, the oldest Reform congregation in the United States, was founded in 1845 by thirty-three German Jews, and like many other New York City houses of worship, its history began in lower Manhattan.[1]

By 1868, Emanu-El members had erected a large Moorish Revival–style building on East 43rd Street and Fifth Avenue. The sanctuary had seating for 1,800 people, the huge organ (a radical break with traditional synagogues) contained 4,840 stops, and there were five arched entryways on Fifth Avenue and two additional entrances on East 43rd Street. The building's nineteenth-century construction cost was $700,000, the equivalent of about $11.3 million today.[2]

The impressive structure was in use until 1927 when construction began on the current landmark building located on the corner of East 65th Street and Fifth Avenue, the site of John Jacob Astor IV's mansion. In that same year Reform Congregation Beth-El on Fifth Avenue and East 76th Street merged with Emanu-El.

Stephen Wise was no stranger to the high-status temple. Indeed, he had forged several personal and professional ties to the venerable congregation during his seven years as B'nai Jeshurun's rabbi in Manhattan. One of Stephen's mentors was Gustav Gottheil, who served as Emanu-El's rabbi for three decades: 1873–1903. In addition, Wise had participated in the congregation's fiftieth anniversary celebration in 1895, and he delivered a guest sermon to Emanu-El's members in May 1900, three months before he left New York City for Portland.[3]

But things did not go well when Wise and the leaders of Emanu-El entered into a public controversy that became ideological and personal in its bitterness and long-lasting impact. Questions still remain about the Wise–Emanu-El dustup of 1905–1906. How and why did the confrontation take place? What were the true goals of Wise and the actual hiring intentions of Emanu-El's leaders? Why did an intra-Jewish community controversy between a rabbi and a congregation receive national attention in the general and Jewish press?

On one level, the episode appeared to be Wise's principled battle for an unrestricted open pulpit where a rabbi, indeed all clergy, would be able to deliver sermons and participate in a myriad of activities free of lay control or supervision and without prior approval from a board of trustees.

If the quest for a free pulpit had been the only issue in the Wise–Emanu-El public confrontation, it would still merit attention because of the controversy's two major personalities: Rabbi Stephen Wise and attorney Louis Marshall (1856–1929), Emanu-El's most prominent lay leader. However, something else was involved when the two men collided with one another. The encounter represented a defining moment in the development of the growing American Jewish community. The clash shaped the leadership style of the twentieth-century

American Jewish community, and Brandeis University historian Jonathan Sarna believes that Wise's strong stand in behalf of a free pulpit "profoundly influenced generations of young Reform rabbis (and some Conservative and Orthodox ones as well) who continued to model the rabbinate on that of Wise."[4]

The clergy-congregation conflict lasted several months and contained moments of mutual attraction between Wise and Emanu-El's leaders that were followed by feigned disinterest on both sides. But the process resumed with on-again / off-again job negotiations, frosty rejections, public denunciations, and long-lasting incriminations. At the end, the exhausting conflict ended in separation, distrust, and alienation. While there is debate about the true agendas and motives of both Wise and Marshall, there is, however, a detailed paper trail of the controversy.

After Wise had concluded the third of his guest lectures in November 1905, a committee of six officers and leaders of Temple Emanu-El visited Stephen at 46 East 68th Street, the Waterman home on the Upper East Side of Manhattan on the last day of that month. The delegation was led by Marshall, the congregation's secretary (the de facto leader of the board of trustees), and included the synagogue president and prominent investment banker James Seligman (1824–1916) and the philanthropist and international business leader Jacob H. Schiff (1847–1920).

The discussion centered on several issues: the possibility that Wise might accept a call to serve as a co-rabbi with Joseph Silverman (1860–1930), Gustav Gottheil's rabbinic assistant, who began his career at Emanu-El in 1888. Wise realized that, unlike Portland, where his predecessor, Jacob Bloch, moved to another city and congregation when Stephen became Beth Israel's rabbi, the forty-five-year-old Silverman would not be retiring or assuming a new position.

The lay committee also explored another area: What were Wise's conditions for a possible position at the temple? Stephen responded with a long list: he had to be unanimously elected by the board of trustees and given an initial three- to five-year contract. In addition, he required a private secretary, and the rabbi wanted to preach three times a month with the proviso that he could invite outside speakers to the Emanu-El pulpit. Such speakers, including Zionists, would include not only other rabbis but also Jews and Christians who could bring an important message to the congregation in the areas of progressive politics, interreligious relations, social welfare, literature, and philosophy. Wise also wanted to establish a downtown branch of the august synagogue in order to reach the large number of new Jewish immigrants.[5]

Stephen's final condition was the most critical and important. Today such a demand would be termed a "game changer" or "dealbreaker": "If I go to Emanu-El, the pulpit must be free while I preach therein. . . . If I accept, I must have an absolutely independent pulpit, not dominated or limited by the views and opinions of the congregation."[6]

The committee's immediate reply stressed that the pulpit of Emanu-El was under the control of the board of trustees. "If that be true," Wise responded, "there is nothing more to say."[7] But as it turned out, there was much more to be said and written; neither Wise nor Marshall, his main antagonist, was prepared to become mute and "go gentle into that good night." Indeed, until then, Wise had never confronted or negotiated with someone as able and formidable as Louis Marshall. For that reason, the Wise-Marshall battle in 1905 and 1906 has been termed the "clash of the Titans."[8]

Marshall was an acknowledged leader of the German Jewish establishment in America. Born to German-speaking immigrant parents in Syracuse, New York, young Louis attended Columbia University Law School, where he received a law degree in 1878. Within a few years, Marshall had become a partner in the prestigious Manhattan firm of Guggenheimer, Untermyer, and Marshall.

He was a rare combination of brilliant attorney, avid nature conservationist, ardent Republican, extraordinary Jewish communal leader, international diplomat, powerful synagogue officer, exemplary family man with a devoted wife and four children, and a superb linguist.[9]

Marshall was a circumspect, conservative, and cautious lawyer, and as the secretary and later president of Temple Emanu-El, he was either unwilling or unable to yield the laity's synagogue leadership to a progressive, precocious, and pugnacious rabbi. Emil G. Hirsch (1851–1923), the leading Reform rabbi in Chicago of the time, said, "Temple Emanu-El lives under Marshall law."[10]

One of the ironies of the acidic Marshall-Wise relationship was the fact that Stephen never learned Yiddish, always relying instead on his powerful command of the English language. Marshall, on the other hand, knew Latin and French as well as German and English and, as an adult, he learned to speak and read Yiddish as a means of better communicating with the growing Jewish population in the United States and the millions of Jews who lived in Eastern Europe.

Although both men grew up in German-speaking upper-class homes, it was Wise, not Marshall, who in later years captured the imagination and the passionate allegiance of many Yiddish-speaking Jewish newcomers to America.

The "masses" may have respected Marshall for his diplomatic and legal skills, but Wise became a beloved figure. One reason for Stephen's success in attracting such loyalty was the perception that his conflict with the Emanu-El leaders represented a struggle for a free pulpit and freedom from the dominance and control of the "uptown" Jewish elite.

Short and rotund in stature—the direct opposite of Stephen Wise in physical appearance—Louis Marshall was a Jewish patrician, a daunting intellectual presence equipped with a keen intellect and a profound commitment to long-established values and principles—American and Jewish. In late 1905, the forty-nine-year-old Marshall was at the peak of his powers.

The clash of Titans—Wise vs. Marshall—had begun with an invitation for Stephen to deliver a series of lectures at Temple Emanu-El in November 1905 along with fourteen other "guest" rabbis. Emanu-El's leaders were searching for a new spiritual leader, and their favorite candidate was Stephen Wise.

Once Wise laid out his demands, Marshall told him that Emanu-El's rabbi could not use the pulpit to discuss Orthodox Judaism, Zionism, or Ethical Culture (an obvious slap at Felix Adler), nor could there be sermons that would convert "the pulpit into a forum of character entirely foreign to the purpose for which the congregation was founded."[11]

Wise's rejoinder was more than a general exposition of his long-held position about the absolute freedom of the pulpit. Instead, Stephen issued a blunt warning that was aimed at several members of the Emanu-El committee, including Marshall himself:

> I have in Oregon been among the leaders of a civic reform movement in my community. Mr. [Moses H.] Moses [a member of the Emanu-El delegation], if it be true, as I have heard it rumored, that your nephew, Mr. Herman, is to be a Tammany Hall [the NYC Democratic Party political machine] candidate for a [New York State] Supreme Court judgeship I would, if I were Emanu-El's rabbi, oppose his candidacy in and out of my pulpit. Mr. [Daniel] Guggenheim, as a member of the Child Labor Commission of the State of Oregon, I must say to you that if it ever came to be known that children were being employed in your mines I would cry out against such wrong. Mr. Marshall, the press stated that you and your firm are to be counsel for Mr. Hyde of the Equitable Life Assurance Society. That may or may not be true, but knowing that Charles Evans Hughes's investigation of insurance companies in New York has been a very great service, I would in and out of my pulpit speak in condemnation of the crimes committed by the insurance thieves.[12]

Wise's remarks revealed he had "done his homework" in preparation for his meeting with the Emanu-El committee. Even though he lived in Portland, Stephen was aware of 1905 Tammany Hall politics as well as the investigation then under way of the New York insurance industry led by Hughes (1862–1948), who was then a special assistant to the US attorney general. In 1906 Hughes was elected New York State governor and was the unsuccessful Republican presidential candidate in 1916. In later years he served as the chief justice of the US Supreme Court.

Once Wise had thrown his rhetorical daggers, he was told "politics is never discussed in the pulpit of Temple Emanu-El." The rabbi's reply was vintage Stephen Wise. He repeated the same ideas many times during his career, sometimes in different forms, to justify and define his commitment to prophetic Judaism:

> The Hebrew prophets were politicians . . . furtherers of civic and national righteousness. As a Jewish minister I claim the right to follow the example of the Hebrew prophets and stand and battle in New York as I have stood and battled in Portland for civic righteousness.[13]

As the tumultuous encounter was ending, Louise Wise, who grew up among Emanu-El's prominent families, is reported to have stood outside the meeting room in her New York City home, looked at her husband, and shaken her head in "scornful negation."[14] Stephen knew she was opposed to his taking the job. But as early as 1900, he had privately expressed his own negative feelings about the possibility of becoming the rabbi of Emanu-El:

> Emanu-El will never get a MAN in its pulpit until the snobs forget the millionairedom long enough to acquire some respect for a man who is not rich, but is some other thing. They must learn that a "call" to Emanu-El is not an "honor" but a burden and responsibility, and that if "honor" there be, it belongs to the God whom congregation and minister should serve.[15]

Two years later, Wise was still thinking, perhaps obsessing about Temple Emanu-El:

> It is to be expected that the trustees . . . will ask me to preach. . . . I cannot conceive of any invitation that would induce me to accept the prospective situation. . . . To be called to Emanu-El as its minister is to be asked to face a responsibility appalling in its magnitude. I never shall shirk any task in life and I would be willing to give every bit of my strength to the task of serving and leading the Jewish community of New York.[16]

It is interesting that Wise's wish to "serve and lead" the New York Jewish community did not include his being the rabbi of Emanu-El.

When he was invited to deliver his guest lectures in November 1905, Wise wrote to Louise,

> Believe me, I am not thinking of the possibilities at Emanu-El to which I look forward with far less joy than to the possibility of the other work, certain to be untrammeled and likelier to be telling! But we shall see.[17]

There is little doubt that in his mind Wise was moving toward the creation of a "Free Synagogue" rather than seeking a rabbinic position at Emanu-El. In his autobiography Stephen wrote,

Leaving Oregon, I said to some intimate friends . . . "I am going to New York to preach some trial sermons at the Cathedral Synagogue. They will call me to be their rabbi. I somehow feel that I will have to decline their call. If I decline it . . . I will go back to New York from Oregon to found a Free Synagogue."[18]

But despite long-standing plans to establish his own congregation, Stephen relished his negative encounter with the temple's trustees and used it to enhance his career.

Following the meeting in the Waterman home, the drama continued the next day, December 1, 1905, when Marshall sent a long letter to Wise that asked whether he would accept an offer of occupying "our pulpit, in conjunction with its present incumbent, Reverend Joseph Silverman." But Marshall's note also contained the stern assertion that

The pulpit should always be subject to and under the control of the Board of Trustees. . . . [This is] not a mere figure of speech, or any empty formula . . . although in the past it has never led to any friction between our rabbis and our Board of Trustees. It does not mean, that the Board . . . will call upon any incumbent of our pulpit, to sacrifice or surrender his principles or conviction.

If there was a severe conflict between the board and the rabbi, Marshall could not have been clearer:

The logical consequence of a conflict of irreconcilable views between the rabbi and the Board of Trustees is that one or the other must give way. Naturally, it must be the rabbi. It goes without saying, therefore that such a juncture, he should have the privilege of resigning.[19]

Two days later Wise crafted a stiff letter to Marshall in response:

Dear Sir: If your letter of December first be expressive of the thought of the trustees of Temple Emanu-El, I beg to say that no self-respecting minister of religion, in my opinion, could consider a call to the pulpit which, in the language of your communication, shall always be subject to, and under the control of, the board of trustees, I am, Yours very truly, Stephen S. Wise.[20]

Although Marshall was the most powerful Emanu-El officer, Schiff told Wise to accept the position: "After you're elected, tell them to go to hell—and I'll back you up." In addition, both Seligman and Guggenheim urged Wise to re-think his refusal. They reminded Stephen that Gustav Gottheil could not have remained at Emanu-El if "we had told him what he could or could not say."[21]

The exchange of letters between Marshall and Wise should have closed the issue, and the various accounts and reports of the November–December 1905 contretemps would have remained buried within the minutes of Emanu-El's board of trustees and in Wise's diary and personal letters. But it was not the end of the matter. In fact, there was more to come.

Upon his return to Portland, Stephen escalated the controversy to a differ-ent level. At the beginning of the New Year, Wise used a Sabbath eve worship service to read a lengthy twenty-two-hundred-word "Open Letter" to the trustees of Emanu-El. It was released to the press, including the *New York Times*, before the synagogue leaders in New York City had a chance to read it. It was Wise's preemptive rhetorical strike against "the millionairedom" led by Marshall.

Wise told his Portland congregation,

> If I am to accept the call to the pulpit of Temple Emanu-El, I do so with the understanding that I am to be free and my pulpit is not to be muzzled. . . . The chief office of the minister . . . is not to represent the views of the congregation, but to proclaim the truth as he sees it. . . . How can a man be vital and inde-pendent and helpful, if he be tethered and muzzled? A free pulpit, worthily filled, must command respect and influence; a pulpit that is not free, howso-ever filled, is sure to be without potency and honor. A free pulpit may some-time stumble into error. A pulpit that is not free cannot powerfully plea for truth and righteousness. . . . The pulpit has done its duty in calling evil and good, in abhorring the moral wrong of putting light for darkness and dark-ness for light. . . . The minister is not to be the spokesman of the congregation, but the bearer of a message to the congregation.[22]

The explosive open letter received extensive coverage in the *New York Times* and in other newspapers, including the Jewish press. *Times* publisher Adolph S. Ochs (1858–1935) was a member of Emanu-El, and his paper car-ried stories about the clash for four straight days in early January 1906. While the *Times*'s staff viewed the controversy as a compelling news story, Ochs had a personal interest in the matter. In 1884 he had married Effie Wise (1860–1937), a daughter of Rabbi Isaac Mayer Wise, and Ochs was concerned not only about his own congregation but the future of the entire Reform Jewish movement in America that his father-in-law had led for many years. After four days of news stories, a harsh anti–Stephen Wise editorial that supported Marshall appeared in the *Times* on the fifth day, titled "Pulpit and Pews":

The views of Rabbi S. S. Wise of Portland, Oregon as to the terms on which he would accept a call to the [Emanu-El] pulpit raise a question which is receiving more or less discussion in the press. . . . His [Wise's] own statement of the case abundantly justifies that organization for declining to accept him as its pastor. He labors to show there is a question of principle involved. . . . Rabbi Wise insists that "my pulpit shall be unmuzzled" . . . that this involves the issue of freedom of thought and speech.

If so, it is within very limited bounds and as to a small field. The rabbi speaks of "my pulpit," but primarily it is not his pulpit; it is that of the congregation, whose affairs are in the charge of the Trustees. . . . If this view be held and acted on, it cannot be said that the preacher has been muzzled. He is entirely free to preach what he wishes for any congregation that is willing to support him. . . . It appears to us that the liberty of preaching is no more sacred than the liberty of listening, especially in a structure and from a minister sustained at the expense of the listeners.[23]

The *American Hebrew*, a leading Jewish newspaper of the time and the editorial voice of the German Jewish community in the United States, was also critical of Wise:

It [the controversy] was not an elevating experience. . . . A discussion that is well calculated to injure the sacred [Jewish] cause it is his [Wise] duty to maintain, it is altogether indefensible and is to be severely condemned. . . . Not that we are disposed to approve of the principle that, "the pulpit shall be subject to and under the control of the Board of Trustees," for a censored pulpit goes against the Jewish grain. . . . But the present-day tendency of the pulpit to discuss everything else under the sun but Judaism, to make of it a public forum rather than a source of spiritual upliftment and the spread of Jewish principles, justifies the restriction of the Trustees. . . . While disapproving of limiting the rabbi's utterances so long as he confines himself within legitimate lines, we are in sympathy with the Trustees in their desire to maintain the pulpit up to the high level of its providence, and to demand that it be Jewish in spirit and in atmosphere, require as much as in dogma.

But the same editorial did not condone the behavior of Marshall and his colleagues:

But in the means they have taken to fill the vacancy in its pulpit, the trustees of Emanu-El have subjected themselves and their congregation to serious criticism. . . . Their method of finding a successor to Rabbi Gottheil has not reflected credit upon themselves or dignity upon the Jewish pulpit, "Emanu-El's next rabbi" has become the perennial theme of the humorist among our people.[24]

During the height of the clash, Wise wrote to Oswald Garrison Villard (1872–1949) to clarify an important point: there were no "doctrinal" differences between himself and Temple Emanu-El. Villard, the grandson of the noted Abolitionist William Lloyd Garrison (1805–1879), was a prominent journalist and an early supporter of the NAACP. Stephen wrote,

> No question was raised as between the board of trustees and myself with respect to the doctrinal position of Emanu-El. . . . I was in substantial agreement with them with respect to the teachings of Reform Judaism. . . . I made the sole stipulation that the pulpit be free and that I not be muzzled. . . . I feel that one of the chief reasons for . . . the loss of moral supremacy of the churches is due to the widespread and largely justifiable belief that the pulpit is not free.[25]

Not content with the *New York Times* coverage of his open letter, Wise published the full text of the document in a booklet along with Louis Marshall's December 1, 1905, missive defining the authority of the temple board in controlling the pulpit. Wise provided an aggressive title for his pamphlet that received wide distribution throughout the United States: "An Open Letter . . . on the Freedom of the Jewish Pulpit." It is likely that Wise wanted his "Open Letter" to be a foundational document of the Free Synagogue he was planning to establish. It was also a way of increasing his profile in the Jewish and American communities.

A week after the publication of the "Open Letter" pamphlet, Stephen notified Congregation Beth Israel that he would resign his rabbinic position at the end of June 1906 and move with his family to New York City.[26]

Despite the icy-cold and white-hot language of the controversy and the passage of time, several major questions still remain. Was there a genuine offer of the Emanu-El rabbinic position to Wise? Did Stephen have any intention of accepting such an offer if it were given? Were Emanu-El's rabbis "tethered and muzzled" on the pulpit? Did Wise use the Emanu-El conflict as a publicity maneuver to enhance his national reputation? Were Wise and Marshall appealing to two separate audiences?

Wise's popular free-pulpit stance resonated with many of the recent Jewish immigrants to America who disdained the German Jewish community in New York City. Orthodox Jews were appalled by the extreme religious reforms of the "uptown" synagogues, especially Temple Emanu-El, while the socialist antireligious elements among the immigrants perceived themselves as victims of the anti–trade union capitalism policies they often experienced from arrogant German Jewish employers. Wise's fiery attacks on the "millionaire-dom" captured the imagination of many immigrants, while Marshall's brusque statements, legal arguments, and aggressive letters played well with a much smaller and wealthier Jewish audience: the group Stephen Birmingham called "Our Crowd" in his 1967 book of the same title.

For Wise,

> The idea of a free pulpit was intimately connected with social justice and social progress. . . . Working tirelessly [in Portland, Oregon] in child labor, gambling and prostitution, sometimes at the expense of his personal safety or career, definitely projected Wise from local to national prominence . . . proving once and for all that rabbis were no longer limited by the confines of their congregation."[27]

In his 1980 study, Sobel asserts, "The question of 'pulpit freedom' was never the substantive issue between Wise and Emanu-El, although Stephen Wise made it appear so, and Louis Marshall, perhaps unwittingly, let him do it."

Sobel, who served as Emanu-El's rabbi between 1962 and 2002, believes,

> It was a legend that fitted well into the ethos of an American Jewish community whose leadership, by the 1920s, would be transferred from German Jews to Eastern European Jews. . . . The legend lingers yet as an embarrassment and source of contempt toward the "Cathedral Synagogue." . . . The evidence suggests that the entire episode was deliberately fabricated by Stephen Wise; that he never intended to accept a call from Temple Emanu-El if offered, and he used the incident to create national publicity for himself. . . . Freedom of the pulpit had always prevailed at Temple Emanu-El; and . . . what Marshall and the other Trustees were talking about . . . had more to do with the designation of rabbis' duties that it had with utterances from the pulpit.[28]

He added, "There is no evidence whatsoever either in the minutes of the Board of Trustees or in any documents from the congregation's founding to the [Wise-Marshall] controversy that would suggest any attempt to censor the content of the sermons preached from the pulpit."[29]

Urofsky believes the entire affair showed "both Wise's best and worst sides. His friends hailed him for having the courage of his principles; his detractors labeled him a publicity seeker. . . . Both were right."[30] In the best of circumstances, Wise would not have accepted the invitation to serve as a co-rabbi at Temple Emanu-El. Stephen was first and foremost a soloist of the first order; he could never share congregational authority with a co-rabbi. Wise created or exploited the controversy to help develop a national image that provided momentum for his ultimate goal at the time: the founding of a "Free Synagogue" where Wise would be the producer, director, and chief actor of the congregation. After thirteen years of leading two historic established congregations—B'nai Jeshurun in New York City and Beth Israel in Portland—it was time for Stephen to become the rabbinic auteur of his own synagogue.

The documentation and primary source material may indicate the accuracy of Sobel's claim that Wise was never serious about the position and that he used the conflict for his own purposes. Indeed, Marshall and his colleagues may have won the "battle" with Wise, but they lost the "war" of public opinion and history.

When Rabbi Joseph Silverman died in 1930, Stephen Wise delivered the eulogy: "All power for Israel, that is to say, all power for righteousness, all power for service throughout his days, he remained unflagging in his zeal for that cause which was interchanged with his life."[31]

Years later Wise and Marshall entered into a period of correct but not cordial relations with one another—a kind of mutual coexistence that included a formal address by Marshall at a Free Synagogue service—but it was never a close relationship. In welcoming the Emanu-El leader, Wise joked that Marshall was "the author and founder of the Free Synagogue."[32]

Marshall and Wise may have become estranged from one another in 1906, but they worked together in later years on a series of important events, including the post–World War I Peace Conference in France, the establishment of the Jewish Agency, and the controversy over Henry Ford's (1863–1947) anti-Semitic publication, the *Dearborn Independent*.

Wise made the most of his conflict with Temple Emanu-El and did what few other people ever achieved: he outwitted, outflanked, and outmaneuvered the master attorney Louis Marshall. Neither man ever forgot the 1905–1906 "Battle at Temple Emanu-El."

Writing about the controversy more than forty years later, James Wise, a dutiful and adoring son, embellished the Emanu-El controversy by using flowery, overblown language, calling it a titanic struggle for religious liberty, freedom of conscience, and social justice. In addition, James went even further and linked his father's conflict with Emanu-El to several heroes of the past:

> That Stephen Wise rejected this fettered pulpit is as truly a part of religious history in America as Roger Williams' struggle for freedom of conscience in Rhode Island, as the anti-slavery crusades of Henry Ward Beecher, as Washington Gladden's rejection of "tainted money" from the elder Rockefeller.[33]

Williams (1603–1683), a Baptist minister in Colonial America and proponent of religious liberty and church-state separation, was forced in 1635 to flee the religiously intolerant Massachusetts Bay Colony for the safer confines of Rhode Island. Congregationalist minister Henry Ward Beecher (1813–1887) was a leader in the Abolitionist movement. His sister, Harriet Beecher (1811–1896), was the author of *Uncle Tom's Cabin*.

Gladden (1836–1918) was a national officer of the Congregationalist Church in the United States and a prominent exponent of the Christian Social Gospel movement. In 1905 he refused a one-hundred-thousand-dollar contribution (about $2.6 million today) to his denomination from John D. Rockefeller (1839–1937).

James Wise may have had an additional reason to link his father to the Beecher family. Calvin Ellis Stowe (1802–1886), Harriet Beecher's husband, identified with ancient Israel, both the land and the Hebrew language. He studied the Bible and the Talmud. Stowe grew a beard, wore a "rabbinical skullcap," and "spoke of Zion and Jerusalem, of the God of Israel, the God of Jacob . . . it might all have been uttered in Palestine by a well-trained Jew in the time of David."[34]

Having "won" his Emanu-El battle in the public opinion arena, Wise moved on. A year later he founded the Free Synagogue in Manhattan. Adolph Ochs's brother-in-law, Jonah B. Wise (1881–1959), the son of Isaac Mayer Wise, was Stephen's rabbinic successor in Portland where he served Congregation Beth Israel between 1906 and 1926. In the immediate aftermath of the Stephen Wise controversy, Temple Emanu-El hired San Francisco–born Judah L. Magnes (1877–1948) as its new rabbi. He was Marshall's brother-in-law and remained with the cathedral congregation until 1910. In 1925 Magnes became the first chancellor and later the first president of the newly established Hebrew University in Jerusalem.

If Stephen Wise made the controversy a public issue and gained a national reputation for his efforts in behalf of a free pulpit, Marshall reacted to the episode in a far different way. Harvard University history professor Oscar Handlin (1915–2011) wrote,

> The incident left its mark upon Marshall. It made him suspicious of rabbinic pretensions to authority; often thereafter he would complain that the clergy were not adequately attentive to spiritual matters and were excessively meddlesome in affairs that did not concern them. The incident also reinforced his instinctive resentment of those who rushed into public proclamations in preference to the quiet, amicable, private adjustment of difference.[35]

Marshall went on to compile a remarkable record of public service achievements, including the presidency of the American Jewish Committee (AJC) between 1912 and 1929. He had been one of the founders of the AJC in 1906. Following World War I, Marshall was a key Jewish leader at the Versailles

Peace Conference, where he pressed for the rights of the millions of Jews in Europe, especially in the former Russian and Austro-Hungarian Empires.

Although Marshall always called himself a "non-Zionist," he died in Zurich in September 1929 while attending an international meeting of the Jewish Agency for Palestine. At that conference, Marshall delivered what was to be his last public address, for which he received a standing ovation from the delegates representing twenty-one countries.[36]

So extensive was Marshall's influence and impact that his death merited front-page coverage in the *New York Times* and his funeral attracted several thousand people to the service as well as many others who lined Fifth Avenue near the temple. It was fitting that Marshall's funeral was the first service to take place in the large new edifice that was planned and built during his temple presidency (1916–1929).

Marshall's honorary pallbearers, an elite Who's Who roster of the era, included former New York State governors Charles Evans Hughes and Alfred E. Smith (1873–1944), New York City mayor James J. Walker (1881–1946), National Association for the Advancement of Colored People leaders James Weldon (1871–1938) and Walter White (1893–1955), Sears, Roebuck chairman of the board Julius Rosenwald (1862–1932), Macy's department store co-owner Nathan Straus (1848–1931), future US Supreme Court justice Benjamin Cardozo (1870–1938), *New York Times* publisher Adolph S. Ochs, Jewish Theological Seminary president Cyrus Adler (1863–1940), mining magnate Daniel Guggenheim (1856–1930), and investment banker Felix M. Warburg (1871–1937). Absent from the published list of pallbearers was Rabbi Stephen S. Wise.[37]

Today the two congregations—Temple Emanu-El on East 65th Street and the Stephen Wise Free Synagogue on West 68th Street—are located opposite one another, separated by the width of Central Park from Fifth to Eighth Avenue. The long-ago dispute between Stephen Wise and Louis Marshall has become an integral part of history embedded within the collective memory bank of each congregation.

The Free Synagogue website describes the clash this way:

> True to its traditions of a free pulpit, a rich religious life, and Jewish-inspired social action, Stephen Wise Free Synagogue builds today on the foundation it has inherited. When Dr. Wise learned that his sermons would be reviewed in advance by the temple's [Emanu-El] board of trustees, he withdrew himself from consideration. In doing so, Rabbi Wise clearly stated his vision from his Portland pulpit, then sent it to the New York Times.[38]

Sobel's opposite view of the controversy represents the Emanu-El perspective:

The members of the Board, through their secretary and spokesman, Louis Marshall, were saying that ultimate Congregational policy rested with the body politic itself . . . in keeping with centuries of well-established Jewish tradition. . . . Wise, for his own reasons . . . chose to distort the issue and the myth was born.[39]

The issue of a free pulpit still resonates more than a century after Wise battled with the leaders of Emanu-El. However, today it is frequently not a lay-led board that inhibits or questions the right of clergypersons to preach provocative sermons or to invite controversial speakers to address their congregations. It is rather a form of protective self-censorship that Stephen Wise would vigorously assail.[40]

If the two protagonists Stephen Wise and Louis Marshall were somehow able to continue the debate today at a neutral undisclosed location inside Central Park, their arguments would be the same as they were in 1905–1906. And since both men knew French, they would agree: Plus ça change, plus c'est le même chose.

Chapter 7

Wise's Very Own Free Synagogue

Although Stephen Wise offered his official resignation to Congregation Beth Israel leaders in January 1906, the rabbi and his family did not leave Portland until October of that year. The subsequent nine months provided ample time for an extended withdrawal process we today call "the long good-bye," the title of a Raymond Chandler novel and a Robert Altman film.

After six years in Oregon, both Stephen and Louise had left their personal marks on the synagogue, the city, and the state. Stephen had become one of the American West's most prominent religious leaders; he seemed to be everywhere: leading Congregation Beth Israel, serving on the Child Labor Commission and the Charities and Corrections Board, acting as an advisor to the Portland mayor and the state governor, and traveling in the region as a dynamic public advocate for the small but growing Zionist movement in the region.

Louise's efforts on behalf of the Visiting Nurses Association and women's suffrage, and her working to repeal the anti-Chinese immigrant legislation affected the entire Oregon population.[1]

More than forty years later Wise wrote,

> To take leave of Oregon with all its precious associations and memories . . . That was most difficult, for in the six years of residence in Oregon I had come to love the state and its people.[2]

When adult children write about deceased parents and early family life, truth is often a casualty. That does not seem to be the case in James Wise's ethereal description of the "Portland years":

> [They] were idyllic. There was the perfect companionship of her marriage, there was the sharing of experience, the interchange of literary and artistic discoveries, the friendship of a few chosen spirits, the simple, ample house almost outside the city limits, the garden with its perennial roses—and Mount

Hood towering in the distance. . . . These were the years and Portland was the place which filled full and made inexhaustible the reservoirs of Louise's spirit. . . .

Louise used to walk on the mountain road . . . with her husband and with us, her two small children; how she helped us to see the wonders of the great woods, and the glory of the Columbia River; and how she wanted no one to harm any living creature, not even the little garter snakes which scurried across our startled path.[3]

The Wise family lived at 233 West 24th Street in Portland, though "in 1931 the streets were renumbered and 233 W 24th Street became 1033 NW 24th Street. That area in NW was a very nice address to have at the turn of the century and it still is."[4]

As often happens when popular rabbis leave a community to move elsewhere, there are pleas from congregation members to reconsider their decision. David Solis Cohen (1850–1928), a prominent Portland lawyer, told Wise,

Nowhere can you do so much good for the principles you have at heart. . . . I put my plea on the broad basis of your opportunity for your people, not only of the west but of the entire country, by making the Beth Israel pulpit reverse the ancient condition, and become the "source of light."[5]

The plea of Solis Cohen carried weight because he was a member of a prominent old-line Philadelphia Jewish family, and after moving from Pennsylvania to Portland in 1878, he became active in many community projects and was one of his adopted city's most respected residents.

There were a series of public events saluting Stephen and Louise as they prepared to leave for New York City. A gala community-wide farewell dinner took place on October 10, 1906, that featured Wise's two political allies, Oregon governor George Chamberlain and Portland mayor Harry Lane, as well as the state's US senators. Wise left a far different Beth Israel synagogue than he had found in 1900; membership had increased, its religious school attracted a larger number of students, and its longtime financial debt had been eliminated. The congregation became one of the nation's most important Reform synagogues, and it was the spiritual home for many of Oregon's political, business, and cultural leaders, including former US senator Joseph Simon (1851–1935) and future governor Julius Meier (1874–1937).

Stephen was pleased and proud of his tenure at Beth Israel. But he became upset when he learned that the congregation's leaders rescinded one of the major changes he had demanded in 1900: rabbinic membership on the board. As Wise was leaving Portland, the officers ruled that future rabbis of the congregation could not participate in board meetings as Wise had done. An embarrassed leadership declared that the reversal of the policy affirmed the fact that Wise's successors could never equal his talent and abilities. But Stephen was not fooled by the board's flattery: "Gentlemen, I see I have wasted six years in Portland." It was another reason Wise wanted to establish his own congregation, where the rabbi would not be perceived or treated as an underling of the laity.[6]

When the Wise family—Stephen and Louise and their two small children—returned to New York City in the autumn of 1906, they needed a place to live. Wise had no job, which meant no income. Although the bruising battle with Temple Emanu-El had added to Stephen's growing national reputation, there was no cash value emerging from the clash with Louis Marshall and his millionairedom associates.

But Louise's older siblings, Leo and Jennie, came to the rescue by inviting the Wises—James and Justine were both under the age of four—to move into the large Waterman townhouse located at 46 East 68th Street on New York City's Upper East Side. In fact, Wise's in-laws turned over much of the brownstone residence to their sister and her family. The second floor contained living quarters for the Wises, the third story was an active and noisy nursery, and the fourth floor served as both Stephen's rabbinic study and bustling office for the future Free Synagogue.

It proved to be a busy, even chaotic time for the residents of 46 East 68th Street. Once Stephen Wise and his family settled into their not-so-temporary home in Manhattan, he set out to fulfill his cherished dream: the establishment of a progressive synagogue that would be distinctive in American religious life. Stephen initiated and received many telephone calls as well as entertained a host of visitors as he once again reentered the active New York City scene. The Reverend Dr. John Haynes Holmes (1879–1964), the Unitarian minister who was to become Stephen Wise's closest Christian colleague for the next forty years, liked to tell the story about a visit he made in 1907 to the Waterman residence:

As he rang the doorbell he heard the loud voices of small children. The youngsters opened the townhouse door and a little boy, James Wise, demanded of Holmes: "Who are you?" The children's nurse was appalled at such rudeness, but the six-year-old child continued his interrogation of the distinguished clergyman. "What do you want? Did you come to see my Daddy or my Mummy?" James' four-year-old sister, Justine, quickly interjected: "Daddy, you silly. He's the only one around here who's important."

But in the following years, because of Louise's leadership in a number of significant causes, "Mummy" also became "important."[7]

The elegant home Julius Waterman gave to his children was demolished in 1920 to make way for a new structure. Today the building next door to where the former Waterman home once stood houses the Dominican Academy, a Roman Catholic high school for girls. Stephen and Louise always remembered 46 East 68th Street: it was the scene of their wedding in 1900 and the tumultuous meetings with the Emanu-El officers in late 1905.

The Wises remained in the Waterman residence for two years before they were able to buy their own Manhattan home at 23 West 90th Street. Much of the money for the real estate purchase came from Louise's inheritance.[8]

In developing plans for the Free Synagogue, Stephen drew upon his own progressive ideals, and he altered how most new congregations are started. The adjective "free" was all encompassing because the pulpit would be unrestricted and open for Wise and guest lecturers. The synagogue would not sell pew seats to wealthy members as a means of raising funds, nor would the congregation collect dues from its members. The Free Synagogue would undertake a program of social welfare projects to aid people in need within the general New York City community. In a radical departure from custom and tradition, the Free Synagogue would depend upon voluntary contributions. Wise called it a "pewless, duesless" congregation.

The process that created the Free Synagogue was a role reversal. Most congregations are founded by laymen and women and not by a rabbi. Usually, a rabbi is selected only after a synagogue has sufficient members and adequate funds to hire a spiritual leader. Because Jewish congregational polity is decentralized and nonhierarchical, each synagogue is an independent entity, a free-standing association of like-minded people who come together to form a *bayt knesset*, the traditional Hebrew term meaning a house of assembly. A synagogue is also a house of study—*bayt midrash*—and a house of prayer or worship—*bayt tefilah*. But Wise reversed the process by first organizing the synagogue himself, and then he began an effort to gain members and funds to support his personal endeavor.

While there were synagogues in existence before 70 CE, the year the Romans destroyed the Second Jewish Temple in Jerusalem, in the years that followed, Jews established hundreds and later thousands of houses of assembly, worship, and study—where Judaism was kept alive and where it survived. The Second Temple's destruction was a cataclysmic event, but it did not mean the end of Jewish life or an abrogation of the Sinai covenant with God. The growth of the synagogue was a remarkable example of religious adaptation. The term "synagogue" comes from the Greek verb συνάγω, "to gather" or "to concentrate." It is also the source of the word "synod."

On Sunday, January 27, 1907, three months after returning from Portland, Wise delivered his first public lecture, at the Hudson Theater on East 44th

Street in Manhattan. In that speech Stephen answered the question, "What is a Free Synagogue?"

> A Jewish society, for I am a Jew, a Jewish teacher . . . It is not a society for the gradual conversion of Jewish men and women to any form of Christianity. We mean to be vitally, intensely, unequivocally Jewish. Jews who would not be Jews will find no place in the Free Synagogue, for we, its founders, wish to be not less Jewish but more Jewish in the highest and noblest sense of term.[9]

Wise was reacting to the criticism he received from several prominent rabbis who questioned his motives and the long-term survivability of such a radical institution. In creating the Free Synagogue, Wise acted as a rabbinic loner, a solo role he relished during his entire career.

Following his inaugural address, Wise embarked on a series of meetings with affluent "uptown Jews." He proved to be an excellent fundraiser: Schiff and two other members of Temple Emanu-El each donated $10,000 (the equivalent today of about $244,000) while Henry Morgenthau, Sr. (1856–1946), the Free Synagogue's first president and a prominent attorney and real estate magnate, added $5,000. Schiff was enthusiastic about the Free Synagogue and its potential to stem the flow of Jews to Felix Adler's humanistic group:

> It should be possible to accomplish through the Free Synagogue movement, within Judaism what the Ethical Culture movement has done without the ranks from which it has sprung.[10]

It was surprising that Wise, despite his well-publicized confrontation with the Temple Emanu-El board, still received support from prominent members of that congregation. Stephen was able to do so for several reasons. Although he loved to deny it, he was very much a part of the Jewish "uptown" establishment that included members of Emanu-El and the Ethical Culture Society. In addition, Louise Waterman grew up in that community as well.

Despite the public image he cultivated, Wise was no wild outsider or barbarian storming the fashionable Upper East Side gates and residences of German Jews. Nor was he offering a demanding form of Judaism to his supporters. On the contrary. Wise's brand of what he like to call "liberal Judaism" represented the basic ideals of the Enlightenment with little or no demand for home ritual, dietary requirements, or traditional Sabbath and holiday observances.

Wise's Free Synagogue promised its members safe, nonconversionary contact with like-minded Christian leaders who were influenced by the Social Gospel movement that Wise was able to adopt and adapt through his commitment to "prophetic Judaism."

The founders of the Free Synagogue saw their new congregation and its very "American" English-speaking rabbi as a vehicle to acculturate younger Jewish immigrants living downtown on the Lower East Side. If some Free Synagogue members did not want to get their own hands dirty working with Yiddish-speaking Eastern European Jews, they were pleased that Wise was reaching out to them by providing educational, religious, and social welfare programs for the immigrant community.

This view reflected Stephen's self-perception as the "people's rabbi," and was similar to the "people's bishop," Henry Codman Potter (1835–1908), the seventh Episcopal bishop of New York, a champion of labor and a supporter of political and social reform, and Edward McGlynn (1837–1900), a New York City Catholic priest who was know as the "people's priest" because of his public commitment to social justice causes. Because of his progressive views and opinions, McGlynn was sometimes at odds with his ecclesiastical superiors.[11]

The Free Synagogue was established at a meeting at the Hotel Savoy on April 15, 1907. The Synagogue's initial membership list included 192 individuals or families. Stephen Wise was unanimously chosen as the congregation's rabbi, and Henry Morgenthau, Sr., was elected president. Charles E. Bloch (1861–1940), Isaac Mayer Wise's nephew, was elected secretary. Bloch, who was born in Cincinnati, headed a family-owned publishing house that specialized in Jewish books. He was a close friend and ally of Wise.

Nathan Straus was chosen as the Synagogue treasurer. Straus was a philanthropist and a longtime supporter of Zionism. The Israeli city of Netanya, established in 1927 on the Mediterranean coastline, was named in his honor. The thirty-three-year-old Stephen Wise was an ex officio member of the congregation's executive committee, a title that understated his influence and leadership.

The synagogue's foundational document was a manifesto reflecting the personality and values of its rabbi:

> The founders of the Free Synagogue resolve that it shall not at any time for any reason impose any fixed pecuniary dues, tax or assessment upon its members, nor shall pews . . . be owned by members; but it shall be supported fully by voluntary contributions.
>
> Believing that Judaism is a religion of perpetual growth and development, we hold, that while loyal to the fundamental teachings thereof, we are and by virtue of the genius of Israel ought to be free to interpret and restate the teachings of Israel of the past in the light of the present, and that each succeeding generation . . . is free to reformulate the truth, first trusting in the providence of the God of our fathers.
>
> Believing that the power of the synagogue for good depends, in part, upon the inherent right of the pulpit to freedom of thought and speech, the founders

of the Free Synagogue resolve that its pulpit shall be free to preach on behalf of truth and righteousness in the spirit and after the pattern of the prophets of Israel.[12]

However, unlike most other congregations, both Christian and Jewish, Wise's new creation did not set out to construct its own building. During the first forty-three years of its existence—1907–1950—the Free Synagogue did not have a permanent home but used an assembly hall, a theatre, a church, a rabbinical school building, and the famous Carnegie Hall as venues. In many ways, Stephen Wise *was* the Free Synagogue.

As he commenced his efforts, Wise recognized that much had changed in New York City during the six years he lived in Oregon. New York's general and Jewish population had increased since 1900. At the start of the twentieth century, the New York City population was 3,437,000, of whom 598,000 were Jews, 17.3 percent of the total number.

Ten years later the population was 4,767,000 and the Jewish figure had more than doubled to reach 1,200,000, about a quarter of the city's inhabitants. One reason for the sharp Jewish increase was the fact that 64.2 percent of all Jewish immigrants whose first US port of entry was New York City remained in the city. The overwhelming majority of such Jews came from Eastern Europe, and they, the "Downtowners," soon outnumbered the older Central Jewish (German, Austrian, Czech) community, the "Uptowners."[13]

An astute Wise sensed the population increase upon his return from Oregon. That is why he envisioned his synagogue linking the two distinct Jewish communities. During the first ten years of the Free Synagogue, Stephen conducted services in both areas of the city: the first public meetings for the Uptowners took place at the Hudson Theatre on East 44th Street and at the Universalist church on West 81st Street.

When Wise commenced the first Free Synagogue services and lectures, he could have launched his new congregation only with the support and participation of his own uptown socioeconomic circle. In fact, that is what he did. But to his credit, the restless and prescient Stephen Wise was not satisfied to restrict his outreach to one specific group: the affluent German Jewish elites.

There were Free Synagogue services and lectures at Clinton Hall, near Grand Street, a site that was more accessible for the Downtowners who lived on the Lower East Side. It was an audacious move for several reasons. Wise, a progressive rabbi with a limited command of Yiddish, conducted Friday evening Sabbath services for new immigrants, most of whom had never heard of Reform or liberal Judaism. In addition, many were "antireligious" because, once in America, they rebelled against the strict Orthodox Judaism they experienced in Eastern Europe, in cities and small towns and villages.

There were a great number of Orthodox rabbis living on the Lower East Side during the first decades of the twentieth century who had the traditional beards and wore skullcaps or yarmulkes. Most of the newly arrived rabbis knew little or no English, and when they did use that language, their obvious accents and limited vocabulary were a source of embarrassment for some. Many immigrant rabbis had been community leaders throughout Eastern Europe, a region rife with anti-Semitism, and they were suspicious of a rabbi like Wise, who professed an interest in interreligious relations of any kind.

For ten years beginning in 1907, Wise continued the downtown Friday night Sabbath services and Sunday night forums. Stephen's intrusion into the Jewish Lower East Side community was met with disgust, hostility, and revulsion on the part of many Orthodox rabbis and laypeople. Wise had no beard and wore no yarmulke, he knew little or no Yiddish, employed a religiously forbidden hand organ during Friday night services, traveled on the Sabbath, did not observe the kosher dietary laws of Judaism, and participated in joint services and programs with Christian clergy.[14]

Stephen's interreligious activities drew criticism not only from Orthodox rabbis but also from Jacob Schiff and Samuel Schulman (1864–1955), a prominent Manhattan Reform rabbi. Schiff was a supporter of the Free Synagogue from its inception, but he withdrew much of his financial contribution (except for the Synagogue's social services programs). At a meeting of the Young Men's Hebrew Association (YMHA) in New York City, he charged, "Christians are still persecuting Jews with atrocious cruelty in Russia. Why then is it seemly for Jews to meet with Christians in common worship in New York? First the atrocities must cease!"[15]

Schiff was concerned about the 1903 anti-Jewish pogrom in the Moldavian city of Kishinev that left 120 Jews dead, 500 injured, and 1,500 Jewish homes and shops in ruins. Outrage over the attacks spurned the creation of the American Jewish Committee in 1906; among the AJC's founders were Schiff and Louis Marshall.

Wise and Holmes, Stephen's closest Christian colleague, attempted to assuage Schiff's anger. They pointed out that Christians in New York City were not engaged in anti-Jewish physical assaults, and Holmes's religion, Unitarianism, advocated religious liberty and opposed bigotry. In a letter to Schiff filled with Wise's usual eloquence, Stephen had a warning for the esteemed banker and philanthropist:

> The synagogue and church can stand together . . . to bring the light of religion to bear upon the tasks and problems of our age. . . . Bear in mind what great damage may be done to the highest interests of American Israel if it should go out . . . that you, as a leader of the Jewish people in America, have taken a

position which meant that you look with disfavor upon the union of Jews and Christians for the furtherance of aims common to the church and synagogue.[16]

Schulman, a lifelong critic of Wise, saw the problem from a spiritual perspective:

If Jews can meet in common worship with the Christians one night in the week, why not every night? If one service can be shared with the Christians, why not all? And then what becomes of historic Judaism?[17]

Schulman had only contempt for Wise: "The way to start a Free Synagogue is to cultivate a voice, place a pitcher of ice water on a stand, and marry an heiress." A week after those sarcastic remarks, the two rabbis met on Fifth Avenue, and Stephen, a nonsmoker, offered a cigar to his rabbinical critic. Louise was surprised by her husband's graciousness. Wise replied, "Well you see, my dear, that was last week."[18]

Schulman was the spiritual leader of Temple Beth-El, and when his congregation merged with Temple Emanu-El in 1927, he became rabbi of the combined synagogue until his retirement in 1934.

Though not a rabbi, Charles Bloch attended a July 1916 Hebrew Union College alumni meeting in Wildwood, New Jersey, where Schulman, who was ordained in Germany, was a guest at the dinner. However, he "devoted his entire time . . . to innuendo and direct attack upon you [Wise]. I am safe in saying they there was not a person there who was not abashed at his outburst."[19]

In time, Wise abandoned the Clinton Hall events. But beginning in 1910 and continuing until 1940, the Free Synagogue services were conducted on Sunday mornings at Carnegie Hall. The rental of the famous hall was not cheap: conducting Sunday services there between October 8, 1911, and May 19, 1912, cost $3,700 (about $90,000 today). The fee also included usage of the auditorium on Rosh Hashanah and Yom Kippur. During that year, 240 congregational members contributed $8,925 (the equivalent of $217,680 today) to the annual budget. In 1916 Stephen earned $10,000 per year (worth about $208,330 today). The size of the rabbinic salary gave "great pleasure" to Charles Bloch.[20]

In another historical example of how the lives and careers of Felix Adler and Stephen Wise intertwined, the Ethical Culture Society leader had first used Carnegie Hall for his Sunday morning meetings for eighteen years beginning in 1892. In 1910 the society's new building was completed, and Adler began delivering lectures and sermons in the new structure located at West 64th Street and Central Park West.

As noted earlier, Stephen was a friend and admirer of Adler. In 1907 Wise called Adler "the one prophetic Jewish voice in the life of the city; Emerson in form, but his spirit that of Isaiah."[21] While a close colleague of John Haynes Holmes, Stephen made clear that one of the reasons he established his congregation was to stem the exodus of Jews from the synagogue to either Ethical Culture or Unitarianism:

> The Free Synagogue is not be an indirect or circuitous avenue of approach to Unitarianism. . . . The largest number of [Free Synagogue] adherents were made up of such as had not only been estranged but actually had come to feel repelled by the unvital character of temple and synagogue institutionalism. . . . It was such Jews, quite a few members of the secular . . . Society for Ethical Culture, whom the prophetic mood of the Free Synagogue recalled and regained . . . once again to the faith of their fathers.[22]

It is an amazing fact that for over forty years Wise was able to create, sustain, and expand the scope of the Free Synagogue without a permanent physical home. But plans were approved in 1940 to erect a building at 30 West 68th Street, and work was scheduled to commence on Monday, December 8, 1941. The Japanese attack on Pearl Harbor the day before, and America's entry into World War II, delayed construction until the postwar period.

It was not until March 1948 that an ailing Stephen Wise, suffering from cancer, witnessed the laying of the cornerstone for the new structure. The current Free Synagogue building was dedicated on January 5, 1950, about eight and a half months after its founder's death on April 19, 1949.[23]

Despite Wise's attacks on the German Jewish establishment during his battle with Temple Emanu-El leaders, he was able to attract Henry Morgenthau, Sr., one of that community's premier figures, to serve as the Free Synagogue's first president. Jacob Schiff was also a member.

The Free Synagogue was the scene of an interesting chapter in American diplomatic history. On April 4, 1911, Morgenthau met New Jersey governor Woodrow Wilson at the Synagogue's fourth anniversary dinner at Manhattan's Hotel Astor. They bonded as friends, and when Wilson was elected US president the following year, he appointed Morgenthau as the US ambassador to the Ottoman Empire, where he served in Istanbul during World War I.[24]

Abram Elkus (1867–1947), a prominent attorney and an early Free Synagogue vice president, succeeded Morgenthau in that ambassadorial position. Morgenthau's son, Henry Morgenthau, Jr. (1891–1967), was secretary of the treasury for twelve years—1933–1945—in the Franklin D. Roosevelt administration and became involved with Wise during World War II. Robert Morgenthau, the ambassador's grandson born in 1919, was the Manhattan district attorney for many years.

Taken a year before his death, Wise (center, standing) with Free Synagogue High School students, c. 1948. Permission granted by the Stephen Wise Free Synagogue Archives.

Wise set up a Free Synagogue Religious School for the congregation's youngsters, and in 1907 he appointed Eugene H. Lehman (1878–1972), a 1902 graduate of Yale University, to serve as the school's director. Under his leadership, student enrollment soared from twenty-three pupils to three hundred two years later, and Lehman also lectured at some of the Free Synagogue's Clinton Hall Sunday night forums. He was popular with the religious school children as well as the downtown adult audiences.

Lehman was a gifted educator who had won several academic prizes at Yale, and he was also an instructor of postbiblical Jewish history at his alma mater. In 1903 *Munsey's Magazine* announced Lehman had won a Rhodes scholarship, but he never attended Oxford University. The reason given was that Lehman was "over age" for the scholarship.

He did enroll at the Jewish Theological Seminary, but was expelled when he wrote a letter to the school authorities that labeled faculty members and students "benighted Talmudists" and hypocrites.[25]

Throughout his career, Wise generally chose able and loyal associates, many of whom worked with the famous rabbi for years, even decades. But

Eugene Lehman was an exception, and in 1912 his relationship with Wise came to a bitter and well-publicized end when he was forced to resign from all Free Synagogue positions.

That spring, Lehman secretly married Madeline T. Davisdburg of Tarrytown, New York, a Westchester County suburb of New York City, but the public announcement of their wedding was not made until September. The news was a surprise to the Religious School faculty, Free Synagogue members, and Wise himself. While some thought Lehman's silence about his marital plans was the cause of his departure from the Free Synagogue, the reality appears to be different.

During the summer of 1912 Wise was on his family vacation, and during that period Lehman, with Stephen's permission, delivered the Free Synagogue lectures at Clinton Hall. When Wise returned in September, he resumed his normal schedule of services and lectures. The situation erupted when Mrs. Lehman told the *New York Times* that members of the Clinton Hall group confronted Wise upon his return and claimed he "had neglected them." She said they charged the rabbi was devoting "too much of his time to politics" and also claimed Stephen was not "regarding them seriously."

According to Lehman's wife, "While they liked him as a rabbi," the Downtowners required a "leader who could be with them, and Mr. Lehman is that man." She added the rebellious group had set up their own organization and wanted to "call it the 'Eugene Lehman League,' but my husband objected. . . . He suggested they call the new organization 'The Prophetic League.'"

She added the breakaway group would leave Clinton Hall for another venue: the University Settlement building also located on the Lower East Side. Madeline Lehman said the new group would not be religious in nature but would focus on "purely educational and social service work." The University Settlement was the original settlement house in the United States.[26]

Mrs. Lehman's outburst and her personal attacks were too much for Wise, and in late September he invited Lehman to meet with him and members of the Free Synagogue's executive committee. At that meeting, Lehman was dismissed from any association with the congregation. Lehman said Wise accused him of "treachery" and acting in a "disloyal" manner.

Stephen's statement to the press was carefully crafted:

> I regret to be under the necessity of saying that Mr. Lehman, for reasons well known to him . . . was unanimously requested by the Executive Committee of the Free Synagogue to withdraw from the work.

In a show of support, the Synagogue leaders praised Wise for his efforts in behalf of the "Downtown Branch" and declared that he will continue his "inspiring" work with all the "magnificent energy which Dr. Wise devotes to all undertakings, within and without the synagogue, with which he is associated."[27]

When Lehman was seventy-six years old, he served for a year as the first president of Monmouth College in New Jersey, now a university. The school newsletter described Lehman as "a man of contradictions. He left a legacy of outstanding achievement, and very human failings."[28]

Lehman never listed his successful, albeit abbreviated Free Synagogue career in his curriculum vitae, nor is he anywhere mentioned in Wise's autobiography. It was an acrimonious controversy for both men.

The episode raises several questions about Wise's leadership style. Why did the *New York Times*, in the closing weeks of the exciting three-way 1912 presidential election involving Woodrow Wilson, William Howard Taft (1857–1930), and Theodore Roosevelt (1858–1919), devote three prominent stories to a local intracongregational personnel matter? The answer seems clear. "Dr. Wise," following his earlier public battle with the Temple Emanu-El trustees, was becoming America's most famous rabbi. He always made news. In addition, having prominent community and business leaders Morgenthau and Schiff as Free Synagogue members ensured extensive press coverage.

Another element in the Lehman affair is that Wise and the executive \committee did not want the Downtown Branch to break away from the supervision and guidance of the Uptowners. They desired the program to continue, but were fearful it would secede and become an independent operation with the possibility of creating additional negative publicity about the Free Synagogue.

Eugene Lehman was an early example of Stephen's skill in spotting talented people and bringing them into his institutions. Yet, like most supervisors in any field of endeavor, Wise did not tolerate what he considered insubordination, or as he termed it, "treachery," from one of his staff, especially from someone like Lehman, who early on acted as a "man of contradictions" with "very human failings."

By 1912 the Free Synagogue was a firmly established institution, and its rabbi was a rising national leader in the religious and political arenas of the United States. Both the institution and Wise were able to afford several days of bad PR, even in the *New York Times*.

More than a hundred years after its founding in 1907, the Free Synagogue's weekly bulletin reminded its visitors and members of the congregation's history and founding values:

Founded in 1907 by Rabbi Stephen S. Wise, one of the most prominent American rabbis of the twentieth century, our "free synagogue" is based on four principles:

Succoth celebration in Booth built
and decorated by the children. Below, Seder Breakfast in the School
with children of two Christian
Churches as guests.

We stress the colorful and
dramatic ceremonials and folk-
ways of our people. The children participate in special services for Rosh Hashanah and Yom
Kippur. Jewish festival observances are made vivid with pa-
geantry and song, and American
patriotic holidays are mean-
ingfully dramatized. Weekly
assembly periods begin with a
prayer service on the children's level.

Customs and Ceremonies

Free Synagogue school customs and ceremonies, Wise and Rabbi Edward Klein, c. 1945.
Permission granted by the Stephen Wise Free Synagogue Archives.

Freedom of the pulpit: anyone who takes the pulpit is free to say what they wish

Freedom of the pew: first come–first served seating at all worship services
Direct, full participation in all social services required by the community
Identification with the Jewish faith and the faith and future of Israel

CONFIRMATION CLASS OF 1945

In the HIGH SCHOOL Department the student is prepared for adult Jewish life. With the knowledge he has acquired in the lower school as a foundation, the contemporary Jewish Scene is explored so that he may make the proper adjustment to Jewish life and general American life in a wholesome and well-balanced manner.

Courses include *Jewish Contributions to Civilization*, *Jewish Literature*, *History of Zionism*, *Jewish Social Ethics*, *The Community and The American Scene*. In addition, students participate in club programs in Dramatics, Debating and Journalism.

A unique feature is our Vocational Guidance Course for Junior and Senior students conducted by experts in cooperation with the Federation Guidance Bureau.

GRADUATES OF THE
CLASS OF 1945

Free Synagogue High School graduation class, 1945; Wise is fifth from the left in back row. Permission granted by the Stephen Wise Free Synagogue Archives.

We have been a vital Reform congregation in the American Jewish community for over a hundred years. Our longstanding connection to Israel is marked by the cornerstone of our building, which comes from the Temple in Jerusalem, presented to Rabbi Wise after World War I. Our pulpit has been open to people of all beliefs including: President Woodrow Wilson, Dr. Martin

Luther King, Eleanor Roosevelt, Bishop Desmond Tutu, Carl Sagan, Justice Louis Brandeis and Albert Einstein.

From its beginnings, Stephen Wise Free Synagogue has been a pioneering institution:

- the first synagogue with a social service department
- among the first synagogues to open a shelter for the homeless
- the first synagogue in the United States to install a female rabbi [Sally J. Priesand]
- the first synagogue to hire a professional Jewish composer and musician [A. W. Binder] as music director, a musical heritage that is present today in our rich repertory of classic and contemporary music.

Behind this striking history lies the belief that liberal Reform Judaism, rooted in traditional Jewish values, is a vital force in the contemporary world and that worship and study are the catalyst for action.[29]

Chapter 8

Why Was the Free Synagogue Different from All Other Synagogues?

In the early years of the Free Synagogue, Wise used his extraordinary energy and talent to create an impressive list of lectures and study topics, a roster of notable guest speakers, a religious school for children, and an innovative congregational social welfare service. In addition, he performed the many pastoral duties of a congregational rabbi, including weddings and funerals. From the outset of its history, the Free Synagogue was a unique institution that included conducting its main services on Sunday mornings instead of the Jewish Sabbath that begins on Friday evenings at sunset.

Wise defended the Sunday services by arguing that many people were required to be at their jobs on Saturday and were unable to participate in synagogue worship. Sundays were usually free of a regular work schedule and was a better day for attending religious services. Wise reflected the views of several other prominent Reform rabbis who made the same decision, including Kaufmann Kohler who in 1874 introduced Sunday morning services to the Chicago Sinai Congregation. Emil G. Hirsch continued the custom that remains today.[1]

In New York City, between 1907 and 1910, it was "Sundays with Dr. Wise" at either the Hudson Theater or the Universalist Church building. However, when in 1910 the Free Synagogue transferred its services to Carnegie Hall, it was a move that allowed Wise to preach for the next thirty years in one of the most famous auditoriums in the world.

On Sundays between 11:00 a.m. and 1:00 p.m., Wise broke free of the traditional form of Jewish worship, including that of his own Reform movement. At Carnegie Hall there was no Torah scroll, the first five books of the Bible that are handwritten on sheepskin in the original Hebrew, a central focus of synagogue services. Most of the Sunday readings or prayers were read in English except for the Kaddish, the mourners' prayer that Wise intoned in a slow sorrowful cadence. The Shema affirming the oneness of God ("Hear O Israel, the

Eternal is our God, the Eternal is One" [Deuteronomy 6:4]), was recited in the original Hebrew.

Each week the Carnegie Hall services attracted crowds that sometimes numbered between two thousand and three thousand people. Stephen's sermons during the Free Synagogue's early years reveal his restive and inquiring intellect that sought to meld a radical view of Judaism with the universal ideals of the Enlightenment, the great authors of world literature, the teachings of science, Progressive American politics, and of course, Zionism. This heady combination allowed Wise to speak on many different themes and subjects and to invite a wide variety of guest speakers.

American Jewish historian Moses Rischin has noted that as the "people's rabbi," Wise "embraced all liberating, noble and just causes, denounced all breaches in the moral law, and strode forth to elevate America, Judaism, and mankind."[2] He rarely, if ever, based his sermons on the weekly Torah or scriptural portion, a traditional mainstay of Jewish preaching. Although committed to Reform Judaism, Rabbi Wise's Free Synagogue was open to all, "inclusive alike of the non-Jew and the Jew."

His admirers perceived Wise as a brilliant spiritual pioneer who made an ancient religion relevant to the twentieth century. However, his foes saw him as an irresponsible, egocentric leader who discarded many fundamental aspects of Jewish liturgy, beliefs, customs, and rituals. The Free Synagogue's universal open-door invitation evoked a negative view of Wise that appeared in a leading American Jewish journal of the time:

An anxiety to preach and teach Judaism and then only to have a Sunday service; the two are hardly compatible. And, of course, our friends the "gentiles are invited to participate." It is difficult to understand what Dr. Wise and his sponsors—Jacob H. Schiff, Adolph Lewisohn, Isaac N. Seligman, Henry Morgenthau . . . really wish to accomplish.

It appears that the Free "Synagogue" will dejudaize its followers and make the "gentiles" "who are invited to participate" still more ignorant of what Judaism really stands for. . . .

They are prophets of Belial [the name of a wicked evil demon who appears in Jewish apocryphal literature as well as in John Milton's (1608–1674) *Paradise Lost*] for they come to lead people to destruction. . . . Such movements . . . have all disappeared for their very foundations were built on the quicksands of fads, whims, and fashion, self-indulgence and self-seeking.[3]

But in the same year, a Jewish visitor from Great Britain had a different and more positive description of Wise:

[He is] an extraordinary man. . . . Just above the medium height, waving shiny black hair, one or two unruly locks constantly demanding attention when Dr. Wise, losing himself in the force of his argument, disintegrates them from the luxuriant growth crown in a head of singular grace, and a Grecian form, a clean-shaven face, capable of denoting and portraying every emotion of the mind, dark piercing eyes, flashing fire and enthusiasm, . . . a black frock coat, low cut collar, and a plain black scarf; singularly expressive hands . . . each individual finger seeming to have a mission of its own.

The language he employs with quotations always apt from the classics . . . authors of all nationalities, playwrights, poets—maintains the fundamental principle of Judaism, and at the same time, makes it a practical religion, suited and possible for any individual who desires to preserve the faith.[4]

In his autobiography, Wise admitted,

We erred, for, as I have long seen, even the form of the Torah, the Scroll of the Law, had become too precious to the tradition of the synagogue to be lightly, indeed on any account, abolished. . . . I made a further mistake in taking it for granted that my unchanging Zionist position was fully understood by those who flocked to the services, not that I for a single moment concealed or minimized my Zionist loyalty. But I failed to make clear . . . the duality of my faith in liberalism as the (religious) expression of the Jewish spiritual genius and in Zionism as the faith and hope for the future of the Jewish people.[5]

When he wrote those words in 1948, he may have been thinking about Henry Morgenthau, Sr.'s, 1919 resignation from both the Free Synagogue presidency and congregational membership. He did so because of his opposition to Zionism, but Wise blamed Morgenthau's defection on the

ill will to Zionism . . . quickened [by] Louis Marshall . . . I owe to myself to add that the personal relations of Morgenthau and myself remained unchanged to the end of his many years.[6]

Wise's sermon and lecture topics are worth noting because they attracted large, appreciative audiences and shocked, even repelled, many others. During the first years of the Free Synagogue, Wise listed every sermon and lecture topic at both Carnegie Hall (Uptown) and Clinton Hall (Downtown). He also noted the attendance at each event as well as the exact amount of money contributed by the audience. For years that information—date, speaker, lecture subject, attendance, and the money collected—was catalogued in Wise's unmistakable bold handwriting.

Even a small sampling of the Free Synagogue's early programming shows the broad scope of Stephen's interests, personal relationships, and commitments. When viewing the attendance figures and the dollar amounts, it is important to note that one 1908 dollar is equal to about twenty-five dollars today.

One pulpit guest was Gifford Pinchot (1865–1946), the chief of the US Forest Service and an avid conservationist. In later years, during the 1920s and 1930s, Pinchot served as governor of Pennsylvania. Other speakers included John Mitchell (1870–1919), the president of the United Mine Workers, and Seth Low (1850–1916), a New York City mayor and president of Columbia University, as well as Washington Gladden and Oswald Garrison.[7]

Two well-known American social workers, Jane Addams (1860–1935) and Jacob Riis (1849–1914), were Free Synagogue guests, as was theologian Walter Rauschenbusch (1861–1918), a founder of the Christian Social Gospel movement. Perhaps the most presciently chosen guest was Thomas G. Masaryk (1850–1937), who spoke to Wise's congregation in the fall of 1907. Following the end of World War I eleven years later, he would become the founder and first president of Czechoslovakia.[8]

Clinton Hall Sermons, 1908–1910 (unless otherwise noted, Wise delivered all the sermons, and the numbers given here are attendance figures along with the money collected at each event). Some of the topics were:

March 22, 1908	Jacob Riis: "The Housing of the Poor" (The Danish-born Riis was a social reformer whose writings and photographs drew national attention to the substandard housing of many poor New York City residents. His best-known work is *How the Other Half Lives*.)
November 20, 1908	"Israel—People and Faith" 475
November 27, 1908	"Henryk Ibsen" 600
December 4, 1908	"Religion of the Heart & the Heart of Religion: Religion and Social Service" 650
February 12, 1909	"Lincoln" 750 (1909 was the one hundredth anniversary of his birth)
April 4, 1909	"Second Anniversary of the Free Synagogue": Speakers included Henry Morgenthau, Sr., Jacob Schiff, Emil G. Hirsch, and Stephen Wise 200
May 2, 1909	"Judaism and Unitarianism" 750
October 3, 1909	"Intermarriage" 800, $66.71—based on Israel Zangwill's play *The Melting Pot*, which dealt with intermarriage and religious and cultural assimilation. An English Jew, Zangwill (1864–1926) is credited with inventing the term "melting pot."
October 17, 1909	"Some Phases of Religious Unrest" $48.05

April 3, 1910	"Marriage and Divorce" 700, $57.40
April 24, 1910	Passover Service: "The Needed Redemption of Israel" 650, $66.15

Clinton Hall Sermons, 1909–1910 included:

December 2, 1909	"Tolstoy" 600
December 9, 1909	"Can Jew and Christian Unite in Worship?" 550

Clinton Hall Sermons, 1911–1912 included:

December 1, 1911	"The Fall of Empire" 600 [Wise noted, "Many turned away"]
January 3, 1912	Dr. Israel Abrahams: "Jewish Principles" 500

Carnegie Hall Sermons, 1911–1912 included:

September 11, 1911	Rosh Hashana Eve: "Israel at Home and Abroad" 1200, $247.00
September 12, 1911	Rosh Hashana Morning: "The Mission of Israel and Missions to Israel" 2400, $539.50
September 20, 1911	Yom Kippur Eve: "Greater Israel: A Plea for Unity" 2200, $520.00
January 5, 1912	"Abolition: The Emancipation Proclamation 50 Years Later" 900, $116.00
January 12, 1912	Yamei Kin, M.D. (1864–1934): "The Awakening of China" 1000, $86.00 (Kin, the first Chinese woman to graduate from an American medical school, was a popular lecturer in the United States.)
January 19, 1912	"What Does the Worker Want?" 1000, $167.00
April 27, 1912	Nahum Sokolow (1859–1936): "The Jewish Renaissance in Palestine" 600, $107.00 (Sokolow was an author and journalist who held many leadership positions in various international Zionist organizations.)

Rosh Hashana and Yom Kippur Services at Carnegie Hall, 2200 at each service, $172.00 and $343.00

October 8, 1912	The Reverend Dr. Lyman Abbot (1835–1922): "Why I Believe in Immortality" 1200, $114.00 (Abbot, a prominent Protestant theologian, was the leader of the US Congregationalist Church. He was a Progressive in politics, but he supported America's entry into World War I.)

Clinton Hall Sermons, 1913–1914 included:

September 5, 1913	"Glimpses of the Holy Land" (Wise made his first visit to Palestine that summer.)
September 12, 1913	Rabbi Henry Cohen (1863–1952): "Immigration at Galveston" (Cohen was a Texas rabbi who facilitated Jewish immigration when Galveston was a major port of entry to the United States.)

Carnegie Hall Sermons, 1913–1914 included:

March 15, 1914	Purim: "The New Anti Semitism" 1300, $244.00
April 5, 1914	"The Right to Work: The Curse of Unemployment" 900, $175.00

Clinton Hall Sermons, 1914–1915 included:

March 7, 1915	Jane Addams: "War and Social Service" 3000, $494.00 (Addams, an acclaimed social worker and the founder of Chicago's Hull House, supported women's suffrage and political reform. She received a Nobel Prize in 1931.)
May 16, 1915	"The Case of Leo Frank" Special Appeal for Frank family 1700, $311.00 (Frank [1884–1915] was falsely accused of murdering a young girl in Georgia. A lynching party took him from his prison cell and hanged him in Marietta, Georgia, but Frank was posthumously pardoned in 1986. His death stunned the American public, caused the exodus of many Jews from Atlanta, and was a catalyst in the founding of the Anti-Defamation League.)

Bronx Branch of the Free Synagogue, 1914 included:

September 30, 1914	Yom Kippur 1000, $95.00

Carnegie Hall Sermons, 1915–1916 included:

December 10, 1915	"Booker T. Washington, American" 1000, $147.00 (Washington [1856–1915], was a groundbreaking African American author, educator, and political advisor who died on November 14, 1915.)
December 17, 1915	"Another Wise Man from the East: Rabindranath Tagore" (1861–1941) 1100, $225.00 (Tagore was an acclaimed Indian author who attracted great interest in Europe and North America.)
December 24, 1915	"Judah Maccabee and Judas Iscariot"
February 11, 1916	"America's Lincoln & Wilson's America" 2200, $321.00
October 20, 1916	John Dewey (1859–1952): "Education on the Social Service" (Dewey was a progressive reformer whose philosophy and pragmatism exerted great influence on American democracy, schools, and education.)

A pioneering Free Synagogue program was a comparative religion lecture series that featured scholars from Columbia, Cornell, Harvard, the University of Pennsylvania, and Union Theological Seminary. Such an interreligious series was a rarity during the first decade of the twentieth century. Wise invited the lecturers to discuss Brahmanism, Buddhism, Christianity, Confucianism, Islam, Judaism, Shintoism, Zoroastrianism, and the religions of ancient Assyria and Babylonia. Penn professor Morris Jastrow (1861–1921) lectured on the latter topic while Richard Gottheil of Columbia spoke on Judaism.

Wise saw himself as a rabbinic bridge between the still insecure "uptown" German Jews who had established themselves in America a generation or two earlier and the "downtown" Jews: the recent immigrants from Eastern Europe. Stephen and the Free Synagogue leaders were eager to set up special programs for the young Yiddish-speaking immigrants, and Wise was pleased to receive support from the likes of "grandees" Schiff and Morgenthau.

But Gottheil had a different view of the encouragement that an altruistic Stephen received from the congregation. About a month after the Wise family returned to New York City from Portland, an apprehensive Gottheil wrote a five-page letter to his former doctoral student. The taciturn and circumspect scholar, himself a member of the uptown German Jewish community, offered a conspiratorial view of why the Free Synagogue leaders were so enthusiastic for Wise to offer downtown English language religious and cultural programs. Although Gottheil mentioned no specific names, the implication in his letter was that Schiff wanted Wise to accelerate the "Americanization" of the Jewish immigrants so that they would not become a public embarrassment or burden to the international banker and his apprehensive socioeconomic group.

In addition, Gottheil believed that such a program of acculturation would also help create an English-speaking workforce that some of the affluent German Jewish manufacturers and factory owners needed. The respected Columbia professor, a recognized leader of the American Zionist movement, believed that Wise's own public Zionist commitment would be muted because of the rabbi's heavy workload: his double duties at uptown and downtown services and programs. Gottheil wrote,

> I almost feel that there is a great deal more individual social and civic virtue below 23rd Street than above it. . . . The people downtown are eager to learn, have not much amusement, have a great deal of time on their hands and are willing to listen to anyone. . . . It would be a clever policy, worthy even of Tammany Hall, to shelve "the dangerous man" [the Zionist advocate Stephen Wise] by giving him work to do downtown. He would be out of harm's reach. . . . The man who finances a movement, no matter what the movement, is, gets a certain right to dictate its policy. . . . [Wise's Free Synagogue's efforts are] are a moral revolt. . . . Felix Adler [the Ethical Culture Society founder] was not an ethical or moral revolt half as much as it was theological one. . . . If it had been a moral revolt only, he would have remained within the Synagogue. . . . That is what you are called upon to do. . . . We have not even the excuse nowadays that Adler had in 1875. We have not to fight superstition or an over zeal for religious observance. On the contrary, we have to fight in-difference and impiety. Not only do most of our people not believe in things religious; they do not believe in things moral. . . . They believe in business and making money . . . This we have to combat.[9]

One of Wise's early guest speakers was Lillian Wald (1867–1940), the inno-vative social worker and director of the famous Lower East Side Henry Street Settlement House that was founded in 1893. She spoke to Free Synagogue members on December 22, 1907, and her subject was the awkwardly worded

"The Utilization of the Immigrant." The Cincinnati-born Wald, herself of German Jewish background, encouraged Stephen to direct his efforts "south of 23rd Street."

Wise later declared,

> These requests were fortified by a meeting held at the Henry Street Settlement, suggested, if not called by Lillian Wald . . . [to establish a downtown Free Synagogue branch] for teaching and influencing . . . those who had not forsaken their Orthodox Jewish moorings and yet were eager to hear the words and the message of an intensely Jewish liberal.[10]

Perhaps because of the Gottheil letter and Wald's personal request, Wise refused to accept Schiff's financial contribution earmarked for the Free Synagogue's work on the Lower East Side. Stephen's refusal is an example of his florid writing style even when refusing a large financial contribution:

> I found it necessary to decline the offer, which included a budget large enough to maintain a planned program of such synagogue activities as I visioned, without calling on me to perform the painful task of securing the needed funds. . . . I would place myself in an intolerable, indeed inexplicable, situation if I preached and conducted religious services exclusively for the masses. . . . This would be doubly true if it were known, as I would insist that it should be known, that the services were subventioned by the well to do, even though the subsidy should come from one of large substance who was a man of deep, traditional Jewish piety. Mr. Schiff, whose judgment was rarely questioned, whose generosity was still more rarely rejected.[11]

The real or imagined battle between uptown and downtown continued for some years. Charles Bloch was wary of granting full and equal Free Synagogue membership to the men and women in the Bronx or on the Lower East Side. He was concerned that the financial support in those two areas of New York City was much lower than at the "main organization" (i.e., the uptown Free Synagogue):

> A serious blunder and the announcement should be withdrawn. . . . If you allow members of the Down-Town Branch all of the privileges of the main organization, then you must allow the same to all of the members of the Bronx Branch and such branches as may be established later. In the course of time, it will be much cheaper to pay $2.00 in the Bronx than $10.00 or $20.00 to the main organization. If you allow these privileges now you will not be able to withdraw them at a later time.[12]

If the bitter public resignation of Eugene Lehman was a difficult moment for the Free Synagogue, it was a different and much happier story with Rabbi Sidney E. Goldstein (1879–1955), who was chosen by Wise in 1907 to direct the Synagogue's Social Service Department the same year Lehman was picked to run the Religious School. Goldstein served in his position until he died, a half dozen years after Wise.

Goldstein, who was ordained at the Hebrew Union College in 1905, was an original in many ways. While at rabbinical school, Goldstein "found little if any understanding or appreciation of social conditions and programs and the movements for social justice."[13] Unlike most of his colleagues of the time, he eschewed serving as a congregational rabbi. During Passover of his senior year, Goldstein delivered a holiday sermon in a Cincinnati-area Reform congregation. He shifted the familiar exodus narrative from the ancient Hebrew slaves to the oppressed American workers of the early twentieth century.

The soon-to-be-ordained rabbi demanded the liberation of laboring men and women from the poor working conditions that existed in many American companies. It was not a popular sermon, and an enraged Kaufmann Kohler, HUC's new president, was present in the synagogue and heard Goldstein's social justice oration. At the conclusion of the service, the leader of Reform Judaism in America rushed from his pew seat and stepped up to the pulpit where he offered an impromptu prayer that asked God to rescue the congregation from Goldstein's sacrilegious remarks.[14]

But Wise added Goldstein to the Free Synagogue staff, where he served for more than four decades. Goldstein once asked Stephen to explain how the two rabbis had been able to work so well together. Wise answered, "In two ways: first, my own inexhaustible patience of spirit; and second your [Goldstein's] own incredible power of endurance."[15]

One of the jewels in the crown of the Free Synagogue was Goldstein and the program he directed. An early congregation publication reflected Wise's view of his congregation's outreach:

> Not charity, but social service, building upon the rock of social justice will be the watchword of the F.S. The essential thing in the religion of Israel . . . is to quicken and keep alive the social conscience, to strengthen and make indissoluble the social bond.[16]

The Social Service Department represented the first time a Jewish congregation had allocated staff personnel and funds to inaugurate and maintain programs for the poor, the orphaned, the homeless, and the physical and mentally ill of New York City. Because nine Jewish men founded New York City's Mount Sinai Hospital in 1852, it would have been natural to focus social

Celebrating the Free Synagogue's twenty-fifth anniversary at Carnegie Hall, April 1932 (left to right): Rabbi Morton Berman, Rabbi Sidney Goldstein, the Reverend John Haynes Holmes, Wise, Synagogue president Joseph Levine, Past President Charles Bloch, Rabbi Jacob X. Cohen. Permission granted by the Stephen Wise Free Synagogue Archives.

welfare services on a medical institution supported by the Jewish community. Instead, Wise and Goldstein concentrated their attention on the municipal Bellevue Hospital in Manhattan, where nearly six thousand Jews a year were admitted as patients, most of them indigent or low-income residents of the city.

Goldstein set up a systematic visitation program that provided social workers and qualified volunteers to work with the Bellevue staff and patients. He also created a program of follow-up visitations once a person was discharged from Bellevue. In 1909 just two years after the founding of the Free Synagogue, Goldstein's Social Service Department had an annual budget of $10,000 (the equivalent of about $250,000 today) and in 1912 that figured had climbed to $15,000 (about $357,000 in today's dollars). Adding Goldstein to his staff and providing him with adequate funds proved to both friend and critic that Stephen Wise was serious about the Free Synagogue's social service program.[17]

Sidney Goldstein also trained Free Synagogue volunteers to engage in projects serving the needs of Jews on the Lower East Side, and he often delivered sermons describing the goals of his program. In 1938 the rabbi was one of the three founders of the National Council of Family Relations and served as the organization's president. He was also professor of social service at Jewish Institute of Religion in New York City, and Goldstein served as chair of the New York State Conference on Marriage and the Family. He was active with the 1948 National Conference on Family Life, the 1950 White House Conference on Aging, and the Tri-State Conference on Family Relations. In addition, he also authored several textbooks on the family.

In *American Jews and Marriage Counseling, 1920–1945*, Jane Rothstein wrote,

> In reaction to rising nationwide divorce rates at the turn of the 20th century, American sociologists and clergymen began educational efforts to keep marriage a healthy social institution. Rabbi Sidney Goldstein, hired in 1907 by Stephen Wise at the Free Synagogue, spearheaded this new initiative among Jews. For him [Goldstein] the moral implications of marriage were more important than the religious ones. He pushed the point in the Reform movement, that rabbis need to be involved with counseling their congregants and the young people in the community about how to create a good marriage, which included economic issues and understanding sexuality. . . . Marriage was an institution that has social ramifications, both for American society and for the Jewish people. He was very much in favor of what he saw as a new development, that marriage is no longer a patriarchal institution, but more of a democratic institution.[18]

Stephen Wise's talent in choosing excellent and loyal associates continued twenty years later when he selected Julius Xenab Cohen (1889–1955), a former civil engineer–turned–rabbi to serve as the Free Synagogue's executive director and associate rabbi. As a young man, Cohen added his exotic middle name to differentiate himself from the many other "Jacob Cohens" in the world.

"J.X.," as his family and colleagues knew him, was born in New York City to immigrant parents from Lithuania. In 1906 Cohen graduated from the Hebrew Technical Institute and began work as a draftsman in Brooklyn. Like many other children of immigrants, Jacob attended night school and earned an engineering degree from Cooper Union in Manhattan. In that era, Jewish engineers often faced anti-Semitic prejudice when they sought employment, but J. X. Cohen found a job with the city of Syracuse's Sewage Waste Department.

Cohen returned to New York City in 1914 and became inspired by Stephen Wise's combination of liberal Judaism and Progressive politics. As part of his religious awakening, Cohen was a founder of the Free Synagogue branch in the Bronx, where he served as the congregation's president. J.X. abandoned the engineering profession and in 1925, at the relatively advanced age of thirty-six, he enrolled as a rabbinic student at the Jewish Institute of Religion, the seminary Wise had established three years earlier.

Cohen was ordained in 1929. Wise recognized J.X.'s talent as a rabbi: a trained engineer who had worked in the real world. Stephen hired him as a Free Synagogue staff member. Over the next two decades, Cohen directed studies of employment discrimination and authored several studies on the subject, including "Jews, Jobs, and Discrimination," published in 1937. Cohen was Stephen Wise's troubleshooter who visited Nazi Germany in 1936 and later traveled to South America in 1941 to gain firsthand knowledge about the Jewish community on that continent.

J.X. was also active in the American Jewish Congress, serving both on its Governing Council and as chair of its National Committee. During his Free Synagogue career, Cohen opposed all forms of bigotry in the business and in-dustrial arena and was a strong supporter of President Roosevelt's New Deal programs. J.X. was also instrumental in strengthening the Jewish chaplaincy programs in New York City's hospitals and prisons.[19]

In 1930 a rumor was brought to Wise's attention that the American Tobacco Company headed by George Washington Hill (1884–1946) had dis-missed all of the company's Jewish employees. Because of his business back-ground, Rabbi J. X. Cohen was assigned to investigate the company's personnel policies. After a ten-week investigation, he told Wise there was no basis for the rumor.

After Wise made Cohen's report public, on February 2, 1931, he received an appreciative letter from Justice Mitchell May (1870–1961) of the Supreme Court of the state of New York:

> I congratulate you on the statement issued . . . relative to the charge that the American Tobacco Company had discharged its Jewish employees. . . . As we demand that justice be done us so we must adhere to the policy not to do injus-tice to others. . . . Sensitive people are prone to believe every rumor . . . of in-tolerance towards them. . . . The said statement was in line with the reputation you have earned of fairness, not only to our people but to all people.[20]

A few years later, there were also charges that the giant tobacco company pursued a pro-Nazi policy because it feared losing the profitable German ciga-rette market that included the popular Lucky Strike brand. Once again, J. X. Cohen investigated the charge and discovered it was baseless and without merit. On July 14, 1934, Wise declared that he accepted at full value the statement made by the American Tobacco Company with respect to its alleged support of the Nazi movement . . . The previous charge was unfair and unjust. It is unthinkable that the ATC should contribute financially or in any other way to the Nazi movement. . . . [The charge is] inexplicable, malicious in character. I accept the personal word of Mr. George Hill, the President of the ATC that the charge is absolutely false.[21]

Edward L. Bernays (1891–1995), the nephew of Sigmund Freud, is considered the "father" of "spin," or modern public relations.

In 1916 Louise Wise continued her own charitable work, taking on the ambitious project of helping Jewish orphans find loving homes and families. She learned that Jewish children left to the care of New York State were routinely placed in asylums because no agency existed to care for them. The rabbi's wife established the Louise Waterman Wise Child Adoption Agency of the Free Synagogue. It was a complex undertaking that involved searching for thousands of Jewish orphans, gaining custody of them, and then placing them in caring Jewish homes throughout America.

In 1917 Louise was enthusiastic after receiving a large financial contribution to her agency:

A red letter day! Adolph Lewisohn [1849–1935; an original Free Synagogue member, a mining executive, art collector, and philanthropist] gave me one thousand dollars to begin my baby-caring work. I can keep twenty babies out of the asylums for a year on that and soon we shall get more and make a big work of it. How I hate those awful asylums where so many poor helpless babies die who might live and ought have the chance such as my babies did.[22]

Three years later she remained enthusiastic, but Louise was also more aware of the problem of finding and rescuing orphans and then placing them in loving homes:

Baby adoption grows almost too big for my strength—yet what joy it was to see one of our babies going away today with a lovely mother looking as rosy and round as an apple. The joy compensates for the sacrifices of time and strength.[23]

Chapter 9

The Year When Everything Changed—The Triangle Factory Fire and the "Subarctic" Waldorf-Astoria Dinner

In 1911 Wise was only thirty-seven years old, but he was already building a reputation for chastising the rich, powerful, and self-satisfied elites of the United States. He was a New York City leader in the Progressive social and political movement that reached its zenith between 1890 and the end of World War I—a movement that changed America and its people.[1]

Wise had an extraordinary speaking ability that evoked powerful responses from his many audiences. Wise's autobiography, *Challenging Years*, was reviewed in the *New Yorker* magazine seven months after Stephen's death in 1949. He was described as

> an Old Testament prophet in a business suit . . . wired for sound, and a mystic as well as a warrior who fought for many causes—the improvement of civic government, Wilsonian idealism in world affairs, labor, the New Deal and Zionism.[2]

The Reverend Dr. John Haynes Holmes, Wise's longtime Christian ally, said of his friend,

> I have heard great orators Robert G. Ingersoll [1833–1899], William Jennings Bryan, [David] Lloyd George [1863–1945], Winston Churchill [1874–1965], but none of them touch Wise for sheer magnificence similar to the prophets of Israel.[3]

The American Jewish Archives, located on the Cincinnati campus of the Hebrew Union College–Jewish Institute of Religion, has gathered some recordings of Wise's sermons. Hearing them today even with the limited audio technology of his era still evinces Wise's rhetorical power. Stephen spoke in a deep baritone voice that enunciated each syllable with great care. He used the same sonorous speaking style when he conducted worship services at the Free

Synagogue and elsewhere. His powerful voice was a key component of his appeal and effectiveness as a religious and political leader.

During much of Wise's career, public leaders did not have the benefit of either radio or television to transmit their messages; it was a period when gifted orators provided their large audiences with popular entertainment, culture, information, and news. Wise's booming voice with its always-compelling message and eloquent phrasing was heard at hundreds of civic and religious meetings advocating Jewish and Progressive causes.

Before Wise, few rabbis had ventured into the American public arena with such prominence and vigor to pursue a broad social justice agenda. Prior to the Civil War, some rabbis, led by David Einhorn (1809–1879), had opposed slavery while others, most notably Morris J. Raphall (1798–1868), joined like-minded Christian ministers in citing certain biblical verses as proof texts to defend the "peculiar institution."[4]

Raphall was Congregation B'nai Jeshurun's spiritual leader between 1849 and 1866. Twenty-six years later Stephen Wise became the synagogue's rabbi. The contrast between the two men who led the same New York City congregation in different eras could not have been greater.

Once the Civil War ended in 1865, most Jewish and Christian clergy were content to perform their traditional tasks: teaching and preaching, performing life cycle events, and in the case of Orthodox rabbis, adjudicating Talmudic questions and guaranteeing that the strict requirements of kashrut (ritual and dietary purity) were met as the American Jewish population expanded during the late nineteenth and early twentieth centuries.

But Wise shattered that comfortable and comforting mold by going far beyond the pious sermons and sweet songs of the synagogue and church. During his career, Wise perfected the art of public rallies, economic boycotts, public relations campaigns that employed print media and the new invention of radio beginning in the 1920s, citizen petition drives, the creation of civil rights organizations, congressional testimonies, interreligious coalitions, face-to-face meetings with public officials including American presidents, and in a sharp break from the docile clergy roles supporting specific political candidates in election campaigns.

On Labor Day in 1909, fifteen years after it became a federal holiday, Wise joined attorney Morris Hillquit (1869–1933), the leader of the Socialist Party in the United States, and Charlotte P. Gillman (1860–1935), an early feminist, women's suffrage supporter, and author, in a public rally supporting the Women's Trade Union League, whose membership included many immigrant workers in New York City's garment manufacturing industry. Wise called for a new era in labor relations:

The synagogue may hope to speak to the workingman only if it first speak for the workingman. . . . The time has come when instead of waging fictitious warfare about the question of the closed shop with labor organizations, there should be an honest and serious attempt to bring about an understanding between capital and labor so there shall be a recognition on the one hand of the right of trades unionism, and on the other hand such adoption of agreement and conciliation as shall virtually make strikes and lockouts and every manner of industrial dispute impossible.[5]

In the same year, Wise joined a large group of prominent leaders in establishing the National Association for the Advancement of Colored People (NAACP). Included in the list of founders were Jane Addams, Roger N. Baldwin (1884–1981), John Haynes Holmes, Emil G. Hirsch, John Dewey, social reformer and muckraking journalist Lincoln Steffens (1866–1936), and Lillian Wald.

Baldwin was also among the founders of the American Civil Liberties Union (ACLU) in 1920 and served as its executive director for many years. The establishment of the ACLU was a reaction to the "Palmer Raids" that followed the end of World War I. Mitchell Palmer (1872–1936) was the US attorney general during the last two years—1919–1921—of the Wilson administration, and he conducted controversial widespread raids in his aggressive search for alleged "radicals and anarchists."[6]

The ACLU itself was the outgrowth of several earlier organizations in the United States that opposed "militarism," the draft, and the armaments race. Before America's entry into World War I in April 1917, Wise was involved in pacifist campaigns along with longtime colleagues including Lillian Wald, Oswald Garrison Villard, Morris Hillquit, George Foster Peabody (1852–1938), Norman Thomas (1884–1968), and Max Eastman (1883–1969). Eastman was a prolific author and political activist who in his early years was a socialist. However, in 1941 he turned away from Progressive causes, and in 1955 he became an original contributing editor of the conservative *National Review*.[7]

A defining moment in the life and times of both the nation and Stephen Wise occurred on Saturday, March 25, 1911. At about 4:40 p.m. an accidental fire broke out at the Triangle Shirtwaist Factory in New York City. The shirtwaist was a popular women's garment of the time that was manufactured in a ten-story building on the corner of Greene Street and Washington Place in Manhattan's Greenwich Village not far from New York University. Nearly all of the six hundred garment employees were Jewish and Italian immigrant women who worked nine hours a day Monday through Friday and an additional seven hours on Saturdays. The women averaged between seven and twelve dollars a week, today's equivalent of between $8,800 and $15,184 in annual wages.

The Triangle Factory owners, Max Blanck and Isaac Harris, were themselves Jewish immigrants from Eastern Europe. Their successful company made them rich men, and they lived an affluent lifestyle on the Upper West Side of Manhattan far from the shabby, overcrowded, and substandard housing of their workers. In 1909 the two owners had beaten back a strike of the company's employees by employing strong-arm tactics to assault and intimidate the workers, most of whom were young women.

In the spring of 1911 the Triangle factory occupied the top three floors of the Asch Building, which also housed some New York University law school classrooms on the lower floors. Blanck and Harris were obsessed that their underpaid and poorly treated employees were stealing finished shirtwaists and selling them on the street to augment their meager wages. To prevent the alleged thefts, the two owners kept their factory exit doors locked so that they could maintain a rigid system of surveillance and prevent pilferage by employees.

When the lethal fire started, Blanck and Harris were in their offices on the top floor. They managed to escape the flames and gain safety by crossing several neighboring rooftops. However, the factory workers on the two floors below were trapped behind locked doors as the fire spread, and although the flames were extinguished within twenty-eight minutes by an alert New York Fire Department, 146 people died in the catastrophe, including 129 women, some of whom leaped to the pavement below to avoid the smoke and fire. The New York City newspapers printed ghoulish pictures of the dead victims lying on the cement sidewalk.[8]

The Triangle fire remains one of New York City's worst human disasters, surpassed only by the September 11, 2001, terrorist attacks that killed nearly three thousand people and the 1904 fire on the steamship *The General Slocum* that sank in the East River when over one thousand passengers died.[9]

On March 26, 1911, a day after the Triangle fire, a bitter and furious Wise spoke at a meeting of the Women's Trade Union League:

> I want the citizens of New York to find out for themselves, through the medium of a committee named at a general mass assembly. If this thing was avoidable, I want to see those responsible punished. If this was due to some corrupt failure to enforce the law, I want to see that determined. And I do not trust public officials to determine it for us; it is our own task to do that for ourselves.[10]

Later that same day, Stephen was the featured speaker at the Holy Trinity Episcopal Church in Brooklyn, the guest of his friend the Reverend John

Howard Melish (1874–1969), a fellow religious and political progressive. Wise told his audience,

> This disaster calls for charity, but more loudly it demands that justice be done to the workers of the nation. The pleasures of the idle rich, however hazardous, are rendered comparatively secure, but the work of the unceasing toilers is surrounded with manifold dangers and endless peril. . . . It is not enough to bewail the fate of those who are lost nor to wring our hands in horror. We stand not before an inscrutable decree of Divine Providence but before the outcome of an unscrupulous degree of human improvidence and human greed. . . . Instead of having safety appliances in a museum, however laudable its purpose, we ought to put in a museum any man who is unwilling to utilize every possible industrial appliance for the safety and security of the toilers.[11]

Philanthropist Anne Tracy Morgan (1873–1952), the daughter of the financier J. Pierpont Morgan (1837–1913), provided the funds necessary to rent the Metropolitan Opera House, and a week later, on Sunday, April 2, at a citywide memorial service in that building, Stephen Wise delivered one of his most compelling and best-remembered speeches. At the event itself, there were emotional and physical tensions between the workingwomen, many of whom had lost friends or family in the fire, and the middle- and upper-class members of Anne Morgan's group, the Women's Trade Union League. The workers wanted justice for the victims' families while the WTUL women, led by Morgan, wanted "reforms."

Jacob Schiff opened the assembly by telling the audience that a large amount of money—seventy-five thousand dollars (about $1.8 million today)— had been raised in the week since the fire; he called the contributions "the public's conscience money."[12] A representative from the Roman Catholic Diocese of Brooklyn spoke representing Bishop Charles E. McDonnell (1854–1921), who was followed by David H. Greer (1844–1919), the Episcopal bishop of New York. Both Christian leaders deplored the large loss of life, and they also affirmed their support for trade unions. Greer declared,

> Hereafter the laws as to fire protection must be enforced, not for a few weeks or a few months but for all time, faithfully, continuously, and effectively. If this is not done the responsibility—the sin—is on the public, on us.[13]

When Greer was finished speaking, many people in the Opera House applauded, but not Wise. In his address, the Episcopal bishop did the expected: he blamed the "public" for the "sin" of the fire and its many deaths. Although Wise respected Greer, he was upset with both his friend's message and the audience's reaction. Whether planned or spontaneous, Stephen took to the stage, quieted the crowd, and then roared:

> Not that! Not that! This is not a day for applause but for contriteness and re-deeming penitence. It is not the action of God, but the inaction of man that is responsible. The disaster was not the deed of God, but the greed of man. This was not inevitable disaster, which could not be foreseen. Some of us foresaw it. We have laws that in a crisis we find are no laws and we have enforcement that when the hour of trial comes we find no enforcement. Let us lift up the indus-trial standards until they will bear inspection. And when we go before the leg-islatures let us not allow them to put us off forever with the old answer, "We have no money." If we have no money for the necessary enforcement of the laws, which safeguard the lives of the workers, it is because so much of our money is wasted and squandered and stolen.[14]

But Wise was not finished:

> This meeting is not summoned in order to appeal for charity on behalf of the families of the slain. What is needed is the redress of justice and the remedy of prevention. The families of the victims ought to be beyond the reach of . . . charity. . . . We ought at least to be willing to give their survivors the justice of economic redress. They need justice, not charity. It is we who need charity for dare we face inexorable justice? . . . The issue is not the open shop, but the closed door, which shuts out the toilers from safety and justice. . . . The life of the lowliest worker in the nation is sacred and inviolable, and, if that sacred human right be violated, we shall stand adjudged and condemned before the tribunal of God and of history.[15]

Wise's thundering remarks stirred the audience, and he received a tumul-tuous tribute, shouts of approval, and cries of excitement. Stephen's friend, Rose Schneiderman (1882–1972), a WTUL leader and feminist, spoke follow-ing the rabbi's remarks. She had been the force behind the failed Triangle workers' strike in 1909. Her remarks were both tearful and sarcastic:

> Public officials have only words of warning for us, warning that we must be in-tensely orderly and must be intensely peaceable, and they have the workhouse just back of all their warnings. . . . The old Inquisition had its rack and its thumbscrews and its instruments of torture with iron teeth. We know what these things are today; the iron teeth are our necessities, the thumbscrews are the high-powered and swift machinery close to which we must work, and the rack is here in the firetrap structures that will destroy us the minute they catch

on fire. . . . The strong hand of the law beats us back when we rise—back to the conditions that make life unbearable. I can't talk fellowship to you who are gathered here. Too much blood has been spilled. I know from experience it is up to the working people to save themselves. And the only way is through a strong working-class movement.

Unlike the earlier orations of Schiff, Greer, and Wise there was no applause when Schneiderman concluded her call to action—only silence.[16] Like Wise and Baldwin, she would also become a founder of the ACLU. Years later Schneiderman served as New York State's secretary of labor from 1937 until 1944, during which time she pressed for equal pay for women and Social Security benefits for domestic workers.

Stephen's bold actions and stirring words inside the Metropolitan Opera House merit analysis because they reveal not only his style and public persona but also his fundamental convictions. Seizing the stage, hushing the crowd, and beginning an oration was pure Stephen Wise. But so, too, were his words. Although there were many rabbis in New York in 1911, Stephen Wise represented that city's Jewish community at the memorial service. This was a role he played many times in his career.

That public profile combined with his charismatic presence allowed Stephen to interrupt a heartfelt round of applause at a solemn memorial meeting. He took command of the opera stage after Bishop Greer concluded his remarks. Within seconds Stephen Wise became the focus of attention. What would he say? How would he say it? Sensing what was to come, it is likely that members of the grieving audience leaned forward in their seats, eager to hear the dynamic rabbi.

Wise jettisoned the conventional talk of charity, whether monetary or emotional, believing it a convenient sop to the victims' families. Stephen demanded something more difficult: justice. And it was not justice in the abstract, but rather he wanted the guilty parties to be punished for the terrible fire. It was not an "act of God" that caused the 146 deaths, but human greed and negligence. Sincere public prayers of piety in a time of crisis were never the answer for Wise. Rather it was a demand for justice in the factories and mines of America, justice for the workers and their families; it was justice in a society that was often craven and criminal in its behavior toward labor. Wise eschewed begging or pleading for charity. Instead, he demanded concrete acts and policies that reflected a just society, a just city, a just state, a just America.

Justice remained a constant theme his entire life. In Stephen's efforts to establish a Jewish state in the Middle East, he did not demand acts of charity from the Great Powers or from the United Nations. He required—he insisted on—justice for the Jewish people. He was aware that individuals, societies, and nations always find it easier to dispense "charity"—prayers, money, sermons—rather than "justice," which demands action, repentance, and most challenging of all, a change in behavior and policies.[17]

Wise's call for justice following the Triangle fire triggered positive responses from three public leaders who played important roles in Wise's later life and career. In 1911 Robert F. Wagner (1877–1949) was the New York State Senate's majority leader, Alfred E. Smith was the State Assembly's majority leader, and Frances Perkins (1880–1965) served as the secretary of the National Consumers League, an organization that advocated for workers' rights and protection.

The three leaders pressed for more and better building codes, regulations of working conditions, the establishment of trade unions, and the prosecution of the guilty exploiters of laboring men and women. In the fire's aftermath, Perkins headed the newly created Committee on Public Safety in New York City, and Smith became the leader of the State Factory Investigating Commission. Sixty out sixty-four proposed New York State laws in the area of public safety and working conditions were passed between 1911 and 1913.[18]

Wagner, Smith, and Perkins—two Catholic men and a Protestant woman—went on to gain national leadership positions, and Stephen Wise was in many ways their conscience and rabbi. All four later became prime champions of President Franklin Roosevelt's New Deal program that emerged in 1933, twenty-two years after the Triangle fire.

Blanck and Harris were indicted for manslaughter and a series of other crimes, but their three-week trial in Manhattan during December 1911, nine months after the fire, resulted in acquittals for both men. A brilliant defense attorney of the period, Max Steuer (1870–1940), convinced a jury that the two owners were unaware that the factory doors were locked. In addition to winning in court, Blanck and Harris received a large insurance settlement—$60,000 (about $1.4 million today), out of which they paid each victim's family a paltry $75 per death (equal to $1,830 today), leaving the owners with a tidy $49,000 (about $1.2 million today) in "fire profit."

But although the factory owners escaped conviction, Wise's call for "justice" instead of "charity" did not go unheeded. After the fire, New York State governor John Alden Dix (1860–1928), a Democrat, established the Factory Investigating Commission (FIC) on June 30, 1911. The commission had extraordinary power to subpoena witnesses, make site visits, and employ a professional staff. Commission members interviewed more than five hundred people in twenty different industries that operated more than three thousand factories in the state.

The commission's negative findings were staggering: many factories lacked fire escapes, and nineteen were infectious, germ-filled workplaces. There was widespread unsanitary food preparation and handling in bakeries. The FIC discovered poor ventilation for many workers, sometimes women employees worked eighteen-hour days, and there were cases of even five-year-old children doing factory work. Only a fifth of the surveyed New York State factories had bathrooms, most of them filthy and disease ridden. State laws were passed requiring factories to install water sprinklers and fire alarms.[19]

On the federal level, in March 1913, just prior to turning the presidency over to Woodrow Wilson, William Howard Taft (1857–1930) signed legislation creating the US Department of Labor. Two decades later when FDR entered the White House, he appointed Frances Perkins as labor secretary, the first female cabinet member in American history. She served in that post until 1945.

Whenever Stephen Wise spoke to an audience or congregation, he chose his words with care, delivering them with a powerful clarity. His sonorous voice and commanding presence conveyed moral authority. During the heyday of the Progressive movement in the years before World War I, Wise believed, falsely as it turned out, that his personal charisma and extraordinary eloquence could convince America's Big Business leaders to join him in pursuing vital social justice goals. This was true following the Triangle fire disaster.

Before the start in 1914 of the "war to end all wars," Wise was active in a host of Progressive causes: workers' rights, poverty, child labor, civil rights (especially as they related to American blacks), and women's suffrage. The self-confident rabbi served on a myriad of organizational boards and committees with leading members of New York City's white Protestant establishment.

In 1911 a blue-ribbon group of wealthy women, mostly wives of bankers and industrialists, established "a free suffrage reading room and library" in Midtown Manhattan "where every woman who shops and lunches can run in between times to put herself straight on the suffrage question if she so desires." The new library's board of managers numbered seventeen women and five men, including Wise.[20]

In the same year the *New York Times* asked Wise and nine other well-known personalities to list the book that had the greatest impact upon them during the past twelve months. In a revealing choice, Wise selected *Daily Bread*, a little-known work by an English poet and author, William Wilfrid Gibson (1878–1962). Wise's description of the book provides an example of Stephen's social justice commitment:

> Simple, sincere, powerful are the glimpses of the life of unprotesting toil and unrevolting misery . . . of the men and women workers in England who spend the whole of their life in toiling for, rather than getting daily bread.[21]

A year before the 1912 US presidential election, Wise became a political ally and personal friend of New Jersey governor Woodrow Wilson, a Progressive Democrat.[22] By 1911 Wise was a religious leader who combined spiritual convictions with a commitment to pursue economic, civil, and human rights for all people.

It was Wilson's idealism and his Progressive programs that compelled Wise in 1911 to switch his political allegiance from the Republican Party to the Democrats. As a six-year-old, Wise marched in torch light parades in support of Winfield Scott Hancock, the 1880 Democratic presidential nominee, but as an adult Stephen had become a Republican, the antislavery party that "saved" the federal Union from destruction. Stephen's support of Wilson marked the end of his support of the GOP.[23]

As the 1912 presidential election neared, American Big Business was under assault from several quarters, led by growing hostility from Progressives and the emerging labor movement. More ominous was the possibility that Wilson, a Democrat, was a favorite to gain his party's nomination, and then win the general election in a three-way race with former president Theodore Roosevelt and the current chief executive, William Howard Taft, also a Republican.

The threat of a president Wilson—with his agenda of a federal income tax, a Federal Reserve System, and antitrust legislation—was threatening to Big Business. America's leading capitalists never forgot that ten years earlier, another Progressive, Teddy Roosevelt, a former New York City police commissioner, had become president following William McKinley's (1843–1901) assassination in Buffalo. But instead of continuing McKinley's pro–Big Business policies, TR mounted a systematic attack on the "trusts," the business and industrial monopolies that dominated America.

The New York State Chamber of Commerce, founded in 1768, was a bastion of Big Business.[24] But in the run-up to the presidential election, the chamber was forced to portray itself as a compassionate organization, in tune with the growing spirit of Progressivism. One way to show the chamber's concern for social and economic justice was to invite Wise to deliver a speech at its gala 143rd annual dinner on November 16, 1911, in the Waldorf-Astoria Hotel in New York City. The dinner attracted four hundred of the richest men in the United States and was a shrewd attempt to convince a skeptical public that Big Business was not deaf to demands for reform—to show that bankers and industrialists "cared" about social justice concerns.

Perhaps chamber leaders believed that the Waldorf-Astoria Hotel setting—the opulent Gilded Age Grand Ballroom—would help mute the forceful rabbinic orator. Or perhaps the presence in the wealthy audience of several prominent Jewish business leaders and financiers, including Jacob Schiff; Paul Warburg (1868–1932); Isidor Straus (1845–1912), the co-owner of Macy's department store, who was to lose his life the following April on the *Titanic*; and Otto Kahn (1867–1934) would intimidate the pro-labor rabbi. Schiff, Warburg, Straus, and Kahn were all original supporters of the Free Synagogue, which may account for Wise's invitation to speak at the dinner.

It is against this historical backdrop that Wise's 1911 speech to the "august assembly" of American capitalists must be viewed. Adding Wise to the speakers' list was not an aberration by Big Business, nor was Stephen's acceptance of that invitation an attempt by the rabbi to gain further public attention. He didn't need it after his public speeches following the Triangle fire.

If Wise believed his personal charisma and extraordinary eloquence would draw the nation's business leaders into supporting the Progressive movement, the dinner provided "the opportunity to face some of America's greatest captains of industry and finance . . . I knew this was a critical occasion, not for the Chamber of Commerce, but for me."[25]

Stephen Wise faced a moral dilemma just moments before he was to deliver one of the most important speeches of his meteoric career: "I could ingratiate myself with this august assembly and lose my soul; I could displease and keep it."[26]

Whatever the reason for receiving a speaking invitation, the handsome, captivating rabbi found himself on the dinner dais as an honored guest. But Wise was nervous and edgy as he waited his turn to speak when he recognized his fellow dais guests and when he heard the speeches that preceded his own remarks.

Sharing the exclusive Waldorf-Astoria podium with Wise were J. P. Morgan, the nation's most successful banker and financier; James J. Hill (1838–1916), the owner of the Great Northern Railroad; Charles Schwab (1862–1939), the owner of Bethlehem Steel; Andrew Carnegie (1835–1919), the US Steel magnate; and Thomas Edison (1847–1931), the world-famous inventor and a one-man business conglomerate.[27]

During the dinner, Morgan offered Wise an expensive Cuban cigar that was custom made for the famous banker. The rabbi accepted the cigar and placed it in his coat pocket. Morgan, lighting up his own cigar, asked whether Wise was going to smoke the expensive gift. Wise told Morgan he didn't smoke. The global financier then asked why the rabbi took the cigar. Wise replied that he would give the cigar to the Free Synagogue janitor who was a smoker. Melvin Urofsky, a biographer of Wise, believes Wise meant no insult. Over the years, Wise always accepted cigars "when offered to him." Later, he would give them to "congregants, friends, or just acquaintances, like the janitor in the synagogue."[28]

Also on the dais were New York City mayor William J. Gaynor (1849–1913); New York governor Dix; Nicholas Murray Butler (1862–1947), president of Columbia University, Wise's alma mater; Elihu Root (1845–1937), US senator from New York and former secretary of state; Lord James Bryce (1838–1922), the British ambassador to the United States; Alabama governor Emmet O'Neal (1853–1922); and the Arctic explorer Admiral Robert Peary (1856–1920).[29]

The dinner audience—all men garbed in elegant tuxedos—included John D. Rockefeller, Jr. (1874–1960), of Standard Oil and William C. McAdoo (1863–1941), the industrialist who owned the new trans–Hudson River train system between New Jersey and New York City. A year later, Butler, Wise's former philosophy professor at Columbia, would become President Taft's vice presidential running mate, and McAdoo would be appointed the secretary of the treasury in the Wilson administration.

Also in the dinner audience were many Wall Street brokers; commodity traders; real estate developers; factory and mine operators; railroad, steamship, and subway proprietors; oil company executives—all members of American's financial elite.

The chamber members were seated at decorated tables adorned by expensive floral displays and bottles of expensive wine. The chamber's official photograph of the 1911 dinner contains no women.[30]

A. Barton Hepburn (1846–1922), husband of one of the board members of the suffragist library in New York City and a past chairman of the Chase Bank, was the Chamber of Commerce president. He delivered introductory remarks that reflected both the defensiveness and the defiance of Big Business:

> Successful builders and managers of industrial enterprises in Canada are knighted. With us they are indicted. . . . It remains to be seen whether [the American] public will receive as good a service at a fair price . . . and whether these segregated corporations [trusts that have been broken up] will continue to contribute . . . to our international trade balance.

Butler was even more combative and increased Wise's anger and anxiety:

> A campaign of education must be undertaken to stop the war on business just as the business men of the country prevented the currency proposal of 1896 [Bryan's populist pro-silver campaign against the gold standard] from becoming a law.

The words of Governor O'Neal were harsh for a Progressive like Wise:

> The people who call themselves progressives are really reactionaries for they are attempting to force upon us laws that were suggested to our fathers [the

Founders of the American Republic] and by them rejected. Unless the heresies are checked, all the forces of Socialism and unrest will be let loose.[31]

Years later Wise remembered that night: "I can feel the audience's subarctic temperatures [a reference to Admiral Peary's recent exploits]."[32]

Even though Stephen Wise was known for his oratorical skills, few in the Chamber of Commerce audience that night were prepared for his blistering assault on the American economic system after the pro-business speeches of Hepburn, Butler, and O'Neal.

Urofsky called Wise's remarks that night "one of his best speeches, although the audience failed to appreciate it, and as much as any talk he ever gave, it summed up his credo as a progressive":[33]

When I have read from time to time of religious noonday meetings held in shops and factories for the wage-earners, I have ventured to observe that the important thing is not so much to bring religious ministrations to the daily toilers—the soldiers of the common good—as to bring it to the captains of industry and commerce, which you are. . . . Yours is the . . . duty . . . of determining . . . the conscience of the nation.

Not only ought . . . business be completely moralized, but we need to ethicize what might be called the processes of creating and production, of distribution and consumption. . . . No business . . . can long endure if it be bound up with the evil of unemployment on the one hand and over-employment on the other, the evil of a man's underwage and a child's toil, and all those other social maladjustments . . . which we lump together under the name of poverty.

The stricken ask not for the occasional tonic of charity, but the daily meat and substance of justice. . . . The conscience of the nation is not real unless the nation safeguards him from the peril of overwork . . . [and] the accidents of industry. . . . Unless we protect women and children in industry, and protect them with half of the thoroughness and generosity with which we . . . have protected infant industries, we have not the right to speak of . . . conserving the opportunity for initiative on the part of the individual as long as masses of individuals are suffered to perish without the opportunity of real life.

The aim of democracy is not to be production of efficient, machine-like men in industry. The first business of democracy is to be the industry of turning out completely effective, completely free and self-determining citizens. . . . Conscience demands that business . . . recognize that articles of incorporation are not to be offered as a substitute for the Decalogue![34]

It was the first and last time he was invited to address the Chamber of Commerce or to ever again share a dais with such prominent "captains of

industry." The audience's negative reaction to his remarks was indeed "subarctic." Bishop's history of the New York State Chamber of Commerce contains
no mention of either the November 16, 1911, dinner or Stephen Wise.

The morning following the dinner, the *New York Times* carried a lengthy
account of the dinner—two and a half columns—describing the event in precise detail. Most of the article centered on British ambassador Bryce's glowing
tribute to the political and economic achievements of New York City and the
United States. By contrast, Wise received a scant thirteen lines in the lengthy
Times story: an accurate reflection of Big Business's icy response to the rabbinical call to conscience.

Until the Chamber of Commerce speech, Wise had often emphasized the
morality of the Progressive agenda in general terms and avoided calls for the
passage of specific legislation or the election of particular candidates. But his
experience at the Waldorf-Astoria dinner and the *New York Times* coverage of
the event convinced Wise that if he wanted to make a difference in addressing
the ills of an expanding industrialized society, more than personal charisma
and soaring oratory were required.

The negative reaction to his speech plus the political opportunities created
by Wilson's election in 1912 were a turning point and moved Wise beyond being a great public speaker. Instead, he became a strong advocate of Progressive
legislation that protected and enhanced the lives of factory workers, women,
children, miners, Jews, Asians, blacks, immigrants, the underemployed and
the unemployed, the elderly, and members of the US armed forces.[35]

As a result of his bitter Chamber of Commerce dinner experience, Wise
became active in the political arena, although never as an aspirant to elective
office. He understood his role to be a morally alert clergyman who campaigned for worthy candidates and legislation.

In the years after 1911 Wise publicly supported specific presidential candidates, including Wilson, Smith, Norman Thomas, and most of all, FDR.
Stephen was a New York State delegate to the long and bitterly divided 1924
Democratic National Convention that revealed the spilt within the party between urban progressives and rural conservatives, some of whom were members of the racist Ku Klux Klan. Thomas, an ordained Presbyterian minister,
ran for the presidency six times as the Socialist Party candidate, and Wise
voted for him in the 1932 election that pitted Roosevelt against the GOP candidate, President Herbert Hoover (1874–1964).

Stephen Wise learned a painful lesson from both the tragic Triangle fire
and the gala Waldorf-Astoria dinner: stirring rhetoric, even charity, may be
necessary weapons, but by themselves they are not sufficient to achieve
Progressive goals and policies in the public arena. The tragic fire in March
1911 and the New York State Chamber of Commerce dinner in November of

the same year changed Wise. He moved from sheer oratory to the more complex tasks of meaningful political action, successful electoral campaigns, and the enactment of Progressive public policies.

Wise always remembered his call for justice uttered inside the Metropolitan Opera House during a memorial service as well as the negative "subarctic" reaction to his speech at the Waldorf-Astoria—the night when for the first and only time he broke bread with the captains of industry.

Chapter 10

The Progressive Warrior

As Stephen Wise neared his fortieth birthday in 1914, he was at the peak of his powers: an extraordinary speaker, becoming one of the nation's most influential clergy, the founding rabbi of the Free Synagogue, and a public advocate of the US Zionist movement, albeit still small in numbers and influence. But there was always more for the energetic and ambitious Stephen Wise to accomplish. In the years before the start of World War I, he became hyperactive in championing a myriad of social justice issues.

Because of his acute built-in personal antenna, Wise was able to pick up the Zeitgeist of his times and act upon it. This was true during the administrations of Theodore Roosevelt (1901–1909), the Republican "trust buster," and Woodrow Wilson (1913–1921), only the second Democrat to be elected to the US presidency following the end of the Civil War; the first was Grover Cleveland (1837–1908), who served two separate terms: 1885–1889 and 1893–1897.

In a 1913 Free Synagogue lecture, Stephen discussed his concept of "civic religion":

> Let us not make a scapegoat of some single political force or organization and thus try to explain away civic inefficiency and righteousness. . . . [They are] made possible by the indifference and lethargy of the multitude who do not care, and moreover, by the inefficiency and incompetence of many of those who set forth to lead the forces of reform.[1]

In the heady days before America's entry into World War I in 1917, Wise believed his Progressive views, including pacifism, were coming to fruition. He was encouraged that Wilson, a former president of Princeton University and the son of a Virginia Presbyterian minister, kept the United States out of war with neighboring Mexico during the tense period of 1916–1917 when Pancho Villa (1878–1923) led an attack against US citizens in Columbus, New Mexico. In that attack, Villa, the Mexican revolutionary leader, lost over a hundred of his fighters. Eight American soldiers and ten US civilians were also killed.

Wise was also confident that the president would not involve the United States in the Great War (World War I) that began in August 1914 and involved Russia, Austro-Hungary, Germany, Great Britain, France, Italy, and Turkey.

As a result of the tragic Triangle fire, other Progressives led by Democrats Robert Wagner and Alfred E. Smith had strengthened their leadership positions in the New York State legislature, and the news was also encouraging in New York City with the 1913 election of the young reformer mayor, John P. Mitchel (1879–1918).

With these Progressive gains in mind, Stephen Wise articulated his concept of why and how religious leaders and institutions must be involved in the public sphere. In 1914 he wrote to one of Mitchel's aides,

> I have been trying to formulate myself just what it is I have in mind when I say as I do that church and synagogue together want to have a large and impressive part in the shaping of the civic life of a community. I need not say . . . that I believe in the wisdom of the wall as between church and state . . . but it is the business of the church and synagogue to have a large part in lifting up the tone of the city's life. The man in the pulpit . . . must speak unafraid in what he believes to be the truth and the right. This may at times involve him in serious disagreement with the officials of the city, for the preacher must dare to speak of wrong when wrong is done by a city's head or heads. It may not be the popular nor the pleasant thing to do, but a man who dares to speak in the name of God must dare to speak nothing less than the truth however much it hurts. . . . I think it also necessary to emphasize that church and synagogue must not limit themselves to fault-finding. While they must dare to speak the truth as regards wrong when wrong is done, they must also and even primarily be generous and appreciative when city officials do their duty finely and faithfully.[2]

During his career, Stephen Wise fought two successful public battles against the corrupt Democratic political organization that was known as Tammany Hall. That term stemmed from an American Indian name, and for over a hundred years it was a strong political force in New York politics.

During its history Tammany Hall was ruled by a series of "bosses" or "grand sachems" who controlled city patronage jobs, building and construction contracts, and appointments to the judiciary; manipulated shady real estate deals; and were linked to brothels, gambling parlors, and saloons. "Sachem" is a Native American term for a powerful leader.

Throughout its history most of Tammany's leadership was Irish, and it exercised electoral power—including the selection of New York City mayors,

district attorneys, and judges—because it was the source and dispenser of
many favors that were given to first- and second-generation Irish Americans.

The name of one grand sachem has entered into the permanent lexicon of
corrupt American politics: William Tweed (1823–1878). For nearly twenty
years beginning in 1858, "Boss" Tweed wielded enormous political and economic power: choosing and controlling candidates, distributing lucrative jobs,
and rewarding loyal allies with influential city committees and commissions.

Tweed was convicted of financial corruption involving millions of dollars,
and he died in a Manhattan jail. However, Tammany Hall continued its infamous role in New York City until the 1960s when it ceased to exist as an effective political force. Wise, Holmes, and other Progressives were vigorous foes
of Tammany Hall.

In 1908, two years after Wise's return to New York City from Oregon, he
had his first battle with Tammany when Grand Sachem Richard Croker
(1843–1922) announced his return to America from exile in his native Ireland.
Croker's friends arranged a gala public dinner in his honor, and among the
guests who attended were a dozen New York Supreme Court judges and a district attorney. Wise, never at a loss for coining an apt phrase, called the Croker
dinner "New York's Night of Shame." Stephen was appalled by the grotesque
spectacle of judges attending a banquet that saluted a corrupt political boss.

The New York City press picked up Wise's phrase, and in its December
1908 issue, *LIFE*, a journal of the era, described the "Night of Shame" in vivid
terms:

> Of course, the judges went to the Croker dinner. A good many, if not all, owed
> their nominations to him. . . . Nobody doubts . . . that gamblers, liquor-sellers,
> and disorderly houses paid tribute to somebody for protection in Croker's
> time . . . and that police captains got rich . . . a part of the Tammany system of
> government. . . . That Tammany and those who managed it, had an immense
> rake-off in Croker's time at the cost of the people . . . All that is shameful,
> Croker cannot possibly escape such shame as belongs to him as a notable head
> and profit-taker of a shameful system. . . . And Rabbi Wise was right in saying
> that it was a shameful night for New York.

The Croker dinner was intended to be the triumphal reassertion of Croker
to leadership of Tammany Hall. But Wise's public attacks prevented that from
happening. Years later, another sachem told Stephen, "Your phrase, 'New
York's Night of Shame,' and the public's reaction to it killed that plan."[3]

In 1915 Wise visited anthracite coal mines in the small town of Lykens,
Pennsylvania, and discovered the perennial problems that American miners
face. He described what he saw in a letter to Louise:

Portland *Daily Oregonian*, cartoon of Wise fighting New York City political corruption, 1908. Permission granted by the Stephen Wise Free Synagogue Archives.

I have seen a coalmine producing about 600,000 tons yearly. . . . But what a sight—the dear little breaker boys, supposed to be 14 or over who stand and separate the coal from the slate, from seven in the morning until 4:30 in the afternoon. Formerly they began at eight or nine years. . . . I'm glad to have seen it all, the dirt and the grime, and the hardship, for it moves me to see more clearly that if this be God's world—and it is—our first business is more justly to distribute the burdens of his children and to apportion their reward.[4]

Eight years later in 1922, Stephen was asked to investigate the New River Coal Company in West Virginia. Leaders of the coal miners wanted an outside observer to gather evidence about the wretched working conditions. Wise was happy to accept the invitation, declaring,

Long before it [the report] is completed, the operators will be sorry they extended the invitation to us. . . . The people of New York are going to get the facts about West Virginia and the brutal assaults on the thousands of miners in America.[5]

A year after the Triangle fire, Stephen was asked to mediate a dispute between labor and management in a Pennsylvania textile factory. He was probably not surprised to learn that young girls worked long hours in the mills; that was bad enough. Making it worse was the fact that the child laborers in dirty, dangerous, and often disease-ridden factories received only two or three dollars per week in wages, less than half the meager salary paid to the ill-fated shirtwaist workers in New York City:

The mill's . . . forelady was receiving six dollars a week for fifty-eight hours of work. . . . The superintendent cursed and even struck some of the women and children . . . which I shall never forget. . . . I was struck by the degrading conditions of the workers, including small children, their inability to win even the most modest wages, which were not sufficient to buy the merest necessities of life. . . . No basic change could be made in the life of the workers until they had won the right to organize and bargain collectively.[6]

The 1979 award-winning film *Norma Rae*, based on the life story of Crystal Lee Sutton (1940–2009), is a cinematic example of art imitating life. Wise would have been disappointed to see how little the textile mills had changed in the sixty-seven years between his visit to the Pennsylvania mill and the making of the movie. In *Norma Rae*, the Jewish union organizer describes the factory that in real life was the J. B. Stevens Company in Roanoke Rapids, North Carolina:

The textile industry, in which you are spending your lives and your substance, and in which your children and their children will spend their lives and their substance, is the only industry in the whole length and breadth of the United States of America that is not unionized. Therefore, they are free to exploit you, to cheat you, to lie to you, and to take away what is rightfully yours—your health, a decent wage, a fit place to work.[7]

In 1915, it was a case of déjà vu for Stephen when there was another street-car workers' strike in New York City. Twenty years earlier when he was the rabbi at Congregation B'nai Jeshurun, Wise supported the striking transit workers, and he did so again in 1915. In a letter to his wife, Stephen made clear his strong pro-labor views and actions:

I hope the [striking] men may win but [I] fear violence. . . . I will not use the "L" [the NYC elevated rail system] or subway during the strike. Am I not right? I will not be served by strike breakers.[8]

Wise, never shy from expressing his views on a myriad of issues, entered into another heated controversy in the spring of 1915 with the release of D. W. Griffith's (1875–1948) film *The Birth of a Nation*. Stephen was furious about the silent movie's harsh portrayal of "Negroes," the term then in popular usage. Other progressives as well as the NAACP leadership joined him in criticizing the three-hour-and-ten-minute film.

On March 30, 1915, Wise; W. E. B. DuBois (1868–1963), the editor of the NAACP publication *The Crisis*; Oswald Garrison Villard, the *New York Post* editor; and other religious and civic leaders met with Mayor Mitchel to protest the anti-Negro elements in the Griffith production. The interracial and inter-religious group urged the mayor to ban the film from New York theaters, but Mitchel rejected their plea, claiming he did not have such censorship power.

However, he told his visitors that because of his personal intervention, two offensive scenes would be cut from the New York City screenings: the attempted rape scene and the efforts employed to force the Lillian Gish (1893–1993) character to marry a "mulatto."

The mayor's response was insufficient for Wise:

If it is true that the Mayor has no power to stop this unexcusably foul and loathsome libel on a race of human beings, then it is true that the [New York City] government has broken down. . . . The film's producers are contemptible cowards. . . . The Negroes in this city have been patient. They have not yet arisen, like the Irish who attacked "The Playboy of the Western World" when they recognized it was as a caricature not as a characterization.[9]

Wise was referring to the 1911 riots in New York City when *Playboy* was performed on stage. Although the play's author, John M. Synge (1871–1909), was himself Irish, others perceived his drama as an attack on the Irish people.

The Birth of a Nation was the first film to be shown at the White House. After the screening, President Wilson reportedly remarked, "It is like writing history with lightning. And my only regret is that it is all too terribly true."[10]

Lillian Wald was fearful about possible violent audience reactions to Griffith's movie:

> It is impossible to measure the potential dangers that threaten us if the production is allowed to go.[11]

The following day a group of Christian clergy led by the Presbyterian minister Charles H. Parkhurst (1842–1933) met with Mayor Mitchel. Parkhurst, an ally of Wise in fighting the corrupt Tammany Hall Democratic organization, differed with his rabbinic colleague. The Protestant pastor said *Birth of a Nation* depicted the Negro "as he was" immediately after the Civil War. He added that slavery's "chains had broken . . . [The Negro] was ignorant as a baby of the way to use [freedom]." Parkhurst told the mayor the film was "exactly true to history."[12]

Wald's concerns were realized on April 17 at Boston's Tremont Theater, when

> 500 negroes [*sic*], headed by W. Munroe Trotter [1872–1934] . . . arrived in a body and tried to buy tickets. The management declared that the house was sold out. . . . Trotter and his friends, among whom were several white men, assumed such an attitude that Manager Schoeffel called in the police, and a squad of 100 hurried to the theater in automobiles. The lobby was cleared without the use of clubs and the performance proceeded. . . . Six arrests were made—[including] Trotter, the Rev. A. W. Fuller, pastor of the People's Baptist Church . . . and Joseph Gould, a white man.[13]

Trotter had graduated magna cum laude from Harvard in 1895, where he also received a graduate degree. He was the first African American to be elected to the Phi Beta Kappa academic honorary society. Trotter later became the editor of the *Boston Guardian* newspaper that served the black community, and he achieved national notoriety by exhibiting a negative "disrespectful" tone toward President Wilson during a White House meeting. Even though had been a supporter of Wilson's election in 1912, the angry president barred Trotter from any future visits or meetings for the remainder of his administration.

The Birth of a Nation was banned in Kansas City, St. Louis, Minneapolis, and Pittsburgh, and the film is credited with spurring the membership growth of the Ku Klux Klan in many parts of the United States.

In May 1919 Wise addressed his fellow members of the National Conference on Lynching at a meeting in Carnegie Hall. Joining Wise were Charles
Evans Hughes, the 1916 Republican candidate for president, former Alabama
governor Emmet O'Neal, and Dr. Emma Howard Shaw (1847–1919). The latter
was a national leader of the women's suffrage movement as well as a physician
and an ordained Methodist minister.

For Wise and O'Neal it was a strange reunion since they had both spoken
eight years earlier at the New York State Chamber of Commerce dinner. Even
though he had espoused a conservative political position at the Waldorf-
Astoria banquet, during O'Neal's years as Alabama's governor—1911–1915—
he supported state legislation that protected child laborers and coal miners.[14]

The National Conference on Lynching, organized by the NAACP, was
committed to combating the growing number of murderous attacks on
American blacks. Lynching had become a serious problem for several reasons:
the emergence of the Klan in many parts of the United States and the spike in
antiblack feelings among whites during World War I that culminated in race
riots in several large US cities, including Chicago and Omaha in 1919 and
Tulsa in 1921.

During World War I many southern blacks migrated to northern cities in
search of better employment opportunities in various war industries. The
surge in population created severe housing problems in urban ghettos that
were further complicated by black military personnel returning from the conflict, who, empowered by their war service, pressed for greater freedom.
Lynching increased as black-white competition for jobs heightened in many
locations.

There were 64 reported lynchings in 1918 and 83 a year later. But because of
poor reporting methods and official suppression of such lethal attacks, the
number was probably much higher. A journal of the time put the number of
lynchings between 1889 and 1919 at 3,224, with 2,834 taking place in the
American South.[15]

Wise believed that lynching in the United States

will be stamped out . . . The time has come when Americans want nothing for
which they must apologize. The stain on our beloved land caused by lynching
must be wiped out. I will not insult those of the negro [sic] race present by
pleading for compassion for your race. . . . There is no such thing as "Jewish
rights" only "human rights." I demand in the name of democracy, justice for
the negro race.[16]

Wise may have criticized the concept of specific Jewish rights, but there is
no doubt that his fervor against lynching, racial and religious bigotry, and
all forms of prejudice was driven by his knowledge of violent anti-Semitic

pogroms in Europe and other attacks upon Jews throughout history. He acted on the premise that an attack on one religious, ethnic, or racial group was an attack on all groups.

Wise was also aware that lynching in America was not limited to blacks; the Leo Frank hanging in 1915 near Atlanta had shaken the American Jewish community's sense of security. The twenty-five-man vigilante gang included a former state governor, a mayor, judges, and many law enforcement officials. As a direct result of Frank's murder, more than half of Georgia's three thousand Jews fled the state in fear.[17]

Another of Stephen Wise's causes was the right of women to vote, and he made numerous speeches throughout the United States in behalf of universal suffrage. In 1908 he wrote that the right of women to vote

appeals to me tremendously. I want women to have fuller, larger, richer lives. Equal suffrage is one of the avenues thereto. That's why I favor it.[18]

In 1915, five years before the constitutional amendment on suffrage became the law of the land, he wrote,

Women must vote, saloons must be closed, all men get a living wage and more, war ended. . . . That's all I want.[19]

Wise's support of Prohibition may today seem puzzling, but it represented a similar position he took in Portland, Oregon, where he witnessed the public dangers, including criminal activity, that erupted inside taverns, bars, and saloons. Wise's negative views about alcohol were shared by other leaders in the Progressive movement, including Jane Addams and Upton Sinclair (1878–1968), the muckraking novelist and 1934 Democratic candidate for governor of California.[20]

Wise believed with many others that the use of alcohol often caused child abuse, poverty, and violent attacks on women. It is sometimes forgotten that the Eighteenth Amendment to the US Constitution—Prohibition—was adopted with the support of Progressives as well as religious conservatives. The law went into effect in 1920 and was not repealed until 1933.

Only four months after Prohibition began, there were already public calls for its repeal, but Wise supported the constitutional ban on alcoholic beverages. In a Free Synagogue sermon at Carnegie Hall on April 11, 1920, Wise declared,

It is an insult to the intelligence and dignity and honor of the American people to keep the liquor issue in the forefront of American life. . . . Enforcement or repeal, but not the cowardly and lawless evasion . . . The American people would visit its wrath upon the heads of any group or party . . . which sought to annul the will of the people.[21]

But Wise was also prescient in sensing that Prohibition would create lawlessness within America, including bootlegging, smuggling, and the rapid rise of organized crime.

As so often happens in times of war, iron and steel factory owners and munitions makers profited from an armed conflict. However, this was not the general rule for labor, especially the American workers who worked long and hard in support of the national war effort but did not share in their companies' large financial gains.

On September 22, 1919, ten months after the Armistice, employees of the US Steel Corporation and several other steel companies went on strike and shut down about 50 percent of the nation's mills. Increased wages, better working conditions, and above all, the right to organize as a trade union were the key issues in the strike. But management was adamant in refusing to meet the strikers' demands, and the steel companies used scab workers, coercion, and physical violence as weapons to break the workers. The situation deteriorated, and in one case, the US Army took control of a chaotic situation in Gary, Indiana, an important steel-producing city.

Adding to the strikers' problems was the fact that most Americans at the time did not support labor or trade unions. In fact, the mill owners capitalized on the widespread Red Scare of the period and labeled the strikers "Reds," "Bolsheviks," or "radical anarchists." "Anti-Red" fever was rampant in the United States in the first years after the Russian Revolution of 1917, and the steel strike collapsed on January 8, 1920. It was not until 1936, during the New Deal, that the United Steel Workers trade union was formed. These were the realities Wise faced in 1919 when he entered into the complex arena of strikes, labor, and steel moguls.

Wise's earlier support of textile workers, coal miners, streetcar operators, child laborers, and abused women in the workplace served as preparation for his monumental battle in 1919 on behalf of the US Steel Corporation workers. Stephen wrote that his involvement in the struggle to organize those workers was "inevitable."[22]

The central issue for Progressives was labor's "right to organize" in the face of a hostile steel company, headed by Judge Elbert H. Gary (1846–1927), the man whose name was given to the Indiana city. Gary, a Chicago judge, remained the president and chairman of the board of USS until his death, and he personified the harsh antilabor policies and actions of his company.

Wise's struggle with Gary began on June 18, 1919, when Wise wrote a letter of support to Samuel Gompers (1850–1925), the president of the American Federation of Labor (AFL). Gompers and his organization backed the steelworkers in their dispute with management. Wise, who was rarely naïve, added in his note,

> Surely the heads of the steel industry will not be idiotic enough to attempt to withstand the organization of their workers. I cannot believe, despite their record, that they would be so Bourbonish.[23]

The Bourbons were French royalists, and the term came to signify extreme or ultrareactionary conservatism. But Wise later admitted he was wrong, and when he saw that the "church and press alike" were indifferent to the steelworkers, he felt compelled to speak out in their defense.

On the first two Sundays in October 1919 Stephen delivered a pair of fiery sermons before large audiences in Carnegie Hall, and the orations represent his strongest anti–Big Business and pro-labor speeches. Indeed, he pushed his beloved principle of a free pulpit to the limit, because the lectures threatened his position as the Free Synagogue's rabbi.

On October 5 Wise delivered a sermon before fifteen hundred people that targeted Gary and his antilabor policies. As he left home for Carnegie Hall that Sunday morning, he told Louise, "My sermon of this morning will light a million-dollar blaze." He placed a provocative title on his remarks: "Who Are the Bolshevists at Home and Abroad?" and the following Sunday he posed another provocative question: "How Ought the Pulpit Deal with the Industrial Situation?"[24]

The following week Wise again attacked Gary and the steel magnates and used one of his most celebrated and lasting phrases. He asserted that Big Steel had "Cossackized and terrorized the workers by means of coercion and violence." "Cossack" was the general designation for roaming armed groups that operated for centuries in southern Russia, Ukraine, and Poland, often carrying out violent attacks upon Jews in the region.[25]

The most infamous and brutal Cossack assault took place in 1648, led by Bogdan Chmielnicki (1595–1657), and is estimated to have killed between one hundred thousand and a half million Jews. Although the exact numbers will never be known, rabbis of the period likened the catastrophe to the Roman destruction of the Holy Temple in Jerusalem sixteen centuries earlier. The Cossack onslaught became an indelible part of Jewish history.

By employing a well-known, highly charged negative term to describe the antilabor tactics of Big Steel, Wise tapped into his audience's collective memory. He also rebuked the wealthy members of his congregation for letting "Gary fight the battle of capitalism for them."[26]

Wise was furious when he learned that half of the steelworkers

> were still working twelve hour days and the employers had resorted to the use
> of the black list and the labor spy as weapons in their industrial war . . . [World
> War I] was won just as much by the workers in the steel-mills of Pennsylvania
> and Ohio as by the American soldiers in France. . . . The heads of a great
> number of industries in America have set out to reverse . . . the gains to the
> workers. . . . .The men in the iron and steel industry are striving for a funda-
> mental right . . . to organize . . . to deal with their employers. . . . Things
> would still be as they were up to five years ago [before the war] . . . if Judge
> Gary and his associates could have averted the pressure of public judgment, of
> public wrath and of public contempt. The Steel Corporation granted nothing
> voluntarily nor will it ever. . . . Mr. Gary and his associates . . . tell us that a
> minority controls a majority. Well, the fact is that a minority always leads, pre-
> cedes, and liberates a majority. . . . I charge the United States Steel Corporation
> with resorting to every manner of coercion and even of violence. . . . If I am li-
> beling the heads of the Steel Corporation, they have the power of redress.[27]

He also learned that US Steel was attempting to pit the Serbian workers
against the Italian laborers in the mills. It was a divide-and-conquer tactic
that Wise described as "racial hatred" of the worst kind.[28] The indefatigable
rabbi repeated his speech later that night before a Brooklyn Civic Forum audience of two thousand people who had gathered in Public School 84 at
Glenmore and Stone Avenues.

At that meeting, Wise roared he didn't know whether his attacks on Gary
and Big Steel would cost him a "beautiful $1,000,000 synagogue but it is nec-
essary for me to speak the truth and, if it is necessary, I am ready to go to
Pittsburgh [America's major steel-producing city] to make the same speech."[29]

As usual, Wise alerted the press in advance of the sermon, and his remarks
were reported not only by the nation's major newspapers but also in places like
Geneva, New York, where the *Daily Times* reported on page one that Wise
characterized Gary and his large corporation as "among the most prolific breeders of Bolshevism . . . If I am libeling them, they know where to
find me."[30]

As a result of the press coverage, Stephen received many letters of both
support and opposition from around the country. However, closer to home,
Wise's attacks on Big Steel sparked angry reactions among some Free
Synagogue members. A Chicago paper noted,

> It appears that a number of [Free Synagogue] members, seven in all, resigned
> their membership during the week. . . . For these reasons . . . Dr. Wise

publicly announced his readiness to step out of his pulpit, if any large part, not
necessarily even one-third, of his congregation decided such a step to be
necessary.[31]

Wise devoted space in his autobiography to the first and only time the Free
Synagogue's policy of an open and free pulpit was "put to the test."[32] Because
Stephen faced a series of congregational resignations from mostly wealthy
members, Wise offered to step down from his rabbinical position.[33]

As a result of Wise's threat to resign, the Free Synagogue's executive committee met to discuss the issue under the leadership of Oscar Straus (1850–
1926), a trusted Wise admirer and ally. Straus, the first Jew to attain
presidential cabinet status (he served as Theodore Roosevelt's secretary of
commerce and labor), and his colleagues refused Wise's resignation and reaffirmed their confidence in their rabbi's leadership. However, the executive
committee did provide a nuanced response to those who believed Wise's anti–
Big Steel attacks reflected upon the entire American Jewish community.
Straus's group asserted the rabbi "speaks not for but to the congregation."[34]
Wise kept his job, but any hope for a successful building campaign was a casualty of the controversy. However, there is doubt whether Stephen Wise actually desired the construction of a Free Synagogue structure.

Perhaps buoyed by the strong support of his congregation's leadership,
Wise continued to play a key role in the steelworkers' strike. In October 1919,
the same month Wise delivered his two anti-Gary sermons, Stephen was a
speaker at a meeting of the Inter-Church World Movement (ICWM), a coalition of thirty Protestant denominations that was established in 1918 thanks to
John D. Rockefeller, Jr., a major financial supporter of the progressive Christian
organization. The ICWM was an "ambitious experiment into interdenomina-
tional cooperative action."[35]

In his speech to the Christian organization, Wise urged the ICWM as part
of its religious mandate to investigate the "facts" of the steel strike. The group
heeded Wise's suggestion, believing such an investigation was justified as an
active and appropriate part of Christian witness and ministry. In 1919 Dr.
Fred B. Fisher (1882–1938), an ICWM leader, declared,

The principles taught and lived by Jesus Christ and entrusted His followers
[should be] the dominating force in the adjustment of industrial relations.[36]

In April 1920 the Inter-Church World Movement issued its report that was
critical of Gary's steel company. Ensley, an associate professor of history at the
University of Evansville in Indiana, has called the ICWM report "a landmark
in the industrial and ecclesiastical history of the United States."[37] Although

efforts were made to suppress the document, it appeared in print three months after the end of the strike. Wise wryly noted, "From that moment on the Inter-Church World Movement was dead. . . . A steel splinter got into its eye."[38]

Wise's efforts in 1911 that prevented Richard Croker from regaining political power was a warm-up drill for a much bigger battle against Tammany Hall that took place twenty years later: the campaign to remove New York City mayor James J. Walker (1881–1946) from office. It was a battle for higher stakes than the skirmish with Croker because it involved a future US president: Franklin D. Roosevelt.

But all that lay ahead for Wise.

Chapter 11

Wise, Wilson, and War

In 1910 Wise was not yet a national religious or political figure, but that began to change when Stephen traveled to Trenton, New Jersey, to make one of his routine speeches. On Sunday, November 6, 1910, Wise addressed the local Young Men's Christian Association (YMCA) just two days before the state's gubernatorial election that pitted Wilson, Princeton University's president, against Vivian M. Lewis (1869–1950), the New Jersey commissioner of banking and insurance. Wise made a startling prediction to his audience:

> On Tuesday the President of Princeton University will be elected governor of your state. He will not complete his term of office as governor. In November 1912, he will be elected President of the United States. In March 1917, he will be inaugurated for the second time as President. He will be one of the great Presidents in American history.[1]

At the time, Stephen's prediction was based on the New Jersey governor's articles and speeches, but Wise trusted his own intuition. In fact, the rabbi did not hear Wilson deliver a public address until February 1911. How and why Stephen Wise abandoned his longtime political home in the pre–World War I Republican Party and built a close personal friendship with Wilson is a classic study of Wise's lifelong ability to gain access to powerful political figures as a means of influencing national and international events. His goals were achieved because Stephen was a superb "talent scout" endowed with the ability to identify potential leaders.

Wise followed up his optimistic forecast with a series of letters to Wilson, one-on-one luncheons, and an invitation for the future president to address the Free Synagogue's anniversary dinner in 1911 at Manhattan's Astor Hotel. Other guest speakers at the event included Senator William Borah of Idaho (1865–1940), the Reverend Dr. John Haynes Holmes, and federal judge Julian

Judge Julian Mack, honorary World Jewish Congress president, Geneva, 1936. Permission granted by the Stephen Wise Free Synagogue Archives.

W. Mack of Chicago (1866–1943), an American Zionist leader. But in Stephen's judgment, "Governor Wilson made the address of the evening."[2]

By 1911 Wise was disenchanted with the Republican Party:

[The GOP] had become hopeless and irredeemable, that it was owned body and soul by the bosses . . . which Colonel [Theodore] Roosevelt had failed to overthrow.[3]

Not everyone in Stephen's immediate family followed his lead and "converted" to the Democrats and the candidacy of Wilson, whom Wise described as "one of the finest figures in our political life for a generation." When news came in June 1912 from the Democratic National Convention in Baltimore that Wilson had gained his party's presidential nomination, Wise "shouted for joy." But not his eleven-year-old son, James:

Tears began to trickle down his cheeks and he said, "That settles Roosevelt, and I prayed for [Champ] Clark." [Clark (1870–1940) was the Speaker of the House of Representatives and Wilson's chief rival for the nomination.] . . . [Jim] called me a turncoat because I had long been a Republican and now was about to vote for the Democratic party. That same night he threatened to pray for Roosevelt, and I said to him, "Don't do that Jim; instead of that, do as I will do—pray that God may give us the best man [women could not vote in 1912], the man best fitted to lead this great nation to honor." Whereupon he added, "That's Teddy all right."[4]

After the New Jersey governor was nominated, Stephen was quick to send an admiring letter to Wilson, and Wise's florid language was similar to the phrasing he was to use many times in the future whenever he congratulated important leaders on their various achievements and victories:

> Member and supporter of the Republican Party though I long have been, I am deeply persuaded that your nomination and election may, by reason of the power of your leadership and the character of service by you to be rendered, bring to pass the re-birth of the Party you represent. . . . I rejoice in your nomination which I ventured throughout the land to urge and to predict at a time when the bosses yet hoped to avert it. . . . You will meet the duties [of the presidency] . . . with deep wisdom, with high courage, with noble purpose.[5]

But as the bitter 1912 campaign among Wilson, TR, and Taft unfolded, Wise was upset that the Democratic Party platform was much weaker than Wilson's announced public positions on key Progressive issues. The platform called for limiting the amount of money corporations could contribute to political campaigns:

> We pledge the Democratic Party to the enactment of a law prohibiting any corporation from contributing to a campaign fund and any individual from contributing any amount above a reasonable maximum. . . . A private monopoly is indefensible and intolerable. We therefore favor the vigorous enforcement of the criminal as well as the civil law against trusts and trust officials, and demand the enactment of such additional legislation as may be necessary to make it impossible for a private monopoly to exist in the United States.

Wilson and his party wanted strong reforms in banking and monetary policy, the creation of a federal income tax and the Federal Reserve, presidential primaries, and the direct election of US senators. Indeed, the Sixteenth Amendment (the income tax) and the Seventeenth Amendment (direct vote for the Senate) were ratified in early 1913 soon after Wilson's electoral victory.

The tariff was a central campaign issue:

> The high Republican tariff is the principal cause of the unequal distribution of wealth; it is a system of taxation which makes the rich richer and the poor poorer; under its operations the American farmer and laboring man are the

chief sufferers; it raises the cost of the necessaries of life to them, but does not protect their product or wages.[6]

But an uneasy Wise expressed concern in his personal journal:

> If the Democratic platform were that of the Progressives, it would be much easier for me. But I cannot help sharing to a very small extent the fear of Holmes [who was supporting TR] and the rest that Wilson may not be strong enough, because no man would be big enough to avoid being influenced, if not dominated, in some degree by the rotten and terrible corrupt bosses of the Democratic Party.[7]

As the presidential campaign neared its end, Wise was not confident Wilson would be elected:

> There are too many conservative people in [Wilson's] entourage and he has not met the issues . . . with the same simplicity and directness which we have come to associate with his public utterances. . . . But unless he begins to strike and strike hard, he will lose the Progressive votes which may go to Roosevelt and even possibly elect him, although the latter is hardly likely.[8]

A week before the election, Wise joined Wilson at a large public rally in Philadelphia, where the Democratic candidate spoke to the crowd for an hour. Stephen wrote,

> He had a fine reception, although one missed the roar which one is accustomed to hear at the Roosevelt meetings. [Wilson] may not command the frenzy of the zealous, but he does command the respect of the thoughtful, which to me is better.[9]

During the presidential campaign, Wilson sought the advice of Louis D. Brandeis (1856–1941), one of America's leading legal minds of that era and a strong critic of monopolies and Big Business. Brandeis, who was called the "people's lawyer," recommended the breakup of all trusts and interlocking corporations, advice that Wilson accepted. Unlike TR, Brandeis and Wilson believed there were no "good" or "bad" cartels or monopolies; they were all "bad."

Brandeis was also skeptical that "regulation" of big trusts could be effective because the regulated companies would work to undermine and influence the government regulators. The Democratic Party believed that the reduction of the trusts' power would increase healthy competition in the marketplace and bring benefit to the general public.

Wilson won the three-way 1912 presidential election against William Howard Taft and Theodore Roosevelt, gaining 41.8 percent of the 14.6 million votes cast. TR was second with 27.4 percent, and Taft, the incumbent, garnered only 23.1 percent. An elated Stephen Wise believed the major Progressive positions he supported would come to fruition within Wilson's New Freedom program, in contrast to Theodore Roosevelt's New Nationalism and Taft's conventional conservative Republicanism.

Wise was pleased with the Wilson-Brandeis stand against Big Business, and the rabbi also believed that Wilson was an idealistic pacifist who would keep America out of war. Indeed, in 1916 Wilson campaigned for a second term on the theme "He Kept Us Out of War." But all that changed less than a year later.

Stephen was elated when Wilson appointed the Kentucky-born Brandeis on January 28, 1916, to serve as a Supreme Court associate justice. Many corporate executives and political leaders opposed the nomination of Brandeis, the first Jew chosen for the high court. Antagonism was strong within the Boston Protestant elite: lawyers, bankers, educators, and others.[10]

Brandeis's nomination resulted in something new in US history: the US Senate's first public confirmation hearings for a Supreme Court justice. The acrimonious process lasted four months. Brandeis's foes focused on his legal philosophy; he was accused of being a "radical," a "socialist," and a "hypocrite."[11]

An interesting aspect of the nomination fight was the personal involvement of two Harvard University presidents. Abbott Lawrence Lowell (1856–1943), who led the university between 1909 and 1933, was a public adversary of Brandeis even though the Supreme Court nominee was a Harvard graduate; indeed his extraordinary academic record remained unmatched for eighty years.

Lowell, who had earlier proclaimed, "I must not drag the name of Harvard into political quarrels," shed that lofty position and opposed Wilson's choice for the court. According to Wise, the Harvard leader "assumed the leadership of the anti-Brandeis forces."[12] Lowell was one of fifty-five prominent Bostonians who were against the nomination.[13] However, over seven hundred Harvard students supported Brandeis.[14]

During his university presidency, Lowell unsuccessfully fought to keep African American students out of the freshman residence halls, and he also failed to impose a quota system that would have limited Jewish enrollment at Harvard to 15 percent.

Countering Lowell was Charles W. Eliot (1834–1926), Harvard's president between 1869 and 1909. Eliot supported Brandeis and opposed limiting the number of Jewish and African American students. He said a rejection of

Brandeis "would be a grave misfortune for the whole legal profession, the court, all American business, and the country."[15]

Two prominent political figures, former president William Howard Taft and former secretary of state and US senator Elihu Root, also opposed Brandeis. However, Stephen Wise was "shocked" when Senator William Borah, his friend and fellow Progressive, voted against Brandeis's confirmation.[16] The final vote came on June 1, 1916: forty-seven in favor and twenty-two opposed. The negative vote was composed of twenty-one Republicans and one Democrat, while three Republicans supported Wilson's choice.

Brandeis was quickly sworn in as an associate justice, and he served with distinction on the Supreme Court until his retirement in 1939. Brandeis died two years later. William O. Douglas (1898–1980) succeeded him on the Court. Brandeis University in Waltham, Massachusetts, founded in 1948, was named in his honor.

When Louis Brandeis retired from the high court at age eighty-three, all his fellow justices except one sent him the "traditional farewell letter" of esteem and appreciation. The lone holdout was the lifelong "virulent anti-Semite," Justice James Clark McReynolds (1862–1946). During a conference of the nine justices, McReynolds "would ostentatiously get up and leave when Brandeis spoke, standing outside until Brandeis had finished and then returning." He was "possibly the most unpleasant fellow ever to sit on the high court."[17]

Wise perceived Brandeis's confirmation as a victory for the Progressive cause that included the rights of labor, women's suffrage and Prohibition, and opposition to lynching, child labor, abuses in the workplace, monopolies and trusts, and all forms of political corruption—exemplified by New York City's Tammany Hall. However, there was another, even larger Progressive issue that Wise was forced to confront during the second decade of the twentieth century—one that would sever his connections and friendships with many Progressive colleagues in the political, religious, and social arenas. That issue was pacifism.

As part of his worldview based upon both the Hebrew prophets and a Jewish version of the Christian Social Gospel, Stephen Wise was an ardent pacifist in the years leading up to World War I. It was a major part of his religious and political credo, as it was for Holmes and many other religious leaders. Wise believed nations could settle their disputes by "mediation or binding arbitration."[18]

As usual, he demanded that America lead by example in preventing war:

In the matter of international relations a democracy must lift itself to the level of the highest moral obligation. Whether it be true or not that a King can do no wrong, a democracy will do wrong unless it will do the right.[19]

Despite his public support for Wilson, Wise was troubled by the president's actions once hostilities began in Europe in 1914. But Wise drew some comfort for his pacifist position when the new president, at the start of his administration a year earlier, chose William Jennings Bryan to serve as secretary of state.

Bryan, the three-time Democratic nominee for the White House, became America's chief diplomat and soon began a program to bring the international community closer through a series of twenty-eight agreements on a host of issues: fishing rights, borders, tariffs, and travel. He believed such pacts would link various peoples and states and reduce the historic reasons for going to war. Bryan, "The Great Commoner," represented not only the pacifist wing of his party but also much of the entire nation.

Once World War I broke out, Bryan was prescient in making his position clear to Wilson:

> It is not likely that either side will win so complete a victory as to be able to dictate terms, and if either side does win such a victory it will probably mean preparation for another war. It would seem better to look for a more rational basis for peace.[20]

Today, a century later and with German Nazism in the public mind, it is important to note that the Germany of World War I, while saturated with brutal Prussian militarism and territorial ambitions personified by the arrogant Kaiser Wilhelm II (1859–1941), was not the Nazi regime led by Adolf Hitler (1889–1945) between 1933 and 1945. Rather, the Berlin-led *Reich* of 1914 was an old-fashioned authoritarian empire that sought its nationalistic *Platz an der Sonne* (place in the sun). That phrase became a fundamental position of Germany's *weltpolitik* (world policy) in 1897 and was perceived as a policy of that nation in World War I.[21]

In addition, there were large numbers of German Americans, including Jews, who maintained strong ties to their "Fatherland," including language, literature, commerce, family, and culture. However, until the US entry into the war in early April 1917, the armed struggle in Europe seemed far away and was often depicted as yet another battle among rival empires: a conflict that Americans of all backgrounds, including Stephen Wise, wanted to avoid.

But a decisive moment came when Wilson and Bryan differed on how to respond to the May 7, 1915, German submarine attack eleven miles off the Irish coastline that sank the British ocean liner *Lusitania* in only eighteen minutes, killing 1,198 passengers, including 128 Americans.[22] Controversy about the incident has continued for nearly a century because the Germans correctly claimed the ship contained hundreds of tons of ammunition and weapons destined for Great Britain's war effort. Bryan had approved the public distribution of a printed warning from the German government a few days prior the *Lusitania*'s fateful journey that began in New York City. The Germans cautioned passengers they were sailing into a war zone where U-boat warfare was taking place.

President Wilson, angry and reacting to intense anti-German feeling in the United States following the loss of the *Lusitania*, imposed strong economic measures against Germany and demanded financial reparations from the Berlin authorities. For Bryan it was an unnecessary, bellicose action that caused him to resign his cabinet post on June 9, 1915. However, Wilson's pressure on the kaiser's government did end the unrestricted campaign of submarine attacks for nearly two years. But a desperate imperial Germany, faced with possible military defeat, resumed U-boat torpedo attacks in February 1917, and two months later, on April 2, the US Congress declared war on Germany.

In 1915 and 1916, Wilson and the Congress began a vigorous military "preparedness" campaign that included increased domestic arms production and other programs aimed at preparing America for possible intervention in the war. Under the National Defense Act of 1916, the US Army strength was increased to 175,000 troops, new warships were ordered, the National Guard personnel total was raised to 450,000, and a Reserve Officers Training Corps (ROTC) was established on college and university campuses. By 1918 and with America engaged in World War I, many additional laws were passed. One key provision of such legislation was the ability of a president to "federalize" state National Guard units in emergencies, an executive power that presidents have employed since 1916.[23]

Wise voiced strong public and private opposition to the president's preparedness projects. On November 15, 1915, Wise wrote to Wilson more in sorrow than in anger:

> From time to time . . . it has been my privilege to write you in order to express my agreement with the things you have said and done. I therefore regard it my duty to tell you how deeply I deplore the necessity under which you have found yourself of accepting and advocating a preparedness program. . . . You will pardon my pointing out that your program, moderate though you believe it to be, will not and . . . cannot satisfy those advocates of military preparedness who will for a time purport to assent to [your program]. . . .
>
> I . . . feel in conscience bound to dissent in pulpit and on platform from your position. . . . I regret this . . . but . . . you will not expect even the most revering of friends [to] remain silent.[24]

In May 1916 New York City was the site of a large parade in support of war preparedness. Wise and only one other member of the city's clergy denounced the parade.[25] A week earlier Wise was part of an American Union Against Militarism delegation that met with Wilson in the White House. The president reassured the pacifist group there was a difference between "reasonable preparedness and militarism." But Wise was unconvinced. He described

> conditions in the Middle West where people are afraid of militarism and complained that army and navy officers had no right to take part in the greater army propaganda because the question was a political one and should be settled by civil authorities.

On the same date a story about Wilson's strong support of the Brandeis Supreme Court nomination appeared on the same newspaper page. The president labeled opposition to his choice for the high court as "intrinsically incredible."[26]

The 1916 presidential election placed Stephen Wise in a difficult situation. Because of his pacifism, he opposed Wilson's preparations for a possible war with Germany. But as a Progressive, he could not return to the Republican Party and vote for Charles Evans Hughes, albeit a friend and former New York State governor. Hughes was antilabor and opposed the principle of an eight-hour workday, claiming it would hurt America's business community. The GOP's chances of regaining the White House improved when Theodore Roosevelt refused the Progressive Party's nomination and backed Hughes.

Wilson and his chief aide, Colonel Edward House (1858–1938), did not want to lose Wise's public support, and perhaps in an effort to keep Stephen from bolting to a possible third-party candidate, the White House floated the idea of the rabbi serving as a member of a presidential commission on Mexico. A flattered Wise was eager to accept and wrote his wife,

> House had proposed my name to the President after Brandeis declined the place on the Mexican Commission. . . . H.M. [Henry Morgenthau, Sr.] told me that when the proposal was mentioned to him, he did not think I would care about it. I could weep over it. Oh for the privilege of having helped little Mexico. . . . The President finally decided it would be unwise to name one Jew after another [the Brandeis nomination], viewing the immense Catholic interests there [in Mexico]. So endeth the near almost Commissioner of peace! . . . Wilson stock is very low at present—therefore I shall come out for him.[27]

But Stephen Wise was edging closer to Wilson's confrontational anti-German position. He wrote Louise in 1916,

> I should like to start a movement to say to Germany: either peace terms now and reparation and security or else war with us![28]

A year later Wise addressed an audience of seventeen hundred people in a Cincinnati church:

[The meeting] was nominally antiwar but actually pro-German [Cincinnati had a large German population]. . . . When I spoke of the submarine warfare as the least of Germany's offendings, . . . about 5 or 6, walked out. I said if you don't agree with me you may go, but when I shall done, one man will be left to agree with me—myself![29]

In 1917 Wise abandoned his previous antiwar position:

Alas for another German victory on the sea [a U-boat attack]! Those ruthless brutes . . . I wish [his son James] were old enough to serve and I young enough.[30]

During January and February 1917, a few months before Wilson asked Congress to declare war against Germany, Wise had crossed his pacifist Rubicon. In speeches at Cornell University and the Free Synagogue, Wise affirmed the "necessity of doing battle against the graver of two evils, the lesser being war and the graver Prussianism."[31]

In late March, only a few days before Wilson's wartime address to the country, Wise declared,

We are on the verge of war. I pray God it may not come, but if it does the blame will not rest upon us, but upon German militarism.[32]

But war did come to the United States. Two years after the *Lusitania* sinking, the Berlin government resumed unrestricted U-boat warfare against shipping. On February 25, 1917, a submarine torpedoed and sank the *Laconia*, a Cunard passenger ship carrying war materiel from New York to Britain. The attack took place just a few miles from the Irish coastline.

Floyd Gibbons (1887–1939), a *Chicago Tribune* reporter on board the *Laconia*, survived the German attack and filed a grim report about it.[33] The ship carried 73 passengers and 216 crew members, and among the 22 fatalities were two Americans. President Wilson, who had campaigned a year earlier on the promise of keeping the United States out of the war, went before Congress on April 2 and asked for a declaration of war against Germany. The president's language was sermonic in style, not surprising given his austere Presbyterian upbringing:

[Germany is conducting] warfare against mankind . . . wrongs . . . which cut to the very roots of human life . . . To such a task we can dedicate our lives and our fortunes, everything that we are and everything that we have, with the pride of those who know that the day has come when America is privileged to spend her blood and her might for the principles that gave her birth and happiness and the peace which she has treasured. God helping her, she can do no other.[34]

The Senate voted 82–6 to go to war, and the House of Representatives tally was 373–50 to enter the fray against Germany. However, the United States did not declare war against the Ottoman Empire, an ally of Germany and the Austro-Hungarian Empire, which controlled much of the Middle East, including Palestine.[35]

Once the United States commenced hostilities with imperial Germany, Wise delivered a passionate and patriotic oration in which he described the war as the "highest and holiest" clash of civilizations. Wise's overheated, apocalyptic rhetoric was a total repudiation of his earlier pacifist position. It is unnerving to read and see the word "holocaust" in Wise's 1917 speech:

> What are we fighting for? My answer to mothers and fathers is—enviable, even glorious is your lot if you give your sons or bless their self-dedication to the highest and holiest of causes in which a people was ever engaged. Remember that you American men and women give your sons to no ordinary war, though outwardly it be war and nothing more. . . . Grimly mocking paradox though it be, we have taken up the burden of war not for the sake of war, but for the sake of peace. . . . We have taken up arms which we shall never ground until the world be made safe in the only way in which the life of nations dwelling together can be made safe, by democracy with peace and healing on its wings.
>
> Remember this is not a war—it is the war. It is the contest of the ages, which we and our allies together can make the last human holocaust, if we be mighty in war and even mightier in the generosities and magnanimities of peace. Your sons have taken up arms not to slay, but to bring the hope of unbroken life to countless generations unborn. As your sons bear fault to battle, be strong mothers and fathers in the knowledge that the sacrificial task unto which they are bent is nothing less than to make the world free. . . . Your readiness to sacrifice may make sacrifice unasked hereafter. . . . It is not too late to save the world, to make and keep the world free, to rebuild an order of life that shall be just and righteous altogether. That shall come to pass if you claim for your sons something better than life, remembering to a man's perdition to be safe, when for the truth he ought to die.[36]

On April 26, 1917, with the United States just three weeks into the war, Wise wrote a paean of praise for Wilson in a letter to Cambridge University professor Israel Abrahams:

Now you can see how wise and great President Wilson has been throughout. Had he gone into War at any other time, he could not have carried the country with him. Now the country stands in virtual unanimity by his side.[37]

But Stephen paid a severe price for his support of America's involvement in World War I, or as it was then called, "The Great War." Wise resigned from the American Union Against Militarism, and he had to confront his pacifist friends and colleagues who were stunned and angered by Wise's pro-war position. Stephen's angry Progressive critics included Oswald Garrison Villard; Crystal Eastman (1881–1928); the sister of Max Eastman; Norman Thomas; and Lillian Wald. They reminded Wise of his antiwar speech a year earlier in which he asserted that no matter who else supported the war, he never would.[38] Wise was shaken by their negative responses, but he did not back down. Indeed, his support of the war went even further than his public rhetoric.

Wise was impressed with the achievements of American industry in both producing and supplying the war materiel necessary to gain military victory; iron, steel, coal, shipbuilding, and other industries contributed to the war effort. Perhaps to prove his support of US participation in World War I or to impress his congregation, Progressive colleagues, and the president, Stephen and James, his seventeen-year-old son, worked during the summer of 1918 as physical laborers in the Luders Marine Construction Company, a Stamford, Connecticut, shipyard.

For six weeks, the two Wises rode their bicycles from the family cottage located at Shippan Point on Long Island Sound to catch an early morning streetcar to the Luders work site. They worked at the shipyard from 7:00 a.m. to 4:30 p.m., and each man received a daily wage of three dollars (about forty-five dollars today). The Wises remained anonymous to the other shipyard employees; Stephen was known as "No. 186." However, their cover was blown when the rabbi asked his foreman for permission to miss two days of work in order to make a speech in Washington. The news leaked out, and the shipyard was soon invaded by a host of journalists and photographers who made the story national news.

The workers praised both Stephen and James for their hard work in contributing to the national war effort. Stephen, always quick to seize what we today call a "photo op," saluted his fellow workers: "I have always respected men who work with their hands. I respect them more than ever today." Wise added he would contribute four weeks of his wages—$76.13 (about $1,145 today)—to the American Red Cross.

The next day Stephen went to the nation's capital to deliver his speech while James traveled to Princeton University to begin his first year of

Wise with son holding sledgehammer beside him, during World War I, Luders Ship Yard in Connecticut, August 4, 1918. ©Corbis Corporation

undergraduate studies. However, many of Stephen Wise's colleagues in the Progressive movement who opposed America's participation in the war saw the shipyard episode as a publicity stunt.[39]

America's entry into the war provided the necessary fresh combat troops that brought about the Armistice nineteen months later. When the war ended in November 1918, Wise recognized that the United States had emerged from being an agrarian-based nation and had become a world power: militarily, economically, and politically.

President Wilson's postwar political idealism was central to his famous Fourteen Points, first articulated in 1918, and his call for a League of Nations that he believed would ensure world peace. Wilson's demand for national self-determination for the peoples of Europe and elsewhere resonated with Wise, and he supported the president's positions, believing they would guarantee Jewish civil and economic rights in Eastern Europe as well as Jewish national rights in Palestine.

However, in the immediate postwar period Wilson faced fierce political opposition regarding American membership in the League of Nations. Wise came down in favor of the president's position because Stephen was a committed internationalist who opposed American isolationism. Wise was attracted to Wilson's strong idealism, but the president was an inflexible leader unwilling to compromise on the League issue. His political rigidity may have been a result of a strict Presbyterian/Calvinist upbringing, and that trait was a severe handicap in his quest for enough Senate votes to guarantee America's full participation in the League of Nations. Wilson's uptight personality may have contributed to the paralyzing stroke he suffered in 1919.

But there was a second reason for Wise's support of Wilson's international agenda. As we shall see in a later chapter, Wilson provided vital backing for Zionism's first international diplomatic victory, the Balfour Declaration that was issued by Britain on November 2, 1917, in the midst of the war.

In 1922, Palestine, no longer controlled by the defeated Ottoman Empire, became a British Mandate as a result of the action taken by the League of Nations. The Mandate stemmed from the United Kingdom's military conquest of the region during the last years of the war. Wise and his fellow Zionists believed that the end of Ottoman control in the Middle East created new positive possibilities for the establishment of a "Jewish commonwealth" in the biblical homeland.

After World War I ended and before the 1920 presidential election, Wise offered a ringing endorsement of Wilson's "greatness." Stephen again used his well-honed rhetorical skill to decry the opposition to Wilson and the League of Nations:

Less than a year ago the moral leadership of the world was in our grasp. We had entered upon the great adventure to save the world, to make and to keep it free, to rebuild an order of life that should be just and righteous altogether. At the critical hour we rendered decisive help, taking our place by the side of England, France, and Italy as deliverers of the world from the horrors of Prussianism. The service was rendered, the sacrifices were made, and for generations we shall pay the tolls. . . .

But all of these services and sacrifices are to be forgotten by Europe and that nothing will be remembered of America, save but at the last moment we shrank from an imperative duty which it was the part of courage and nobleness to accept. As Americans, we have the right to demand that the presidential election of next November [1920] be forgotten for a moment, and the world's need of peace and healing be remembered for more than a moment.

But world justice be not sacrificed in the interest of partisan advantage. Our appeal is to America at its highest. The America of Washington and Lincoln, of Roosevelt and Wilson—the America of Lexington and Gettysburg and Chateau-Thierry—the America of noblest vision and faith and great illusion. If the League of Nations be not helped by America to come to pass, it is not President Wilson who will have been defeated, but America—not America, but the world—not mankind alone, but mankind's hope of peace and justice.

The achievements of the President, his great services, the unequalled clarity and power with which he molded and applied the ideals of America—all these things many of my fellow Americans for a time seem, alas, to forget. The real difficulty of the situation has been that the President thinks straight, that he is an honest man, that he does not resort to political subterfuge, that he will not indulge in political equivocation, and the President is blamed on these grounds. When in truth it is because of these things that he ought to be held up to the youth of the nation for honor, and above all for the honor of emulation.

The President is not unerring, but his place in history is secure. He has done great things and will stand as one of the mightiest figures of a mighty epoch.[40]

Chapter 12

From A (Americanism) to Z (Zionism) and Everything in Between . . . A Rebel with Lots of Causes

Throughout his career, Stephen Wise possessed an abundance of physical stamina, political talent, public relations skills, and religious passion: it was a potent combination that enabled him to achieve his goal of becoming a leader in American as well as Jewish life. From 1907 until his death in 1949, his primary job was serving as the senior rabbi of the Free Synagogue in New York City, and although Wise had two excellent associate rabbis in Sidney Goldstein and Jacob X. Cohen, Stephen performed most of the many duties of a congregational rabbi: baby namings and officiating at circumcision ceremonies, Confirmation services for young people, supervising the synagogue religious school, weddings, pastoral visits to the sick and infirm in homes and hospitals, funerals and gravestone dedications.

But as an active political Progressive, Wise also devoted enormous energy to confront America's domestic issues and concerns and to challenge both public and private corruption. At the same time, he became a powerful force in the complex and fractious global Zionist movement in the decades before the state of Israel achieved its independence in 1948.

During the crucial 1930s and 1940s, friends and foes both recognized Stephen Wise as the premier American Jewish leader who had personal access to President Franklin Roosevelt, key members of the FDR administration, congressional leaders, and State Department officials. Many of the latter group were perceived as both anti-Zionist and anti-Semitic. Indeed, those two decades represented the greatest opportunities and challenges of Wise's entire life.

In addition to the Free Synagogue, Wise founded and led three other institutions that are among his most enduring achievements: the American Jewish Congress (AJCongress) that began its formation process in 1915, the Jewish Institute of Religion (JIR) in 1922, and the World Jewish Congress (WJC) in 1936.

For most men and women, a single successful endeavor in life is often sufficient. Perhaps by reason of strength, some individuals are able to work effectively in two separate professional areas, but Stephen Wise—forever rest-less, creative, egotistical, dynamic, ambitious, eloquent, contentious, and forceful—moved from one public arena to another and to another and to yet another. We employ the hackneyed image that describes an engaged, hyperac-tive person simultaneously burning both ends of a single candle. However, that description does not apply to Stephen because he possessed a large num-ber of personal and professional candles to set aflame, all at the same time.

There is a more apt metaphor to describe Wise's extraordinary career: Sir Walter Scott's (1771–1832) words from *Marmion*, canto 6, stanza 17: "Oh what a tangled web we weave . . ." Stephen's life was indeed a tangled web, and only he knew its numerous particulars, priorities, problems, pitfalls, and possibili-ties. It was Wise himself who created a personal web with complicated path-ways that allowed him to move within the complex maze that was his life.

Nothing was more tangled than his ambivalent, often hostile relationship to the Reform Jewish movement. Wise, both in practice and belief, always re-mained "in" the group, but he was never "of" the movement. He preferred the term "liberal Judaism" to describe his religious commitment rather than "Reform," the official name.

But whatever the word, for many years Stephen engaged in a series of con-troversies with the three major bodies of the Reform establishment: the Hebrew Union College (HUC), the movement's rabbinical seminary in Cincinnati; the Union of American Hebrew Congregations (UAHC), the con-gregational body of hundreds of Reform synagogues; and the Central Conference of American Rabbis (CCAR)—all organizations founded by Rabbi Isaac Mayer Wise during the second half of the nineteenth century.

There were major reasons for Stephen's constant conflicts and quarrels with many of his Reform rabbinical colleagues: he detested their anti-Zionist beliefs, their sterile views on the need for religious social action, and their op-position to some Progressive policies. Wise's battles with the Reform move-ment began early in his career. In July 1901 he was twenty-seven years old and living in Portland, Oregon, when he attended his first CCAR national con-vention, the annual gathering of Reform rabbis that took place that year in Philadelphia.

Wise had met Theodor Herzl in Switzerland during the Second Zionist Congress in 1898, and three years later, the extraordinary, life-changing im-pact of that encounter still remained fresh for the young rabbi. Wise was pleased when the CCAR convention delegates were presented with a resolu-tion expressing support for Herzl's emerging Jewish national movement. The CCAR president, Rabbi Joseph Silverman of New York City's Temple Emanu-El, called for its rejection:

The Conference [is being asked] to co-operate with the Zionists in the colonization of Palestine. We deem it inadvisable for this body to consider this question at this time.[1]

Perhaps because Stephen had not yet achieved leadership status among his
colleagues, Wise's response to the resolution was muted, unlike his later,
slashing personal attacks on anti-Zionist rabbis:

S. S. Wise said that a real vital question was involved in Zionism. . . . The aim
of Zionism was to make Palestine a homestead for homeless Jews. He thought
that a thoughtful study of Zionism should be made by the Conference and that
it ought not to be hastily or contemptuously dismissed.[2]

The CCAR members took no action on the controversial resolution, and in
good bureaucratic fashion, they called instead for a study paper on Zionism to
be offered at the 1902 meeting. It was the last time Wise was so tepid in his defense of Zionism at a CCAR meeting.

Sixteen years later, in June 1917, an anti-Zionist resolution was debated at
the CCAR convention in Buffalo, New York. It stated that because Judaism
was solely a religious faith, the Reform rabbinate looked "with disfavor upon
the new doctrine of political Jewish nationalism."[3] The CCAR president that
year was Rabbi William Rosenau (1865–1943) of Baltimore, who supported
the anti-Zionist declaration.

Wise opposed the resolution, and he worked with fellow Zionist Max
Heller in the preparation of a minority statement that asserted,

There is nothing in the effort to secure a . . . home for the Jews in Palestine
which is not in accord with the principles and aims of Reform Judaism.[4]

A lengthy, contentious debate took place on the convention floor between
the pro-Zionist and anti-Zionist rabbis. The clash marked the high-water
mark—the "CCAR Battle of Gettysburg"—for anti-Zionist dominance within
the Reform movement. As usual in such moments of drama, Wise delivered
an eloquent oration. Even his foes were forced to listen to Wise's fiery words,
because by 1917 Stephen was emerging as a national Jewish leader—a rabbi
with entree to the White House and President Wilson. In his 1917 speech Wise
blasted the CCAR and its anti-Zionist members:

In the twenty years' history of the Conference [since the First Zionist Congress
in 1897] there has never been an attempt made to compel any one to accept

Zionism as the lawful and permissible interpretation of liberal or reform Judaism. But year after year we have heard Zionism attacked. You are making reform Judaism proscriptive of us who are Zionists.

Perhaps you feel you have the right, perhaps you feel Zionists are a menace to liberalism and Judaism, but I warn you to be mindful of the Conference. If you pass this [anti-Zionist] resolution, no matter how you water or mitigate it, the moment you say that we who are Zionists are anti-religionists, that we are enemies of religious Judaism, that moment we must regretfully yet with absolute conviction say, "We can stay no longer within the Conference."

I stand here today not as a Zionist, but as a reform rabbi. I would not have you say that a reform teacher or rabbi has forfeited the right to be a teacher . . . because he has subscribed to the Zionist platform. I appeal not for Zionism, but for the inclusiveness and comprehensiveness of liberal Judaism.

Will liberal Judaism, after a century of distinguished and outstanding history, make the monumental blunder of saying to men who love and serve it, "We bid you go forth"? I ask this not for the sake of Zionism, but that the honor and dignity and noble history of reform Judaism shall not be marred and undone now.[5]

Although Wise threatened to resign from the CCAR, he did not leave the organization. The floor debate, highlighted by Wise's sharp rhetoric, resulted in a compromise resolution that pleased neither side. While it did not affirm Stephen's position, the compromise CCAR resolution lacked the earlier anti-Zionist language and was adopted by a vote of 68–20.[6] The statement included the bland assertion that Reform rabbis looked "with disfavor upon any and every un-religious or anti-religious interpretation of Judaism and of Israel's [the Jewish people's] mission in the world." The polarized rabbinic group meekly offered the pious hope that all Jews would "work together in a spirit of harmony and concord."[7]

It was natural that Wise, a leading Reform rabbi, directed much of his fire at his liberal colleagues, but many Orthodox Jews were also early opponents of the Zionist movement. Their criticism of Herzl and others was not based upon the central idea of Jewish peoplehood but rather on the premise that Zionists sought to create a Jewish commonwealth through secular and political efforts and not by spiritual or religious means. Indeed, a tiny minority of Orthodox Jews today still rejects Zionism and the very existence of the modern state of Israel. Other foes of Zionism were Jewish socialists who identified themselves as members of a universal international working-class proletariat devoid of any national, ethnic, or religious particularism.[8]

By 1917 a battle-scarred Wise had soured on the Reform rabbinical association as a possible pro-Zionist ally, except for colleagues like Max Heller.

During the next thirteen years Stephen attended only one CCAR convention. However, after 1917 the "anti-Zionist supremacy in the Reform movement had passed."[9] But a number of liberal rabbis, including Rosenau, continued to oppose Zionism for another thirty years. However, once the state of Israel achieved independence in 1948, anti-Zionism within the entire American Jewish community weakened, ceasing to exist as a significant force following the 1967 Six-Day War in the Middle East.

But Zionism was not the only reason Wise battled with his rabbinic colleagues. At the 1909 CCAR meeting in New York City, Wise was angered by a drawn-out, tedious speech of Rabbi Solomon Foster (1878–1966) of Newark, New Jersey, that minimized the possibility of any significant synagogue role in America's social justice concerns. Foster's address, titled "The Workingman and the Synagogue," contained many references drawn from the Jewish tradition that celebrated the value of labor, but he did not believe rabbis and synagogues should be involved in strikes, trade unions, and other workforce issues.

The New Jersey rabbi, who also opposed Zionism, urged his colleagues to avoid taking sides in labor controversies. For Foster, the appropriate role was to encourage working men and women to become connected to synagogue life and Judaism. In his sixty-page speech, he avoided recommending any positive action to support the labor movement.[10]

This insipid approach to America's critical problems was anathema to the Progressive, pro-labor Stephen Wise. He assailed Foster's call for synagogue neutrality in labor disputes and berated his CCAR colleague with a depreciating mixture of satire and substance:

[Foster's address is] platitudinous pomposity. . . . I want to protest against the very careful irrelevancy . . . in this Conference. . . . I pass over to [Foster's] three fundamental principles: the synagogue cannot deal with the workingman; the synagogue cannot attract the workingman; the synagogue has no word for the workingman. . . . The synagogue must have an open door and a free pulpit. . . . You can't get the workingman to respect the synagogue . . . unless its pulpit is free. . . . You may ask me, "What have you done about the synagogue and the workingman?" I will tell you what I did. I was asked last summer to have a part in the bakers' strike in New York. . . . I did not talk about general principles. I went down and found Jewish bakers, treated almost like slaves. I told their Jewish masters it was an outrage. And that strike was settled by the strikers gaining . . . every single point for which they had contended. They did not ask enough. . . . They asked for the minimum. And it was given to me to present their claim to their employers.

We must be true to Judaism. The synagogue deals with this world. . . . A year ago it was said in one of the Jewish seminaries, "It is alright to speak about

great moral principles, but you must not apply them." That is a new idea to me.
We are told the rabbi may deal with these things, but not as a representative of
the synagogue. Why not? If the synagogue has laid down these principles [in
favor of labor and workers], why should we not speak out and deal frankly and
fairly as men?[11]

Solomon Foster never forgot Stephen Wise's blistering public attack. As a
rabbinical student in 1960 I conducted intown Sabbath morning services in
Philadelphia for Congregation Knesseth Israel, which had moved its school
and sanctuary to the city's suburbs. Rabbi Foster by then was eighty-two years
old and attended my weekly services. In May of that year, I had the congregation sing "Ha-Tikvah," Israel's national anthem, to commemorate the Jewish
state's twelfth Independence Day.

Foster was livid. He pulled me aside after the service and shouted, "Young
man, I never want to hear that song again during a Jewish service. The blame
for all this lies in the fact you are attending the seminary founded by Stephen
Wise. You have made a great mistake!"

I reminded Foster of the HUC-JIR merger: "Now we are one school."

Foster snapped, "No. No. The real Reform seminary is in Cincinnati, not
New York." Foster appears by name in a Philip Roth novel.[12]

Stephen's lifelong battle with the Hebrew Union College leadership that
began as a student in the 1890s, described in an earlier chapter, was never fully
resolved until 1948, when a cancer-stricken Wise, facing death, agreed to
merge the Jewish Institute of Religion, his New York City rabbinical school,
with the Cincinnati-based HUC. One major reason he agreed to the union of
the two institutions was the 1947 election of Rabbi Nelson Glueck (1900–1971)
as HUC's fourth president. It was the first time a committed Zionist was chosen to lead Reform Judaism's seminary.

Because Wise did not attend HUC as a student and, instead, received private rabbinical ordination in Vienna, he never felt any loyalty to the school
whose faculty and administration he considered religiously vapid, disengaged
from the general society's problems, and anti-Zionist. In typical fashion,
Stephen developed his own strategies in an attempt to dominate and perhaps
control both the HUC and the CCAR.

Three days before attending the 1914 CCAR convention in Detroit, Wise
wrote to Louise about his plans to bypass the HUC faculty and administration
and influence the student body in a personal way:

The recent [Hebrew Union College] graduates made me their guest of honor at
the luncheon yesterday. . . . This is certain—if I will give the time, the

Conference [the Reform rabbinical group] will be in my hands with the possibility of directly and immediately of affecting the younger men.[13]

Wise was intent on going over the heads of the anti-Zionist faculty and administration dominated by Kaufmann Kohler and David Philipson (1862–1949), a prominent Cincinnati Reform rabbi and a lifelong adversary of Wise. The plan was a simple one: if the students become advocates of Zionism, the Reform movement of the future would belong to Wise. By 1914, there were a growing number of young rabbis and seminarians who supported the Jewish national movement, and Wise moved forward to create an endowed lectureship at Hebrew Union College for a prominent Zionist professor—a project that fit into Stephen's long-range plans.

At the convention, Wise was authorized to set up and chair a CCAR lectureship at the Cincinnati seminary.[14] However, HUC president Kohler—the same rabbi who had officiated at the funeral of Wise's father and at Stephen's wedding—was given veto power over the choice of lecturers:

The selection of the lecturers must ultimately rest with the Faculty of Hebrew Union College, naturally in cooperation with the Executive Board of the Conference.[15]

Wise chafed under this provision and attacked the HUC and the CCAR in a letter to Heller. Wise wanted the sole executive power to choose the person for an important teaching position that had the potential to shape the thinking of future Reform rabbis:

[Kohler's] conditions . . . leave no freedom of thought or action and accord us only the right to raise funds . . . [but] my own determination to serve the Conference shall not be neutralized by the littleness and the meanness that for a long time under certain unhappy inspirations have had too large a part in the councils of the Central Conference.[16]

Herman believes Wise's "main complaint," although not overtly stated, was the anti-Zionism of the era that was embedded in the HUC and the CCAR. But when things did not go well for either Stephen's master plan or for the proposed lectureship, a frustrated Wise resigned as the chair of the CCAR Lectureship Committee. He complained to Heller,

The conditions imposed by the [Conference] Executive Committee constitute an intolerable and most impertinent limitation upon our freedom.[17]

Perhaps the only surprising thing about Wise's irate resignation is that he chose to employ the word "limitation" instead of his being "muzzled," the colorful term he used to describe his confrontation years earlier with the board of Temple Emanu-El in New York City. But Stephen Wise had one more arrow in his quiver to aim at the despised HUC and CCAR leaders.

In late 1914 Professor Horace Kallen (1882–1974) of the University of Wisconsin, a rabbi's son and one of Wise's closest Zionist colleagues, was invited to address the HUC students on "The Meaning of Hebraism" (a code word in that era indicating a Zionist perspective). But as the time neared for his lecture, Kohler sent Kallen a curt telegram that disinvited him:

> The authorities of Hebrew Union College resent [your speaking invitation] and have commanded me to cancel said invitation because of your views [Zionism], which they oppose.[18]

On December 23, 1914, an angry Wise wrote again to Max Heller in New Orleans, expressing his fury at the abrupt cancellation of a Zionist professor's speaking invitation:

> Is there nothing to be done to end once and for all that bigoted attitude which stifles every expression of opinion that differs from the gentlemen of the College who are still living in 1840, including Kohler and Philipson?[19]

As a result of the Kallen cancellation, Wise and Heller demanded a special meeting of the HUC Board of Governors. They were granted their request, and the agenda for the meeting scheduled for February 15, 1915, focused on the abandoned lectureship, the need for academic freedom, and the Kallen fiasco. But as in all such encounters, Wise had several additional goals in mind.

First, he wanted a blue-ribbon "commission appointed . . . [to make] a careful study of the College situation for ultimate report thru the Board of Governors to the Union" [the Union of American Hebrew Congregations, the parent body of Reform Judaism]. Wise expressed "shock" that the HUC board was "absolutely independent" of the UAHC, even though "the Union supplies the funds and then [the HUC board] erect themselves into an independent institution. It is beyond my understanding."

Like a chess master, Wise was two or three moves ahead of his rivals in this bureaucratic clash. He knew if such an investigative commission were established, he was certain to be one of its members. That position would allow Wise to influence HUC policy on Zionism. The Free Synagogue, with its collection of affluent and prominent lay leaders—all Wise loyalists—had recently joined the UAHC, and Wise wanted to shift the balance of power vis-à-vis the

HUC away from Cincinnati and closer to New York City and to Wise's powerful cohort of friends and associates.[20]

In what was later called a "concordat," Wise and Heller on one side and Kohler and Philipson on the other reached a three-point agreement. A total conflict was averted, but the agreement was not a peace treaty; it was only a temporary cease-fire. The concordat's three points were

> The President of the College shall alone prescribe who may speak in the Chapel. . . . Dr. Kohler agreed that he had no objection to addresses on Zionism being delivered in the College building outside the Chapel. . . . Dr. Kohler further agreed that students may preach on Zionism or may refer to the subject in their Chapel sermons provided the sermons are religious in tone and otherwise unobjectionable to him.[21]

With Kohler holding such a powerful veto, it did not take long for the shaky agreement to collapse. Heller's son James (1892–1971) was the first HUC rabbinical student to be barred from speaking about Zionism. Although the matter was soon resolved and called a misunderstanding, Wise was "greatly disturbed about the whole thing . . . This matter is very grave. It is such a flagrant breach of faith."[22]

Wise's continuing battles with Kohler, Philipson, and other HUC authorities ended with Wise withdrawing from the field of combat. By 1915 he understood he had little or no chance of having the HUC and the CCAR fall into his hands, as he had earlier outlined to his wife. Wise recognized he could not take over the firmly controlled institutions of Reform Judaism: the Hebrew Union College and the Central Conference of American Rabbis. He wrote a letter to Max Heller filled with a large dose of egotism and sharp-pointed attacks upon both Kohler and Philipson, who represented

> milk and water emasculated Judaism, which is the sad survivor of the German-Jewish Reformation. I feel as you do closer to our Orthodox brothers who are Jews than to our Reform colleagues many of whom have fundamentally ceased to be Jews. . . . I am perhaps differently circumstanced from any other man in the Conference. . . Because of my physical strength and perhaps resolute will, it is given to me to reach annually a very large number of Jewish communities throughout the country . . . fifty to seventy-five of the largest cities. . . . It lies within my power to speak over their heads [Kohler and Philipson] . . . and make myself felt in a perhaps not wholly insignificant way. . . . Is it then worth my while to make the same painful, toilsome, heart breaking effort year after year in an attempt to redeem [the CCAR and HUC] from itself which chooses to remain unredeemed? . . . If the men want to

accept Philipson as their leader . . . so be it. I have no desire in the world to fight him. I am indifferent to him . . . and all their comrades, but I abhor and loathe the things for which they stand.[23]

It is remarkable that on the eve of World War I and as Wise solidified his personal relationships with President Wilson and Supreme Court justice Brandeis, Stephen still had enough time and energy to move against the Hebrew Union College in Cincinnati. For Wise, HUC represented the socioeconomic elitism and the anti-Zionism of Jews whose families came to the United States during the nineteenth century from German-speaking areas of Europe.

But as Wise and his colleagues began the effort in 1915 to establish a broad-based American Jewish "congress," Stephen added another target to his list: the American Jewish Committee (AJC), an organization founded in 1906 in reaction to the murderous anti-Jewish pogroms three years earlier in Kishinev, Moldavia, a region of tsarist Russia. For many years the AJC espoused an anti-Zionist position, and many of its leaders were members of New York City's Temple Emanu-El, including Louis Marshall, who served as AJC president from 1912 until his death in 1929. Cyrus Adler, another Wise adversary, succeeded Marshall as the committee's president.

From the outset, AJC leaders saw themselves as the Jewish establishment in America, an organization that was proud of its special expertise, political influence, and skill in international relations. The American Jewish Committee was a handy, easy-to-identify foe for Wise. The committee—its very name reeked of a small, controlling group rather than a large, democratically based organization—was, in Stephen's view, a self-appointed/self-anointed aristocracy that perceived its role as the unelected leadership cadre of American Jews.

Wise opposed the American Jewish Committee and worked instead to establish a broad-based democratic organization anchored to Zionism as a liberating force for the Jewish people, an organization that was also committed to social justice within the United States. Stephen over the years expressed public contempt toward the aristocratic AJC and the spiritually uninspiring HUC—two institutions that for him symbolized everything wrong with "American Israel," as Stephen preferred to call the US Jewish community.

Wise was not alone in his negative feelings about the AJC. In 1916 Kallen, of German Jewish background himself, had harsh words for the committee in a letter to Brandeis:

They distrusted the rank and file. They were afraid of the publicity. They were afraid of having their "Americanism" impugned. . . . The class as a whole

Mrs. Sol Rosenbloom
Prof. H.M. Kallen

Two Zionist colleagues of Wise: Pittsburgh philanthropist Mrs. Sol (Celia) Rosenbloom and Professor Horace M. Kallen, c. 1934. Permission granted by the Stephen Wise Free Synagogue Archives.

showed distrust of democracy, fear of frankness, a consciousness of moral and social security. They insisted that whatever could be done, could be done quietly, by wire pulling, by use of the influence of individuals, by the backstairs methods of the "Sh'tadlan" of the Middle Ages and of the Russian ghetto.[24]

A *Sh'tadlan* was an intermediary figure in Europe who represented the Jewish community in its contacts with the often anti-Semitic secular and religious authorities. The sh'tadlan's job was to act as a negotiator with the powers that be to protect the vulnerable and fearful Jewish inhabitants of a region or locality. But by 1914 with the onset of World War I, European Jews needed much more than a sh'tadlan to provide for their security.

The Great War shifted Wise's focus away from the HUC and the CCAR. The conflict created both a crisis and an opportunity for Wise and his Zionist associates. The hostilities were taking place in areas of Europe where nine million Jews lived in combat zones under dangerous conditions. Adequate food, shelter, medical supplies, and physical protection were imperative to ensure the survival of the threatened communities.

In addition, Wise anticipated that the end of the war would bring historic changes for the Jewish people. He believed a clearheaded analysis was needed of "the entire Jewish situation in regard to the change of the condition of the world after the war."[25]

As early as August 1914 and the outbreak of World War I there were calls for a coalition of American Jewish organizations, a "congress" that would be effective in dealing with the new realities created by the war. However, Stephen's Temple Emanu-El nemesis, AJC president Louis Marshall, rejected the idea of a Jewish congress, believing that his own organization was best equipped to handle all foreign affairs issues affecting Jews. Marshall sneered, "The problems with which we have to deal are so delicate in nature that the mob cannot grapple with them."[26]

The AJC's monopoly on international concerns was broken, however, when Wise and others enlisted the efforts of a new and unexpected ally to counter Marshall's influence. Louis Brandeis was the intellectual and social equal of Marshall and the other AJC leaders. As a result, the AJC could not dismiss Wise's campaign, endorsed by Brandeis, to create a congress of American Jews supportive of Zionism.

Recruiting Brandeis to the cause of Zionism and the congress is a remarkable story that has been well documented by Melvin Urofsky in his volume *Louis D. Brandeis: A Life.* Brandeis was the high-profile personal catalyst that energized and aided Wise and others in their battles against the anti-Zionism that dominated much of the top echelon of American Reform rabbis and lay leadership during the early years of the twentieth century. Without Brandeis's guidance, Wise and his colleagues might have remained ineffective in enlisting "American Israel" to support the Jewish national movement.

It is questionable if Wise by himself could have defeated the strong anti-Zionist position of many American Jewish leaders. As noted above, Stephen attempted, but failed to gain personal and programmatic control of either the CCAR or the HUC. Nor was he able to curb the American Jewish Committee's dominance in international affairs. But Brandeis, as a Zionist leader, represented a serious rival of the AJC's self-proclaimed hegemony over the American Jewish community.

Born in Louisville, Kentucky, in 1856, Brandeis graduated from high school at age fourteen, and six years later he was first in his graduating class at Harvard Law School. Brandeis remained in Boston after his Harvard years and gained a national reputation as a Progressive Democrat and a superb attorney with a careful, judicious style in both his personal and professional life. He seemed an improbable mentor to the fiery Stephen Wise, yet their productive relationship of fire and ice endured until Brandeis's death in October 1941.

Brandeis was an assimilated, nonobservant Jew who was not an active participant in any phase of American Jewish life, not even within the Reform movement, whose leaders were often similar to his own family background. As sometimes happens, a single event can trigger a profound change in the trajectory of a person's life and career.

In 1910, fifty-four-year-old Brandeis, well settled in his Boston legal profession, became the chairman of an arbitration board during a New York City garment workers' strike. It was the first time the taciturn attorney had directly encountered members of the Eastern European Jewish community, many of whom were immigrants and laborers in the clothing industry.[27]

Brandeis was impressed with the workers' intellectual vitality, their devotion to his own democratic ideals, and their shared passion for social justice. These were "different" Jews from those of Brandeis's own socioeconomic class. His contact with the "Jewish masses" had a great impact upon the brilliant Harvard-trained "people's lawyer," and Brandeis began a self-examination of his own Jewish identity and the problems not only of the New York City garment workers but also of Jews throughout the world. After his experience in New York City, the future Supreme Court justice and American Zionist leader declared,

> [Jews] possessed . . . a deep moral feeling [and] a deep sense of the brotherhood of man.[28]

Brandeis's growing interest in Zionism and Judaism was heightened in 1910 when Jacob de Haas (1872–1937), the editor of the Boston *Jewish Advocate* newspaper, interviewed him about low-cost savings bank insurance for workers, one of Brandeis's major proposals to curb the power of private insurance companies. De Haas had recently arrived in the United States from Britain, . where he served as Herzl's secretary in London.[29]

During the interview, de Haas asked if Brandeis was related to Lewis Dembitz (1833–1907), a prominent Louisville, Kentucky, lawyer. When Brandeis replied he was Dembitz's nephew, de Haas said, "Dembitz was a noble Jew," a man who practiced traditional Judaism and had been an early supporter of Herzl's Zionist movement. Unlike many of his family members, Dembitz studied Torah; he was religiously observant and knowledgeable of Jewish religious texts. Dembitz authored *Services in Synagogue and Home* in 1892, and years earlier he translated Harriet Beecher Stowe's *Uncle Tom's Cabin* into German.

In addition, Lewis Dembitz, a strong abolitionist, had been a delegate to the 1860 Republican Convention that nominated Abraham Lincoln as its presidential candidate.[30] In tribute to the memory of his uncle, Brandeis changed his original middle name from "David" to "Dembitz."[31]

After the 1910 de Haas interview, the intellectually curious Brandeis began reading more about Zionism and other Jewish subjects. Brandeis explored the movement's goals and concluded he could support them, and two years later Brandeis joined the Federation of American Zionists (FAZ).

Louis Brandeis did not become an active Zionist as part of a bandwagon effect—on the contrary. At the time Brandeis had his personal epiphany about Jews, Judaism, and Zionism, the latter movement was at low ebb in the United States. In a nation that had about three million Jews, the Zionist organizations had only twelve thousand active members and a deficit budget of $12,000 (about $293,000 in today's dollars), and no one wanted to be the organization's president.[32]

As Brandeis immersed himself more and more into the study of Jews and Judaism, thanks to people like de Haas, he "thought himself into Jewish life" as a mature adult. In a very real sense, Brandeis "became" a Jew in his mid-fifties, but it was not through participation in synagogue life, home rituals, or holiday celebrations.[33]

Central to that personal transformation was Brandeis's belief that he and other Jews could best support American democracy and social justice by being better Jews, as he defined the meaning of that identity. Brandeis wrote, "The twentieth-century ideals of America have been the ideals of the Jew for more than twenty centuries."[34] Brandeis declared, "Zionism is the Pilgrim inspiration and impulse all over again."[35]

In March 1913 Brandeis appeared on a speaker's platform in Boston with Nahum Sokolow, a European Zionist leader.[36] Within eighteen months, Brandeis was the leader of the American Zionist movement.

The major event in elevating Brandeis, the "outsider," to that position was an emergency Zionist conference at Manhattan's Hotel Marseilles on August 30–31, 1914, at the start of World War I. The European headquarters of the Zionist movement was in Berlin, but Chaim Weizmann (1874–1952), a key leader of the movement, resided in England. Weizmann, loyal to Britain, wanted nothing to do with Germany, his adopted country's prime enemy. Complicating matters was the Ottoman Empire's alliance with Germany, as well as its control over Palestine.

At the start of the war in 1914, the United States remained neutral. As a result, American Zionists believed their organization could best function as the movement's operational headquarters during the war. Recognizing the problems created by the conflict in Europe, de Haas and Louis Lipsky (1876–1963), the executive director of the FAZ, sent a telegram to Brandeis inviting him to attend the emergency meeting.[37] Brandeis accepted the invitation and presided at the conference that marked a turning point for him and American Zionism.

While at the Hotel Marseilles, Brandeis received a cram course about Judaism and Zionism from his new colleagues. He learned a great deal of facts and history in a short time, but the internal organizational frictions surprised

Leaders and staff of the Federation of American Zionists in New York City, 1915; first row: Henrietta Szold, Wise, Jacob de Haas, Robert D. Kesselman, Louis Lipsky, Charles A. Cowen, Shmaryahu Levin, Rabbi Meyer Berlin; second row: Blanche Jacobson, Adolf Hubbard, A. H. Fromenson. Permission granted by the Stephen Wise Free Synagogue Archives.

Brandeis, as did the lack of a systematic structural plan and a tiny budget with a large deficit. However, the conference participants were also surprised: it was clear that Brandeis intended to take charge of American Zionism as an active, involved leader.[38]

Brandeis established the Provisional Executive Committee (PEC) for General Zionist Affairs. One of the PEC's tasks was to collect relief funds in the United States for endangered overseas Jewish communities. Nine months after the emergency fund was set up, $170,000 (about $3,953,000 today) was raised, much of it coming from many small contributions—a result of having the well-known, high-profile Brandeis as the American Zionist leader.[39] In his new role, Brandeis appointed Rabbi Stephen Wise to the PEC two weeks after the Hotel Marseilles conference concluded.

On April 25, 1915, Brandeis delivered a long (over five thousand words), detailed speech to the Eastern Conference of Reform Rabbis in Boston. In his address, which was more akin to a legal brief, Brandeis first outlined the precarious physical and psychological status of Jews in Europe and then described the urgent need for an active Zionist movement to ameliorate that dire situation and to strengthen Jewish identity and self-esteem throughout the world.

Stephen Wise and many other American Jews adopted the central themes of that speech. Brandeis's words to the Reform rabbis represent his coming of age as both a Jew and a Zionist:

> Let no American imagine that Zionism is inconsistent with Patriotism. . . . Multiple loyalties are objectionable only if they are inconsistent. . . . Every Irish American who contributed towards advancing home rule was a better man and a better American for the sacrifice he made. Every American Jew who aids in advancing the Jewish settlement in Palestine, though he feels that neither he nor his descendants will ever live there, will likewise be a better man and a better American for doing so. . . .
>
> The Jewish spirit, the product of our religion and experiences, is essentially modern and essentially American. Not since the destruction of the Temple have the Jews in spirit and in ideals been so fully in harmony with the noblest aspirations of the country in which they lived. . . .
>
> Indeed, loyalty to America demands rather that each American Jew become a Zionist. Let us therefore lead, earnestly, courageously and joyously, in the struggle for liberation. Let us all recognize that we Jews are a distinctive nationality of which every Jew, whatever his country, his station or shade of belief, is necessarily a member. . . .
>
> Organize, Organize, Organize, until every Jew in America must stand up and be counted, counted with us, or prove himself, wittingly or unwittingly, of the few who are against their own people.[40]

Looking back a century after Brandeis's "conversion" to Zionism, several things are clear. The Kentucky-born Jew never intended to move from the United States to live in the Holy Land. His support of the Jewish national movement was not the result of anti-Semitic persecution, but rather Brandeis believed that while American Jews were fully participating citizens of the American Republic, millions of other Jews required "a land, a home of their own."[41] Also important was Brandeis's belief that the renewal of Jewish life everywhere in the world could best be achieved through Zionism.

Echoing Brandeis was Richard Gottheil, who was careful to separate living in the Jewish homeland from supporting the Zionist movement:

> We believe that such a home can only naturally . . . be found in the land of the fathers . . . [but] we hold that this does not mean that all Jews must return to Palestine.

Even Wise in the formative years of the Jewish national movement took a position similar to Brandeis. He supported the creation of a little Jewish principality within . . . Palestine . . . [The American Jew] longed for no Palestine. . . . [He] gives his allegiance to this land which alone can satisfy his very passion for liberty.[42]

Brandeis's brilliant intellectual powers and personal stature, his emphasis on "Americanism," his demand for organizational discipline and efficiency, and his careful analysis of difficult problems changed American Zionism. He insisted on organizational structures, fiscal transparency, delegation of duties, and a systematic approach to raising funds and enrolling new members. Despite his almost illegible handwriting and his duties after 1916 as a member of the high court, Brandeis's leadership was vital to the growth of American Zionism in the United States. Brandeis energized Zionism and made it a powerful and permanent factor of American Jewish life.

Unlike most Zionists, including Wise, who saw the movement as an integral part of their Judaism, Brandeis said he came "to Zionism . . . through Americanism . . . Zionism is essentially a movement of freedom, a movement to give the Jews more freedom, a movement to enable Jews to exercise the rights now exercised by practically every other people in the world."[43]

But for many Jews of his day, Brandeis still remained an outsider who was not religiously knowledgeable or personally observant. He lacked a traditional emotional attachment to the Jewish community, and his personality was cool and often aloof. But Wise saw something quite different in the character and personality of Brandeis: a throwback to the biblical Hebrew prophets.[44] Indeed, in the 1930s, it was President Franklin Roosevelt who referred to Brandeis as "Isaiah."[45] Stephen Wise had at last discovered his new hero and mentor, and Zionism had found an unexpected but important leader in America.

Outsiders who become leaders are not unknown in Jewish history. The biblical Moses was raised as an Egyptian in Pharaoh's royal court until he witnessed the murder of a Hebrew slave. The assimilated Herzl discovered his Jewish identity as a result of the anti-Semitism he witnessed during the Dreyfus trial in Paris.

After a complex series of delaying tactics and other stalling efforts, the American Jewish Committee leaders facing Brandeis's leadership were compelled to accept a new reality: the creation in June 1915, at a large American Zionist meeting in Boston, of an "American Jewish Congress."[46] But there were ill will and raw feelings on both sides. Wise described Cyrus Adler, a prominent AJ Committee leader and chancellor of the Jewish Theological Seminary, as "a longtime violent implacable foe of the Congress."[47]

Stephen conceived and organized the American Jewish Congress as a national organization that was the antithesis of the American Jewish Committee.

He insisted on a broad-based membership, unlike the committee, one that would appeal to the large number of Eastern European Jews in the United States. It was no accident that Wise chose a similar name—the American Jewish Congress—and the identical initials—AJC—of the group he abhorred. It was a decision that often resulted in confusion about the positions, policies, and identity of the two organizations.

Once plans for the AJCongress were under way, Brandeis and others wanted Wise to assume direct leadership of the new organization, but the increasingly famous (and always ambitious) rabbi demurred, saying, "I am a clerical. . . . I am an ultra-liberal, and . . . I am a New Yorker."[48]

But there was another reason for Stephen's unusual diffidence. At first, Wise wanted the American Jewish Congress to become a public battering ram that would force the major Jewish groups to support Zionism and other "democratic" Jewish causes. But Brandeis, the prudent attorney, had a different strategy—one that we today call "containment."

Brandeis believed that once Zionism as a movement became stronger in the United States and attracted a greater number of followers, the anti-Zionist Reformers in Cincinnati (Hebrew Union College) and New York (the American Jewish Committee) would become isolated and their power weakened. Wise reluctantly agreed with Brandeis, and he began a new way to undermine the credibility of his arch-foes Kohler, Philipson, and Marshall.

Stephen made the Brandeis connection between Americanism and Zionism a central part of his own personal philosophy. The team of Wise and Brandeis excited many American Jews and weakened the religious and communal monopoly of Wise's two main adversaries: anti-Zionist Reform rabbis and the American Jewish Committee. In a January 1916 Free Synagogue sermon, Wise declared,

I know that I can be a loyal American. Zionism is not a religion. It is not un-American. But it is touched by the spirit of religion.[49]

Four months later Wise returned to the same theme:

That Zionism is irreligious, it is left in the main for religionless Jews to assert. That Zionism is un-American is an indictment drawn up principally by Americans . . . of dubious if not infirm loyalty.[50]

This line of attack on anti-Zionism could not have succeeded without the Jewish community's belief that being a supporter of Zionism did not impinge upon being a loyal American. Brandeis, an assimilated Jew, endorsed a winning, easy-to-remember formula that asserted, "To be good Americans, we must be good Jews; to be good Jews, we must become Zionists."[51]

Brandeis's statements became a critical component in the acceptance and then the embrace of Zionism by the overwhelming majority of American Jews. In addition, Brandeis's imprimatur and standing as a celebrated lawyer guaranteed Wise and his colleagues access to the White House, the State Department, and other power centers of the US government. That access only grew once Brandeis took his seat as an associate justice of the Supreme Court in 1916.

During World War I, Wise had a simple agenda when he traveled to Washington to meet members of the Wilson administration: provide physical security and food for the imperiled European Jews and the growing Jewish community in Palestine. On one of his trips to press his case, he wrote Louise,

> It [the work in Washington] is hard and wearing, but I should feel that I were perfidious as a Jew and disloyal as an American not to have my part, such as it is, in guiding the superbly democratic passions of the representative body of Israel in America.[52]

The partnership between Wise and Brandeis came just in time, because in 1917 it was needed in order to achieve Zionism's first major diplomatic victory.

Chapter 13

The Making of a Presidential Zionist

Stephen Wise's commitment to Zionism was the ultimate "lodestar" of his life. That zeal ran through every fiber of his being, and as previously noted, it was inspired first by his father and then by Wise's life-changing 1898 encounter with Theodor Herzl at the Second Zionist Congress. It gained strength when Stephen collaborated with Columbia University professor Richard Gottheil in establishing the embryonic Federation of American Zionists in 1897, and Wise's fervor for the Jewish national movement intensified during his fierce personal battles with anti-Zionist rabbinical colleagues whom he despised. Wise's Zionist enthusiasm culminated with his close working relationship with Louis Brandeis, and it was on constant public display during his numerous bitter controversies within the World Zionist Organization. The most passionate cause in Stephen's life always began with the letter "Z."

Louis Lipsky offered an accurate description of Wise and his lodestar:

> The most sacred of all causes which he served was the Zionist Movement, in which was included not only the ideal of a Jewish State in Palestine but the re-birth of the Jewish nation. . . . Jewish rights everywhere, Jewish democracy, Jewish survival . . . It was resistance and protest all along the line against Jewish inequality; it was Jewish pride and dignity.[1]

Wise, a rabbi's son, admired President Woodrow Wilson, the son and grandson of Presbyterian ministers who instilled in the future president a thorough knowledge of the Hebrew Bible, the sacred scripture that Christians call the "Old Testament." In his rambling autobiography, Wise titles one chapter, "Woodrow Wilson: Leader and Friend."[2]

Wilson's childhood family memories focused on the Civil War and the devastation the conflict brought upon his native Virginia and many other parts of the defeated Confederacy. He grew up in a society and a state that had waged four years of war against the federal Union and suffered enormous damage—all in support of the fabled Lost Cause.

Perhaps that is one reason, among many others, for Wilson's strong commitment as the US president to the principle of "self-determination" for all peoples, especially minorities like Armenians and Jews. He may have perceived himself as a member of a minority people that had fought for but lost its own attempt at self-determination. Memories of the Civil War may have also shaped Wilson's anathema to anti-southern Republicans and northern-based industrial trusts, monopolies, industries, and corporations.

The former group enacted many post–Civil War Reconstructionist policies that from Wilson's point of view unduly punished the South. The latter group supplied much of the financial, economic, and industrial power that was required to crush the Confederacy.

Once the Democratic New Jersey governor won the presidency in 1912, Wise was in close personal contact with both Wilson and his chief aide, Colonel Edward House. The rabbi pressed the president on a number of issues, including support for home rule for Ireland, American opposition to the persecution of Jews in tsarist Russia, US diplomatic recognition of the new Republic of China founded in 1910 by Dr. Sun Yat-sen (1866–1925), a White House backing of the Progressive domestic agenda that included championing trade unions and the rights of labor, and countering the rise of Big Business monopolies.

Wise believed America's leader must denounce Tsar Nicholas II's (1868–1918) cruel anti-Jewish policies: "What right have the Allies even to expect the sympathy of American Jews with their cause as long as Russia fails to make any pronouncement with regard to the Jewish question?"[3]

Wise, who had access to the Oval Office because of his early support of Wilson's presidential aspirations, was pleased when the president chose Brandeis for the Supreme Court in 1916. There were, however, two major issues that revealed significant differences between Wilson and his favorite rabbi: the status of "Negroes" in American society and the extensive war preparedness program that began two years before the United States entered the war.

Wise raised the issue of "tensions among Negroes, due to a sense of being driven back to further segregation under a Democratic administration." In that era the Republicans were identified as the party of President Abraham Lincoln, who issued the historic Emancipation Proclamation during the Civil War and pressed for the adoption of the Thirteenth Amendment to the US Constitution that outlawed slavery. At the same time, the Democrats were still seen by many as the political face of the defeated Confederacy that instituted discriminatory regulations and laws against the freed black slaves and their descendants in the American South: the anti-Negro party of "Jim Crow."

Wise described Wilson's view of Negro rights:

> "We have merely continued the policy of the former [Taft] administration, but the mere fact that it is the Democratic party causes all this vociferous protest" . . . [Wilson] spoke as a true Southerner when he added, "White people do not wish to work in too close proximity to the Negro."

When Stephen asked the president to do more in this area, Wilson replied,

> "I have given orders that the thing [racial segregation] be changed. . . . I must first gain the leadership of my party and then I can do a great deal more." He [Wilson] went on to speak of the great pressure from the West as well as the South not to give the Negro any place in the government. I found him weaker on this subject than any other.[4]

But in reality, Wilson's postmaster general, Albert Burleson (1863–1937), and treasury secretary, William McAdoo, racially segregated their federal departments, and Wilson failed to nominate blacks as US ambassadors to Haiti and Santo Domingo, diplomatic posts that had traditionally been given to African Americans. Despite Wilson's reply to Wise, he did not "change . . . the thing" (racial segregation) during his years as president.[5]

Although Wise had great affection and esteem for Wilson, Stephen never abandoned his commitment to civil rights nor condoned the Wilson administration's racial policies. But Wise did jettison his pacifism position once the United States entered into war against Germany in April 1917. In a complete turnaround, Stephen became one of the president's strongest wartime supporters among America's religious leaders. In a letter to Wilson, Wise affirmed his support for America's involvement in the war:

> The time has come for the American people to understand that it may become our destiny to have part in the struggle which would avert the enthronement of the law of might over the nations.[6]

But Wise's greatest success with Wilson came later that same year when the president affirmed the British government's public statement in favor of a "national home for the Jewish people" in Palestine—a document that became known as the Balfour Declaration. During the spring and summer of 1917, amid World War I, Weizmann in London and Brandeis and Wise in the United States engaged in a complex diplomatic effort: pressing the London

government to support the establishment of a Jewish commonwealth following the Ottoman Empire's military defeat and its loss of several Middle East
provinces, including Palestine.

As a result of the war, the political situation in the Middle East had
changed. Britain replaced Turkey as the ruling power in Palestine, and Zionist
leaders recognized London's central role in shaping the future of postwar
Palestine. But complicating American support for Britain's role in the Middle
East was the fact that in 1917 the United States did not declare war against the
Ottoman Empire, even though it was a Central Power ally of Germany, the
Austro-Hungarian Empire, and Bulgaria. As a result, the United States had
limited diplomatic leverage in the region.

That same year Weizmann became the president of the British Zionist
Federation. For the next thirty years he remained a preeminent leader of the
world Zionist movement, and in 1948 he became Israel's first president. A
skilled and charming diplomat, Weizmann cultivated personal relationships
with many British political leaders, including Arthur J. Balfour (1848–1930),
who was prime minister between 1902 and 1905.

The two men first met one another in 1906, and they are reported to have
had this famous conversation:

> "Mr. Balfour, suppose I was to offer you Paris instead of London, would you
> take it?"
>
> "But Dr. Weizmann, we have London," said Balfour.
>
> "True, but we had Jerusalem," replied Weizmann, who knew that most
> Anglo-Jewish grandees scorned Zionism, "when London was a marsh."
>
> "Are there many Jews who think like you?"
>
> "I speak the mind of millions of Jews."[7]

Weizmann and his associates worked for three years with various British
officials in an attempt to secure London's public support of Zionism.[8] But despite the leadership of Lloyd George and Balfour, delay followed upon delay,
and Weizmann grew fearful of failure and impatient with the slow pace of
negotiations.

But Weizmann and his colleagues were successful in their efforts to gain
British support for Zionism. On November 2, 1917, the now-historic Balfour
Declaration was issued in the form of a letter from Balfour, who was then serving as the UK foreign minister, to Lord Walter Rothschild (1868–1937), a
prominent English Jewish leader:

> His Majesty's government view with favour the establishment in Palestine of a
> national home for the Jewish people, and will use their best endeavours to

facilitate the achievement of this object, it being clearly understood that nothing shall be done which may prejudice the civil and religious rights of existing non-Jewish communities in Palestine, or the rights and political status enjoyed by Jews in any other country.[9]

There are many published studies of how and why the Balfour Declaration came into being, as well as what the declaration meant and did not mean. Few documents in history have been so carefully analyzed and its few words so carefully parsed. Some scholars attribute the declaration to the personal diplomatic skill of Weizmann, a respected chemist who taught at the University of Manchester. Weizmann became a British subject in 1910 and contributed his scientific talents to the production of the chemical acetone, a vital ingredient for Britain in the manufacture of cordite explosives.

However, others saw the declaration as a British attempt to enlist American Jewish support in making certain the United States would commit itself to the war by sending its troops into battle alongside Allied forces. Other students of the period believe the declaration was intended to gain Jewish support as a buffer against postwar French colonial designs in the Middle East—that is, Lebanon and Syria.

One of the Balfour Declaration's most public supporters was Winston Churchill, whose statue in the form of a bronze bust is today on public display in Jerusalem even though in 1922 it was Churchill as British colonial secretary who led the effort to partition the original Palestine by creating "Trans-Jordan," today's Hashemite Kingdom of Jordan.

Britain's support for the Zionist enterprise was based on several other factors, including the need to protect British control of the vital Suez Canal, the water shortcut to India. Another factor was predicated upon a grand wartime strategy that opposed continued Ottoman Turkish rule in Palestine or German influence in the vital oil-producing region. Although the United States was not at war with the Turkish Empire, Great Britain, America's chief ally, was in a military struggle with Turkish forces in the Middle East.

Sometimes overlooked in the debate about Britain's diplomatic and military motives is the fact that David Lloyd George and Arthur Balfour were both believing Protestant Christians who took the Scriptures seriously, especially the inextricable Jewish attachment to the Holy Land and the centuries-old belief in the physical return of Jews to their biblical homeland.

Wise described a Lloyd George encounter in London with Jewish Parliament members who opposed the prime minister's pro-Zionist position, believing that their own status in Britain would be undermined. The Jewish legislators were aware that English king Edward I (1239–1307) had expelled Jews from England in 1290, and the official lifting of the ban did not occur until 1656. As a result, even as successful politicians elected to Parliament, many Jewish M.P.s still felt insecure in Britain.

The story goes that the wartime prime minister read several biblical passages to the apprehensive group, verses about the restoration of the Jewish people to Zion:

> Triumphantly, he [Lloyd George] closed with these words . . . "Now gentlemen, you know what your Bible says. That closes the matter."[10]

While London was the center of Zionist diplomacy in 1917, the "real" Zionists, the Jews who lived in the Holy Land, were facing a desperate situation. The Ottoman Turks who still controlled Palestine confiscated Jewish property, disarmed Jewish communities, and threatened to deport fifty thousand "Russian" Jews from Palestine because they were considered wartime enemies of the Turkish Empire. The US consul in Jerusalem, Otis Glazebrook (1845–1931), an Episcopal clergyman and a former Princeton Seminary professor, warned the Wilson administration that "a great blow" was coming, a catastrophe that would undermine "the religious aspirations of the Jews throughout the world," and would weaken the "message of hope . . . that has let them to once more feel the national spirit."[11]

In the face of the deteriorating situation of Jews in Palestine and his own stalled diplomatic efforts in London, a discouraged Weizmann sent an urgent message to Brandeis in October 1917 asking him to enlist Wilson's support for the proposed declaration. Weizmann wrote, "I have no doubt that the amended text of the declaration will be again submitted to the President [by Prime Minister Lloyd George and Foreign Secretary Balfour] and it would be most invaluable if the President would accept it without reservation and would recommend the granting of the declaration now." Just as Weizmann predicted, the two British leaders sought American support of their declaration.

But Brandeis and Wise had not been idle even before they received Weizmann's message. In June 1917, two months after America entered the war, Wise met with Wilson, who told the rabbi,

> You know of my deep interest in Zionism. . . . Whenever the time comes, and you and Justice Brandeis feel that the time is ripe for me to speak and act, I shall be ready.[12]

Woodrow Wilson's position on Zionism was a combination of presidential Realpolitik and personal religious commitment. Wise soon discovered that the American President had an intense interest in the Zionist efforts to build a Jewish commonwealth. That interest stemmed from his belief in the Jewish people's central role in the divine economy as understood by a staunch Presbyterian like Wilson: "To think that I, a son of the manse [a minister's child] should be able to help restore the Holy Land to its people."[13]

The time was ripe four months later, and House sent the president a pro–Balfour Declaration memo that reflected the views of Brandeis and Wise. Wilson carried the memo with him for a period of time before informing House on October 13, 1917,

> I find in my pocket the memorandum you gave me about the Zionist Movement. I am afraid I did not say to you that I concurred in the formula suggested by the other side [Britain]. I do, and would be obliged if you would let them know it.[14]

But the president chose not to immediately inform Secretary of State Robert Lansing (1864–1925) that he "concurred" with Lloyd George and Balfour regarding Zionism and the contents of the declaration. Lansing only learned of Wilson's position on December 14, and he felt humiliated by the delay in being informed about such an important diplomatic development.

Lansing, who succeeded Bryan as secretary of state, was not personally close to Wilson, and he had a negative view of both the Balfour Declaration and Zionism. In a December 13 letter to Wilson, Lansing wrote,

> My judgment is that we should go very slowly in announcing a policy for three reasons. First, we are not at war with Turkey and therefore should avoid any appearance of favoring taking territory from that Empire by force. Second, the Jews are by no means a unit in the desire to reestablish their race [sic] as an independent people; to favor one or the other faction would seem to be unwise. Third, many Christian sects and individuals would undoubtedly resent turning the Holy Land over to the absolute control of the race [sic] credited with the death of Christ.
>
> For practical purposes, I do not think that we need go further than the first reason given since that is ample ground for declining to announce a policy in regard to the final disposition of Palestine.[15]

The next day Lansing received a brief note from Wilson that seemed to retract the president's earlier support for the declaration:

> The President returned me this letter at Cabinet Meeting. December 14, 1917, saying that very unwillingly he was forced to agree with me, but said that he had an impression that we had assented to the British declaration regarding returning Palestine to the Jews.[16]

Lansing saw the letter as a vindication of his own anti-Zionist position and a negation of Wilson's supposed support of the Balfour Declaration. A kind of limbo ensued, with the British government taking a public position while President Wilson's chief diplomat maintained that the president had not endorsed the London document endorsing the Zionist goal.

The impasse was not ended until the fall of 1918, when Wilson wrote to Wise on the eve of the Jewish High Holidays. The last sentence of the presidential statement reflects the Woodrow Wilson who was once a professor at Wesleyan University and later the president of Princeton University:

> I have watched with deep and sincere interest the reconstructive work which the Weizmann Commission has done in Palestine at the instance of the British Government, and I welcome an opportunity to express the satisfaction I have felt in the progress of the Zionist Movement in the United States and in the Allied countries since the declaration by Mr. Balfour on behalf of the British Government, of Great Britain's approval of the establishment in Palestine of a national home for the Jewish people, and his promise that the British Government would use its best endeavors to facilitate the achievement of that object, with the understanding that nothing would be done to prejudice the civil and religious rights of non-Jewish people in Palestine or the rights and political status enjoyed by Jews in other countries. I think that all America will be deeply moved by the report that even in this time of stress the Weizmann Commission has been able to lay the foundation of the Hebrew University of Jerusalem with the promise that that bears of spiritual rebirth.[17]

Wilson's linking of Zionism with his Christian beliefs was complementary to Brandeis's linkage of Zionism with Americanism. In addition, the influence of both Wise and Brandeis played a significant role in Wilson's public support of Zionism. Wise was effusive in his praise of Wilson's support of Zionism in general and the Balfour Declaration in particular. In 1922, when the League of Nations awarded Britain the Palestine Mandate, Wise wrote to the former president,

> Jewish history, which is the history not of a day but of centuries, will never fail to make mention of the great and generous service which you were ever ready to render to the cause of a national homeland for the Jewish people . . . who will hold you in honor and in gratitude for all generations as one of the great, wise and helpful friends of Israel.[18]

Former president Theodore Roosevelt also supported a "national home for the Jewish people." In a Carnegie Hall address on October 28, 1918, just two weeks before the Armistice and the collapse of the Ottoman Empire, TR declared that Palestine must "be made a Jewish state."[19]

But President Wilson's 1918 High Holiday statement did not silence the anti-Zionist elements within the State Department. Allen W. Dulles (1893–1969), a nephew of Robert Lansing—who in later years became director of the US Central Intelligence Agency—headed the State Department's Near East Division in the early 1920s. Dulles was also the grandson of John Watson Foster (1836–1917), who served as President Benjamin Harrison's (1833–1901) secretary of state. Allen's brother was John Foster Dulles (1888–1959), who was secretary of state in the Dwight Eisenhower (1890–1969) administration. In 1922 Allen Dulles wrote,

> Ex-President Wilson is understood to have favored the Balfour Declaration, but I do not know that he ever committed himself to it in an official and public way.[20]

Dulles and many of his State Department colleagues of the time saw Zionism as a British Mandate and a European issue, one that did not involve American national interests. They believed US concerns in the Middle East should focus on American Christian missionary endeavors and philanthropy, trade, and maintaining the treaty rights gained during the Ottoman rule of the region. During the 1920s, the decade between the Wilson and Franklin Roosevelt administrations, Dulles urged caution regarding the Middle East, espousing a basic hostility to Zionism:

> To commit the [US] Government to the support of Zionists at this particular moment would be especially unfortunate.... [We] should avoid any action which would indicate official support of ... either the Zionists, the anti-Zionists or the Arabs.[21]

As often happens, an American president's public position on a particular international issue sometimes embarrasses, surprises, or upsets many government officials. That is what happened when Wilson supported Zionism and endorsed the Balfour Declaration.

It was a recurring troubling situation that Wise and other Jewish leaders confronted for decades: a US president or the Congress articulates a policy favorable to Zionism, but it is opposed in private or sometimes in public by the professional diplomats in the State Department. The Wilson-Lansing disagreement in 1917–1918 was a preview of what was to come in later years, especially during the tumultuous 1930s and 1940s.

Wise believed there was an entrenched anti-Zionist "cabal" within the US State Department that morphed into anti-Semitism among some senior diplomats and Foreign Service officers. He was not wrong, and how he confronted such adversaries consumed much of Wise's time and energy in the years leading to Israel's independence.[22]

Chapter 14

Wise and the 1919 Paris Peace Conference

In an address before a joint session of Congress on January 8, 1918, President Wilson outlined fourteen specific "points" or war aims of the United States. It was perhaps the most important speech of his entire career, and he presented it in his usual sermonic style. Growing up in his father's Presbyterian church in Staunton, Virginia, influenced young Woodrow in many ways, including the stern manner in which he often delivered his public speeches. Wilson's oratory was a dramatic change from the flamboyant populist oratory of fellow Democrat William Jennings Bryan, who ran unsuccessfully for the White House in 1896, 1900, and 1908. The last of the Fourteen Points was Wilson's call to establish a League of Nations as an international body entrusted with maintaining the postwar peace and preventing future armed conflicts:

> A general association of nations must be formed under specific covenants for the purpose of affording mutual guarantees of political independence and territorial integrity to great and small states alike.[1]

Wilson also called for "open agreements" or treaties among the world's nations, liberal economic trade policies, free and unfettered ocean navigation, and adjustment of European national borders that would negate any territorial gains made by Germany and its allies during the war. The vanquished Habsburg Austro-Hungarian Empire was to be broken up into a group of independent national states that would reflect the American president's demand for "self-determination" by all peoples. The empire's last kaiser, Karl I (1887–1922), lost both his royal status and power in 1918 after reigning for only two years following the 1916 death of his great-uncle, the legendary emperor Franz Joseph. Most historians describe Karl as a weak and vacillating ruler.[2]

Poland, Yugoslavia, and Czechoslovakia were three of the new post–World War I states. The latter nation had Stephen's friend, Thomas Masaryk, as its first president. The Prussian-dominated German Empire collapsed when

Kaiser Wilhelm II of the House of Hohenzollern abdicated in 1918 and fled Berlin, his capital city, to find safety in Holland, where he lived for another twenty-three years.[3]

On November 6, 1917, during the same week the Balfour Declaration was issued, the Bolsheviks, led by Vladimir Lenin (1870–1924), overthrew the huge Russian Empire led by Wilhelm's cousin, Nicholas II, the last House of Romanov tsar. The new "proletariat" regime executed the entire royal family on July 17, 1918, in Yekaterinburg along with several members of the tsar's personal staff. Among the dead were Nicholas's wife, their son, and four daughters, including the Grand Duchess Anastasia (1901–1918). Many people believed she had somehow survived the killings, but Anastasia did not escape the executioner's bullets, despite the later claims of several imposters and a 1956 motion picture starring the famed Swedish actress Ingrid Bergman (1915–1982).[4]

The defeated Ottoman Empire, the "Sublime Porte" based in Istanbul, lost most of its Middle East possessions, including modern-day Israel, Jordan, Lebanon, Iraq, and Syria. But the victorious Allies permitted the sultan to rule a small imperial entity until the empire was overthrown in 1922 by Mustafa Kemal Ataturk (1881–1938), who established the Turkish Republic.[5]

One of Wilson's points demanded the end of colonialism on the part of various powers, including Britain and France, a proposal that was not met with cheers in either London or Paris. In fact, the Fourteen Points were at first minimized, even dismissed as naïve idealism by America's allies. France's wartime prime minister Georges Clemenceau (1841–1929) mockingly noted that God in the Bible had offered only Ten Commandments, four less than the Presbyterian American president.[6]

Even with the public and private criticisms, Wilson's views represented the only comprehensive list of war aims of the Allies. The Fourteen Points served as the basis of both the postwar peace conference in Paris and the final agreement that emerged in 1919 from those deliberations: the Versailles Peace Treaty. Despite the treaty or perhaps because of its provisions, the post–World War I period was a time of extraordinary violence, change, and upheaval that culminated with World War II, which began twenty years later in 1939.

When the Armistice was signed on November 11, 1918, nine million Jews lived in Eastern Europe. Like many other peoples in that region, they had endured great hardships and extensive "collateral damage" during the four years of hostilities: civilian deaths and injuries, loss of property, physical devastation of both urban and rural areas, widespread hunger, disease, geographical dislocation, and family separations. However, when the armed combat concluded, Stephen Wise expressed enthusiasm about President Wilson's Fourteen Points, especially number five, which called for national self-determination:

A free, open-minded, and absolutely impartial adjustment of all colonial claims, based upon a strict observance of the principle that in determining all such questions of sovereignty the interests of the populations concerned must have equal weight with the equitable claims of the government whose title is to be determined.[7]

Stephen saw a rare opportunity for European Jews to achieve a measure of freedom and security after centuries of anti-Semitic persecution and discrimination. Jewish communities in Eastern Europe had their own schools, language, religion, culture, and a self-perception that constituted a Wilsonian "national entity." After the enormous suffering during the war, Jews throughout the world were hopeful that they would be among the beneficiaries of the American president's idealistic principle of self-determination in both Europe and within the growing Jewish population in Palestine. Brandeis said the Paris peace conference was "the most auspicious moment in the history of the Zionist movement."[8]

The conference began in January 1919 just two months after the Armistice, and it involved delegates from thirty-two countries as well as hundreds of journalists who reported on the historic event. They were joined by a host of consultants and specialists attached to many of the delegations. Among such advisers were historian Arnold Toynbee (1889–1975) and economist John Maynard Keynes (1883–1946) from Britain, and State Department official Allen Dulles, journalist Walter Lippmann (1889–1974), and historian Samuel Eliot Morrison (1887–1976) from the United States.

The French delegation included author Anatole France (1844–1924) and future prime minister Leon Blum (1872–1950). Among that group was Ho Chi Minh (1890–1969) from Indo-China/Vietnam. Also attending the peace conference were other national leaders: Jan Christian Smuts (1870–1950) of South Africa; Edvard Benes (1884–1948), who succeeded Thomas Masaryk as the Czechoslovakia president in 1936; Greek prime minister Eleftherios Venizelos (1864–1936); and Iranian Mohammad Mossadegh (1882–1967). Thirty-four years later, in 1953, Allen Dulles was the CIA director who engineered the coup that removed Mossadegh as his country's prime minister.[9]

There were also representatives in Paris from a myriad of ethnic and national groups who were intent on achieving the goal of self-determination for their peoples, sometimes at the expense of other like-minded competing groups in the Balkans, Eastern Europe, Asia, and the Middle East.

The peace conference lasted about six months and was dominated by the victorious "Big Four" political leaders: Wilson from the United States, Clemenceau of France, David Lloyd George of Britain, and Vittorio Emanuele Orlando (1860–1952) of Italy. The latter had the least influence, and he departed the conference before the diplomats, consultants, and wordsmiths had completed their work. The Italian leader was upset that his nation's post-war territorial gains would be far less than demanded.

When Wilson arrived in Paris on December 14, 1918, it was already clear that the idealism expressed in his Fourteen Points was a thin public veneer that covered up the always-present national and ethnic self-interests that pervade most peace conferences. Nevertheless, an optimistic Wise wrote his son from London in late 1918, "The European world looks to him [Wilson] above all men for deliverance from militarism."[10] But Franklin Roosevelt, the assistant secretary of the navy, had a different, more realistic view of the peace conference:

> President Wilson's gallant appeal . . . meant little to the imagination or the hearts of a large number of so-called statesmen who gathered in Paris to assemble a treaty of so-called peace in 1919. I saw that with my own eyes. I heard that with my own ears. Political profit, personal prestige, national aggrandizement, attended the birth of the League of Nations, and handicapped it from its infancy.[11]

That was the cynical setting in which the various Jewish delegations convened in Paris. There were representatives from Britain, France, South Africa, Canada, Poland, Rumania, Russia, and Ukraine, along with written petitions from Jewish communities in Greece, Transylvania, and Bukovina.

However, the most important and influential delegation was from the United States. It had not been easy to assemble a delegation. The American Jewish delegates included Stephen Wise, Julian Mack, Cyrus Adler, Louis Marshall, and Felix Frankfurter (1882–1965): a charismatic rabbi, a respected judge, a gifted academic leader, a superb attorney, and a brilliant Harvard Law professor and future US Supreme Court justice. Frankfurter acted as Brandeis's eyes and ears at the peace conference.

Mack, Wise, and Frankfurter were selected at an American Jewish Congress meeting in Philadelphia's Independence Hall in December 1918. There had been two earlier meetings in 1916 that were divisive. One reason for the discord was the American Jewish Committee's demand that any attempt to create a "congress" be postponed until the end of the war.

But Wise and his Zionist allies, including Brandeis, opposed the committee's call for delay, and the organizing plans moved forward. The congress was established to serve as a temporary coalition of many American Jewish groups with the goal of working in unity during the crisis of World War I. The "temporariness" ended in 1922 when the AJCongress was permanently established under Wise's leadership. But the American Jewish Committee agreed to join the peace conference delegation, with Marshall and Adler as its representatives. Judge Mack headed the entire delegation, with Marshall serving as the deputy. Interestingly, the Union of American Hebrew Congregations chose not to participate in the American Jewish Congress meeting or the peace conference.[12]

Stephen wanted Brandeis to be part of the American Jewish delegation, believing his presence would provide the brilliant Zionist leader an opportunity to participate in the important deliberations that would affect the Jewish people throughout the world. But Wilson did not agree with Wise:

> If he comes here [to Paris] he will have to resign from the bench. It would not be easy for me to secure Senatorial confirmation of another great liberal, even if I could find one. . . . Dr. Wise, I need Brandeis everywhere, but I must leave him somewhere.[13]

Prior to sailing for France, Mack articulated the two major goals he would pursue at the peace conference: international support of the growing Zionist enterprise in Palestine and full "national rights" for Eastern European Jews. The Chicago judge called for

> justice for the Jew in all those lands of Eastern Europe . . . justice for the Jew in those lands in which justice has heretofore been denied.[14]

The overall goal of all the various Jewish delegations that traveled to Paris in 1919 was to defend and enhance Jewish interests at the peace conference.[15] That the question of Jewish rights should appear on the agenda of an international diplomatic assembly was not a novelty; it had been brought before every significant European congress since 1815.[16]

But Mack believed the 1878 treaty that emerged from the congress of Berlin was "faultily worded" regarding the civil and religious rights of Jews, especially in the Balkans and in Rumania. Indeed, Rumania failed to carry out the treaty's provisions regarding minority rights. Mack described Jews as "men and women without a country . . . who must have equal civil, political, religious, and national rights."[17]

But by 1919, the status of European Jews had changed from the previous century. No longer could they be dismissed and treated as a pariah people as had been the custom of the past. Wise wrote,

> The position of the Jews in respect to the Peace Conference of 1919 is a very different thing from the status of Jewry in 1878 [the Treaty of Berlin Conference]. . . . Jews have greatly and nobly served in the armies of the world.[18]

Stephen was correct. Historians estimate that 1.5 million Jews served in the Allied and Central Power armies during the war. This number included a half million men in the tsar's armed forces—most of them drafted into service, while as many as 100,000 German Jews, many of them volunteers, fought for their kaiser and "Fatherland." There were fifty Jewish generals in the Italian Army, and the total number of all Jewish military deaths between 1914 and 1918 was about 140,000, most of them within the ranks of the ill-equipped and poorly led Russian Army. A postwar survey indicated that 12,000 German Jewish soldiers were killed during the war.[19]

In addition, a "Jewish Legion" was attached to the British Army and numbered about 5,000 troops, many of them Palestinian Jews. World War I Legion members included two future Israeli prime ministers—David Ben-Gurion (1886–1973) and Levi Eshkol (1895–1969)—and the second president of Israel—Yitzhak Ben-Zvi (1884–1963).[20]

The forty-four-year-old Wise, accompanied by his wife, spent five weeks in London and Paris during December 1918 and January 1919. It marked Stephen's debut on the global stage as a major leader of the world Jewish community. While in London he met with Chaim Weizmann, who was the same age as Wise. The American rabbi found the Zionist leader either unable or unwilling to press the British government for greater support of Jewish rights in either Palestine or Eastern Europe. Stephen was also upset that Weizmann did not understand or even accept the "reality" that, after the war, the American Zionist movement led by Justice Brandeis had a major role to play—much more than providing financial support:

> The Zionist movement in Europe admits that there is a Zionist movement in America . . . but if [our] remittances for any reason should cease to float into the coffers of London or Paris, we should speedily be cut off from London or France. Our friends there do not know us, do not believe in us, and do not believe in the reality of our Zionism.[21]

During his London visit, Wise also met with Arthur Balfour and assured him that the American Zionist leadership was supportive of a possible postwar British Mandate over Palestine that would include London's commitment to carry out the provisions of the 1917 declaration bearing the foreign secretary's name.[22] Three years later, in 1922, the League of Nations awarded Britain control of the Holy Land—a situation that lasted until the modern state of Israel declared its independence on May 14, 1948.

While in Britain, Stephen attended a gala banquet where he met with prominent Arab leaders, including Emir Faisal (1883–1933) and the legendary British military officer T. E. Lawrence (1888–1935), who had led the fight

against the Turks in the Middle East. Faisal would later become the king of
Greater Syria and Iraq. Lord Walter Rothschild—to whom the Balfour
Declaration was addressed—hosted the dinner. An irate Louise Wise was excluded from the banquet with the Arabs and "Lawrence of Arabia" because
she was a woman. Forced to dine alone in a London cafeteria while her husband met with the various dignitaries, Louise wrote her son,

> Princes and lords, who only have male persons at dinner, the princes of Arabia
> not being civilized as yet.[23]

Although Stephen was critical of Weizmann's apparent disregard of the
American Zionist movement, Wise understood that the famed chemist was
the key figure in achieving the Balfour Declaration. Wise was also aware that
Weizmann, who was born in an Eastern European shtetl (a small Eastern
European Jewish village), had the strong emotional and political backing of
millions of Jews throughout the world.

On January 3, 1919, on the eve of the Paris Peace Conference, Weizmann
gained another diplomatic victory in addition to the Balfour Declaration:
Faisal's public support of Zionism. The joint agreement between a prominent
Zionist official and a leading Arab political figure was never carried out, but it
remains a milestone in modern Middle Eastern history. Faisal, a Hashemite
and the great uncle of the late Jordanian king Hussein (1935–1999), declared,

> We Arabs . . . look with the deepest sympathy on the Zionist movement. Our
> deputation here in Paris is fully acquainted with the proposals submitted yes-
> terday by the Zionist Organisation to the Peace Conference, and we regard
> them as moderate and proper. We will do our best, in so far as we are con-
> cerned, to help them through; we will wish the Jews a most hearty welcome
> home. . . . I look forward, and my people with me look forward, to a future in
> which we will help you and you will help us, so that the countries in which we
> are mutually interested may once again take their places in the community of
> the civilised peoples of the world.[24]

After his meetings in London, Wise left for Paris in January 1919 with
Louise to attend the peace conference. He was "optimistic" about the "political
situation" regarding Jewish aspirations in both Eastern Europe and Palestine
because of Wilson's leadership. On February 4 he wrote an effusive letter to
Max Heller:

> The most hopeful thing of all is the attitude of our President. . . . He is our
> friend and he will stand by us to the end. . . . A Jewish Palestine is taken for

granted throughout the Allied peoples in just the same way as a renascent Poland or a reorganized Serbia. Surely that is nothing less than a God-given miracle.[25]

It would not be the last time Wise placed great trust in an American president. He was equal in his praise of Franklin Roosevelt during the 1930s and 1940s.

The weeks that Stephen spent at the peace conference revealed the deep fissures among the Jewish representatives. Members of the anxious and apprehensive French delegation, still reeling from the infamous anti-Semitic Dreyfus affair, affirmed an intense Gallic loyalty. They believed they were completely integrated into the French nation, including its history and culture, and they could not comprehend how other Jews could fail to be as "patriotic" in their own countries. To them the word "Jew" possessed only religious significance, and they perceived the outspoken demands of Eastern European Jews for national self-determination as not only unjustified but dangerous as well. The French Jews were also opponents of Zionism.

The historian Eugene See (1864–1936) and the archaeologist Salomon Reinach (1858–1932) represented the French Jewish community at the conference. Both professors feared that the Jewish claims made at the international meeting could be disastrous for Jews of Eastern Europe and even endanger the security of Western European Jews like themselves. The French delegation sought only civil, political, and religious rights for their Eastern European brothers and sisters, but rejected any demand for Jewish "national" rights.[26]

The British Jewish delegation was also wary of pressing for "national" rights for their co-religionists in Eastern Europe. A tense standoff developed between the two opposing camps—the "secure" French and British Jews on one side and the "nationalistic" Eastern European Jews on the other. The deadlock was not broken until March 16, 1919, when the full American Jewish delegation arrived in Paris.

Months earlier, on Sunday, December 6, 1918, Wise, Mack, and Marshall, along with Bernard G. Richards (1877–1971), the American Jewish delegation's secretary, met with Wilson at the White House. The reason for the meeting was to make certain that the post-Armistice agenda of the upcoming American Jewish Congress assembly in Philadelphia did not conflict with the programs and policies Wilson would present at the upcoming peace conference in Paris.

The four Jewish leaders gave the president a detailed report of the status of Eastern European Jews with special emphasis on the dire situation in Poland and Rumania. The Bucharest government's denial of rights to its Jewish population, despite the Treaty of 1878, was reiterated at the White House meeting.

The group also presented Wilson with its proposals for aiding the Jews in Palestine.

After the White House meeting concluded, Wise stayed behind for a few minutes to have a personal conversation with the president. Stephen told Wilson of "some of the difficulties the Jewish delegations had begun to face in Paris" and appealed to Wilson:

> "Mr. President . . . World Jewry counts upon you in its hour of need and hope." Placing his hand on my shoulder, he [Wilson] quietly and firmly said, "Have no fear, Palestine will be yours."[27]

In late February, Wilson returned to Washington for a brief visit and then set sail again for Europe on March 5. While the president was still in the capital, Wise and his colleagues had another Sunday White House meeting with Wilson on March 2, 1919. Wilson gave his visitors an update on the peace conference and assured the Jewish delegation that "the Allied nations, with the fullest concurrence of our own government and people, are agreed that in Palestine should be laid the foundation of a Jewish commonwealth." Wise was delighted with Wilson's support of Zionism, but he worried: "I wish I might be assured that the Jewish people will be equal to the opportunity."[28]

The following day, the *New York Times* reported on page one, "President Gives Hope to Zionists." In the same story Stephen tackled head-on a prevalent canard that Bolshevism in Russia was a "Jewish" movement:

> Rabbi Wise said that Bolshevism was not a Jewish phenomenon. Admitting that a considerable number of Jews held office under the Bolsheviks, it must be remembered that these Jews who have returned to Russia included many of the "all but crucified exiles." . . . "I consider it a grave wrong against a whole people to speak of Bolshevism and the Russian Jew as if these were interchangeable terms," continued Dr. Wise. "Even though a handful of Bolshevist leaders may be perfidious outcasts, the great leaders among the Russian Jews are against Bolshevism. Are all Jews to be damned because a few Jews are damnable?"[29]

A few months earlier, Marshall had composed a comprehensive Jewish "Bill of Rights" that Wise and his colleagues wanted included in any peace treaty. In fact, they called Marshall's document "irrepealable." In it, Marshall was careful to clarify the concept of "national rights." Wise did not advocate the establishment of an *imperium in imperio*, but rather the concept signified those basic rights that might be accorded to all other religious and ethnic groups living in chaotic Eastern Europe.

The lengthy Bill of Rights emphasized the physical security needs of Jews, the importance of language freedom (the right to use Yiddish or Hebrew), and the right to observe the Jewish Sabbath (Saturday) without penalty or discrimination.[30] When Wilson received a copy of the Bill of Rights, he responded with a vague statement expressing his "sympathy to the incontestable principle of the right of the Jewish people to equality of status everywhere."[31]

Although President Wilson voiced "sympathy" for Jewish rights, it was not true of a man who would reside in the White House ten years later. On April 18, 1919, Cyrus Adler met with Herbert Hoover in Paris, and the results were not reassuring. At the time Hoover was serving as the head of the peace conference's Supreme Economic Council, whose task was to present the economic requirements necessary to ensure peace following World War I. In 1917 Wilson had appointed Hoover, a mining engineer by training and education, to lead the US Food Administration.

The Iowa-born Quaker's task was making sure that the American troops had the necessary quantity and quality of nourishing food, and Hoover achieved fame for advocating sparse diets for the American civilian population. The strategy was called "Hooverizing" America's wartime national menu. In his meeting with Adler, Hoover said,

> That strong Jews in America and elsewhere ought to be factors in preventing the Jews in Poland from continuing the mistakes they are making in causing a political division [within the new independent nations] . . . That the Jews ought to insist on political equality and religious liberty. That it is a profound error to introduce the words "national rights" into the discussion . . . a most serious mistake.[32]

Allen Dulles, a member of the American delegation in Paris, also opposed any special treaty rights for the Jews of Europe:

> If we endeavor to set [the Jews] up as a privileged community, they will be subject to oppression on the part of the people who are not ready for so radical a change.[33]

Before the American Jewish delegation could confront the criticisms of Hoover and Dulles, Mack worked first to meld the Jewish delegations into a unified group. And it was Marshall, Wise's bitter foe from the Temple Emanu-El controversy years earlier in New York City, who worked to guarantee there "would be no open conflict with regard to those subjects [national rights] as to which there was a disagreement."[34]

Wise left Paris for the United States in late January 1919, and while at sea he learned that his forty-eight-year-old brother, Otto, had died on January 23. The grieving family deferred the funeral until Stephen returned. Two years before, during the momentous month of November 1917 (the Balfour Declaration and the Russian Revolution), Stephen's mother, Sabine Fischer Farkashazy Wise, died on the twenty-eighth of that month. She was eighty-one years old.

Back in New York City, Wise presented his Free Synagogue congregation with an analysis of the Jewish aims and goals at the peace conference. He was hopeful that he, Mack, Adler, Marshall, and Frankfurter could "bring order out of the Jewish chaos, and better yet, make it possible for Jews everywhere and under all circumstances to reorder Jewish affairs."[35]

Because Wise, Mack, and Frankfurter were identified as strong Zionists, it was left to Marshall, the president of the "non-Zionist" American Jewish Committee, to placate the hypersensitive and fearful French Jewish community. He had a personal meeting with Israel Levi (1856–1939), the acting chief rabbi of France. Marshall reassured the rabbi that the provisions of the American Jewish Bill of Rights were "almost identical" with the positions of the French and British delegations. Marshall pointed out that "Easterners are those [Jews] most nearly concerned" with their national rights.

Marshall told Rabbi Levi it was

> necessary to lay aside his preconceived notions and approach the question with an open mind . . . [Eastern European Jews] approach the question with more knowledge than we. . . . We must not deal with the matter as though they were not capable of forming a judgment and perhaps of being right.[36]

Wise approved of such personal meetings because he was convinced that the prominent American Jewish representatives who were close to President Wilson, the dominant figure in Paris, were the only ones capable of obtaining national rights for Eastern European Jews:

> [It] is the truth that the most significant Jewish community in the world today is part of that nation which has become the most potent in the world councils and most eager to inaugurate the era of reparation to the Jew in the only form in which the Jew demands reparation for centuries of Wrong And Hurt By Him Endured—Namely, Justice.[37]

The lengthy and complex Polish Minorities Treaty approved at the peace conference was the model for other nations, including Albania, Latvia, Lithuania, Greece, and Rumania. In fact, every newly created nation was required to accept a minorities treaty as the "price" for gaining independence. Wise, a self-described "friend of Poland," was hopeful that this country with its large Jewish population would grant to the very considerable Jewish minority within the Polish republic that measure of self-determination which is wholly compatible with national loyalty and makes in truth for the strongest federation.[38]

The Polish treaty promised Jews and other minorities in Poland a full set of rights. But in later years Wise became disappointed and angered that the Polish government and several other independent nations created after World War I failed to meet their human rights obligations.

The charming and talented Polish prime minister Ignacy Paderewski (1860–1941), who was also an acclaimed concert pianist, opposed the Minorities Treaty. During the peace conference Paderewski did not specifically attack the document's provisions that granted rights and protections to Polish Jews and other minorities in his country. In 1939 on the eve of World War II, the total Polish population numbered about 37 million people, 10 percent of whom were Jews.

Paderewski focused instead on the fact that France, Germany, Great Britain, and even Lenin's Russia had no special treaties for their minority populations because it was assumed the "major" nations did not need any special safeguards to protect their diverse populations. The assumption proved to be both false and fatal: Nazi Germany's "War against the Jews" and Joseph Stalin's (1878–1953) murderous policies in the Soviet Union are but two examples of such an erroneous belief.

Paderewski declared that Poland would grant the same rights to its minorities that the Western powers granted to their minority groups. But the pianist-political leader also assured the Big Four that his country was ready to accord all its diverse peoples the same rights the proposed League of Nations might demand in the future.

If Paderewski's opposition was somewhat disingenuous and oblique, Ioan Bratianu (1864–1927), the Rumanian prime minister, attacked both Wilson and Clemenceau by asserting that the Minorities Treaty represented a negative reflection upon his country's record in fulfilling the provisions it assumed in 1878. The Rumanian leader's criticism of the Minorities Treaty differed from Paderewski's subtle opposition. Bratianu warned that if foreign powers (i.e., the United States and France) meddled in the internal affairs of a state, it would embroil the peoples of the world in further turmoil.

When Clemenceau criticized Bratianu's position, the Rumanian leader took to the peace conference floor again and replied,

The fact that a part of Rumania's citizens [Jews and Hungarians] will be granted and guaranteed special rights by a foreign Power(s) will make fragile the foundations of the State in question.[39]

Wilson was also angered by Bratianu's outburst and reminded the Rumanian (and other European leaders), "If we agree to these additions of territory (Rumania gained land—Transylvania—from Hungary as part of the peace treaty), we have the right to insist on certain guaranties of peace." For the US president, protecting minorities was not meddling in the internal affairs of a state, but rather it was an effort to maintain peace and stability among peoples and nation-states.[40]

In addition to enhancing the rights of Eastern European Jews, Wise had another hope for the Paris Peace Conference—perhaps the one closest to both his head and heart. In describing that aspiration, Wise employed his usual eloquence:

> The question before the peace conference is not whether there shall be a Jewish Palestine, but what form that Jewish Palestine shall take politically and how best it can be developed from within and safeguarded from without. . . . The future of the Jewish commonwealth the world cannot shape. The event must rest in the hands of the Jewish people. . . . It will be not the least of the glories of the peace conference to have framed the charter of hope for the Jewish people, to have at one and the same time proclaimed to the Jew freedom in all lands, and above all, freedom to rebuild the waste places and to make the Holy Land of an earlier day rich with fulfillment of prophetic promises of justice and righteousness.[41]

Despite the fruitful March 1919 meeting with Wilson in Washington and Mack's successful campaign to unify the Jewish delegations in Paris, there were many difficulties and obstacles at the peace conference. In the face of the public opposition of Paderewski and Bratianu and the not-so-visible hostility of other national leaders to the issue of minority rights, the Jewish delegations presented their positions to the Big Four in May 1919 as the conference neared its conclusion. Thanks to Wilson and others in the US delegation, many of the Jewish goals were incorporated into the final wording of the Polish treaty.

While that treaty and others like it were not faithfully followed in the years between the two World Wars, many of the themes, concerns, topics, and subjects debated in 1919 formed the basis for the UN human rights declarations that were adopted in the post–World War II period. For that reason, it is important to analyze what Marshall, Wise, Mack, and others achieved in 1919.

The Polish treaty's twelve Articles can be divided into six major categories.

Article 2 assures that all inhabitants in Poland are guaranteed protection of life and property. The racial, religious, national, or linguistic backgrounds of a nation's citizens are of no concern.

Articles 3–6 guarantee that no one should be excluded from Polish citizenship on account of race, language, or religion. In addition to the large Jewish population in Poland, there were many Germans, Austrians, Hungarians, Russians, Ruthenians, and White Russians within the new nation's borders.

Articles 7 and 8 provide Polish citizens who differ in race, language, or religion equality before the law, and they are to enjoy equal civil and political rights. Minorities in Poland are also given the right to establish and control "at their own expense, charitable, educational, religious and social institutions." Article 9 guarantees that the minorities in Poland can use an "equitable share" of public funds for "educational, religious or charitable purposes."

Articles 10 and 11 were written for Jews, and they are named in the treaty. Although the term "national rights" was rejected at the peace conference, Jews, unlike other minorities, however, were given control of their own schools. In addition, Jews were not to suffer any discrimination or persecution because they observe the Sabbath on a day different from Christians (i.e., Sunday).

The final article limits the legal process of protecting minority groups. If they believe there is any "infraction" of their rights, only a member of the "Council of the League of Nations" could submit the question to arbitration. Individuals or separate minority communities are not permitted to take such a step alone.[42]

Marshall and Mack spent almost six months in Paris attempting to bring unity to the diverse Jewish delegations and then pressing the Big Four to adopt the Bill of Rights that was presented to President Wilson in Washington. At the end of the conference, many Jewish leaders, including Wise, were convinced that the Minorities Treaty had

> at last absolved the Jews of Eastern Europe from the serious disabilities from which they have for so long suffered and will forever end the grave abuse of the past. They [the Treaties] will enable Jews as well as other minorities to live their own lives and to develop their own culture. . . . A better era is now dawning.[43]

However, that was not the view expressed by some vocal members of the diverse American Jewish Congress when the organization met at the Bellevue Stratford Hotel in Philadelphia on May 30, 1920, about a year after the conclusion of the peace conference. When Judge Mack called upon the indefatigable Marshall to report to the four hundred delegates on the Paris meeting, a near riot ensued. One of the delegates, Benjamin Zuckerman of New York City, jumped from his seat and screamed in Yiddish that Marshall and Mack and by implication Wise as well had "betrayed the Jewish race [sic]" at the conference. Things got much worse on the convention floor, and Mack had to call upon uniformed members of the Jewish Legion to remove about a dozen protesting delegates from the hall.

Emotions remained white-hot later that day when Wise chaired a session where he was compelled to bang the gavel many times without calming the angry crowd who believed their leaders had deceived and failed the Jewish people. Wise shouted, "You will sit down and come to order!" When Wise was unable to quiet the AJCongress assembly, he threatened "to adjourn this session and abandon the Congress [that he had created] for all time." Some order was restored, and Marshall was able to read his report. But the damage was done, and the "temporary" Congress was disbanded and replaced by a "permanent" American Jewish Congress.

The entire ordeal lasted twelve hours. Louis Marshall and Jacob Schiff, two leading officers of the wartime AJCongress, refused to join the newly constituted organization. Stephen was not upset by their departure, and he celebrated the birth of a "democratic" national Jewish group. However, the final formation of the American Jewish Congress did not conclude until 1922. But at last Wise had not only his Free Synagogue but he also played the dominant rule in his own national organization.[44]

The Versailles Peace Treaty, signed on June 28, 1919, even with its elegant language and clear promises of minority rights, was a failure in preventing national, ethnic, and religious strife. German leaders believed that the peace treaty severely punished their defeated nation and created the widespread belief that their country's honor must be restored. Germany had to admit its guilt for World War I, surrender the Alsace-Lorraine region to the French, and pay $32 billion (about $456 billion today) in reparations.

The Versailles Treaty was assailed by Fascists in Italy led by Benito Mussolini (1883–1945) and by Hitler and his Nazis in Germany. The two dictators created violent totalitarian movements that destabilized any hopes for a lasting peace on the blood-soaked European continent. In addition, the spirit of revanche and explosive national rivalries were widespread in other parts of Europe, and twenty years after the peace conference concluded, another and even more catastrophic global conflict began.

If Wise, Mack, Marshall, Adler, and Frankfurter had "betrayed" their fellow Jews in Paris, the other conference participants including the Big Four political leaders "betrayed" any hope for a lasting peace in Europe.

Following the peace conference, Wilson campaigned throughout the United States in support of US membership in the League of Nations. While speaking in Pueblo, Colorado, on September 26, 1919, the president suffered a paralyzing stroke—a physical condition that rendered him out of commission for the remainder of his second term.

When the international organization became a reality in 1920, it was an ineffectual guardian of world peace. One major reason for the league's weakness was the US Senate's action on November 19, 1919, that rejected America's membership in the new body. A two-thirds affirmative vote of the Senate was required, but Wilson and his supporters were able to garner only fifty-five "yea" votes, while Republican senators Henry Cabot Lodge of Massachusetts (1850–1924), Hiram Johnson (1866–1945) of California, and Wise's friend William Borah of Idaho opposed league membership. The "anti" position received thirty-nine negative votes.[45]

The Senate's rebuff of the League of Nations was a crushing defeat for the ailing President Wilson, despite the pro-league efforts of Stephen Wise, former president William Howard Taft, and many other religious and political leaders.

Following Wilson's stroke, few persons were permitted to see the ailing president, and his physical setback marked the end of Wilson's active leadership. His wife, Edith (1872–1961), shielded him from public view until the end of his term in office on March 4, 1921, and during that time she made numerous decisions in her husband's name.

Many believe Wilson should have authorized Vice President Thomas R. Marshall (1854–1925) to assume presidential powers, but that did not happen. One result of Wilson's stroke was the enactment in 1967 of the Twenty-Fifth Amendment to the US Constitution that provides for an orderly transition of power in such situations.

Woodrow Wilson died on February 3, 1924, and two years later, on the seventieth anniversary of his birth, Stephen Wise broadcast a eulogy for his hero that contained criticism of America's failure to join the League of Nations, Wilson's great dream. In his radio address Wise declared,

The American Pantheon is wide and spacious and its occupants are comparatively few. . . . [Wilson] wrought wise and statesmanlike things for America. He prepared America for the terrible ordeal [the US involvement in World War I]. . . . More than anyone else the people of England, France, and Italy trusted him. . . . Then came the end [of the war] and the beginning of peace. . . . [There] was acclamation and homage [for Wilson] that did not last . . . because America tragically failed Wilson . . . in the councils of peace [unlike] the days of war.[46]

Chapter 15

Stephen Builds His Very Own Seminary

Conventional wisdom has it that in 1915, a bitter and petulant Stephen Wise realized he had failed in the battle to dominate the administration, faculty, and student body of the anti-Zionist Hebrew Union College in Cincinnati, and, as a result of his defeat, he decided instead to establish his own seminary in New York City. Similar to the Free Synagogue, Wise would also control the Jewish Institute of Religion (JIR), the name he gave to the new rabbinical school. The accepted story posits the theory that Stephen compensated for his HUC loss by creating his own personal "academic sandbox."

While there is some truth in this account, the reality, like many other aspects of Wise's life and career, is more complex and complicated. As early as 1909, the egotistical thirty-five-year-old rabbi was already exploring the possibility of setting up a rabbinical seminary. In a letter to Louise he wrote,

> A lovely young boy [an HUC student] came to me yesterday from Cincinnati, he is so unhappy at the College. The boy is dejected and sullen. Now, Madam, please hold your breath while I tell you something. Why shouldn't I have a school for the training of Jewish ministers? . . . The practical experience, training and discipline, they could get under me! I am just aflame with the idea and I will do it and you'll help me.[1]

Once Wise returned to New York City in 1906 after his half dozen years in Portland, Oregon, he intensified his efforts to become the premier Jewish leader in the United States. He commenced that endeavor a year later when he founded the Free Synagogue. It was a necessary first step in his campaign, but a single Manhattan-based congregation was not sufficient to achieve his long-range goals of advancing and leading American Zionism and the domestic social justice agenda.

Wise, the master organizer, always knew that his plans required not only the support of prominent (and affluent) laypeople but also his ability to influence future generations of Reform rabbis. That is one reason why he earlier had invested considerable time and energy in his unsuccessful campaign against the entrenched powers at the Hebrew Union College. It is possible he may have defeated his arch foes—Kohler and Philipson—but Stephen's personal involvement in Progressive politics, the advent of World War I and America's entry into the conflict in 1917, his work with Louis Brandeis to lead American Zionists, the intricate diplomatic campaign to gain President Wilson's support for the pro-Zionist Balfour Declaration, and Stephen's attendance at the lengthy and exhausting Paris Peace Conference in 1919 all combined to delay the establishment of the JIR. But in 1920 Stephen was at last ready to create his "school for the training of Jewish ministers."

Stephen was proud of his extraordinary oratorical skills and his abilities as a public leader, but Wise was aware he was not a Jewish scholar even though he earned a doctorate in Semitic studies at Columbia University. However, he recognized and respected gifted scholars in any field of study, and he wanted such individuals to teach at his proposed seminary. Even as Wise demanded a free pulpit for rabbis at the Free Synagogue, he made *lehrfreiheit* (German for "academic freedom") a centerpiece of the Jewish Institute of Religion.

In the summer of 1920, Wise began his search for potential JIR staff members, including the future school's scholar-president. He conducted several interviews with thirty-nine-year-old Rabbi Mordecai Kaplan (1881–1983), a Jewish Theological Seminary faculty member. Stephen wanted Kaplan to serve as the rabbinical school's president. It was a logical choice for many reasons. At the time, Kaplan was already considered one of the leading theologians and creative thinkers in the Jewish community.

He was born into a Lithuanian rabbinic family and came to the United States when he was eight years old. Kaplan, a gifted religious leader, was a Columbia University student of the American pragmatist John Dewey.

Like Wise, Kaplan was a rabbi's son, and he also received a Ph.D. from Columbia, where he studied philosophy and sociology, including the teachings of Felix Adler. He served as a congregational rabbi at New York City's Kehilath Jeshurun synagogue, and was a founder in 1912 of the Young Israel Orthodox religious movement. However, because of his evolving beliefs, Kaplan broke from the group and was later declared by some Orthodox rabbis to be a "heretic."

On June 12, 1945, leaders of an Orthodox rabbinic organization, Agudat HaRabbanim, met at a Manhattan hotel and burned a siddur or Jewish prayer book that Kaplan had compiled. Kaplan was placed in *herem*, a Jewish form of excommunication.[2]

In 1922 he made history when Judith, his eldest daughter, celebrated the first Bat Mitzvah in America. In 1934 at age fifty-four, he published "Judaism as a Civilization," and it remains a basic document for the Reconstructionist movement he established. During his long life Kaplan influenced generations of rabbis and laypeople with his teachings and writings. In 1968, forty-eight years after his encounter with Wise regarding the JIR presidency, Kaplan founded his own Reconstructionist rabbinical school that is located in the Philadelphia area.

Kaplan described the exploratory meetings with Wise in his diary:

> I went to see Wise and after a few interviews with him we seemed to feel that ultimately he might get the funds for a Rabbinical Training School of which I would be given charge.[3]

Kaplan flirted with the idea of accepting Wise's offer, but he "ultimately" chose to remain at the Jewish Theological Seminary for the rest of his long and distinguished career.

At that same time he was offering Kaplan the top JIR position, Wise also consulted with Richard Gottheil, his Columbia University mentor, and his childhood friend George Kohut.[4] Both men encouraged Stephen to move ahead with the project. On November 2, 1920, a special Free Synagogue committee meeting was convened to consider Wise's plan to establish a liberal Jewish seminary in Manhattan. The report of the meeting encapsulates several major factors in JIR's creation. Wise and his lay group believed that the Hebrew Union College had lost its luster when the school's founder, Isaac Mayer Wise, died in 1900. Stephen wrote,

> Cincinnati's glory had largely departed. Only immovable buildings and local piety or patriotism had kept the college in Cincinnati. . . . In addition, Cincinnati was no longer an intellectual, religious, demographical or cultural center of the American Jewish community. . . . [Hebrew Union College] offered its students an inadequate experimental station. New York had uniquely become such a station, with its great Jewish population, made up of representatives of virtually every Jewish community on earth.[5]

The official minutes were even more critical of the Cincinnati Reform seminary:

> Hebrew Union College had outgrown whatever usefulness it may have originally had. . . . It no longer attracted . . . the finest of our American youth and those it did attract, were but poorly trained to fill the pulpits of forward-looking, progressive American congregations. . . . There was an urgent and insistent demand for [a new rabbinical school].[6]

At the JIR organizational meeting, Wise stressed something novel for the American rabbinate:

A new group of men [there were no female Reform rabbinical students until 1968] with a different type of training must be developed. . . . These men must be college graduates before they should be admitted into the professional school. . . . The Rabbinate as a profession must be placed on the same plane as any other profession such as Medicine or Law. . . . The old practices of granting subsidies as bait to prospective rabbis must be discontinued. . . . A fee [tuition] should be charged. . . . Such a new plan would measurably raise the choice of the Rabbinate as a profession to a new level.

The meeting also reflected Wise's own self-importance:

There was no organization or group . . . prepared or qualified to create such an institution as the Free Synagogue, in view of its past achievements and its ideals for the future.[7]

The committee agreed that a minimum of $30,000 (about $347,000 in today's dollars) was required to ensure a September 1922 opening of the JIR, although the "publicly stated" goal was $50,000 (about $578,000 today):

An effort would be made to procure pledges from friends of the Free Synagogue and of Dr. Wise as a leader throughout the country.[8]

Wise and his Free Synagogue colleagues wanted to upgrade the rabbinic profession by insisting that every JIR student hold a college degree. For decades the HUC had enrolled young boys, including high school students, in its program that allowed the youngsters to attend both the rabbinical school and the University of Cincinnati. Wise opposed such "early recruiting," claiming teenagers were not "old enough or mentally mature enough to make a life commitment" to the rabbinate. In addition, Stephen opposed providing financial subsidies as "bait" to attract financially poor students to the seminary. But, of course, there was always the major reason for establishing the JIR as an alternative to HUC:

The Cincinnati Seminary . . . had shown a deep-seated intolerance of Zionist advocacy. . . . Zionism seemed an intolerable refutation of Reform Judaism. But it never seemed to suggest itself . . . that anti-Zionism was a still graver refutation of the fundamentals of Judaism.[9]

Wise and his Free Synagogue leaders exhibited extraordinary chutzpah (Yiddish for cheek, nerve, and impudence) in seeking to break the Reform rabbinic education monopoly that the Hebrew Union College had maintained since its founding in 1875. To bolster his proposal, Stephen noted that Europe supported "five superior (liberal) seminaries . . . in Breslau, two in Berlin, Budapest and Vienna."[10]

Thanks to the generosity of such prominent contributors as Adolph Lewisohn, Abram Elkus, and Bertha Guggenheimer (1857–1927), the new seminary's budget was secured for two years. A five-story building was constructed at 40 West 68th Street in New York City in 1923 that housed both the Free Synagogue's offices and the JIR. Not until 1950 was a separate Free Synagogue structure erected next door to the original building. The JIR edifice remained in use until 1979, when a new facility was opened in the Greenwich Village area of lower Manhattan near New York University.

The JIR, with Wise as the school's acting president, opened its doors to rabbinical students in 1922, and it maintained its precarious independent existence until 1948 when it merged with the HUC. An astute Kaplan early on had identified the need to "get the funds" for the seminary, and that was always a difficult problem for Wise, the school's chief and sometimes only fundraiser. For a quarter century Stephen was constantly soliciting funds for his impoverished institution. He became JIR's "schnorrer in chief." The derisive Yiddish term describes a person who begs or beseeches others for money.

However, Wise was able to secure several significant contributions, including a grant from Mrs. Guggenheimer that provided a JIR graduate or faculty member a year of study in British Mandate Palestine. Two years after the school opened, Hannah S. Heyman (1851–1928) contributed $163,000 (about $1.8 million today). But such gifts were the exception, and Wise was compelled to juggle an uncertain budget that often failed to meet the needs of his seminary.[11]

For the first five years of JIR's existence, Stephen held the title of acting president, but in 1927 he abandoned the search for an outsider and became the school's official chief executive, a post he held until the school ended its independent existence. Dr. Lee K. Frankel (1867–1931), the head of the United Hebrew Charities of New York and also vice president of the Metropolitan Life Insurance Company, was the first chairman of the JIR Board of Trustees. He was followed by Stephen's longtime Zionist colleague, Julian Mack, and in 1937 New York City judge Joseph M. Levine (1883–1963) became board chairman. Levine also served as the Free Synagogue president between 1930 and 1945, and he was the last surviving founding member of the Free Synagogue.[12]

From the outset, Wise and his associates wanted the JIR to have a cooperative relationship with the Reform Jewish congregational body, the Union of

American Hebrew Congregations (UAHC). Stephen did not want his school to be an "orphan" with no official connection with Reform Judaism. The JIR founders also wanted the UAHC to provide needed financial support. The amount proposed was $45,000 (about $577,000 today) annually for three years. In return, the UAHC would provide one-fifth of the JIR Board of Trustees, a minority of the total board membership. But, of course, in such an arrangement, Wise demanded total freedom for his rabbinical school while still receiving needed UAHC dollars.[13]

In 1921 Abram I. Elkus, president of the Free Synagogue, presented the plans for the new seminary, but UAHC leaders dashed any hope of collaboration when they, along with the HUC officials, unanimously rejected any link to the JIR. Wise was not surprised by the UAHC's total rejection. In 1922 he wrote,

As I expected it has come to pass. . . . [It] is a notice of war. I have done my best and my conscience is clear. We have done all that could be done. The truth is perhaps we should never have expected that there would be any attempt on the part of those in authority [at the UAHC] to foregather with us. . . . But we shall go on. If I live, the Institute will be established.[14]

As a result, the Jewish Institute of Religion was always forced to be a free-standing independent school with no endowment and no financial help from the UAHC. Wise soon became pessimistic about his seminary's future. In a January 1928 letter to Rabbi Morton Berman (1899–1986), a member of JIR's first graduating class, Stephen lamented,

I am desperately worried about the Institute. If we don't get $10,000 this year from the graduates I shall seriously consider discontinuing the Institute. This is not for publication, but it will have to be done. There is no other way. . . . I have no right to go on even though I stay alive unless I have some assurance that the work can be carried out. At present I have not.[15]

But money was only one of the problems Wise confronted in maintaining his rabbinical school. The first, as mentioned above, was the constant need to raise basic operating expenses. The second problem, linked to the first, was the recruiting and retention of full-time faculty members. Often a JIR professor was lured away to another school.

One such case involved Professor Salo W. Baron (1895–1989) considered the greatest Jewish historian of the twentieth century. Baron left his teaching position in Vienna in 1926 to teach at the JIR, but within three years, he moved to Columbia University where he achieved international fame as an expert witness during the Adolf Eichmann (1906–1962) trial in Israel.[16]

Other renowned scholars who taught at the JIR included Israel Abrahams; Ismar Elbogen (1874–1943), who fled his native Germany in 1938; Mordecai Kaplan; Joshua Loth Liebman (1907–1948), the author of the best-selling book *Peace of Mind*; Ralph Marcus (1900–1956), who later moved to the University of Chicago; Julius Obermann (1888–1956), who went on to teach at Yale University; James Parkes (1896–1981), a British pioneer in Christian-Jewish relations; Gershom Scholem (1897–1982), whose academic field was Jewish mysticism and who later taught at the Hebrew University in Jerusalem; Shalom Spiegel (1899–1984), who became a Jewish Theological Seminary faculty member; Harry A. Wolfson (1887–1974), a Harvard University professor; and Jerusalem-born David Yellin (1864–1941).[17]

However, Stephen was able to hire several excellent full-time professors, three of whom were my own teachers as an HUC-JIR student: biblical scholar Harry M. Orlinsky (1908–1992); JIR's longtime dean, Henry Slominsky (1884–1970); and Talmudist John Tepfer (1898–1988). One of JIR's most famous faculty members was the Talmudist Chaim Tchernowitz (1871–1949), who began teaching there in 1923, a year after the school opened.

Wise's distinguished faculty, both full- and part-time, was, in sports parlance, an all-star team. The professors' intellectual talents and academic firepower were so great that students complained that "what we needed was *aleph bes*," the ABCs or simple basics of rabbinic study.[18] In addition to the outstanding professors, Stephen also brought many political, labor, Zionist, religious, literary, social work, and community leaders to address the students.[19]

Because of Wise's personal charisma and JIR's location in the heart of New York City, the school had no problem attracting excellent rabbinical students. As part of his efforts to upgrade the rabbinic profession, Wise never employed the terms "ordination" or *s'micha* when a student completed his JIR studies. He preferred the term "graduation." Stephen enjoyed interviewing prospective students for his rabbinical school and commented to a colleague that "I spent one of the happiest moments of my life" meeting candidates for the rabbinate: "Not one of these boys would have dreamed of going to Cincinnati. . . . I almost tremble at the immensity of the task before us."[20]

In 1922 Stephen's son, James, was a member of the first class that enrolled in his father's seminary. For a time, it appeared James would be the eighth generation of Wises who became rabbis. But Jim, like Felix Adler, another famous rabbi's son, rejected the rabbinate because he said he lacked the faith required for a spiritual leader.

His son's decision in 1926 pained Stephen, even creating headlines in the press. The *New York Times* reported that Wise was "grieved" by his son's decision, and Stephen gave a painful interview even as he "paced back and forth" and spoke in a sorrowful voice. James sent his father a telegram from Minneapolis declaring he would always remain a Jew and "serve my people, Israel."

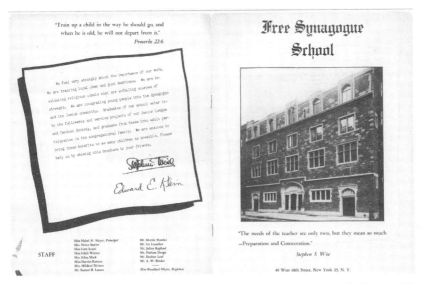

Jewish Institute of Religion building and Free Synagogue School, New York City, c. 1945. Permission granted by the Stephen Wise Free Synagogue Archives.

A disappointed Wise accepted and praised his son's choice. It seemed that "intellectual scruples and doubts . . . stand in the way [of James entering the rabbinate]. . . . The only decent and honorable thing to do is to reach the decision that he has reached, however much I regret it."[21]

The first class "graduated" in 1926 without James Wise. When the last group became rabbis in 1949, over two hundred men had studied at JIR under the leadership of Stephen Wise; many of them became prominent leaders in the Jewish community. His "boys" were devoted to Wise; some even tried to imitate his oratorical elegance and rabbinic style, but Stephen always told them to be themselves in their careers.

On Thursdays, Wise would meet with his students and describe his busy week of activities, meetings, and projects. On Friday mornings, students conducted worship services in the small synagogue/chapel located on the fifth floor of the JIR building. After a nervous student delivered his sermon before "Dr. Wise," the master preacher offered his evaluation of a student's sermonic skills. Even when Wise was critical of a sermon, everyone knew he offered such rebukes from a warm, caring heart. He loved his students, and they returned the affection many times over.

But as we shall see in a later chapter, the JIR continued to be a severe financial problem for Wise, and after the end of World War II, it appeared the school was headed for extinction as an independent institution.

Chapter 16

The 1920s—A Busy "Normalcy"
Decade between Wilson and Roosevelt

The Roaring 1920s were a severe letdown for Wise after the heady days of the previous decade when he helped gain President Wilson's support of the Balfour Declaration and the postwar aspirations of Jews in Eastern Europe. During the same period Stephen worked with Louis Brandeis to solidify the Zionism movement in the United States.

But between 1920 and Franklin Roosevelt's winning presidential campaign in 1932, Wise, an ardent Wilsonian Democrat, had to endure three Republican administrations led by men he considered mediocrities: Warren G. Harding (1865–1923), Calvin Coolidge (1872–1933), and Herbert C. Hoover. Little wonder that Stephen described his mood in the 1920s as "slightly dispirited."[1]

He may have been "dispirited," but he was also engaged in an extraordinary number of critical issues and historical events that affected the United States, the Zionist movement, the Jewish people, interreligious relationships, and the international family of nations.

The politically astute Wise recognized that American voters in 1920, fatigued by the war effort and the tumultuous Progressive era, sought a return to what the Grand Old Party and Harding called "normalcy." It was a potent winning term that encompassed American isolationism, US opposition to the League of Nations, and nativist hostility toward recent immigrants coming from Asia (mainly Chinese) and Eastern and Southern Europe (mostly Jews and Roman Catholics).

On October 7 of that year, a depressed Stephen wrote to Richard Gottheil in Paris,

> Things are rather dull and uninspiring in America just now. Harding is an impossible person, and yet he is inevitable as President. He is a person without even an elementary understanding of the rudiments of English, to say nothing of the rudiments of national international policy. His nomination is the

greatest insult ever leveled at the American people . . . and they will make him President.[2]

Wise's prediction came true a month later when US senator Harding of Ohio and Massachusetts governor Coolidge, his vice presidential running mate, crushed the Democratic ticket of James M. Cox (1870–1957), the governor of Ohio, and the youthful thirty-eight-year-old Franklin D. Roosevelt. The GOP candidates received 60.3 percent of the vote while the Democrats won only 34.1 percent.

During the campaign, Harding ignored Cox and instead attacked Wilson's Progressive domestic record and his internationalist foreign policies. In a historic coincidence, both Harding and Cox had been Ohio newspaper publishers, and the latter's name endures today in the telecommunication industry. Despite the Democratic electoral debacle, Wise remained confident that Roosevelt, a former assistant secretary of the navy and New York State senator, had a promising political future.

The recent deaths of his brother and mother in 1917 and 1919 added to Stephen's despondency and were reminders of his own mortality when he turned fifty in 1924. On a happier note, Wise officiated at his daughter's wedding in June 1927. Justine, a second-year law student and the editor of the *Yale Law Journal*, married Yale law professor Leon Arthur Tulin (1901–1932).[3] A year later, shortly before she took the bar exams, Justine gave birth to Stephen Wise Tulin.

Arthur Tulin died of leukemia in 1932, and in March 1937 Justine, by then a justice of the Domestic Relations Court of New York City, married attorney Isadore ("Shad") Polier (1906–1976). Once again, her father officiated at her wedding.[4] The Poliers had three children, Trudy, Jonathon, and Michael. The latter child died in 1944; he was only six months old.[5] Justine died in 1987 at age eighty-five and was survived by her three children, five grandchildren, and two great-grandchildren.[6]

Stephen's son, James, married Louise Joan Hahn in July 1923, but the couple was divorced five years later. James's wife "obtained an uncontested divorce . . . on the ground of desertion." Custody of young Stephen, the couple's three-year-old son and another namesake of his grandfather, was given to the child's mother, and James Wise was directed to pay two hundred dollars a month (about twenty-six hundred dollars today) for the support of mother and child.[7]

James later married Elizabeth Halle Kraus on November 27, 1929, and the couple had two daughters, Halle and Deborah. But that marriage also failed; after a dozen years of marriage, James was again divorced.[8] James Waterman Wise, an author and art dealer who wrote on Jewish and Zionist themes, died in 1983. He was eighty-one years old and was survived by his three children and four grand children.[9]

During the 1920s, Stephen Wise's peripatetic travels throughout the United States in support of social justice concerns, Zionism, and the urgent need to raise funds for the Jewish Institute of Religion, his financially endangered rabbinical seminary, depleted much of his physical and emotional strength.

Wise had suffered a serious "nervous breakdown" years earlier when he was a congregational rabbi in Portland, Oregon, but he recuperated and even intensified his work schedule when he moved back to New York City in 1906. But as Wise undertook more responsibilities and extensive travel, his body paid a price.

But there was sometimes more to his travels than public speeches. To the outside world, it appeared Stephen had a picture-perfect marriage to Louise, his wife for forty-seven years until her death in 1947. But Wise had dalliances with adoring women. One of the best known of Stephen's sexual conquests was Helen Lawrenson (1908–1982), the managing editor of *Vanity Fair* in the 1940s and later an *Esquire* magazine contributor.

In her autobiography, *Stranger at the Party*, Lawrenson recounts the first time she met Wise. In 1930, she was a twenty-two-year-old Vassar graduate and aspiring journalist when she interviewed Stephen following his speech on the Syracuse University campus:

He was one of the most powerful orators of our time and . . . I thought he was the most MALE man I had ever seen. So when I went up to his suite in the Hotel Syracuse to do a routine interview . . . I told him how much I admired him. The next thing I knew, he had toppled me backward on the sofa and was making love to me . . . WITH MY GLOVES ON. Before I knew what hit me, it was over. . . . [Later] as he was sitting on the sofa and I stood before him, he put his hands on my shoulders and tried to force me to my knees. 'Kneel before me in prayerful attitude, my darling,' he said. . . . I knew what he wanted me to do. I didn't comply—at that time. 'At least you'll admit I have guts,' he said, adding, with no undue modesty that he believed every dynamic man has a powerful sex drive and should make the most of it.

Three years later as a *Vanity Fair* staff member, Lawrenson went to Wise's office on West 68th Street for another interview:

and whoops! There I was on my back again, this time on a long table in his office with Wise reciting in Hebrew: "Lift up your heads, oh ye gates, and be lifted up, ye everlasting doors, and the King of Kings shall come in" [Psalm 24:9]. I don't know Hebrew, but he translated it for me when I asked.[10]

In a *Time* magazine interview, Lawrenson mentioned several other lovers in addition to Wise. They included presidential adviser Bernard Baruch (1870–1965), Harlem gangster Ellsworth Raymond "Bumpy" Johnson (1905–1968), aviator Charles Lindbergh (1902–1974), publisher Conde Nast (1873–1942), and novelist John O'Hara (1905–1970).[11]

Even a brief sampling of Wise's letters from 1921 reveals his frenzied pace and compelling need to speak in all parts of the United States, in large cities as well as small towns:

> I got to Philadelphia at 10:20 PM [after speaking earlier that evening in Mount Holly, New Jersey], but it would have been very difficult to take you [daughter Justine] back to Bryn Mawr [College] and still get the midnight train which I did for New York. . . . [12]

> It is very late at night and I am to be off [from Selma, Alabama] early Saturday morning for Meridian [Mississippi]. . . . The [Selma] Temple was jammed, people sitting on the steps and many, many turned away—the address on "The Jew in Fiction and Fictions about Jews" . . . am riding from Baton Rouge to Greenville, Mississippi. Left at six this morning and just had breakfast at one—seven hours with nothing but an orange. . . . As soon as I arrived [in Baton Rouge], I was taken to the State House where the Governor, John Parker [1863–1939] . . . awaited me. . . . He told me that when T.R. [Parker was a close friend of Theodore Roosevelt] had Booker T. Washington at his table, he [Parker] wrote—"We have been friends, but I can never again sit at a table with a man who eats with a nigger." What a character![13]

> After speaking last night at Durham, I motored 26 miles to Raleigh . . . to the Negro school, 300 young people, more sympathetic and responsive than the youth at Yale or Cornell.[14]

Stephen's itineraries of the period reveal that America's most prominent rabbi craved public and private adulation, and he journeyed almost everywhere to receive it. He also needed the speaking fees to augment his Free Synagogue salary. Most travel in the United States during the 1920s was limited to noisy railroad trains and slow-moving buses and automobiles. Roads in many parts of America were often only gravel, dirt, or clay, and usually consisted of two narrow driving lanes.

Stephen's international trips included British Mandate Palestine in 1922—the second of three visits during his life to the land of Israel, the last coming in 1935. Wise also traveled to Europe to recruit faculty members for his seminary and to participate in Zionist congresses; each journey required time-consuming transatlantic passenger ship voyages. Among his continental destinations during the 1920s were Basel, Berlin, Breslau, Cologne, Geneva, London, Paris, and Vienna.

During the 1920s, Wise visited many large cities, including Boston, Chicago, Cleveland, Denver, Miami, New Orleans, and Pittsburgh, and he addressed smaller-sized audiences in Cherry Vale, Topeka, and Hays in Kansas; Butler and Elizabethtown in Pennsylvania; Sanford, Florida; Portland, Maine; Savannah, Georgia; Albany, New York; Charleston, West Virginia; and Athens, Alabama. One can only imagine Wise's travel schedule if there had there been interstate highways, high-speed trains, and jet travel during his lifetime.

However, the physical and psychological pressures were debilitating for someone even as strong as Wise. In July 1921 following a medical operation, Stephen went on vacation in New Hampshire, but his recovery was slowed by a serious ailment. A concerned Louise wanted her husband to return to Manhattan where his personal physician could treat him, but Wise rejected her plea:

> I am not at all well. . . . In any event going to New York is out of the question . . . for if I had to go now it would not be an easy matter. I should practically have to go on a stretcher.[15]

In 1922 the Travelers Insurance Company refused to increase his life insurance coverage because of poor physical condition. Friends and colleagues urged Wise to slow down and reduce his travel and workload. A 1926 physical examination revealed the fifty-two-year-old rabbi had liver and heart problems as well as tonsillitis and bursitis. Stephen's tonsils were removed that year, and his physicians prescribed a change in diet, more rest, sleep, and exercise.[16]

In December 1929, Stephen's half-sister, Ida, was killed when an automobile struck her in Boston. Complicating Stephen's problems was the haunting memory of his father's fatal heart attack thirty years earlier in 1896.[17]

During the 1925 Zionist Congress in Vienna, Wise paid a "visit" to the office of Sigmund Freud, the famed psychoanalyst. It remains unclear whether Stephen sought psychological help from Freud or whether it was, as described in a newspaper article, a chance to discuss contemporary Jewish issues.

Freud asked the famous American rabbi to list the four greatest contemporary Jews. Wise replied: "Oh, that is easy. Einstein, Ehrlich, Freud, and Brandeis." Albert Einstein was the world's most famous theoretical physicist. He was in the United States in 1933 when Hitler came to power, and Einstein never returned to Germany. Paul Ehrlich (1854–1915) won a Nobel Prize in 1908 for his pioneering work in immunology and chemotherapy. Three of Wise's "Four Wise Men" were born in Germany or the Austro-Hungarian

Empire. Brandeis's parents settled in Kentucky after leaving Prague, now the capital of the Czech Republic.

The bemused psychoanalyst wondered if his "visitor/patient" should be added to the quartet. Wise answered, "No, no, no, no you cannot include me." Freud offered his professional insight into Stephen's response: "If you had said 'no' once, I would believe you, but four 'nos' leads me to suspect that you protest too much." Wise is reported to have smiled and later told a reporter, "I have gotten a free psychoanalytic reading from the great authority on the subject."[18] In time he recovered his energy and pressed forward to meet his numerous commitments and responsibilities. However, in October 1930 Stephen collapsed from "acute indigestion" at the Hotel Half Moon on Coney Island in New York City. Wise was admitted to Manhattan's Doctors Hospital for an "indefinite stay." The rabbi's physician and personal friend, Dr. Dudley Schoenfeld, attributed the collapse to "overwork . . . [and said his patient's hospital stay] would not be a short one . . . We believe that he is merely suffering from overwork and we wish to keep him under close observation."[19]

The news report failed to mention that Schoenfeld (1893–1971) was a prominent psychiatrist and psychoanalyst and likely treated Wise for more than "overwork." In 1932 Schoenfeld achieved national fame as a psychiatric consultant following the famous kidnapping in New Jersey of the young son of Charles Lindbergh and his wife, Anne Morrow (1906–2001).[20]

On December 26, 1930, two months after his "indigestion," Stephen wrote to a friend in Portland, Oregon, describing the seriousness of his illness:

> I had an attack . . . that laid me low, and which I think got my doctors pretty well scared. . . . They put me in a hospital . . . for complete rest for a few weeks. Since then I have been in Atlantic City [Wise's favorite recovery location], have not done a stitch of work worth mentioning, except to dictate a few letters.[21]

But Stephen also encountered professional problems as well as suffering physical and psychological disorders. One such setback was Henry Morgenthau, Sr.'s, resignation from the Free Synagogue because of his strong opposition to Zionism. Morgenthau was a founder of the Synagogue in 1907 and served as its first president until 1917. That leadership position provided him an opportunity to meet Woodrow Wilson, who was impressed with Morgenthau. In 1913 Wilson as president appointed him the US ambassador to the Ottoman Empire.

But by 1919 and at the end of his diplomatic tour in Istanbul, Turkey, Morgenthau had soured on Zionism and become a vocal opponent of the Jewish national movement. Morgenthau wrote,

We can have a Jewish revival in this country, which is our Zion, and not Palestine.

I have no objection to the founding of a Jewish university in Palestine. I think it is a fine thing. But when we realize the opportunities that the men who sit at this table have had in this country, it seems a stupid and ridiculous notion not to admit that this is the Promised Land. . . . We Jews cannot accept the foolish argument that you must have Zionism to keep the Jews as Jews. We must have something, but it is not Zionism.[22]

Wise countered his friend's critique with a Free Synagogue sermon that was later printed for wide distribution. However, the differences between the two men were irreconcilable, and Morgenthau resigned from the Free Synagogue. A stunned Wise wrote,

I cannot quite bring myself to believe that because I deemed it my duty to reply earnestly and vigorously to your terrible arraignment of Zionism and Zionists . . . you should wish to end your connection with the Free Synagogue.[23]

But Morgenthau was irate because he led the Sunday morning Free Synagogue service at Carnegie Hall in March 1919. However, he was unaware that Wise was meeting that morning with Wilson at the White House in an effort to gain the president's support for Zionism at the peace conference. Morgenthau wrote, "My resignation must stand, and my interest in the Free Synagogue cease." Despite his anger, Morgenthau always affirmed the principle of the freedom of the pulpit, a major element in the founding of the Free Synagogue.[24]

When Morgenthau died in 1946 at age ninety, his funeral took place in New York City's Temple Emanu-El. Wise did not speak at the service, nor was he among the many honorary pallbearers, even though that honor was accorded to Wise's closest Christian colleague, John Haynes Holmes, and to Julian Morgenstern (1881–1977), the Hebrew Union College president.[25]

In March 1923 there were plans to merge the Free Synagogue and the Central Synagogue with Stephen as its senior rabbi. The latter institution, located at East 55th Street and Lexington Avenue in New York City, is a historic landmark because of its distinctive Moorish architecture. While the lengthy merger discussions were under way, Wise needed to raise funds to build a Synagogue House near Central Park at 40 West 68th Street. To further complicate the merger negotiations, Wise conducted his weekly Sunday service at Carnegie Hall on West 57th Street and Seventh Avenue. Despite the three Manhattan venues for the congregations, plans were announced "to erect a synagogue which will be one of the largest and costliest in America."[26]

Although Central Synagogue did not have the pedigree or socioeconomic status of Temple Emanu-El, a successful merger would have been a coup for Wise. In a letter to Mack, Stephen listed his fundamental demands for that to happen:

> Freedom of the pulpit, including [rabbinic] membership in the Executive Committee; unassigned pews; and voluntary dues. If a stodgy old group such as 55th St. can accept this, I think we are reasonably safe.[27]

But after two years of talks, the plans were ended. Wise was not unhappy:

> As for the terminating of the merger, I think it is best from every point of view. We really had no choice in the matter. Our good friends would not move forward in the matter of a building program, and we could not possibly go on in this way. . . . Relations [between the two synagogues] are to continue to be really of the happiest type.[28]

President Harding, the man whom Wise described as "an impossible person," unexpectedly died in San Francisco on August 2, 1923. To this day there is conspiratorial speculation that he was either murdered because of his well-known extramarital affairs or he committed suicide in the face of his administration's Teapot Dome bribery corruption scandal. However, most observers believe the fifty-seven-year-old Harding died of congestive heart failure, perhaps brought on by excessive drinking, heavy smoking, poor diet, and lack of exercise.[29]

Vice President Coolidge received the sad news while vacationing in Plymouth, Vermont. His father, a notary public, administered the presidential oath of office to his son. A kerosene lamp offered the only light for the ceremony, and the image of father and son is an iconic part of American history.[30]

Following the president's death, Wise was hopeful the anti-Progressive policies of the Harding administration might be muted or even reversed with Coolidge in the White House. Unlike his predecessor, Coolidge, a man of few words, was honest in both his public and private conduct. But his most famous quotation left little doubt for Wise and other Progressives about "Silent Cal's" domestic priorities and agenda soon after his election to a full four-year term in 1924. In an address to newspaper editors Coolidge declared, "The chief business of the American people is business."[31]

New York governor Alfred E. Smith and Franklin D. Roosevelt asked Wise to be an alternate New York State delegate during the 1924 Democratic National Convention (DNC) that took place that year in Manhattan's Madison Square Garden. It was the first Democratic Convention in Manhattan since 1868. Even though Stephen believed clergy should not hold a public political position, he accepted his friends' invitation. Smith and FDR wanted the famous rabbi to use his national influence against the Ku Klux Klan. Both Smith and Roosevelt were certain the KKK would be a major divisive issue at the convention.[32]

The many Democrats who opposed immigration and "urban America" were upset that the convention was in New York City. Wise defended the choice, and in a letter to the *New York World* newspaper, he detected in the attacks on the nation's largest city more than a whiff of anti-Semitism, anti-Catholicism, and anti-immigrant feeling:

> New York and the rest of the country do not know and understand each other . . . New York thinks that the rest of the country is not quite American. The country holds that New York is no longer America. . . . New York is not a landing-place for Europe, but a power-house of American idealism.[33]

Wise offered a public prayer at the convention on June 26, 1924:

> Almighty God and Father, give Thy merciful guidance to this gathering of the Sons and Daughters of our beloved Nation, that together we may greatly serve the highest and noblest interests of our Country. Help us to be brotherly and forbearing to one another, but dauntlessly resolute for the right. May we battle for truth, not for advantage, for public honor and not private gain, for the privilege of service and not the glory of victory. Unless the Lord build the house, they labor in vain who build it. So let this mighty gathering help to build the house of a righteous and peace furthering Nation; and in the unity of our fellowship and the bond of our abounding fulfillment of the prophecy, "For Mine house shall be called the house of prayer unto all peoples." And Thine, O Father, be the honor and the praise and the glory, forevermore.[34]

The DNC that year was a wild, raucous, and bitter event that required 103 ballots before a presidential nominee was chosen. In that era, a nomination needed the votes of two-thirds of the delegates, not a simple majority. One of the two front-runners—William G. McAdoo, Wilson's treasury secretary and the former president's son-in-law, was the champion of the "dry" or Prohibition wing of the Democratic Party. He was supported by the rural southern and western, mostly Protestant, delegates who opposed the coalition of northern Progressives, many of them Catholics and Jews. There were no black delegates at the 1924 convention. McAdoo's chief opponent was Smith, who had been elected New York governor in 1922. Wise supported Smith, a Roman Catholic, who at that time was a Progressive political leader and an opponent of both the Klan and Prohibition.

As Smith and Roosevelt had predicted, the major storm cloud at the

Democratic gathering was the issue of membership in the Ku Klux Klan. McAdoo was either unwilling or unable to disassociate himself from his Klan supporters and delegates. During the mid-1920s, the racist group was at the peak of its political power and had thousands of members, including numerous elected officials. The KKK in addition to being anti-black was also anti-Catholic and anti-Semitic. Wise and other Progressive convention delegates backed an anti-Klan resolution, but to ensure passage it did not mention the hooded group by name. However, even with that major concession, the delegates adopted it by a margin of only one vote.

The highlight of the Democratic Convention—or as it was called, the "Klanbake"—was Roosevelt's speech in behalf of Smith's candidacy. FDR was stricken three years earlier with polio in Campobello, Canada, and because the paralysis of his lower body prevented him from walking on his own, most political observers believed Roosevelt's once promising public career was finished.

But he surprised people by moving on a pair of crutches and carrying the weight of heavy metal braces on his legs. FDR reached the convention lectern and placed Smith's name in nomination for president. He called the New York governor the "happy warrior," a nickname that remained with Smith the rest of his life. It was an exciting moment for the delegates and marked Roosevelt's return to active politics.

After sixteen days that included fistfights on the convention floor, on the 103rd ballot, the Democrats selected a compromise nominee: John W. Davis (1873–1955), a bland former US solicitor general, ambassador to Britain, and House of Representatives member from West Virginia. Wise was little impressed with Davis, a conservative Democrat, and he flirted with the idea of voting in November for the Progressive Party's presidential candidate, Senator Robert LaFollette (1855–1925) of Wisconsin.

Wise was angry about the Klan's influence at the DNC:

> To unmask the Klan is to destroy it. . . . Not one member of the Klan had the courage to stand up at the National Democratic Convention and defend it. . . . The Klan is not so much a menace to America, which is secure . . . as it is blasphemous in the Christlessness of its repudiation of all that is fundamental in Christianity.[35]

A few weeks before the 1924 presidential election, Stephen spoke to an audience of five thousand people and ripped into the Protestant clergy who feared to attack the Klan:

> [Wise] denounced the organization [the KKK] as unwholesome and hurtful to the spirit of America. Only when . . . members of the Protestant ministry

"speak out against this betrayal of America" would he desist from attacking it. . . . "The Protestant clergy for the most part . . . are silent on the Klan."[36]

As Election Day neared, Stephen told Holmes he was looking for "the light which somehow does not seem to come."[37] In a letter to Mack, Wise expressed concern about "the whole mixed character" of the Progressive Party:

> [LaFollette's supporters are] pro-Germans, anti-British, anti-Leaguers, pro-Sovietists, anti-Socialist Liberals and illiberal Socialists. . . . I cannot endure LaFollette's European policy, and I am still more intolerant of the gang which surrounds him.[38]

In a letter to Newton D. Baker (1871–1937), Wilson's secretary of war, Stephen expressed his electoral unease:

> Even if I should vote for Davis, I would be most sorely tempted to leave the Democratic party. . . . I derived little comfort and hope from the Madison Square Garden affair in July.[39]

In the end, a reluctant Wise voted for Davis, who was defeated by Coolidge. The Republican ticket gained 54 percent of the vote, and the lackluster Davis but 28.8 percent, while LaFollette won 16.6 percent. Thirty years later in 1954, a year before he died, Davis appeared before the US Supreme Court in the historic *Brown v. Board of Education* school segregation case as a lawyer representing the state of South Carolina. Davis argued in favor of the "separate but equal" principle for public schools. When the high court, led by Chief Justice Earl Warren (1891–1974), unanimously ruled the doctrine unconstitutional, a distraught Davis returned his attorney's fee to South Carolina.[40]

If in 1924 Wise was a wavering Democrat, during the same year he was an unambiguous foe of the restrictive immigration legislation that carried the names of Congressman Albert Johnson of Washington (1869–1957) and Senator David Reed of Pennsylvania (1880–1953), both Republicans. The object of their legislation was to ban all Asians from entering the United States and to restrict immigration from Southern and Eastern Europe.

Johnson said his bill was written to block "a stream of alien blood, with all its inherited misconceptions" from entering America. Johnson, a racist, anti-Semite, and nativist, was also the leader of a eugenics association that backed sterilization of the mentally ill, and he opposed interracial marriage.[41]

Reed, the Senate sponsor of the bill, represented "those of us who are interested in keeping American stock up to the highest standard–that is, the people who were born here." Southern and Eastern Europeans, he believed, "arrive sick and starving and therefore less capable of contributing to the American economy, and unable to adapt to American culture."[42]

The bill's exclusionary provisions outraged Wise:

> Is it not violative of a spirit of American fair-play to insist that America open wide its doors to some peoples and virtually shut them in the face of other peoples who have made their contribution to the building up of America?[43]

Stephen also employed sarcasm to express his opposition:

> Were Jesus and his twelve disciples on earth today, they would have to cast lots as to which one of them would have the privilege of coming to the United States under the Johnson bill quota system.[44]

The 1924 legislation that both houses of Congress overwhelmingly adopted—there were only nine negative votes in the Senate—did not place the same strict limits on newcomers from Latin America. The restrictive quota system of that era was aimed at Asia and selected regions of Europe.

One of the strongest congressional opponents of the Johnson-Reed bill was Emanuel Celler (1888–1981), a freshman Democratic representative from New York City. For the next forty years, Celler fought to repeal the 1924 law, and he succeeded in 1965 when he joined with Democratic US senator Philip Hart (1912–1976) of Michigan to enact the more liberal 1965 immigration act that bears their names.

Even though one of the goals of the Johnson-Reed legislation was to limit the number of Jews coming to the United States, Samuel Gompers, the president of the American Federation of Labor, a friend of Stephen Wise and himself a Jewish immigrant, favored the bill because it blocked an influx of cheap labor.[45]

Two years after the immigration law went into effect, Wise wrote a letter to Holmes with the proviso that it be released only after both of them were dead. Stephen was appalled that during the public debate on the immigration act, some German Jews in the United States agreed with Johnson and Reed about the inferior nature and status of Eastern European Jews. In his plaintive letter, Stephen, the child of Central European parents whose mother tongue and culture were German, lamented that

> Jews have infinitely much to learn in the way of tolerance to one another. He concluded, ". . . after all, the most distinguishing trait of the Jew, which is the capacity for sacrificial effort, is to be found chiefly in the Russian Jew."[46]

Less than ten years after the passage of the restrictive immigration act, many desperate European Jews attempted to flee the Nazi regime that came to power in 1933. Wise pressed American government officials for greater Jewish immigration, but the Johnson-Reed legislation limited the number of refugees who could find safety in the United States. Had the gates of entry been open during the 1930s and 1940s, many more Jews could have been saved.

Instead, the victims of Nazism confronted a restrictive US immigration quota system that negatively affected Jews. Refugees from Hitler faced passive and active bureaucratic red tape, deliberate delays, and a pervasive anti-immigrant feeling in America and within a State Department that controlled entry visas. There was continuous widespread anti-Semitism even during World War II when the United States was engaged in a global war against the murderous anti-Jewish Nazi regime.

But anti-Semitism in the 1920s was not limited to the halls of Congress. In addition to immigration quotas, limits were often placed on the number of Jewish students enrolled in many American colleges and universities, including the elite Ivy League, as well as medical, dental, law, and other graduate schools. My father graduated from the University of Pittsburgh Dental School during the mid-1920s, but he always remained resentful that Pitt's policy in those years was to limit the number of qualified Jewish applicants in each class to 10 percent. In 2012, Emory University officials in Atlanta were forced to apologize for the Jewish quota system that existed in its dental school between 1948 and 1961.[47]

There were also restrictive housing practices in the United States that barred Jews from purchasing or renting certain real estate, and most high-level executive suites of corporations were closed to Jews. Some public accommodations, including luxury hotels and upscale restaurants, refused to serve Jews, and obstacles were erected that blocked fair employment in many industries, particularly engineering, and membership in professional clubs. That was one reason many Jews were self-employed in pre–World War II America.

Wise, well aware of the systemic anti-Semitism of the 1920s, aimed his criticism at one of the most important and influential sources of American anti-Semitism: Henry Ford (1863–1947), the world famous automaker.

In 1919 Ford purchased the *Dearborn Independent*, then an obscure newspaper that carried the name of the Michigan headquarters city of his automobile company. For the next eight years, the weekly publication reflected the bigoted views of Ford and several of his closest associates.

One of the paper's chief targets was the so-called International Jew, a sinister figure cited as the root cause of World War I. Ford's paper focused on the Warburg family and its financial branches in New York and Germany. The *Dearborn Independent* also attacked financier Bernard Baruch and the Federal

Reserve System established in 1913 during the Wilson administration, cited as an evil creation of the alleged global "Jewish banking conspiracy." On the cultural front, the Ford publication paper ripped into the jazz music of the American black community and "Jewish-produced" Hollywood films.

In 1921, the *Dearborn Independent* printed the infamous anti-Semitic *Protocols of the Elders of Zion*. By that year, the *Protocols* was well documented and exposed as a complete forgery created by the Russian tsar's secret police in 1905 to foment virulent anti-Semitism. The fraudulent document described an alleged secret cabal of Jewish leaders who plotted to control the world. Despite the fact that the scurrilous *Protocols* was denounced as a vicious and dangerous anti-Jewish forgery, the *Independent* went ahead and published the discredited document. Ford's fame gave credibility to the defamatory document.[48]

The paper attracted the attention of anti-Semites throughout the world, including Adolf Hitler in Germany. In fact, Ford is the only American mentioned by name in Hitler's book *Mein Kampf* (My Struggle) that was published in 1925. Anti-Semitic articles from the *Independent* were translated into German and other languages during the 1920s and were used to "prove" that Nazis were not alone in their pathological hatred of Jews and Judaism.

Hitler said, "You can tell Herr Ford that I am a great admirer of his. I shall do my best to put his theories into practice in Germany. . . . I regard Henry Ford as my inspiration."[49]

Stephen Wise was quick to criticize both Ford and his newspaper. A 1920 *New York Times* article carried the headline, "Wise Denounces Ford as 'Contemptible Liar,'" and the full story represented Stephen at the peak of his condemnatory power:

"He Is as Guilty of Pogroms as Any Murderer in Poland," Says Rabbi.

"God help Henry Ford, God forgive him," cried Rabbi Stephen S. Wise before a crowded meeting in the Bronx last night. In answer to the Detroit manufacturer's charges against the Jews, quoted from The Dearborn Independent, the speaker hurled invective after invective, and finally called Ford "the most contemptible little liar that ever lived."

"His main charge," Rabbi Wise said, "is that the Jews aim to control the world. No sane, truthful man could say that of the Jew, hunted like a dog in Poland and treated as a spy in the Ukraine. Ford would have the world believe that Boshekiki and Jews are the same, and in destroying one would destroy the other. He is as guilty of pogroms himself as any murderer in Poland."

The American sense of fair play, however, can be trusted to take care of Ford, Rabbi Wise concluded. He declared that Ford was trying to debase the spirit of America, but that his "blood-stained hands will fall impotent at his sides."[50]

In January 1921, 119 leading Americans "of Gentile birth and Christian faith" signed "The Perils of Racial Prejudice," a joint statement that labeled anti-Semitism as un-American. Among the signers were President Woodrow Wilson, former president William Howard Taft, William Jennings Bryan, Nicholas Murray Butler, Paul Cravath (1861–1940), Clarence Darrow (1857–1938), Robert Frost (1874–1963), Samuel Seabury, Ida Tarbell (1857–1944), and the presidents of Williams, Oberlin, and Dartmouth Colleges and Princeton, Cornell, and Syracuse Universities.[51]

In 2000 the Simon Wiesenthal Center in Los Angeles issued "The Attack on 'Jewish Hollywood': A Chapter in the History of Modern American Anti-Semitism" that described Ford's prejudice and bigotry:

> Characterizing Prohibition-era whiskey as "nigger gin" and jazz as "Yiddish moron music," Henry Ford's *Dearborn Independent* fused, crudely but effectively, the racism and anti-Semitism animating this anti-modern critique. "As soon as the Jews gained control of the 'movies,'" Ford observed, "we had a problem . . . It is the peculiar genius of that race to create problems of a moral character in whatever business they achieve a majority." About producers "of Semitic origin," Ford's newspaper also observed that "many . . . don't know how filthy their stuff is—it is so natural to them." The movies deployed Jewish "cleverness" to "camouflage the moral filth" of "the monkey talk, jungle squeals, grunts and squeaks and gasps" of African American popular culture.[52]

Many Americans, Jews and Christians, refused for years, even decades, to buy Ford products. There was also a public outcry, led by Wise, that deplored Ford's crude anti-Jewish tirades. By 1925 the *Independent* had a weekly circulation of 900,000.

But Wise was not the only foe of Henry Ford. Sigmund Livingston (1872–1946), a founder and longtime chairman of the Anti-Defamation League, organized a public campaign of opposition to Ford's publication. Aaron Sapiro (1884–1959), an attorney and an activist leader of American farmworkers, was outraged by the *Independent*'s attacks in 1924 on Jewish community organizers in the agricultural community. The Ford newspaper named Sapiro the kingpin of a Jewish plot to exploit the farmers of America.[53]

Sapiro brought a libel suit against Ford and his paper in the US District Court in Detroit and told *Time* magazine,

> Henry Ford has made one of the greatest contributions ever made by any man. That is mass production. It amounts to first rate genius. But just as I am color blind, Henry Ford has blind spots in his intellect. In my opinion he is mentally

unsound on certain questions of race and religion. He has a streak of bigotry on that side of his mind that is totally foreign to his industrial ability.[54]

During the same month, Wise praised Sapiro in a Free Synagogue sermon:

I offer the homage of my reverence to a man ready to face the richest and, in some senses, the most powerful man on earth [Henry Ford], and say, "You may libel me, but you shall not lie about my people."[55]

On October 30, 1927, Sapiro presented a Free Synagogue guest sermon in Carnegie Hall. He told Wise's congregation, "Only persons who are specifically named in the defamatory remarks may bring suit against the defamer."[56] Although he was legally correct, many people believed Sapiro represented the entire Jewish people in his court case against Henry Ford.

Sapiro's libel suit went to trial in Detroit, but the auto magnate did not testify because he suffered an auto accident, and Ford's doctors at the Michigan hospital named in his honor felt their famous patient was not able to appear in court. The trial came undone when a reporter interviewed one of the jurors, and the judge declared a mistrial.[57]

However, behind the scenes, Ford contacted Louis Marshall and requested that the prominent attorney and American Jewish Committee president write a public apology for him. Ford issued the mea culpa Marshall had composed, and in a full retreat, the famous automaker retracted his anti-Semitic views. In December 1927 he ended publication of the *Dearborn Independent.*

Ford said he was "mortified" to learn the *Protocols* were forged, declared he was "fully aware of the virtues of the Jewish people," and offered his "future friendship and good will." The industrialist always claimed he never read the articles in his newspaper and placed the blame for the anti-Semitic views on his underlings. Marshall called Ford's statement "humiliating."

In his public statement written by Marshall, Ford apologized to Jews "everywhere" for articles defaming them. He declared that he was unaware of what his employees were publishing in his name and that he never intended anyone to believe that Jews were behind an international conspiracy to destabilize world governments and financial institutions. The statement marked the first time anyone apologized for anti-Semitism in writing. That it came from Ford, who for years had told the press in detail what his intentions were in demonizing the "International Jew," was all the more extraordinary. That it was ghostwritten was concealed from the public.

But anti-Semites throughout the world remained convinced that Ford had not recanted. Others chose to believe Ford because the statement's profession of "friendship and good will" matched his public image as an imaginative tinkerer, marketing genius, and loveable grandfather. When Ford shut down the *Independent*, he settled with those who had sued him for libel, and he believed such acts assured the public of his sincerity. His public apology confirmed the widespread perception of Ford as kind, gentle, and generous, enabling him to disown his publication without taking responsibility for it.[58]

While many Jews and Christians were satisfied with Ford's retraction and the demise of his newspaper, Wise was concerned about the negative long-term effects and the lasting damage created by the anti-Semitic attacks. Stephen feared that Ford's apology would not heal the wound his publication had inflicted upon Jews and Judaism.[59]

Wise's worry was not unfounded because old hatreds and bigotry often remain within a person. Ford opposed America's entry into World War II, and he blamed the conflict once more on "international bankers," well-known code words for "Jews." In 1938 the automaker received the Grand Cross of the German Eagle from Nazi Germany. The Nazi award incensed many Americans, including Eddie Cantor (1892–1964), the singer, songwriter, and actor. Cantor told *Time* magazine,

> Mr. Henry Ford, in my opinion, is a damned fool for permitting the world's greatest gangster to give him this citation. Doesn't he realize that the German papers, reporting the citation, said all Americans were behind Naziism [*sic*]? Whose side is Mr. Ford on?[60]

However, when his grandson, Henry Ford II (1917–1987), nicknamed "Hank the Deuce," assumed control of the company in 1945, he began a life-long campaign to reach out to and support both the American Jewish community and the state of Israel. His positive efforts helped erase much of his grandfather's negative impact. In addition, he played a major role in the development of the philanthropic Ford Foundation.[61]

Throughout his career, Wise was careful not to make his stirring demands for justice, equality, and fairness a special plea from a Jewish leader. Rather, he accused his bigoted adversaries, including Henry Ford, for failing to live up the highest ideas of Americanism or Christianity. Stephen eschewed "begging" for Jewish rights and freedoms. Rather, he cast his lofty rhetoric in universal terms that all Americans could identify and understand: the Bible, the Declaration of Independence, the Constitution, the Bill of Rights, and Progressive legislation. Wise often linked his calls for justice to the words of US presidents George Washington, Thomas Jefferson, Abraham Lincoln, and of course, Woodrow Wilson and Franklin Roosevelt.

In 1929 Wise was the major speaker at an interreligious celebration commemorating the 150th anniversary of Washington's encampment in Morristown, New Jersey, during the Revolutionary War:

We are gathered to invoke the presence, not the memory of Washington. . . .
The men of this generation apprehend more fully his excellent qualities than
any since he lived and his memory is so alive that he is present in all but
actuality.[62]

A year earlier the Daughters of the American Revolution (D.A.R.) placed
Wise's name on its list of dangerous Americans. Stephen cited Washington in
his public response:

Their ancestors [the D.A.R.] crossed the Delaware with Washington; mine
crossed the Red Sea. Their ancestors wrote the Declaration of Independence;
mine the Ten Commandments. I have no patience with those persons who believe that to be one hundred percent American one must be a Protestant
American.[63]

Years later the Reverend Dr. Martin Luther King, Jr. (1929–1968), employed a similar strategy. Like Wise, he, too, was a champion of his own community, but King also spoke in eloquent terms about America living up to its
historic commitment to human rights, equality, and justice. For both men—
Wise and King—such an approach was more effective than demanding the
same noble goals as a Jewish or black supplicant coming before the general
American public.

Wise's lack of "patience" with people who claimed only a "Protestant
American" can be a full citizen of the United States was not mere rhetoric. In
1928, it had a distinct political meaning because Governor Alfred E. Smith of
New York became the Democratic Party's presidential nominee. A year earlier
it appeared that Calvin Coolidge would be the GOP standard-bearer. He had
completed Harding's shortened presidential term and in 1924 the New
Englander won four more years in the White House.

Political tradition permitted him to run for a second full term, but the
president ended such speculation when he announced at a 1927 press conference, "I do not choose to run for President in 1928." When the stunned reporters asked Coolidge if he had anything more to add, the taciturn president
replied with a single word, "No," and left the room.[64]

Wise and other Democrats were hopeful their party could regain the presi-
dency after two devastating defeats. To no one's surprise, Stephen supported
Smith, who had been denied the nomination four years earlier at the infamous
"Klanbake" convention.

Stephen and other Progressives were irate after eight years of greedy Big
Business Republican administrations, exemplified by the Teapot Dome corruption scandal that involved high government officials, bribery, and sweet-
heart, no-bid contract deals for oil companies in the American West. At the

same time, there was also concern among Democrats that the prosperity of the 1920s would trump any voter discontent with the GOP.

While Wise was critical of the Republicans, he was also disapproving of his own party:

> We [the Democrats] are so fearful of annoying the few who will never trust the Democratic Party that we alienate the many who might and ought to trust our party. . . . The control of Government by business, which has come to pass in the current [Coolidge] and preceding [Harding] administrations, is the most disheartening spectacle of a generation.[65]

Stephen viewed unemployment as a "moral problem," and he employed a vivid phrase that still resonates today:

> [The Republican] policy of government aiding the possessing classes with the alleged hope that such aid would trickle down to the masses became almost a state doctrine, while the numbers of unemployment and their suffering mounted.[66]

The 1928 Democratic Convention was held in Houston, Texas, in late June—the first time the party had met in the South since the Civil War. It was far different than the marathon meeting four years earlier. Smith, a Roman Catholic and an opponent of Prohibition, was nominated on the first ballot. During the same month, the Republicans, meeting in Kansas City, Missouri, also chose a nominee on the first ballot: Commerce Secretary Herbert Hoover.

Wise was pleased with Smith's nomination but had doubts about his chances of winning the White House. In a letter to a friend he wrote:

> how happy . . . that I was among the earliest of his [Smith's] non-political friends to believe in him, to hope for him, and to support him.[67]

Three weeks before the election he confided to Holmes (who knew his own presidential candidate, Norman Thomas, would lose):

> I am just as sure as you are that my candidate is going to be [defeated in November]. But if you knew what is happening in the South, where I was on Sunday, you'd go on the stump for Al [Smith] to stem the tide of hideous religious bigotry that is engulfing the nation.[68]

Wise was referring to the strong anti-Catholic feelings that existed within many Protestant denominations. There were fears that Smith would take orders from the pope in Rome. Some bigots spread the rumor that the pontiff was planning to move into the White House if the New York governor became the president. Smith was the first Catholic presidential candidate in US history, and Stephen also recognized some unease among many Jewish voters regarding the Democratic candidate for the White House.

Wise needed no reminder of

what my people had suffered at the hands of the Roman Catholic Church in other days and centuries. I was not unmindful of that. I could not be. My answer was . . . to remember that America meant a new start in the life of the world. If America was to mean to me nothing more than the perpetuation of the past, then the promise of America would come to naught.[69]

Wise appealed

to Americans to vote as Americans, and not as Jews and Catholics and Protestants . . . I shall vote with equal satisfaction for three men of three different Churches [sic] . . . Smith [a Catholic], [Franklin] Roosevelt [an Episcopalian for New York governor] and [Herbert] Lehman [a Jew for lieutenant governor].[70]

On Monday evening, October 15, near the end of the 1928 campaign, Stephen delivered a radio address supporting Smith that was heard throughout the United States. Wise's theme was "Religious Tolerance and the American Idea." Stephen attacked religious prejudice and urged voters to live up to the nation's highest ideals of fairness and justice when they cast their ballots.

Following the network broadcast, Stephen received a large amount of hate mail, but many listeners were moved by the rabbi's passionate attack on bigotry. A typical response came from Jack Marco, a Jewish resident of Champaign, Illinois, and the owner of a scrap iron business. He wrote to Wise,

A few words to let you know we heard both your speeches over the radio and want to say we enjoyed them so much that someday I want to shake your hand and tell you in person what we really think of your speech.[71]

Millard E. Tydings (1890–1961), the chairman of the Democratic National Committee Speakers Bureau, sent a letter to Wise thanking him for "a courageous, forceful and candid speech."[72] Tydings was a US senator from Maryland between 1927 and 1951.

The 1928 election was another easy victory for the Republican Party. Hoover captured forty states and 444 electoral votes while Smith carried eight states and only 87 electoral votes. The popular vote was devastating for dejected Democrats like Wise. Hoover won 58.2 percent of the vote (21.4 million votes) and Smith captured only 40.8 percent and 15 million votes.

Wise wrote a friend in Portland, Oregon,

> The character of the rout saddens me. I cannot help feeling that the debacle is really a thrust by the older Protestant folk of America against us inferior newcomers—Catholics and Jews, Irish, Italians, Russians and all the rest; I am disheartened.[73]

In a letter written the day after the election, the savvy Wise reminded Smith of their friendship and offered some rabbinic consolation:

> You made a brave fight. . . . "Not failure but low aim is a crime," you battled with valor. . . . I shall always remember with joy and pride that I stood at your side and fought under the banner of your leadership. . . . A happier day for America may yet dawn.[74]

However, there were several hopeful signs despite the huge defeat. Smith won about 6.5 million more votes than Davis in 1924, and FDR and Lehman were elected governor and lieutenant governor in New York State.

Wise may have been "dispirited" during the 1920s, but when the decade ended with the stock market crash on October 29, 1929, and the start of the Great Depression, the entire nation joined Wise in despair and gloom. However, in 1932, Franklin Roosevelt would hold those new Democratic votes won by Smith and add 7.8 million more and cruise to victory over a discredited President Hoover in the first of FDR's four successful presidential campaigns.

Not content with affecting national elections, Wise made New York City's corrupt Tammany Hall Democratic organization a special target in the 1920s. A corrupt mayor, James J. Walker, was forced from office in the 1930s because of the persistent attacks of Wise and Holmes.[75]

As a product of Tammany Hall, Walker had worked his way up the electoral ladder, and in 1925 he was elected mayor. Four years later he was reelected, defeating both Fiorello LaGuardia (1882–1947) and Norman Thomas. Debonair and natty to his manicured fingertips and his shoe tops with spats, Walker was dubbed "Beau James" and "Gentleman Jimmy" by his admirers. He was a popular celebrity as the prosperous Roaring Twenties came to an end.

Part of his charm was the fact that he composed a well-known song in 1905: "Will You Love Me in December as You Do in May?"[76] The 1957 Hollywood film *Beau James* starred Bob Hope in the title role. The glossy movie biography presented an inaccurate perspective of the devious, corrupt mayor who was forced to resign his office.

During his years in city hall, Walker had extramarital affairs and left his wife to marry a showgirl: Betty Compton (1904–1944). It was an act that drew the public condemnation of Cardinal Joseph Hayes (1867–1938) of the Archdiocese of New York. At first, the jaunty, jolly mayor appeared to weather the ecclesiastical criticism and his sexual infidelities. However, his personal popularity and expensive lifestyle plummeted with the 1929 stock market crash that led to the Great Depression.

Worse yet, Gentleman Jimmy became the target of an investigation by the City Affairs Committee headed by Holmes and Wise. The committee discovered widespread financial graft and bribery. The charges against Walker included not only fiscal malfeasance and the acceptance of bribes for political favors but also his appointment of "unqualified politicians" in various city agencies, including the vital Health and Hospital Departments. Wise and Holmes also charged that unemployed workers in New York City were cheated out of their benefits by dishonest city officials. Law-abiding citizens "were being swindled out of millions of dollars by excessive condemnation awards when property owners were represented by 'political' counsel."[77]

There were also charges that some New York City women who did not pay protection money to the police to avoid arrest were imprisoned for being prostitutes. When informed of the trumped-up charges against the hapless females, Walker's response was that he was "more or less shocked."[78] Perhaps the mayor's flippant remark was the inspiration eleven years later when the corrupt French police chief in the 1942 film *Casablanca* discovered that gambling was taking place at Rick's Café: "I'm shocked, shocked to find that gambling is going on in here!"

On March 17, 1931—St. Patrick's Day and Stephen's fifty-seventh birthday—Wise and Holmes visited New York governor Franklin D. Roosevelt at his mother's home on East 65th Street in Manhattan. Because of Roosevelt's later success as winner of four terms as president, it is largely forgotten that FDR won the 1928 New York State gubernatorial race by only 28,950 votes out of a total vote of 4,351,135: a victorious margin of .006 percent. FDR won his close race for governor by running as a Progressive Democrat.[79]

Roosevelt's GOP opponent, Albert Ottinger (1878–1938), was the first Jew to run for the governorship in New York State. FDR's 1928 running mate for lieutenant governor was another Jew, Herbert H. Lehman (1878–1963), who beginning in 1932 served four terms as governor, and later was a US senator between 1950 and 1957.

At their meeting with the governor, the rabbi and the minister handed FDR a four-thousand-word document that listed ten serious counts of misconduct and corruption—all aimed at Mayor Walker. Wise and Holmes urged Roosevelt to use his executive state power to dismiss Walker from his office. Under the state charter, a governor had the power to "suspend the mayor, or remove the mayor for incompetence or neglect of duty on specific charges."[80]

After their joint presentation and believing that Roosevelt agreed with their demand, Wise and Holmes made ready to leave the second-floor study of the polio-stricken governor. But then it was FDR's turn to speak, and it soon became an ugly confrontation:

I have listened to you. Now you sit down and listen to me.[81]

An angry FDR spoke to the two clergymen for thirty minutes. It was a severe tongue lashing, and a stunned Wise, who had first met Roosevelt twenty years earlier, was angered by his "friend's" criticism of him and Holmes and the role of religious leaders in public life.

Roosevelt's position was that although he had little regard for Walker, he did not want to antagonize Tammany Hall, whose delegate votes he would need at the 1932 Democratic National Convention to gain the party's presidential nomination. Roosevelt had disdain for "Beau James" and had ridiculed Walker the same month as his meeting with Wise and Holmes:

Our little Mayor can save much trouble in the future by getting on the job, cleaning his own house and stopping wisecracks. If he does not do all this he can have only himself to blame if he gets into trouble.[82]

A month later, in April 1931, Gentleman Jimmy faced a series of serious charges and was humiliated when he faced Judge Samuel Seabury's (1873–1958) rigorous questioning about financial and political wrongdoing.[83] Seabury was the head of a commission that investigated corruption in New York City courts and within the Police Department.

As the charges became known to the public, Walker at first dismissed them with a wisecrack or joke because the evidence did not link him to corrupt actions. When asked to explain how as New York City's mayor he was able to live the high life, including visits with his mistress to the French Riviera, California, and Florida, Walker replied that his good fortune came from having generous and loving friends.[84]

Seabury also later led a commission to investigate Walker that was established by FDR and approved by the New York State legislature. The conscientious Seabury and his staff questioned more than two thousand witnesses, and the evidence revealed systemic corruption in many city departments, including the police and judiciary. The investigation involved 2,260 private witnesses and 175 testimonies that were taken in thirty-seven public sessions. Seabury and his staff assembled fifty-two thousand pages of sworn testimony and hundreds of thousands of documents.[85]

But by mid-March 1932 Walker still retained his post, and in two separate letters Wise and Holmes demanded the governor remove a pair of other corrupt public officials from office: a Queens County surrogate court clerk and a local sheriff. Roosevelt not only refused to act, but on March 30 he also issued a stinging attack upon the integrity and motives of both Wise and Holmes. It appeared to be a follow-up to FDR's verbal assault made a year earlier on the same two troublesome clergymen:

> You care more for personal publicity than for good government. . . . You two gentlemen have deliberately requested the Governor of this State to disregard [a] fundamental of justice. . . . of American Constitutions and laws. . . . Let me tell you two gentlemen straight from the shoulder that . . . a rushing into print early and often, with extravagant language, causes many of our decent citizens to doubt your own reliance on law, on order and on justice. . . . The time which you two gentlemen now spend in bringing charges and asking your Governor to perform unconstitutional functions and to ignore the principles of representative government could be more profitably spent.[86]

Wise and Holmes responded to FDR two days later. They, too, engaged in a salvo of angry rhetorical flourishes in defense of their motives:

> You know perfectly well what we meant in our appeal. . . . So far as the public record shows, you have done nothing. . . . You purport to be profoundly shocked at our request for the removal of a public official. . . . Your statement on this question is a patent evasion of the issue. It has support neither in law nor in morals. We have refrained from reference or reply to the graceless innuendos, the covert sneers, the gratuitous personal advice contained in your letter. . . . Your language . . . constitutes a perversion of truth and must have been written . . . to deceive the public. . . . We crave no privilege higher than that of holding up your hands in the battle for righteousness. . . . Your hands, alas, are not raised against the enemy. On the contrary, we find them raised against those forces making for righteousness which we have striven, however imperfectly, to represent.[87]

But Governor Roosevelt dismissed the attack of Wise and Holmes "with finality":

If they would serve their God as they seek to serve themselves, the people of the City of New York would be the gainers.[88]

However, the general public was losing patience with Roosevelt's continual refusal to act in the case of Mayor Walker. In May 1932 Walker once again confronted Seabury face-to-face, who had clear, incriminating evidence that linked the jovial mayor to fiscal wrongdoing. It was a damaging encounter for the cornered Walker.

But FDR still did not remove the mayor from office, claiming he had not received any official documents about Walker's alleged wrongdoing. Seabury soon provided the governor with the evidence and the sworn testimony of the corrupt mayor, placing FDR in a public bind. The Democratic National Convention was scheduled to begin in Chicago on June 27, and because Roosevelt had not yet clinched the nomination, he needed the Tammany Hall votes in the convention. FDR was worried about one of his major opponents, Al Smith, who still attracted many New York State delegates. However, time and the public's patience were running out for both FDR and Walker. Wise and Holmes used their congregational pulpits to demand that Walker be removed from his position.[89]

On June 21, 1932—fifteen months after the bitter meeting between Roosevelt and the two clergymen—FDR acted. He transmitted the charges assembled by Seabury and his staff to the mayor and demanded a quick response. "Beau James," playing for even more time, told the governor he was traveling to the Democratic Convention in Chicago. Once back in the city, Walker promised to answer FDR's request.

As Roosevelt pushed to gain the 1932 Democratic presidential nomination, the Walker albatross remained around his neck. A member of Roosevelt's trusted inner circle and the future secretary of the interior, Harold L. Ickes (1874–1952), a Progressive Republican who supported Theodore Roosevelt in the 1912 presidential election, warned FDR,

> While many independents and Republicans are favorably inclined toward you at this time I find they are not prepared to make up their minds until you have passed upon the case of Mayor Walker.[90]

The astute Roosevelt understood his problem and spent three precious postconvention weeks in August when he personally interrogated Walker in Albany. Both men had a lot at stake. Walker might lose his coveted job, and FDR needed to appear strong and confident to a nation that was sizing him up as a possible president who had the ability to confront the problems of the Great Depression.

Wise with New York City mayor Fiorello LaGuardia, c. 1945. Permission granted by the
Stephen Wise Free Synagogue Archives.

Roosevelt was well prepared for the questioning of the mayor, and the
governor even insisted on evening sessions to speed up the process.[91] This
time there was no escape for the mayor or for the Democratic presidential
nominee. Like a clever boxer, Walker bobbed and weaved during the severe
questioning, and Roosevelt was at the same time flooded with pleas from
Gentleman Jimmy's supporters to allow Walker to continue as New York
City's mayor. As the hearings neared their end, and hardly acting as a profile
in courage, FDR again refused to move against the popular Tammany-backed
mayor.

But Roosevelt was soon relieved of taking any executive action against
Walker. On September 1, 1932, about two months before the presidential election, the mayor resigned his office, boarded an ocean liner with Betty Compton,
and sailed to Europe.[92]

Wise and Holmes were vindicated, and the Progressive Fiorello LaGuardia,
who in 1934 would be elected NYC's mayor, said it best: "When Rabbi Wise
talks about mayors, there is usually a run on Atlantic steamship accommodations."[93] As a sign of the tension created by Walker's resignation and without her husband's knowledge, a fearful Louise Wise "hired a detective at the

height of the controversy to follow him [Wise] and guard against physical assault."[94]

One direct result of the clash with FDR was Holmes's permanent distaste for Roosevelt; it was a case of complete alienation. Wise, who thrived on his personal access to powerful political leaders, was not to meet FDR again until 1936, when he supported the president's reelection. But in 1932, Stephen, like his Christian colleague, was not a Roosevelt fan or supporter, even though he had voted for him in the 1928 and 1930 gubernatorial elections in New York.

In a letter to his friend Felix Frankfurter, Wise complained that FDR had "no deep-seated convictions . . . no bed-rock . . . he is all clay and no granite. We shall have another four years such as we had under Harding, Coolidge and Hoover." Stephen voted for Norman Thomas in the 1932 presidential election.[95]

Wise felt betrayed and disappointed by FDR, and on January 26, 1932, he wrote to his friend George Foster Peabody:

> I now feel I have been grossly misled by his [FDR] personal charm and by the winsomeness of a pseudo-liberalism. . . . He has no deep convictions concerning social justice. . . . It would seem to me to make very little difference whether Hoover or Roosevelt is in the White House. I repeat that I consider Hoover preferable, for at least he has the merit of being outspoken in his capitalist philosophy, whereas Roosevelt poses as a liberal and acts, and will always act, when the test comes as a representative of the capitalistic group, whatever his speech or pose may be.[96]

Wise's surprising statement that "I consider Hoover preferable" to FDR in the 1932 race for the White House seems out of character, both politically and personally. Twenty years earlier Stephen had abandoned the Republican Party to support Woodrow Wilson, and he remembered that Hoover had not been helpful to the Jewish delegations at the 1919 Paris Peace Conference. By January 1932 it was clear that as president, the Iowa Quaker's incompetent policies had failed to ameliorate the disastrous Great Depression that began in 1929.

But when Wise wrote Peabody, Stephen was working to have President Hoover appoint Benjamin N. Cardozo (1870–1938), the chief judge of the New York State Court of Appeals, to succeed Oliver Wendell Holmes, Jr. (1841–1935), on the Supreme Court. Justice Holmes's retirement from the bench came after serving more than thirty years on the high court. Cardozo, a respected judge and a close friend of Wise, was of Sephardic Jewish (Spanish-Portuguese) background and traced his family roots to the 1492 Jewish expulsion from the Iberian Peninsula.

Once news of the Holmes retirement became public, Wise traveled to Washington to confer with Senator William Borah, who was persuaded that Cardozo was the best-qualified judge in America. The Republican senator from Idaho was most supportive and promised to press the candidacy with Hoover. When Borah met with the president, Hoover was wary of choosing a second Jew to join Brandeis on the Court. He told Borah, "There is a great deal of anti-Semitism in this country. New York already has two justices on the Supreme Court."

The president suggested that the appointment would be politically easier if Brandeis stepped down and was replaced by Cardozo. Borah reassured him there was no religious issue and indicated that choosing Cardozo could enhance the president's battered reputation. Hoover, with a difficult election in the fall, perhaps thought he might win some votes in key states with large Jewish populations. Or perhaps the president was convinced Cardozo was the best person for the job.

Whatever the reason or motive, Hoover nominated the New York judge and the US Senate unanimously approved the appointment. Wise was delighted, but Justice Cardozo served only six years on the Court before he died in 1938, the victim of a heart attack and a stroke. He was sixty-eight.[97]

Walter Lippmann, the leading political columnist of the era, was even harsher on FDR than Wise:

It is well known in New York, though apparently not in the West, that Governor Roosevelt had to be forced into assisting the exposure of corruption in New York City. . . . For Franklin Roosevelt is no crusader. He is no tribune of the people. He is no enemy of entrenched privilege. He is a pleasant man who, without any important qualifications for the office, would very much like to be President.[98]

Although Wise did not vote for the "pleasant man" in the 1932 presidential election, FDR defeated Herbert Hoover by 7 million votes. Wise's candidate, Norman Thomas, received about 900,000 votes, and William Z. Foster (1881–1961), the Communist Party's candidate, attracted 102,000 voters, including literary figures Theodore Dreiser, John Dos Passos (1896–1970), and Sherwood Anderson (1876–1941). Foster's vice presidential running mate was James W. Ford (1893–1957), the first African American in history to appear on a presidential ballot. Ford was the Communist Party's VP candidate again in 1936 and 1940.[99]

Neither Wise nor FDR forgot their public battle in 1931 and 1932 over the political fate of Mayor Walker. But the next time these two leaders encountered one another, the issue was no longer something as simple as New York

City politics. January 30, 1933, was FDR's fifty-first birthday, but it was also the date Adolf Hitler became Germany's Nazi chancellor, which changed the relationship between Roosevelt and Wise as they confronted the radical evil emanating from Berlin. How the two men dealt with that challenge was the last and most important chapter of an often ambivalent thirty-year relationship between Roosevelt, a political Titan, and Wise, a religious giant, that is uncommon in American history.

In that fateful year of 1933 when both Roosevelt and Hitler gained power in their countries, Stephen Wise was not only a leader in Progressive political causes but he had also become America's best-known rabbi, the role he had long pursued.

Chapter 17

Some of the Rabbi's Best Friends Really Were Christians

Building new and constructive relations between Jews and Christians was a major part of Wise's career. He did this by fostering interreligious cooperation to achieve Progressive social justice issues and by speaking at hundreds of public events in churches, assemblies, conventions, and Christian seminaries. Wise also developed positive personal relationships with many members of the Christian clergy in addition to John Haynes Holmes.

However, Stephen was no rabbinic Pollyanna about the history of Christian-Jewish relations; he knew the grim teachings and realities of what historian Salo Baron has termed the "lachrymose" history of Jewish encounters with the followers of Jesus. But Wise believed that the pluralistic nature of the American religious experience and the collective self-esteem that Zionism offered the Jewish people were transformative forces for purposeful change.

Stephen was always alert to stereotypes and caricatures of Jews and Judaism. That is why he became a major critic of the celebrated Hollywood director Cecil B. DeMille (1881–1959) and the moviemaker's epic 1927 silent movie *The King of Kings*. The film described the last days of Jesus, and much of it reflected the complex, tense interplay between Joseph Caiaphas, the Jerusalem Temple's high priest, and Pontius Pilate, the cruel Roman governor of ancient Judea.

That relationship is a central feature in the New Testament account of Jesus's crucifixion. It is always the key feature in Christian Passion Plays and has been used to foment anti-Judaism. In those productions, the Jewish high priest is, with very few exceptions, portrayed as venal and keen for Jesus's death as he manipulates and badgers the supposedly weak, milquetoastlike overlord of the Roman occupation.

But Pilate, the Roman procurator or military governor, was neither weak nor powerless. It was only Pilate and not the Jewish leaders who had the authority to carry out capital punishment in the terrifying form of crucifixion.

Caiaphas, the subservient high priest, was a political appointment of the Roman authorities and served at the bidding of the conquerors of Judea.

In 36 CE, Pilate's cruelty, especially his mistreatment of Jews and Samaritans, caused Vittellius, his superior stationed in Syria, to remove him from office. Pilate was forced to make a disgraceful and humiliating return to Rome.[1]

Because he owed his religious position to the Romans, a submissive Caiaphas collaborated with them on many issues. His job was to satisfy his foreign masters by maintaining law and order among the various groups and sects within the restive Jewish population living under Roman occupation.

Dr. Eugene Fisher, an American Catholic scholar, questions the claim that Caiaphas and the Temple priesthood were the authentic "Jewish leaders":

> Eager to please their Roman superiors, they would zealously seek to bring to the attention of Pilate even the slightest hint of rebellion. . . . They were not the truly religious leaders of the day, [unlike] the Pharisees. Rather the individuals involved [including Caiaphas] . . . had sold out to Rome . . . and represented no more than their own selfish interests.[2]

Because of that historical reality, Wise zeroed in on DeMille's false cinematic version of the Caiaphas-Pilate connection. He was also outraged that the film evoked the infamous deicide charge of "Christ-killers"—that Jews, because of their alleged "crime," are to be forever punished by God. Although deicide was never an official teaching of the Catholic Church, the odious charge was repudiated on October 28, 1965, by the world's bishops at the Second Vatican Council. The Declaration *Nostra Aetate* (In Our Time) no. 4 included this sentence: "The Jews should not be presented as rejected or accursed by God as if this followed from Sacred Scripture."[3]

A Simon Wiesenthal Center report of 2000 reiterated the criticism Wise had made seven decades years earlier:

> Despite the rise of the Hollywood moguls, Jewish characters did not fare well. In 1927—coincident with the appearance of *The Jazz Singer*, the first talking picture in which Al Jolson sang in blackface—DeMille released *The King of Kings*, which still ranks as the most blatant film rendition ever made of the Jews-killed-Christ myth. For ethnic verisimilitude, DeMille raided the New York Yiddish theater for Rudolph and Joseph Schildkraut to play the chief villains, Caiaphas and Judas, and cast as extras in the mob scenes Orthodox Jews from the Boyle Heights neighborhood of Los Angeles. A devout Episcopalian who harbored grudges against his Jewish former partners both in the movie business and in the Julian Oil Scandal of the 1920s, DeMille was delighted rather than dismayed by the hackles his film raised in the Jewish community.

On the other hand, he inoculated himself against Catholic criticism of his depiction of Jesus by having Jesuit Father Daniel Lord offer sunrise Mass on the set every day.[4]

The Schildkrauts were well-known actors, and in retrospect, DeMille created what we today call a "dog whistle" for his movie audience. That is, by using "foreign" Jews—Rudolph (1862–1930), who was born in Turkey, and his son Joseph (1896-1964), in Vienna—the film director was sending a prejudicial message that the most negative characters and the worst foes of Jesus were, in fact, "the Jews," the dreaded "other."

Wise demanded that the film's producers make significant changes in the movie. Stephen feared that if *The King of Kings* was shown in parts of Europe, it could ignite anti-Jewish riots. He warned, "The blood of the Jews will be upon the heads of the producers of 'The King of Kings.'"[5] Complicating the issue was the fact that DeMille's British-born mother, Matilda Samuel (1853–1923), was Jewish, and some of the film's producers were Jews. Rabbi Edgar Magnin, Los Angeles's leading rabbi of the period and a personal friend of DeMille, offered strong support for the movie:

[I] knew the "King of Kings" would be a success. Hearty congratulations to you. . . . I believe the picture will exercise a spiritual and wholesome effect upon all who will have the privilege of witnessing it.[6]

Of course, Wise was not deterred by Jewish movie producers, his rabbinical colleague's warm praise of the film, or the fact that DeMille's mother was a Jew. In a Free Synagogue sermon, he warned about the potential dangers "if they attempt to show the picture in Eastern or Central Europe." He labeled the film as "this Oberammergau of Hollywood."[7]

A few positive changes were made for screenings in New York City. However, because of Wise and other Jewish critics, including the Anti-Defamation League, then a part of B'nai Brith, the Jewish fraternal organization, the movie was not exhibited in Eastern Europe.[8]

Three years later, in 1930, Wise condemned the "real thing": the Oberammergau Passion Play (OPP) that is performed every ten years in the picturesque Bavarian village fifty-six miles south of Munich. In 1634 the faithful residents of Oberammergau, overwhelmingly Roman Catholic, escaped the worst ravages of the plague that swept parts of Europe that year. In gratitude for their deliverance, they vowed to present a Passion Play about the last days in the life of Jesus of Nazareth. The OPP has been called the "Grandparent" of all other Passion Plays in the world, including DeMille's 1927 film.

The villagers kept their vow, and by 1930, the play—performed by the townspeople on a large outdoor stage with elaborate costumes and special music—had become an international event that hundreds of thousands of people attended every ten years at the start of a new decade. Henry Ford was one of the celebrities who traveled to Germany and viewed an OPP performance that year.

As a critic of the Oberammergau Passion Play, Wise aimed some of the strongest language of his career at the Bavarian religious epic:

> The play is like a poisonous influence on the hundreds of thousands of Christians who see it, bringing the confirmation of every prejudice, the deepening of every bitterness and the justification of every manner of ill will against the Jews.
>
> The actors who portray the roles of Judas, Caiaphas and the mob are represented as typically Jewish. . . . The actors who portray the roles of Mary, Jesus and his disciples are represented as Nordic Teutons. . . . The play encourages the audience to forget that Jesus and all his disciples were Jews. . . . Only when Christians cease teaching that the Jews killed Jesus, and teach instead that Jesus and His disciples were all Jews, will true good-will be obtained among Gentile and Jew.[9]

More than eighty years later, thanks to the work of both Christian and Jewish scholars, Passion Play officials in Germany, and the efforts of the American Jewish Committee and the Anti-Defamation League, some positive changes have been made in the staging, costumes, and script of the Oberammergau Passion Play.

But the criticisms of Wise and others continued to swirl around the stage and movie versions of Andrew Lloyd Webber and Tim Rice's *Jesus Christ Superstar* of the 1970s, and the 2005 Mel Gibson film, *The Passion of the Christ*. Many critics have charged the depictions of the Jewish people and their religion in those productions contain negative images, biblical inaccuracies, and distortions of historical reality.

In almost every Passion Play, Jesus and his followers, all of them Jews, appear radiant, inspiring, and joyful while the rest of the Jewish people, especially the Temple's religious leaders, are portrayed in a sinister manner—caricature-like, with dark, ugly costumes and fearsome visages. It is a simple case of "good guys" vs. "bad guys," even though all the guys except for the Romans were members of the Jewish community of the time.

On December 20, 1925, the Sunday before Christmas, Stephen preached a Free Synagogue sermon before three thousand people in Carnegie Hall. Wise focused on a 1922 book written in Hebrew: *Jesus of Nazareth*, by Joseph Klausner (1874–1958) of the Hebrew University in Jerusalem. An English

version of the volume translated by Herbert Danby appeared in 1925 and attracted public attention. A literary footnote: Klausner was a great-uncle of
Amos Oz, the prize-winning Israeli novelist.

Danby (1889–1953) was an Anglican priest who served as the canon of
Jerusalem's St. George's Cathedral between 1923 and 1936. He was an excellent Hebraist who also provided an English translation of the Mishnah that
remains a standard reference work. The Mishnah, a basic rabbinic text, is the
first written compilation of the Jewish oral religious tradition, and was re-
dacted during the third century.

Following his years in Jerusalem, Danby returned to his native Britain and
became a professor of Hebrew at Oxford University. He is credited with intro-
ducing important Hebrew language texts to English readers.

Klausner and Danby represented the "modern" religious scholarship of the
late nineteenth and early twentieth centuries. In 1906, Albert Schweitzer's
(1875–1965) book *The Quest of the Historical Jesus* appeared. The author, a
German-French Lutheran pastor, achieved world fame and won the 1952
Nobel Peace Prize as a physician working in Gabon, Africa. He was also a
theologian and a world-class organist.

Schweitzer wrote,

> The Jesus of Nazareth who came forward publicly as the Messiah, who
> preached the ethic of the kingdom of God, who founded the kingdom of
> heaven upon earth and died to give his work its final consecration never
> existed.[10]

In his book, Klausner presented Jesus as an authentic Jew, a gifted teacher
and a religious figure who offered hope to his distressed people suffering under the Roman occupation. The Hebrew University professor asserted that
Jesus was a reformer of Judaism, but he rejected the belief that Jesus was God,
the Son of God, or divine as expressed in the Trinity. Nor was Jesus the
Messiah because "the kingdom of heaven" has not yet arrived, and Jesus's
death by crucifixion was a Roman form of execution, not an act of Jewish capital punishment. Klausner saw Jesus as a Jewish teacher of morality and a master of the traditional parable, and not the founder of a new religion. The
establishment and spread of Christianity came after his death.

In his Free Synagogue sermon, Stephen presented views on Jesus that were
similar in many ways to both Klausner and Schweitzer. In his address, he
made four major points:

1. Jesus was a man, not divine or a myth.
2. Jesus was born, lived, and died as a Jew. He was not a Christian.
3. Jews have not repudiated Jesus the Jew, including many of his teachings.

4. Christians have, for the most part, not adopted and followed the teachings of Jesus.[11]

Wise had been stressing these points for many years before his fateful sermon in December 1925. Three years earlier, Wise spoke at a forum at the Union Theological Seminary in New York City, a prominent Protestant divinity school. A student asked Stephen the question that has been hurled at Jews for centuries: "Why don't Jews accept Jesus Christ?" Wise waited for the room to grow quiet as the tense audience awaited his reply. Wise said, "We take Jesus seriously. Do you Christians?" There was no response. He added, "The religion of Jesus is not Christianity. Christianity is a substitute for the religion of Christ. I am not anti-Christian; I am ante-Christian."[12]

He described a "most grievous error that was common among the masses of Christendom in America, the idea that there was no basic relation between the Jews and Jesus other than that they had crucified him, as Christians would put it!"[13]

The heart of his 1925 sermon contained these paragraphs:

Jesus was a Jew in every sense. . . . It is absurd to deny that fact historically. . . . All Jesus did was to simplify. He placed the accents of religion with rightful and far-reaching emphasis upon the essentials. . . .

If Jesus returned today, he would find greed and unbrotherliness as great blotches on the canvas of Christian life. He taught love and brotherliness. Where are they today? . . . Because Christendom has renounced Jesus in fact, shall we continue to deny him now that we his brother Jews, are free to face his life and teaching anew?[14]

Wise's Carnegie Hall speech created a public firestorm that erupted into a major crisis, one of the worst in Wise's life. The day following his sermon, the New York City newspapers covered the story of how the most famous rabbi in America spoke in positive terms about Jesus five days before Christmas.

The *Sun's* headline on the story put Stephen on the defensive:

Wise Declares All Jews Must Accept Jesus; Rabbi Says Nazarene, Despite Old Hebraic Teachings, Is Not a Myth.[15]

By Monday afternoon, twenty-four hours after the sermon, the president of an Orthodox rabbinic group in the United States condemned Wise for his remarks and placed Stephen in *herem*, a form of excommunication from the Jewish people.[16]

Two Yiddish-language newspapers, *Der Morgen Journal* and the *Tagblatt*, both representing traditional Jewish views and opinions, attacked Stephen for leading "the younger generation to the baptismal fount." The Union of Orthodox Rabbis called Wise's sermon "a manoeuvre toward baptism." The Young Israel Orthodox religious organization, which Wise helped create with Mordecai Kaplan in 1912, called him a "menace to Judaism."[17]

In his autobiography written a quarter century later, Wise repeated his basic theme:

> Whatever I believe with respect to the imputed miracle of his birth, his mother, Mary, was a Jewish woman. He was reared and taught as a Jew. He worshiped in the synagogue. He spoke no language save Hebrew, the harsher Hebrew [Wise was referring to Aramaic] of the Galilean country in which he grew up and of the synagogue in which he preached.
>
> Jesus did not teach or wish to teach a new religion. . . . It would be absurd to imagine that Judea, the little dependency of mighty Rome, possessed and exercised the power of slaying [capital punishment].[18]

The 1925 controversy further escalated when a group of Methodist Episcopal clergy in Philadelphia praised Wise for his sermon because in it he declared Jesus was an actual person and not a "myth." One clergyman objected to Wise's views because the rabbi did not accept the "full divinity" of Jesus, but a fellow pastor said, "There is no need to go back to the beginning of time in order to split theological hairs."[19]

Edwin Knox Mitchell (1854–1934), dean of the Hartford Theological Seminary, jumped to a false conclusion and called Wise's sermon a "noble and courageous thing in accepting the moral and spiritual leadership of Jesus." The liberal Protestant preacher Harry Emerson Fosdick (1878–1969) called Wise "the best Christian in New York."[20]

The overwhelming majority of Reform rabbis in the United States supported Wise and his perspective on Jesus. Rabbi William Fineshriber (1878–1968) of Philadelphia's Knesseth Israel Congregation told Stephen, "Be ye of good courage, neither thou be dismayed and forgive them for they know not what to say." Rabbi Nathan Krass (1880–1949) of Temple Emanu-El in New York declared,

> A small group of ignorant fanatical Jews passed a bigoted, vicious, nasty resolution condemning a rabbi who has given his life in the service of Israel. [They and] the so-called liberal rabbis who attack Dr. Wise . . . ought to be ashamed of their inexcusable conduct.[21]

One of those "so-called liberal rabbis," Samuel Schulman, the rabbi of Temple Beth-El in Manhattan and a longtime opponent of Wise, criticized his more famous Reform colleague:

Rabbi Wise's remarks were entirely uncalled for. . . . It does not help religion much to make such superficial, sensational and facetious statements as those in which Rabbi Wise indulged.[22]

Another Reform rabbi, George Solomon (1873–1945) of Temple Mickve Israel in Savannah, Georgia, had a different kind of criticism. He was more upset by who delivered the Carnegie Hall sermon and less by its contents:

The controversy is very regrettable. It is, to my mind, an aftermath of the results of sensational publicity, which has always been characteristic of Dr. Wise's policy. He is a very able and gifted man, but I fear success has made him think more of the continued glory of Stephen S. Wise than of the cause which he is serving. . . . The business of the preacher in his pulpit is to confine himself to his own faith. . . . It has come about that many a so-called synagogue or church is nothing more than a gathering place, catering to the whims and fancies of the crowd.[23]

Louis Marshall's smug remarks about the Wise sermon perhaps reflected the hurt he still felt from the battle the two men had fought with one another nearly twenty years earlier about the freedom of the pulpit:

I am sure Dr. Wise did not intend to express any opinion looking to apostasy. It is regrettable that he has been misunderstood and misinterpreted both by Jews and non-Jews. It merely proves how circumspect a preacher must be when those whom he addresses have varying points of view. The unfailing consequence is a war of polemics, which is always deplorable.[24]

In his autobiography Wise remembered the attacks:

I know not which was more hurtful—the acceptance of me as a brother and welcoming me into the Christian fold or the violent diatribe of a fellow rabbi.[25]

But the crisis for Wise was more than being assailed by Orthodox Jews and saluted by most Reform rabbis and some Christian religious leaders. In 1925 Wise was the chairman of the United Palestine Appeal (UPA), a fund-raising campaign in behalf of the growing Jewish community in the biblical homeland.

His critics within the Orthodox community called for Wise's resignation as the head of such an important philanthropic institution that had set a goal of raising $5 million in 1925 (worth about $66 million today). The embattled Wise sought a meeting with Orthodox critics, and his request was accepted. A downcast Stephen arrived for the encounter wearing a skullcap for the occasion.

The atmosphere at the meeting was tense; an American Jewish historian wrote it was "not unlike that which prevailed at the religious court in Amsterdam [in 1656] when [Baruch] Spinoza [1632–1677] was summoned to answer charges of heresy."[26] The meeting did not go well, even though Wise explained to his detractors that his sermon was not a call for Jews to "accept Jesus as a teacher." After the session concluded and their guest departed, the hundred-plus Orthodox rabbis unanimously demanded that Wise give up his UPA chairmanship. Stephen was not surprised:

> The Orthodox, of course, do not like me and they have been trying to get rid of me for twenty years. I never gave them a good enough chance to decapitate me, but when I seemed to have said that Jews must accept Jesus and embrace Christianity, they felt their day had come.[27]

Wise resigned his UPA post, making clear he was angered by the personal attacks:

> [By] passing a verdict of condemnation against a man on hearsay evidence, without hearing of witnesses . . . [my] thirty years and more of service to Jewish life in all its aspects . . . should . . . have outweighed misleading head-lines of a newspaper report of what I said. . . . I am not prepared to permit any word or act of mine to be used to the hurt of the Zionist cause. If the [UPA] Executive Committee accepts my resignation I mean to continue to serve in the ranks of a cause which I have sought to serve throughout my ministry.[28]

Wise was urged by many people and organizations to withdraw his resignation. Some rabbis preached sermons supporting Wise's perspective of Jesus, and liberal Christians, perhaps influenced by Schweitzer and other theologians, affirmed the Jewish roots of their faith and the "Jewishness" of Jesus. But Monsignor Joseph H. McMahon (1862–1939) of the Church of Our Lady of Lourdes on West 142nd Street in New York City provided Wise's enemies with additional ammunition:

> There can be no everlasting peace on earth until everyone accepts the teach-ings of Jesus. . . . We . . . have entered Christ's Church and . . . we understand Scripture and comprehend the meaning. The eye of the Jew is still folded.[29]

In 1910 both Wise and McMahon were listed as honorary vice presidents of a New York City committee that pressed for women schoolteachers to receive equal pay for equal work. Another name on that list was Dorothy Dix (1861–1951), the author of a syndicated personal advice column that appeared in many newspapers.[30]

Harry M. Orlinsky, a Bible professor at Hebrew Union College–Jewish Institute of Religion, recounted an important episode during Stephen's "Jesus crisis." The Mizrahi Zionist organization hosted a luncheon in late December 1925 to honor Gedalia Bublick (1875–1948), *Der Morgen Journal*'s editor and the man who castigated Wise in several of his editorials.

The luncheon took place at a well-known Manhattan kosher restaurant. During the meal, the door opened and an uninvited guest interrupted the festivities. It was Stephen Wise. The eating stopped as the tension rose in the crowded restaurant. Once the initial shock wore off, Wise was given a seat and offered some food.

"I did not come here to eat," Wise said. When the meal in honor of Bublick concluded, Stephen arose and in his usual imperious style demanded the right to speak:

> Did you think, gentlemen, that you are going to honor my friend, my comrade in arms, my fellow Zionist Gedalia Bublick, without my participation? True, Bublick wrote what he did about me, and we have had and will have some differences of opinion. What friends do not? But, gentlemen, please remember: BUBLICK opinion is not yet PUBLICK opinion!

Wise then went over to Bublick and hugged him. The Mizrahi luncheon group rose from their chairs and applauded Wise, some with tears in their eyes.[31]

Wise also received strong support from Jewish leaders in Palestine, including David Yellin, the vice mayor of Jerusalem. An unofficial poll conducted after Wise's sermon showed that 190 of 205 of American Zionist leaders did not want him to resign his UPA position. Among those supporting Wise was Reform Rabbi Abba Hillel Silver (1893–1963) of Cleveland, who twenty years later would become Wise's chief antagonist within the Zionist movement.

The ten days following the Jesus sermon indicated that Wise had the support of most American Jews, including many rabbis. Secure in that knowledge, Stephen issued a public statement rejecting any claim that he asked Jews "to accept the teachings of Christianity." But because of the seriousness of the charges made against him, Stephen added,

> I did say that Jesus was an historic being, not a myth; a man, not a god; a Jew not a Christian. . . . I stand exactly where my fathers have always stood in unequivocal denial of the uniqueness or divinity of Jesus. What a mournful commentary upon the infinite hurt which the Jew has suffered at the hands of

Christendom, that a Jewish teacher cannot even at this time speak of Jesus, his completely Jewish background and his ethical contribution to his time and all time, without being hailed as a convert to Christianity or misunderstood by some of his fellow-Jews.[32]

But it was Nathan Straus who threw the most important lifeline to Stephen Wise in the midst of the rabbi's "Jesus crisis." Five days after Wise delivered his sermon, Straus wrote a letter of strong personal support that included a half-million-dollar contribution to the United Palestine Appeal and an additional $100,000 to build the Nathan and Lena Straus Welfare and Relief Center in Jerusalem that would also provide office space for Hadassah, the women's Zionist organization that was established in 1912. The $600,000 in 1925 would be the equivalent of about $8.5 million today.

Straus encouraged Wise to continue leading the UPA:

I can hardly believe the newspaper reports that a lot of rabbis . . . should condemn a man like you, with your record and your position, without giving you a chance to explain what you meant. They should have known that no word would ever come out of your mouth that would not have the effect of making Jews still stronger Jews and better Americans, and that, if you said anything at all about Christianity, it would only be order to remind Christians, as you and I always do, that the first thing for them to do is be just to Jews.[33]

The crisis ended two weeks after it began. On January 3, 1926, the United Palestine Appeal's executive committee met in Manhattan's Hotel Pennsylvania and by a vote of 59–9 refused Wise's resignation. A chastened Stephen was grateful for the vote of confidence:

Words cannot convey how deeply I am moved by the expressions of confidence and trust which have come to me the past fortnight. . . . [I tendered my UPA resignation] not because of any fear of censure, but because of my instinctive unwillingness to endanger or hurt, even in the slightest degree, the cause of Zionism. . . . It would have been the most grievous hour of my life if you had concluded otherwise. . . . I have felt confident . . . that . . . ultimately the sanity and justice of Jewish opinion would make itself felt and this save American Israel [the US Jewish community] from perpetuating a deep injustice against a fellow-Jew.[34]

Stephen ended his rare expression of humility and thankfulness with a dramatic flourish by uttering two powerful words from the biblical book of Jonah (1:9): *Ivri anochi* (I am a Hebrew!) that drew enthusiastic applause from the executive committee members. A headline in the Philadelphia Jewish paper summarized the crisis in five words: "Dr. Wise Vindicated by Zionists."[35]

The brief but intense clash was akin to a lightning flash that illumines an unexplored landscape. The crisis revealed the divisions within the growing amorphous American Jewish community that in 1925 numbered more than 2.5 million people. Orthodox leaders, many of them newcomers to America from Europe, were suspicious of any Jewish public or even private discussions about Jesus, the New Testament, the Trinity, or Christianity. Their wariness reflected shared memories of Christian persecution, pogroms, and prejudice often justified in the name of Jesus. In addition, some of the most rabid foes of Jews throughout history were Jewish converts to Christianity.

For many Orthodox Jews, that history was embedded in their collective memory bank. They were not certain that the safety and security of Jews in the United States would be any different from their bitter European experiences. Wise's well-publicized sermon triggered a combination of anger and fear—anger that a prominent rabbi would discuss such a toxic subject in public and fear that Stephen had provided permission for young Jews to abandon traditional Judaism.

Strong support for Wise came from rabbis and laypeople who felt more at home in America, people who interacted on a regular basis with Christians in a myriad of ways—politically, culturally, educationally, socially, and economically—a situation that was either rare or impossible in many parts of Europe. "Dr. Wise" was the personification of the Jewish experience in the United States: a charismatic orator with a mastery of the English language and a Jewish leader engaged in all aspects of American life, including culture, politics, history, religion, and national values. Stephen, a Columbia University Ph.D. graduate, was sure footed and at ease with Christians. He was a new type of rabbi—without a beard, a Yiddish accent, or a yarmulke—a person who challenged and threatened many Orthodox Jews.

But Wise's 1925 sermon about Jesus based on Klausner's study did not break new ground. In fact, the great philosopher and physician Moses Maimonides (1135–1204) viewed Jesus as a Jewish teacher whose task was to prepare the world for the coming of "King Messiah." Maimonides was aware of the pain that Jews experienced for centuries as Christianity attempted to supersede Judaism.

Maimonides believed, however, that Christianity was a necessary element, but not sufficient by itself to bring about the Messianic era. In his important work, Mishneh Torah (*Hilchot Melachim* 11.4), Maimonides wrote,

> But the human mind has no power to reach the thoughts of the Creator, for his thoughts and ways are unlike ours. And all these things of Jesus the

Nazarene . . . there is no [purpose] but to straighten out the way for the King Messiah, and to restore all the world to serve God together [and follow] the Torah's laws.[36]

If curious Jews expressed any interest in learning about Jesus, Christianity, and the New Testament, they were many times rebuffed with a popular saying: "What was good in Jesus's teachings was not new and what was new was not good."

But since 1925, an increasing number of Jews have studied and written about Jesus in a serious way. In his book *Two Types of Faith*, the philosopher Martin Buber asserted, "From my youth onwards I have found in Jesus my great brother."[37]

In 1963, almost forty years after Wise's controversial sermon, another well-known rabbi, Maurice N. Eisendrath (1902–1973), who served as president of the Union of American Hebrew Congregations (now the Union for Reform Judaism) between 1943 and his death, told a huge UAHC convention audience,

> Needless to say, Jews never can and never will accept Jesus as the Messiah or as the Son of God, but, despite this constant reality, there is room for improved understanding and openness to change in interpreting Jesus as a positive and prophetic spirit in the stream of the Jewish tradition. . . . [Jewish scholars need to examine] our own statements, our own facts, our own interpretations of the significance of the life of Jesus, the Jew.[38]

In more recent years, New Testament professors David Flusser (1917–2000) of the Hebrew University, Samuel Sandmel (1911–1979) of the Hebrew Union College–Jewish Institute of Religion, Michael Signer (1946–2009) of the University of Notre Dame, Michael Cook of HUC-JIR, Amy-Jill Levine of the Vanderbilt Divinity School, David Fox Sandmel of the Catholic Theological Union, Jon Levenson of the Harvard Divinity School, and others have provided many students, including Christian clergy and rabbis, with an authentic Jewish understanding of Jesus and the development of early Christianity.

However, in 1925 Wise did not have such a group of Jewish scholars to buttress his remarks about Jesus. But he did have the extraordinary friendship and support of his Christian colleague, John Haynes Holmes, who supported and sustained Stephen during the "Jesus crisis."

Holmes and Wise were an odd couple: a patrician preacher and a Progressive prophet. Holmes's paternal ancestors arrived in what is now Massachusetts in 1620, and the Haynes family came to Boston in 1635. Nearly three centuries later, Holmes graduated from Harvard College in 1902, and two years later he completed his studies at the Harvard Divinity School. Always a liberal in his religious beliefs, Holmes served a Dorchester church near Boston until 1907 when he was called to lead New York City's Church of the Messiah, then located at East 34th Street and Park Avenue.[39]

Holmes was uncomfortable with the church's name because he did not view Jesus as the Messiah. In 1918 the Unitarian house of worship changed its name to the Community Church, and its redbrick building stands today near its original location. Following his death in 1964, Holmes's remains were placed under the main aisle of the church sanctuary.

The two men first met in 1907 when Wise established the Free Synagogue, and they remained devoted colleagues until Stephen's death forty-two years later. That special friendship is described in Carl Hermann Voss's 1964 book *Rabbi and Minister: The Friendship of Stephen S. Wise and John Haynes Holmes.*

Their two congregations grew in membership under the leadership of their gifted preachers and community leaders. Wise and Holmes became national leaders in interreligious cooperation, social justice concerns, race relations, human rights, civil liberties, trade unionism, and civic government issues.

By 1933 they were popular public figures. A Broadway comedy, *She Loves Me Not*, had one of the characters, a newspaper editor, yelling instructions to his reporters into several telephones. To one reporter the editor shouted, "Call Rabbi Stephen Wise and get a statement." To a second he screamed, "Get John Haynes Holmes on the phone and have him dictate a paragraph."[40]

In 1910 the two clergymen joined with Frank Oliver Hall (1860–1941) of the Universalist Church, and together they established joint Sunday night Union Services that were sponsored by their three congregations. Wise and his two Christian colleagues agreed that during the joint services,

No word be uttered, no prayer be offered up, no hymn be chanted that did not include within itself the spirit of the three congregations worshipping together. . . . But none of us did or would abate one jot or tittle of our respective positions, of our several loyalties. . . . There entered only those elements to which all of us together might without reluctance assent.[41]

As noted earlier, Holmes and Wise, personal friends and professional colleagues, were instrumental in removing the corrupt New York City mayor James Walker from office. Holmes and Wise opposed Tammany Hall and worked together in the establishment of the National Association for the Advancement of Colored People in 1910.[42]

Their views on most domestic issues were generally congruent, but Wise and Holmes disagreed on one major issue during their four-decade friendship: pacifism. An earlier chapter depicts how the two religious leaders differed in 1917 when the US Congress declared war on imperial Germany. Wise abandoned his previous antiwar position and supported America's entry into the conflict led by his friend, President Woodrow Wilson.

Holmes remained opposed to all military involvement. He made his position clear in a 1915 sermon:

War is never justifiable under any circumstances. . . . Never will I take up arms against a foe. And if, because of cowardice or madness, I do this awful thing, may God in his anger strike me dead, ere I strike dead some brother from another land![43]

In the late summer of 1917, Holmes attended the American Unitarian Association meeting in Montreal. Former president William Howard Taft chaired the convention, and he denounced Holmes for failing to support the US war effort. Taft called for a resolution urging "the war must be carried to a successful conclusion to stamp out militarism in the world." Holmes, the strong pacifist, was outvoted, and Taft's pro-war resolution was adopted, 236–9.

Holmes returned from Montreal exhausted and ill, but Wise praised his colleague's courage for holding fast to his pacifist principles. Despite their differences on the war, that November Wise and Holmes led their two congregations in a joint Thanksgiving service.[44]

Just as the Free Synagogue membership increased under Wise, by 1930, so, too, Holmes's Community Church had more than eighteen hundred members from thirty-four countries. Holmes wrote, "We are a public not a private institution—a community church in the true sense of the word."[45]

Years later, the two religious leaders once again found themselves in opposing camps. Holmes, a disciple of Mohandas Gandhi's (1869–1948) doctrine of nonviolence, remained steadfast in his opposition to war, even in the face of Nazism, fascism, and Japanese militarism. It was a position Wise respected but could never endorse. Many of Holmes's Christian friends and clergy colleagues disassociated themselves from him. But not Wise.

Holmes's pacifism was also attacked in the media. On January 13, 1942, *PM*, a liberal New York City newspaper, printed a cartoon by Theodore Geisel (1904–1991), who later achieved worldwide fame as "Dr. Seuss," the author of many children's books. *PM*'s publisher and editor was Ralph Ingersoll (1900–1985), and department store heir Marshall Field III (1893–1956) of Chicago was the paper's chief financial supporter. During World War II, Geisel drew nearly four hundred cartoons for *PM*; almost all of them were anti-Nazi, anti-isolationist, and anti-Japanese. His drawings also assailed anti-Semitism and antiblack racism.[46]

Geisel's cartoon featured Holmes's quotation, "The Unhappy People of Japan Are Our Brothers," and a caricature-like Japanese soldier holding a knife and a decapitated head. When the newspaper received many letters supporting Holmes's pacifist position, Geisel responded with an angry editorial:

> In response to the letters defending John Haynes Holmes . . . sure, I believe in love, brotherhood and a cooing white pigeon on every man's roof. I even think it's nice to have pacifists and strawberry festivals . . . in between wars. But right now, when the Japs are planting their hatchets in our skulls, it seems like a hell of a time for us to smile and warble: "Brothers!" It is a rather flabby battlecry. If we want to win, we've got to kill Japs, whether it depresses John Haynes Holmes or not. We can get palsy-walsy afterward with those that are left.[47]

It got even worse for Holmes. During a White House meeting, President Roosevelt asked Wise, "Can't you do anything with John Haynes Holmes? What's the matter with him?" Stephen responded, "John Haynes Holmes believes that war is the greatest of evils. He obeys his conscience and his God in opposing war under any and all circumstances."

The president laughed and replied, "Well, that's all right. So do I—BUT!"[48]

During their forty-two years of friendship and collaboration on many issues, the loyal Wise never turned his back on his Christian colleague. The Holmes-Wise bond of mutual respect and understanding still remains the benchmark, the gold standard, the model by which all interreligious relationships must be judged.

Chapter 18

The Rabbi Who Couldn't Say "No"

Because of Stephen Wise's worldwide fame, he received numerous invitations to speak at public meetings, colleges, universities, seminaries, high schools, synagogues, and churches; to write articles for various newspapers and journals; and to add his name in support of a particular cause, organization, or committee. Despite the enormous physical and psychological demands he made upon himself, Stephen honored many of those requests.

During his rabbinic career of fifty-six years, Stephen exhibited a zest for all things religious and political. Because he broadly defined those terms, his enthusiasm allowed him to become involved in almost every aspect of American society. He was a human version of today's 911 emergency number: if there was a crisis, conflict, confrontation, or controversy, individuals and groups contacted Rabbi Stephen Wise for help.

In addition to conducting weekly Free Synagogue services (when he was in New York City and not traveling), he maintained a crushing schedule of attending meetings, conferences, assemblies, rallies, dedications, graduations, conventions, and other public gatherings—many of them overseas.

Like any speaker, Wise enjoyed appearing in front of large, appreciative audiences: it was an exhilarating experience because the energy flowed both ways. By addressing appreciative audiences, Stephen received public affirmation of his opinions, views, and positions on a host of issues. His listeners were excited to hear one of the world's greatest orators in person.

But there was also another reason for his heavy lecture schedule. For many years, the Wise family employed a cook, maid, and governess when James and Justine were youngsters. Louise and Stephen sent their children to a series of private schools—Ethical Culture and Horace Mann in New York City—and prestigious colleges and universities—Princeton, Bryn Mawr, Radcliffe, Barnard, Yale, and Cambridge in Britain. The family spent many summer vacations at their Lake Placid home in the Adirondack Mountains, and there were trips to Europe before World War I.

Wise family Adirondack Mountain vacation lodge, c. 1925. Permission granted by the
Stephen Wise Free Synagogue Archives.

The Wises also contributed money to a number of charities, including
Louise's donations to Hadassah, the women's Zionist organization, and
Stephen's financial support of the *Habimah* (Hebrew for "stage") Theater in
Palestine. Because his Free Synagogue salary did not cover the costs of the
family's lifestyle, the lecture circuit, albeit filled with endless travel, provided
Wise with the necessary additional income.[1]

During his career, Stephen established and headed four major institutions:
the Free Synagogue (1907), the Jewish Institute of Religion (1922), the American Jewish Congress (1922), and the World Jewish Congress (1936).

A talented self-publicist, Wise left a huge public record that covered almost
every aspect of his life. Even a few examples, a thin slice of life from Stephen
Wise's life and times, reveal his extensive interests as well as his reputation as
an indefatigable force of nature who worked for human, political, and civil
rights for all people, his beloved Zionist movement, liberal Judaism, the
Progressive public policy agenda with emphasis on trade unionism, protection of child laborers, and women's suffrage. In addition to Zionism, he was
also a champion of national independence movements that included Armenia,
China, Czechoslovakia, India, and Ireland.

Robert Louis Stevenson Adirondack Memorial Society cottage, c. 1925; Wise is second from the right. Permission granted by the Stephen Wise Free Synagogue Archives.

John Haynes Holmes described his hero, Mohandas Gandhi, in reverent religious terms, even equating the Indian leader with Jesus. While Wise backed Gandhi's political efforts to create an independent India, Wise differed with Gandhi on the question of the right and necessity of Jews having their own independent state—a position that Gandhi opposed. Even an admiring Holmes was unsuccessful in changing his Indian hero's anti-Zionist position.[2]

Stephen Wise backed Armenian independence. That support put Wise at odds with the new Turkish Republic established following the breakup of the Ottoman Empire at the conclusion of World War I:

> The threatened extinction of Armenia is the condemnation of the Allies. The saving of Armenia might well become the glory of America and England and those of the Allies who are not wholly lost to a sense of solemn obligation to wronged Armenia . . . the denial to Armenia of the opportunity of creating a national State.[3]

As early as 1912, years before he became the famous "Rabbi USA," Wise began receiving letters from Jews who felt they or their friends and families were victims of anti-Semitism. On May 12 of that year Max Levy wrote to Stephen complaining that when a Jewish high school student in Passaic, New Jersey, was elected to a student government office, the school authorities attempted to invalidate the election. Their efforts failed, but Levy wanted to alert Wise to the episode because Stephen was scheduled to speak at the school.

On November 4, 1924, Jacob Podell sent a letter to Wise reporting an anti-Semitic incident at Erasmus Hall High School in Brooklyn. However, Podell did not want his name to be mentioned if the rabbi investigated the school's actions. Stephen's secretary wrote to Podell that

> he [Wise] is entirely ready to take up the matter but he can and will not do anything unless you permit your name to be used in connection with the complaint. You cannot expect Dr. Wise to peddle about anonymous charges.[4]

On November 8, Podell wrote that Wise should meet with the student to "secure confirmation first hand . . . because the Rabbi is a clearing house for any and all attempts to injure the name of the Jewish people in this city and country." Two days later, Wise asked Podell "to bring the boy to see me" at the Free Synagogue House in New York City. The matter was soon resolved, and the school rescinded its anti-Jewish action.

In January 1925 the *Jewish Forum* printed a "Symposium" titled "Is the Jewish Boy or Girl Handicapped in the Business, Literary or Professional World?" The publication's editor, Isaac Rosengarten (1887–1961), wanted Wise to contribute a "brief statement" on the theme. Stephen wrote,

> I have no doubt whatever that the Jewish boy or girl is very seriously handicapped in the so-called literary or professional world. . . . The young Jew has not the same opportunity of an academic career as the non-Jew. . . . Some of these selfish, contemptuous Jews are themselves responsible. Jews, who at the head of law offices and businesses houses, refuse to give employment to Jews . . . serve to enfeeble morale and break the moral fiber.[5]

Stephen publicly and privately attacked discrimination in housing, real estate, employment, education, and voting. In 1925 Wise assailed real estate companies and agents who discriminated against Jews. One of his targets was Colonel L. J. Campbell, the son of the president of Youngstown Sheet and Tube Company. Campbell lost a leg during World War I and had been gassed by the Germans. Seven years after the conflict ended, Campbell came to Boca Grande, a small "exclusive" resort community in southwestern Florida not far from Fort Myers. For years it had been the winter playground of such famous families as the Lodges, DuPonts, and Cabots.

In the mid-1920s as Campbell was recuperating from his war wounds, he saw great potential in Boca Grande and began a targeted sales campaign that included these paragraphs:

CHARLOTTE HARBOR REALTY COMPANY,
Sales Rep., L. J. Campbell, Florida

The winter colony at Boca Grande is composed of people of charm and distinction. Yale has always been well represented. There is property here avail-
able for winter homes at very reasonable prices. . . . There are no free bus rides
or ballyhoos; there are no Jews; there is no Chamber of Commerce. . . .

Boca Grande remains a desirable vacation destination, but today because
of antidiscrimination legislation and attacks on restrictive real estate cove-
nants it is no longer the exclusive preserve of Campbell's "people of charm and
distinction" (i.e., white Christians). In recent years, it has been the winter resort for the presidential Bush family.[6]

On December 13, 1927, Ernest P. Bicknell (1862–1935), a national leader of
the American Red Cross, wrote to Wise and asked him to write an article for
youngsters that would appear in a Junior Red Cross publication. Three days
later Stephen dashed off a piece he must have known would be "little noted nor
long remembered." Yet he responded to Bicknell's request with a column that
was quintessential Stephen Wise—a combination of flowery language, mixed
with a touch of universalism and an attack on bigotry:

[The Junior Red Cross reflects] the oneness of our common life. . . . Whatsoever race or faith or speech, and above all, as a symbol of that oneness . . . we
labor together, labor in the spirit of love for the service of humankind.[7]

Three months later, in early March 1928, the leaders of the American
Clothing and Furnishings Credit Bureau, a professional group with many
Jewish members, complained to Wise about an article in the *Brooklyn Eagle*,
an influential newspaper of that era. At one time the *Eagle*, which was published between 1846 and 1955, was the most popular afternoon daily in the
United States. Walt Whitman (1819–1892) was the paper's editor for two years
beginning in 1846.

Because of the paper's history and influence, concerned bureau leaders
claimed the *Eagle* engaged in anti-Semitism when it described a "fence" who
had engaged in some shady business dealings with the identifying words
"Polish Jew." The bureau leaders were upset and charged the paper was perpetuating the anti-Semitic canard that Jews, especially those from Poland,
were dishonest. They asserted that such an unwarranted religious and ethnic
description denigrated the entire Jewish people. Wise agreed and fired off a
note to the paper's editor demanding a full retraction with an apology, and the
Eagle was quick to comply.

On May 16, 1925, Mrs. Jose Estrago wrote to Wise indicating she wanted a
job interview at the New York Public Library. But she was informed by an

employment agency that the library does "not consider any Jewess" for staff positions. Wise called for an investigation of the library's hiring practices.

But Wise did exercise some restraint about the use of his name even when a cause was worthwhile and important. On March 8, 1928, a week after the *Brooklyn Eagle* incident, Stephen received a formal request from John Collier (1884–1968), a leader of the American Indian Defense Association, asking the Free Synagogue rabbi to join with other prominent national leaders in signing a joint letter to the *New York Times.* The letter urged President Coolidge to veto a congressional bill that in Collier's words was a Republican "bid for New Mexico's electoral vote" in the 1928 election. Collier believed the Rio Grande Conservancy bill would be an "admitted and gross violation of the Constitution."

The legislation called for the removal of eleven thousand acres of Pueblo tribal lands to be used for commercial development. The law would result in exploitation and "spoliation," something Collier was certain would never happen if the land were owned by "white men" and not Native Americans.

The proposed letter to the *Times* contained detailed financial statistics that proved what an "outrageous bill" it was. Collier urged a presidential veto because the bill was based upon "fiction of the wildest sort," and a "new form of confiscation of land against all Indians."

Among the American Indian Defense Association's board members were several friends of Wise: Barnard College dean Virginia Gildersleeve (1877–1947), who in 1945 was the only female member of the US delegation at the San Francisco founding conference of the United Nations; George Foster Peabody, banker, philanthropist, and the creator of the journalism award in his name; Lillian Wald; and William Allen White (1868–1944), the Progressive editor of the *Emporia Gazette* in Kansas.

Although Stephen supported the goals of the association and believed Coolidge should veto the bill, he refused to add his name to the letter because, as he wrote to Collier on March 12, "I cannot sign a letter with a lot of figures of which I know nothing." Wise wanted more precise details—more facts about the bill and the actual situation on the ground in New Mexico—before he would allow his name to be used in a public statement.[8]

But Stephen did not forget the American Indian cause. Collier became commissioner for the Bureau of Indian Affairs in the FDR administration from 1933 to 1945, and in May 1935 Wise wrote to him,

> Some of us came to Washington and did what we could to have a part in the fight [to protect the rights of the American Indian and to secure redress for past wrongs]. Is it really true some Congressional idiots are now fighting you? ... Is there anything that "we fellers" can do in New York? ... You

[Collier] have come pretty near being the salvation of the Indians, even though
you may not believe in that terribly ecclesiastical thing.[9]

Wise delivered the eulogy at Samuel Gompers's funeral in New York City
in late 1924.[10] A month later, on January 29, 1925, Stephen received a letter of
thanks from the American Federation of Labor, the trade union organization
that Gompers founded years earlier. The AFL leadership complimented Wise
for the "remarkable sermon at the funeral services of our revered and beloved
President, Samuel Gompers."

In May 1932 Wise was asked to serve as a labor arbitrator along with
Columbia University Law Professor Joseph Chamberlain (1877–1951) and
Progressive journalist Milton Mayer (1908–1986). The Associated Brick
Masons sought an increase in their wages, and the three-member panel
awarded the bricklayers an hourly wage of $1.65 ($27.10 in today's dollars) and
$13.20 per day ($220 today).[11]

Stephen was also active in international relations. In 1923 the Lausanne
Treaty was signed in Switzerland between the Allies of World War I and the
new Republic of Turkey led by Kemal Ataturk. The treaty established Turkey's
national borders and ended the state of hostilities. The United States was not a
signatory to the agreement because Congress did not declare war on the
Ottoman Turkish Empire in April 1917.

After four years of debate, the Lausanne Treaty came before the US Senate
for ratification. Wise, 110 Episcopal bishops, and many other religious and political leaders opposed the treaty because, in their view, it failed to protect
non-Muslim minorities—mostly Christians and Jews—within Turkey. Treaty
opponents also supported Armenian independence, and they were shocked by
the Turkish attack on Armenians in 1915 that is today considered an act of
genocide. Senate members were concerned that the new Turkish Republic did
not recognize the validity of US passports issued to naturalized Turkish
American citizens. Significant opposition focused on the fact that Standard
Oil was in favor of the treaty's ratification. Big Oil, it was believed, would gain
concessions that would provide it with commercial benefits in Turkey.

Wise lobbied against passage of the treaty, and he contacted several key
Democratic senators, including Burton K. Wheeler of Montana (1882–1971),
Royal Copeland of New York (1868–1938), and Claude Swanson of Virginia
(1862–1939). Stephen urged Wheeler to "investigate the integrity of motives
behind the Lausanne Treaty . . . You should oppose ratification."

On January 18, 1927, the US Senate, in executive session, voted 50–34 in
favor of the treaty, but fell short of the necessary two-thirds majority. Wise
and the other treaty foes were pleased, but two years later the Senate approved
the Lausanne Treaty.[12]

Between 1927 and the outbreak of World War II in 1939, Turkey and the United States entered into several new agreements that met many of the objections that Wise and others had raised. Chief among the accords was the 1930 Treaty of Ankara that the Senate approved without debate.[13]

Wise received many honors, including a number of honorary degrees. In 1919, on the eve of the Paris Peace Conference, he was presented with the French Legion of Honor Medal for his efforts during World War I.[14] In 1933 Bates College in Maine awarded him an honorary doctorate, as did Roanoke College in Virginia a year later.[15] Following his visit to Roanoke, Wise continued his tour by speaking to audiences in small towns:

> Rabbi Stephen S. Wise has accepted an invitation to speak at the Bluefield, West Virginia Association of Retail Credit Men's annual dinner Thursday evening. Afterwards he will address the graduating class of Beaver High School. On Friday morning he will speak to students of Concord College, Athens, as the final lecture in a Lyceum course at that institution.[16]

In his book describing the collegial relationship between Stephen Wise and John Haynes Holmes, Carl Hermann Voss (1911–1995) chose a single eight-day period—November 20–28, 1927—to illustrate how Stephen pushed himself to meet a lengthy series of public commitments. Voss could have chosen almost any other week during Wise's life to make the same point. It is little wonder that the famed rabbi suffered several physical and emotional breakdowns during his career.

On Sunday morning, November 20, Wise conducted the weekly Free Synagogue service in Carnegie Hall before the usual large audience and discussed how to achieve a successful marriage and avoid divorce. That afternoon he traveled from Manhattan to Cranford, New Jersey, in Union County where he spoke to the town's Community Forum on "The Best and the Worst in American Life." In the evening Stephen was back in New York City inside Holmes's Community Church where he addressed the theme "Directions for American Life."

The next morning he met with Professor Salo W. Baron to discuss the rabbinic curriculum at the Jewish Institute of Religion. Later that day, Wise consulted with an engineer, Julius Fohs of Houston, Texas (1884–1965), about the possibility of discovering oil in Palestine. That evening, he spoke at a gala dinner at Manhattan's Savoy Plaza Hotel in support of the Social Service Division of the Free Synagogue, which was directed by Stephen's associate, Rabbi Sidney Goldstein.

On Tuesday, November 22, 1927, Wise met first with the Synagogue's women's group, then he officiated at a wedding, which was followed by lunch at the Harvard Club where he met with the executive vice president of the American Unitarian Association. That afternoon Stephen returned to his study on West 68th Street, and among Wise's visitors that day to discuss community issues was Janet Avery Dulles (1891–1969), the wife of John Foster Dulles. They were the parents of Cardinal Avery Dulles (1918–2008), a famous convert to Catholicism from his family's Presbyterian roots.

That evening, Stephen attended a dinner at the Yale Club hosted by Henry A. Atkinson (1877–1960) of the Committee on Religious Rights and Minorities, where special attention was given to the deteriorating situation of the Romanian Jewish community.

Wednesday morning Wise conferred with one of his closest colleagues in the American Zionist movement: Judge Julian Mack. In the afternoon Stephen went to the Bankers' Club in Manhattan where he met with the board of directors of the new Hebrew University in Jerusalem. That evening Stephen attended two dinners. The first was an event sponsored by the Church Peace Union at the Commodore Hotel, and the second dinner, hosted by the philanthropist Maurice Wertheimer (1886–1950), took place at the upscale Sherry's Restaurant in Manhattan where plans were discussed for the Jewish Agency in Palestine.

Thursday was Thanksgiving, and the two congregations, Wise's Free Synagogue and Holmes's Community Church, conducted their tenth-annual joint holiday service led by the rabbi and the minister. On Friday, November 25, Wise took a train to Jamestown, New York, to address a public meeting about Henry Ford and his anti-Semitic publication, the *Dearborn Independent*. That evening he boarded an overnight sleeper to Chicago, arriving in time to speak the next day to the Windy City's Culture Club on "The Best and Worst in American Life." On Sunday morning, Stephen exchanged pulpits with Rabbi Louis Mann (1890–1966) of Chicago. Mann delivered the Free Synagogue sermon in Carnegie Hall while Stephen spoke to thirty-five hundred people at Temple Sinai on "Do We Need a New Religion?"

That afternoon, still in Chicago at Temple Sinai, he addressed the congregation's forum audience. He focused on Ford's apology and retractions regarding Jews and Judaism. Then Wise was driven to suburban Wilmette that evening for yet another public lecture.

On Monday morning, November 28, he spoke to twelve hundred people at Northwestern University in Evanston on "The College Student in America." Wise attended a working luncheon at the Standard Club in downtown Chicago where he sought to raise funds for the JIR rabbinical school. That evening Stephen was back on a train headed for Milwaukee to participate in a debate on Zionism.[17]

There were three major crises during the 1920s that demanded Wise's

time, talent, and energy. The first was the 1926 labor strike at the garment factories in Passaic, New Jersey, and a year later he was involved in the celebrated
Sacco and Vanzetti anarchist case in Massachusetts. In 1928 Stephen inter-
vened during an ugly chapter in American history: a medieval blood libel incident in Massena, New York, a small town near the US-Canadian border.

In the mid-1920s, Passaic, New Jersey, located about sixteen miles from
Manhattan, was the site of several textile mills, including Botany Worsted
Mills and Fortstmann and Huffman Company. The owners of the clothing
factories opposed all attempts to organize their workers into a trade union.

In the autumn of 1924, Justine Waterman Wise was a senior at Barnard
College in New York City, and after graduation the following year she would
enter Yale Law School. She conducted a survey for the American Jewish
Congress to gather information about the lives of women workers who had
been hurt on the job. Justine was also interested in determining whether
women received appropriate financial compensation for their job-related
injuries.

To gain firsthand knowledge, Justine Wise and a friend, Bertha Paret, became employees in one of the Passaic textile factories. Emulating her father
and brother who six years earlier had worked anonymously in a Connecticut
shipyard, Wise's daughter, using only two-thirds of her name—"Justine
Waterman"—became a quilter in a cotton mill and received $18 a week (about
$240 today). A few months later Justine requested that the Central Employ-
ment Bureau of the textile mills move her to a woolen mill where she would
become a floor manager and earn $22 a week.

But her identity was revealed when the owners' well-developed spy system
noticed that Justine's hands were not callused enough for a factory worker's.[18]
Once Justine's famous last name became known, she was told to leave Passaic
at once. If she did not, Stephen Wise's daughter would be arrested. She bravely
continued working in the sweatshop while she gathered more information
about the poor working conditions in the Passaic mills.

Justine shared her experiences and data with her father and Holmes. She
cited the "starvation wages" and the embedded spy system that intimidated
workers. The mill owners had contempt for their workers calling them "a dull
herd of 'foreigners,' mere cogs in a profit-making machine with the result of a
ruthless and relentless system of exploitation." Wages were cut for the Passaic
factory workers, with many mothers compelled to work on the night shift
while husbands and fathers worked during the day.[19]

Wise and Holmes both injected themselves into the Passaic strike. The
Christian pastor addressed a cheering group of workers when he brought relief funds from his Community Church congregation to aid the strikers. The
police wanted to prevent Holmes's appearance, but the American Civil

Liberties Union, which Holmes helped establish in 1917, blocked a shutdown of the rally. The minister called his appearance with the strikers a "genuinely thrilling time."[20]

Wise offered his own support when he delivered a fiery sermon. He called the intransigent mill owners "breeders of communism and fomenters of revolt." A few Synagogue members resigned from the congregation, but one Free Synagogue member, Harry Myers of Passaic, the strikebound community, presented a check for $25,000 (about $333,000 today), fulfilling his building campaign pledge. Meyers was the first Jewish attorney to practice law in Passaic, and he was the president of a local mortgage company. Meyers told Wise that he disagreed with both the strikers and the sermon, but he still made a large contribution to Wise's synagogue.[21]

In January 1926, forty-five hundred workers went out on strike demanding better working conditions, the right to organize into a trade union, and increased wages. Wise, Holmes, and "Justine Waterman," then a Yale Law School student, all supported the strikers. While they backed the Passaic workers from New York City and New Haven, the on-the-ground labor organizer was Albert Weisbord (1900–1977). Weisbord received his undergraduate degree at City College of New York, where he was elected to the Phi Beta Kappa academic honorary society. In 1924 he graduated from Harvard Law School. Although he supported Senator Robert LaFollette, the Progressive Party's 1924 candidate for president, Weisbord became a communist the same year.

He was a superb speaker, and his radical political positions represented a distinct threat to the Passaic mill owners. They refused to negotiate with him, and the AFL leadership worried that they, too, would be tarred with the radical red brush. As a result, Weisbord was removed from the Passaic strike. Stephen admired Weisbord's firebrand organizing skills, but the rabbi thought he was ineffective, even naïve in his efforts in behalf of the strikers.[22]

Justine Wise's responses to the anti-Weisbord attacks delighted her father. He could not have said it better. She rallied the strikers with these words, and her picture in the New York newspapers pleased her father:

> You will hear much of the menace of the violence of the "Reds" or Bolshevism, but it is Forstmann and Huffman, the Botany and their kind, that constitute the gravest menace to the peace and lawfulness of Passaic and of our country. No outside agitator, however radical, can be as menacing to the life and ideals of America as the interests which invoke our flag solely to protect their profits.[23]

Wise assembled a four-person mediation committee that was acceptable to the striking workers, but the mill owners rejected his offer. The latter group termed the strike "a Communist demonstration, led by professional Communists . . . to give the textile workers a schooling in Revolution."[24] Besides Stephen, the committee included John Lovejoy Elliot (1868–1942), the leader of the Hudson Guild, a Manhattan community center; Paul Underwood Kellogg (1879–1958), the editor of the social work publication *Survey*; and the Episcopal priest and social activist John Howard Melish, rector of Brooklyn's Trinity Church. Wise was disappointed that recruiting a member of the Christian clergy was the most difficult task in forming his labor mediation panel.

Wise pressed William Green (1873–1952), the AFL's mild-mannered president, to become engaged in settling the bitter Passaic dispute. The strike dragged on for over a year, but after the cautious AFL leadership entered the fray, the owners gave in, the workers were permitted to organize, and the strikers were rehired. However, even in the midst of America's prosperity of the time, labor failed to win a wage increase. One result of the Passaic strike was the further radicalization of John Haynes Holmes, Stephen Wise, and "Justine Waterman."

It was no surprise that Wise and Holmes became involved with the famous Sacco and Vanzetti case. Both religious leaders saw the two murder trials in Massachusetts as an egregious example of anti-immigrant prejudice combined with a miscarriage of justice topped off with specific anti-Italian bigotry and prejudice.

Although much has been written about the controversy, a brief description of the events will illustrate why Wise, Holmes, and a host of religious leaders, intellectuals, and celebrities from all over the world injected themselves into the Sacco-Vanzetti affair. Among the many people supporting the innocence of the two men were John Dos Passos, Albert Einstein, Felix Frankfurter, Edna St. Vincent Millay (1892–1950), Katherine Anne Porter (1890–1980), George Bernard Shaw (1856–1950), Upton Sinclair, and H. G. Wells (1866–1946). The author Anatole France compared the trials in America to the anti-Semitic case of Alfred Dreyfus a quarter century earlier in France.

Nicola Sacco (1891–1927), a shoemaker, was born in Italy and came to the United States in 1908. Bartolommeo Vanzetti (1888–1927), a fisherman, left his native Italy for the United States also in 1908. It was the era of anarchism in both Europe and the United States. Luigi Galleani (1861–1931) was the leader of one group of Italian anarchists who used violent means to express their hatred for capitalism and the abuses that the despised system carried out against working men and women.

Two murders were committed in Braintree, Massachusetts, on April 15, 1920. The victims, both shot dead, were delivering the cash payroll of a local company. The fatal shootings took place a year after the bombing of US attorney general A. Mitchell Palmer's Washington, DC, home. Antianarchist emotions in America ran even higher after the Braintree murders.

Sacco and Vanzetti were charged with the crime. There were two well-publicized trials following by a special advisory review committee appointed by Massachusetts governor Alvan T. Fuller (1878–1958). A controversial judge, Webster Thayer (1857–1933), presided at both trials, and the defense attorneys and supporters of Sacco and Vanzetti accused him of anti-Italian prejudice and improper judicial conduct. The defendants were found guilty and in 1927 were sentenced to death.[25]

During the controversy, Wise delivered a Free Synagogue sermon titled "Law versus Justice in the Sacco-Vanzetti Case." Stephen also spoke about the case to students and faculty of the Yale Law School, where his daughter was a student. Holmes appealed to Fuller, but to no avail. After seven years of imprisonment and trials, the two men, judged innocent by much of the world, were executed in the electric chair on August 23, 1927.[26]

For Wise, the Sacco-Vanzetti case, the 1924 antievolution Scopes "monkey trial" in Tennessee, and Henry Ford's anti-Semitic publication, the *Dearborn Independent*, were proof that America was experiencing a turbulent, painful, and prejudice-filled period as the country moved from being a white Protestant agricultural nation to a multiethnic, multireligious, and multiracial industrial society with a growing, diverse population.

The case never disappeared from public view. In 1977 Massachusetts governor Michael Dukakis and the Democratic Party's presidential nominee in 1988, declared, "Any disgrace should be removed from their [Sacco and Vanzetti] names." But Dukakis did not grant a posthumous pardon, since that would have been a public admission that the two anarchists were, in fact, guilty of the murders.[27]

In September 1928 Wise became involved in an anti-Semitic incident that took place in Massena, New York, a small town of eighty-five hundred residents near the US-Canadian border. Massena's Jewish community of about a hundred people was shaken when it was accused of requiring the blood of a Christian child in the baking of the unleavened bread (matzo) that is eaten during the spring Passover festival: it was the obscene "blood libel" canard that has been used against Jews for centuries, including in the 1913 Mendel Beilis (1874–1934) trial in tsarist Russia. For Wise, it was shocking that the infamous charge would be hurled at Jews in the United States.[28]

On September 22, 1928, two days before the Day of Atonement—Yom Kippur—a four-year-old Christian girl, Barbara Griffiths, wandered off into a wooded area close to her home in Massena. When she did not return to her parents that evening, the Griffiths family became alarmed and asked the authorities to find her. It was reported later that the Massena police force included Ku Klux Klan members who assumed "the Jews" had kidnapped young Barbara as part of their religious ritual.

They gained that false belief from Albert Comnas, an immigrant from Salonika, Greece, who owned a café in Massena.[29] When the search group and the local police took a "break" at the coffee shop, Comnas suggested that "the Jews" had abducted the four-year-old girl for a human sacrifice rite in advance of the upcoming Jewish holiday. That the blood libel is linked to Passover and not Yom Kippur made little difference to Comnas or the police. The anti-Semitic charge is literally an old story. Geoffrey Chaucer (1343–1400), author of the *Canterbury Tales*, accused the "cursed Jewes" of infanticide in "The Prioress's Tale."

The ugly rumor quickly spread and soon involved the New York State Police. One of the troopers, Corporal Harry M. McCann, of Troop B, believed Comnas's accusation. He visited the home of Morris Goldberg, a member of the Massena Jewish community, to gather information about the alleged Jewish religious practice.

McCann asked Goldberg whether Jews used the blood of a Christian child for ritual purposes. Goldberg replied he was unfamiliar with such a ritual and doubted it took place in America. He suggested McCann check with the rabbi of Massena's Adath Israel congregation for more extensive and accurate information.

The state police officer then ordered Rabbi Berel Brennglass (1876–1966) to appear at police headquarters for questioning. Brennglass had come to Massena in 1918 and served his congregation until 1941. The rabbi did as he was requested, and once he arrived at the headquarters late that Saturday afternoon, he sharply criticized McCann, saying it was "shameful" for even asking "such a foolish and ridiculous question." For the next hour Brennglass denounced the odious blood-libel slander charge even as an angry crowd milled about outside the police facility.

The next afternoon, around 3 p.m. and a few hours before the start of Yom Kippur, the missing child was found alive and well, and was returned to her parents. Unfortunately, Barbara Griffiths's safe homecoming did not end the matter. It was claimed "the Jews" returned young Barbara from her "captivity" only because Rabbi Brennglass became frightened under questioning. In reality, the rabbi gave a stern historical lesson to the police about the total falsity of the blood libel.

Nonetheless, Massena's mayor, W. Gilbert Hawes, called for a boycott of the Jewish stores and businesses in town. On September 25, three days after the girl's disappearance and return, Jacob Shulkin (1881–1964), a prominent member of the local Jewish community, sent a letter to Wise in New York City asking for help in quelling the ugly outburst of raw anti-Semitism.

Stephen immediately entered the controversy by writing Shulkin,

I cannot tell you how shocked and pained I am by the story . . . of even the faintest intimations of a rumor of ritual murder. . . . This thing must be cleared up and cleared up immediately and fully. . . . We shall not rest content until there be the most ample and unequivocal apology.[30]

The same day Wise wrote to Hawes and pointed out

what a hideous thing it is that this ancient and unspeakable libel should be resurrected in our country, with all the incalculable damage that it might do . . . No intelligent, decent person has ever given credence to this charge which has been exposed whenever made . . . and laid to rest by the heads of the Christian Churches. . . . I should be very glad . . . to have a full statement from you . . . and also word with respect to the course that you intend to pursue.[31]

Wise contacted New York governor Al Smith, who was engaged in his presidential campaign against Herbert Hoover. Stephen also wrote to Major John A. Warner (1886–1963), the state police commander, a Harvard graduate and an accomplished concert pianist. Wise was irate:

I take it for granted that you will send for the trooper [McCann], secure the fullest statement from him . . . and see to it that such action follow as will make clear to the citizenship of Massena that this awful charge is completely and contritely withdrawn as far as [McCann] is concerned.[32]

Louis Marshall, the president of the American Jewish Committee, also pressed for a full and speedy apology from the mayor and the state trooper. Governor Smith was appalled that the ancient blood-libel canard existed in his state, but he could only rebuke the mayor. However, as governor, he demanded that McCann be disciplined and punished for his anti-Jewish actions. The trooper was

indefinitely suspended and reprimanded for the part he played in the questioning of Rabbi Bcrel Brennglass in Massena, NY, on September 22. McCann was suspended "for gross lack of discretion in the exercise of his duties and for conduct unbecoming an officer."[33]

Wise and Smith later held a joint news conference in Albany in which the governor condemned bigotry and officially apologized to the Massena Jewish community. Wise closed the press conference with his usual elegant language. The Massena incident was a bitter reminder that it was necessary for all Americans to banish religious intolerance and bigotry and all their hateful consequences and to be firm and resolute against everything that savors of injustice between faith and faith, people and people.[34]

At first, Mayor Hawes was reluctant to issue a public apology for his own and the town's anti-Semitic actions, but the national Republican establishment pushed him to do just that. He expressed his regrets "clearly and unequivocally" in a letter to Wise that Stephen released to the press.[35]

A Jewish resident of Massena, Harry Clopman (1914–2013), who was fourteen years old in 1928, said the pressure on Hawes was enormous and the mayor finally issued a full public apology. In 2012, Clopman, who was born in Massena and owned a furniture and appliance store in the town, said, "That man was never the same after that."[36]

In a letter to George Gordon Battle (1868–1949), Wise thanked the prominent New York attorney for his "fine and generous [legal] service . . . by taking so helpful a part at the hearing" dealing with the Massena anti-Semitic episode.[37]

As for the missing girl, Barbara Griffiths married and had three children, six grandchildren, and one great-grandchild. In October 2012, at age eighty-eight, she told a reporter, "I don't remember anything directly." During the same month, the Massena Public Library sponsored a public discussion of the blood-libel incident.[38]

Wise was proud of his many battles against all forms of anti-Semitism, but in later years he rarely if ever publicly referred to the Massena events of 1928. Nor did the ugly response to the little girl's disappearance shake Stephen's oft-proclaimed bedrock conviction that his beloved America was truly "different" from the anti-Jewish toxicity and poisons of Europe. And it was in Europe, not the United States, that Wise soon faced his greatest challenges: the onslaught of Nazism that culminated in the Holocaust.

Chapter 19

For Zion's Sake I Will Not Hold My Peace, and for Jerusalem's Sake I Will Not Rest

Following the end of World War I in 1918, the Zionist movement in the United States grew rapidly in both membership and influence. The collapse of Ottoman Turkish rule in Palestine, the issuance of the Balfour Declaration in London, and the international San Remo, Italy, conference in April 1920 that committed Great Britain to work for "the establishment in Palestine of a national home for the Jewish people" provided hope for Wise, Brandeis, and many other Jewish leaders. After centuries of corrupt and inefficient Ottoman control, they looked forward to the potential benefits and opportunities of the British Mandate in the Holy Land.

Two weeks after the conclusion of the San Remo conference, the Zionist Organization of America held its national convention in New York City, which featured a huge parade on Fifth Avenue that drew fifty thousand spectators and a gala evening session at the Metropolitan Opera House that reflected the optimistic spirit in the aftermath of the "war to end all wars." The meeting attracted eleven hundred delegates, including several prominent Orthodox rabbis as well as Supreme Court justice Louis Brandeis, Stephen Wise, and Abba Hillel Silver, a twenty-seven-year-old Reform rabbi from Cleveland whose fiery orations in English and Yiddish captivated his enthusiastic audiences.

The NYC gathering was a prelude to the 1921 World Zionist Congress in Karlovy Vary, the Czech name for the German Carlsbad, located in the newly created republic of Czechoslovakia. The United States sent thirty-nine delegates to that meeting, the largest American delegation up to that time. The congress urged the immediate opening of Palestine by the British government to Jewish immigration and the major improvement of public utilities, sanitation, transportation, health services, and a host of other items aimed at strengthening the Yishuv, the Hebrew term for the growing Jewish population in the Holy Land. In 1920 the Yishuv numbered sixty thousand; in 1948 it was more than six hundred thousand. A newspaper reporter was impressed with the New York City meeting:

On the dais, where Dr. Stephen S. Wise presided, flanked by Julius Simon [1875–1969], the Zionist delegate from London; Justice Louis D. Brandeis, Dr. Harry Friedenwald [1864–1950] and other officials of the Zionist organization, [were] Rabbi [J. D.] Jurman of [Waterbury] Connecticut [1869–1927] . . . [and other] white bearded rabbis, in their black Sabbath clothes and their skull caps. Their turn came to speak. Was it criticism? These uncompromising Orthodox rabbis pleaded rather for the mutual co-operation between the old and the new generations in the task at hand, acknowledging in full the latter's right to a strong voice in the affairs of the restored Holy Land.[1]

In the decades after World War I, Wise, an acknowledged leader of the Zionist movement, "presided" over and frequently dominated many such meetings. He used his extraordinary talents to advance the cause of establishing a Jewish state in the Middle East, yet it would be a mistake to view those efforts as either easy or unchallenged. Like most revolutionary or national liberation movements, Zionism, especially in the 1920s and 1930s, was filled with internecine bitterness, fierce personality clashes, and profound policy differences.

Because of his high-profile personality and imperious style, Wise was often the center of numerous controversies and battles; he was never exempt from attack, criticism, ridicule, or even hatred from some of his colleagues. But many other Zionist leaders received the same treatment, including Brandeis, Weizmann, Vladimir Jabotinsky (1880–1940), David Ben-Gurion, Menachem Begin (1913–1992), and Golda Meir (1898–1978).

There are several reasons why the movement in the three decades between 1918 and 1948 (the year that the state of Israel achieved its independence) had internal dissension, angry resignations of major leaders, votes of no confidence, convention floor fights over personalities and policies, and many other negative events. The Jewish national liberation movement, rooted and anchored in the ancient teachings and beliefs of Judaism, was a late-nineteenth-century arrival on a global stage already filled with a large number of other nationalisms all vying for media attention, increased funds, popular support, and hopefully political success.

But modern Zionism beginning with Theodor Herzl in the mid-1890s was compelled to move quickly to achieve its goals in the face of virulent anti-Semitism in many countries, two global wars, Nazism, fascism, communism, the Great Depression, the post–World War I Arab Awakening, and the mass murder of six million Jews during the Holocaust.

The window of possible peace between Jews and Arabs that was opened briefly with the 1919 Faisal-Weizmann agreement was quickly slammed shut. While Wise and other Zionist leaders focused most of their attention on anti-Semitism in Europe, hatred of Jews and Judaism also existed within Muslim countries. Despite the state of Israel's current peace treaties with Egypt and Jordan, there is still no permanent peace in the region.

In addition, the high hopes of the 1917–1920 period for fair and sympathetic British rule in Palestine were dashed as London pursued the usual tactics of a colonial power: divide and conquer the subject peoples. Britain made conflicting promises to Jews and Arabs, attempted to repress or control the leadership of both peoples, and even encouraged tension and friction between Jews and Arabs. Finally, in the face of two seemingly irreconcilable forces and claims, the British abdicated responsibility and in May 1948 gave up its Palestine Mandate. They left the two peoples to fight one another in a series of bloody and costly wars.

But for Wise, there were also adversaries inside the Zionist movement as well as among British government leaders. That is because Zionism from its very outset was extraordinarily diverse. It has never been monolithic, nor have its leaders marched in a lock step of uniformity. Rather, Zionism is a complex national liberation movement that contains a wide range of political, religious, social, economic, and cultural ideas and policies. Zionism is akin to the biblical Jewish "tent of meeting" that has ample room under its roof for many different conflicting views.

Like other national movements, Zionism cannot be reduced to a mere slogan or catchphrase. Successful national movements—and Zionism is one of them because it succeeded in creating the modern state of Israel—are often remembered by later generations in glowing terms, as if they were always destined and assured of victory. But history does not operate in an unimpeded positive line, nor do leaders of such efforts always work together as dedicated comrades and friends, an integrated team filled with unbounded mutual respect for one another.

The eighteenth-century American colonists' struggle to break free from British royal control is rife with personal hatreds and significant policy and philosophical differences. The signers of the Declaration of Independence in 1776 were divided on several key issues, most notably the continuation of human slavery in the new nation. John Adams (1735–1826) and Thomas Jefferson (1743–1826), the second and third US presidents, were competitors, rivals, and antagonists. As every American schoolchild knows, Adams and Jefferson both died on the same day, July 4, 1826, exactly fifty years after the Declaration of Independence was ratified in Philadelphia. Indeed, the last words Adams uttered were, "Thomas Jefferson survives." Adams in Massachusetts could not have known that, in reality, Jefferson had died a few hours earlier in Virginia.

Alexander Hamilton (1755–1804), the first secretary of the treasury, and Aaron Burr (1756–1826), America's third vice president, loathed one another, and their animosity resulted in an 1804 pistol duel in Weehawken, New Jersey, that resulted in Hamilton's death. It is often forgotten that in 1786 Jefferson and Patrick Henry (1736–1799) were bitter foes in their home state when they opposed one another regarding the legislature's historic adoption of Jefferson's Virginia Statute for Religious Freedom.[2]

But the profound differences among the pioneering Zionist leaders represented more than the usual divisions that always exist among talented and ambitious leaders of a national movement. For European Zionists like Chaim Weizmann, the hope of an independent Jewish state was more than a lofty goal. They perceived it as a personal life-or-death cause. Theodor Herzl, the sophisticated, charismatic Viennese journalist and playwright, was prescient in recognizing the precariousness of Jewish physical existence in Europe. He became disillusioned with the anti-Semitic "clamor against the Jews" and concluded, "We shall not be left in peace." Tragically, he was correct when he wrote his 1896 analysis of the grim situation, *Der Judenstaat* or *The Jewish State*.[3]

Weizmann and other European Jews saw Zionism as their own means of liberation and deliverance—physically, psychologically, nationally, spiritually, and culturally—from a European continent that over the centuries had become saturated with hatred of Jews and Judaism. Zionism was their collective life preserver, their dream of salvation in a sea of bigotry and violence, and they staked their lives on the success of their monumental efforts to end eighteen hundred years of Jewish homelessness, powerlessness, and dispersion. Less than thirty years after Herzl's death, the Nazis came to power in Germany and ultimately the Holocaust occurred. Hitler made Zionism an imperative for a people's survival.

It was different in the United States, where support for Zionism before 1933 was often expressed within the American context and experience. America was a land where Jews felt more at home and secure than in any other country of the world. American Zionists, including Stephen Wise, Richard Gottheil, Louis Brandeis, Julian Mack, Felix Frankfurter, Horace Kallen, and Abba Hillel Silver, albeit different from one another in their personalities, fervor, and commitments, did not feel or believe their own existence as human beings and as Jews ultimately depended upon the success of their movement.

Brandeis, as noted in an earlier chapter, linked his practical Zionism with pragmatic Americanism. The Supreme Court justice had no intention of physically moving to Palestine, nor did most of the other American Zionist leaders.

But there was another basic reason for the differences between the two brands of Zionism: American and European. Weizmann and many of his allies grew up in pre–World War I Eastern Europe, a region where millions of

Jews lived. The case of Poland's Jewish population is similar to other countries in the region. Most Jews perceived themselves not as "Polish Jews," but rather as "Jews living in Poland." Their separate language (Yiddish), religion, history, culture, music, education, literature, food, and dress all provided the inner sources of "national" strength required to endure and survive within hostile societies.

In contrast, the most important American Zionists before World War II were Brandeis and Wise, and neither man was fluent in Yiddish. Neither the Wise or Brandeis family was part of the huge Eastern European Jewish immigration to the United States that took place between 1881 and 1924. For some leaders in Europe, their full-time occupation, their primary profession, was the Zionist movement. An exception was Weizmann, a chemist, who taught at the University of Manchester for many years while devoting much of his time to the Zionist cause. But the major American leaders of the movement had their own separate day jobs.

Brandeis served as a member of the US Supreme Court. Wise led the Free Synagogue, the Jewish Institute of Religion, and the American Jewish Congress. Silver was the rabbi of a large Cleveland congregation, Mack was a federal judge in Chicago, Frankfurter was a Harvard Law School faculty member and a well-known US government attorney, and Kallen and Richard Gottheil were university professors.

The two Zionist blocs, European and American, also had differing views on the impact of the Balfour Declaration. Once Britain issued the declaration with the support of President Wilson, Brandeis assumed—falsely as it turned out—that the political battle to create a Jewish state had been won. The justice believed that Zionism's main task after 1917 was a practical one: the step-by-step, systematic, businesslike development of an effective infrastructure in Jewish Palestine—that is, nation building: agriculture, industry, governance, health, water, electricity, commerce, education, housing, transportation, and communication.

Weizmann rejected the Brandeisian view. He stressed that the Balfour Declaration for which he labored so long was only the beginning of the political campaign needed to achieve Zionist goals. He, too, pressed for a step-by-step campaign, but one different from Brandeis and his American followers, including Wise. Weizmann stated,

> A state cannot be created by decree, but by the forces of a people and in the course of generations. Even if all the governments of the world gave us a country, it would only be a gift of words. But if the Jewish people will go build Palestine, the Jewish State will become a reality—a fact.[4]

Brandeis and Weizmann met one another for the first time in London in 1919. Brandeis visited Palestine later during the same trip, where he was both impressed and depressed. He was moved by the exuberant spirit of the Zionist *halutzim* (pioneers) who were engaged in agricultural and environmental reclamation work and developing the first kibbutzim (collective communities) and *moshavim* (cooperative villages). But Brandeis was dismayed by the presence of physical diseases, including malaria, and the absence of adequate financial oversight within the Zionist movement both in Palestine and Europe. But Weizmann and his associates rejected Brandeis's emphasis on "technical" issues and fiscal orthodoxy. A major clash between the two Zionist leaders was inevitable and, in fact, dominated the Zionist Organization of America meeting in Cleveland in June 1921.

Weizmann used a pithy statement to define his differences with Brandeis: "There is no bridge between Pinsk [a Belarus city near the village of Motol, his birthplace] and Washington [Brandeis's]."[5] Urofsky described the distinctions:

The Americanized leadership [Brandeis-Wise-Mack] lacked "yiddishkeit," a true feeling for things Jewish. . . . They failed to see the great spiritual and emotional aspects of Zionism, and instead reduced the movement for restoration to a passionless abstraction, a charity.[6]

In one of his speeches, Wise expressed the differences between American and European Zionists in the simplest terms:

The European and American points of view, as far as they are two, are not to be merged into one point of view. . . . If there is a difference, and I deny there is a difference, . . . it lies in this: Some of our brothers, just as well-meaning, just as devoted as we are . . . are for Zionism first and for Zion second. We Americans are for Zion first, and for Zionism second. In other words, not Zion for the sake of Zionism, but Zionism for the sake of Zion.[7]

Stephen wanted first to secure a safe haven, a "national home," a "commonwealth" for endangered Jews—Zion—and only then could Zionism come to full flower as a new, dynamic component of Jewish civilization. First, a "Jewish state" à la Herzl, then the various political parties, policies, programs, procedures, platforms, and plans could emerge after Zion was restored, not the other way around.

Stephen Wise perceived the Jewish national liberation movement and the emergence of a Jewish state to be the self-fulfillment of an entire people. Without Zionism, Jews remained incomplete and unable to reach their full collective human potential. That goal could only be achieved by a physical flesh-and-blood reunion, a national rootedness with the land of Israel, and not merely a spiritual or cultural return to the biblical homeland. Wise drew upon the writings of his Ph.D. thesis subject, Solomon ibn Gabirol. For Stephen, a restored Zion, a Jewish state, was necessary for the Jewish people to fully "enjoy the bliss to which ibn Gabirol points" for an individual.

Wise and his idol, Brandeis, were angered by the disdain that Weizmann and others in Europe exhibited toward them and their US colleagues. Wise complained that Continental leaders saw America primarily as a source of constant cash for the Zionist movement, a rich but immature Jewish community that had little or no role to play in the great decisions that needed to be made.

That is why the Brandeis followers, including Wise, broke with the Europeans and their American disciples at the tumultuous Cleveland convention that Chaim Weizmann attended as an "observer." It was a decisive clash between him and Brandeis for leadership and the proverbial hearts and minds of the two hundred thousand American Zionists.

Weizmann was hardly a neutral onlooker in Cleveland as he pressed for a special Zionist Foundation Fund, Keren Hayesod, that would hopefully collect $25 million by 1925. The fund was to be a combination of personal gifts and financial investments. Such a commingling of vitally needed funds was an anathema to the practical fiscal beliefs of Brandeis. The Supreme Court justice saw Weizmann's Keren Hayesod plans as irresponsible and even the work of a "trickster."[8]

But Brandeis also opposed Weizmann's personal leadership style, in addition to his lack of organizational skills. The floor fight on the Keren Hayesod issue turned into a vote of confidence on Brandeis's concept of Zionism and his leadership. The European Zionists, products of highly ideological societies, represented the various sociopolitical aspects of the movement: socialist, secular, religious, labor, and capitalism—all filled with emotional imperatives and a sense of urgency. They heeded the words that British prime minister David Lloyd George told the Zionist representatives at the Paris Peace Conference:

You have to take your chance now, because the political world is in the state of the Baltic Sea before it freezes. As soon as it is frozen, nothing can be moved, and one has to wait a long time until a second opportunity arises.[9]

However, despite the urgency described by Lloyd George, in Cleveland Brandeis and his American followers, including Wise, stressed systematic "pragmatism," organizational efficiency, and transparency in budget matters, and they expressed less concern about party platforms and the purity of various Zionist ideologies. Brandeis thought the Balfour Declaration had won

Zionism's political battle. All that was required was the physical development of Palestine.

Weizmann felt differently, asserting that much more political and practical work was needed to fulfill the Zionist goals. He arrived in the United States in April 1921 and received a tumultuous welcome from American Jews. In the run-up to the June Zionist Organization of America meeting in Cleveland, the charismatic chemist and Zionist leader attacked Brandeis's lack of emotional connection to millions of Jews in Europe. Weizmann exuded Yiddishkeit to his very fingertips, while Brandeis lacked such a link with the masses of Jews who daily faced severe anti-Semitism in many areas of Europe and fervently prayed for the establishment of a Jewish commonwealth in Palestine.

Weizmann offered a passionate, "Pinsk" form of Zionism while Brandeis offered a businesslike, "Washington" version of the movement.[10] It was a false choice because the Zionist movement needed both "Pinsk," the emotional driving force of highly dedicated men and women, as well as "Washington," a systematic effort that required transparent fiscal policies and specific pragmatic programs such as eradicating malaria in the Holy Land. Even though Wise attempted to be a mediator, a peacemaker between Weizmann and Brandeis, he was unsuccessful.

The critical issue in Cleveland that focused on the creation of the Keren Hayesod fund in America became a vote of confidence in Brandeis's leadership. The vote, 153–71 in favor of Weizmann's proposal, marked the end of the Brandeis era of US Zionism that began in 1914. The rupture revealed the fissures, ire, personal animosities, and mutual suspicion that separated the Americans and Europeans.[11]

After the vote, Mack, the president of the Zionist Organization of America, addressed the convention and sadly announced that thirty-seven members of the ZOA Executive Committee resigned en masse. As their names were read out loud—one by one—it seemed to be the death knell of American Zionism. Some of the delegates wept openly as Mack spoke.[12] Following the rupture in Cleveland, Louis Lipsky, a Weizmann disciple, became the functional leader of American Zionists and served as the ZOA president between 1922 and 1930.[13]

Those leaving with Brandeis included Wise, Mack, Silver, Frankfurter, Mary Fels (1863–1953), Kallen, Max Heller, and Nathan Straus. As part of its coverage of Brandeis's seventy-fifth birthday ten years later, the Jewish Telegraphic Agency retold the story of the Cleveland schism.[14]

Although Wise departed from the Weizmann-dominated movement in 1921, Stephen, like Brandeis, did not leave Zionism. The rabbi continued to work with those who had gained control of the American organization. But he believed that Lipsky lacked administrative competence, and Stephen was distrustful of Weizmann's admiration for all things British.

However, Wise maintained his relationship with the man who later became Israel's first president. At the same time, "Dr. Wise's" stature grew, and in time he became an iconic hero for millions of Eastern European Jews. Stephen was a link between the two competing Zionist groups of Pinsk and Washington. One Weizmann supporter told Stephen,

> I want you to know that even in the time we voted down your motion, personally we admired and loved you as we always have.[15]

Four years after the traumatic Cleveland debacle, Wise returned in triumph to Zionism, his lodestar. On April 2, 1925, Stephen addressed a special ZOA meeting in the Metropolitan Opera House that marked the opening of the Hebrew University in Jerusalem.

Wise started his remarks that evening in the New York City opera house with these words: "Mr. Chairman and fellow Zionists." The audience quickly erupted into cheers and applause and Stephen, the prodigal son, received a standing ovation.

> Not one of us . . . ever stepped out of the ranks of Zionism. We stood outside while other men [Lipsky and his associates] took up the burden. . . . The business of every Zionist in America is to take his place once again . . . and . . . give their complete and unequivocal support to every agency and instrumentality of our Zionist movement, remembering the critical hour has come. . . . We who for too long were among the builders may not stand outside the gates, but must return as I have returned tonight within the gates, and become a soldier in the arms of our common cause.[16]

Wise had "come home."

Following his Cleveland victory over Brandeis, Weizmann moved to increase the leadership ranks of the Jewish Agency, the internationally recognized organization that supported the Yishuv. Weizmann, a shrewd and talented diplomat, wanted to enlist prominent Jews, known as "non-Zionists," who did not share the ideology but nonetheless were committed to strengthening the Jewish national endeavor in British Mandate Palestine. One of Weizmann's major goals was the recruitment of American Jewish Committee president Louis Marshall, Felix Warburg, and other officers and members of the officially non-Zionist AJC.

Weizmann began his campaign on February 17, 1924, with a large dinner at the fashionable Hotel Astor in Manhattan. At age fifty he was well prepared for the task of attracting wealthy Jews to work for the restoration of a Jewish commonwealth in the land of Israel. Weizmann earned a Ph.D. in chemistry from the Swiss University of Fribourg, and after moving to Britain he had taken on the style, dress, and mannerisms of upper-class England.

Weizmann was an imposing figure, with a large, bald head, a trimmed goatee, well-tailored suits, a top hat, and a walking stick. In some ways he physically resembled Vladimir Lenin, but, of course, the two men had completely different political views. A British diplomat once said that Chaim Weizmann could "charm a bird down from a tree."

Marshall, the chair of the special dinner meeting, told his fellow non-Zionists that the Balfour Declaration and the British Mandate meant that "we have no right to be different [from the Zionists in the building of Jewish Palestine]. . . . Indifference can do us a thousand times more than harm than all the Ku Klux Klans and Henry Fords."[17]

Weizmann's carefully nuanced response to Marshall was an attempt to assuage any fears about the alleged parochialism and narrow "nationalism" of the world Zionist movement: "[We] will create a center of Jewish learning and Jewish culture in a country where our sacred traditions still exist and continue to exist." He stressed economic and cultural development in Palestine and assured his affluent audience that "new visions and new ideas may come forth once more from Palestine, and the word of God from Jerusalem"—a carefully crafted paraphrase of a traditional synagogue prayer, "For out of Zion shall go forth the Torah and the word of God from Jerusalem."[18]

The event was a love fest between the wealthy German American Jews in the audience and the brilliant, elegant, Eastern European Zionist leader. It still took five additional years of hard work on Weizmann's part, but in 1929 at a Zionist Congress in Zurich he succeeded in his campaign. He signed an agreement of cooperation, a "pact of glory," with Marshall that provided a 50 percent leadership role within the Jewish Agency for the once hated "non-Zionists." It was the American Jewish leader's last official act before he unexpectedly died at the Zurich meeting.[19]

Not surprisingly, Stephen Wise was opposed to the entire plan of enlarging the Jewish Agency's membership to include "non-Zionists." He was especially irate by Weizmann's plan to grant so much control of the agency to Marshall and others. He wrote that such a scheme

> meant a serious compromise with the basic principles of Zionism. A philanthropic, economic, cultural or spiritual interest in Palestine was laudable and helpful. But it was not Zionism. . . . Against those tendencies and the personalities who embodied them, I placed myself in resolute opposition.[20]

Wise was also angered that two of his longtime adversaries—Marshall and Weizmann—had joined forces. Stephen's ire went to extremes. In 1926 he declared, "[I] would give one thousand Warburgs for one Bialik. Warburg gives out of his surplus, while Bialik gives out of his soul." Hayim Nachman Bialik

(1873–1934) has been called the "poet laureate" of modern Hebrew, and his writings became part of the basic Israeli and Jewish literary canon.[21]

Wise attended the 1927 World Zionist Congress in Vienna and soon discovered tension inside and outside the meeting hall. Anti-Semitic gangs roamed the streets of the Austrian capital shouting "Juden raus!" (Jews get out!), and delegates needed armed police protection when they traveled to and from their hotels to attend the congress sessions.

Inside the hall, Wise was furious over Weizmann's timidity in criticizing Great Britain's restrictions on the Yishuv and the infusion of non-Zionists into Jewish Agency leadership positions. Stephen demanded strong political action against the British government, but an angry Weizmann rejected Wise's criticism. The delegates faced another vote of confidence regarding Weizmann's leadership, and the London-based Zionist leader won the vote as he had done earlier in Cleveland. Lipsky and other Americans backed Weizmann, and an incensed Wise resigned his important Political Committee chairmanship. Stephen quickly left Vienna and returned to New York City.[22]

As the 1920s ended, Wise remained a vocal opponent of what he considered Weizmann's weakness and passivity toward Britain. The Zionist movement and the Yishuv careened from crisis to crisis: anti-Jewish Arab riots in 1929 and 1936 in Palestine, a 1930 British "White Paper" that restricted Jewish immigration and land purchases, and other setbacks. Wise intensified his public criticism of Weizmann in 1930 by writing a book with Jacob de Haas, *The Great Betrayal*, that was critical of Britain's polices in Palestine.

At the same time, Stephen continued to consult with his mentor, Brandeis. But after the 1921 defeat in Cleveland, the justice never again assumed personal direction of American Zionism. Nor could Lipsky or Emanuel Neumann achieve Brandeis's public stature. In his autobiography, Wise paid tribute to the modern "Isaiah":

Our guiding spirit and our constant and unfailing counselor . . . He was our leader in the most critical years of American Jewish history . . . when America had become supremely important in the leadership of world affairs. . . . No one could have known Brandeis without recognizing that he was touched by the quality or genius of prophecy.[23]

The first three months of 1933 were a momentous time for Wise: the Nazis led by Adolf Hitler came to power in Germany on January 30, and Franklin Roosevelt was sworn in as the US president on March 4. It was not long before Wise and the entire world recognized that the two men, so different in background and policies, would dominate the global stage as inevitable and implacable enemies. In a quirk of history, Roosevelt and Hitler were both still leading their nations when they died a dozen years later less than three weeks apart. The American leader suffered a fatal cerebral hemorrhage in Warm Springs, Georgia, on April 12, 1945, and the Nazi Fuhrer committed suicide in his underground Berlin bunker on April 30.

Those turbulent twelve years presented Stephen with the greatest challenges, the climax of his entire career. In 1936 at age sixty-two he wrote a friend,

> I confess that for the first time in my life I shrink from what lies before me—U.P.A. [United Palestine Appeal], Z.O.A. [Zionist Organization of America], [American Jewish] Congress, [Free] Synagogue, [Jewish] Institute [of Religion].[24]

But Stephen could not and did not "shrink" from his duties and responsibilities. Indeed, he devoted the last twenty years of his life to meet his greatest challenges.

Chapter 20

The Historic Encounter Begins
between the President and the Rabbi

Everything that Wise had done during the first sixty years of his life was preparation for his historic encounters with Franklin Roosevelt between 1933 and
1945, the years of the Great Depression, the New Deal, World War II, the
Holocaust, and the final push for a Jewish state in the Middle East. Whether
fair or not, any judgment of "Rabbi USA" must ultimately focus on his personal relationship with the thirty-second American president and their thirteen face-to-face meetings.

Wise and Roosevelt were both golden princes of their families who were
doted over by strong mothers. Sara Delano Roosevelt (1854–1941) was a major
influence in Franklin's life, even surpassing that of his wife, Eleanor, who was
Theodore Roosevelt's niece and FDR's distant cousin. Even though Sara opposed her son's marriage, it took place in New York City on March 17, 1905.
Because Eleanor was an orphan, TR "gave away" the bride, who detested her
mother-in-law's overbearing and controlling behavior. Sara cast a constant
shadow over both Eleanor and Franklin until her death.

Sabine Fischer Wise, the haughty daughter of a Hungarian Jewish baron,
provided Stephen with the aristocratic bearing and mien that was a central
feature of Wise's public persona. The self-doubt that Stephen suffered as a
youngster was offset by his mother's wealthy family background and her regal
style. As a result, Sabine's son was never destined to be an "ordinary" rabbi.

James Roosevelt, FDR's father, died when the future president was eighteen, and Stephen was twenty-two when he lost his father. Because Sara was a
widow for forty-one years and Sabine for twenty-one years, the two women
remained major influences in their sons' lives.

FDR graduated from Harvard College in 1903, attended Columbia University's law school, and passed the New York Bar exam in 1907. Wise's undergraduate and Ph.D. degrees were also from Columbia. Both Roosevelt and
Wise would today be called alpha males; they were handsome and charismatic
leaders, physically active and sexually attractive, superb orators, fellow New

Yorkers, and highly ambitious. Their talented wives, Eleanor and Louise, although products of the repressive Victorian Age, were able to establish their own international reputations that featured dedicated public service. Eleanor and Louise also shared something else: Franklin and Stephen were both womanizers.

Sara and Sabine lived long enough to see their beloved sons achieve extraordinary leadership positions: at his mother's death at age eighty-seven, Franklin had been elected US president for the third time. When Sabine died at seventy-nine, Stephen was emerging as a global Jewish leader and a significant force in American politics. In addition, her son was a friend of President Wilson and Supreme Court justice Brandeis.

The complex and ambivalent Wise-Roosevelt relationship began on September 8, 1914, when Wise learned that the thirty-two-year-old assistant secretary of the navy with a celebrated last name residing in Hyde Park, New York, in Dutchess County was planning to run for the US Senate. Wise, sensing something promising in the would-be candidate, wrote an encouraging letter to Franklin D. Roosevelt:

> I want you to know how glad I am that you have decided to present your name at the primaries in connection with the United States Senateship. Nothing could be better for the Administration of the Democratic Party that you should be elected. . . . The Party needs a clear-minded, high-hearted genuinely democratic leader such as you are, in the Senate, and I shall rejoice to do all I can on your behalf.[1]

Wise may have been fulsome in his praise of Roosevelt, but FDR was already a known quantity and a rising Democratic star. Four years earlier in 1910, at age twenty-eight, Roosevelt eked out a narrow win (15,708–14,568) over John F. Schlosser (1848–1916), the Republican incumbent, for a New York State Senate seat representing Dutchess County.

FDR's salary as an elected official was $1,500 (about $36,600 today), and most members of the state legislature viewed their elective office as a part-time position. As a result, they spent little time in Albany, the state capital. However, young Roosevelt promised his constituents he would devote 100 percent of his time serving as their state senator, and he was reelected two years later.[2]

Early in his administration, Woodrow Wilson recognized the potential political significance of an up-and-coming Democrat named Roosevelt, and in 1913 the president appointed FDR as assistant secretary of the navy. A year later, the scion of the famous family sought his party's US Senate nomination in New York. Despite support from Wise and other Progressives, FDR failed to win the primary.

James Gerard (1867–1951), who returned from his ambassadorial post in Berlin to run for office, easily defeated FDR by a two-to-one margin (138,815–63,879), but Gerard lost the general election to Republican James W. Wadsworth (1877–1952). It was the first time US senators were chosen by direct popular voting. The 1914 primary was Roosevelt's sole election defeat, aside from being the vice presidential nominee on the losing national Democratic ticket in 1920.[3]

In 1921, the summer following the losing 1920 election, Roosevelt developed poliomyelitis during a summer vacation on Campobello Island in Canada and quickly became paralyzed and was unable to walk on his own. He likely contracted the dread disease while swimming in fetid lake water. Sara Roosevelt wanted her only child to retire to Hyde Park and live out the rest of his life as a genteel country squire, albeit physically disabled. But Eleanor and Louis M. Howe (1871–1936), FDR's longtime political adviser, urged him to reject the idea of permanently retreating to the family estate. Most New Yorkers believed FDR's political career was over, but it did not turn out that way.

Wise and FDR worked together in 1924 in a futile attempt to secure the nomination for Al Smith, but they were more successful four years later in 1928 when the colorful New York governor was chosen to run against Herbert Hoover. Smith lost the presidential race, but FDR was narrowly elected to succeed Smith in Albany. Roosevelt's winning margin in the gubernatorial race was a slim 1 percent or twenty-six thousand votes out of a total of 4.2 million ballots.[4]

He was easily reelected in 1930 (at the time the Empire State had two-year terms for its chief executive). Wise backed Roosevelt's two winning races, but their relationship soured in 1932 as a result of the Mayor James Walker scandal described earlier. The bitter fallout resulting from the controversy remained a sore point for both men.

Because of Stephen's robust public support of Roosevelt's New Deal policies, it is often forgotten that Wise did not support FDR's 1932 bid for the White House, voting instead for Socialist Norman Thomas. But when FDR defeated Hoover, Wise put aside his differences, and on November 17, 1932, he and John Haynes Holmes wrote the president-elect a warm congratulatory letter:

> We feel that we wish to tender you our congratulations and good wishes upon your triumphant election to the Presidency. . . . We trust that, whatever have been the differences between us with regard to civic affairs [Mayor Walker's resignation], you may feel free to call upon us for whatever service it lies within the power of American citizens to render their government and President.[5]

It took a month, but on December 16 the president-elect responded in a friendly way, but FDR did not paper over his differences with the two clergymen:

> That is a mighty nice letter of yours and I honestly appreciate the spirit in which it was written. Some day I should much like to talk with both of you because I am confident that your ultimate objectives and mine in the cause of better government are the same. I have never differed with you in that objective, though as you know, I feel very strongly that you were using methods last year which would hurt rather than help the objective. If you will let me, I will gladly talk over with you my feelings for this.[6]

A cagey Roosevelt knew that Wise eagerly sought a personal meeting, especially when FDR wrote about conferring "some day." However, the president delayed that "some day" for three years. He never forgot his public quarrel with Wise and Holmes regarding Walker or the rabbi's 1932 vote for Thomas. However, it was not until January 12, 1936, that Wise finally entered the FDR White House, the rabbi's first visit to the executive mansion since the Wilson administration. It had been a long wait, and things had greatly changed for both Roosevelt and Wise in the years since 1932.

Despite the American upper class's consuming hatred of him, Roosevelt was riding high in public approval in 1936, and he looked forward to winning a second presidential term. His innovative policies, the New Deal, while not ending the Great Depression, gave millions of Americans hope for the future.

It was FDR's "image of human warmth in a setting of dramatic action which made people love him . . . Roosevelt gained his popular strength from that union of personality and public idealism which he joined so irresistibly to create so profoundly compelling a national image."[7] Once FDR began his New Deal policies and programs, especially during his first one hundred days in office, Stephen Wise underwent a political conversion, similar to what he had experienced in 1912 when Woodrow Wilson, another progressive Democrat, won a presidential race:

> He [Roosevelt] rewon my unstinted admiration, and I spoke of him everywhere I went with boundless enthusiasm. . . . [In April 1934 Stephen wrote to a friend] If ever a man deserved to be loved for his enemies he has made, it is F.D.R. I am looking forward to the fight in 1936. . . . We will have the prettiest fight of the century.[8]

The long-deferred conversation between the president and Wise in January 1936 started out on an awkward note, but it soon became warmer as the men discussed the upcoming presidential election and other topics of mutual interest and concern.

Holmes broke with FDR over the Walker resignation controversy and never voted for Roosevelt in any presidential election. Wise wrote to his Christian colleague in an attempt to explain why he sought a meeting with the president and why he supported FDR:

> I wanted you to know of my meeting with the President. . . . Despite his bitter attack on us, I was giving my full moral support to the Administration, despite its obvious shortcomings and its multitudinous defects. . . . It was not easy to go there [the White House], for no man in public life has ever attacked us as he [Roosevelt] did. Still, I could not permit personal rancor or resentment on my part to stand in the way of giving my support to him. . . . There was no reference to the past [Mayor Walker] in our conversation. We resumed where we had left off before the break. I am perfectly sure that the President will be eager to see both of us again whenever we are ready for a visit.[9]

It is hard to believe that FDR and Wise "resumed where we had left off before the break." Each man nursed wounds from their public clash, but Stephen had a more important item on his agenda than reconciliation with Roosevelt. He wrote to Holmes about his favorite villains who "surrounded" FDR:

> I might help him [the President] see the light and the right about the Nazi situation. Excepting for Brandeis and Frankfurter, he has been surrounded by timorous Jews. . . . I really was sorry for the President. . . . He has not quite wholly been converted from his faith in the present social system. But the reactionaries may yet achieve even that notable victory.[10]

Less than two weeks after his meeting in the White House, Wise and his wife heard a radio speech by Al Smith that tore into Roosevelt, his fellow New Yorker, as well as the New Deal. Smith, still angry he did not receive the Democratic presidential nomination four years earlier, criticized the legislation of Roosevelt's first term, believing the new laws were too radical. The "happy warrior" that FDR and Wise supported in 1924 and again in 1928 became a member of the anti-Roosevelt Liberty League. Smith urged Democrats to "take a walk" if the president was nominated to run for a second four-year term.

When the broadcast was over, Wise told Louise, "Al Smith is dead." Stephen later wrote to Felix Frankfurter,

> Both of us believed in Al, trusted him and served him. . . . We now can see how lightly rooted was his philosophy of social justice, and that the moment it

collides with those interests which have come to overwhelm them it evaporates.[11]

The White House meeting in early 1936 solidified Stephen's support of FDR's candidacy. On September 24, 1936, in the midst of the battle for the White House, "Rabbi USA" issued a press statement that was classic Wise—an eloquently worded expression of praise:

> Roosevelt already belongs to the tradition of our great American Presidents. . . . It was Roosevelt who saved American democracy at a time when its ideals were in greatest peril. . . . It was Roosevelt who saved the American people from . . . acquiescent despair or violent revolt. . . . [He] saved the American democracy for the well-being of all mankind.[12]

A month later he reaffirmed his support in a lengthy letter to the *New Republic* that included his usual attack of conservatives whom Wise loved to call "Tories":

> Let it not be thought that the results of the awful years associated with the name of President Roosevelt's predecessor . . . were entirely averted or completely healed the moment President Roosevelt came to office. Even to this day the consequences are still being borne, despite the courage of the nation's leadership and the incredible patience of millions of almost too long enduring Americans. . . . American democracy withstood its ultimate test, and, thanks to the vision . . . of President Roosevelt . . . the democratic way of life was reborn. However imperfectly and inadequately, foundations were laid for a juster order of life. . . . I do not believe that President Roosevelt consciously set out to avert a revolution. It is to his lasting honor and it will be perhaps to his immortal fame, that on the one hand he averted a revolution of ruthless destruction and on the other hand inaugurated what the ages may yet call an era of "revolutionary justice" for the American democracy. . . . Naturally, there have been mistakes and blunders in the course of such years as have made it necessary for the President day after day to reach momentous decisions and to act in relation to problems of farthest-reaching consequence. . . . The President has had to face and still faces the challenge of the ruthless Tories who demand security for themselves and for the value of their securities but . . . are unconcerned about the life and well-being of the millions of these workers who together with their families constitute our America. These dragged America down, these with unappeasable selfishness and incredible unwisdom dragged America down to the level of 1929. I do not say that the President substituted a paradise in 1933–36 for the Coolidge-Hoover concocted inferno of 1925–33.

But the President has helped us to save ourselves. That is his great and imperishable achievement![13]

On Election Day, Roosevelt won 65 percent of the vote and forty-six states while Landon carried only Vermont and Maine. FDR's margin over the GOP candidate was 11 million votes, and 85 percent of American Jews backed the president. That percentage climbed even higher in 1940 and 1944.[14]

On January 15, 1937, five days before FDR's second inaugural, Wise became alarmed when he learned that Colonel Jozef Beck (1894–1944), the Polish foreign minister, had labeled his nation's 3.5 million Jews "superfluous." Even though Jews constituted ten percent of the total population and had lived in Poland for centuries, Beck declared they must leave Poland.

In his letter to Roosevelt, Stephen urged FDR to address Beck's outrageous comment by adding this sentence to the upcoming inauguration address: "Nor will the American democracy ever hold any faithful law-abiding group within its border to be superfluous." FDR did include Wise's suggested wording in his speech and thanked Stephen in a January 23 letter:

> Yours of January fifteenth came just in the nick of time—i.e. when I was going over the final draft of the Inaugural speech. Your sentence, as you will have noticed, was included verbatim![15]

Wise's enthusiasm for FDR reflected the American Jewish community's emotional and political support for Roosevelt. There were many reasons for that positive, even passionate, feeling. Wilson and Hoover may have appointed Brandeis and Cardozo to the Supreme Court, but FDR selected many Jews as his personal advisers, notably White House counsel Samuel I. Rosenman (1896–1973), David K. Niles (1888–1952), and Benjamin V. Cohen (1894–1983). In 1939 Felix Frankfurter was chosen to succeed Justice Cardozo on the Supreme Court.

FDR's Hyde Park neighbor Henry Morgenthau, Jr., served as secretary of the treasury for twelve years, and David E. Lilienthal (1899–1981) headed the Tennessee Valley Administration (TVA) beginning in 1941. Five years later he was picked to be chairman of the newly created Atomic Energy Commission (AEC). Another Jewish appointee was labor expert Anna M. Rosenberg (1902–1983), who played a major role in the War Manpower Commission and was FDR's personal representative in Europe during World War II, where she analyzed how US troops could be utilized more effectively.

The Roosevelt administration was the first time in American history that so many Jews were prominent and visible members of a president's circle of advisers. Their work in important government positions, including

Morgenthau's treasury cabinet post, paved the way for the post–World War II proliferation of Jews, Democrats and Republicans, who were elected and not appointed to public office.

In addition, American Jews welcomed the pro-labor policies of the New Deal, especially the National Industrial Recovery Act passed in 1933 and the National Labor Relations Act of 1935. Many Jews in that period belonged to the International Ladies Garment Workers Union and the Amalgamated Clothing Workers Union. David Dubinsky (1892–1982), an FDR confidant and supporter, was a longtime leader of the ILGWU, and Sidney Hillman (1887–1946) and Jacob Potofsky (1892–1979) were Amalgamated Union presidents. Wise worked with all three union leaders, and he invited Potofsky and Hillman to speak to JIR students—hands-on lessons for future rabbis in promoting social justice.[16]

American Jews were aware that European financial crises and economic downturns in the past had frequently led to increased anti-Jewish and anti-Semitic outbursts within a society. Roosevelt's programs that were enacted during the Great Depression—including Social Security, statutory minimum wages, the Federal Deposit Insurance Corporation, the Fair Employment Practices Committee, the Securities and Exchange Commission, and a host of other laws—were hailed by members of the Jewish community, many of whom were either newcomers to the United States or first-generation Americans. They looked to the friendly Roosevelt administration to strengthen their political and employment security, civil liberties, religious freedom, and economic opportunities.

A New York Republican judge, Jonah J. Goldstein (1886–1967), quipped that Jews lived in three worlds or *velten* in Yiddish: *die velt* (this world), *yene velt* (the world to come), and Roosevelt.[17] During the 1944 presidential campaign, Rabbi Abba Hillel Silver, a Republican, sought to have the Democrats and the GOP "compete" for Jewish votes. Silver was concerned that Roosevelt, knowing the Jewish vote was in the bag for him, felt no urgency or electoral need to advance the Zionist cause.[18]

Wise also realized the serious risks attached to the Jewish enthusiasm for FDR and the public visibility of his Jewish advisers. Roosevelt's anti-Semitic detractors branded his program the "Jew Deal" while Joseph Goebbels (1897–1945), the Nazi propaganda minister, vilified FDR, calling him "that Jew Rosenfeld."[19]

Even more worrisome to Stephen than the high number of Jews in the Roosevelt administration was his fear that US opposition to Nazism and the nation's possible entry into armed conflict against Hitler would be perceived by the American public as "a Jewish war" or "America fighting for the Jews," and not an existential battle to preserve freedom, democracy, and liberty. Wise's concerns were not unfounded.

Fifty years after World War II, Schlesinger wrote,

> FDR well understood that it would be fatal to let the war be defined as a war to save the Jews. He knew he must emphasize the large and vital interest all Americans had in stopping Hitler, and that is what he did.[20]

During the 1930s, Charles Lindbergh expressed his admiration for Nazi Germany, and a Detroit-based Catholic priest, Charles Coughlin (1891–1979), broadcast a weekly national radio program heard by millions of listeners that was filled with anti-Semitic venom. Representative John Rankin (1882–1960) and US senator Theodore Bilbo (1887–1947), both Mississippi Democrats, openly denounced Jews on the floor of Congress.

On September 11, 1941, two months before the Japanese attack on Pearl Harbor and Hitler's declaration of war against America, Lindbergh, a major figure in the isolationist America First organization, delivered a speech in Des Moines, Iowa, titled "Who Are the War Agitators?" Lindbergh answered his own question and identified the three groups "pressing this country toward war . . . the British, the Jewish [community] and the Roosevelt Administration." In the same address Lindbergh employed the usual anti-Semitic stereotypes and canards: "[The Jewish people have a] large ownership and influence in our motion pictures, our press, our radio and our government." However, he did criticize Nazi Germany's anti-Semitism: "No person with a sense of the dignity of mankind can condone the persecution of the Jewish race in Germany."[21]

But the Des Moines speech and his pro-Nazi public activities, which included receiving a special "Fuhrer Medal" in October 1938 from Field Marshal Hermann Goring (1893–1946) in Berlin, permanently damaged Lindbergh's once positive public image. Wise detested Lindbergh, as did President Roosevelt, who considered him a strong Nazi sympathizer.[22]

Wise and other Jewish leaders had another major problem during the 1930s and 1940s. Many members of the US political, military, economic, academic, cultural, and media elite, especially during World War II, made a clear distinction between a total American commitment to defeat Nazism and fascism and an equally strong effort to save the Jewish people from mass murder. The two causes were often not congruent.

Stephen's admiration for Roosevelt grew stronger during the 1930s. In fact, Wise publicly supported FDR's controversial plan in 1937 to increase the number of justices on the Supreme Court. The president, after his smashing electoral victory the previous fall, felt stymied by the conservative justices who blocked some New Deal programs. Shortly after his second inauguration, FDR made a legislative proposal to add one new justice to the court for every sitting justice who was seventy years and six months in age. The limit of new judges would be six, bringing the maximum total number to fifteen justices.

Roosevelt's congressional foes, including some Democrats, opposed the plan, and it received tepid public support. Four months after it was proposed, the plan died in the US Senate when it was sent back to a committee by a vote of 70–20.

However, because FDR served as president for a dozen years, he was able to choose eight new justices, and those appointments provided some judicial support for the New Deal. But the court-packing scheme consumed much of FDR's political capital, and it gave political ammunition to those who perceived Roosevelt as a dictatorial tyrant.

It is interesting that Wise, perhaps blinded by his admiration for the president, used extremely harsh words to describe opponents of the Court proposal:

> The resurrected federalists of our day, treasonable to every ideal of democracy and every vision of the people, rose as one man to pillory the President for the Court Plan. . . . It was a conflict of forces for and against the program of social justice as presented by Roosevelt, I supported the President, and took issue with the Bar Associations, local and national, who led the opposition.[23]

Because the Great Depression affected all of American society, the economic plight of millions of people was the centerpiece of FDR's first two terms in the White House. However, by 1940 the focus of the Roosevelt administration had shifted almost entirely to the aggressions and threats of the Axis powers—Germany, Italy, and Japan—and the outbreak of World War II in September 1939.

In 1940, three years after FDR's attempt to pack the Supreme Court with additional justices, Roosevelt broke with American political tradition with the announcement he was open to a draft from his party to run for an unprecedented third term. His action set off another controversy that saw some of the president's closest allies oppose his election.

Chief among such dissenters was James A. Farley (1888–1976) of New York, who was postmaster general between 1933 and 1940. But more importantly, Farley, a leading Roman Catholic layman, was also the chairman of the Democratic National Committee and a longtime FDR adviser. Another anti-third termer was vice president John Nance Garner (1868–1967) of Texas. But Roosevelt was drafted, and he went on to defeat Republican Wendell L.

Wise with FDR's postmaster general James A. Farley and Elizabeth Farley, New York City, c. 1939. Permission granted by the Stephen Wise Free Synagogue Archives.

Willkie (1892–1944) of Indiana, although the margin of victory was less than the 1936 victory over Landon.

Not surprisingly, Wise backed FDR's reelection in 1940. Stephen believed the defeat of France in May earlier that year and the growing perception that America would soon be drawn into World War II in both Europe and Asia was reason enough to back the man who had "done most to fortify the nation against successful aggression."[24] Once again, Stephen mounted a strong attack on the president's opponents:

> The talk about Rooseveltian dictatorship and the third term or bureaucratic despotism surely gave infinite comfort to the enemy—and the enemy was then Hitler-Mussolini totalitarianism. . . . The Founding Fathers fully debated the third term possibility and omitted any rule on this point in our Constitution. . . . Washington [wrote] in a letter to [Marquis de] Lafayette [1757–1834] in 1788, "that the nation should not thus deny itself of a particular resource if circumstances required."[25]

The Constitution's Twenty-Second Amendment, ratified in 1951, limited the number of presidential terms to only two.

During the election Wise became upset with an old foe: the *American Hebrew* newspaper, which consistently assailed Wise on many issues. In 1932 the paper's editor had criticized Wise's public leadership:

> The time has come for some foresight to throttle the personal ambition of an oratorical demagogue who, to gratify his craving for the limelight and the tinsel glory of a spurious leadership, is willing to lead his people into a pitfall. . . . [Dr. Wise is] a rabbinical rajah.[26]

In 1940 Stephen was angry that the paper supported Willkie against FDR and had "deliberately twisted" some of Stephen's remarks. A few days before the election, he wrote to Henry Morgenthau, Sr., that the *American Hebrew* "should be sharply rebuked for this bit of cheap electioneering, which does the Jewish people no good . . . [It is] attempted coercion by well-to-do Jews against the so-called (popular) 'Jewish vote' for the President."[27]

FDR's fourth and final presidential campaign in 1944 did not evoke the same passion as the 1940 presidential campaign. It took place in the midst of World War II, the third-term tradition had been shattered four years earlier, and Americans were eager to bring the terrible conflict to an end under Roosevelt's leadership.

Although the president was clearly ill in 1944, he defeated another New York governor, Republican Thomas E. Dewey, by a 3.6-million-vote margin. FDR won 432 electoral votes, but only 53 percent of the vote. However, nine out of ten Jewish voters supported Roosevelt. A still-admiring Wise addressed a Madison Square Garden Democratic rally that year where he declared that FDR's reelection was essential "to secure a just rightful and enduring peace."

In the same speech Wise dismissed public concern about the president's health:

> Some of our Republican friends seem to feel that President Roosevelt will not live or survive the term of office. . . . What they really dread is not his mortality, but his immortality . . . in the fellowship of Washington and Jefferson, Jackson and Lincoln, Cleveland and Wilson.[28]

FDR had served only eighty-five days of his fourth term when he died on April 12, 1945. Because the new president, Harry S. Truman of Missouri (1884–1972), had almost no contact with Wise or other prominent American Jewish leaders, Stephen's days of regular access to the Oval Office were over. A biblical verse best describes Wise's last four years of his life vis-à-vis President Truman: "Now arose a new king, who knew not Joseph" (Exodus 1:8).

But as we shall see in a later chapter, Truman did, in fact, know Jews, especially Edward (Eddie) Jacobson (1891–1955) of Kansas City, the new president's former clothing store partner and army companion from World War I. Often overlooked is the fact that Jacobson played a critical role in the struggle to achieve a Jewish state.[29]

Indeed, on May 14, 1948, it was Harry Truman who granted the new state of Israel immediate American diplomatic recognition eleven minutes after Israeli independence was proclaimed in Tel Aviv by Prime Minister David Ben-Gurion. When Jacobson thanked Truman for his efforts in behalf of Israel, the president exclaimed, "I am Cyrus! I am Cyrus!"[30] Cyrus was the sixth-century BCE Persian king who allowed Jews to return to Israel following the Babylonian destruction of the Holy Temple in Jerusalem.

Franklin Roosevelt's New Deal, its achievements, and its lasting impact upon America represented the culmination of Wise's decades-long dedication to social justice. He was a quintessential early-twentieth-century American Progressive, but Stephen's commitments were rooted to a religious base: the Hebrew Bible, especially the Prophets.

In 1942, after a White House meeting with the president, an adoring Wise was not embarrassed to cite the Psalms as a way of saluting FDR. Stephen wrote,

> Thank God for Roosevelt. We ought to distribute cards throughout the country bearing just four letters, TGFR, and as the Psalmist would have said, thank Him every day and every hour.[31]

Although Roosevelt always resented and remembered Wise's 1932 vote for Thomas, Stephen was not a socialist. Nor was Stephen ever a communist or a Bolshevik, although his anti-Semitic enemies threw that charge at him. A Progressive counterpart in the Christian community besides John Haynes Holmes was the Protestant theologian Reinhold Niebuhr (1892–1971), a Union Theological Seminary faculty member who impressed Wise:

> I spoke at a symposium [in Abba Hillel Silver's Cleveland congregation] . . . and heard an address by Niebuhr which was a tour de force. There is not another man in America who could have done it.[32]

Niebuhr was a leading anti-Nazi clergyman and a strong supporter of Zionism and the state of Israel. In December 1940 during the Battle of Britain, Wise, Niebuhr, and Union Theological Seminary president Henry Sloane

Coffin (1877–1954) publicly called for American aid to the beleaguered United Kingdom.[33]

Progressivism had achieved a great deal since the days of William Jennings Bryan, Theodore Roosevelt, Lincoln Steffens, Roger Baldwin, Louis Brandeis, Woodrow Wilson, Lillian Wald, Jane Addams, and others. Though he sometimes differed with his Progressive colleagues, Wise never weakened his commitment to the cause of American social justice and universal human rights. But after 1933, his central concern was the security and existential survival of the Jewish people. It was that battle that will forever define the life and times of Stephen Wise.

Chapter 21

Confronting Nazism in the 1930s

In the years leading up to the fateful events of January 30, 1933, in Berlin, Wise had been one of the few voices in America predicting the terrifying impact of Nazism upon the Jewish people. But in the early 1930s, Stephen was still receiving confident words from German Jewish leaders, including Rabbi Leo Baeck (1873–1956), who called the surging Nazi movement an "internal" matter that would abate and fade away.[1]

Even as late as 1931, Wise remained somewhat hopeful about the situation. In December of that year he wrote to Ismar Elbogen, a well-known German Jewish professor:

> We are aghast over things as they are developing in your country. Perhaps it fairer to say we are nauseated by the things we read. . . . I can hardly bring myself to believe that Germany will lapse into the madness to which Hitler invites it, though when a people is hungry and suffering it is not difficult to incite them to wrong doings and wrong thinking.[2]

He grew apprehensive as Hitler attracted more and more voters to his Nazi movement in the series of German elections before 1933. But once Hitler legally became chancellor in January 1933 as the result of a political deal, Stephen rejected the positive reports he continued to receive from Jews in Germany. He abandoned any optimism and worked to alert Americans to Nazism's dangers.

Hitler's rise to power permanently changed Wise and radically altered his set of priorities. Stephen was forced to devote almost all of his time, talent, and energy to counter not only the vicious state-sponsored anti-Semitism emanating from Berlin but also the not-so-polite anti-Jewish sentiments and policies embedded within the highest levels of the US government.

As a result, Wise focused on three basic objectives: increasing the number of Jewish refugees who could enter the United States, building public and political support for a Jewish state in the land of Israel, and combating the brutal attacks upon defenseless Jewish communities in Europe.

Although outwardly defiant in attacking the "New Germany," in 1933 a despondent Wise sought the advice of Brandeis. The reserved and taciturn Supreme Court justice was unusually blunt, and as it turned out, accurate as well:

> The Jews must leave Germany: There is no other way. [Wise] interposed the question, "How can 585,000 people be taken out of Germany?" Before I could again record my doubt about the unlimited difficulties, he more fully and less categorically added . . . , "I would have the Jews out of Germany. They have been treated with deepest disrespect. I urge that Germany shall be free of Jews. Let Germany"—and these were his [Brandeis's] only stern words, self-respecting rather than vindictive—"share the fate of Spain . . . no Jew must live in Germany."[3]

Spain expelled its Jews in 1492, and historians believe that event was a major factor in Spain's decline as a world power.

On March 29, 1933, Wise wrote to Julian Mack

> I do not give a penny for the counsel of the Berlin people. They have been saying for years there is no Gefahr [danger] of Hitler's coming to power. They have no judgment and certainly they can have no objective judgment now.[4]

Stephen early on recognized that the ultimate Nazi goal was radically different from even the worst anti-Jewish movements of past centuries. In April, he wrote to a friend in Portland, Oregon,

> It is a war of extermination that Hitler is waging; and it is a deliberate thing planned since the 25th of February 1920, when the Hitler program was first issued.[5]

Wise was referring to the date when Hitler in Munich issued the basic "Twenty-Five Points" of the nascent Nazi Party that at the time had only sixty members. Point Four read, "Only a national comrade can be a citizen. Only someone of German blood, regardless of faith, can be a citizen. Therefore, no Jew can be a citizen."[6]

Stephen's Free Synagogue sermon during Passover in 1933 was typical of his nonstop obsession with Nazism. He demanded Christian condemnation of the anti-Jewish policies of the new German government:

They [German Jews] are a people crucified and crucifixion is not too strong and terrible a term. . . . Where are they who are faithful to Christianity? The spectacle of nineteen hundred years ago is in a very real sense less tragic than the spectacle of this Easter/Passover. For these who crucify a people still invoke his [Jesus's] name while they betray him, while they despise him, while they crucify him and his people "anew."[7]

On April 30, three months after Hitler came to power, Wise traveled to Yale University at the invitation of William Lyon Phelps (1865–1943), a famous author and professor of English literature. Stephen's topic was "Ten Important Novels of the Last Twelve Months—Good Thoughts in Bad Times."

Phelps added a small statement to the public announcement: "Dr. Wise will also briefly comment on the Jewish Situation in Germany." Although Stephen used every public appearance in those "Bad Times" to "comment on the Jewish Situation in Germany," his remarks were rarely "brief."

By November 1933 Wise expressed his frustration with FDR:

[The President is] immovable, incurable and even inaccessible excepting to those of his Jewish friends whom he can safely trust not to trouble him with any Jewish problems.[8]

But Wise and the Jewish community in the United States also instinctively knew that FDR represented their most effective shield, perhaps their only defense against the Nazis even when the president was forced in the 1930s to walk a fine line of supposed US noninvolvement and neutrality even as the world moved toward war.

In the momentous year of 1933, Roosevelt made a surprising and unlikely choice to serve as the American ambassador in Berlin: University of Chicago history professor William E. Dodd (1869–1940). Dodd was not a career foreign service officer, nor was he a political colleague of the president. Shortly before he left for his duties in Nazi Germany, Dodd met with Wise, Felix Warburg, and several other Jewish leaders in New York City. They expressed concern to the newly appointed ambassador about the anti-Jewish programs of policies of the Berlin regime.[9]

Later that year, by chance, Dodd and Wise were on the same transatlantic ocean liner en route to Europe. During their voyage, they had more than a half dozen discussions about the true intention of the Nazis and of the ambassador's role in representing America in Berlin. On the one hand, Wise was pleased that Dodd was a strong "liberal" supporter of FDR. However, Wise was concerned that Dodd was not fully aware of the Nazis' hatred of Jews:

I suggested the greatest service he could render his own country and Germany
would be bell the truth to the Chancellor [Hitler], to make clear to him how
public opinion, including Christian opinion . . . turned against Germany. . . .
I asked [Dodd] time and time again that he do just two things: get the truth to
Hitler about American feeling, and get the truth to F.D.R.[10]

Wise was fearful the American ambassador was "being lied to" by German
officials. He wrote to Dodd on July 28, 1933, from Geneva:

How I wish I could share your optimism. . . . However . . . things are becoming graver and more oppressive for German Jews from day to day.[11]

In fact, an agitated and upset Wise wanted to fly from Zurich to Berlin to
"tell [Dodd] the truth which he would not otherwise hear." But Dodd refused a
meeting with the famous rabbi in the Nazi capital. Wise's picture had appeared many times in Nazi publications, including the Nazi newspaper
Volkischer Beobachter and *Der Sturmer,* the personal publication of Julius
Streicher (1885–1946), the rabid anti-Semite. Dodd was rightly worried that
an "unpleasant incident" might happen to Wise if he came to Germany.
Stephen remained in Zurich to participate in a planning meeting to create the
World Jewish Congress.[12]

Wise's most public anti-Nazi activities began early, a few weeks after Hitler
gained power in Berlin. It included a call for a boycott of German goods and
products in reaction to the Nazi-sponsored April 1, 1933, boycott of all Jewish
stores, shops, and professional services in Germany. His idea caught on, and
boycott committees were established in Belgium, Canada, France, Great
Britain, Mexico, and Poland.[13]

On March 19 the American Jewish Congress (Wise was its honorary president) sponsored a meeting at the Hotel Astor in Manhattan to develop plans
for a national boycott rally against Nazi Germany. There was an overflow
crowd inside the meeting hall, and another fifteen hundred people stood outside in the street. The boycott proposal received overwhelming and enthusiastic support from the large and noisy audience, with only two people present
who publicly opposed the idea. One was retired judge Joseph Proskauer (1877–
1971), the president of the Federation of Jewish Philanthropies, who later
served as the American Jewish Committee's president between 1943 and 1949.
The other dissenter was James N. Rosenberg (1874–1970), a well-known corporate attorney and artist.

Proskauer warned the angry assemblage they would be "causing more
trouble for the Jews in Germany by unintelligent action [the boycott]." The
judge added, "Don't let anger pass a resolution which will kill Jews in

Germany." The audience, eager to take action against Nazi Germany, roundly booed and hissed both Proskauer and Rosenberg.

When Wise rose to speak, he sarcastically welcomed Proskauer and Rosenberg, to their "first [American Jewish] Congress meeting." Stephen offered a resolution supporting the boycott rally that was easily approved. But he cautioned, "I am afraid of meetings we cannot control. We want neither Communist nor Socialist nor Revisionist [an extreme wing of the Zionist movement] meetings. We want Jewish meetings."[14]

On the Friday before the massive rally, Wise and the AJCongress president, Bernard S. Deutsch (1884–1935), conferred with State Department officials in Washington. "Throughout the day," Stephen received messages from the German foreign ministry in Berlin, promising "if the protest meeting [on the following Monday] were abandoned and there were no more telling of atrocity tales [of violence against Jews], there would be some moderating of anti-Jewish measures."[15] In addition, Secretary of State Cordell Hull (1871–1955) received a report from Germany that the physical attacks on Jews "may be considered virtually terminated." Wise was both unconvinced and unmoved. He refused to cancel the rally.[16]

However, on Sunday, March 26, Stephen received a telephone call at his home from the German Embassy in Washington. The Embassy official again urged Wise to call off the rally. In return, he was assured there would be an "amelioration" of anti-Jewish acts in Germany. The call came shortly before the rabbi departed for Carnegie Hall to lead the weekly Free Synagogue service where his sermon would focus on the anti-Nazi rally.

The conversation with the German official left Wise in an uneasy state of mind with a "sense of terrible responsibility." Stephen once again called on Brandeis for advice. The seventy-seven-year-old justice's response was, "Go ahead and make the protest as good as you can."[17]

It was not only the Nazi government that wanted the rally canceled. A lengthy message from Berlin was received from Julius Brodnitz (1866–1936), the president of the awkwardly named "The Central Association of German Citizens of the Jewish Faith." The cumbersome German, *Centralverein deutscher Staatsbürger jüdischen Glaubens*, speaks volumes about the apologetic self-understanding of German Jews. Brodnitz wanted Wise to halt plans for the rally, claiming it would result in the "stirring of emotions . . . against Germany." He assured Stephen the "German Government is permanently and successfully engaged in assuring peace and order to all citizens without discrimination."

Wise correctly understood that the Nazi regime forced Brodnitz and his organization to convey such lies. At the same time Stephen was receiving reports from other Jews in Germany that accurately described the brutal actions of the Nazis. A Berlin lawyer transmitted a message from Zurich:

It was only foreign protests, especially that of America, which prevented even more happenings, a greater number of kidnappings and bloody beatings and possibly one big pogrom.[18]

The huge Madison Square Garden rally took place as scheduled on Monday, March 27, 1933. The crowd both inside and outside the arena numbered fifty-five thousand, and the NBC Radio network carried the proceedings throughout the country. Similar rallies took place in other American cities, and the *New York Times* reported that "More Than 1,000,000 in All Parts of the Nation Also Will Assail Hitler Policies."

Wise, the chairman of the rally, had assembled an impressive roster of speakers, which included former New York governor Al Smith, US senator Robert F. Wagner (who was born in Germany and came to the United States when he was eight years old), New York City mayor John P. O'Brien (1873–1951), American Federation of Labor president William Green, Episcopal bishop William T. Manning (1866–1949), Methodist bishop Francis McConnell (1871–1953), the Reverend Dr. John Haynes Holmes, and a representative of Cardinal Patrick Joseph Hayes. New York governor Herbert H. Lehman was invited to speak but declined, citing the need to be in Albany for state business. Wise saw Lehman's unconvincing excuse as one more sign of "timorous Jews."

Inside Madison Square Garden, Stephen presented four public demands to the German government, which he knew the Nazis would totally reject:

1. A "cessation" of all anti-Semitic activities and propaganda.
2. The "abandonment" of all anti-Jewish discrimination and an end to the "exclusion" of Jews from the economic life of Germany.
3. The "protection" of all Jewish life and property.
4. No "expulsion of Ost-Juden" (Eastern European Jews) who lived in Germany prior to 1914.[19]

The rally in one sense was hugely successful. It marked the first time the American Jewish community joined by its political and religious allies held a mass meeting in defense of their rights and freedom. The American Jewish Congress event became the model for many other such gatherings in future years. Some were in support of Israel, Soviet Jewry, and civil and human rights for many groups within American society. Years earlier Stephen Wise had fought for a free pulpit for clergy, and in 1933 he established the public rally as a means of highlighting a specific issue.

Stephen believed the massive New York City turnout prevented "one big pogrom" against German Jews on April 1, 1933:

When the Nazi regime considered the strength of the American Jewish Congress indictment uttered by leading American citizens, Catholic as well as Protestant, it took heed of that warning and realized the Reich would endanger its position in the eyes of the world if it resorted to a Jewish pogrom.[20]

That may or may not have been true, but the rally, despite its size and publicity, failed to improve the situation of German Jews or hinder the Nazis' anti-Semitic campaign. However, Wise said, "We must speak out," and "if that is unavailing, at least we shall have spoken." Tragically, "a Jewish pogrom" did take place five years later: Kristallnacht in November 1938.

Two months after Lehman's refusal to attend the Madison Square Garden rally, Wise saw further evidence of Jews who were either unable or unwilling to recognize the ominous situation in Nazi Germany. In May 1933 the American Jewish Committee convened a meeting to plan its strategy in light of the new realities in Germany. Sol M. Strook (1873–1941), an AJC officer, was stunned by several of the responses he received:

> It is somewhat disappointing to me to receive a letter from one gentleman that he could not come tonight because he had to go out to dinner. It is equally disappointing, and possibly more so, to receive a letter from another gentleman saying he is not interested in this because "I have too many other things that take my time and action."[21]

But many other people besides Rabbi Baeck in Germany and the United States were also wrong about Hitler. They falsely perceived that the Nazi leader with his cartoonlike mustache and comedic middle name of Schicklgruber was a passing political phenomenon. George S. Messersmith (1883–1960) was the US consul in Berlin between 1930 and 1934. Because he sent lengthy detailed reports to the State Department, he was nicknamed "Forty-Page George." The consul described the first months of Nazi rule as a time of ugly violence directed against Jews as Hitler increased his control of all sectors of German life, including an "absolute" censorship of the press.

But on June 26, 1933, five months after Hitler gained power, Messersmith reported to Undersecretary of State William Phillips (1878–1968), "There is every evidence that they [the Nazi rulers] are becoming constantly more moderate." But he also warned the "pressure from the bottom (newly empowered Nazi party members and brown shirted Storm Troopers) is becoming stronger all the time. . . . Goring and Goebbels in particular no longer seem so moderate."[22]

Messersmith soon realized the "moderation" he sensed was unreal, and he finally recognized the intention of the Nazi regime was to make Germany into

Rabbi Stephen Wise addressing anti-Nazi protest rally, Battery Park, NY on May 10, 1933.

Wise in New York City's Battery Park leading one of the world's first anti-Nazi rallies, May 10, 1933. Permission granted by the Stephen Wise Free Synagogue Archives.

the "most capable instrument of war that there has ever existed." Messersmith is best remembered today as the American consular official in Berlin who issued Albert Einstein a visa in 1933 to enter the United States.

Phillips, a career diplomat, was one of several major State Department officials in the 1930s and 1940s who detested Jews. He traced his family roots to the Massachusetts Bay Colony, and Phillips received both his undergraduate and law degrees from Harvard. His wife was a childhood friend of Eleanor Roosevelt, and it was FDR, not Secretary of State Hull, who personally appointed him as the most important US diplomat.

Phillips, suave and elegant in both speech and appearance, was the quintessential white Anglo-Saxon Protestant, a leading member of the socioeconomic class that dominated the American government for generations. He labeled a Boston business associate as "my little Jewish friend." Phillips liked to visit Atlantic City, but was upset that

the place is infested with Jews. In fact, the whole beach scene on Saturday afternoon and Sunday was an extraordinary sight—very little to be seen, the whole beach covered by slightly clothed Jews and Jewesses.[23]

Phillips was not alone in his abhorrence of Jews. Wilbur J. Carr (1870–1942), the State Department official in charge of the consular service, used the pejorative anti-Semitic term "kikes" and once described Detroit as a place of "dust, smoke, dirt, Jews." Like Phillips, Carr also liked to spend time in Atlantic City. When walking on the famous Boardwalk, he was upset to see only a "few Gentiles." An American Jewish Committee official said that Carr was "a trickster, who talks beautifully and contrives to do nothing for us."[24]

But Breckinridge Long (1881–1958), a Princeton graduate, was the best-known State Department official of the period who loathed Jews. It was Long, a leading Missouri Democrat and another friend of the president, who in 1940 and 1941 headed twenty-three of the department's forty-two divisions. In June 1940 at the time of the Nazi blitzkrieg in Western Europe, Long wrote a secret memo describing how the United States could systematically block the number of visas issued to people (mainly Jews) who were fleeing Nazism. Long was clear in his intention:

We can delay and effectively stop for a temporary period of indefinite length the number of immigrants into the United States. We could do this by simply advising our consuls to put every obstacle in the way and to require additional evidence and to resort to various administrative advices, which would postpone and postpone and postpone the granting of visas.[25]

By late September 1940 an upset Eleanor Roosevelt learned of Long's memo and his bureaucratic plans to block the entry of Jewish refugees into America. She urged her husband to meet with Long and "get this cleared up quickly."[26]

She had a twenty-minute conversation with her husband that revealed the depth of her feeling about Jewish refugees:

> If Washington [the State Department] refuses to authorize these visas immediately, German and American émigré leaders with the help of their American friends will rent a ship, and in this ship will bring as many of the endangered refugees as possible across the Atlantic. If necessary the ship sill cruise up and down the East Coast until the American people, out of shame and anger force the President and the Congress to permit these victims of political persecution to land.[27]

When Long spoke with the president in the White House on October 3, 1940, he persuaded FDR to adopt a restrictive immigration policy. The State Department official provided Roosevelt with the fraudulent warning that most of the refugees, including Jews, eager to enter the US were German agents and spies. Long was successful in overcoming Eleanor's concern, and in his diary, a jubilant Long wrote,

> I found that he [FDR] was 100% in accord with my idea. The President expressed himself as in entire accord with the policy which exclude persons about whom there was any suspicion that they would be inimical to the welfare of the United States.[28]

Long and his associates did indeed set up "obstacles" for Jews and others who applied for a visa. This was Long's labyrinth that a frightened and desperate Jewish refugee faced:

Visa Application (five copies)
> Birth Certificate (two copies; quotas were assigned by country of birth)
> The Quota Number must have been reached (This established the person's place on the waiting list to enter the United States.)
> A Certificate of Good Conduct from German police authorities, including two copies respectively of the following:
> Police dossier
> Prison record
> Military record
> Other government records about the individual

1. Affidavits of Good Conduct (required after September 1940)
2. Proof that the applicant passed a Physical Examination at the US Consulate
3. Proof of Permission To Leave Germany (imposed September 30, 1939)
4. Proof that the prospective immigrant had Booked Passage to the Western Hemisphere (required after September 1939)
5. Two Sponsors ("affiants"); close relatives of prospective immigrants were preferred. The sponsors must have been American citizens or have had permanent resident status, and they must have filled out an Affidavit of Support and Sponsorship (six copies notarized), as well as provided:
   • Certified copy of their most recent Federal tax return
   • Affidavit from a bank regarding their accounts
6. Affidavit from any other responsible person regarding other assets (an affidavit from the sponsor's employer or a statement of commercial rating)[29]

Incredibly but not surprisingly, the visa quotas for German and Austrians were never fully filled. The official records indicate that between 1933 and 1943 there were more than four hundred thousand unfilled entry visas for people living in Nazi-occupied Europe.[30]

Many State Department colleagues recognized a streak of paranoia in Long, who believed he was the victim of "the communists, extreme radicals, Jewish professional agitators, [and] refugee enthusiasts." Wise was clearly included in the latter two groups.[31]

With adversaries like Phillips, Carr, and Long operating in the State Department during the 1930s, it was a difficult struggle for Wise and others both in and out of the government to increase the number of Jewish refugees able to enter the United States. Despite this generally gloomy history, it should be noted that America admitted 250,000 Jews between 1933 and 1945.

FDR always presented a Janus-like persona to Wise. When a "sanitized" edition of Hitler's manifesto, *Mein Kampf*, appeared in the United States, Roosevelt, who knew the German language, noted,

This translation is so expurgated as to give a wholly false view of what Hitler is and says—the German original would make a different story.[32]

On November 13, 1935, FDR wrote a letter to New York governor Herbert Lehman that described Roosevelt's examination of the visa issue for refugee Jews, the legal limits of the 1924 Immigration Act (Johnson-Reed), and his presidential order to the State Department that German Jews seeking admission to the United States should receive "the most generous and favorable

Free Synagogue School Activities and Projects, Wise with the School Choir, and a Purim holiday costume party including a boy dressed as Hitler, 1945. Permission granted by the Stephen Wise Free Synagogue Archives.

treatment possible under the laws of this country."[33] Roosevelt's order would have meant more if he had deleted the last six words of his letter to the Jewish governor of New York. There was little or no "generous and favorable treatment" of Jewish refugees.

During the 1930s there was another community in Europe that required Roosevelt's assistance in gaining admission to the United States as refugees. On November 13, 1936, a few days after FDR's reelection, White House press secretary Stephen Early (1889–1951) sent a memorandum to Missy Marguerite LeHand (1898–1944), the president's private secretary. Early urged Roosevelt to make no public appeal on behalf of persecuted German Christians, many of whom were anti-Nazis. Early, along with State Department officials, believed such an appeal would be an inappropriate expression of FDR's preference for one group of refugees (Christians) over other groups (Jews). In the mid-1930s, isolationism, widespread unemployment, and restrictive immigration laws inhibited both talk and action about increasing the number of either Christian or Jewish refugees coming to America. The memo shows that the president accepted Early's negative recommendation.[34]

As Wise approached his sixtieth birthday in 1934, and faced his greatest fight of his entire life, he lamented, "The awful thing is to stand utterly impotent in the presence of impending danger and disaster."[35]

A pensive Wise, c. 1935. Permission granted by the Stephen Wise Free Synagogue Archives.

I wish I could go on and on fighting, but for the first time in my life I feel that it will be good when the fight is over, seeing that one can do so little. If only one might be sure that the fight that we have tried to put up will be fought with un-abated courage and without compromise . . . [36]

The public never heard such depressing thoughts from Wise, who consistently projected both the image and the reality of an untiring anti-Nazi warrior battling for the lives of his endangered people:

We shall fight like hell! . . . And I will . . . I shall . . . let loose an avalanche of demands for action by Jewry. I have other things up my sleeve. . . . I shall be free to speak as I have never spoken before. And, God helping me, I will fight.[37]

However, Stephen was always careful to couch his public anti-Nazi criticism in terms that went beyond attacking the blatant anti-Semitism of Hitler and his National Socialists. Stephen denounced Nazism as a direct threat to democracy, freedom, and liberty, and he was also critical of Benito Mussolini's Fascist rule in Italy.

On September 25, 1935, Stephen was a major speaker at a Madison Square Garden rally in New York City sponsored by the American League Against War and Fascism. His remarks that night were aimed primarily at Italy and its armed invasion of Ethiopia:

Fascism means war. Democracy means peace. Fascism means aggression. Democracy means national self-respect and respect for others. . . . The choice is between freedom and enslavement. Between peace and war . . . Choose ye this night whom ye shall serve.[38]

In his January 1936 meeting with Roosevelt, Wise was appalled to learn that Max Warburg (1867–1946) had written to FDR from his family's financial headquarters in Hamburg indicating, "The situation in Germany is so hopeless that nothing can be done." Yet at the same time Warburg was working with Hjalmar Schacht (1877–1970), the Nazi minister of economics, in a fruitless effort to help the German Jewish community.

Wise was furious with Warburg for "dispiriting" Roosevelt. Stephen also felt the famous financier was "naïve" to be working with a Nazi cabinet minister.[39] Stephen believed a great deal could be done to aid persecuted Jews, including an economic boycott of Germany. He wanted Roosevelt to speak out publicly about the Nazis' anti-Semitic campaign that had deprived German Jews of their citizenship, their livelihoods and professions, and their property, and would ultimately deprive them of their lives if they could not or did not leave Germany.

The day after his meeting with FDR, an irate Wise wrote to Albert Einstein in Princeton:

Max Warburg and his kind do not really desire to help. This is doing exactly what the Nazi government would wish him to. The President threw up his hands as if to say, "Well, if Max thinks nothing can be done, then nothing can be done." . . . Brandeis told me that the President would have acted [against Hitler] in March 1933, if it had not been for the Warburg family. . . . These great philanthropists are our deadliest enemies and a fatal curse to the security and honor of the Jewish people.[40]

The 1936 Summer Olympic Games were held in Berlin, and the Nazis successfully made the German capital into "a warm, hospitable place" for the large influx of foreign visitors, especially members of the Western media. Most journalists described Berlin as a "mild and tolerant" city. However, one astute American journalist, Paul Gallico (1897–1976), writing in the *Washington Post*, saw through the gauzy subterfuge and wrote,

> The anxious Germans are rehearsing for the next war right next door to where the athletes are . . . practicing to win the great peace Games of 1936.[41]

The Berlin Games are best remembered today for the four gold medals won by Jesse Owens (1913–1980), the African American sprinter. But at the time, the Nazi propaganda campaign achieved great success with a series of positive stories about Germany's openness and hospitality, and some of those accounts reached FDR.

In a meeting with Wise, Roosevelt said that visitors returning from the Olympics "tell me that they saw that the synagogues were crowded and apparently there is nothing wrong." A stunned Wise responded that the Nazis did not "let foreigners see anything wrong in their relations of the [German] people to the Jews." Stephen was concerned that "tourists had made an impression on him [Roosevelt]." Wise requested Frankfurter to prepare a special report for the president describing the grim reality behind the Olympic propaganda façade.[42]

Less than two years later, the pogrom that Wise feared took place. On the night of November 9–10, 1938, the Nazi government ordered a wide physical attack upon the Jews of Germany and Austria, a nation that had been annexed to Hitler's Reich in March of that year. Shortly before midnight on the ninth, Heinrich Muller (1900–1945?), the Gestapo chief, sent a message to the police throughout the country: "In shortest order, actions against Jews and especially their synagogues will take place in all Germany. These are not to be interfered with." As a result of Muller's order, the police did not arrest the roaming thugs, but rather the Jewish victims instead.

Nazi gangs damaged about 7,500 Jewish businesses, shops, and stores; 267 synagogues were burned; ninety-one Jews killed; cemeteries, schools, and hospitals were destroyed. Thirty thousand Jewish males were arrested and sent to what the world learned to call "concentration camps." The well-organized massive pogrom was called Kristallnacht, the Night of Shattered Glass.[43]

Among those sent to the Dachau concentration camp was Rabbi Hugo B.

Schiff (1892–1986), who fled Germany in 1939 with his wife, Hannah, and set-tled in Alexandria, Virginia. Schiff led Congregation Beth El and was my childhood rabbi.

Incredibly, Goring ordered the battered and defenseless Jewish communi-ties to pay insurance companies the cost of damages. German and Austrian Jews were forced to pay a collective punitive fine of one billion Reich marks (the equivalent of about $400 million in 1938). And, of course, the owners of destroyed or damaged Jewish-owned businesses were forbidden to collect any insurance payments to cover the costs of the extensive damage. Wise and other Jewish leaders recognized there was no longer any hope for the survival of Jews in Germany and Austria.[44]

On November 15, 1938, Jews were forbidden to attend German schools, they faced a curfew on their daily activities, and a month later they were barred from most public places. The final blow was the "Aryanization," the forced expropriation of whatever was left of Jewish property.

The American media, including the nation's most prominent newspapers, widely covered Kristallnacht, and President Roosevelt issued a statement of condemnation at a press conference on November 15, five days after the pogrom:

> The news of the past few days from Germany has deeply shocked public opin-ion in the United States. . . . I myself could scarcely believe that such things could occur in a twentieth-century civilization.[45]

FDR recalled Ambassador Dodd to Washington for a "report and consul-tation" and extended the visas of the twelve thousand German Jewish refugees who were then in the United States. However, the United States did not take any retaliatory economic sanctions or political action against Nazi Germany or break diplomatic relations with Berlin. Nor did Kristallnacht's horrors pry open the gates of America to allow more Jewish refugees to enter the United States.

Wise had kept Roosevelt and the White House fully informed as the terri-ble Kristallnacht events took place. However, Stephen faced a painful but self-created dilemma. Kristallnacht vindicated Wise's often-criticized public campaign of protests and activities against the Nazis. He rang the alarm bell early and often about the lethal Nazi plan for Jews. At the same time, he placed enormous trust in Franklin Roosevelt, who, although he spoke the right words of condemnation, took little or no action to save Jewish lives.

Although the president decried Kristallnacht, he announced there would be no change in America's harsh immigration laws. Strict numeric quotas would remain in place, effectively closing the nation's doors to the large number of Jews seeking refuge in the United States. But some courageous American leaders pressed for increased immigration. Following Kristallnacht, in February 1939, Senator Wagner and Representative Edith Nourse Rogers (1881–1960), a Massachusetts Republican, cosponsored a bill permitting twenty thousand German Jewish children, a modest number, to enter the United States as nonquota immigrants. Eleanor Roosevelt unsuccessfully urged her husband to support the bipartisan Wagner-Rogers bill. Anti-Semites and isolationists attacked the legislation, as did the Daughters of the American Revolution, and the bill died in committee.

FDR's cousin, Laura Delano Houghteling (1893–1978), whose husband was the US commissioner for immigration and naturalization, opposed the Wagner-Rogers legislation, declaring, "Twenty thousand charming children would all too soon grow into 20,000 ugly adults."[46]

After November 9–10, 1938, a depressed Wise once again put the best face, the most positive spin on FDR, but it was a difficult task:

I would be the last person in the world to minimize the act of the President, whose word and deed have been beyond praise, but in all that has been said and done he has only expressed the heart and voiced the will of the American people.[47]

Stephen's description of Roosevelt expressing the "heart" and "will of the American people" was, in a bitter ironic way, a valid description of the United States in November 1938: a nation that was still suffering the negative effects of the Great Depression. At that time, a Gallup poll found that four of five Americans, 80 percent of the population, were opposed to allowing more immigrants to enter the United States.[48]

As *Fortune* magazine, the business journal of the Henry Luce (1898–1967) publishing empire, rhetorically inquired,

Would Herr Hitler and his German-American Bunds be safe in the joyful conclusion that Americans don't like the Jews much better than the Nazis?[49]

As the 1930s came to an end, the situation of Jews in Europe became even more dangerous. Various projects, conferences, and programs were suggested. They all ended in failure and revealed the inadequate responses of the Western nations, especially the United States and Great Britain, as well as exposing the disarray among Jewish leaders and their organizations.

In April 1938 Roosevelt created the President's Advisory Committee on Political Refugees. The term "refugees" was code language and almost always referred to Jews attempting to escape Nazism. The committee's announced mission was to coordinate and improve the rescue efforts of various religious and private organizations. Because the group was to act outside of government agencies, it lacked any real power or effective White House backing.

The original Jewish members of the toothless committee were Treasury Secretary Henry Morgenthau, Jr., and presidential advisor Bernard M. Baruch. Wise was troubled by both selections because neither man represented any significant sector of the American Jewish community. Stephen was soon made a committee member, but Roosevelt neglected the group and relied instead on the State Department (i.e., Long and his anti-Jewish colleagues).[50]

Because no high-profile political leader wanted to chair the new committee, the Roosevelt administration turned instead to James G. McDonald (1886-1964). Born in Ohio and educated at Harvard, McDonald was the chairman of the Foreign Policy Association from 1919 until 1933, when he was appointed the League of Nations High Commissioner for Refugees Coming from Germany. However, he soon became frustrated with the inability or unwillingness of various nations to admit Jews who were desperate to escape Hitler. McDonald resigned his position in 1935.

Because his mother was German, McDonald learned her language and was able to speak candidly *auf Deutsch* with Nazi officials in Germany, including Hitler, both before and after January 30, 1933. In early April of that year, McDonald met with two Nazi Party officials. It was a chilling preview of what was in store for the Jews, and once back in the United States, he discussed the disturbing encounter with Wise and James Warburg:

> I looked forward to an informing analysis of the Nazi economic program. Instead, after we discussed it for ten or fifteen minutes, both Daitz and Lüdecke [Werner Daitz (1884-1945) and Kurt G. W. Lüdecke (1890-1960)] drifted back to the subject of the Jews, which seems to be an obsession with so many of the Nazis. . . . The casual expressions used by both men in speaking of the Jews were such as to make one cringe, because one would not speak so of even a most degenerate people. When I indicated my disbelief in their racial theories, they said what other Nazis had said, "But surely you, a perfect type of Aryan, could not be unsympathetic with our views." . . . I had the impression that they really do set unbelievable store by such physical characteristics as long heads and light hair.

McDonald also reported on his meeting with Hitler:

> "I will do the thing that the rest of the world would like to do. It doesn't know how to get rid of the Jews. I will show them" . . . Thus Hitler's rabid remarks confirm that he was determined to "cleanse" Europe of the "Jewish problem," as foreshadowed in his book "Mein Kampf."[51]

In addition to being a strong advocate for Jewish refugees, McDonald was also a fearless adversary of Nazism and a public champion of Zionism. In 1948, despite the objections of Defense Secretary James V. Forrestal (1892–1949) and Secretary of State George C. Marshall (1880–1959), President Truman appointed McDonald the first US representative, later ambassador, to the state of Israel. He served in that post until 1951.

There was one more futile attempt to aid Jewish refugees prior to World War II. In March 1938 President Roosevelt called for an international conference to confront the refugee (Jewish) problem: "to facilitate the emigration from Germany and Austria of political refugees." In July, four months after the *Anschluss* destroyed an independent Austria and swept it into Hitler's Reich, representatives from thirty-two countries, thirty-nine private rescue and relief groups, plus more than two hundred journalists flocked to Evian-les-Bains on the south shore of Lake Geneva, near the Swiss border.[52]

Myron C. Taylor (1874–1959), a former US Steel executive, was the conference president, and McDonald was his chief adviser. The State Department officials did not want the famous Dr. Wise as a member of the US delegation. Instead, the most prominent American Jew at Evian was Congressman Sol Bloom (1870–1949), a New York City Democrat.

Stephen publicly criticized the choice of Bloom, labeling him "the State Department's Jew," a charge that Long used to his own advantage when he responded and called Bloom a "representative of America."[53] US newspaper reporters at Evian were critical of the entire conference because the delegates

> vied with one another in deploring the plight [of Jews in Europe] . . . but provided no brass tacks . . . for facilitating emigration . . . Evian emulated a famous region [the proverbial road to hell] paved with good intentions.[54]

As Wise had predicted, the Evian Conference changed nothing, and the status quo remained intact: restrictive immigration policies in the United States and Britain, widespread negative attitudes toward Jewish refugees in many nations, and the American public's lack of commitment to "remake Europe" despite the rise of Nazism.[55] In addition, the British delegation, acting on orders from Prime Minister Neville Chamberlain (1869–1940), rejected any attempt to discuss increased Jewish immigration to Palestine or to have the subject on the conference agenda.

The hostile Australian response was typical of many other nations: "As we have no real racial problem, we are not desirous of importing one," declared Lieutenant Colonel T. W. White (1888–1959), his country's minister for trade and customs and a delegate at Evian. In December 2010, Australian foreign minister Kevin Rudd, and a former prime minister, formally apologized in Jerusalem for his nation's conduct at the infamous 1938 Conference.[56]

Wise was disgusted by the charade at Evian, calling it a "dismal failure."[57] In private he complained, "Evian was a gesture which meant little. . . . One might have expected more from an administration that pretends sympathy."[58] Berlin, of course, was delighted with the ill-fated meeting. "Nobody wants them" was the headline in the *Völkischer Beobachter*.[59]

Goldie Meyerson attended the Evian meeting as an observer. Better known today as Golda Meir, she served as Israel's fourth Prime Minister between 1969 and 1974. She was outraged by the conference and told the press about being in

> the ludicrous capacity of the [Jewish] observer from Palestine, not even seated with the delegates, although the refugees under discussion were my own people. . . . There is only one thing I hope to see before I die and that is that my people should not need expressions of sympathy any more.

Weizmann described the Jewish quest for an escape from Nazism: "The world seemed to be divided into two parts—those places where the Jews could not live and those where they could not enter."[60]

In July 1979 Vice President Walter Mondale represented the United States at an international conference on Indo-Chinese refugees. He lamented the failure of the Evian conference forty-one years earlier:

> At stake at Evian were both human lives—and the decency and self-respect of the civilized world. If each nation at Evian had agreed on that day to take in 17,000 Jews at once, every Jew in the Reich could have been saved. As one American observer wrote, "It is heartbreaking to think of the . . . desperate human beings . . . waiting in suspense for what happens at Evian. But the question they underline is not simply humanitarian. . . . It is a test of civilization."[61]

Simon E. Sobeloff (1894–1973) challenged Wise after the conclusion of the ill-fated Evian Conference. Sobeloff, a respected judge from Baltimore, Maryland, would later serve in the Eisenhower administration as the US solicitor general. In a personal letter he questioned Wise,

> Are plans being made by [Jewish organizations] to bring to bear upon the government of the United States the full weight of their combined influence with a view, for example, to having the consular agents of this country [Long and his State Department associates] adopt a less obstructive attitude in dealing with applications for visas? Until now, despite expressions of sympathy by Washington officials, there has been no abatement in the harsh insistence by

our consuls abroad upon difficult conditions in excess of legal requirements with respect to immigration visas. . . . We have . . . the anomalous picture of the president calling the nations into conference at Evian to consider the problem number permitted by our laws.[62]

The decade of the 1930s was a period of constant despair and continuing disappointments for Wise. Initially exhilarated by Franklin Roosevelt's domestic New Deal, Stephen inevitably came to see the president in more realistic terms, especially as it related to international relations and the desperate situation of Jews in Europe. On April Fool's Day, 1938, he expressed his bitter inner thoughts to the author Ludwig Lewisohn (1882–1955). Wise's private words reveal a disillusioned leader who recognizes that his world and his people are facing a catastrophic disaster:

> I am not hopeful at all that there is such a thing as a Christian conscience to be aroused. That prostitute [Austrian cardinal Theodor] Innitzer [1875–1955] selling himself into the arms of Hitler, and Canterbury [Archbishop Cosmo Gordon Lang (1864–1945)] thanking God for the "peaceable invasion of Vienna" . . . This is what our Christian brothers mean by the glory of non-resistance.
>
> But . . . we Jews are still worse. We do not care. We give one tenth of one hundredth of one percent of our possessions and we think we have done our duty. . . . I almost despair of doing anything for our people because our people simply wish to go on, to live from day to day, and from hand to mouth without feeling, without sacrificing. In that way no people can live.[63]

Innitzer was an infamous Christian leader in 1938 who warmly welcomed the Nazi takeover of Austria by offering the stiff-armed Nazi salute, "Heil Hitler." The Vatican later criticized his actions.[64]

Archbishop of Canterbury Lang, accused of being an appeaser of dictators, believed the September 1938 Munich Agreement negotiated by Chamberlain merited a day of thanksgiving in Britain because there was a "lifting of the cloud" of war.

Wise's final crushing event of the decade came just four months before the start of World War II. On May 13, 1939, the S.S. *St. Louis* sailed from Hamburg, Germany, for Havana, Cuba. On board the German ocean liner were 937 anxious German Jews attempting to escape Nazi persecution. It is often forgotten that other ships had taken the same route earlier and successfully discharged their passengers in Cuba's capital. Not so for the ill-fated *St. Louis*.

Eight days before departure, the corrupt Cuban government informed the Hamburg-Amerika Line, the ship's owner, that it had scrapped the previous immigration documents and required new visas. Only twenty-two Jewish passengers had obtained the necessary new documents, and they were, in fact, permitted to land in Havana. Cuba's president in 1939 was Fernando Bru (1875–1946), but real power resided with the military strongman, Fulgencio Batista (1901–1973), who a year later became president, a position he held until Fidel Castro overthrew his regime in 1959.

The image of more than 900 refugees denied entry into Cuba attracted extensive media attention, especially in the United States. The Jewish relief agency, the Joint Distribution Committee, sent Lawrence Berenson (1891–1970) to begin negotiations with the Cuban authorities. Berenson, an attorney, had close ties with the Havana government. But the talks collapsed even though huge bribes were offered to both Bru and Batista.

The Jews on board the ship cabled the White House asking for support, but the matter was referred to the State Department. Citing America's strict immigration laws, US officials led by Breckinridge Long and his colleagues prevented the *St. Louis* from docking in Florida. The ship finally turned away from Florida and slowly sailed slowly back to Antwerp, Belgium.

The *St. Louis* passengers ended up in Britain (287), France (224), Holland (181), and Belgium (214). Tragically, many of those who returned to the continent were murdered during the Holocaust. The US government has always maintained that President Roosevelt never issued a specific or executive order blocking the entry of the *St. Louis* passengers. A year earlier following Kristallnacht, Undersecretary of State Sumner Welles wrote to the British ambassador to the United States that

> the President stated there was no intention on the part of his government to increase the quota of German nationals. It was my strong impression that the responsible leaders among American Jews would be the first to urge that no change in the present quota for German Jews be made.[65]

Throughout the ordeal, the ship's captain, Gustav Schroeder (1885–1959), behaved in a compassionate manner with high ethical standards. He treated his distraught Jewish passengers with dignity and kindness and made many attempts to save them from Nazi terror. Because of his efforts, on March 11, 1993, Schroeder posthumously received the "Righteous Gentile" award in Jerusalem from Yad Vashem, Israel's Holocaust Memorial Center.

The *St. Louis* ordeal compelled Methodist bishop James Cannon, Jr. (1864–1944), of Virginia to write a letter to the *Richmond Times-Dispatch*. Cannon, a controversial religious figure, had been a national leader in support of Prohibition and was involved in questionable financial dealings. He had also expressed distaste for Catholics and Jews, but the spectacle of the *St. Louis* moved him deeply:

The press reported that the ship came close enough to Miami for the refugees to see the lights of the city. The press also reported that the U.S. Coast Guard, under instructions from Washington, followed the ship . . . to prevent any people landing on our shores. And during the days when this horrible tragedy was being enacted right at our doors, our Government at Washington made no effort to relieve the desperate situation of these people, but on the contrary, gave orders that they be kept out of the country. Why did not the President, Secretary of State, Secretary of the Treasury, Secretary of Labor and other officials confer together and arrange for the landing of these refugees who had been caught in this maelstrom of distress and agony through no fault of their own? . . . The failure to take any steps whatever to assist these distressed, persecuted Jews in their hour of extremity was one of the most disgraceful things which has happened in American history and leaves a stain and brand of shame upon the record of our nation.[66]

The August 1939 issue of the Nazi publication *Der Weltkampf* gloated upon American hypocrisy:

We are saying openly that we do not want the Jews while the democracies keep on claiming that they are willing to receive them—and then leave the guests out in the cold! Aren't we savages better men after all?[67]

In 1979 Gordon Thomas and Max Morgan Witts wrote *Voyage of the Damned*, a best-selling account of the *St. Louis*. That voyage has become both the symbol and the symptom of America's prewar anti-Jewish refugee policy. The sight of hapless Jews returning to Europe after seeing the shore lights of Florida depressed Wise. He had hoped that Berenson's connections with Cuban leaders and the possible intervention of the Roosevelt administration would save the refugees.

Stephen Wise knew Berenson; they had been allies in 1928 during the unsuccessful attempt to defeat Weizmann's US supporters who controlled the Zionist Organization of America.[68]

Despite the disappointing *St. Louis* episode, Wise remained a strong public supporter of Roosevelt. Stephen was especially proud of one of the administration's signature achievements: Social Security. That New Deal legislation mandated sixty-five as the age when Americans were eligible to receive benefit payments—the age of retirement from the active workplace, shop, office, or factory, the beginning of life's so-called golden years.

When World War II began on September 1, 1939, sixty-five-year-old Stephen Wise was already in failing health, but instead of retirement from the public arena, the last ten years of his life brought him and the world a global war, the mass murder of six million Jews, and the feverish struggle for an independent Jewish state. They all demanded Wise's greatest emotional, physical, spiritual, and psychological strength, and he wondered whether he had such energy.

Stephen wrote to a personal friend in Chicago,

> What with the tragic Palestinian situation [the 1939 British White Paper restricting Jewish immigration] and the really rising tide of anti-Semitism everywhere, I do not know what to do! . . . Last night after Carnegie Hall was refused to the so-called Christian Front, made up of Coughlinites, they marched up and down 57th Street, shouting, "Hang Rabbi Wise to a flagpole! Lynch Rabbi Wise!"—Thousands of them and the police didn't even intervene.[69]

On November 1, 1939, some admiring friends presented Wise with a Jacob Epstein (1880–1959) sculptured bust "which looks as though I were a man of 87 with a running nose."[70]

However, Stephen's major health problem was far more serious than a "running nose." In June 1938 he began X-ray therapy to reduce an enlarged spleen, and during the last tumultuous decade of his life, Wise's physical condition continued on a downward spiral that culminated with the cancer that ended his life in April 1949.

There never were any golden years for Stephen—no senior quality time with his wife, children, and grandchildren; no time to write a detailed

Judge Julian Mack, Wise, Polish senator Rafal Szereszowski, and World Jewish Congress leader Nahum Goldmann, Geneva, 1936. Permission granted by the Stephen Wise Free Synagogue Archives.

comprehensive autobiography or to spend time with his faithful Free Synagogue members. There was no time to savor the world literature he loved or to delve into the numerous texts and teachings of the Jewish tradition, no time to engage in stimulating intellectual encounters with colleagues from a myriad of disciplines and professions, no time to enjoy the accolades of an adoring public.

Chapter 22

Wise's Wars Within and Without

Stephen Wise was a master builder. During his early career, he helped establish the American Civil Liberties Union, the National Association for the Advancement of Colored People, and the Zionist Organization of America, and in later years he founded the Free Synagogue, the American Jewish Congress, and the Jewish Institute of Religion. He was a longtime supporter of women's suffrage and trade unions.

In 1936 Wise was a major figure in the creation of yet another major institution: the World Jewish Congress (WJC). When the 1919 Paris Peace Conference concluded, the Comite des Delegations Juives, a coalition that had pressed for national and civil rights at the Conference did not dissolve. Leo Motzkin (1867–1933), the Comite's secretary, convened a meeting in 1927 in Zurich that drew sixty-four representatives from thirteen countries—a kind of peace conference alumni reunion. Wise was one of the four conveners of what was then called the Council on the Rights of Jewish Minorities.

The rise of Nazism in the 1920s within the weak German Weimar Republic combined with the news that Jews in Eastern Europe, especially in Poland and Romania, faced serious problems that threatened those communities gave urgency to the efforts of Wise, Motzkin, and others. But the creation of a global Jewish organization that would address and combat anti-Semitic persecution, discrimination, and the other major difficulties Jews encountered during the interwar period met strong opposition from some predictable foes.

Once again the American Jewish Committee, led by its president Louis Marshall and later by his successor, Cyrus Adler, rejected the idea of a World Jewish Congress. Similar criticism also came from like-minded organizations in Britain, France, and Germany. Wise expected, perhaps even welcomed such familiar adversaries, and he constantly attacked those who were fearful of an international Jewish body. By pushing back against his critics, Stephen enhanced his already formidable reputation in Eastern Europe and among recent Jewish immigrants to the United States.

Spanish Jewish leader Dr. Ignacio Bauer and Wise at the founding meeting of the World Jewish Congress, Geneva, Switzerland, 1936. Permission granted by the Stephen Wise Free Synagogue Archives.

The WJC planning process accelerated in the early 1930s because of the ominous reports coming out of Germany. The Council on the Rights of Jewish Minorities set up headquarters in Geneva and chose Nahum Sokolow as its president and Motzkin as secretary. Julian Mack and Stephen Wise were the council's two vice presidents. The fact that the latter two officers were from the United States provided hope there would be significant financial and political support from the large American Jewish community, which numbered five million people.

Adler was a vigorous foe of any world council, comite, committee, conference, or congress. It was the same type of argument used against Wise and Brandeis twenty years earlier when the American Jewish Congress came into being. Adler argued that Jews should not air their problems and issues in public, and he believed Jewish security and rights were best handled through non-public "back channels" with people like himself working with the appropriate governments. Critics argued that a "World Jewish Congress" would by its very assertive name give ammunition to anti-Semites who claimed that Jews were the secret leaders of a cabal that controlled various governments, banks, and the media.

When Adler addressed the 1933 convention of the Union of Orthodox Jewish Congregations, he clearly had Wise in mind:

Two European delegates at the WJC meeting, Geneva, 1936. Rabbi Samuel Danzig of Romania on right was killed in Auschwitz in 1944. Permission granted by the Stephen Wise Free Synagogue Archives.

I do not believe that we Jews are helped by congresses and meetings and speeches and resolutions; I think we are often harmed by them and I certainly do not believe that we are helped by a constant endeavor of one community to settle the other community's affairs.

Adler disapproved of boycotts, parades, and mass meetings as "measures for bringing relief to the Jewish sufferers in Germany." The five hundred delegates to the American Jewish Committee's 1935 Annual Meeting unanimously adopted a resolution disapproving the establishment of the World Jewish Congress.[1]

A furious Wise condemned Adler and all those who echoed his "intemperate and abusive" critique of the proposed new international Jewish organization:

If we are not strong enough and brave and wise enough to meet together in the sight of men to consider what can be done to lighten the burdens laid upon our people, then in truth we do not deserve a better fate. . . . But the time is short. The need is great. The work presses.[2]

Six months after the American Jewish Committee's 1935 action, Wise intensified his attack on Adler, who was also the head of the Jewish Theological Seminary in Manhattan and Dropsie College of Hebrew and Cognate Learning in Philadelphia. Stephen specifically mentioned those two US cities and ended his verbal assault with one of Woodrow Wilson's favorite terms:

Judge Julian Mack with American WJC delegates, Geneva, 1936. Permission granted by the Stephen Wise Free Synagogue Archives.

The Jewish people are not . . . governed from afar without the consent of the governed. The Jewish people believe in democratic government. . . . It would be easier to let a half-dozen men in Philadelphia and New York tell us how to think and what to do, [but] we of the American Jewish Congress believe we are too old, too wise, too learned and too confident to surrender the right of self-government and self-determination.[3]

In a letter to Brandeis, Stephen further expressed his contempt for the opponents of the proposed WJC:

It is against that sort of thing—the [New York City] Park Avenue Stadtlanut [Court Jews] that the World Jewish Congress may yet prove to be an effective protest. I am even of the hope that the Congress . . . may intervene and express the feeling of the Jewish world with power.[4]

Despite the protests from Adler and others, including the editor of the *American Hebrew* newspaper, the World Jewish Congress was officially established in Geneva on August 8, 1936. Wise's organizational creation required a decade of planning, involving Jewish communities in over thirty countries. Stephen delivered the opening address and was chosen to serve as chair of the WJC Executive and Nahum Goldmann (1895–1982) headed the Administrative Committee.

From its inception, the WJC's most serious priority was fighting to save Jewish lives—one person, one community, one country at a time—from the horrors of Nazism, but Wise had few illusions about the new organization:

Wise with novelist Sholem Asch on his right, Geneva, 1936. Permission granted by the Stephen Wise Free Synagogue Archives.

What do we expect of a World Jewish Congress? We answer: "No miracles." . . . It will not solve all, or most, nor even many of the involved problems of the Jewish people.[5]

Nonetheless, in the face of radical evil—Nazism—he believed an activist multinational instrumentality was required.

But there were several other important events for Wise in 1936. On August 7 the British government established the Royal Commission on Palestine under the leadership of Earl William Peel (1867–1937). Twenty years after the issuance of the Balfour Declaration, it was clear that Great Britain was either unwilling or unable to honor that commitment. For Wise, it was a "great betrayal," the title of a 1930 book he and Jacob de Haas coauthored. In it Wise denounces the "direction of British policy, namely, to curtail Jewish aspirations in Palestine, assure doom of the idea of a national home, and tolerate Arab harassment of Jewish pioneers."[6]

Peel and his colleagues heard testimony from both Chaim Weizmann and Haj Amin al-Husseini (1898–1974), the pro-Nazi grand mufti of Jerusalem, and commission members visited Palestine to gain firsthand knowledge about the actual situation on the ground.

In July 1937 the Peel Commission issued its findings; the chief feature of the report called for the partition of the country into a Jewish and an Arab state, with the possibility of a "compulsory population exchange" of the two peoples. This was the first official governmental endorsement of partitioning Palestine. The report also supported the validity of Jewish land purchases in

Wise in discussion with WJC delegate, Geneva, 1936. Permission granted by the Stephen Wise Free Synagogue Archives.

Palestine, and it recommended a land corridor between Jaffa and Jerusalem under British control.

Arab leadership, led by the grand mufti, totally rejected any partition plan, but the Peel proposal drew a divided response from Jewish leaders. Once again, Wise was pitted against Chaim Weizmann. Stephen attacked the commission's partition idea, while Weizmann was willing to accept only a portion of Palestine as the Jewish national home. Wise wrote to Brandeis, "I am sick of the whole business. I never dreamed we would fare so badly at Britain's hands."[7] He declared,

> We transformed the waste into a high civilization, investing energy, substance and life in the process, and this [the Peel Commission report] is our recompense.[8]

But the most important and influential supporter of partition was not Weizmann but David Ben-Gurion, the Jewish Agency chairman. The pragmatic future Israeli prime minister, living in Palestine and not in either London or New York, wrote,

> The compulsory transfer of the Arabs from the valleys of the proposed Jewish state could give us something which we have never had, even when we stood on our own during the days of the First and Second Temple. . . . We are being

given an opportunity which we never dared to dream of in our wildest imagination. This is more than a state, government and sovereignty—this is a national consolidation in a free homeland. . . . If because of our weakness,
neglect or negligence, the thing is not done, then we will have lost a chance
which we never had before, and may never have again.[9]

Two decades later and ten years after Israel achieved its independence,
Ben-Gurion wrote,

Had partition [the Peel Commission partition plan] been carried out, the history of our people would have been different and six million Jews in Europe
would not have been killed—most of them would be in Israel.[10]

The World Zionist Organization meeting that summer in Switzerland
backed the concept of partition by a vote of 300 in favor and 158 against. But it
did not matter because Britain scrapped the partition recommendation in
1938, mainly because of Arab opposition.[11] In November 1947 the UN General
Assembly approved a partition plan, and in 1948 a Jewish state was established
in part of Palestine following the end of the British Mandate.

The controversy surrounding the Peel Report was another sign that, during the 1930s, Wise participated in and led too many organizations. At the
same time he was "present at the creation" of the WJC in Switzerland in 1936,
he was also vigorously campaigning for FDR in the US presidential campaign.
Wise, an inveterate letter writer, complained to Rebekah Kohut (1864–1951), a
Jewish educator and the wife of Alexander Kohut, one of Wise's early teachers,

Despite the American Jewish Committee, and it has acted filthily . . . we shall
have a dignified and impressive . . . assembly [thirty-two countries and more
than two hundred delegates for the establishment of the World Jewish
Congress].
    After comes the Hebrew University meeting for a few days . . . and then the
Executive of the Zionist Organization almost to the day of my home going,[12]

An overcommitted Wise took on even more responsibility in 1936 when he
became editor of *Opinion*, the weekly publication he had established five years
earlier. The magazine provided Wise with one more megaphone to reach the
pubic in addition to his weekly Free Synagogue sermons, radio speeches, and
constant mentions in both the Jewish and the general press.

Opinion's first editor was James, Stephen's son. While studying at Cambridge University, James Wise wrote *Liberalizing Liberal Judaism*, a critique of
Reform Judaism of the 1920s. James was a 1921 Phi Beta Kappa graduate of

Stephen and Louise on board the S.S. *Leviathan*, 1932. Permission granted by the Stephen Wise Free Synagogue Archives.

Columbia University. As *Opinion*'s editor, he steered the magazine leftward and alienated some of the journal's supporters.

Publishing a weekly magazine in the depth of the Great Depression was a costly business, and finally in 1936 Stephen took over the editorship himself and converted *Opinion* into a monthly publication. The elder Wise continued in the editor's chair until his death in 1949. It was one more project that demanded Stephen's fundraising time and energy.[13]

For Wise, traveling to and from Europe in the 1920s and 1930s meant sailing on ocean liners. The voyages may have been luxurious, but they took precious time away from Stephen's many commitments. Regular commercial air travel to Europe from the United States did not become a reality until 1939 when the now-defunct Pan American Airways began service with its famous Clipper flights.

When Stephen returned in 1936 from the World Jewish Congress meeting in Switzerland, he visited Roosevelt at the president's Hyde Park, New York, home. Stephen and other Jewish leaders in the United States, Europe, and Palestine became alarmed when the British government announced plans to severely limit Jewish immigration to the Holy Land. The proposed White Paper restrictions were denounced as the Mandate Power's capitulation to the recent Arab-led anti-British and anti-Jewish riots in Palestine.

Although there were oppositional voices within Britain, including some members of Parliament, Wise recognized that the new immigration policy, if carried out, would bar Jewish victims of Nazism from finding haven in the Yishuv. Wise appealed directly to "the Chief" to express American displeasure with the British White Paper plan.

During his Hyde Park visit with FDR, Wise focused on the proposed White Paper, and he was able to gain a tangible victory that benefitted the Jewish people. However, there were not many such achievements.

FDR did intervene, and British leaders recognized the danger in upsetting their delicate relationship with Roosevelt, who was on the verge of an easy re-election. As a result of FDR's message to London, more than fifty thousand mostly German and Austrian Jews legally entered Palestine. It is likely they would have been killed during the Holocaust.[14] Of course, Roosevelt saw the domestic political benefits of his action, even though he had no worries about the allegiance of the overwhelming majority of American Jewish voters. They remained among FDR's most ardent supporters each time he ran for president.

Stephen claimed responsibility for the successful FDR pressure on London, and by 1936 Wise was "the pre-eminent Jew in America, and his contacts with those in power had wrought great things."[15] On October 12, 1936, Stephen wrote to Dr. Harry Friedenwald (1864–1950), a Baltimore physician and Zionist leader,

> As a result of seeing the President a few days ago, I now know that his intervention saved the situation, at least temporarily.[16]

Wise was correct, but a much bigger and less successful battle came three years later when the British Parliament approved a restrictive White Paper that limited Jewish immigration to Palestine to seventy-five thousand people for a period of five years, or only fifteen thousand refugees per year. The vote in London on May 24, 1939, was 268–179, and among those who criticized the action were the archbishop of Canterbury, Cosmo Gordon Lang (whom Wise had attacked a year earlier for praising the Munich Agreement with Hitler), and former prime minister David Lloyd George.

But the sharpest condemnation of the White Paper came from an "embarrassed" Winston Churchill, who a year later would become Britain's wartime prime minister:

[I] could not stand by and see solemn engagements entered into before the world [the 1917 Balfour Declaration] set aside for reasons of administrative convenience or—it will be a vain hope—for the sake of a quiet life.[17]

But unlike his action in 1936, this time Roosevelt did not intervene with the London government, and the White Paper went into effect only months before the start of World War II.

If FDR's appointment of William Dodd as ambassador to Nazi Germany in 1933 was "nonpolitical," that description did not fit Roosevelt's choice in 1938 when he picked Joseph P. Kennedy (1888–1969) to serve as America's envoy to Great Britain. The wealthy Kennedy, a leading Roman Catholic layman, was a banker, shipbuilder, financier, and film producer. In 1934 he served as the first chairman of the Securities and Exchange Commission and later was the initial chairman of the US Maritime Commission. The Irish-American Kennedy, a strong FDR supporter, was a public critic of Great Britain's centuries-old anti-Ireland campaign. Besides his Irish heritage, FDR had another reason to dispatch Kennedy to London: to remove him from any chance of nabbing the 1940 presidential nomination for himself. But to the president's surprise, Kennedy fell in with the Chamberlain-led appeasers and the aristocratic British anti-Semites led by the famous Virginia-born Lady Nancy Astor (1879–1964). He was fearful that the alleged Jewish media power would press America into a war with the Nazis.[18]

Even though Kennedy was born in Boston, was a Harvard College graduate, and his father-in-law, John F. Fitzgerald (1863–1950), served as the city's mayor, Kennedy felt excluded from the white Anglo-Saxon Protestant elite class in the Massachusetts capital. As a result, he moved his large family to New York City, where he felt more accepted within the local power structure.

Wise was the first to pay a formal visit to the new US ambassador in London. He was impressed with Kennedy's brusque, direct manner. Stephen wrote to FDR,

I know you will be glad to hear, though probably you will have heard it before this, that J.K. [Kennedy] has already made a very good impression. These Britishers will hear, of course, in private, language from him to which their dainty ears are not accustomed.[19]

More importantly for Wise, who was attempting to influence British policies in Palestine, Kennedy also seemed committed to pressuring the London government. Wise wrote to his Zionist colleagues in the United States,

J.K. is going to be very helpful, as he is keenly understanding, and there is just enough Irish in him to make him sympathetic to those of us who resent the

British promise [to permit Jewish immigration to Palestine] that is in danger of being broken.[20]

But Kennedy was quixotic about addressing Zionism and the Jewish refugee problem. He was convinced if he could arrange a face-to-face personal discussion with Hitler, the Nazi dictator would, for a financial price, allow Jews to leave the Third Reich. He did not get his wish, and a Hitler-Kennedy meeting never took place. In addition, Kennedy angered the State Department in November 1938 when he leaked the Roosevelt administration's plans to resettle European Jews in a proposed "United States of Africa," in Portuguese Angola—a scheme that required $300 million to create a refuge for Jews escaping Nazism.

The day the story broke in the *New York Times*, FDR held a press conference and was asked about the African plan. Roosevelt replied he "could not comment on the report because I know nothing of what is happening in London." The White House was upset that Kennedy was "negotiating on his own with the British Government."[21]

But Kennedy's leak about the Angola settlement plan was not as bizarre as it appeared. In 1943 in the midst of World War II, FDR created the secret "Project M" (for Migration). The project was to present the president with possible options to settle refugees, mainly Jews, in areas of the world with low-density population and promising agricultural land. Proposals included the Orinoco River in Venezuela, Costa Rica, Mexico, Haiti, and Brazil—any place, it seemed, but America or Palestine.[22]

The architect of the administration's clandestine resettlement plans was Isaiah Bowman (1878–1950), a professional geographer who was the president of Johns Hopkins University between 1935 and 1948. He studied at Harvard and was a Yale faculty member early in his career, and later served as the president of the American Geographical Society. Bowman was a "territorial adviser" to President Wilson at the 1919 Paris Peace Conference, and his expertise was useful in defining borders of the new Europe that emerged following World War I.

He served the Roosevelt administration in the same capacity and supported the idea that the global Jewish population should be "thinned out" to avoid Christian/Gentile antagonisms. FDR agreed with Bowman and spoke of the "slow amalgamation" of Jews into the general populations of the world.

On November 2, 1938, a week before Kristallnacht, Roosevelt wrote to the famed geographer,

Frankly what I am rather looking for is the possibility of uninhabited or sparsely inhabited good agricultural lands to which Jewish colonies might be

sent. . . . All this is merely for my own information because there are no specific plans on foot.[23]

Bowman responded with a twenty-six-page memo that listed areas in
Africa, South America, Asia, and Australia as possible sites for Jewish resettlement. The famed geographer noted the cost for the program might be as high
as $500 million. FDR thanked Bowman for his memo.[24]

A Johns Hopkins faculty member, Owen Lattimore (1900–1989), called
Bowman a "notorious anti-Semite." In the anticommunism scare following
World War II, Lattimore was falsely accused of being an agent of the Soviet
Union and indicted for perjury in his testimony before a congressional com-
mittee. A federal judge later dismissed the perjury charges.

Christian Parenti, reviewing Neil Smith's book *American Empire:
Roosevelt's Geographer and the Prelude to Globalization*, notes that Bowman

> helped draw up the modern border of Europe, helped shape America's non-
> committal policy toward Jewish refugees from Nazism, and ran Johns
> Hopkins University and the Council of Foreign Relations. In all these capaci-
> ties, he sought to harness ideas to the larger project of American commercial
> and political power on a global scale. But what strikes one most is Bowman's
> opportunism: He was to the right of Roosevelt but subtly changed positions so
> as to always be in favor. He spent his life in the cloistered comfort of Ivy League
> universities and the inner sanctums of the executive branch. He was a stone-
> cold racist and anti-Semite who let Jews burn and talked of brown people in
> the global south as "smaller peoples" in need of control and guidance. One of
> his last acts of accommodation just before his retirement and early death was
> to passively allow a Hopkins colleague and social acquaintance, Owen
> Lattimore, to be red-baited by McCarthy and driven out of a job. It was the
> perfect, politely brutal end to Bowman's career, which is to say his life.[25]

Bowman made certain that "Project M" was a time-consuming project
that required experts on refugees, transportation, agriculture, climate, agron-
omy, infrastructure, education, housing, and other special studies. Whether
by design or not, he was able to defer any change in America's immigration
policy, especially as it impacted upon Jews. Bowman opposed any increased
Jewish population in Palestine, and he was a public foe of the Zionist movement. Many scholars believe Bowman had an outsized influence on FDR's
thinking about Jewish refugees, Zionism, and other key issues. Another academic participant in the presidential "Project M" was Henry Field (1902–
1986), a well-known anthropologist.

As early as November 1938 following Kristallnacht in Germany and

Austria, a shocked Roosevelt personally proposed resettling Jews in under-populated areas of South America and Africa. He believed it was politically impossible to increase the US immigration quotas on refugees including Jews. FDR wanted the world's democracies to take in the threatened Jewish population. On April 4, 1938, even before the November pogrom, he told Arthur Sweetser (1888–1968), an American who was a League of Nations official,

> Why not get all the democracies to share the burden? . . . There are . . . 14, 16 million Jews in the whole world, of whom about half are already in the United States. If we could divide up the remainder in groups of 8 or 10, there wouldn't be any Jewish problem in three or four generations.[26]

In May 1943 Roosevelt and Churchill lunched together in the White House. FDR believed there needed to be a solid bloc of Arab nations in the Middle East that would geographically surround the growing Jewish presence in Palestine. But Churchill took a different stance and "cussed out" the Arabs who were not making a significant contribution to the total Allied war effort. The British prime minister even spoke of Trans-Jordan (today's Kingdom of Jordan) that he had helped create in 1922 as a potential Jewish center.[27]

In early February 1939, when Britain convened a joint Jewish-Arab confer-ence in London on the future of Palestine, Kennedy cabled Secretary of State Hull that he had requested Wise, who was in the British capital, to "come in tomorrow to see if I can get any definite reactions or thoughts and will send them to you. Is there any angle on this that you wanted covered [the Jewish-Arab conference] or have any suggestions to make to [Lord] Halifax" [Edward F. L. Wood (1881–1959)]? Halifax was the British foreign minister between 1938 and 1940.[28]

Hull's icy response to Kennedy's cable revealed the FDR administration's "cautious" Palestine policy in 1939, seven months before the start of World War II.

> [We do not have] any suggestions which you might make to Halifax on the Palestine question. . . . I must say in strict confidence that I feel we should be cautious about being drawn by the British into any of their preliminary pro-posals in advance of any final plan which they may decide upon for a solution of the Palestine problem. . . . I am confident you will bear the above observa-tions in mind and keep us promptly advised.[29]

Kennedy followed Hull's instructions. As expected, the London confer-ence on Palestine ended in failure on March 17, 1939. No agreement was reached, and the British government, led by Neville Chamberlain, moved to issue its White Paper that sharply restricted Jewish immigration. But unlike 1936, FDR did not challenge London's policy.

On May 9, 1939, Wise, Brandeis, Frankfurter, US senator Robert Wagner, White House aide Ben Cohen, and William Green, the AFL president, met with Roosevelt. They urged FDR to use his influence to block Britain's harsh restrictions on Jewish immigration to Palestine. The president was able to delay the vote on the White Paper in the British Parliament for a few days, but the policy was adopted in London on May 17. As a result, Roosevelt was able to shift the blame for the failure from himself to Kennedy.[30]

In a revealing historical sidelight, on August 4, 1939, Hull's "Jewish wife" (she was actually an Episcopalian) was the subject of a conversation between FDR and Democratic senator Burton Wheeler, a New Deal supporter from Montana. Hull, the timid secretary of state, was always fearful his "Jewish" wife would be a target for anti-Semites who would claim—quite falsely—that he favored increasing the number of Jewish refugees entering the United States.

Rose Frances Hull's (1875–1954) father, Isaac Witz, was an Austrian Jew who married a Christian woman. Rose Frances was born in Staunton, Virginia, which was also Woodrow Wilson's birthplace. Her brother, Julius Witz, served as Staunton's mayor in the late nineteenth century. Recalling his meeting with Roosevelt, Wheeler wrote,

> I said to the President someone told me that Mrs. Hull was a Jewess [*sic*], and I said that the Jewish-Catholic issue would be raised. He [Roosevelt] said, "Mrs. Hull is about one quarter Jewish." He said, "You and I Burt are old English and Dutch stock. We know who our ancestors are. We know there is no Jewish blood in our veins, but a lot of these people do not know whether there is Jewish blood in their veins or not."[31]

Joseph Kennedy returned to the United States in November 1940, more than a year after the start of World War II. He had hoped to be the Democratic presidential nominee, but instead threw his support to FDR when the president allowed himself to be "drafted" for an unprecedented third term. But because of his undisciplined actions and controversial statements in London, Kennedy was suspect within both the State Department and the White House. He never again played a major role in public service or diplomacy.

A suspicious American Jewish community believed Kennedy was an anti-Semite because of his pro-Nazi sentiments and public remarks. On June 13, 1938, a few months after his arrival in London, Kennedy met with Herbert von Dirksen (1882–1955), the German ambassador to Britain. Von Dirksen reported to Nazi authorities in Berlin that Kennedy had said, "It was not so much the fact that we want to get rid of the Jews that was so harmful to us, but rather the loud clamor with which we accompanied this purpose. [Kennedy] himself fully understood our Jewish policy."[32]

After the Kristallnacht pogrom, Kennedy was concerned that violent actions against Jews created adverse publicity for Germany in the United States and elsewhere. He confided to an aide in the American Embassy in London that Jews "spoil everything they touch. Look what they did to the movies."[33]

The anti-Semitism attributed to Joseph Kennedy played a key role in the 1960 US presidential election when his son John F. Kennedy (1917–1963) personally rejected his father's positions regarding Jews and Zionism's creation: the state of Israel. In fact, when JFK authorized the sale of Hawk missiles to Israel in August 1962, he was the first American president to sell weapons to the Jewish state. Neither Truman nor Eisenhower had ever done so.[34]

Wise had to be upset with Joseph Kennedy. He had initially believed, "J.K. is going to be very helpful . . . and . . . sympathetic [to the Zionist cause]." Stephen hoped Kennedy would become an important partner in countering the influence of the anti-Semitic white Anglo Saxon Protestants inside the US government, especially at the State Department. But Kennedy's personal animus to Jews and Judaism was proof that being an Irish American Catholic did not mean that person was automatically an ally of Wise and the American Jewish community.

It was another disappointment for Wise. His battles with the State Department, his uneasy and complex relationship with the president, and his never-ending clashes within the Zionist movement took their physical and emotional toll. But there was to be no relief for Wise as the 1940s began.

Chapter 23

Put Not Your Trust in Presidents

Once World War II began on September 1, 1939, Stephen Wise faced the greatest challenge of his entire career. Everything he had achieved during the first sixty-five years of his life was a prelude to the final denouement: the fight to save Jews during the Holocaust and the struggle to establish "Zion," an independent Jewish state in the biblical homeland.

Stephen's success or failure was inextricably bound up in his relationship with one person: President Franklin D. Roosevelt. The two leaders were New Yorkers, Democrats, politically astute, superb orators, Ivy League graduates, and charismatic, larger-than-life figures. They knew they were playing on one of the greatest stages in world history as the United States led the momentous and successful battle against totalitarianism: German Nazism, Italian Fascism, and Japanese militarism. But Wise and Roosevelt were also participants in tragic events that resulted in the slaughter of millions of innocents and the near-destruction of the Jewish people.

Everything that had gone before in the sometimes tense relationship between the rabbi and the president played a role as two ill, slowly dying men— the polio-stricken American commander-in-chief suffering from extreme hypertension and the world's best-known Jewish leader with polycythemia (an enlarged spleen), an inoperable double hernia, and ultimately fatal stomach cancer—met face-to-face with one another thirteen times between 1933 and 1945.

Incredibly, there are no pictures of the two of them together at any of those personal encounters. Yet there are thousands of photographs of FDR greeting senators, members of the House of Representatives, cabinet members, state governors, mayors, ethnic leaders, religious leaders, labor leaders, county commissioners, journalists, foreign dignitaries, political allies and foes, educators, members of the US armed services, ordinary voters, and a myriad of other individuals and groups. But there are none of President Roosevelt meeting with Rabbi Wise.

Although it has been many years since they were major figures in the arena of world history, the controversy surrounding their relationship has intensified. Following Roosevelt's death, some of his closest advisers and aides publicly extolled FDR and wrote about his record of achievements. With the passage of time, others have rallied to "defend" Roosevelt's record toward Jews, refugees, and Zionism. Chief among them are historians Arthur M. Schlesinger, Jr. (1917–2007), Richard Breitman, Allan J. Lichtman, and William vanden Heuvel.[1]

An entire intellectual and publishing industry has developed with a single thesis: beginning in 1933 when both he and Adolf Hitler came to power, Franklin Roosevelt recognized that America would eventually have to fight anti-Semitic Nazi Germany. He skillfully prepared the United States for that epic conflict during the 1930s, and when America entered the armed conflict in December 1941, FDR became a forceful and successful wartime leader.

Roosevelt, it is argued, acted with single-minded, laserlike intensity as the commander-in-chief of the greatest military force in history, and because of his extraordinary efforts, FDR forced the "unconditional surrender" of America's enemies. All other issues—including the fate of Jews confronting Nazism and the Zionist enterprise in Palestine—had to be subordinated to that supreme goal.

FDR's supporters maintain that the best assistance he could have given to saving Jewish lives was achieving military victory over Nazism as quickly as possible: Roosevelt's assertion that winning the war was the best way to save Jews—"rescue through victory." His supporters concede that defeating Hitler came at a great human cost: the Shoah (Holocaust) that resulted in millions of Jewish deaths at the hands of the German Nazis and their collaborators in many countries.

In addition, Gypsies (Romani), gays, anti-Fascists, the mentally infirm, and other "inferior" groups were also targets of a Nazi killing machine that was much larger and more lethal than previously believed. The actual number of murdered Jews may be nearer to seven million instead of the long-accepted figure of six million.[2]

It is argued that Roosevelt, instead of being unconcerned or uncaring about a Nazi-led genocide that targeted Jews, was a vigorous leader who rallied an isolationist and economically depressed America to fight a long, multi-continent war against the archenemies of Jewish survival.

It was Roosevelt who mobilized every sector of American society to crush totalitarianism. It was Roosevelt who expanded the size of the US military from a paltry 458,000 in 1940 to more than 12 million men and women in 1945—an extraordinary effort, completed in only a few years, that was imperative if the Axis powers were to be defeated.[3]

Finally, the FDR aficionados assert, Roosevelt did all that he was able to do to save Jewish lives, including his creation in January 1944 of the War Refugee Board that rescued an estimated two hundred thousand Jews. Could FDR have done more? Of course, but without his strong, steady leadership, the war would have gone on longer. Tragic as it may sound decades later, in the early years of World War II there was a possibility that with increased German military conquests, more Jews would be murdered in the deepest reaches of the Soviet Union, on the British Isles, in Jewish Palestine, and even in the United States and Canada.

The counterarguments offered by historians, journalists, and others are equally passionate. Chief among such critics are Arthur D. Morse (1920–1971), Rafael Medoff, and David S. Wyman. They have analyzed the same critical time period—1933–1945—and reached negative conclusions about Roosevelt's behavior as president and his commitment to Jewish survival and security.

FDR's critics agree with his defenders that from the time he entered the White House, he was sympathetic to the unfolding titanic struggle to save the West, especially Britain and the United States, from Nazi tyranny. However, as a charming but supremely cunning national leader, Roosevelt harbored and deliberately hid his latent anti-Jewish beliefs as well as his lack of support for the goals of Zionism.

Critics make a serious charge: FDR harbored deep-seated anti-Jewish prejudices. He spoke pejoratively about people with "Jewish blood," and Roosevelt agreed with the need for a restrictive Jewish quota system in many fields of endeavor. Historian Frank Friedel noted,

> The feelings of Roosevelt [about Jews] were to surface in November, 1941, when he remarked at a cabinet meeting that there were too many Jews among federal employees in Oregon.

He backed Jewish admission quotas at Harvard, his alma mater, and feared that a large concentration of Jews in one profession or industry was a threat to his own ethnic group's hegemony in American society, including politics, culture, law, medicine, education, literature, music, industry, and finance.[4]

FDR's critics reject the oft-heard excuse that his anti-Jewish sentiments were relatively mild and did not affect his policies as the American president. It is argued that many members of his socioeconomic class shared such sentiments, and Roosevelt's prejudices were a "product of his times."

But Roosevelt detractors do not believe he was merely a polite cultural anti-Semite. Rafael Medoff asserts that FDR's tepid and inadequate response to the plight of European Jewish refugees was "based on the idea of [the US] having only a small number of Jews." Medoff said that defenders of Roosevelt seek "to rescue Roosevelt's image from the overwhelming evidence that he did not want to rescue the Jews."[5]

> FDR was a man who always had one eye cocked on historians who would someday assess his role in history. He tried to cover his historical tracks, using unrecorded telephone conversations and unrecorded private interviews. As a result, the Roosevelt papers, too, are not as rich as one would hope.[6]

As president, FDR's critics believe that he was either unable or unwilling to use the extraordinary power of the office and his own political capital to pry open the American gates of entry in order to admit a larger number of Jewish refugees fleeing Hitler. Instead, Roosevelt wanted to "thin out" and "acculturate" a Jewish minority in America, always believing that white Anglo Saxon Protestants were the fittest people on the planet.

FDR's detractors further argue that he employed several convenient excuses to justify the limited number of Jewish refugees who entered the United States. One explanation was the 1930s economic Great Depression. It was feared that skilled "foreign" Jews would take scarce jobs away from the vast number of American unemployed. The president also used the threat of increased anti-Semitism in the world if a Jewish state was established in Palestine or if Jewish refugees entered the United States in large numbers.

FDR was aware that isolationism was rampant in the America of the 1930s, and Jews were frequently perceived in the general society as an international people with a broad global agenda. It is charged that Roosevelt hid behind the harsh immigration laws of the 1920s and made no effort to circumvent, amend, repeal, change, or ameliorate them. He did not fire Breckinridge Long and other anti-Semites in the State Department or similar-minded officials who held important positions in various branches of the American government.

But instead, critics allege Roosevelt did more than tolerate the policies and beliefs of Long, Bowman, and others. He emotionally and intellectually supported them in their anti-Jewish policies and canards—bigotry that resulted in closed minds, closed hearts, and closed gates of refuge.

For anti-FDR historians, Roosevelt was a deceptive president in his dealings toward Jews and Zionism. He was a public anti-Nazi who condemned homegrown anti-Semites like Charles Coughlin and Charles Lindbergh, and he captured the voting enthusiasm of American Jews through his domestic New Deal programs.

But the other FDR was that of a duplistic national leader with entrenched anti-Jewish feelings who appointed but a single Jew to his cabinet (Henry

Morgenthau, Jr.) and only a few others to his White House staff. Behind the president's cocked head and jutting chin, the engaging smile and unmistakable voice, the perpetually lit cigarette held in an elegant holder and the famous crushed fedora hat, was a man with a profound distaste and dislike for Jews as a people and a lack of sympathy for Zionism.

If one accepts the validity of such criticism, FDR failed on many counts: he did not save enough Jewish lives in Europe and North Africa, he did not enlarge the opportunity for desperate refugees to enter America, and he failed to offer effective support for Zionism that would have allowed many more Jews to enter Mandate Palestine if Roosevelt had only exerted increased pressure on key British leaders who were in no position to counter their great American ally in the White House. Instead, Roosevelt offered tepid public backing, at best, for the rebirth of a Jewish state in the Middle East. FDR denigrators see him as a grudging, restrictive, and deceptive leader during his dozen years as president of the United States.

It is clear that beginning in late 1942 Roosevelt was aware of the Nazi plan to murder millions of Jews:

> He was privy to far greater information than the ordinary citizen. . . . He had spent nearly an hour [in July 1943] with Jan Karski [1914–2000], a [Catholic] leader in the Polish underground who had traveled to London and Washington to report on the terrible events he had witnessed in Poland. . . . Karski had seen the inside of the Belzec concentration camp . . . where thousands of Jews were being gassed. "I am convinced," Karski told Roosevelt, "that there is no exaggeration in the accounts of the plight of the Jews. Our underground authorities are absolutely sure that the Germans are out to exterminate the entire Jewish population of Europe."[7]

In his meeting with the president, Karski may have believed he was bringing Roosevelt new evidence about the Nazi mass murders. But four months earlier, on March 17, 1943, FDR received similar information

> about the Nazi death machine from a variety of sources, including the State Department, Treasury Department, his own personal network of informants led by [journalist] John Franklin Carter [1897–1967], private relief and Jewish organizations, and the Office of Strategic Services [the predecessor of the CIA].[8]

During his time in the United States, Karski also met with Felix Frankfurter, but the Polish emissary failed to convince the Jewish Supreme Court justice of the Nazi mass murders: "I did not say that he [Karski] was

lying, I said that I could not believe him. There is a difference." In the years following World War II, Karski taught at Georgetown University, was awarded
honorary Israeli citizenship, and received Yad Vashem's Righteous Gentile
Award.[9]

As we move further and further away from the era of Roosevelt, the pro
and con positions regarding the 32nd US president grow more entrenched and
strident. This is not likely to change, but will intensify in the years ahead.

Interest in the complex Roosevelt-Wise relationship will also increase in
the future for several reasons. The 1930s and 1940s were the both the nadir
(the Holocaust) and the apex (the creation of the state of Israel) of modern
Jewish existence, and Stephen Wise was intimately involved in both events.
Because the United States is perceived to be the freest and most powerful
Jewish diaspora community in history, how that community's preeminent
leader interacted with America's major leaders remains of great interest.

Wise's defenders recognized his shortcomings, but still lauded him as a
leader who

> spent himself in the titanic struggle against Nazism. He hounded and harried
> US Government leaders who sought to sit on reports of anti-Jewish atrocities
> for fear of provoking public opinion in America. He importuned President
> Roosevelt to extend every possible aid on American shores to Jewish refuges
> from Hitler. . . . The destruction of 6,000,000 Jews was the supreme sorrow of
> his life . . . a picaresque and gallant fighter . . . who faced the challenging years
> with courage and dignity and without fear.[10]

Interest in Wise and Roosevelt will remain high because today's American
Jewish community is haunted by the perceived "failures" of Stephen and others to save more Jews between 1933 and 1945. A sense of guilt for the past catastrophe and responsibility for the present dangerous period permeates the
thinking of contemporary American Jewish leaders.

Although today they operate in a far different era than the first half of the
twentieth century, they still look to Wise as a model of what gifted leaders can
achieve and build: Jewish self-esteem, social justice engagement, full participation as Jews in American society, and the democratization of religious and
community life. But today's leaders, disturbed by Wise's alleged errors and
failures, are obsessed with fear they are "not doing enough" to guarantee
Jewish security and survival throughout the world.

Wise's extraordinary persona will always fascinate the public because it is
unlikely we shall ever again see such a centralization of personal influence and
power in a single rabbi. Nor are we likely to see an American Jewish leader
stake so much emotion and time for so long on maintaining his ambivalent
personal friendship with an American president, no matter the cost.

That relationship with FDR that Wise proudly touted especially to his Jewish audiences could never be a balanced one because one of the parties was the president of the United States, "the most powerful person in the world." Roosevelt was always careful to refer to Stephen as "Dr. Wise" in all his written correspondence, and he used the same terminology in public. But in private conversations, FDR had another name for the famous rabbi: "Stevie." For his part, Stephen consistently referred to the president as "the Chief" or "the Skipper."

> Calling Wise "Stevie" made the American Jewish Congress leader feel he was a personal friend of the most powerful man on earth. "The president glad-handed Zionist leaders," Prof. [Selig] Adler [1909–1984] recalled. "He would pacify his Jewish visitors with promises . . . but then failed to put these pledges into the executive pipeline."[11]

Although the terms "Chief" and "Stevie" reveal a great deal about how Roosevelt and Wise viewed one another, several documents written during World War II illustrate the parameters and limits of that relationship more vividly.

The first was a February 9, 1944, letter from FDR to Wise. In it the president condemned both Hitler's anti-Semitism and, by inference, American anti-Semites, although he did not specifically name Coughlin, Lindbergh, or the pro-Hitler German-American Bund led in the prewar period by Fritz Kuhn (1896–1951).

Stephen treasured FDR's note. It was "a letter I shall always cherish":

> The attempt by Adolf Hitler and the Nazi party to rule Germany, to rule Europe and then to rule the Western World, was based on two brutal devices: organized terror and organized anti-semitism. . . . Some of the sources of anti-semitism in this country was created to serve Hitler's purposes. . . . Whoever condones or participates in anti-semitism plays Hitler's game. There is no place in the lives or thoughts of true Americans for anti-semitism.[12]

The letter was a follow-up to Roosevelt's statement read at the July 17, 1942, Madison Square Garden rally sponsored by the American Jewish Congress in which the president promised "to hold the perpetrators of these crimes to strict accountability in a day of reckoning which will surely come. . . . [Winning the war] will bring the Jews and oppressed peoples in all lands the four freedoms which Christian and Jewish teachings have largely inspired."[13]

Although condemning anti-Semitism was never difficult for Roosevelt, it is, however, perhaps no surprise that FDR did not include in his address to the rally or in his private letter to Wise even a brief positive reference to Zionist achievements and aspirations in Palestine or the American government's plans to save endangered Jews. But, in fact, the 1942 presidential statement came two months after the highly publicized Zionist "Biltmore Program" in May that urged, "Palestine be established as a Jewish Commonwealth." Roosevelt failed to mention that pivotal event in modern Middle Eastern history.

The same omissions occurred in a later message from FDR to Wise that was read at a mass demonstration in New York City's Madison Square Park on July 31, 1944:

> Please express to those gathered at the meeting to protest the deportations and cruelties visited upon the remaining Jewish community of Europe my feelings of abhorrence of these desperate acts of the enemy. I repeat to all concerned my earlier warning that those who participate in these acts of savagery shall not go unpunished.[14]

The president's 1944 private letter to Wise was composed during the formation period of the War Refugee Board, a US government rescue program that Roosevelt personally authorized. Yet FDR failed to mention the board, something he created by executive order.

In November 1944, less than a week before the US presidential election, a still adoring Wise spoke at an FDR rally at Madison Square Garden. It is vintage Stephen—lavish in his warm praise of Roosevelt, even though Wise knew of FDR's lassitude and indifference toward increased Jewish immigration, the president's welcome but tardy rescue effort in Europe, and his lack of strong support for Zionism. Yet even as an obviously ill FDR ran for a fourth term, Stephen remained a dedicated cheerleader for the president's reelection.

Roosevelt's death may have ended the Chief-Stevie connection, but the public's fascination with that historic, complicated relationship has only grown with the passing years.

Roosevelt's extraordinary political ambitions and his often-enigmatic presidential style of leadership are now well documented. But a further analysis of Wise's ambitions and his desperate need to be a "friend" of the president is required. What drove him to hang on so long to that friendship, even when it became clear it was a one-way street that greatly benefitted Roosevelt and not Wise?

For decades Stephen Wise sought the mantle as the premier leader of the American Jewish community. By the 1930s he had finally gained that position after a long, carefully honed career as an antiestablishment rabbi, the man who would not be "muzzled" by the rich, insecure German Jews who dominated American Jewish life in the early twentieth century.

Brash and brilliant are adjectives that describe Wise's early career—a rabbi thoroughly at home in America; a lonely Zionist among Reform rabbis; a master of the English language; a magnificent orator; a dynamic force for social justice, democracy, liberty, and freedom; and a champion of the free pulpit. But as Stephen aged, he slowly and inescapably became what he had once so fearlessly attacked as a young man: a *Hofjude* or court Jew, the quintessential frequently obsequious representative of the Jewish establishment.

No one was more aware of his metamorphous from fiery iconoclast to somber icon than Wise himself. In September 1942 when he was cognizant of the Nazi mass murders of Jews and in almost daily contact with US government officials, a depressed Stephen wrote to his longtime Zionist ally, Supreme Court justice Felix Frankfurter:

> I have been in Washington twice this week. . . . I don't know whether I am getting to be a Hofjude, but I find that a good part of my work is to explain to my fellow Jews why our government cannot do all the things asked or expected of it.[15]

In his struggle against Nazism and the demands for more Jewish immigration, Stephen Wise never neglected his lifetime commitment to Zionism. During the 1930s and 1940s, he was vindicated in his long-held belief, "Zion, before Zionism." Hitler and his deadly "War against the Jews" confirmed Wise's obsession to achieve an independent Jewish state; for him, that came before any discussion about the rebirth of the Hebrew language, the renaissance of Jewish culture, or the political, economic, religious, and social structure of the desperately desired "Jewish commonwealth." Based upon his successful encounters with President Wilson a generation earlier regarding Zionism, Wise believed he could replicate his achievements with Roosevelt, another Democratic chief executive.

But unlike Wilson, an idealistic son of a Presbyterian minister firmly rooted in the Bible, Roosevelt was a supreme pragmatist who shifted his positions frequently or kept his true beliefs hidden from his associates and the general public. Wilson physically cracked under the strain of his rigid views and suffered a severe stroke, while Roosevelt relished the game of puzzling and confusing his allies and his foes on a host of issues. Stephen Wise tried to play the game with the wily FDR with only limited success. But in truth, few people did well in effectively dealing with Roosevelt.

In his autobiography, Stephen asserted he always "kept the President informed of the facts concerning Zionism and Palestine." That may be so, but FDR always avoided direct public support of "a free and democratic Jewish Commonwealth in Palestine."[16]

Stephen continually put the best face on the president, who, beginning in
1933, "saved the American democracy for the well-being of all mankind."[17]
Wise claimed Roosevelt "grasped what was occurring [regarding Zionism and
the deteriorating situation in Europe for Jews] with more feeling and understanding than . . . so-called 'friends' of the administration." Stephen portrayed Roosevelt as well intentioned and well motivated, and he placed the
blame for American indifference and inaction, not on the president himself,
but on FDR's Jewish advisers (always unnamed by Wise) "who had access to
the President . . . [but] failed accurately to interpret either the true mood or
determination of Jews in Palestine or the tragic plight of their brother Jews in
Hitler Europe." Wise also charged FDR was misled by "the indifference if not
hostility of certain gentlemen in the State Department."[18]

There is no doubt which Jews Stephen had in mind: they included Samuel
Rosenman, David Niles, Ben Cohen, the Warburgs, Henry Morgenthau, Jr.,
and others. They were always the "bad guys," while Louis Brandeis, Felix
Frankfurter, and of course, he were the "good guys."

The descriptions of Presidents Woodrow Wilson and Franklin Roosevelt
in Wise's autobiography are revealing. Wilson receives twenty pages of praise,
while the FDR chapter is four pages shorter. But that is not the only difference
in the treatment of the two presidents; there is a significant contrast in substance and tone. Wilson is portrayed in glowing terms as an "idealist," a
"leader and friend" who "had a touch of the quality of Lincoln." Wise praised
Wilson as instrumental in the issuance of the pro-Zionist Balfour Declaration
in 1917 and a force for Jewish rights in Europe after World War I.[19]

Stephen is more circumspect and nuanced in his assessment of Roosevelt.
While fulsome in his praise of the New Deal and the FDR domestic agenda,
Wise is less so about the fight on behalf of Jewish refugees and Zionism.
However, if his White House idol failed to live up to Stephen's hopes, it was
never Roosevelt's fault: it was Britain, the State Department, or the weak Jews
around the president. But even Wise perceived that FDR had no special affection for Jews. Instead, Stephen links Roosevelt's "friendliness to Jews" not as a
case of "token pro-Jewishness but of his Americanism."[20] The concluding
paragraph of Wise's unpublished draft of his autobiography is remarkably
weak in his assessment of FDR:

The record of Franklin D. Roosevelt is what it is. History will do him justice,
though his detractors cannot. He was the embodiment of his country's ideals
as he understood them and strove to put them into practice. Not failure but
low aim is crime, said Lowell. Roosevelt rarely aimed low. If he sometimes,
rarely enough, did aim low, he acted not for advantage nor out of fear. It is in
his rendezvous with destiny that he was equal to its measureless and majestic

responsibility. Woe to them who vainly sought and seek to divert this heroic figure from his definitely appointed rendezvous.[21]

That damning section does not appear in *Challenging Years*, but a whiff of Wise's criticism of FDR still remains in the published volume:

> I do not wish to have it understood that Roosevelt was particularly a friend of the Jewish people. He was a friend of man and men.[22]

Stephen Wise constantly excused FDR's lack of passion for Zionism or the president's unwillingness to allow more Jewish refugees to find haven in the United States. It was never really the president's fault. But, of course, it was.[23]

Melvin Urofsky asks the right questions about FDR:

> Where is the moral response of the man who showed such compassion for the ill-housed, the ill-clothed, and the ill-fed? . . . Did Jews expect too much from him? Did they believe that if any democratic society could live up to its most humanitarian aspirations, then the America of Franklin Roosevelt would?[24]

Chapter 24

Wartime Crises That Will Forever Define Wise

Because Stephen Wise wore so many leadership hats and was involved in numerous issues, it is necessary to focus on the six most significant crises in the 1930s and 1940s by which history will judge him. The half dozen crises (and there were others) were serious and in some cases catastrophic, but a strategic question must first be addressed. Could Wise, working within the American establishment, or other Jewish leaders working outside the parameters of the White House, State Department, and Treasury Department, have been able to achieve different results?

One need not be a Wise apologist or a Wise critic to recognize the temper of the times in the United States and the limitations under which he labored. Hitler and his Nazi collaborators in many European countries made the persecution and mass murder of Jews their paramount goal. Historian Lucy S. Dawidowicz (1915–1990) correctly titled her book, *The War against the Jews: 1933–1945*. That genocidal war consumed not only the political and emotional energies of the Nazis but it drained off vital scarce war materiel as the conflict neared its end in 1944 and 1945.

The Nazi German regime and its armed forces diverted trains, trucks, tires, ammunition, gasoline, personnel, food, and other precious sinews of war to carry out the Shoah, even as Germany was losing its "other" war against the Western Allies and the Soviet Union. Nothing, not even impending military defeat, deterred Nazis from killing Jews until V-E Day in May 1945.

In addition, the large American Jewish community residing on a vast continent far from the battlefield and the death camps was generally fearful in asserting itself as a significant political force. The community's leaders, including Wise, recognized the latent, sometimes virulent anti-Semitism of the era, and above all, he was aware of the single-minded dedication of the total American society to achieve the overarching goal of winning the war—a broad-based public commitment that seemed to leave no room for such "side issues" as the destruction of the Jewish people in Europe.

Nor was there a sovereign Jewish state in existence during World War II. The Yishuv was, only after a struggle, ultimately allowed to contribute troops qua Jews to the Allied cause, but the "Promised Land" of Palestine had restrictive Jewish immigration under the British Mandate, and of course, there was no independent Israel Defense Force.

But between 1933 and 1945 in the United States there were mass rallies, marches, articles and reports in the American news media, parades, staged pageants, news conferences, public calls to increase the number of Jewish refugees able to enter the United States, demands to repeal the harsh 1939 British White Paper on immigration to Palestine, and demands for Allied planes to bomb the railroad lines near the Auschwitz-Birkenau death camp in Poland.

However, the American Jewish community did not have much political/ electoral influence in Washington during the 1930s and 1940s because FDR and every other political leader knew that Jews overwhelmingly supported Roosevelt in the voting booth. Wise and his colleagues faced entrenched anti-Jewish and anti-Zionist foes in the State Department and elsewhere within the government who systematically blocked the entry of Jewish refugees to the United States and opposed the growth of the Jewish community in Palestine.

However, despite these painful realities, it is still fair to question the actions of Wise—America's preeminent Jewish leader—as he confronted the major crises of the World War II / Shoah period. The argument about Wise and his record continues unabated more than seven decades later.

The first crisis began with a telegram. One of the initial persons hired to staff the World Jewish Congress's Geneva office was Gerhard M. Riegner (1911–2001), a Berlin-born Jewish lawyer who fled Germany for Switzerland in 1933. On August 10, 1942, he sent a now historic telegram to Samuel Sidney Silverman (1895–1968), the head of the British Section of the World Jewish Congress and a Labour member of the British Parliament. The Riegner Telegram was one of the first reports that described in detail the ultimate aim of Germany: the mass murder of Jews.

Riegner's message remains frightening reading:

Received alarming report stating that, in the Fuehrer's Headquarters, a plan has been discussed, and is under consideration, according to which all Jews in countries occupied or controlled by Germany numbering 3½ to 4 millions should, after deportation and concentration in the East, be at one blow exterminated, in order to resolve, once and for all the Jewish question in Europe. Action is reported to be planned for the autumn. Ways of execution are still being discussed including the use of prussic acid. We transmit this information with all the necessary reservation, as exactitude cannot be confirmed by us. Our informant is reported to have close connexions with the highest

German authorities, and his reports are generally reliable. Please inform and consult New York.[1]

Riegner's reference to "New York" meant the WJC's president, Stephen Wise. Two days earlier, on August 8, Riegner visited the US consulate in Geneva. It was a Saturday, and the consul was away from his office on a weekend Alpine summer skiing trip. The thirty-one-year-old Riegner met with another young man, US vice consul Howard Elting, Jr. (1907–2001), a former Princeton University head cheerleader.

A distressed Riegner asked Elting to convey to the State Department the horrific news that Hitler had both the intention and the means to murder every Jew in Europe who lived under German occupation. The WJC official had gained his information from Dr. Eduard Schulte (1891–1966), a German industrialist who lived near the Auschwitz death camp, but for business reasons he visited neutral Switzerland on a regular basis. Because Schulte had contacts with high-echelon Nazi officials, he was able to gain accurate knowledge about the Nazi Final Solution to the so-called Jewish Question.

In his memoirs written many years later, Riegner recounted that he was dazed and stunned when he received Schulte's information and nervously paced the shore of Lake Geneva not sure whether the news was true. But he believed Schulte and wanted the US State Department to learn of the devastating report in addition to the World Jewish Congress leadership in London and New York.

Elting was at first doubtful about the Nazi mass-murder plan, but there was something in Riegner's manner that resonated positively with the American official. He considered the WJC official both "serious and balanced."[2]

After speaking with his Jewish visitor, Elting sent the following message to the American legation in Bern headed by Leland Harrison (1883–1951), a Harvard graduate:

> This morning Mr. Gerhard M. Riegner, Secretary of the World Jewish Congress in Geneva, called in great agitation. He stated that he had just received a report from a German business man of considerable prominence, who is said to have excellent political and military connections in Germany and from whom reliable and important political information has been obtained on two previous occasions, to the effect that there has been and is being considered in Hitler's headquarters a plan to exterminate all Jews from Germany and German controlled areas in Europe after they have been concentrated in the east (presumably Poland). The number involved is said to be between three and a half and four million and the object is to permanently

settle the Jewish question in Europe. The mass execution if decided upon would allegedly take place this fall.[3]

We now know the program for the mass execution of millions of Jews was officially decided on January 20, 1942, at a conference that included fifteen top Nazi Party and government officials. The infamous Reinhard Heydrich (1904–1942), the head of the German Security Service apparatus and the *Reichsprotektor* of Bohemia and Moravia, chaired the conference in a mansion in Wannsee, a fashionable Berlin suburb.

Heydrich, who was later assassinated in Prague on May 27, 1942, by two Czech partisans, was implementing the policy directive of Hitler. British historian Richard J. Evans writes, "It is clear that the mass murder of . . . Jews . . . was above all, a reflection of Hitler's own personal desires and beliefs, repeatedly articulated both in public and in private."[4] SS Lieutenant Colonel Adolf Eichmann recorded the minutes of the Wannsee Conference. While Schulte may not have known the precise details of the conference, the information he shared with Riegner in Geneva accurately reflected the decisions made at that ominous meeting.[5]

The American legation in Bern forwarded the Riegner and Elting messages to the State Department, but Harrison added a paragraph that questioned the accuracy of Riegner's information:

> CONFIDENTIAL: Legation note: Legation has no information which would tend to confirm this report which is, however, forwarded in accordance with Riegner's wishes. In conversation with Elting, Riegner drew attention to recently reported Jewish deportations eastward from occupied France, protectorate and probably elsewhere. The report has earmarks of war rumor, inspired by fear and what is commonly understood to be the actually miserable conditions of these refugees who face decimation as result physical maltreatment and scarcely endurable privations, malnutrition and disease.

Baltimore City College maintains online primary source material that relates to the activities of Elting, Riegner, and Harrison during the fateful summer of 1942.[6] The messages were received in Washington by Yale graduate Elbridge Durbrow (1903–1997), a career Foreign Service official and the director of the department's European Division. In the late 1950s, Durbrow served as the US ambassador to South Vietnam.

Durbrow dismissed the veracity of Riegner's information, labeling it "fantastic" and recommended it not be publicly released or sent on to Wise. After Secretary of State Hull and Undersecretary Sumner Welles (1892–1961),

Wise with FDR's treasury secretary, Henry Morgenthau, Jr., c. 1946. Permission granted by the Stephen Wise Free Synagogue Archives.

another graduate of an Ivy League college (Harvard), read the telegram, they instructed the US diplomats in Switzerland to limit their messages to only those subjects or matters with "definite American interests." Clearly, the Nazi German mass murder of Jews was not included in that category.[7] Welles was the great-nephew of Radical Republican US senator Charles Sumner of Massachusetts (1811–1874), a leading proponent of post–Civil War Reconstructionism in the defeated Confederacy.

Unknown to the State Department, Wise also received the telegram, thanks to Silverman in Britain. However, the message did not arrive in New York from London until August 28, nearly three weeks after Riegner met with Elting. The anxious WJC official did not know for several weeks whether his important information actually reached the United States.

In early September, a depressed Wise traveled to Washington to present the terrible news to Welles, the one high-level State Department official considered friendly to Jewish and Zionist concerns. But, of course, Welles already had received the same information.

Welles requested Wise to withhold any public release of Riegner's telegram until US officials were certain the Schulte information was accurate. Welles was wary because of the World War I false atrocity stories that described the ruthless "Huns" and their "cadaver factories" in Belgium.

Wise agreed to the undersecretary's request for public silence. It was a great mistake by Wise, who too willingly acceded to the wishes of US government officials, especially the "friendly" Welles. During the period of his public silence, on September 4 an anguished Wise wrote to Frankfurter:

> My heart is so full that I just must write to you. . . . I want you to share the knowledge of this horror. You may think of something that could be done. . . . Welles tried to be reassuring. He seems to think that the real purpose of the Nazi government is to use Jews in connection with war work. . . . A moment ago another message came from Berne, saying that in the past days one hundred thousand Jews have been killed in Warsaw, and that their corpses are being used to make soap. . . .
>
> I was tempted to call up Henry [Morgenthau, Jr.] . . . and ask him to put it before the Chief [FDR], just that he might know about it, even though, alas, he prove to be unable to avert the horror. . . . The Chief ought to know about it. . . . One somehow feels that the foremost and finest figure in the political world today should not be without knowledge of this unutterable disaster which threatens and may now be in the process of execution.[8]

But twelve weeks went by before Wise had a second meeting with Welles on November 24, 1942, when the State Department official sadly confirmed the truth contained in the Riegner telegram. Wise and his son James heard the grim news:

> I hold in my hands documents which have come to me from our legation in Berne. I regret to tell you, Dr. Wise, that these confirm and justify your deepest fears. . . . For reasons you well understand, I cannot give these to the press, but there is no reason why you should not. It might even help if you did.[9]

It is estimated that nearly two million Jews were killed between August and November 1942, the period when the United States investigated the accuracy of Riegner's report.

Following his meeting with Welles, Wise quickly called a news conference, and on the day before Thanksgiving, November 25, 1942, the American press reported the Nazis were murdering millions of Jews. The *New York Times* headline was "Wise Gets Confirmations" and noted that Stephen had "deliberately waited confirmation" before he went public.

There was the expected shock and horror at the news. Sunday, December 13 was declared a "Day of Mourning," and on November 26, Wise invited "the aid of any Christian organization ready to speak out on behalf of the Jewish victims." Few Christian leaders accepted Wise's invitation. The *Times* story on page 16 also listed the greatly diminished Jewish populations of a dozen European nations, including Germany, Austria, and Poland.[10]

But the American public's attention was then focused on the Anglo-American invasion of North Africa earlier that month and the climatic battle of Stalingrad in the Soviet Union that was taking place at the same time.

Worse still, the Roosevelt administration's policies and actions regarding Jews did not change. On the contrary. On December 2, 1942, Wise wrote to FDR asking the president "to speak a word which may bring solace and hope to millions of Jews who mourn, and be an expression of the conscience of the American people."[11]

Wise appealed to Roosevelt:

> As the recognized leader of the forces of democracy and humanity to initiate the action which . . . may yet save the Jewish people from utter destruction.

FDR was, as usual, ambiguous in his response. He only promised that America would assist persecuted Jews as "the burden of war permits."[12]

On January 21, 1943, the State Department instructed the American legation in Bern to cease transmitting any further information from Riegner. Treasury Secretary Morgenthau, who was slowly discovering his suppressed Jewish identity and emerging as an activist regarding the saving of Jews, realized there were to be no "more stories of atrocities which might provoke more mass meetings and more public protests."[13]

Stephen's acquiescence to Welles's request to refrain from immediately releasing the telegram's contents has drawn enormous criticism. In 1968 Nobel Peace Prize winner Elie Wiesel wrote,

> What did American Jews do to aid their brothers in Europe? . . . By the time Stephen Wise (whom I consider a very great man and a very great Jew) talked with Under-Secretary Sumner Welles he already knew of Hitler's "Final Solution." Welles asked Wise not to reveal this information until it was proved conclusively true, and Wise consented. He gave no information to the press. Wise knew that two million Jews had already been exterminated. How could he pledge secrecy? . . . Was he not driven mad by this secret? How could other Jewish leaders pledge silence? How it is they did not cry out in despair?

The more important, the more disturbing question is . . . What happened after Rabbi Wise was released from his pledge? Not much. Not much at all . . . Did he proclaim hunger strikes? . . . Did they organize daily marches to the White House? They should have shaken heaven and earth. . . . Taken in by Roosevelt's personality; they in a way became accomplices to his inaction.[14]

However, Urofsky disagrees:

Wiesel has read the tactics of the antiwar protests of the sixties back to an earlier and far different time. World War II was not Vietnam, when this nation stood bitterly divided over the rightness and righteousness of American foreign policy. . . . One can argue that Wise and other Jews should have done more, although exactly what the "more" should have been remains difficult to define; but the protest tactics suggested by Wiesel would have accomplished little if anything in 1942.[15]

Wise's news conference based upon the Riegner telegram sparked a nasty public debate between Stephen and Charles Clayton Morrison (1874–1966), the editor of the *Christian Century*, an influential Protestant journal. Morrison did not believe Wise's figures about the number of Jews murdered by late 1942 nor did he accept the claim that such information had been verified by the State Department. The *Christian Century* charged that the famous rabbi had exaggerated and made false statements.

An angry Wise wrote a letter to the magazine that appeared in its January 13, 1943, issue:

I cannot quite understand that you should seem to be spiritually unconcerned about the tragic fate of the people whose gift to the world you purport to revere and worship. . . . [The *Christian Century* takes] a frankly or disguisedly anti-Jewish attitude whenever it deals with Jewish subjects.[16]

A second crisis for Wise began in the summer of 1940 and involved one of Stephen's most skilled and formidable adversaries: Hillel Kook, a twenty-five-year-old Lithuanian-born Palestinian Jew (1915–2001). He was the nephew of Rabbi Abraham Isaac Kook (1865–1935), the Ashkenazi chief rabbi of British Mandate Palestine between 1921 and his death fourteen years later. As a youngster in Palestine during the 1930s, Hillel became a follower of Vladimir Jabotinsky, the leader of the Revisionist Zionists, and he joined the Irgun Ha-Tzvai ha-leumi b'eretz Yisrael (the National Military Organization in the Land of Israel). A fellow member of the combative Irgun was Menachem Begin, the sixth prime minister of modern Israel.

In July 1940 the Irgun leadership sent Kook to the United States, where he chose to be known as "Peter Bergson" in honor of the French Jewish philosopher, Henri Bergson (1859–1941). Kook assumed the name of his favorite philosopher because he did not want to embarrass his famous rabbinic family. Bergson's aggressive agenda included fundraising in America for his organization and the development of a public information campaign about the immediate need to save threatened Jews in Europe, the creation of an independent Jewish state, as well as the establishment of a "Jewish Brigade" composed of Palestinian Jews to fight Nazism as part of the British armed forces.

Bergson was a talented practitioner of issue-focused public relations. He attracted entertainment celebrities, American political leaders, artists, academics, authors, and others to his cause. They included US congressmen Will Rogers, Jr. (D-California; 1911–1993), Joseph C. Baldwin (R-New York; 1897–1957), and Andrew Somers (D-New York; 1895–1949), senators Guy Gillette (D-Iowa; 1879–1973) and Elbert Thomas (D-Utah; 1883–1953); the actress Stella Adler (1901–1992); and Bergson's chief ally, the writer and journalist Ben Hecht (1893–1964).

Bergson placed two hundred advertisements (many of them full-page) in the *New York Times* and other US newspapers between 1940 and 1944. The ads demanded American action to save Jews from Hitler with headlines like "Help 4,000,000 People from Becoming Ghosts."[17] Bergson also established a number of organizations in the United States: the American Friends for a Jewish Palestine, the American League for a Free Palestine, the Organizing Committee of Illegal Immigration, Emergency Committee for the Rescue of European Jewry, the Hebrew Committee of National Liberation, and the Committee for a Jewish Army of Stateless and Palestinian Jews.

On March 9, 1943, Bergson and his colleagues staged a huge multimedia three-act pageant in Madison Square Garden produced by Billy Rose (1899–1966) and written by Hecht and Moss Hart (1904–1961) titled *We Will Never Die*, a review of Jewish history and a tribute to the two million Jews in Europe already known to have been killed by the Nazis. Thanks to Hecht, film stars Edward G. Robinson (1893–1973), a former Hebrew Union College rabbinical student, and Paul Muni (1895–1967), a star of the Yiddish theater, narrated the spectacle, and Kurt Weill (1900–1950), a Berlin cantor's son and a refugee from Nazism, provided the music.

It is estimated that forty thousand people saw the Madison Square Garden production, and Bergson arranged for additional performances in Washington, DC, and four other American cities. Eleanor Roosevelt, Supreme Court Chief Justice Harlan Fiske Stone (1872–1946), five other high court justices, and remarkably, three hundred members of the US Congress saw *We Will Never Die* in the nation's capital.[18]

Stephen Wise and many other leaders of the Jewish establishment, including Zionist organizations, publicly opposed Bergson for several reasons. He represented an extremist militant Irgun political philosophy that was anathema to most American Jews. It was feared that Bergson's high-profile calls for US action on behalf of Jews would increase American anti-Semitism in the midst of World War II. But perhaps Bergson's greatest "crime" was his extraordinary effectiveness in attracting large support.[19]

Wise was a public opponent of both Bergson and the Irgun. A year after the end of the war, Begin directed the most famous Irgun operation: on July 22, 1946, his group blew up a section of the King David Hotel in Jerusalem housing the British military and intelligence headquarters. Nearly a hundred people were killed, most of them British officials and military. Many Jewish leaders, including Wise and Ben-Gurion, condemned the Irgun's actions.[20]

Many of Bergson's supporters were not Jewish, and in addition to the American political leaders he had recruited, the young Palestinian Jew also attracted such luminaries as Melvyn Douglas (1901–1981), Frank Sinatra (1915–1998), Jerry Lewis, Jimmy Durante (1893–1980), Dean Martin (1917–1995), and Danny Thomas (1912–1991). Along with celebrity performers, Bergson enlisted composer and conductor Leonard Bernstein (1918–1990), radio newscaster Lowell Thomas (1892–1981), author Dorothy Parker (1893–1967), and Protestant theologians Reinhold Niebuhr and Paul Tillich (1886–1965).

Wise's reaction to Bergson was shameful. Stephen said the Revisionist movement in Zionism was "fascism in Yiddish or Hebrew" and "a disaster to the Zionist cause and the Jewish people."[21]

Thanks to Peter Bergson, a year after the Pearl Harbor attack, four major US newspapers carried a two-page "Proclamation on the Moral Rights of the Stateless and Palestinian Jews," signed by fifteen hundred prominent Americans, including Langston Hughes (1902–1967), Humphrey Bogart (1899–1957), Aaron Copland (1900–1990), Eugene O'Neill (1888–1953), and Senator Harry S. Truman, all pledging that "we shall no longer witness with pity alone . . . the calculated extermination of the ancient Jewish people by the barbarous Nazis."[22]

The British Embassy in Washington joined with some American Jewish leaders in an unsuccessful attempt to deport Bergson. His military draft status was questioned, along with his organizations' finances, but nothing illegal was found.[23]

Wise's bitter opposition to Bergson was personal, ideological, and generational. Stephen in the 1940s was the ultimate establishment leader who operated behind closed doors in the White House Oval Office and within governmental "corridors of power." He depended upon personal charisma and an international reputation to achieve results in contacts with presidents, prime ministers, and other high public officials.

It was disgraceful that Stephen, the president of the American Jewish Congress, Zionist Organization of America, and the World Jewish Congress, told US leaders that Bergson was "as equally as great an enemy of the Jews as Hitler, for the reason that his activities could only lead to increased anti-Semitism."[24]

The Hebrew-speaking Bergson represented something new and threatening. The young Palestinian Jew was forty-one years younger than Wise and was able to marshal supporters in ways we today consider normal, especially after the civil rights struggle and the Vietnam War protests: huge entertainment pageants, marches, newspaper ads, congressional resolutions, and the public support of celebrities and public officials—all designed for maximum impact upon American public opinion. Much to Wise's dismay, on November 9, 1943, Bergson was successful in achieving a joint congressional resolution, albeit nonbinding, to save Jews in Europe. Senator Gillette and Representative Baldwin were the bipartisan sponsors. The resolution read,

> Whereas the Congress of the United States, by concurrent resolution adopted on March 15 of this year, expressed its condemnation of Nazi Germany's "mass murder of Jewish men, women, and children," a mass crime which has already exterminated close to two million human beings, about 30 per centum of the total Jewish population of Europe, and which is growing in intensity as Germany approaches defeat; and Whereas the American tradition of justice and humanity dictates that all possible means be employed to save from this fate the surviving Jews of Europe, some four million souls who have been rendered homeless and destitute by the Nazis: therefore be it resolved, that the House of Representatives recommends and urges the creation by the President of a commission of diplomatic, economic, and military experts to formulate and effectuate a plan of immediate action designed to save the surviving Jewish people of Europe from extinction at the hands of Nazi Germany.[25]

The congressional resolution angered Wise. It is reported that Stephen personally confronted Bergson at the end of 1943 and asked the young Palestinian Jew, "Who empowered you?" Bergson's response made clear the sharp differences between himself and Wise:

> We represent the conscience of the Hebrew nation. We represent ourselves. You are an American clergyman and a member of the Democratic Party. . . . On the day on which one square yard of Palestine will be free, I shall be there as a citizen, and abide by the decision of whoever will be the government of the Hebrew people. . . . Whereas you will then continue to be an American clergyman, member of the Democratic Party.[26]

Nearly seven decades later, Seymour D. Reich, a leader of several major Jewish organizations, wrote, "The time has come to acknowledge, unequivocally, that Rabbi Wise and his colleagues were wrong. . . . [Rescuing Jews] was their obligation, and they failed."[27]

Wise's third crisis was also directly related to Peter Bergson. Drawing upon his rabbinic uncle's fame and respected name, Bergson organized a large rabbis' march on Washington to demand that Roosevelt and his administration take immediate action to save the Jews of Europe. The march sponsors were Bergson's Emergency Committee to Save the Jewish People of Europe and the rabbinic Va'ad ha-Hatzala (Rescue Committee). In retrospect, the march on Wednesday, October 6, 1943—three days before Yom Kippur—was historic because it involved many of the leading Orthodox rabbis of the twentieth century, including Naftali Carlebach (1889–1967), father of Rabbi Shlomo Carlebach (1925–1994); Moshe Feinstein (1895–1986); Charles Kahane (1905–?), father of Rabbi Meir Kahane (1932–1990); Avraham Kalmanowitz (1891–1964); Eliezer Silver (1882–1968); and Joseph B. Soloveitchik (1903–1993).[28]

Over four hundred rabbis from around the United States, almost all of them Orthodox, arrived by train in Washington. Many rabbinic marchers were recent Yiddish-speaking immigrants to the United States and were not fluent in English. However, they were keenly aware of their personal deliverance from the Nazi killing machine in Europe. All the rabbis wore either hats or yarmulkes, and many had beards and long black coats: a clear visible presence in the nation's capital.

The rabbis first walked the short distance from Union Station to the Capitol building. Once there, they were received by Vice President Henry A. Wallace (1888–1965) and several congressional leaders, including Senators Alben Barkley (D-Kentucky; 1877–1956), Charles McNary (R-Oregon; 1874–1944), W. Warren Barbour (R-New Jersey; 1888–1943), and Sam Rayburn (D-Texas; 1882–1961), the Speaker of the House of Representatives. McNary had been Wendell Willkie's vice presidential running mate in the 1940 election, and Barkley later served as US vice president between 1949 and 1953.

Following their Capitol visit, the rabbinic group traveled by "chartered streetcars" to the Lincoln Memorial, when they read Psalm 22 and prayed for the welfare of President Roosevelt, the members of America's armed forces (six hundred thousand of whom were Jews), and their threatened brothers and sisters in Nazi-occupied Europe. They recited the Kaddish, the Jewish mourners' prayer, and then sang "The Star-Spangled Banner."

The four hundred–plus rabbis next marched to the White House with a petition to be presented to the president, but they were unsuccessful in that effort. The marchers were told that Roosevelt could not meet them because of the "pressure of other business." But, in fact, FDR slipped out a White House back door to attend an army public event. In his place, Roosevelt dispatched presidential secretary Marvin H. McIntyre (1878–1943) to receive the rabbis' petition demanding presidential action to rescue Jews.

While standing in front of the White House, many rabbis wept as they prayed for the safety of the Jews who each day in Europe faced Nazi execution-ers. One of those sobbing across the street from 1600 Pennsylvania Avenue was twenty-two-year-old Arthur Hertzberg (1921–2006), who in 1943 received his rabbinic ordination at the Jewish Theological Seminary of America. He may have been the only Conservative rabbi in the group, and there were no Reform rabbis among the marchers.

Following the war, Hertzberg served as a US air force chaplain and became a congregational rabbi in New Jersey, Columbia University professor, noted author, and an American and World Jewish Congress official. In 2003 Hertzberg remembered the march he had made sixty years earlier with his rabbinic father:

> This was a different kind of rabbinic gathering. These rabbis were not clean-shaven or well-dressed. They were avowedly East European. They represented not "American types" from the posh synagogues. On the contrary, they might just as well have been the rabbis whom Hitler was then putting in death-camps along with their congregants. They were standing at the gate of the White House begging the president to see them and to do something for the Jews who were being slaughtered by the tens of thousands.
>
> I could not get up to the fence of the White House so I had to look on from the park across the road. Eventually someone [presidential secretary McIntyre] came out of the White House. He took a letter from the rabbis to the president, but the president himself never greeted them. We were soon told that several of his Jewish advisers had told FDR that these immigrant rabbis were not the official leaders of the Jewish community. The people who had put them up to this gesture, such as Peter Bergson and his Emergency Committee to Save the Jewish People of Europe, were opponents of the Jewish establishment.
>
> All of us who had been there that day left feeling very bitter; America was our last great hope. If the president of the United States could not take the lead in this effort, or more precisely, if he chose not to be identified with the kind of activist effort that the rabbis were requesting, where could we now go? Was there some other address for our outcry? Or was the outcry being raised at the wrong time? These questions are still being debated to this very day. I continue to feel that the rabbis were right to go that day in 1943 to the gate of the White House. They were right. Those who advised Franklin D. Roosevelt not to see them continue to bear their shame.[29]

At a news conference following the march, Methodist Bishop James Cannon, Jr., urged "all quotas of all countries be made 'elastic' enough to admit oppressed people." Representative Andrew Somers declared the "homeless Jew must be cared for."[30]

In another appalling example of his fear of losing access to FDR and his coveted leadership status, Wise called the march "the orthodox rabbinical parade" and a "painful and even lamentable exhibition." He criticized the organizers labeling them as "stuntists" and said the rabbis insulted "the dignity of [the Jewish] people." Stephen and other establishment Jews were concerned that the sight of four hundred Old World rabbis would increase anti-Semitism in America.

Inside the White House itself, FDR counsel Samuel Rosenman advised his boss to avoid any personal meeting or encounter with the rabbis. William D. Hassett (1880–1965), another presidential aide, wrote in his diary that Rosenman "said the group behind this petition [is] not representative of the most thoughtful elements in Jewry. Judge Rosenman said he had tried—admittedly without success—to keep the horde from storming Washington. Said the leading Jews of his acquaintance opposed this march on the Capitol." Hassett wrote that Rosenman described them as "a group of rabbis who just recently left the darkest period of the medieval world."[31]

It is little wonder that Roosevelt felt no need to meet with the Orthodox "horde." The Jewish vote for his upcoming fourth term in 1944 was securely in his pocket, and FDR was armed with criticism of the march from Wise on the outside and from Rosenman on the inside. The march was viewed as a failure at the time; "most of the press, with the exception of the local papers, ignored the visit."[32]

Wise's fourth crisis—the creation of the US government's War Refugee Board (WRB) in 1944—was not the result of a specific event like the rabbis' march or a single telegram from Riegner in Geneva. Rather, the WRB was the result of Wise's constant pressure on Roosevelt and Secretary of the Treasury Morgenthau's painfully slow self-discovery of his Jewish identity, a process that ultimately moved the FDR cabinet member to demand presidential action to save his fellow Jews in Europe.

By December 1942, four months after Wise and the State Department both received Riegner's grim information, FDR was also fully aware of the Nazi Final Solution. On December 8, a high-level Jewish delegation headed by Wise met with Roosevelt at the White House. It was a desultory encounter, and it marked the only time during World War II that the president met with a group of Jewish leaders to confront the Nazi mass murders taking place in Europe.

Besides Wise, the delegation included Rabbi Israel Goldstein (1896–1986), the president of the Synagogue Council of America; Adolph Held (1885–1969),

the Jewish Labor Committee president; Henry Monsky (1890–1947), the B'nai
Brith president; Orthodox rabbi Israel Rosenberg (1875–1956), the leader of
the Agudath Harabonim (the Association of Rabbis); and American Jewish
Committee president Maurice Wertheim (1886–1950).

Like his AJC presidential predecessors Louis Marshall and Cyrus Adler,
Wertheim was a product of the German Jewish establishment in the United
States. Wertheim was married to Henry Morgenthau, Sr.'s, daughter, and the
AJC leader was the father of the historian Barbara W. Tuchman (1912–1989), a
niece of Treasury Secretary Morgenthau. But despite Wertheimer's multiple
connections and relationships, and Wise's leadership, the meeting with FDR
was a failure.

Held wrote a detailed report of the Oval Office meeting and noted that the
Jewish leaders spent only twenty-nine minutes with the president, who consumed twenty-three of those precious minutes with his well-known banter
and a few jokes while smoking his omnipresent cigarette. However, Wise was
able to present the president with a twelve-page memorandum demanding
immediate action by the United States to save as many Jews as possible. The
memorandum urged Roosevelt to

> raise your voice in behalf of the Jews of Europe . . . warn Nazis that they will
> be held to strict accountability for their crimes . . . [There is] verification of re-
> ports concerning the barbarities against the inhabitants of countries overrun
> by Hitler's forces. To these horrors has now been added the news of Hitler's
> edict calling for the extermination of all Jews in the subjugated lands, . . .
> Already almost two million Jews . . . have been cruelly done to death, and five
> million more Jews live under the threat of a similar doom. . . . We are of the
> belief that you can speak the word and take such action as will strike fear into
> the hearts of the enemies of civilization and at the same time bring hope and
> faith to their victims.
>
> In this spirit, we appeal to you, Mr. President. Speak the word! Institute the
> action![33]

A disappointed Held wrote,

> Rabbi Wise did not read the details but simply said: "Mr. President, we also
> beg to submit details and proofs of the horrible facts. We appeal to you, as head
> of our government, to do all in your power to bring this to the attention of the
> world and to do all in your power to make an effort to stop it."
>
> The President replied: "The government of the United States is very well
> acquainted with most of the facts you are now bringing to our attention. Unfor-
> tunately we have received confirmation from many sources. Representatives of

the United States government in Switzerland and other neutral countries have given up proof that confirm the horrors discussed by you. We cannot treat these matters in normal ways. We are dealing with an insane man—Hitler, and the group that surrounds him represent an example of a national psychopathic case. We cannot act toward them by normal means. That is why the problem is very difficult.

"At the same time it is not in the best interest of the Allied cause to make it appear that the entire German people are murderers or are in agreement with what Hitler is doing. There must be in Germany elements, now thoroughly subdued, but who at the proper time will, I am sure, rise, and protest against the atrocities, against the whole Hitler system. It is too early to make pronouncements such as President Wilson made, may they even be very useful. As to your proposal, I shall certainly be glad to issue another statement, such as you request."

Apparently, at the end of this quotation the President must have pushed some secret button, and his adjutant appeared in the room. His eyes and broad shoulders showed determination. We rose from our seats, and, as we stood up, the President said: "Gentlemen, you can prepare the statement. I am sure that you will put the words into it that express my thoughts. I leave it entirely to you. You may quote from my statement to the Mass Meeting in Madison Square Garden some months ago, but please quote it exactly. We shall do all in our power to be of service to your people in this tragic moment."

The President then shook hands with each of us, and we filed out of the room.[34]

Roosevelt was referring to the statement he gave Wise to be read at the Madison Square Garden rally in July 1942. But as Held reported, FDR made no promises about any plan or program to save Jews other than winning the war.

However, Wise kept demanding action, even suggesting the use of monetary bribes to rescue Jews in occupied Europe. In early 1943 Stephen learned from Riegner that seventy thousand Jews in France and Romania, including ten thousand children between the ages of two and fourteen, could be saved "if we could get funds into Switzerland." The endangered Jews would be "moved to Hungary, where there was as yet no organized campaign of destruction." The money would be held in escrow at the American legation in Bern until war's end for the Nazi individuals aiding the rescue efforts.[35]

In July 1943 Wise met again with Roosevelt and explained the proposed plan. He also told the president, "Our armies will see to it that these Nazi mercenaries shall not live to reap the benefit of their hostage-holding, blackmailing plan."

To Wise's delight and astonishment, FDR replied, "Stephen, why don't you go ahead and do it?" Wise wrote that Roosevelt then called Morgenthau on the telephone and said, "This is a very fair proposal which Stephen makes." The US government approved the project and authorized the payment of $170,000.

But State Department officials and the British Foreign Office delayed and "sabotaged" the program until December 18. Wise wrote that bureaucratic "bungling and callousness" prevented saving "thousands of Jewish lives."[36] In fact, Riegner reported that during the five-month delay, four thousand of the Jewish children "had been sent in sealed box cars to the death camps." A furious Morgenthau looked into the delay and discovered "the full extent of obstruction and double-dealing practiced by Long and his [State Department] cohorts."[37]

On April 19, 1943, a second international conference on refugees took place in Hamilton, Bermuda; the first was at Evian in France in 1938. In a chilling historic coincidence, the 1943 date marked the first night of Passover, the Jewish holiday commemorating the ancient Israelite exodus from Egyptian slavery.

But April 19, 1943, was also the first day of the Warsaw Ghetto Uprising, when thousands of entrapped Polish Jews, mostly young people, began an armed guerilla-style urban battle with crude weapons against German general Jürgen Stroop (1895–1952) and his elite SS troops. The outnumbered, outgunned, and physically weakened Jews battled for six weeks before the well-equipped Nazi forces destroyed the ghetto and killed most of the Jewish fighters. A proud Stroop wrote a book, *The Warsaw Ghetto Is No More*, and after the war was hanged as a war criminal in Poland.

The April 1943 wartime meeting in Bermuda lasted twelve days and involved the United States and Great Britain. US representative Sol Bloom (D-New York), the chairman of the House Foreign Affairs Committee, was a member of the American delegation as he had been at Evian five years earlier. Representative Emanuel Celler (D-New York) and a fellow Jew called Bloom a "sycophant of the State Department."[38]

The assertive and demanding Wise was, of course, not appointed to the US group. However, Stephen and his colleagues did submit a memorandum to the Bermuda conference participants about rescuing Jews.

Supreme Court justice Owen J. Roberts (1875–1955) turned down FDR's invitation to serve as the head of the American group. The president accepted Roberts's decision with a jovial response: "I fully understand, but I am truly sorry that you cannot go to Bermuda, especially at the time of the Easter lilies! After my talk with you, the State Department evidently decided (under British pressure) that the meeting should be held at once instead of waiting until June." FDR did get Princeton University president Harold W. Dodds (1889–1980) to lead the American delegation.[39]

Nothing substantive emerged from the Bermuda Conference; indeed, no final statement was even issued. The entire enterprise was perceived as a response to the mounting pressure in the United States and the United Kingdom to save Jewish lives and increase immigration to both countries. David Wyman has called the conference a "façade for inaction."[40]

Only about 21,000 Jews were admitted to the United States during the war years when the immigration quota was 191,000. Bermuda, like Evian, was a failure even when it was clear by 1943 that Nazi leaders were determined to kill every Jew under their control. Both Wise and Bergson denounced the Bermuda Conference; the latter called it a "mockery."

But predictably, Bloom termed the conference a "success" when he told eight hundred Jewish women at a Waldorf-Astoria Hotel luncheon, "As a Jew I am perfectly satisfied with the results of Bermuda."[41]

But Wise's proposal about using bribes to save Jewish lives accelerated within Morgenthau's Treasury Department. Josiah E. DuBois, Jr. (1913–1983), a Morgenthau assistant and a graduate of the University of Pennsylvania Law School, prepared a comprehensive memorandum describing the tragic Jewish condition in Europe as well as detailing the State Department's systematic pattern of blocking refugee immigration to the United States and various other anti-Jewish tactics. DuBois's accusative memo, titled "Report to the Secretary on the Acquiescence of This Government in the Murder of the Jews," charged, "It is the policy of this Government to take all measures within its power to rescue the victims of enemy oppression who are in imminent danger of death and otherwise to afford such victims all possible relief and assistance consistent with the successful prosecution of the war."

A troubled Morgenthau was reticent to present DuBois's harshly worded memo to the president, but the Treasury official threatened to resign his position and expose the Roosevelt administration's anti-Jewish actions to the press. Finally, Morgenthau reached the conclusion that DuBois's document must be given to FDR for executive action, but he gave it a more nuanced title: "Personal Memo to the President."

On Sunday, January 16, 1944, the secretary; the Treasury Department's general counsel, Randolph Paul (1890–1956); and another Morgenthau assistant, John W. Pehle (1910–1990), a Yale Law School graduate, met with FDR. The damning memo outlined the "incompetence, delay and even obstruction of a variety of rescue efforts" by the State Department. Morgenthau and his associates believed the State Department was guilty of "acquiescence in Germany's mass murder of Jews."[42]

FDR had a derogatory nickname for his treasury secretary: "Henny Penny." But this time, the often-docile Morgenthau was adamant, and Henny Penny got some positive results. Six days later, on January 22, Roosevelt authorized the establishment of the War Refugee Board with Pehle as its first director and DuBois its general counsel. Pehle proved to be an effective leader, and as the war neared its end, the board is credited with saving the lives of two hundred thousand Jews as well as twenty thousand people who were not Jewish.[43]

Stephen's proposal to President Roosevelt about using monetary bribes to save lives ultimately led to the creation of the War Refugee Board, one of the few positive achievements of the FDR administration involving Jews. But as Pehle later said,

> Looking back at the Board, I recognized that it was too late when it was established and the resources available were too small to deal effectively with the problem. But we were able to change the policy of the United States, and we were able to help the private agencies, and we were able to change the moral position of the United States in this area.[44]

The War Refugee Board also sent the Swedish diplomat Raoul Wallenberg (1912–1947?) to protect the Jews of Budapest, and the agency funded his efforts in the Hungarian capital. His adversary in that difficult and dangerous endeavor was Adolf Eichmann, who was in Budapest at the same time. The skillful Wallenberg was able to save a significant number of Jewish lives, including that of Tom Lantos (1928–2008), who later served as a member of the US Congress. The Soviet Army captured Wallenberg in 1945 and charged him with being a spy. It is believed he died in a Moscow prison in July 1947.[45]

Stephen Wise's fifth crisis focused on the proposed Allied bombing of Nazi death camps, especially Auschwitz located in Poland. The decision by the United States and Great Britain not to bomb Auschwitz or the rail lines leading to the camp remains a fiercely debated and well-documented issue. Historians, political leaders, and military experts have written numerous articles and books on the subject, and they remain divided about the feasibility and the effectiveness of bombing the infamous Nazi death camp.

The issue became critical for Wise and other Jewish leaders in April 1944 when Rudolf Vrba (1924–2006) and Alfred Wetzler (1918–1988), two Slovakian Jews, escaped from Auschwitz and gave the Czechoslovakian government-in-exile detailed information about the size, deadly purpose, and means of operation at Auschwitz and the neighboring Birkenau camp located about three miles away. The two escapees also presented an actual label from a container of the deadly Zyklon-B gas used at Auschwitz.[46]

Their report reached the Geneva WJC office, and Riegner transmitted the data via the British Foreign Service to Wise and others in New York. Weizmann in London and Ben-Gurion in Jerusalem also received the Vrba-Wetzler report as well as Pehle at the newly created War Refugee Board in Washington.

On June 29, 1944, Pehle wrote John J. McCloy (1895–1989), the assistant secretary of war, urging an air attack on Auschwitz. The request was rejected.

McCloy, a Harvard Law School graduate, later served as the US High Commissioner in postwar Germany, World Bank president, and a member of the Warren Commission in 1963 that investigated President John Kennedy's assassination. Doris Kearns Goodwin believes that

> though McCloy was not an anti-Semite like Breckinridge Long, he shared some of the stereotypes and prejudices against Jews held by many men of his generation and social milieu, including a suspicion of any information coming from Jewish sources.[47]

Two months later, the World Jewish Congress led by Wise pressed the US military to use heavy bombers to destroy the rail lines and other targets, including the crematoria and gas chambers in the death camp.

Aerial attacks became possible in 1944 because the US Air Force was using airfields in and around the eastern Italian city of Foggia, an area captured in 1943 from the Germans. Bombers from Foggia had the capability of reaching Poland, and official military records indicate that four US air attacks took place within five miles of Auschwitz in late November and December 1944. The target was a synthetic oil and rubber factory in Oswiecim, the Polish name for Auschwitz.

On August 9, 1944, the World Jewish Congress, with Wise as its president, advocated an attack on Auschwitz. The organization wrote to McCloy:

August 9, 1944
Hon. John J. McCloy
Under Secretary of War
War Department
Washington, D.C.

My dear Mr. Secretary:

I beg to submit to your consideration the following excerpt from a message which we received under date of July 29 from Mr. Ernest Frischer of the Czechoslovak State Council through the War Refugee Board:

"I believe that destruction of gas chambers and crematoria in Oswiecim by bombing would have a certain effect now. Germans are now exhuming and burning corpses in an effort to conceal their crimes. This could be prevented by destruction of crematoria and then Germans might possibly stop further mass exterminations especially since so little time is left to them. Bombing of

railway communications in this same area would also be of importance and of
military interest."

Sincerely yours,

A. Leon Kubowitzki, Head, Rescue Department

After the war, Kubowitzki (1896–1966) became an Israeli diplomat and
took the name Kubovy. The WJC received McCloy's response five days later:

14 August 1944

Dear Mr. Kubowitzki:

I refer to your letter of August 9 in which you request consideration of a proposal made by Mr. Ernest Frischer that certain installations and railroad centers be bombed.

The War Department had been approached by the War Refugee Board,
which raised the question of the practicability of this suggestion. After a study
it became apparent that such an operation could be executed only by the diver-
sion of considerable air support essential to the success of our forces now engaged in decisive operations elsewhere and would in any case be of such
doubtful efficacy that it would not warrant the use of our resources. There has
been considerable opinion to the effect that such an effort, even if practicable,
might provoke even more vindictive action by the Germans.

The War Department fully appreciates the humanitarian motives which
promoted the suggested operation, but for the reasons stated above it has not
been felt that it can or should be undertaken, at least at this time.

Sincerely,

John J. McCloy

Assistant Secretary of War[48]

McCloy's position that "doubtful efficacy" of the proposal "would not warrant the use of our resources" was the argument also used by Archibald
Sinclair (1890–1970), the British secretary for Air, in response to Weizmann's
request to bomb the crematoria and train lines near the camp. Ben-Gurion in
Mandate Palestine was at first not in favor of the bombing, but by July 1944 after digesting the Vrba-Wetzler report, "B-G" changed his position and advocated an attack.

Incredibly, McCloy worried that an Allied bombing mission might make
the Germans more "vindictive" in their actions against their Jewish prisoners.
However, by 1944 the Auschwitz-Birkenau death camp complex was operating
at "full capacity," murdering more than 500 Jews per hour, according to Vrba

and Wetzler. Between May 15 and July 9 that year, about 438,000 Hungarian Jews were sent to Auschwitz on 147 deportation trains that could have been used by the Germans elsewhere in Europe when the Soviet forces were driving westward and the Anglo-American forces had landed in France on D-day, June 6, 1944.

Holocaust scholar Michael Berenbaum has written,

> We know that, in the end, the pessimists won. They argued that nothing could be done, and nothing was done. The proposals of the optimists, those who argued that something could be done, were not even considered. Given what happened at Auschwitz-Birkenau during the summer of 1944, many have seen the failure to bomb as a symbol of indifference. Inaction helped the Germans achieve their goals and left the victims with little power to defend themselves. The Allies did not even offer bombing as a gesture of protest.[49]

Several years before his death, former South Dakota US senator George S. McGovern (1922–2012), the 1972 Democratic presidential nominee, gave an interview about the possibility of bombing Auschwitz. During the war McGovern was a crewmember of the 455th B-24 Liberator bomber group based at Cerignola near Foggia. Official records show that in late 1944, American bombers, B-24s and B-17 Flying Fortresses, made a series of attacks on the synthetic oil and rubber plant near the death camp.

The US military described the target:

> The target is located app. 32 miles west of Krakow and app. 20 miles southeast of Katowice and forms with the rubber plant to the east, one area. . . . The oil refinery covers an area of approximately 1100 x 1200 yds and the synthetic rubber plant an area of approximately 1800 x 1200 yds. The plants were owned and operated by the I.G. Farben Trust of Frankfurt, Main. To the south and west of the target, a concentration and labor camp [Auschwitz-Birkenau] exists which indicates forced and foreign labor at these plants.[50]

On December 26, 1944, McGovern participated in a raid that dropped fifty tons of bombs on the targeted factory. Three days earlier the Soviet Air Force destroyed over half the SS barracks at Birkenau. Four months before, on August 20, another American bomber group attacked the same factory and dropped 1,336 bombs. In that attack, P-51 (Mustang) fighters piloted by members of the African American "Tuskegee Squadron" escorted the US bombers.

McGovern agreed with the critics: "I attended every briefing that the air force gave to us. I heard everyone, from generals on down. I never heard once mentioned the possibility that the United States air force might interdict against the gas chambers." McGovern said if his commanders had asked for volunteers to bomb the death camp, "Whole crews would have volunteered. . . . There is no question we should have attempted . . . to go after Auschwitz. . . . There was a pretty good chance we could have blasted those rail lines off the face of the earth, which would have interrupted the flow of people to those death chambers, and we had a pretty good chance of knocking out those gas ovens."

McGovern was a lifelong supporter of FDR: "Franklin Roosevelt was a great man and he was my political hero, but I think he made two great mistakes in World War II": the forced internment of Japanese Americans in 1942 and the decision "not to go after Auschwitz . . . God forgive us for that tragic miscalculation."[51]

Critics of the US/UK "no-bomb" policy concede that bombing raids on or near Auschwitz-Birkenau would have killed Jewish prisoners, many of them already destined for the gas chambers. They further admit that the Germans would have repaired the rail lines or used other transportation to move Jews to Auschwitz. However, Wise and the leaders of the World Jewish Congress believed an attack on the camp in late 1944 would have been a clear signal to the Germans that the Allies were aware of the mass murders taking place and would have boosted morale for the Jews trapped there.

Elie Wiesel has written that he heard the bombs going off near Auschwitz in August 1944 when Allied planes bombed the I. G. Farben plant: "We were no longer afraid of death; at any rate, not of that death. Every bomb filled us with joy and gave us new confidence in life."[52] A bombing attack would have signaled to Wise and other Jewish leaders that the US recognized and understood the moral issues of the war, not simply the strategic ones.

Doris Kearns Goodwin has written,

Jan Karski and Elie Wiesel were later [years after the war] given a chance to see some of the aerial reconnaissance photos taken in those [American air force] flights. "It was the saddest thing," Karski recalled. "With a magnifying glass we could actually read the names and numbers of the Hungarian Jews standing on line waiting to be gassed. Yet McCloy claimed the target was too far away."[53]

Once again Wise and his World Jewish Congress were unable to effect a significant change in the policies of the Roosevelt administration.

Wise's sixth and last important crisis during the Roosevelt administration came in March 1945, a month before FDR died. On January 20, two days after his fourth presidential inauguration, the ailing president left Washington for Yalta in the Crimea to participate in the "Big Three" Conference. Eleanor had asked to go with Roosevelt to the meeting, but he chose their daughter Anna

(1906–1975) instead. FDR worried that the First Lady would attract her own media coverage and perhaps create serious press problems. Eleanor was humiliated by her husband's rejection.

Roosevelt made the difficult trip by air, sea, and land to the Black Sea port, where he joined Winston Churchill and Joseph Stalin. The Big Three had first met in Tehran, Iran, between November 28 and December 1, 1943. By early 1945, the end of the long war in Europe was finally in sight.

On January 30, Roosevelt celebrated his sixty-third birthday on his way to Yalta, but he had diminished strength and vigor. The conference took place between February 4 and 8, and FDR and his entourage did not return to Newport News, Virginia, until February 26. It was a grueling month of travel, intense negotiations, and the debilitating illness of Harry Hopkins (1890–1946), the president's most trusted aide.[54]

Wise hoped that the question of a postwar Jewish commonwealth in Palestine would be part of the Big Three's agenda, but it was not. Indeed, there was no action taken about increasing Jewish immigration to Palestine following the mass murders in Europe. The British opposed any changes in their restrictive policy.

However, during his month away from Washington, FDR did discuss Zionism and the future of Palestine, but not with a Jewish leader. The president had a personal meeting on February 15 with King Ibn Saud of Saudi Arabia (1876–1953). The encounter took place on board the *Quincy*, a US Navy cruiser, anchored in the Suez Canal. The meeting shattered Wise's long-held belief that FDR was a champion, albeit timidly, of the Zionist enterprise.

Worse still for Wise was Roosevelt's address to Congress on March 1, 1945. In that speech, FDR was forced to sit as he delivered his remarks. The president's physical condition had deteriorated badly, and for many Americans it was the first time they saw their once-vibrant, buoyant leader drained of stamina and energy. He devoted most of his speech to the results of the Yalta Conference.

But it was the few words uttered by Roosevelt near the end of his report that alarmed Wise and other Jewish leaders; words that sparked the rabbi's last confrontation with his "good friend" in the White House:

> I learned more about the whole Arabia [Middle East] problem, the Moslem problem, the Jewish problem, by talking with Ibn Saud for five minutes than I could have learned in an exchange of two or three dozen letters.[55]

Two weeks later, on the Ides of March, Wise had a fateful final White House meeting with Roosevelt. The president, less than a month from his death, continued his balancing act: affirming his support for Zionism and the

goal of a Jewish commonwealth in Palestine against the results of his recent
meeting with Ibn Saud, the ruler of an oil-rich kingdom whose "black gold"
the United States required to sustain its robust industrial economy.

Roosevelt found the Saudi monarch intractable on the question of any
Jewish immigration to the Holy Land, even in the wake of the Nazi wartime
mass murders. FDR was candid with Wise and admitted,

> I had a failure. The one failure of my mission was Ibn Saud. Everything went
> well [at Yalta], but not that, and I arranged the whole meeting for the sake of
> your cause. . . . I have never so completely failed to make an impact upon a
> man's mind as in his case.[56]

But, as he had done so often, after the meeting Wise offered an upbeat perspective of the president. On March 17, Stephen's seventy-first birthday, the
New York Times carried a story describing the forty-five-minute meeting two
days earlier. Wise praised FDR's support of Zionism:

> I [Roosevelt] made my position on Zionism clear in October. That position I
> have not changed and shall continue to bring about its earliest realization.

The president was referring to his letter sent during the 1944 election to
Senator Robert F. Wagner of New York indicating presidential backing for the
Democratic Party platform supporting "the opening of Palestine to unrestricted immigration . . . to result in the establishment of a free and democratic Jewish Commonwealth."[57]

In his autobiography written three years later, Wise reverts back to form
and attacks the "usual suspects," those who are responsible for FDR's acknowledged "failure" to change Ibn Saud's positions on Jews, Zionism, and immigration to Palestine. For Stephen, it was always the misguided advisers in the
State Department and the White House who rendered poor advice. It was
never the president's fault:

> He [FDR] told me at great length the story of his purpose to make the Near
> East leaders understand the miracle the Jewish rebuilders had wrought in
> Palestine. . . . Nothing but good would come of the continuation and the emu-
> lation in neighboring [Arab] lands of their toil and sacrifice for a great ideal
> [Zionism]. . . . If . . . he felt a sense of failure in respect to his most recent mis-
> sion to the ruler of Saudi Arabia to secure his assent to the development of
> Palestine, it was only because he attached too much importance to the power
> of that medieval ruler in determining the fate of Palestine on the poor advice
> of some counselors in our State Department and in the Foreign Office in

England. . . . He had already planned for another . . . more effective method of approach to the problem, the solution of which was bound to be the establishment of a free and democratic Jewish Commonwealth in Palestine.[58]

We will never know what Roosevelt's "more effective method of approach" to the Middle East might have been, because he died four weeks after meeting with Wise. Finding such an "approach" would be left to someone else: the new US president, FDR's running mate, Harry S. Truman.

Today we know more about the FDR–Ibn Saud meeting, and it was even worse than Wise suspected. In 1972 the FDR Presidential Library in Hyde Park, New York, released previously classified documents. One repudiated the claim that Roosevelt "asked Ibn Saud to admit more Jews to Palestine. Instead, Roosevelt is represented as agreeing that survivors of the Nazi holocaust might be resettled in the lands from which they were driven, particularly Poland."[59]

Franklin Roosevelt's death ended the most controversial and significant chapter in Stephen's life and career. But none of the complexity, ambiguity, anger, or differences in the FDR-Wise relationship were hinted at in the rabbi's tribute to Roosevelt:

I remember as early as March 1933, how his soul rebelled at the Nazi doctrine of superior and inferior races! . . . More than any American since Lincoln he brought the common man back to the remembrance and conscience of all Americans. . . . Our country was bereft as it had not been since April, 1865, when another emancipator passed out of the presidency into history.[60]

But perhaps Wise's true feelings were better expressed when his daughter, Justine, and her husband, Shad Polier, dined with the Roosevelts at the White House on Saturday night, February 13, 1943. Joining them were the explorer Admiral Richard E. Byrd (1888–1957) and his wife, Marie.[61]

During the dinner FDR asked Justine to convey his "affectionate regards" to her famous father. When Wise received Roosevelt's best wishes, he was not impressed. In a moment of candor, he lamented, "If only he would do something for my people."[62]

Chapter 25

The Last Years Were Not the Best Years of His Life

When World War II ended in 1945, Stephen Wise was emotionally and physically depleted by his years of efforts at the White House, the State Department, and the Treasury Department, as well leading the American and World Jewish Congresses, his rabbinical seminary, and various Zionist organizations. Yet the aging and ailing rabbi still remained the preeminent leader of a postwar American Jewish community that had been transformed as a result of the war. Because much of European Jewry was destroyed during the Holocaust, the United States became the home of the largest, most powerful, and most influential Jewish community in the world.

Nearly six hundred thousand Jewish men and women served in the US armed forces, and the returning veterans, many of whom had participated in combat, provided a new self-confidence and sure-footedness within a once insecure and timid population that had a constant fear of anti-Semitism and prejudice in housing, employment, and education.

Before the war, most Americans who were not Jewish perceived anti-Semitism as erecting barriers of discrimination or simply telling anti-Jewish jokes to one another. But with war's end the American public soon learned the deadly extent of Nazi anti-Semitism. "Holocaust" and "Shoah" had not yet entered the lexicon as terms describing the mass murder of six million Jews, but eyewitness accounts, including those of General Dwight D. Eisenhower (1890–1969), the Supreme Allied Commander in Europe, and thousands of American soldiers confirmed what many government, media, and religious leaders had known for years: the Nazi ideological belief in "racial purity and superiority" nearly resulted in the physical annihilation of the Jewish people.

When the veterans came home to America after V-E Day and V-J Day, they were presented with the extraordinary opportunities and benefits of the GI Bill of Rights. The 1944 congressional legislation provided discharged military personnel with low-interest business loans and low-cost housing mortgages as well as tuition and living expenses for students enrolled in professional and vocational schools, colleges, and universities.

The 2.2 million men and women, including many Jews, who utilized the GI Bill were able to enter the American middle class—something that many of them prior to the war had thought impossible or unlikely. The implementation and positive results of the GI Bill are today considered one of the nation's greatest success stories.[1]

The ghastly reports and eyewitness accounts from the many concentration and death camps in Europe drove Jewish leaders to intensify their demands for a Jewish state in Palestine. They recognized the truth of the cliché: "It's now or never." In early May 1942, only five months after the United States entered the war, six hundred delegates, including Chaim Weizmann, David Ben-Gurion, Abba Hillel Silver, and Stephen Wise, put aside their long-standing differences and assembled in New York City's Biltmore Hotel. After five days of intense meetings, they unanimously agreed upon the "Biltmore Program" that called for a "Jewish Commonwealth" in the biblical homeland, a Jewish army composed of Palestinian Jews, and an end to the 1939 British "White Paper" that restricted immigration to the land of Israel.

It was an extraordinary historic break with the past practice of Jewish leaders who frequently spoke about an ambiguous "Jewish national home" in Palestine or an undefined "Return to Zion." The Nazi assault on Jews, Britain's anti-Jewish policies, and a recognition that the future postwar period represented the last real possibility of establishing an independent Jewish commonwealth were major factors in the adoption of the Biltmore Program. The delegates recognized that the defeat of Germany and the terrifying results of Nazi anti-Semitism would be one final, never-to-be-repeated opportunity for Zionism to achieve its goal. It was a time for action. Michael Oren described the program's historic importance:

> Zionist representatives approved an eight-point plan that, for the first time, explicitly called for the creation of a "Jewish Commonwealth integrated in the structure of the new democratic world." Gone were the proposals for an amorphous Jewish national home in Palestine, for carving out Jewish cantons and delineating autonomous regions with an overarching Arab state. Similarly, effaced was the long-standing Zionist assumption that Palestine's fate would be decided in London. Instead, the delegates agreed that the United States constituted the new Zionist "battleground" and that Washington would have the paramount say in the struggle for Jewish sovereignty. Henceforth the Zionist movement would strive for unqualified Jewish independence in Palestine, for a state with recognized borders, republican institutions, and a sovereign Army, to be attained in cooperation with America.[2]

Although they voted in favor of the Biltmore Program, the two old lions, Weizmann and Wise, once bitter rivals in the Zionist movement, opposed the

Wise, future Israeli prime minister David Ben Gurion, and Nobel Prize winner Dr. Albert Einstein, New York City, 1939. Permission granted by the Stephen Wise Free Synagogue Archives.

statement. Both men still believed in the efficacy of the high-level diplomatic negotiations with political leaders in Britain and the United States they had engaged in for decades. Weizmann cherished his major role in pressing Britain to issue the Balfour Declaration in 1917; Wise relished his access to the highest levels of the American government, and he treasured the statements of support for Zionism from Presidents Wilson and Roosevelt.

As a result, Weizmann and Wise, both born in 1874, were out of step in many ways with the younger, more militant Zionist leaders who in the 1940s were led by David Ben-Gurion in Palestine and Abba Hillel Silver in the United States. The Biltmore meeting ended one era of Zionism and began a frenzied six-year period that ended in May 1948 with the creation of the independent state of Israel. The Biltmore Program defiantly called for "unqualified Jewish independence in Palestine," a sovereign Jewish state.

Shortly after the Biltmore Conference concluded, Wise wrote to Frankfurter expressing his misgivings:

It is very easy for some of the grand Zionist statesmen [Ben Gurion and Silver] to urge us to smash England. . . . But if England goes, everything is lost; if England wins, we still have a chance re [sic] Palestine and a Jewish future. . . . Weizmann's attitude has not been feeble or cowardly, as is alleged, but wise. . . . I am personally very fond of Ben-Gurion . . . but I cannot help feeling that in this hour Weizmann's course . . . is one of higher statesmanship.[3]

But both Wise and Weizmann were wrong on two counts. Zionism required much more than old-fashioned diplomacy of high-profile leaders like themselves. And the two aging warriors underestimated the vigor and impatience of people like Ben Gurion and Silver who correctly sensed a historic opportunity and acted upon it.

One reason for Stephen's unhappiness with the Biltmore Program was the aggressive leadership of Silver, a key ally of Ben-Gurion, the political leader of Palestinian Jewry. In fact, Rabbi Silver became the dominant American Zionist leader after Biltmore, and in that role he repeatedly denigrated, insulted, and criticized Wise.

The Silver-Wise battle has been termed as another clash of the Titans. In 2004 Kenneth Libo and Michael Shakun described the intense rivalry between the two famous Reform rabbis. Silver publicly condemned Wise for placing too much trust in Roosevelt's leadership and Stephen's dependence on FDR's goodwill regarding Zionism and the survival of the Jews in Nazi-occupied Europe. In Silver, Wise had met his match and more. The former was a brilliant orator in both English and Yiddish. Above all, the Cleveland rabbi represented independent Jewish action and was insistent that "there is but one solution for national homelessness. . . . Enough! There must be a final end to this, a sure and certain end (i.e., a Jewish State in Palestine)."[4]

At a Zionist congress in December 1946 in Europe, leaders of Hadassah, the women's Zionist organization with broad-based membership and support in the United States, begged Silver to appoint Wise to an honorary position without any power: chairman of the World Zionist Organization's Actions Committee. Silver's one-word response was "No!" In a brutal series of internecine battles, Silver was triumphant over Wise. Silver took no prisoners and ultimately assumed the sole leadership position within American Zionism.

When Wise once encountered Silver in a corridor, he pleaded, "Rabbi Silver, I am an old man, and have had my moment in the sun. You are a young man and will have your proper share of fame. It is not necessary for you to attack me." Silver walked away without a word.[5]

A defeated and angry Wise resigned from the Zionist Organization of America and denounced the new leaders. But his criticism was mostly a stroll down Zionism's memory lane. He did not want to substitute Zionism of the present imperiling regime [Silver] of the ZOA for the Zionism of Weizmann, Brandeis, Nordau and Herzl.[6]

Wise accused the "regime" of gaining power through a voting procedure he termed "caucus bondage." However, just as he done in 1921 when the Brandeis forces were defeated by Weizmann, Stephen still promised "to serve Zion and Zionism."[7]

During the 1930s and 1940s Wise's public leadership position, something he coveted, was anchored to his oft-proclaimed personal "friendship" with President Franklin Roosevelt. While that relationship was troubled and complex, the two men did together share decades of New York State history that began thirty years earlier. But Stephen did not have such a bond with Harry Truman, a Missourian, who was at first dismissed as an "accidental" president following FDR's death.

For Wise and other Jewish leaders, Truman was an unknown who had his own ties to the Jewish community, especially in Kansas City and St. Louis. As a US senator, Truman had supported the pro-Zionist statements of Peter Bergson, but he was never a leader in pressing for a Jewish commonwealth or state in Mandate Palestine.

But in his typical fashion, Wise warmly praised the new occupant of the Oval Office with flattering language. Soon after FDR's death, Stephen sent a letter to the new president praising Truman's "will and capacity greatly to serve our country."[8]

Indeed, Wise met with the president on April 20, 1945, just eight days after Truman became the nation's leader. The famed rabbi, however, was but one of nineteen visitors to the White House that day. Truman saw the cabinet members he inherited from Roosevelt as well as the American delegates to the upcoming San Francisco Conference that would establish the United Nations, the successor to the ineffectual League of Nations.[9]

Again, as was his practice following an Oval Office meeting, a pleased Wise told the press that Truman was a supporter of the Balfour Declaration and was prepared to back the efforts to establish a Jewish state. But in reality, Truman simply affirmed FDR's less than full-throated support for Zionist aspirations.

In 1962 Truman remembered his meeting with Wise during the first days of his presidency:

I recall that, a few days after I took office as President, in April 1945, Rabbi Stephen Wise came to see me in the White House to talk about the plight of the Jews in Europe and about the work that was then going forward to save them and the need of a Jewish Homeland in which they might be sheltered. I

was for a Jewish Homeland then and I am for it now. I could foresee difficulties
in the way of establishing that Homeland, but no difficulty was as great as the
moral disgrace of failing to establish it.

Truman remembered that Stephen "was just as polite as he could possibly
be." The new president told Wise that he "knew all about the history of the
Jews . . . [and] the Arab point of view . . . The United States would do all that it
could to help the Jews set up a homeland."[10]

Almost three years after his meeting with Wise, Truman had a private, un-
publicized meeting on March 18, 1948, in the White House with Chaim
Weizmann. The president met the Zionist leader after a personal request from
Eddie Jacobson. On May 14 Truman quickly granted US diplomatic recognition to the newly established state of Israel eleven minutes after the Jewish state
declared its independence. The president rejected the recommendations of the
State Department headed by Secretary George C. Marshall, Truman's personal
hero; James Forrestal, Truman's defense secretary, also articulated Marshall's
position. Both men reflected Roosevelt's negative response to Zionist goals and
opposed Truman's immediate diplomatic recognition of the new Jewish state.

Harry Truman often overruled the advice of "the 'striped pants' boys . . .
the career fellas in the State Department," and he was always proud of his role
in the rebirth of Israel after two thousand years.[11]

However, the new president maintained a "correct," but not a warm or cordial, relationship with "Roosevelt's rabbi," and an angry Truman later refused
to see Silver in any future meeting because during a White House meeting, the
fiery rabbi from the Midwest had pounded his fist on the president's desk demanding support for the creation of a Jewish state. Interestingly, there is not a
single mention of Truman in Stephen's autobiography.[12]

Following his initial meeting with Truman, Stephen and Louise traveled
by train from New York City to San Francisco and were "observers" at the
founding conference of the United Nations. However, Wise was concerned
that the various Jewish representatives would mill around the conference's
venue "giving out daily statements contradicting one another, and getting in
each other's way."[13]

Fifty nations sent delegates to the meeting that began on April 25, 1945,
and ended on June 26 when President Truman signed the founding document
along with other world leaders. Because the state of Israel did not gain its independence until 1948, Eliahu Elath (1903–1990) of the Jewish Agency represented the Yishuv in an unofficial capacity. In addition to Wise, Joseph Proskauer
and Jacob Blaustein (1892–1970) of the American Jewish Committee attended
the conference, and they successfully pressed to ensure that the UN Charter
included international human rights guarantees.

Wise with Gerhard Riegner and Nahum Goldmann, Zeilsheim, Germany displaced persons camp, 1946. Permission granted by the Stephen Wise Free Synagogue Archives.

In mid May, a nine-page memorandum in the Russian language was submitted to the Soviet delegation in San Francisco dealing with the protection of Jewish rights in Mandate Palestine. Wise attempted to personally deliver the document to USSR foreign minister Vyacheslav Molotov (1890–1986), but he was unsuccessful. Nonetheless, Stephen was confident the memorandum would ultimately reach top Soviet officials in Moscow, including Joseph Stalin.[14]

Despite the efforts of the American Jewish Committee officials, Wise, and others, Elath later wrote that the Jewish impact in San Francisco was minimal because of the rivalries among the various Jewish delegates.[15] Elath was later to serve as Israel's first ambassador to the United States, and during the 1960s he was the president of the Hebrew University.

In 1946 Wise visited displaced persons (DP) camps in Germany. The haggard survivors of Hitler's Final Solution cheered him wildly. In fact, "Stephania" had been a password in the Jewish underground in Nazi-occupied Europe. The word meant "America," and the Hebrew plural "Stephanim" was a code word for "dollars." The ailing seventy-two-year-old Stephen was overcome with emotion during his visit to a camp and said in a tearful voice, "This I do not deserve."[16]

However, back in the United States, Silver continued to show Wise little mercy even after he had won the battle for control of the American Zionist movement. The battle between the two famous Reform rabbis was both personal and ideological, a constant occurrence among Zionist leaders beginning with Herzl and his critics. Wise still relied on his extensive government contacts in Washington—Sumner Welles, members of Congress, and the Truman White House. It was akin to Weizmann's trust in the British governmental authorities regarding the creation of a Jewish state.

Silver and his followers won because he demanded a more aggressive policy, especially after the catastrophe in Europe during the Nazi years. The Cleveland rabbi, a Republican, always distrusted the wily Roosevelt and the behind-the-scenes maneuvering of Wise and Nahum Goldmann, Stephen's longtime Zionist ally in Washington.

The two rabbis differed in politics, geography, and strategy. Silver was a Republican who led a large Reform congregation. He was a political ally of Robert A. Taft, the prominent GOP senator from Ohio (1889–1953). Both rabbis had the ability to move audiences to cheers and tears and to impress even the most jaded governmental officials and members of the media.

After a grueling series of organizational fights within the Zionist movement, including the Biltmore Program, Silver was victorious. The final battle took place in 1947 when a weary Wise was forced to resign a key leadership position in the Zionist movement. It was a difficult moment for him professionally and personally.

However, the differences between Silver and Wise were also more than personal or stylistic. Soon after the war, a nearly bankrupt Great Britain begged the United States for a large financial loan. The once proud and haughty British Empire was diplomatically weak and at the fiscal breaking point. The loan issue was a divisive point among all Americans in 1946, especially within the Irish community, and it also polarized American Jewish leaders.

Silver despised the anti-Jewish British policies in Mandate Palestine and publicly opposed London's loan request. Wise, who sixteen years earlier had published "*The Great Betrayal*" that denounced the United Kingdom's actions in Palestine, supported American assistance to its battered ally. Adding to Silver's anti-British feeling was Ernest Bevin (1881–1951), Britain's foreign secretary, who loathed Zionists, opposed the creation of a Jewish state, and was accused by many, including Richard Crossman (1907–1974), a fellow Labour Party leader, of being an anti-Semite.[17]

Silver did not want the United States to aid a nation whose policies toward Jews and Zionism he considered morally bankrupt. But Wise felt differently. Stephen urged Congress to pass the loan legislation even though Britain

has wrought grievous injury to the Jewish population of Palestine . . . I shall
not permit my abundantly justified indignation . . . to change . . . my support,
as an American, of the British loan.[18]

The $4.34 billion (about $52 billion today) loan was approved at an interest
rate of 2 percent. Britain made its final repayment sixty years later in 2006.[19]

The weary British public and its fatigued wartime leaders wanted to abandon their difficult League of Nations Mandate responsibilities in Palestine. In
addition to the expense of maintaining armed forces and a civil administration, it was evident that the United Kingdom was either unable or unwilling to
satisfy the opposing irreconcilable demands of Jews and Arabs, and the British
failed to pacify the country.[20]

Although Wise and Silver battled one another for control of American
Zionism, in the mid-1940s, the movement's most important and dynamic
leader was Ben-Gurion, the leader of the Yishuv and the Jewish Agency. He
believed that what the Jews in Palestine actually did on the ground would ultimately decide whether modern Zionism, a movement that arrived late on the
world stage, would succeed or fail. Ben-Gurion preached a single concept:
"Independence!" He was in effect "Mr. Inside" of the movement, having arrived in 1906 in Ottoman-ruled Palestine from Poland as a twenty-year-old.

The skilled chemist-diplomat, Dr. Chaim Weizmann, was Zionism's "Mr.
Outside," the London-based leader who eloquently addressed commissions,
presidents, premiers, prime ministers, conventions, congresses, and the world
media. His often-criticized link to Britain was both personal and tragic because his son Michael (1916–1942), a Royal Air Force fighter pilot, had been
killed in action over the Bay of Biscay during the war.[21]

Michael's first cousin, Ezer Weizman (1924–2005), was also a pilot first
with the RAF and later served as chief of the Israeli Air Force. Weizman (who
deleted the second "n" from his last name) was Israel's seventh president, between 1993 and 2000.[22]

While fighting fellow Zionist Silver and joining forces with Chaim
Weizmann, Wise became involved in a fierce battle with a group of thirty-six
Reform US rabbis who in 1942 formed the anti-Zionist American Council for
Judaism (ACJ). Three of its founders were long time foes of Wise: William
Fineshriber and Louis Wolsey (1877–1953), both of Philadelphia, and David
Philipson of Cincinnati. The council strongly rejected both the concept and
the creation of a Jewish state.[23]

When the February 1942 convention of the Central Conference of American Rabbis adopted a resolution by a vote of 64–38 calling for a separate "Jewish
Army" in Palestine to fight Hitler, three dozen irate rabbis believed such an
"army" was a form of self-segregation instead of full Jewish integration into

the Allies' armed forces. But their real issue was fear that a muscular Zionism "would confuse the attitude of America towards the Jew . . . [The anti-Zionists did not want] to be identified with the concept of the Jew as a national group . . . who wishes to build up an army of his own under his own flag."[24]

Wise was pleased that his years of Zionist efforts bore fruit when the Jewish Army resolution was adopted. By 1942 Stephen was no longer a lone voice among Reform rabbis. Many prominent rabbis supported the Jewish national movement, including Solomon B. Freehof of Pittsburgh (1892–1990), who declared at the 1942 CCAR meeting,

> The Zionist movement . . . brought together into one land, Jews from everywhere . . . see each other now for the first time since that ancient day when they parted from each other in Palestine 2000 years ago.[25]

The similar initials and names of the American Jewish Congress (strongly Zionist and led by Wise), the American Jewish Committee (officially "non-Zionist" until the creation of Israel in 1948), and the American Council for Judaism (strongly anti-Zionist) frequently confused both the Jewish and the general American public.

Before the inception of the ACJ, Wise's Reform anti-Zionist foes were generally individual rabbis who rejected any "national" aspects of Jewish identity; they defined being a member of the Jewish people in solely religious terms. Wise had battled with his anti-Zionist rabbinic colleagues since the late 1890s, but he became especially concerned when the American Council for Judaism attracted not only rabbis but also a number of influential laypeople, notably Sears Roebuck executive Lessing J. Rosenwald (1891–1979), to its leadership ranks.

Rosenwald provided money for the organization and was able to present the anti-Zionist case to Presidents Truman and Eisenhower, Secretaries of State Dean Acheson (1893–1971) and George Marshall, and other high US government officials.[26]

Wise was furious with the anti-Zionism of the group, but he was also angered when anti-Semitic officials within the State Department and in the media cited the council's positions as "proof" that American Jews did not support the Zionist program. Wise made certain the public knew that the council represented a tiny fraction of the total American Jewish community. It is estimated that, in 1948, there were only fourteen thousand ACJ members. Stephen wrote to Silver on November 15, 1944,

> I considered, as I believe you do, the conduct of [William] Fineshriber and [Louis] Wolsey to be treasonable to every high Jewish interest.[27]

Wise had special contempt for the anti-Zionist American Council for Judaism once the state of Israel gained its independence:

> Unless it [the ACJ] wish to sever itself from the body and soul of the Jewish people, [it] has no right to offer a platform for an impoisining declaration against the Jews of America and the State of Israel. We know well the world will never identify these cowardly persons with the heroic enterprise of the Jewish State. These, whether they hire or are hirelings, have chosen the ignoble way of self-obliteration at a time when self-redemption lay within their unheroic grasp.[28]

Nonetheless, the ACJ attracted important lay leaders and significant money, and was a public voice that vigorously opposed Zionism, labeling it "Jewish tribalism" and "anti-Enlightenment." The council leaders believed that Zionists like Wise had gained major control of US Jewish institutions, including rabbinical seminaries and congregational bodies. However, the group lost many members and became weaker when Israel was established in 1948, and weaker still following the June 1967 Six-Day War in the Middle East.

In addition to the ACJ leaders who believed Wise was too militant in his "political" Zionism, Stephen was also criticized at the other extreme by the followers of Peter Bergson as described in an earlier chapter. For them, Wise's brand of Zionism was linked too closely to Franklin Roosevelt and Wise's other alleged "friends" in the US government, particularly Sumner Welles, the undersecretary of state.

On yet another front, in early 1947 Wise attacked the leadership of the Federal Council of Churches. In 1950 it became the National Council of Churches with headquarters at 475 Riverside Drive in Manhattan, and its member organizations include many Protestant and Eastern Orthodox church bodies.

The council had invited the German Lutheran pastor Martin Niemoeller (1892–1984) to present a series of lectures in the United States. Niemoeller today is best remembered as the presumed author of the anti-Nazi statement, "First they came for the Communists . . . ," composed after the war. However, some historians dispute Niemoeller's authorship.[29]

Wise wrote a sharply worded letter to Dr. Samuel McCrea Cavert (1888–1976), the council's general secretary:

> When Hitler launched the movement destined to become the most disastrous in human history, Rev. Mr. Niemöller became his enthusiastic supporter. He went to the unbelievable length of hailing Nazism as "an instrument approved by God." From 1933 to 1937 . . . Niemoeller was neutral and silent. Not until

1937 did he find his tongue and then only with respect to the threatened regimentation of the . . . Churches of Germany. He paid the penalty of his opposition . . . by being sent to concentration camps where he suffered no more than other victims and far less than thousands of Jewish residents of concentration camps who, unlike Niemoeller, never emerged alive. . . . In 1939 he volunteered his services to, and in, Hitler's navy. . . . The record is that neither before nor after his incarceration in concentration camps did Niemoeller speak one word of protest against one of the foulest crimes in history.[30]

Until his death in 1949, and despite the public attacks from Silver, the American Council for Judaism, and the Irgun-sponsored Bergson group, a physically weakened Wise was still able to maintain many of his leadership positions in American Jewish life when there was a race against time to achieve a Jewish state in the years immediately after World War II. Stephen never ceased in his efforts to achieve a free democratic Jewish state.

Wise remained the Free Synagogue's senior rabbi, although in May 1943 in the midst of the war, the congregation's leaders gave him a "leave of absence for the duration" that enabled Stephen to devote more of his time to work in behalf of Zionism and the rescue of Jews from Nazism.[31] Rabbis Sidney Goldstein and J. X. Cohen continued in their roles at the Free Synagogue, and Rabbi Edward Klein (1913–1985), a JIR graduate, was added to the staff. Klein became the senior rabbi following Stephen's death, and remained with the congregation until his own passing.

In the immediate postwar period, Wise remained a dominant force in both the American and the World Jewish Congresses. Indeed, his last overseas trip came in 1948 when he presided at the WJC meeting in Switzerland. That assembly, the first since the war, was a bittersweet event for Wise and the delegates who were haunted by "the mass slaughter of millions of our fellow Jews."[32]

At the founding of the WJC in 1936, Wise wrote,

Delegates from Poland represented a great Jewry. . . . In the things that matter in Jewish history—piety, learning, devotion, integrity—a Jewry then estimated of three million, three hundred thousand. In 1948, barely one hundred thousand Jews remained alive in Poland.[33]

Wise and his WJC colleagues were also unhappy that representatives from the Soviet Union were not permitted to attend the meeting. Banning such international travel was a key part of the Stalin regime's anti-Jewish policies. The battle to free Soviet Jews from the restrictions imposed upon them was a long one that only ended with the collapse of the USSR decades later. However, in

Louise Waterman Wise at the WJC meeting in Geneva, 1936. Permission granted by the Stephen Wise Free Synagogue Archives.

1948 the WJC representatives gave a rousing, joyous welcome to David Remez (1886–1951), the state of Israel's first minister of transportation.[34]

During the first postwar years, Wise also continued to serve as president of the Jewish Institute of Religion. In 1945 Wise launched a $1 million drive to guarantee the continuing independent existence of his beloved seminary. He enlisted Albert Einstein to serve as the campaign's honorary chairman. But the effort was able to raise only a paltry $60,453 because most of the Jewish philanthropic money in those years went to aid the survivors of the Holocaust. A distraught Wise complained,

> What can I do? The congregations are not supporting me. Our graduates are not as loyal to the school as they should. . . . I've reached the end of my tether.[35]

There had been some earlier unsuccessful attempts to bring about cooperation among the JIR, UAHC, and HUC. In 1929 a resolution about the JIR was introduced at the congregational body's convention. Ten years later, there were negotiations for the merger of the two rabbinical schools, and a compromise agreement was hammered out by 1941. But the war and the creation in 1943 of the American Council for Judaism prevented a merger. Wise, in the twilight of his life, was adamantly opposed to linking his seminary to any consortium that represented an anti-Zionist position.

However, in 1945 HUC awarded Stephen an honorary degree, and at the ceremony in Cincinnati he was lauded specifically for his leadership in the Zionist movement. In 1946 a UAHC convention unanimously called for greater cooperation between JIR and HUC, something that had taken twenty-four years to achieve. Two years later, a physically weakened Wise "retired" from the JIR presidency and was named president emeritus of the combined seminary that chose Nelson Glueck as its president in 1947. The latter was a world-famous archaeologist and a supporter of Zionism. Wise and Glueck personally met in Stephen's office in May 1946, with the younger man promising Stephen that the JIR would remain a viable New York City seminary. Glueck's election removed several barriers for Wise, and facing a fiscal crisis, Stephen agreed to the merger.

In 1948 it became a reality, and the leaders of the two schools issued a joint statement that promised

> freedom for faculty and students alike . . . This united institution shall continue to maintain schools in Cincinnati and New York, with Nelson Glueck as president and Stephen S. Wise and Julian Morgenstern as presidents emeriti. Upon this union we invoke the blessing of God.[36]

Wise delivered a poignant "Farewell Address" to his JIR students at the rabbinical school's 1948 graduation ceremonies:

> This be my last word to you if we never meet again. God speak not to you chiefly or alone, but through to your congregation, to your people, to American Israel. I part with you in sorrow but with limitless hope and with deep affection for you, my dear boys. And I pray that the God of our fathers may bless you, bless you now and always.[37]

Today, Hebrew Union College–Jewish Institute of Religion is an international academic institution offering a wide variety of programs. In addition to its rabbinical school, the College-Institute includes schools of graduate studies, education, Jewish nonprofit management, sacred music, and biblical archaeology. HUC-JIR has four major campuses: Cincinnati, New York City, Los Angeles, and Jerusalem.

David Ellenson, the school's chancellor and former president, a native of Virginia, completed his rabbinic studies at the New York school and is a graduate of William and Mary (the same college Thomas Jefferson attended). Ellenson, like Wise, earned his Ph.D. from Columbia University. Aaron Panken, Ellenson's successor as HUC-JIR's president, was also a rabbinical student at the New York school and received his doctorate from New York University. It is mandatory for all HUC-JIR rabbinical, cantorial, and religious education students to spend their first year of study in Jerusalem—all facts that would greatly please Stephen Wise.

Louise Waterman Wise hard at work at WJC meeting, Geneva, 1936. Permission granted by the Stephen Wise Free Synagogue Archives.

The death of Wise's wife on December 10, 1947, from pneumonia shattered Stephen. Louise Wise was a devoted partner of her husband and a powerful civic and philanthropic force in her own right; Louise was not merely "Mrs. Stephen S. Wise." She established the adoption agency in New York City that bore her name and also provided needed Manhattan housing in the 1930s and 1940s for European Jewish refugees fleeing from Hitler. During World War II, Louise's leadership was central when she and many volunteers from the American Jewish Congress women's division welcomed 250,000 Allied military personnel at the organization's hostel in New York City.

Louise's funeral drew more than a thousand people to 40 West 68th Street, the building that housed both the JIR and the Free Synagogue offices. Wise did not officiate, but instead Stephen sat with his family and amid the mourners. Dr. David Petegorsky (1915–1956), the American Jewish Congress executive director, offered the eulogy:

> Her life was a restless passionate pursuit of justice, beauty and truth. . . . She knew and felt profoundly that the world would never be molded in the image of God and His purpose unless it rested on those foundations. . . . [Louise Wise] was certain that active participation in causes which served justice and truth could transform those of ill will or no will to persons of good will.[38]

A year earlier, Wise, Silver, and Goldmann had planned to visit Palestine, but Britain denied entry visas to the prominent Jewish leaders, fearing their presence would create problems for the Mandate authorities. About a week later, Louise was chosen to receive the prestigious Order of the British Empire (OBE) because of her wartime work in behalf of British military personnel. In a carefully worded letter of refusal, the once-pampered and overprotected daughter of a wealthy Manhattan family asserted that she could not accept such an honor from a nation that had, in her opinion, disgracefully broken its public promises to support Jewish aspirations and hopes in Palestine.[39]

In honor of his seventy-fifth fifth birthday, March 17, 1949, twelve hundred people attended a gala dinner in Wise's honor at the Hotel Astor in New York City. Slowed by advancing age, an enlarged spleen, and a stomach cancer that eventually ended his life a month later, Stephen still delivered a powerful speech that summed up his credo and life's work. He concluded his emotional address by lifting his fist and yelling, "I'll fight! I'll fight!" The dinner guests gave the famous rabbi an extended standing ovation.[40]

A day earlier in an interview with the *New York Times*, he struck a progressive internationalist note that reflected Woodrow Wilson's vision of the world. Wise spoke positively about how Americans

> moved forward from the isolation of my youth, out of which it was difficult to move our country before the first World War, in an understanding of our relation to the political and, above all, economic problems of the nations.[41]

In the same interview Stephen offered a rebuttal of the charges raised by the American Council for Judaism. Wise attacked the idea that when American Jews support the state of Israel, they are somehow being disloyal to America. Stephen reaffirmed Louis Brandeis's position on the same theme:

> Let no one dare to hint at the "dual allegiance" of the American Jewish community. . . . The very loyalty of American Jewish citizens imposes upon them the obligation of maximum helpfulness to those Jews within the State of Israel who have suffered, endured and toiled in order to be free to rebuild collectively their own life.[42]

One of his last public acts was to travel to Waltham, Massachusetts, in late March 1949 to congratulate Dr. Abram L. Sachar (1899–1993), the president of Brandeis University, the newly established Jewish-sponsored school named in honor of the first Jew on the Supreme Court and an early leader of American Zionism.

On March 27, a day after his Brandeis visit, Wise delivered the final address of his life at the Ford Hall Forum in Boston, where he had first spoken in 1908. Forty-one years later, Wise's topic was "My Challenging Years: A Seventy-Fifth Birthday Address." An emotional Stephen told the large audience, "I have lived to see the Jewish State. I am too small for the greatness of the mercy which God has shown us." Sensing he was near the end of his life,

Wise concluded by reciting a benediction in Hebrew, something he had refrained from doing in thousands of other public addresses.[43]

Once back in New York City, on March 30 he was admitted to Lenox Hill Hospital on Manhattan's Upper East Side. He underwent surgery on April 7 to remove a "malignant stomach ailment," but the cancer was unchecked. Shortly before he died, he had a private bedside conversation with his grandson, Stephen Wise Tulin, an Oberlin College student and the son of Justine Wise and her late husband, Abe Tulin. On Tuesday, April 19, Stephen went into a coma. Surrounded by his family, he died at 4:00 p.m.[44]

Chapter 26

The Final Bow

Although the sociologist Erving Goffman (1922–1982) published his influential book *The Presentation of Self in Everyday Life* in 1959, ten years after Wise's death, during a long public career Stephen always grasped and acted upon Goffman's basic idea that

> in social interaction, as in theatrical performance, there is a front region where the "actors" (individuals) are on stage in front of the audiences. This is where the positive aspect of the idea of self and desired impressions are highlighted. There is also a back region or stage that can also be considered as a hidden or private place where individuals can be themselves and get rid of their role or identity in society.[1]

Although Wise, as an adult, may have still suffered from the childhood inferiority complex described in a previous chapter (his "back region or stage"), there is little doubt about his effective use of the "front region" where Stephen consciously projected a commanding and forceful persona. It is no surprise that Wise carefully planned his own funeral service to create the "desired impressions" for his adoring public one last time.

However, as Stephen faced his own mortality, he did not neglect the "back region" of his life. A few months before his death Wise wrote to his children, James and Justine:

> When something happens to me, Ed [Klein] knows about the things I prefer for the [funeral] service.
>
> Ed, of course, is to have charge of the service, whether at the Synagogue House or in Carnegie Hall, where I preached for thirty years and with which I became associated during the stronger years of my life. . . .
>
> In view of the large part which the [American Jewish] Congress and Zionism have had in my life, I think just as in the case of Mummie [Louise], I

Sculpture of Wise by Robert Berks in Free Synagogue, New York City, 1957. Permission granted by the Stephen Wise Free Synagogue Archives.

would like to have Dave [Petegorsky] to speak the word of farewell if he were equal to it. Dave has grown very dear to me. He knows what it is that I most deeply care for: the State of Israel and freedom and justice for Jews everywhere. . . .

I would like a prayer or reading of a poem by my beloved friend [John Haynes] Holmes.

You won't see this while I am alive. When you do see it, I beg you to understand that my release, whenever it comes, is a great mercy. I am far from well and comfortable. . . . I hate to leave you both and Shad [Justine's husband] and Helen [James's wife] and my precious grandchildren, but I feel the time is drawing very near for me to go Home. . . . It will mean the reunion of my spirit with that of Mummie's. . . . I want my dust to be placed in the niche wherein she lies.

All love forever to you who have taken such wonderful care of me. . . . You will love and care for each other always.

Into the Hand of God, I commend my spirit. May he continue to vouchsafe me His grace and mercy.[2]

On April 22, 1949, three thousand mourners crowded into Carnegie Hall for his funeral, while another fifteen thousand people stood outside in the rain. President Truman called Wise "a valiant fighter in the cause of righteousness and good will." Chaim Weizmann, recently elected the first president of Israel, said,

America and Israel have sustained in his death an irreparable loss, but for both of them as for countless men and women of the democratic faith throughout the world he will long continue as a living and effective force for good. I have lost one of my dearest friends, the Jewish people one of its most illustrious sons.[3]

In the turbulent fifty-six years of his rabbinate, Wise influenced many lives, movements, and organizations. It was appropriate that A. Philip Randolph (1889–1979), the founder and president of the Brotherhood of Sleeping Car Porters, was among the first public figures to express sorrow following Wise's death. A leading black theologian, Howard Thurman (1899–1981), the dean of Boston University's Marsh Chapel and Martin Luther King, Jr.'s, mentor, captured Wise's life and influence:

I knew a man who was like one of the ancient prophets.

There was something of the eternal in the rolling sound of his majestic voice. . . .

There was something dazzling about the burning brilliance of his mind. When one listened to his words, there were moments that seemed to be all light, and all the little dark caverns of one's prejudices and fears melted away. . . .

He was the authentic embodiment of a dream. He lived it, he talked it and thought it, until at last the magic of its power became to many what it was to him. . . .

It is not difficult to believe that in years to come, when some daring dreamer sees a deeper meaning and a greater glory in an ancient faith and calls others to walk therein, they will feel a strange new courage feeding the hidden fires of their dreams . . . when some gaping wrong cries aloud for righting . . . there will be moving across the horizon of their minds the spirit to which this great man gave himself with such unyielding devotion.[4]

Wise's funeral began with Rabbi Klein reading Psalms 90 and 144 in the original Hebrew. The first psalm contains verses that befit someone who has attained seventy-five years of age:

> The days of our years are threescore years and ten, or even by reason
>   of strength fourscore years;
> yet is their pride but travail and vanity;
> for it is speedily gone, and we fly away.

Wise likely chose the second psalm because it encapsulated his own life as a warrior for justice, but also as a human being who recognized the limitations of earthly life:

> Blessed be the Lord my Rock, who traineth my hands for war, and my fingers for battle. . . . Lord, what is man, that Thou takest knowledge of him? His days are as a shadow that passeth away.

Wise's Christian colleague, the Reverend Dr. John Haynes Holmes, read selections from John Milton's *Samson Agonistes* and Matthew Arnold's (1822–1888) *Rugby Chapel*. Rabbis Sidney Goldstein and J. X. Cohen assisted in the service, and David Petegorsky's tribute included these words:

> He was a simple man who dared to remain simple in an age which rewarded cunning and cold calculation and deceit. He was man of profound faith and piety, and he dared to retain his faith in a world which mocked and seemed to disapprove any faith. He was man overflowing with love, and he dared to continue to love during a generation when hate and prejudice and ill-will stalked the earth and crept into the hearts of millions. . . . [He had] an overflowing love . . . for his people Israel, his country America, his family, his friends, his associates, for ordinary and humble men and women. . . .
>
> History will inscribe Stephen Wise among the truly great men of our era. It will record that he was a pioneer, a fearless crusader, in every worthwhile field of social concern; in the cause of justice and freedom for all men and for all peoples; for public morality and social welfare; for the deepening of religion and the extension of knowledge; for international peace and understanding.[5]

Wise's casket draped with both the American and Israeli flags was driven slowly from Carnegie Hall through the Manhattan streets that Stephen had known since his childhood, and the procession attracted a large crowd as it traveled through Harlem. When the hearse completed the twenty-mile journey to Hastings-on-Hudson and entered Westchester Hills Cemetery, Wise was placed in the family mausoleum next to his wife.

A few days after the funeral, James and Justine received a letter of sympathy from Albert Einstein, who wrote,

> He helped the Jewish people to maintain dignity and to win their independence. . . . I consider it a blessing to have been close to him personally. For it is due to the few of his stature that one does not completely despair of man. His deep, moral influence will continue although he is no longer among us. This knowledge will be a real comfort in your sorrow.[6]

In addition to his wife, son, and daughter, Stephen had six grandchildren. His expensive lifestyle included a home in the Adirondack Mountains of New York State, and the Wise family lived in various upscale residences in Manhattan. Stephen sent Justine and James to expensive private schools and colleges, including Bryn Mawr, Princeton, and Yale Law School.

His Free Synagogue salary was not excessive, and Wise earned needed extra income from his numerous appearances on the lecture circuit. The gross estate value of the famed rabbi was $273,455 (worth about $2.5 million today), and the net amount was $140,865 (about $1.3 million). The money was left to his children.[7]

At first glance, evaluating the life and times of Wise appears to be an uncomplicated task. He was a Titan, the most prominent Jewish leader of his era, a dynamic advocate of Zionism, a strong supporter of American Progressive politics, and an early foe of Hitler and Nazism. But such a limited description would be a mistake because there are many conflicting opinions and negative views of Wise.

Happily for historians, Wise, a well-known public figure for over fifty years, left behind a huge number of letters, sermons, magazine articles, newspaper interviews, speeches, public statements, and several books, including an autobiography that was hastily written near the end of his life. Stephen attracted extraordinary attention because he was a rarity: a rabbi who confidently walked in America's corridors of power, the nation's important political and social circles, where he interacted personally with mayors, governors, members of the US Congress, Supreme Court justices, cabinet members, prominent Christian clergy, foreign leaders, and especially with American presidents Woodrow Wilson and Franklin Roosevelt.

Because Stephen was unafraid to take political positions, he publicly supported and opposed a large number of candidates for a myriad of elective offices. At the same time Wise demanded justice and freedom for the Jewish people, he also made the same demands for all peoples who suffered discrimination and prejudice. He was a champion of what we today know as civil, economic, and human rights.

Wise's powerful speaking voice, his striking physical appearance, and his eloquent command of the English language were rare for his time, especially when compared to most of his fellow rabbis and Christian leaders. Few orators during his lifetime could command a stage and deeply move an audience as Stephen repeatedly did for more than a half century.

He also employed the new medium of the radio to deliver his many messages. When he died in 1949, television was literally in its infancy, and if he were alive today, there is little doubt Stephen Wise would be the master of all forms of electronic social media and networking.

However, it is an incomplete picture of the man and his times if the focus is solely on his public style, his zest for controversy and debate, his campaigns to gain access to the politically powerful, his oratorical prowess, and his personal charisma.

Wise must also be judged by another set of weights and measures, another set of scales, another set of criteria. How well did Stephen Wise succeed in achieving the three goals that were the foundation of his lengthy public career? Identifying Wise's basic ideals and goals is easy, but more difficult is the question: Was he able to gain his objectives as an American, a Jew, and a rabbi?

He believed that being fully Jewish and fully American was not incompatible. He was often confronted with the question whether one could be both Jewish and American. Wise's lifelong answer was a thunderous "Yes!"

Interestingly, Cardinal Richard Cushing (1895–1970), the archbishop of Boston, faced a similar question, and he echoed Wise's forceful commitment to America. The cardinal answered the charge hurled at Alfred E. Smith during the New York governor's unsuccessful 1928 presidential campaign:

> Can a Roman Catholic President faithfully follow the US Constitution or will America's chief executive place Church laws and Vatican policies above everything else?

In 1951 during the Korean War, Cushing struck a theme he repeated many times. If the word "Jewish" is substituted for "Catholic," Wise could have uttered the cardinal's strident statement:

> Love of God and love of country are linked together in the heart of every true Catholic American citizen. Patriotism, the noblest of human virtues, burns as brightly in the heart of the American Catholic as it does in the heart of any neighbor. . . . Yes, America, we love thee, and we are ready, if necessary, to

pour out the last drop of our blood in its defense. . . . We defy anyone to disprove the loyalty of Catholics of the United States, to the government under which we live.[8]

Wise, working with Louis Brandeis, was committed to making Zionism an authentic, integral part of American Jewish life. Zionism, for Stephen, was not a bizarre, quaint, impractical idea, but rather he wanted it to be an essential component of the self-perception and self-identity of Jews in the United States. One of his principal aims was to enlist the entire Jewish community, especially those who were "liberal" Jews, to the cause of the Zionist movement.

Wise's third great goal was the belief that it was incumbent for American Jews to participate in all phases of US political life as full citizens and not as pleaders or beggars bowing low at the entry gates of the powerful and influential. That is one reason he emphasized gaining personal access to political leaders, including the occupants of the White House. Stephen believed all Americans had the absolute right to vote, including women and blacks, and every American had the absolute right to commend or condemn political candidates and office holders, including Stephen's fellow Jews.

Wise demanded that the United States fulfill and make real the highest aspirations of the American experiment in democracy. Because he loved America with passion and devotion, Wise insisted that his adopted nation live up to its professed ideals of "liberty and justice for all." Stephen perceived America, not as an extension of the divided and troubled Europe he and his family had fled, but as something exceptional in human history that merited his total commitment and support.

Historians employ the German term *Sitz im Leben*, or "sitting in life," as a basic working component for their work and research. The phrase requires later generations when writing about the past to understand the religious, cultural, political, economic, and social settings and the specific time frames in the life of a person or a nation.

Sitz im Leben is a warning not to apply contemporary attitudes, knowledge, or values onto a previous era. Although we may know "how things turned out" in the past and while we may have applied the required principle of *Sitz im Leben* to our study, we are not exempt or excused from rendering judgment on a historical figure.

This is especially true in evaluating the career of Stephen Wise. He was born in Budapest within the Catholic-dominated Austro-Hungarian Empire that shaped many of the values and much of the culture of his parents and grandparents. Religious anti-Judaism and racial anti-Semitism were prevalent in the nineteenth century, even as imperial leaders led by Kaiser Franz Joseph struggled to preside over a disparate group of competing nationalities and religions: Austrians, Bosnians, Croatians, Czechs, Germans, Hungarians, Italians, Poles, Romanians, Serbians, Slovaks, Slovenes, and Ukrainians. The empire included not only Roman Catholics but also millions of Orthodox Christians, Jews, and Muslims. It was a tinderbox that ultimately exploded in August 1914, setting off World War I.

Wise always feared such turmoil, and he worked to ensure a harmonious relationship among the world's religious, ethnic, and racial communities. It is no accident that Stephen's idol, modern Zionism's founder Theodor Herzl, and a product of the empire's two capital cities of Budapest and Vienna, sought to protect Jews by physically removing them from the European political chaos and its bastard child, anti-Semitism.

It also explains why Wise was such a fervent advocate of the League of Nations and later the United Nations. He believed that the Jewish people living as a minority within the diaspora or in an independent Jewish state could exist safely and thrive only within a strong international family of nations that guaranteed freedom, security, and stability for all peoples.

When he was seventeen months old, his family took Stephen from a Europe soaked with anti-Judaism and anti-Semitism to a fledgling republic; in 1875 the United States was barely a century old when the Wise family arrived in New York City. But for young Wise the American democracy recovering from a horrific Civil War became the embodiment of his personal worldview: a free nation composed of many different kinds of people, all citizens equal under the law who were constitutionally guaranteed personal liberty and freedom of conscience and religion. During Stephen's lifetime the United States experienced enormous population growth and became a global industrial, military, and political power while still retaining its agricultural base.

In the same years, the American Jewish community expanded in size, influence, and leadership, and the United States entered into a progressive era that was a vital part of Stephen Wise's life and work.

Although there is basic agreement about the major goals and values of Stephen Wise, there are sharply differing opinions about his success in achieving them. During the first two decades following Wise's death, the conventional view was that he was the premier American Jewish leader during the first half of the twentieth century. This positive judgment was frequently articulated by Wise's devoted and admiring rabbinic students, who by the 1950s and 1960s had attained positions of influence within the Jewish and general American communities.

Rabbi Louis I. Newman (1893–1972) of Congregation Rodeph Shalom in Manhattan, the same congregation Rabbi Aaron Wise had served years earlier, offered a tribute on the tenth anniversary of Stephen's death that was typical of the praise showered upon Wise:

[He was] a tempestuous, indomitable man who bestrode the American Jewish world. . . . [Wise has] an imperishable place in the hearts of those who knew him . . . a Promethean figure.[9]

However, Arthur Morse, with his 1968 book *While Six Million Died*, was among the first to raise critical questions about the Roosevelt administration's actions and inactions regarding Jews between 1933 and 1945. As the number of books and studies on that controversial subject increased, the role of Stephen Wise, "FDR's rabbi," was analyzed more closely.

During the late 1970s, questions were publicly raised about the American Jewish community's responses to Nazism and the Holocaust. There was a pervasive sense of guilt ("Not enough was done") among many leaders, even though most of them had no positions of authority in the 1930s and 1940s and others were not alive in that era.

Often when inquiries were raised about the actions of FDR and Wise during the Holocaust, the questioners found both men guilty and any further analysis or exploration was abruptly ended with the two words, "Never again!" Support for the embattled state of Israel and the long, difficult campaign to free Soviet Jewry dominated American Jews even as they looked back in time and perceived weakness in the leaders of an earlier era.

By 1981 the American Commission on the Holocaust was established to explore the actions and inactions of the American Jewish community during those horrific dozen years between 1933 and 1945. The chair of the thirty-three-member commission was Arthur J. Goldberg (1908–1990), a former Supreme Court justice and President John F. Kennedy's secretary of labor. However, the commission ended its work within a year without reaching a consensus. It reflected the sharp and bitter differences that were emerging in the American Jewish community about its leaders and their behavior during the dark period of the Shoah.[10]

Rabbi Alexander M. Schindler (1925–2000) was born in Germany. He came to the United States in 1937 and later saw combat in Europe as a member of the US Army ski troopers. A graduate of Hebrew Union College–Jewish Institute of Religion and later the president of the Union of American Hebrew Congregations and chairman of the President's Conference of Major Jewish Organizations, Schindler presents a balanced summation of both Wise and his chief adversary, Abba Hillel Silver:

Unfortunately, Abba Hillel Silver's preeminence was overshadowed by subsequent events. In this he shared the fate of Stephen S. Wise, his archrival and the other rabbinic titan of his time. Their greatness was eclipsed by their successes. . . . They succeed gloriously, but only to be quickly replaced . . . by the leaders of the newborn Jewish state [i.e., David Ben-Gurion, Golda Meir and Chaim Weizmann]. . . .

The American Commission on the Holocaust formed in September of 1981 with Arthur Goldberg as chair was riven by internal dissension within the year and did little to modify this perception. At worst, American Jewish leaders of the period are portrayed as impotent, or even criminality culpable in their inability to halt or slacken the genocidal onslaught. [Critics claim that Jewish leaders during World War II] ignored or sacrificed rescue efforts for the sake of building the Jewish community in Palestine and transforming the Yishuv into a state. [Wise and Silver labored] in an historical context dramatically different from own [and that] considerably softens the harsh judgment of their failures even as it amplifies our appreciation of their triumphs.

Schindler used a graphic image to describe the work of both Wise and Silver and to smooth over their bitter personal rivalry:

In their Zionism Stephen S. Wise and Abba Hillel Silver were united. . . . [Their] rivalry was a functional partnership. Together, they hitched their dreams to the great draft horse of America. Silver, the militant, swept Great Britain and other obstacles out of her path. Wise, the diplomat, fed and groomed the beast, thereby helping non-Zionists to hop on the wagon. Eventually, the mighty horse did its labor. Then other Jewish leaders took over the reins.[11]

In 1985 David S. Wyman, the grandson of a Protestant minister, published *The Abandonment of the Jews: America and the Holocaust, 1941–1945*, in which he charged that the FDR administration did not exercise its political authority and military power to save the lives of European Jews during the Holocaust or to force Britain to admit more Jews to Mandate Palestine.

Raphael Medoff, Wyman's associate, followed up with a series of books that are critical of Stephen's relationship with Roosevelt and the failure of Wise to save Jewish lives. David Kranzler (1930–2007), who describes the rabbis' 1943 march in Washington, DC, in *Thy Brothers Blood: The Orthodox Jewish Response during the Holocaust*, is also critical of Wise.

The critics charge that Wise was blinded by his admiration for FDR, who cleverly and cynically used his friendship with "Stevie" to deflect criticism while doing little to rescue Jews from Hitler's grip. Medoff, Kranzler, and others are harsh in their condemnation of Wise. Medoff wrote,

Wise was unquestionably the most prominent and influential Jewish leader of his time. . . . Wise is perhaps the most enigmatic figure in the complicated

history of American Jewry's relationship with President Roosevelt and its response to the Holocaust. His career is a study in contradictions.

Wise championed the democratization of Jewish communal life in defiance of the old guard Jewish establishment, then came to resemble the establishment he once fought. He passionately advocated Zionism at a time when
most of his fellow-Reform rabbis were anti-Zionist, then wavered on Jewish
statehood when the Roosevelt administration backtracked on it. Wise enjoyed
unprecedented access to the White House, yet repeatedly failed to secure presidential action on matters of Jewish concern.

Most of all, Wise privately recognized that FDR was doing far less than he
could to aid Europe's Jews during their darkest hour, yet he could not bring
himself to publicly challenge Roosevelt's policies.[12]

Wise, it is charged, had become what he had so hated early in his career: a
"court Jew," the quintessential establishment figure who valued his hard-won
leadership position and personal relationship with FDR far more than actually helping his fellow Jews.

In 2008, criticism of Wise came from a surprising source, Rabbi David
Ellenson, speaking as the president of Hebrew Union College–Jewish Institute
of Religion at a Holocaust conference in New York City, asked, "In the 1930s, it
was Wise who led the rallies against Hitler, so why did he fail so horribly in the
1940s?" Wise had an "absolute and complete love" for President Franklin D.
Roosevelt, and an aversion toward the Zionist leader Ze'ev Jabotinsky, and the
Bergson Group, whose leaders were followers of Jabotinsky. His dislike "helped
blind him" to the need for more activism. Ellenson brushed aside concerns
that Jewish activism during the 1930s and 1940s would have provoked an anti-
Semitic backlash. "Jewish leaders have an obligation to be sufficiently flexible
and imaginative to deal with unprecedented situations," Ellenson said, especially when the lives of millions of people are at risk.[13]

A more positive view of Stephen Wise appears in Richard Breitman and
Alan J. Lichtman's 2012 book, *FDR and the Jews*:

Roosevelt reacted more decisively to Nazi crimes against Jews than did any
other world leader of his time. . . . His compromises might seem flawed in the
light of what later generations have learned about the depth and significance of
the Holocaust. . . .

The American Jewish community was divided both over how much they
could accomplish politically and how they should go about it. . . . That's the
critical thing. . . . We tend, today, to look back and say he didn't do this or he
didn't do that. The people who lived in his world saw him against the context

of who else was there. And they appreciated the fact that he was better than his predecessors and his rivals.[14]

The authors take the position that no Jewish leader of that era, even one as gifted as Wise, or a united American Jewish community was capable of overcoming the forces both within and without the US government that actively resisted attempts to rescue Jews, to open the gates of immigration to the United States and Palestine, or to take other positive steps that Wise and his colleagues constantly requested.

They argue that anti-Semites occupied key positions within the State Department and in Congress, and the high unemployment rate created by the Great Depression in the 1930s made increased Jewish immigration and rescue difficult if not impossible.

The conclusion of Melvin I. Urofsky's 1982 biography of Wise reflects the change in the public perception of "Rabbi USA":

> Wise was the last of a generation of titans in American Jewish life, people who by the force of their personalities and will shaped the Jewish community into a self-respecting, self-reliant force. Such individuals are no longer on the scene, for American Jewry, like American society, has matured to the point where no one person can exert the influence of a Wise or a Brandeis or a Louis Marshall.... [Wise] was no saint.... He had his share of failings, his ego and temper at times got the best of him, and on occasion he could be maddeningly self righteous, assured that he alone knew what was right.[15]

He correctly notes,

> Wise rarely pushed Roosevelt, this did give the administration the option to ignore Jewish pressure without fear of political retribution or public controversy.... For all the pious statements, the Western democracies bore out Hitler's prediction that they would not lift a finger to save the Jews. In light of this reality, Stephen Wise and his fellow American Jews, despite all their efforts, could accomplish very little.[16]

In any judgment of Wise, it must be remembered that he was both a product and a victim of his time, and he must ultimately be judged on two levels: strategic and tactical. During his entire public career Wise operated with a top-down mentality that dominated his overall strategy. It needs to be repeated that the American Jewish community between 1874 and 1949 was constantly wary of making specific "Jewish" demands, qua Jews, upon the larger

American society. When such demands were made, the American Jewish leaders preferred to be part of a large coalition of like-minded organizations or individuals who were not Jewish—that is, Christian church bodies, labor unions, civil libertarians, and political leaders.

It did not matter whether the "Jewish" calls were for economic freedom, church-state separation, overcoming bigotry and discrimination, increased immigration, or support for Zionism. The Jews of Wise's era frequently walked on collective egg shells fearful of an anti-Semitic backlash. As a result of their collective diffidence, they looked for someone who could vigorously represent them in what was for many Jews a new and still strange country. Wise even at the end of his life was the de facto surrogate who embodied in his language, appearance, and style what many Jews yearned to be.

However, Wise became trapped in his strategic stately role. He wanted to be perceived as the noble, omnipresent, indispensible person whose leadership was required for every important Jewish or American issue. And he fought, sometimes with excessive malice, to protect his position at the top of the American Jewish ladder.

But Wise's top-down strategy that had been effective for more than thirty years blinded him to the significant changes that were under way in the 1930s and reached their zenith in the 1940s within both the American and Jewish communities. He continued to operate within his strategic leadership bubble; he did not emerge or escape from it, nor did he want to change his imperious style.

While sitting atop a pinnacle of acclaim and adulation, Stephen Wise made several major tactical errors that will forever stain his place in history. In August 1942 he shamefully failed to act when he first received Gerhard Riegner's telegram confirming the reality of the Nazi Final Solution. Wise willingly sat on that terrible information for several months before going public with the monstrous news that Hitler planned to physically annihilate the Jewish people through a program of mass murder. Because Wise was too entangled with the Roosevelt administration and too enamored of FDR personally, he chose not to sever that relationship when he received the fateful telegram from Geneva.

Few would argue today that the tepid American and international public reaction to that news would have been different in August 1942 than it was three months later in November. But Wise would have shown Roosevelt, the State Department, and other government officials that they did not control or "own" him, which, in reality, they did. Stephen's lack of courage in alerting the world as early as possible about Hitler's goal of genocide haunted him because he knew the FDR administration had manipulated him. It was a blunder of the first order. We have the right to ask Senator Howard Baker's famous question: "What did [Stephen Wise] know and when did he know it?"

Wise also failed to give credibility or support to the efforts of Peter Bergson when the young Palestinian Jew carried out an effective public relations campaign to demand concrete American action to save the Jews of Europe and to support Zionist aspirations. Instead of cooperating in possible rescue attempts—perhaps futile, perhaps not—a mean-spirited Wise perceived Bergson as a direct threat to his hard-won leadership position. Stephen failed to recognize and harness the energy that Bergson brought to the anti-Nazi and Zionist effort.

Instead, Wise chose to belittle Bergson and showed himself to be a vindictive and jealous man who placed more importance on his leadership role than strengthening the cause of preserving Jewish lives. It is telling that Wise, who in 1933 organized huge anti-Nazi rallies at Madison Square Garden, was either unable or unwilling (clearly the latter) to recognize and support the same kind of public events when they were led a decade later by Bergson.

Wise's disgraceful attacks on Bergson helped marginalize rescue efforts. "Dr. Wise's" criticism of Bergson provided cover to anti-Semites, both in and out of the US government, who were pleased to discredit any attempt to employ American power to save Jewish lives.

Another inexcusable failure of leadership took place in October 1943 when Stephen assaulted both the integrity and the importance of the Orthodox rabbis' march on Washington. Just as he did with Bergson, Wise refused to share his leadership position with the desperate rabbis who sought the president's aid. Instead, Wise ridiculed and defamed the hundreds of marchers who exercised their rights by demanding strong executive action to save their fellow Jews in Europe.

A jealous Wise had neither the heart nor the wisdom to share his status with either Bergson or the marching rabbis. Wise clearly was no team player; instead, he was a soloist who brooked no competition.

Finally, there is the argument that Wise, operating in a time so different from our own era, did the best he could when any public criticism of President Roosevelt and his administration would be perceived as weakening, even sabotaging the war effort against Nazism. The same argument goes on to stress the need to "understand" that Wise faced systematic anti-Semitism in the America of the 1930s and the 1940s.

But even when we know the hostility and obstacles that Wise faced, we cannot "understand" his lack of courage and his inability to transcend, even sacrifice his own position for a larger goal: a supreme effort to save human lives. To whom much is given, much is expected. Because his beloved Jewish people gave him their precious trust and profound love, they had the right to expect much more from him. Did they receive that kind of selfless leadership from Stephen Wise during their darkest moment in history? The answer is no.

One thing, however, is certain. More than sixty-five years after his death, "Rabbi USA" continues to occupy the familiar position he so loved and coveted: center stage and the focus of attention and controversy in the public arena. It is a situation unlikely to change.

Notes

CHAPTER 1

1. Carl Hermann Voss, ed., *Stephen S. Wise: Servant of the People: Selected Letters* (Philadelphia: Jewish Publication Society of America, 1969), 231–32.
2. Ibid., xvii.
3. "S/S Gellert, Hamburg America Line," Norway Heritage, http://www.norwayheritage.com/p_ship.asp? sh=gelle, accessed September 29, 2014.
4. Bill Bell, "Rabbi Stephen Wise Four Thousand Years a Jew," *New York Daily News*, April 21, 1999.
5. Steven T. Katz, ed., *The Shtetl: New Evaluations* (New York: New York University Press, 2007), 43, 86, 241.
6. Alex J. Goldman, *Giants of Faith: Great American Rabbis* (New York: Citadel Press, 1964), 180.
7. *Jewish Encyclopedia*, s.v. "Weiss, Joseph Hirsch," http://www.jewishencyclopedia.com/#, accessed August 25, 2014.
8. "Israel Jacobson," New World Encyclopedia, http://www.newworldencyclopedia.org/entry/Israel_Jacobson, last modified April 26, 2014.
9. "The First Hungarian Jewish Reform Community," Sim Shalom Progressive Jewish Congregation, Budapest, Hungary, http://www.sim-shalom.org/history/the-first-hungarian-jewish-reform-community/, accessed September 29, 2014.
10. Melvin I. Urofsky, *A Voice That Spoke for Justice: The Life and Times of Stephen S. Wise* (Albany: State University of New York Press, 1982), 1–2.
11. Glenn R. Sharfman, "Jewish Emancipation," Encyclopedia of 1848 Revolutions, http://www.ohio.edu/chastain/ip/jewemanc.htm, last modified October 20, 2014.
12. Michael K. Silber, "Hungary: Hungary before 1918," YIVO Encyclopedia of Jews in Eastern Europe, http://www.yivoencyclopedia.org/article.aspx/Hungary/Hungary_before_1918#id0exuak, last modified August 26, 2010.
13. "Rev. Dr. Aaron Wise," *American Jewess* 2, no. 9 (1896): 482–87, http://quod.lib.umich.edu/a/amjewess/taj1895.0002.009/38:14?page=root;rgn=main;size=100;view=image.
14. Ibid.
15. Goldman, *Giants of Faith*, 196. She is buried in the Holy City, but her grandson did not set foot in Zion—the land of Israel—until 1913.
16. "Rev. Dr. Aaron Wise."
17. *Jewish Encyclopedia*, s.v. "Wise, Aaron," http://www.jewishencyclopedia.com/#, accessed August 26, 2014.

18. Mark A. Raider, "Stephen S. Wise and the Urban Frontier: American Jewish Life in New York and the Pacific Northwest at the Dawn of the 20th Century," *Quest: Issues in Contemporary Jewish History, Journal of Fondazione CDEC*, no. 2 (2011): 229.

19. Urofsky, *Voice*, 2–3.

20. *Jewish Encyclopedia*, s.v. "Fischer, Moritz," http://www.jewishencyclopedia.com/#, accessed August 26, 2014.

21. Urofsky, *Voice*, 3.

22. Ibid.

23. Noah Wiener, "The Shema' Yisrael Monotheistic Jewish Amulet Discovered near Carnuntum," Bible History Daily, August 15, 2014, http://www.biblicalarchaeology .org/daily/biblical-artifacts/the-shema'-yisrael/.

24. "Virtual Jewish World: Budapest, Hungary," Jewish Virtual Library, http://www .jewishvirtuallibrary.org/jsource/vjw/Budapest.html, accessed on July 28, 2014.

25. "Dohany [sic] Street Synagogue," Hidden Treasures of Budapest / Jewish Quarter, http://www.greatsynagogue.hu/gallery_syn.html, accessed September 30, 2014.

26. Bela Adalbert Vago, "Internal Life during the 19th Century," Jewish History of Hungary, http://www.porges.net/JewishHistoryOfHungary.html#The%20Emancipation%20Pe- riod, %201867-1914, accessed October 1, 2014.

27. Michael K. Silber, "Hungary: Hungary before 1918," YIVO Encyclopedia of Jews in Eastern Europe, http://www.yivoencyclopedia.org/article.aspx/Hungary/Hungary _before_1918#id0exuak, last modified August 26, 2010.

28. Carl E. Schorske, *Fin-De-Siècle Vienna: Politics and Culture* (New York: Vintage, 1981), xxvii.

29. Ilsa Barea, *Vienna* (New York: Alfred A. Knopf, 1966), 270, 280.

30. Ibid., 275–81.

31. Hilde Spiel, *Vienna's Golden Autumn: From the Watershed Year 1866 to Hitler's Anschluss, 1938* (New York: Weidenfeld and Nicolson, 1987), 196–97.

32. Ibid., 162.

33. Howard M. Sachar, *A History of Israel: From the Rise of Zionism to Our Time*, 2nd ed. (New York: Alfred A. Knopf, 1996), 37.

34. Ibid., 47.

35. Louis L. Snyder, *Encyclopedia of the Third Reich*, 1st ed. (New York: McGraw-Hill, 1976), 222.

36. Spiel, *Vienna's Golden Autumn*, 49.

37. "AJC Welcomes Name Change to Vienna Street Honoring Prominent Anti-Semite," American Jewish Committee, April 20, 2012, http://www.ajc.org/site/apps/nlnet/content2 .aspx? c=7oJILSPwFfJSG&b=8479733&ct=12487799#sthash.VoBcpsyE.dpuf.

38. Peggy Noonan, "The War That Broke a Century," *Wall Street Journal*, July 26–27, 2014.

39. Ronald Harwood, "The Lost Worlds of Joseph Roth," *Jewish Quarterly*, no. 196 (Winter 2004), http://www.jewishquarterly.org/issuearchive/article466c.html?articleid=47; see also http://www.nybooks.com/articles/archives/2014/nov/06/joseph-roth-genius -exile/.

40. Daniel Barry, "Exhibition: 'Doomsday—Jewish Life and Death in World War I, Vienna,'" Centenary News, http://www.centenarynews.com/article?id=1392, accessed October 1, 2014.

41. "Rev. Dr. Aaron Wise," 484–86.

42. Willis Rudy, *The College of the City of New York: A History 1847–1947* (New York: City College Press, 1949), 308.

43. C. Morris Horowitz and Lawrence J. Kaplan, "The Estimated Jewish Population of the New York Area, 1900–1975," Berman Jewish Databank, http://www.jewishdatabank .org/studies/details.cfm?StudyID=511, accessed September 12, 2014.

44. *Jewish Encyclopedia*, s.v. "Statistics," http://www.jewishencyclopedia.com/articles /13992-statistics, accessed September 2, 2014.

CHAPTER 2

1. Urofsky, *Voice*, 4.
2. Sydney Strong, ed., *What I Owe to My Father* (New York: Henry Holt and Company, 1931), 161–66.
3. Stephen S. Wise, *Challenging Years* (New York: Putnam, 1949), 3.
4. Irving Howe, *World of Our Fathers: The Journey of the East European Jews to America and the Life They Found and Made* (New York: Schocken Books, 1983), 200–202.
5. "America's First Immigration Center," the Battery Conservancy, http://www .castlegarden.org, accessed September 22, 2014.
6. Robert M. Seltzer, *Jewish People, Jewish Thought: The Jewish Experience in History* (New York: Macmillan, 1980), 630.
7. Ibid., 643.
8. "Our Senior Rabbis through the Years," Central Synagogue, *Our Archives*, http://www .centralsynagogue.org/about_us/archives/our-senior-rabbis-through-the-years, accessed September 3, 2014.
9. "PS15, "The Roberto Clemente School," http://www.ps15.org, accessed August 27, 2014.
10. *New York Times*, January 2, 1973.
11. Urofsky, *Voice*, 5.
12. Ibid., 79.
13. Wise, *Challenging Years*, xii.
14. Carl Hermann Voss, *Rabbi and Minister: The Friendship of Stephen S. Wise and John Haynes Holmes* (Cleveland: World Publishing, 1964), 31–33.
15. Jerry Klinger, "Richard Gottheil, The Reluctant Father of American Zionism," *Jewish Magazine*, November 2007, http://www.jewishmag.com/118mag/richard_gottheil /richard_gottheil.htm.
16. "Timeline: Life of Isaac Mayer Wise, 1819–1900," http://americanjewisharchives.org /collections/wise/view.php?id=2463, accessed October 1, 2014.
17. Cyrus Arfa, *Reforming Reform Judaism: Zionism and the Reform Rabbinate, 1885–1948* (New York: University Publishing Projects, 1985), 1–3.
18. *American Israelite*, January 24, 1879.
19. Melvin I. Urofsky, *American Zionism from Herzl to the Holocaust* (Garden City, NY: Anchor Books, Anchor Press/Doubleday, 1976), 85.
20. Samson Raphael Hirsch, *Horeb: A Philosophy of Jewish Laws and Observances*, trans. Isidore Grunfeld, 7th ed. (Brooklyn: Soncino Press, 2002), 460–61.
21. *Central Conference of American Rabbis Yearbook*, vol. 7 (1897), 12.
22. *Hebrew Union College Journal* 4 (December 1899): 45–47.
23. Urofsky, *Voice*, 8.
24. Wise, *Challenging Years*, 38–40.
25. William Knight, ed., *Memorials of Thomas Davidson: The Wandering Scholar* (Boston: Ginn and Co., 1907), 16–20.
26. Gaynell Hawkins, "Thomas Davidson, Teacher," *Southwest Review* 13 (1928): 334.
27. Urofsky, *Voice*, 9.
28. Justine Wise Polier and James Waterman Wise, eds., *The Personal Letters of Stephen Wise* (Boston: Beacon Press, 1956), 74–75.
29. Jacob Katz, ed., *Toward Modernity: The European Jewish Model* (Piscataway, NJ: Transaction Books, 1987), 50.

30. "Synagogue," Vienna: Now or Never, http://www.wien.info/en/sightseeing/sights/from -s-to-z/synagogue, accessed September 11, 2014.

31. *Jewish Encyclopedia*, s.v. "Jellinek, Adolf."

32. Katz, *Toward Modernity*, 56–57.

33. http://halakhah.com/pdf/nezikin/Shevuoth.pdf.

34. Sarah Pessin, "Solomon Ibn Gabirol [Avicebron]," in Edward N. Zalta (ed.), *The Stanford Encyclopedia of Philosophy*, Summer 2014 ed., http://plato.stanford.edu/archives/sum2014/entries/ibn-gabirol/.

35. *Selected Religious Poems of Solomon Ibn Gabirol*, trans. Israel Zangwill (Philadelphia: Jewish Publication Society of America, 1923), xv.

36. Urofsky, *Voice*, 13–14.

37. Ibid., 14.

38. Stephen S. Wise, *The Improvement of the Moral Qualities: An Ethical Treatise of the Eleventh Century by Solomon Ibn Gabirol, Printed from a Unique Arabic Manuscript, Together with a Translation and an Essay on the Place of Gabirol in the History of the Development of Jewish Ethics* (New York: Columbia University Press, Macmillan Company, Agents, 1901), 1–5.

39. Polier and Wise, *Personal Letters*, 158 (emphasis added).

40. Urofsky, *Voice*, 14.

41. Fred MacDowell, "An American Chief Rabbi Proposed in 1862? Also, Squabbling Over Who Was or Wasn't an Ordained Rabbi, and by Whom. Isaac Leeser Confronts I. M. Wise," On The Main Line, August 17, 2010, http://onthemainline.blogspot .com/2010/08/american-chief-rabbi-proposed-in-1862.html.

42. Urofsky, *Voice*, 14–15.

CHAPTER 3

1. Sandee Brawarsky, "A History of Congregation B'nai Jeshurun, 1825–2005"; B'nai Jeshurun, "A Century of Judaism in New York: B'nai Jeshurun 1825–1925," 2005, http://www.bj.org/Articles/a-history-of-bj-1825-2005/.

2. *New York Times*, April 21, 1887.

3. *New York Times*, March 24, 1886.

4. *New York Times*, March 12, 1934.

5. *New York Times*, April 20, 1894.

6. *Rochester Democrat and Chronicle*, January 23, 1895.

7. Theodore Dreiser, *Sister Carrie, Jennie Gerhardt, Twelve Men* (New York: Library of America, 1987), 378.

8. Wise, *Challenging Years*, 56.

9. Louis Lipsky, *Memoirs in Profile* (Philadelphia: Jewish Publication Society of America, 1975), 194.

10. *New York Times*, March 31, 1896.

11. *New York Times*, April 3, 1896.

12. Urofsky, *Voice*, 16.

13. Wise, *Challenging Years*, 32.

14. "First Zionist Congress: Basel 29–31 August 1897," Herzl Museum Jerusalem, Israel, http://www.herzl.org/english/Article.aspx?Item=544, accessed September 15, 2014.

15. Carl Hermann Voss, "The Lion and the Lamb," *American Jewish Archives* 20, no. 1 (April 1969): 5.

16. Isaiah 1:27.

17. Klinger, "Reluctant Father of American Zionism."

18. Arfa, *Reforming Reform Judaism*, 7.

19. Wise, *Challenging Years*, 31–32.
20. Seltzer, *Jewish People*, 630, 635, 697.
21. Wise, *Challenging Years*, 27.
22. "Second Zionist Congress: Basel 28–31 August 1898," Herzl Museum Jerusalem, Israel, http://www.herzl.org/english/Article.aspx?Item=539, accessed September 15, 2014.
23. Voss, *Servant of the People*, 8.
24. Urofsky, *Voice*, 23.
25. Sachar, *History of Israel*, 59–63.
26. Ibid.
27. Louis Lipsky, *A Gallery of Zionist Profiles* (New York: Farrar, Strauss and Cudahy, 1956), 147.
28. Floyd L. Herman, "Some Aspects of the Life of Stephen S. Wise to 1928" (master's thesis, Hebrew Union College–Jewish Institute of Religion, 1964), 130.
29. Matt Plen, "A. D. Gordon: The Religion of Labor-Zionist Thinker Who Advocated a Return to Nature," http://mobile.myjewishlearning.com/israel/Jewish_Thought/Modern/Secular_Zionism/AD_Gordon.shtml, accessed September 2, 2014.
30. A. James Rudin, *Israel for Christians: Understanding Modern Israel* (Philadelphia: Fortress Press, 1983), 32, 39.
31. Rachael Gelfman Schultz, "Religious & Religious Zionists Believe That the Jewish Return to Israel Hastens the Messiah," My Jewish Learning, http://www.myjewish learning.com/israel/Jewish_Thought/Modern/Religious_Zionism.shtml?p=0, accessed August 26, 2014.
32. Voss, *Servant of the People*, 14–15.

CHAPTER 4

1. Urofsky, *Voice*, 25–26.
2. Nanette Stahl and Judy A. Schiff, "A Great Assemblage: An Exhibit of Judaica in Honor of the Opening of the Joseph Slifka Center for Jewish Life at Yale," Sterling Memorial Library, Manuscripts and Archives, Fall 1995, http://www.library.yale.edu/exhibition/judaica/.
3. Guido Kisch, "Two American Jewish Pioneers of New Haven: Sigmund and Leopold Waterman," *Historical Judaica* (1942): 16–37.
4. *New York Daily Tribune*, October 14, 1854.
5. Joe Rooks-Rapport, "Louise Waterman Wise," Jewish Women: A Comprehensive Historical Encyclopedia, March 1, 2009, Jewish Women's Archive, http://jwa.org/encyclopedia/article/wise-louise-waterman, accessed on October 2, 2014.
6. James Waterman Wise, *Legend of Louise: The Life Story of Mrs. Stephen S. Wise* (New York: Jewish Opinion Publishing Corporation, 1949), 9–10.
7. Urofsky, *Voice*, 27.
8. *New York Times*, January 18, 1897.
9. *New York Times*, April 26, 1933.
10. "The Pittsburgh Platform 1885," Declaration of Principles, October 27, 2004, http://ccarnet.org/rabbis-speak/platforms/declaration-principles/.
11. Benny Kraut, *From Reform Judaism to Ethical Culture: The Religious Evolution of Felix Adler* (Cincinnati: Hebrew Union College Press, 1979), 181, 219–20.
12. Ibid., 156.
13. Polier and Wise, *Personal Letters*, 17.
14. Wise, *Legend of Louise*, 22–23.
15. Urofsky, *Voice*, 28.
16. Polier and Wise, *Personal Letters*, 23–24.

17. Ibid., 16.
18. Ibid., 25.
19. Elaine S. Friedman, "Congregation Beth Israel," Oregon Encyclopedia, http://www
.oregonencyclopedia.org/articles/#page=1&index_name=oep&search
_text=congregation+beth+israel, accessed August 28, 2014.
20. Ibid.
21. Urofsky, *Voice*, 28–29.
22. Ibid., 29.
23. Polier and Wise, *Personal Letters*, 20.
24. Urofsky, *Voice*, 30.
25. Voss, *Servant of the People*, 13.
26. Herman, *Some Aspects of the Life of Stephen S. Wise to 1928*, 4.
27. Voss, *Servant of the People*, 11–12.
28. Polier and Wise, *Personal Letters*, 21.
29. Urofsky, *Voice*, 31.
30. Polier and Wise, *Personal Letters*, 55–56.
31. Ibid., 74.
32. Ibid., 75.
33. Ibid., 67.

CHAPTER 5

1. Julius J. Nodel, *The Ties Between: A Century of Judaism on America's Last Frontier* (Portland, OR: Congregation Beth Israel, 1959), 89–90.
2. "About the Club," Arlington Club, http://www.thearlingtonclub.com/club/scripts/library/view_document.asp?GRP=11700&NS=PUBLIC&APP=80&DN=house-rules, accessed September 9, 2014 .
3. Urofsky, *Voice*, 35.
4. Raider, *Stephen Wise and the Urban Frontier*, 88.
5. Polier and Wise, *Personal Letters*, 71.
6. Ibid.
7. Urofsky, *Voice*, 35.
8. Polier and Wise, *Personal Letters*, 70.
9. Jacob Voorsanger, *Divre Yeme Emanuel, The Chronicles of Emanu-El: Being an Account of the Rise and Progress of the Congregation Emanu-El* (Charleston, SC: Nabu Press, 2010), 3.
10. Nodel, *Ties Between*, 88.
11. Polier and Wise, *Personal Letters*, 72.
12. Ibid.
13. Ibid., 75–76.
14. Urofsky, *Voice*, 33.
15. Voss, *Rabbi and Minister*, 47.
16. Gary P. Zola, *The Americanization of the Jewish Prayer Book* (New York: Central Synagogue, 2008), 9.
17. Richard Sarason (professor of rabbinic literature and thought, Hebrew Union College–Jewish Institute of Religion) in discussion with the author, June 25, 2012.
18. James Waterman Wise [Analyticus], *Jews Are Like That* (New York: Brentano's, 1928), 86.
19. Polier and Wise, *Personal Letters*, 59.
20. Urofsky, *Voice*, 40–41.
21. Ibid., 41.
22. Wise, *Challenging Years*, 7–8.

23. Voss, *Rabbi and Minister,* following 128.
24. Wise, *Challenging Years,* 9.
25. Ibid., 9–10.
26. *Proceedings of the New York State Conference of Charities and Correction at The Sixth Annual Session,* New York, November 14–16, 1905, 12–15, http://books.google.com /books?id=B3QXAAAAYAAJ&pg=PA16&dq=1905+new+york+conference+on +charities+and+corrections&hl=en&sa=X&ei=tfwuVN_ADe7gsAS5yYHwCg&ved =0CDgQ6AEwAQ#v=onepage&q=1905%20new%20york%20conference%20on%20 charities%20and%20corrections&f=false.
27. Wise, *Challenging Years,* 8.
28. Ibid.
29. Ibid.
30. Ibid., 109–10.
31. Neil Gabler, *An Empire of Their Own: How the Jews Invented Hollywood* (New York: Anchor New Edition, 1989), 282.
32. Wise, *Challenging Years,* 110.
33. Urofsky, *Voice,* 44–45.
34. Leonard J. Mervis, "The Social Justice Movement and the American Reform Rabbi," *American Jewish Archives* 7, no. 2 (June 1955): 203.
35. Peter C. MacFarlane, "The Unmuzzled Dr. Wise," *Colliers* 49 (June 1, 1912), 37.
36. Wise, *Legend of Louise,* 7–9.
37. Ibid., 29–31.
38. Ibid., 27.
39. Fred Rosenbaum, *Cosmopolitans: A Social and Cultural History of the Jews of the San Francisco Bay Area* (Berkeley: University of California Press, 2009), 180–81.
40. Ibid., 195.
41. *San Francisco Call,* April 30, 1908.
42. Franklin Hichborn, *The System: As Uncovered by the San Francisco Graft Prosecutors* (San Francisco: The Press of the James H. Barry Company, 1915), 451.
43. Urofsky, *Voice,* 39.
44. Wise, *Challenging Years,* 37.
45. Urofsky, *Voice,* 40.
46. Wise, *Challenging Years,* 37.

CHAPTER 6

1. Ronald B. Sobel, "A History of New York's Temple Emanu-El: The Second Half Century" (doctoral thesis, New York University, 1980), 132.
2. Ibid., 64.
3. Ibid., 132. In the autumn of 1905, Wise was invited to deliver three guest lectures at Temple Emanu-El.
4. Jonathan D. Sarna, *American Judaism: A History* (New Haven, CT: Yale University Press, 2004), 251.
5. Urofsky, *Voice,* 52.
6. Voss, *Rabbi and Minister,* 55.
7. Wise, *Challenging Years,* 84–86.
8. Mark A. Raider, "The Aristocrat and the Democrat: Louis Marshall, Stephen S. Wise, and the Challlenge of American Jewish Leadership," *American Jewish History* 94, nos. 1–2 (March–June 2008): 91–113.
9. Jonathan D. Sarna, "Two Jewish Lawyers Named Louis," *American Jewish History* 94, nos. 1–2 (March–June 2008): 1–19.

10. Wise, *Challenging Years*, 83.
11. Urofsky, *Voice*, 53.
12. Voss, *Rabbi and Minister*, 55–56.
13. Urofsky, *Voice*, 53.
14. Wise, *Legend of Louise*, 35–36.
15. Polier and Wise, *Personal Letters*, 88–89.
16. Ibid.
17. Ibid., 108.
18. Wise, *Challenging Years*, 82.
19. Sobel, *History of New York's Temple Emanu-el*, 144–45; see also Charles Reznikoff, ed., *Louis Marshall, Champion of Liberty: Selected Papers and Addresses* (Philadelphia: Jewish Publication Society of America, 1957), 831–32.
20. Wise, *Challenging Years*, 89.
21. Urofsky, *Voice*, 53–54.
22. Sobel, *The History of New York's Temple Emanu-el*, 135; see also Urofsky, *Voice*, 55.
23. *New York Times*, January 11, 1906; see also Voss, *Servant of the People*, 25–34.
24. *American Hebrew*, January 12, 1906.
25. Voss, *Servant of the People*, 33–34.
26. Voss, *Rabbi and Minister*, 57.
27. Mordechai Ben Massart, "A Rabbi in the Progressive Era: Rabbi Stephen S. Wise, Ph.D. and the Rise of Social Jewish Progressivism in Portland, Or., 1900–1906", (doctoral thesis, Portland State University, 2010), 97.
28. Sobel, *History of New York's Temple Emanu-El*, 138–40.
29. Ronald B. Sobel (senior rabbi emeritus, Congregation Emanu-El), in discussion with the author, September 23, 2013.
30. Urofsky, *Voice*, 54.
31. Jewish Telegraphic Agency, July 30, 1930.
32. Urofsky, *Voice*, 57.
33. Wise, *Legend of Louise*, 35.
34. Edmund Wilson, *A Piece of My Mind: Reflections at Sixty* (Garden City, NY: Doubleday, 1958), 90–91.
35. Reznikoff, *Louis Marshall*, xix.
36. Sobel, *History of New York's Temple Emanu-El*, 373.
37. *New York Times*, September 23, 1929.
38. Stephen Wise Free Synagogue, "About Us: History," September 8, 2014, http://www.swfs.org/welcome/history/, accessed October 5, 2014.
39. Sobel, *History of New York's Temple Emanu-El*, 145–46.
40. James Rudin, "The First Fight for a Free Pulpit," *Reform Judaism* (Fall 2014/5774): 66–67.

CHAPTER 7

1. Wise, *Legend of Louise*, 31.
2. Wise, *Challenging Years*, 94.
3. Wise, *Legend of Louise*, 31–33.
4. Anne LeVant Prahl (curator of collections, Oregon Jewish Museum) in discussion with the author, June 19, 2012.
5. Urofsky, *Voice*, 57.
6. Nodel, *Ties Between*, 97.
7. Voss, *Rabbi and Minister*, 83–84.
8. Urofsky, *Voice*, 73–74.
9. Wise, *Challenging Years*, 96.

10. Moses Rischin, *The Promised City* (Cambridge, MA: Harvard University Press, 1962), 242.
11. Wise, *Challenging Years*, 95, 98, 102; see also *Free Synagogue Pulpit*, "Social Service and the Free Synagogue," December 15, 1907, 49.
12. Urofsky, *Voice*, 62.
13. Paul Ritterband, "Counting the Jews in New York, 1900–1991: An Essay in Substance and Method," *Jewish Population Studies / Papers in Jewish Demography* 28, no. 29 (Jerusalem: Avraham Harman Institute of Contemporary Jewry, 1997), 199–228.
14. Urofsky, *Voice*, 63.
15. Ibid., 66.
16. Ibid.; see also Voss, *Rabbi and Minister*, 109–11.
17. Voss, *Rabbi and Minister*, 111.
18. Ibid., 81.
19. Charles Bloch to Stephen Wise, July 12, 1916, Stephen Wise Free Synagogue Papers.
20. Free Synagogue Board Minutes, November 7, 1916; see also Free Synagogue Board Minutes, June 19, 1911.
21. Rischin, *Promised City*, 242.
22. Wise, *Challenging Years*, 96–98.
23. *New York Times*, March 16, 1957.
24. Peter Balakian, *The Burning Tigris: The Armenian Genocide and America's Response* (New York: HarperCollins, 2003), 220.
25. *New York Times*, October 8, 1912.
26. "A Haven on the Lower East Side," University Settlement, http://www.university settlement.org/us/about/history/, accessed October 5, 2014.
27. *New York Times*, October 8; October 12; October 13, 1912.
28. "Growing Pains," unknown author, *Monmouth University Newsletter*, Summer 2008, 14–17, http://www.monmouth.edu/uploadedFiles/Content/University/about-monmouth/Monmouth_Magazine/Magazine_PDFs/MUSummer2008.pdf.
29. "Hashavua" (The Week), *Stephen Wise Free Synagogue Sabbath Newsletter*, August 10, 2012.

CHAPTER 8

1. "Sundays at Sinai," Chicago Sinai Congregation, http://www.chicagosinai.org/services/services/, accessed October 2, 2014.
2. Rischin, *Promised City*, 243.
3. *Hebrew Standard*, April 19, 1909.
4. "By an English Jew," *Jewish Chronicle* [London], November 5, 1909.
5. Wise, *Challenging Years*, 97.
6. Ibid., 105.
7. Urofsky, *Voice*, 66.
8. Wise, *Challenging Years*, 106.
9. Richard Gottheil to Stephen Wise, Stephen Wise Free Synagogue Papers, November 7, 1906.
10. Rischin, *Promised City*, 242; see also Marjorie N. Feld, *Lillian Wald: A Biography* (Chapel Hill: University of North Carolina Press, 2008), 78.
11. Wise, *Challenging Years*, 102–3.
12. Charles Bloch to Stephen Wise, Stephen Wise Free Synagogue Papers, December 8, 1914.
13. Sidney E. Goldstein, *The Synagogue and Social Welfare: A Unique Experiment* (New York: Bloch, 1955), 10. See also Urofsky, *Voice*, 68.

14. Urofsky, *Voice*, 68.
15. Ibid., 69.
16. *The Free Synagogue Report 1907–1908*, Stephen Wise Free Synagogue Papers.
17. Urofsky, *Voice*, 69.
18. Jane Rothstein, "American Jews and Marriage Counseling, 1920–1945, " *Tablet: A New Read on Jewish Life*, December 16, 2003, http://tabletmag.com/jewish-arts-and-culture /books/794/conference-calls.
19. *Encyclopedia Judaica*, s.v. "Jacob X. Cohen." See also Sadie Alta Cohen, *Engineer of the Soul: A Biography of Rabbi J. X. Cohen* (New York: Bloch, 1961).
20. "Mitchell May to Stephen Wise," Stephen Wise Free Synagogue Papers, February 19, 1931.
21. Stephen Wise Free Synagogue Papers, July 14, 1934; see also Edward L. Bernays, *Biography of an Idea: Memoirs of Public Relations Counsel Edward L. Bernays* (New York: Simon & Schuster, 1965), 397.
22. Wise, *Legend of Louise*, 47.
23. Ibid., 51.

CHAPTER 9

1. Urofsky, *Voice*, 106, 109.
2. *New Yorker*, November 26, 1949, 133.
3. John Haynes Holmes, *I Speak for Myself: The Autobiography of John Haynes Holmes* (New York: Harper & Row, 1959), 93–94, 99.
4. Bertram W. Korn. *Eventful Years and Experiences* (Cincinnati: American Jewish Archives, 1954), 128, 147.
5. *American Hebrew*, December 24, 1909.
6. Voss, *Rabbi and Minister*, 182–83.
7. Max Eastman, *Reflections on the Failure of Socialism* (New York: Devin-Adair, 1955), 113.
8. Hope Nisly, ed., "Remembering the Triangle Factory Fire," Cornell University Industrial and Labor Relations School, http://www.ilr.cornell.edu/trianglefire/, last modified January 1, 2011.
9. *New York Times*, June 16, 1904.
10. Voss, *Rabbi and Minister*, 114.
11. Ibid.
12. Ibid., 115.
13. Urofsky, *Voice*, 94.
14. Ibid.
15. Wise, *Challenging Years*, 62–64.
16. Leon Stein, *The Triangle Fire* (New York: Lippincott, 1962), 141–47, 196–97.
17. Urofsky, *Voice*, 94–95.
18. Hope Nisly, ed., "Legacy of the Triangle Fire," Cornell University of Industrial and Labor Relations, http://www.ilr.cornell.edu/trianglefire/legacy/index.html, last modified January 1, 2011.
19. Ibid.
20. *New York Times*, November 14, 1911.
21. *New York Times*, January 11, 1912.
22. Wise, *Challenging Years*, 164–65. During most of his adult life, Wise had been a Republican—the "party of Lincoln" and political reformer President Theodore Roosevelt (1858–1919).
23. Ibid., 3–4, 162–65.

24. Joseph B. Bishop, *The Chronicle of One Hundred and Fifty Years: The Chamber of Commerce of the State of New York* (New York: Charles Scribner's Sons, 1918), 213.
25. Wise, *Challenging Years*, 60.
26. Ibid.
27. *New York Times*, November 17, 1911.
28. Urofsky, *Voice*, 98–99.
29. *New York Times*, November 17, 1911.
30. Ibid.
31. Ibid.
32. Wise, *Challenging Years*, 60.
33. Urofsky, *Voice*, 99.
34. *New York Times*, November 17, 1911.
35. Urofsky, *Voice*, 98.

CHAPTER 10

1. *New York Times*, January 16, 1913.
2. Urofsky, *Voice*, 106.
3. Wise, *Challenging Years*, 10–12.
4. Polier and Wise, *Personal Letters*, 147–48.
5. *New York Times*, May 19, 1922.
6. Wise, *Challenging Years*, 64–65.
7. Internet Movie Data Base, *Norma Rae*, http://www.imdb.com, accessed August 27, 2014.
8. Polier and Wise, *Personal Letters*, 57.
9. *New York Times*, March 31, 1915.
10. John Steinle, "D. W. Griffith," *Senses of Cinema*, no. 40 (July 2006), http://sensesof cinema.com/2006/great-directors/griffith/; see also William R. Keillor, "The Long-Forgotten Racial Attitudes and Policies of Woodrow Wilson," Professor Voices: Commentary, Insight and Analysis, March 4, 2013, http://www.bu.edu/professorvoices /2013/03/04/the-long-forgotten-racial-attitudes-and-policies-of-woodrow-wilson/.
11. Jewish Women's Archive, "Lillian Wald," http://jwa.org/womenofvalor/wald, accessed on October 7, 2014.
12. Richard Schickel, *D. W. Griffith: An American Life* (Montclair, NJ: Limelight Editions, 2004), 285–86.
13. *New York Times*, April 18, 1915.
14. R. B. Rosenberg, "Emmet O'Neal," Encyclopedia of Alabama, http://www.encyclo pediaofalabama.org/face/Article.jsp?id=h-1585, last modified November 7, 2013.
15. "New Phases of the Fight against Lynching," *Current Opinion*, July 1919, http://www.old magazinearticles.com/National_Conference_on_Lynching_article#.UUyMIaWVjLY, accessed October 3, 2014.
16. *New York Times*, May 7, 1919.
17. Athan Theoharis and John Stuart Cox, *The Boss: J. Edgar Hoover and the Great American Inquisition* (Philadelphia: Temple University Press, 1988), 45.
18. Polier and Wise, *Personal Letters*, 124–25.
19. Ibid., 151. Floyd Herman noted that "this short statement, revealed the full extent of his [Wise's] liberalism" (*Some Aspects of the Life of Stephen S. Wise to 1928*, 113).
20. James Linn, *Jane Addams: A Biography* (Urbana-Champaign: University of Illinois Press, 2000), 366; see also *New York Times*, November 26, 1968.
21. *New York Times*, April 12, 1920.

22. Wise, *Challenging Years*, 66.
23. Ibid., 67.
24. Stephen S. Wise, "Who Are the Bolshevists at Home and Abroad?" and "How Ought the Pulpit Deal with the Industrial Situation?" Free Synagogue Pulpit, *Sermons and Addresses by Stephen Wise*, Vol. 5, *1918–1920* (New York: Bloch, 1920), 97–103, 103–20.
25. *New York Times*, October 6, 1919.
26. Wise, *Challenging Years*, 66.
27. Ibid., 68–69.
28. Ibid., 66.
29. *New York Times*, October 6, 1919.
30. *Geneva* (NY) *Daily Times*, October 6, 1919.
31. *Reform Advocate*, October 18, 1919.
32. Wise, *Challenging Years*, 70–71.
33. Wise, *Free Synagogue Pulpit*, 118.
34. Wise, Challenging Years, 71.
35. Brian C. R. Zugay, *The Interchurch World Movement and the Scientific Survey of American Religious Architecture, 1919–1924* (Sleepy Hollow, NY: Rockefeller Archives, 2010), 1.
36. Philip C. Ensley, "The Interchurch Movement and the Steel Strike of 1919," *Labor History* 13, no. 2 (1972): 217–30, http://www.tandfonline.com/doi/abs/10.1080/0023656720 8584202?journalCode=clah20#.VDQwwEttdZA, last modified July 3, 2008; see also Brian C. R. Zugay, *The Interchurch World Movement and the Scientific Survey of American Religious Architecture, 1919–1924* (Sleepy Hollow, NY: Rockefeller Archives, 2010).
37. Ensley, "Interchurch Movement."
38. Wise, *Challenging Years*, 71.

CHAPTER 11

1. Wise, *Challenging Years*, 161.
2. Ibid., 163.
3. Ibid., 164.
4. Ibid.
5. Ibid., 165–66.
6. Democratic Party Platforms: "Democratic Party Platform of 1912," June 25, 1912. Online by Gerhard Peters and John T. Woolley, *The American Presidency Project*, http://www.presidency.ucsb.edu/ws/?pid=29590.
7. Voss, *Rabbi and Minister*, 124.
8. Ibid.
9. Ibid.
10. Melvin I. Urofsky, *Louis D. Brandeis: A Life* (New York: Pantheon, 2009), 440.
11. Urofsky, *Brandeis*, 438. Although anti-Semitism was not overt, there was opposition based upon Brandeis's religion; see Phillipa Strum, *Louis D. Brandeis: Justice for the People* (New York: Schocken, 1984), 293–94.
12. Wise, *Challenging Years*, 172.
13. *New York Times*, February 12, 1916.
14. *New York Times*, February 29, 1916.
15. Urofsky, *Brandeis*, 457.
16. Wise, *Challenging Years*, 171.
17. Urofsky, *Brandeis*, 388, 479.
18. Urofsky, *Voice*, 134.
19. *New York Times*, February 10, 1913.

20. Richard Hofstadter, *The American Political Tradition: And the Men Who Made It* (New York: Vintage, 1989), 260.

21. *New York Times*, October 14, 1914.

22. *New York Times*, May 8, 1915.

23. Joshua Reuben Clark, Jr., "Emergency Legislation Passed prior to December, 1917, Dealing with the Control and Taking of Private Property for the Public Use, Benefit, or Welfare, Presidential Proclamations Executive Orders Thereunder, Including January 31, 1918, to Which Is Added a Reprint of Analogous Legislation since 1775," Washington, DC, Government Printing Office, 1918, http://books.google.com/books?id=CGj _5WJx_ToC&printsec=titlepage#v=onepage&q&f=false.

24. Voss, *Servant of the People*, 68.

25. *New York Times*, May 15, 1916.

26. *New York Telegram*, May 8, 1916.

27. Polier and Wise, *Personal Letters*, 159–60.

28. Ibid., 160.

29. Ibid., 162.

30. Ibid., 165.

31. *New York Times*, January 4, 1917.

32. Urofsky, *Voice*, 138.

33. *Chicago Tribune*, February 26, 1917.

34. *New York Times*, April 3, 1917.

35. Spencer C. Tucker, ed., *The Encyclopedia of Middle East Wars: The United States in the Persian Gulf, Afghanistan, and Iraq Conflicts* (Santa Barbara, CA: ABC-CLIO, 2010), 1480.

36. Stephen S. Wise, "What Are We Fighting For?" [speech], ca. 1918, Library of Congress, "American Leaders Speak: Recordings from World War I and the 1920 Election, 1918–1920," http://memory.loc.gov/ammem/nfhtml/nfhome.html.

37. Voss, *Servant of the People*, 77.

38. Urofsky, *Voice*, 138–39.

39. Voss, *Rabbi and Minister*, 153; see also *New York Times*, July 27–28, 1918; August 18, 1918.

40. Stephen S. Wise, "President Wilson," [speech], ca. 1918, Library of Congress, "American Leaders Speak: Recordings from World War I and the 1920 Election, 1918–1920," http://memory.loc.gov/ammem/nfhtml/nfhome.html.

CHAPTER 12

1. *Central Conference of American Rabbis Yearbook*, XI (1901), 76.

2. Ibid., 81.

3. Ibid., XXVII, 132.

4. Ibid.

5. Ibid., 139–40.

6. Arfa, *Reforming Reform Judaism*, 23.

7. Herman, *Some Aspects of the Life of Stephen S. Wise to 1928*, 52.

8. Michael Oren, *Power, Faith, and Fantasy: America in the Middle East, 1776 to the Present* (New York: W. W. Norton, 2007), 352.

9. Urofsky, *Voice*, 123.

10. *Central Conference of American Rabbis Yearbook*, XIX (1909), 432–94.

11. Ibid., 16ff.

12. Philip Roth, *The Plot against America* (Boston: Houghton Mifflin, 2004), 33.

13. Polier and Wise, *Personal Letters*, 140–41.
14. *Central Conference of American Rabbis Yearbook*, XXIV (1914), 83.
15. Ibid., 84.
16. Herman, *Some Aspects of the Life of Stephen S. Wise to 1928*, 29.
17. Ibid., 31.
18. Ibid., 33.
19. Ibid.
20. Ibid., 36.
21. *Minutes of the Board of Governors, 1875–1955*, Hebrew Union College–Jewish Institute of Religion, February 23, 1915.
22. Herman, *Some Aspects of the Life of Stephen S. Wise to 1928*, 38.
23. Ibid., 43.
24. Urofsky, *Voice*, 124–25.
25. Ibid., 125.
26. Ibid.
27. James Wise, *Jews Are Like That*, 17.
28. Oren, *Power, Faith, and Fantasy*, 354.
29. Urofsky, *Louis D. Brandeis*, 399.
30. John E. Kleber, ed., *The Kentucky Encyclopedia* (Lexington: University of Kentucky Press, 1992), 259.
31. Ben Halpern, *A Clash of Heroes: Brandeis, Weizmann, and American Zionism* (New York: Oxford University Press, 1987), 65.
32. Urofsky, *Louis D. Brandeis*, 403.
33. James Wise, *Jews Are Like That*, 18.
34. Ibid.
35. Michael Feldberg, "Louis D. Brandeis and American Zionism," Jewish Federations of North America, http://www.jewishfederations.org/page.aspx?id=53583, accessed October 8, 2014.
36. Urofsky, *Voice*, 118.
37. Paul C. Merkley, *The Politics of Christian Zionism: 1891–1948* (New York: Routledge, 1998), 75.
38. Urofsky, *Louis D. Brandeis*, 405; see also Urofsky, *American Zionism from Herzl to the Holocaust*, 165–66.
39. Urofsky, *Louis D. Brandeis*, 423.
40. "The Jewish Problem and How to Solve It," *The Supreme Court*, December 2006, http://www.pbs.org/wnet/supremecourt/personality/sources_document11.html.
41. James Wise, *Jews Are Like That*, 19.
42. Oren, *Power, Faith, and Fantasy*, 352–53.
43. *Boston Post*, September 28, 1914.
44. Urofsky, *Voice*, 118.
45. James F. Simon, *FDR and Chief Justice Hughes: The President, the Supreme Court, and the Epic Battle over the New Deal* (New York: Simon and Schuster, 2012), 259.
46. *New York Times*, June 21, 1915.
47. Wise, *Personal Letters*, 90. Adler remained a public adversary and critic of Wise.
48. *American Israelite*, April 1, 1915.
49. *New York Times*, January 24, 1916.
50. *New York Times*, May 1, 1916.
51. Urofsky, *Voice*, 122.
52. Polier and Wise, *Personal Letters*, 148.

CHAPTER 13

1. Lipsky, *Gallery of Zionist Profiles*, 148–49.
2. Wise, *Challenging Years*, 161–81.
3. Andrew Preston, *Sword of the Spirit, Shield of Faith: Religion in American War and Diplomacy* (New York: Anchor, 2012), 272.
4. Wise, *Challenging Years*, 172–73.
5. Richard Wormser, "Segregation in the US Government (1913)," *The Rise and Fall of Jim Crow*, 2002, http://www.pbs.org/wnet/jimcrow/stories_segregation.html.
6. Voss, *Servant of the People*, 74.
7. Simon Sebag Montefiore, *Jerusalem: The Biography* (New York: Vintage, 2012), 410.
8. Jonathan Schneer, *The Balfour Declaration: The Origins of the Arab-Israeli Conflict* (New York: Random House, 2010), 339.
9. "The Balfour Declaration," Yale Law School, Lillian Goldman Law Library, *The Avalon Project, Documents in Law, History and Diplomacy*, http://avalon.law.yale.edu/20th _century/balfour.asp, accessed September 29, 2014.
10. Wise, *Challenging Years*, 190.
11. Oren, *Power, Faith, and Fantasy*, 356.
12. Wise, *Challenging Years*, 189.
13. Preston, *Sword of the Spirit*, 287.
14. Arthur S. Link, ed., *The Papers of Woodrow Wilson*, Vol. 44 (Princeton, NJ: Princeton University Press, 1983), 371.
15. US Department of State, Papers Relating to the Foreign Relations of the United States. The Lansing Papers, 1914–1920 (in two volumes), Vol. 2, US Government Printing Office, 1914–1920, http://digital.library.wisc.edu/1711.dl/FRUS.FRUS19141920v2, 71.
16. Ibid.
17. Wise, *Challenging Years*, 194.
18. Ibid., 197–98.
19. William Griffiths, ed., *Newer Roosevelt Messages*, Vol. 3 (New York: Current Literature Publishing Company, 1919), 1004.
20. Frank Manuel, *The Realities of America-Palestine Relations* (Washington, DC: Public Affairs Press, 1949), 280–84, 291–92.
21. Oren, *Power, Faith, and Fantasy*, 423–24.
22. Voss, *Servant of the People*, 252.

CHAPTER 14

1. *New York Times*, January 9, 1918.
2. *The Guardian*, January 19, 2004.
3. Lamar Cecil, *Wilhelm II: Emperor and Exile, 1900–1941* (Chapel Hill: University of North Carolina Press, 1996), 292.
4. *Wall Street Journal*, July 10, 2012.
5. Andrew Mango, *Ataturk: The Biography of the Founder of Modern Turkey* (New York: Overlook Press, 2002), 394.
6. Kenneth C. Davis, *Don't Know Much about History* (New York: Harper, 2012), 314.
7. *New York Times*, January 9, 1918.
8. Preston, *Sword of the Spirit*, 287.
9. Peter Grose, *Gentleman Spy: The Life of Allen Dulles* (Boston: Houghton Mifflin, 1994), 45.
10. Polier and Wise, *Personal Letters*, 171.
11. Frank Freidel, *Franklin D. Roosevelt: The Ordeal* (Boston: Little Brown, 1954), 3.

12. Luigi Luzzatti, *God in Freedom: Studies in the Relations between Church and State* (New York: Macmillan, 1930), 756–57; see also Urofsky, *Brandeis*, 490–93.

13. Wise, *Challenging Years*, 178–79. But Brandeis did made a brief visit to the peace conference in the spring of 1919 while en route to Palestine.

14. Julian W. Mack, "Jewish Hopes at the Peace Table," *Menorah Journal* 5, no. 1 (1919): 3.

15. Nathan Feinberg. *La Question des minorities a la Conference de la Paix de 1919–1920 et l'action juive en faveur de la protection international des minorities* (Paris: Rousseau & Cie, 1929), 33.

16. James Parkes. *The Emergence of the Jewish Problem* (London: Oxford University Press, 1946), 104.

17. *Menorah Journal* (February 1919): 3–4.

18. Stephen S. Wise, "What Will Come Out of the Peace Conference?" *The Maccabean: A Magazine of Jewish Life and Letters* 32 (1919): 29.

19. Leo Lowenstein, ed., *Die Judischen Gefallenen, The Jewish Roll of Honor Commemorating the 12,000 German Jews Who Died for Their Fatherland in World War I*, Reich Association of Jewish Combat Veterans, 1932, http://www.germanjewishsoldiers.com/epilogue.php.

20. Oren, *Power, Faith, and Fantasy*, 363.

21. Urofsky, *Voice*, 155. It was a foretaste of the future problems that grew up between the two Zionist giants: Wise and Weizmann.

22. Ibid., 155–56.

23. Ibid., 155.

24. Chaim Weizmann, *Trial and Error: The Autobiography of Chaim Weizmann* (New York: Schocken, 1966), 246–47; see also Sachar, *History of Israel*, 121.

25. Voss, *Servant of the People*, 85.

26. Oscar Janowsky, *The Jews and Minority Rights (1898-1919)* (New York: Columbia University Press, 1933), 261.

27. Wise, *Challenging Years*, 197.

28. Urofsky, *Voice*, 157.

29. *New York Times*, March 3, 1919.

30. *The Maccabean*, March 1919, 57–63.

31. Janowsky, *Jews and Minority Rights*, 328.

32. Moshe Davis, "The Human Record: Cyrus Adler at the Peace Conference, 1919," *Essays in American Jewish History* (Cincinnati: American Jewish Archives, 1958), 475–76.

33. Grose, *Gentleman Spy*, 65.

34. Reznikoff, *Louis Marshall*, 554.

35. *Free Synagogue Pulpit*, 1920, 55.

36. Janowsky, *Jews and Minority Rights*, 295.

37. *Free Synagogue Pulpit*, 1920, 54.

38. Ibid., 54–55.

39. Feinberg, *La Question des minorities*, 98.

40. Ibid., 167.

41. *Free Synagogue Pulpit*, 1920, 58.

42. Parkes, *Emergence of the Jewish Problem*, 120–23.

43. Janowsky, *Jews and Minority Rights*, 389–90.

44. *New York Times*, May 31, 1920.

45. *New York Times*, November 20, 1919.

46. *New York Times*, December 28, 1926.

CHAPTER 15

1. Polier and Wise, *Personal Letters*, 131.
2. Zachary Silver, "The Excommunication of Mordecai Kaplan," *American Jewish Archives Journal* 62, no. 1 (2010): 21–48, http://americanjewisharchives.org/publications /journal/PDF/2010_62_01_00_silver.pdf.
3. Herman, *Some Aspects of the Life of Stephen S. Wise to 1928*, 63.
4. Urofsky, *Voice*, 183.
5. Wise, *Challenging Years*, 130.
6. Herman, *Some Aspects of the Life of Stephen S. Wise to 1928*, 64–65.
7. Ibid., 64.
8. Ibid., 65.
9. Wise, *Challenging Years*, 131–32.
10. Ibid., 131.
11. Hannah Heyman correspondence, 1924–1927, *Jewish Institute of Religion Records*, Series A, Office of the President, 1921–1950, MS19, Folder 11, American Jewish Archives, Cincinnati.
12. Jewish Telegraphic Agency, August 19, 1963.
13. Urofsky, *Voice*, 184.
14. Ibid., 185.
15. Ibid., 190.
16. Jewish Telegraphic Agency, April 15, 1961.
17. Urofsky, *Voice*, 187; see also Wise, *Challenging Years*, 136–138.
18. Philip S. Bernstein, "Stephen S. Wise: Some Personal Recollections," *Central Conference of American Rabbis Journal* 11 (April 1963): 6–7.
19. Urofsky, *Voice*, 187.
20. Ibid., 186.
21. *New York Times*, April 27, 1926.

CHAPTER 16

1. Urofsky, *Voice*, 174.
2. Polier and Wise, *Personal Letters*, 100–101.
3. *New York Times*, June 4, 1927.
4. *New York Times*, March 27, 1937.
5. Voss, *Rabbi and Minister*, 319.
6. *New York Times*, August 2, 1987.
7. *New York Times*, October 16, 1928.
8. *New York Times*, August 10, 1941.
9. *New York Times*, November 30, 1983.
10. Helen Lawrenson, *Stranger at the Party* (New York: Random House, 1975), 44.
11. *Time*, April 14, 1975.
12. Polier and Wise, *Personal Letters*, 186
13. Ibid., 188.
14. Ibid., 190.
15. Urofsky, *Voice*, 234.
16. Ibid., 234–35.
17. Ibid., 235–36.
18. David Schwartz, "The Genius of Stephen Wise," *Canadian Jewish Chronicle*, March 24, 1944.
19. *New York Times*, October 28, 1930.

20. *Pittsburgh Press*, February 1, 1935.
21. Voss, *Servant of the People*, 169.
22. Henry Morgenthau, Sr., *All in a Lifetime* (Garden City, NY: Doubleday and Page, 1922), 292–95.
23. Voss, *Servant of the People*, 106–7.
24. Florence Reif Richman, "Heritage," *About SWFS*, 2006, http://ecc.swfs.org/About /Heritage.
25. *New York Times*, November 28, 1946.
26. *New York Times*, April 16, 1923.
27. Voss, *Servant of the People*, 121.
28. Ibid., 129.
29. "American President: A Reference Resource: A Life in Brief," Miller Center, University of Virginia, http://millercenter.org/president/harding/essays/biography/1, accessed October 6, 2014.
30. *New York Times*, August 3, 1923.
31. *New York Times*, January, 18, 1925.
32. Polier and Wise, *Personal Letters*, 199.
33. *New York World*, June 8, 1923.
34. Official Report of the Proceedings of the Democratic National Convention held in Madison Square Garden, New York City, June 24–July 9, 1924, 227, http://archive.org /details/officialreportp00greagoog.
35. Voss, *Servant of the People*, 128.
36. *New York Times*, October 20, 1924.
37. Urofsky, *Voice*, 180.
38. Voss, *Servant of the People*, 125–26.
39. Ibid., 127.
40. Sydnor Thompson, "John W. Davis and His Role in the Public School Segregation Cases—A Personal Memoir," *Washington & Lee Law Review* 52, nos. 5–6 (1995): 1679, http://scholarlycommons.law.wlu.edu/wlulr/vol52/iss5/6.
41. Dennis Wepman, *Immigration: From the Founding of Virginia to the Closing of Ellis Island* (New York: Facts on File, 2002), 242.
42. Maldwyn Allen Jones, *American Immigration* (Chicago: University of Chicago Press, 1960), 277; see also George M. Stephenson, *A History of American Immigration: 1820–1924* (New York: Russell & Russell, 1964), 190.
43. *New York Times*, March 9, 1924.
44. *New York Times*, January 7, 1924.
45. Samuel Gompers to John Harkey Reiter, April 28, 1921, Harold K. Thompson Collection, Hoover Institution Archives, Stanford University, http://www.cwalocal4250.org /politicalaction/binarydata/The%20Voice%20of%20Labor.pdf.
46. Voss, *Servant of the People*, 138–39.
47. *New York Times*, October 6, 2012.
48. *Encyclopedia Judaica*, 2nd ed., Vol. 6, 297.
49. Michelle Wehrwein Albion, ed., *The Quotable Henry Ford* (Gainesville: University of Florida Press, 2013), 205–6.
50. *New York Times*, November 30, 1920.
51. Deborah Lipstadt, "*The Protocols of the Elders of Zion* on the Contemporary American Scene: Historical Artifact or Current Threat?" In Richard Allen Landes and Steven T. Katz, eds., *The Paranoid Apocalypse: A Hundred-Year Retrospective on the Protocols of the Elders of Zion* (New York: New York University Press, 2011), 172–85.
52. Harold Brackman, "The Attack on 'Jewish Hollywood': A Chapter in the History of Modern American Anti-Semitism," Simon Wiesenthal Center, 2000, http://www.lib .washington.edu/subject/History/BI/hist498-glenn/art2.pdf.

53. Robert S. Rifkind, "Confronting Antisemitism in America: Louis Marshall and Henry Ford," *American Jewish History* 94, nos. 1–2 (2008): 83.

54. *Time*, March 28, 1927.

55. *New York Times*, March 21, 1927.

56. Aaron Sapiro, "An Experience with American Justice," *Free Synagogue Pulpit* 8, no. 5 (1927–1928): 10–12.

57. Rifkind, "Confronting Antisemitism in America," 83.

58. Victoria Saker Woeste, "Apologies and Atonement," Huffington Post, August 1, 2012, http://www.huffingtonpost.com/victoria-saker-woeste/apologies-and-atonement _b_3678095.html.

59. Rifkind, "Confronting Antisemitism in America," 85.

60. Albion, *Quotable Henry Ford*, 198.

61. Alan D. Kandel, "Ford and Israel," *Michigan Jewish History* 39 (Fall 1999): 13–17.

62. *New York Times*, December 2, 1929.

63. *New York Times*, April 20, 1928.

64. *Milwaukee Sentinel*, August 3, 1927.

65. *Challenging Years*, 113.

66. Ibid., 115.

67. Voss, *Servant of the People*, 155.

68. Ibid., 159.

69. Wise, *Challenging Years*, 114.

70. Voss, *Servant of the People*, 160.

71. Jack Marco to Stephen S. Wise, American Jewish Historical Society Archives, P-134, New York, October 26, 1928.

72. Millard E. Tydings to Stephen S. Wise, American Jewish Historical Society Archives, New York, October 18, 1928.

73. Voss, *Servant of the People*, 161.

74. Ibid., 162.

75. Ibid., 174, 200.

76. Urofsky, *Voice*, 241.

77. Wise, *Challenging Years*, 16–17.

78. Conrad Black, *Franklin Delano Roosevelt, Champion of Freedom* (New York: Public Affairs, 2003), 213.

79. *New York Times*, November 8, 1928.

80. Wise, *Challenging Years*, 16.

81. Voss, *Rabbi and Minister*, 275–76.

82. Frank Freidel, *Franklin D. Roosevelt: The Triumph* (Boston: Little Brown, 1956), 256; see also Elliott Roosevelt, ed., *FDR: His Personal Letters*, vol. 3 (New York: Duell, Sloan & Pearce, 1947–1950), 186–87.

83. *New York Times*, April 30, 1931.

84. Friedel, *Franklin D. Roosevelt*, 295.

85. Urofsky, *Voice*, 246.

86. *Public Papers of Franklin D. Roosevelt, Forty-Eighth Governor of the State of New York, 1932* (Albany: J. B. Lyon Company, 1931–39), 287–93.

87. *New York Herald Tribune*, April 2, 1932.

88. *New York Herald Tribune*, April 3, 1932.

89. Urofsky, *Voice*, 246.

90. Freidel, *Franklin D. Roosevelt*, 296, 334.

91. Ibid., 335.

92. Urofsky, *Voice*, 248–49.

93. Wise, *Challenging Years*, 18.

94. Wise, *Legend of Louise*, 43.

95. Urofsky, *Voice*, 254–55.
96. Voss, *Rabbi and Minister*, 278.
97. Wise, *Challenging Years*, 149–51; see also Urofsky, *Voice*, 239–40.
98. *New York Herald Tribune*, January 8, 1932.
99. "US Presidential Elections: Leftist Votes," http://www.marxistsfr.org/history/usa/government/elections/president/timeline.htm, accessed October 13, 2014.

CHAPTER 17

1. Flavius Josephus, *Antiquities*, trans. William Whiston, book 18 (Nashville: Thomas Nelson, 1998), 4.12.
2. Eugene J. Fisher, *Faith without Prejudice* (New York: Paulist Press, 1977), 75–76.
3. James Rudin, *Christians and Jews: Faith to Faith* (Woodstock, VT: Jewish Lights, 2010), 97–101.
4. Brackman, "Attack on 'Jewish Hollywood,'" 4.
5. *New York Times*, December 5, 1927.
6. Scott Eyman, *Empire of Dreams: The Epic Life of Cecil B. DeMille* (New York: Simon and Schuster 2010), 245.
7. *New York Times*, December 5, 1927.
8. Urofsky, *Voice*, 177–78.
9. *New York Times*, May 19, 1930.
10. Albert Schweitzer, *The Quest of the Historical Jesus: First Complete Edition*, John Bowden, ed., W. Montgomery et al., trans. (Minneapolis: Fortress Press, 2001), 478.
11. Voss, *Servant of the People*, 132.
12. Voss, *Rabbi and Minister*, 100.
13. Wise, *Challenging Years*, 281.
14. *New York Times*, December 21, 1925.
15. *New York Sun*, December 21, 1925.
16. Urofsky, *Voice*, 196.
17. *New York Times*, December 22; December 29; December 30, 1925.
18. Wise, *Challenging Years*, 281–82.
19. *New York Times*, December 22, 1925.
20. Stephen Prothero, *American Jesus: How the Son of God Became a National Icon* (New York: Farrar, Straus & Giroux, 2001), 236.
21. *New York Times*, December 28, 1925.
22. Urofsky, *Voice*, 196.
23. *New York Times*, December 27, 1925.
24. Reznikoff, *Louis Marshall*, 2:828–29.
25. Wise, *Challenging Years*, 283.
26. Judd Teller, *Strangers and Natives* (New York: Delacorte, 1968), 78.
27. Urofsky, *Voice*, 197.
28. *New York Times*, December 25, 1925.
29. Urofsky, *Voice*, 198–99.
30. Grace C. Strachan, *Equal Pay for Equal Work* (New York: B. F. Buck & Co., 1910), 18.
31. Harry M. Orlinsky, "The Legacy of Stephen Wise," *Founders' Day Addresses* (Cincinnati: Hebrew Union College–Jewish Institute of Religion, 1978), 22–23.
32. *New York Times*, December 31, 1925.
33. *New York Times*, December 26, 1925; see also Urofsky, *Voice*, 201.
34. Jewish Telegraphic Agency, January 3, 1926.
35. *Jewish Exponent*, January 8, 1926.
36. Rudin, *Christians and Jews Faith to Faith*, 128–29.

37. Maurice Friedman, *Martin Buber's Life and Work, The Early Years*, vol. 1 (Detroit: Wayne State University Press, 1988), 361.
38. Jewish Telegraphic Agency, November 18, 1963; see also *Time*, November 29, 1963.
39. Voss, *Rabbi and Minister*, 76.
40. Ibid., 285.
41. Wise, *Challenging Years*, 286–87.
42. Voss, *Rabbi and Minister*, 102–3.
43. Paul Sprecher, "John Haynes Holmes," Dictionary of Unitarian and Universalist Biography, November 11, 2002, http://uudb.org/articles/johnhaynesholmes.html.
44. Voss, *Rabbi and Minister*, 150.
45. Sprecher, "John Haynes Holmes."
46. War Monuments No. 4, *PM Magazine*, January 13, 1942, Dr. Seuss Collection, MSS 230. Special Collections & Archives, University of California San Diego Library, http://libraries.ucsd.edu/speccoll/dswenttowar/#ark:bb8499185p.
47. *PM*, January 21, 1942.
48. Voss, *Rabbi and Minister*, 309.

CHAPTER 18

1. Urofsky, *Voice*, 75–77.
2. Stephen S. Wise, "Gandhi, The Jews and Zionism," Jewish Virtual Library, October 30, 1931, http://www.jewishvirtuallibrary.org/jsource/History/WiseGandhi.html; see also Moshe Davis, *America and the Holy Land*, vol. 4 of *With Eyes toward Zion* (Westport, CT: Praeger, 1995), 73.
3. *The New Armenia*, May 1923; see also *New York Times*, October 18, 1915.
4. Stephen Wise Free Synagogue Papers, November 6, 1924.
5. *Jewish Forum*, January 12, 1925.
6. Stephen Wise Free Synagogue Papers, October 23, 1923.
7. Stephen Wise Free Synagogue Papers, December 19, 1927.
8. Stephen Wise Free Synagogue Papers, March 12, 1928.
9. Voss, *Servant of the People*, 202–3.
10. Jewish Telegraphic Agency, December 16, 1924.
11. Stephen Wise Free Synagogue Papers, May 19, 1932.
12. Merrill D. Peterson, *Starving Armenians and the Armenian Genocide, 1915–1930 and After* (Charlottesville: University of Virginia Press, 2004), 147–49; see also *New York Times*, January 19, 1927.
13. John A. DeNovo, *American Interests and Policies in the Middle East: 1900–1939* (St. Paul: University of Minnesota Press, 1963), 238–39.
14. *New York Times*, January 6, 1919.
15. Jewish Telegraphic Agency, May 30, 1934.
16. Jewish Telegraphic Agency, May 29, 1934.
17. Voss, *Rabbi and Minister*, 240–41.
18. Urofsky, *Voice*, 232–34.
19. Voss, *Rabbi and Minister*, 232–33.
20. Ibid., 234.
21. Urofsky, *Voice*, 233.
22. Ibid., 232.
23. Voss, *Rabbi and Minister*, 233.
24. *New York Times*, March 6; March 8, 1926.
25. Felix Frankfurter, "The Case of Sacco-Vanzetti," *The Atlantic*, March 1927.
26. Voss, *Rabbi and Minister*, 238–39; see also Urofsky, *Voice*, 203.

27. *New York Times*, July 19, 1977.
28. Maurice Samuel, *Blood Accusation: The Strange History of the Beiliss Case* (New York: Alfred A. Knopf, 1966).
29. Saul S. Friedman, *The Incident at Massena* (New York: Stein and Day, 1978), 61–62.
30. Voss, *Servant of the People*, 157.
31. Ibid., 157–58.
32. Urofsky, *Voice*, 207–9.
33. Samuel J. Jacobs, "The Blood Libel Case at Massena—a Reminiscence and a Review," *Judaism: A Quarterly Journal of Jewish Life and Thought* 28, no. 4 (Fall 1979): 465–74.
34. Urofsky, *Voice*, 208.
35. *New York Times*, October 5, 1928.
36. Julie Grant, "Massena's History Still Tied to the 1928 'Blood Libel' Incident," February 14, 2012, North Country Public Radio Regional News, http://www.northcountry publicradio.org/news/story/19305/20120214/massena-s-history-still-tied-to-1928 -blood-libel-incident.
37. Voss, *Servant of the People*, 159.
38. *The Forward*, October 26, 2012.

CHAPTER 19

1. *New York Globe & Commercial Advertiser*, May 11, 1920.
2. "Bill of Rights in Action," *Constitutional Rights Foundation* 26, no. 1 (Fall 2010), http:// www.crf-usa.org/bill-of-rights-in-action/bria-26-1-the-virginia-statute-for-religious -freedom.html.
3. Theodor Herzl, *The Jewish State* (New York: Dover Publications, 1988), 73.
4. Barnet Litvinoff, ed., *The Letters and Papers of Chaim Weizmann*, vol. 1 (Piscataway, NJ: Transaction Publishers, 1983), 301.
5. *Canadian Jewish Chronicle*, September 23, 1921.
6. Urofsky, *Voice*, 163.
7. *Buffalo Courier*, November 28, 1920.
8. Urofsky, *Brandeis*, 538.
9. Sachar, *History of Israel*, 139.
10. Ibid., 142.
11. Urofsky, *Voice*, 163.
12. Urofsky, *Brandeis*, 541–42.
13. *New Palestine*, June 27, 1930.
14. Jewish Telegraphic Agency, November 13, 1931.
15. Emanuel Neumann, *In the Arena* (New York: Herzl Press, 1976), 47.
16. *New York Times*, April 3, 1925.
17. Urofsky, *Voice*, 214.
18. Ibid.
19. Jewish Telegraphic Agency, September 24, 1929.
20. Wise, *Challenging Years*, 306–8.
21. Matthew M. Silver, *Louis Marshall and the Rise of Jewish Ethnicity in America: A Biography* (Syracuse, NY: Syracuse University Press, 2013), 511.
22. *New York Times*, October 1, 1927.
23. Wise, *Challenging Years*, 198–200.
24. Voss, *Servant of the People*, 215.

CHAPTER 20

1. American Jewish Historical Society Archives, P-134, September 9, 1914.
2. Bill Samuels, "Lost Century," New Roosevelt Initiative, www.newrooseveltinitiative
.com/lost-century/2, accessed October 7, 2014.
3. "NY US Senate D Primary," *Our Campaigns*, http://www.ourcampaigns.com/Race
Detail.html?RaceID=164609, accessed October 6, 2014; see also John Macgregor
Burns, *Roosevelt: The Lion and the Fox*, vol. 1 (Norwalk, CT: Easton Press, 1956), 32–34,
57–60.
4. *New York Times*, November 8, 1928.
5. Wise, *Challenging Years*, 217.
6. Ibid., 217–18.
7. Arthur M. Schlesinger, Jr., *The Coming of the New Deal* (Boston: Houghton Mifflin,
1959), 567.
8. Wise, *Challenging Years*, 218.
9. Voss, *Rabbi and Minister*, 295–96.
10. Polier and Wise, *Personal Letters*, 232–34.
11. *New York Times*, January 27, 1936; see also Urofsky, *Voice*, 257.
12. Wise, *Challenging Years*, 219–20.
13. Stephen S. Wise, "How They Are Voting: IV," *New Republic*, October 20, 1936.
14. L. Sandy Maisel and Ira Forman, eds., *Jews in American Politics* (Lanham, MD: Rowman
and Littlefield, 2001), 153.
15. Wise, *Challenging Years*, 223.
16. Urofsky, *Voice*, 187.
17. Marc Dollinger. "Die Velt, Yene Velt, Roosevelt: The Legacy of Jewish Liberalism in
American Political Culture," *American History* 26, no. 3 (September 1998): 599–605.
18. Zvi Ganin, *Truman, American Jewry and Israel* (Teaneck, NJ: Holmes and Meier, 1978),
13–14.
19. William J. vanden Heuvel, "America, Franklin D. Roosevelt and the Holocaust," Fifth
Annual Franklin and Eleanor Roosevelt Distinguished Lecture, Chicago, Illinois,
October 17, 1996, newdeal.feri.org/feri/wvh.htm.
20. *Newsweek*, April 18, 1994.
21. *New York Times*, September 12, 1941.
22. *New York Times*, April 29, 1941.
23. Wise, *Challenging Years*, 222, 224.
24. Ibid., 229.
25. Ibid., 228.
26. *American Hebrew*, July 8, 1932.
27. Stephen Wise Free Synagogue Archives, November 1, 1940.
28. Wise, *Challenging Years*, 231.
29. Michael T. Benson, *Harry S. Truman and the Founding of Israel* (Westport, CT: Praeger,
1997), 124–29.
30. Oren, *Power, Faith, and Fantasy*, 500–501.
31. Richard Breitman, "Roosevelt and the Holocaust," in Verne W. Newton, ed., *FDR and
the Holocaust* (New York: St. Martin's Press, 1996), 117–18.
32. Voss, *Servant of the People*, 221.
33. *New York Times*, December 30, 1940.

CHAPTER 21

1. Urofsky, *Voice*, 260.
2. Ibid., 261.
3. Wise, *Challenging Years*, 237.
4. Voss, *Servant of the People*, 182.
5. Ibid., 185.
6. "Nazi Party Platform," United States Holocaust Memorial Museum, http://www
.ushmm.org/learn/timeline-of-events/before-1933/nazi-party-platform, accessed September 23, 2014.
7. *Free Synagogue Weekly Bulletin*, April 25, 1933.
8. Erik Larson, *In the Garden of the Beast: Love, Terror, and an American Family in Hitler's Berlin* (New York: Crown, 2011), 28.
9. Ibid., 37.
10. Voss, *Servant of the People*, 191–92; see also Larson, *In the Garden of the Beast*, 42.
11. Larson, *In the Garden of the Beast*, 79.
12. Ibid., 80.
13. World Jewish Congress, *Unity in Dispersion: A History of the World Jewish Congress* (New York: World Jewish Congress, 1948), 28.
14. *New York Times*, March 20, 1933.
15. Wise, *Challenging Years*, 244.
16. *St. Petersburg, Florida Independent*, March 27, 1933.
17. Wise, *Challenging Years*, 244–45.
18. Ibid., 248.
19. *New York Times*, March 27, 1933.
20. Wise, *Challenging Years*, 250.
21. Frederick A. Lazin, "The Response of the American Jewish Committee to the Crisis of German Jewry, 1933–1939," *American Jewish History* 68 (March 1979): 303–4.
22. Larson, *In the Garden of the Beast*, 33–35.
23. Richard Breitman and Alan M. Kraut, *American Refugee Policy and European Jewry, 1933–1945* (Bloomington: Indiana University Press, 1988), 36–37.
24. Larson, *In the Garden of the Beast*, 30–31.
25. Doris Kearns Goodwin, *No Ordinary Time* (New York: Touchstone/Simon & Schuster, 1994), 173.
26. Ibid.
27. Andy Marino, *A Quiet American: The Secret War of Varian Fry* (New York: St. Martin's Press, 1999), 47.
28. Fred L. Israel, ed., *The War Diary of Breckinridge Long, Selections from the Years 1939–1944* (Lincoln: University of Nebraska Press, 1966), 134–35.
29. http://www.ushmm.org/museum/exhibit/online/stlouis/teach/supread.htm.
30. Arthur D. Morse, *While Six Million Died* (London: Secker & Warburg, 1968), 60–61.
31. Steven Lehrer. *Wartime Sites in Paris: 1939–1945* (New York: SF Tafel Publishers, 2013), 303; see also http://www.pbs.org/wgbh/amex/holocaust/peopleevents/pande AMEX90.html.
32. Richard Breitman, *Official Secrets: What the Nazis Planned, What the British and Americans Knew, 1933–1945* (New York: Hill and Wang, 1998), 24–25.
33. Letter, Franklin D. Roosevelt to Herbert H. Lehman, November 13, 1935; Folder, President's Official File 133: Immigration 1933–1935, Franklin D. Roosevelt Library, Hyde Park, New York.
34. Memo, Stephen Early to Marguerite LeHand, November 13, 1936; Folder, President's Official File 133: Immigration, 1936–1941, Franklin D. Roosevelt Library, Hyde Park, New York.

35. Voss, *Servant of the People*, 179.
36. Ibid., 183–84.
37. Polier and Wise, *Personal Letters*, 221.
38. Stephen Wise Free Synagogue Archives, September 25, 1935.
39. Wise, *Challenging Years*, 219.
40. Voss, *Servant of the People*, 208.
41. Deborah E. Lipstadt, *Beyond Belief: The American Press and the Coming of the Holocaust 1933–1945* (Boston: Free Press, 1986), 79–83.
42. Shlomo Shafir, *The Impact of the Jewish Crisis on American-German Relations, 1933–1939* (Ann Arbor: University Microfilms International, 1971), 593–94.
43. *New York Times*, November 11–14, 1938; see also Maria Mazzenga, ed., *American Religious Responses to Kristallnacht* (New York: Palgrave Macmillan, 2009), and Martin Gilbert, *Kristallnacht: Prelude to Destruction* (New York: HarperCollins, 2006).
44. "Kristallnacht: A Nationwide Pogrom, November 9–10, 1938," *Holocaust Encyclopedia*, http://www.ushmm.org/wlc/en/article.php?ModuleId=10005201, accessed September 30, 2014.
45. Wise, *Challenging Years*, 264.
46. Richard Cohen, "Muffling the Drums of War with Iran," *Washington Post*, October 1, 2012.
47. Wise, *Challenging Years*, 265.
48. Urofsky, *Voice*, 303.
49. Saul S. Friedman, *No Haven for the Oppressed* (Detroit: Wayne State University, 1973), 31–32.
50. Henry L. Feingold, *The Politics of Rescue: The Roosevelt Administration and the Holocaust, 1938–1945* (New Brunswick, NJ: Rutgers University Press, 1970), 21–26.
51. Richard Breitman, Barbara McDonald Stewart, and Severin Hochberg, eds., *Advocate for the Doomed: The Diaries and Papers of James G. McDonald, 1932–1935* (Bloomington: Indiana University Press in Association with the United States Holocaust Memorial Museum, 2007), 48.
52. Feingold, *Politics of Rescue*, 22–44.
53. Urofsky, *Voice*, 305.
54. *Washington Star*, July 13, 1938.
55. Lipstadt, *Beyond Belief*, 97.
56. "1938 Conference Still Haunts Australia," *Christian Today*, January 9, 2012, http://au.christiantoday.com/article/1938-evian-conference-still-haunts-australia/10769.htm.
57. *New York Times*, July 4, 1938.
58. Urofsky, *Voice*, 305.
59. *Perspective: Journal of the Beth Shalom Holocaust Memorial Centre* (Newark, Notts. Nottinghamshire, England) 1 (1998): 1.
60. *Manchester Guardian*, May 23, 1936.
61. *New York Times*, July 28, 1979.
62. Rafael Medoff, *FDR and the Holocaust: A Breach of Faith* (Washington, DC: David S. Wyman Institute for Holocaust Studies, 2013), 80.
63. Voss, *Servant of the People*, 225.
64. Richard Bonney, ed., *Confronting the Nazi War on Christianity: The Kulturkampf Newsletters, 1936–1939* (Oxford: Peter Lang, 2009), 352–53.
65. David Morrison, *Heroes, Antiheroes and the Holocaust: American Jewry and Historical Choice* (New London, NH: Milah Publishing, 1995), 128.
66. Morse, *While Six Million Died*, 228.
67. Arthur D. Morse, "Voyage to Doom," *Our Heritage Vision* (2005–8), http://paperpen.com/heritage/350/look/look2.htm.

68. Urofsky, *Voice*, 218.
69. Voss, *Servant of the People*, 233.
70. Ibid., 236.

CHAPTER 22

1. *New York Times*, April 8, 1940.
2. Urofsky, *Voice*, 294.
3. Jewish Telegraphic Agency, June 21, 1932.
4. Voss, *Servant of the People*, 213.
5. Urofsky, *Voice*, 301.
6. Voss, *Servant of the People*, 169.
7. Urofsky, *Voice*, 286.
8. *New York Times*, July 9, 1937.
9. Shabtai Teveth, *Ben-Gurion and the Palestinian Arabs: From Peace to War* (New York: Oxford University Press, 1985), 180–82.
10. Tom Segev, *One Palestine Complete* (New York: Henry Holt, 1999), 414.
11. Urofsky, *Voice*, 287.
12. Voss, *Servant of the People*, 215.
13. Urofsky, *Voice*, 252–54.
14. Ibid., 284.
15. Ibid.
16. Voss, *Servant of the People*, 216.
17. *New York Times*, May 25, 1939.
18. Jacob Heilbrun, "The Patriarch: Joseph Kennedy Sr.'s Outsized Life," Daily Beast, November 21, 2012.
19. David Nasaw, *The Patriarch: The Remarkable Life and Turbulent Times of Joseph P. Kennedy* (New York: Penguin, 2012), 286.
20. Ibid., 286–87.
21. Ibid., 362.
22. Ibid.
23. Morse, *While Six Million Died*, 237.
24. Ibid.
25. John Stanton, "Human Terrain System Meets the Bowman Expeditions," *El Enemigo Común*, January 29, 2009, http://elenemigocomun.net/2009/01/human-terrain-system-meets-bowman-expeditions-armytradoc-embroiled-another-controversy/.
26. *New York Times*, May 1, 2009.
27. Monty Noam Pentkower, *The Holocaust and Israel Reborn: From Catastrophe to Sovereignty* (Champaign-Urbana: University of Illinois Press, 1994), 151–52.
28. Nasaw, *Patriarch*, 386.
29. Ibid.
30. Ibid., 389.
31. Irwin F. Gellman, *Secret Affairs: Franklin Roosevelt, Cordell Hull, and Sumner Welles* (Baltimore: Johns Hopkins University Press, 1995), 25.
32. Nasaw, *Patriarch*, 311.
33. Seymour M. Hersh, *The Dark Side of Camelot* (Boston: Little Brown, 1997), 63–64.
34. Abraham Ben-Zvi, *John F. Kennedy and the Politics of Arms Sales to Israel* (New York: Frank Cass Publishers, 2002), 52.

CHAPTER 23

1. *New York Times*, March 9, 2013.
2. *New York Times*, March 2, 2013.
3. "Active Duty Military Personnel—1940–2011," *Information Please Database*, http://www.infoplease.com/ipa/A0004598.html, accessed August 28, 2014.
4. Frank Freidel, *Franklin D. Roosevelt, A Rendezvous with Destiny* (Boston: Back Bay Books, 1991), 296.
5. *New York Times*, March 8, 2013.
6. Selig Adler, Moshe Davis, and Robert Handy, eds., *America and the Holy Land: A Colloquium* 1st ed. (Jerusalem: Institute of Contemporary Jewry and the Hebrew University of Jerusalem, 1972), 12.
7. Goodwin, *No Ordinary Time*, 454.
8. Map Room Papers; Mr 203 (12); Sec. 1; *OSS Numbered Bulletins*, March–May 1943, Franklin D. Roosevelt Presidential Library, Hyde Park, New York.
9. "Jan Karski about His Meeting with Supreme Court Justice Felix Frankfurter, 1943," YouTube video, 8:57, created by Claude Lanzmann during the filming of *Shoah*; used by permission of the United States Holocaust Memorial Museum and Yad Vashem, the Holocaust Martyrs and Heroes' Remembrance Authority, Jerusalem, http://www.youtube.com/watch?v=7YVTfG_qE2Y, last modified on September 5, 2012.
10. Albert Vorspan, *Giants of Justice* (New York: Crowell, 1960), 113–14.
11. *News Review*, New South Wales, Australia Jewish Board of Deputies, May 14, 2009.
12. Wise, *Challenging Years*, 227–28.
13. Ibid., 227.
14. Jewish Telegraphic Agency, August 1, 1944.
15. Voss, *Servant of the People*, 250.
16. Wise, *Challenging Years*, 232.
17. Ibid., 230.
18. Ibid., 224–25.
19. Ibid., 179.
20. Ibid., 229.
21. American Jewish Historical Society Archives, Stephen Wise Papers, P-134.
22. Wise, *Challenging Years*, 232.
23. James Macgregor Burns, *Roosevelt: The Soldier of Freedom* (New York: Harcourt Brace, 1970), 396.
24. Urofsky, *Voice*, 331.

CHAPTER 24

1. Christopher R. Browning, "A Final Hitler Decision for the 'Final Solution'—The Riegner Telegram Reconsidered," *Oxford Journals: Holocaust and Genocide Studies* 10, no. 1 (1996): 3–10; see also http://www.flickr.com/photos/nationalarchives/7751738690/lightbox/.
2. Urofsky, *Voice*, 318.
3. Walter Laqueur and Richard Breitman, eds., *Breaking the Silence* (New York: Simon and Schuster, 1986), 148, 152, 270–72; see also Brace Pattou, "Howard Elting, Jr. (1907–2001)," Bevier-Elting Family Association, http://www.b-efa.org/elting/bio_howard_elting_jr.htm, accessed September 2, 2014.
4. Richard J. Evans, *The Third Reich at War* (New York: Penguin Press, 2009), 240.
5. *The Origins of the Final Solution* (Lincoln: University of Nebraska Press, 2009), 309, 411.
6. "US State Department Receives Information from Switzerland Regarding the Nazi Plan to Murder the Jews of Europe," 3–5, http://www.google.com/url?sa=t&rct=j&q=&esrc

=s&source=web&cd=1&ved=0CCAQFjAA&url=http%3A%2F%2Fwww.baltimorecity
college.us%2Fourpages%2Fauto%2F2008%2F9%2F25%2F1222349884865%2Fth%2520
Holocaust%2520Primary%2520Sources.doc&ei=W3dBVKPmK4qQsQTPhoL4Aw&
usg=AFQjCNHb_ceKBp0dy_TEEK_TYJJleGx99w&bvm=bv.77648437,d.cWc.

7. Urofsky, *Voice*, 319.
8. Voss, *Servant of the People*, 248–49.
9. Wise, *Challenging Years*, 275–76.
10. *New York Times*, November 26, 1942.
11. Voss, *Servant of the People*, 253.
12. Kenneth Libo and Michael Shakun, "Clash of the Titans: Abba Hillel Silver and Stephen S. Wise, Part 3: The War Years," *Cleveland Jewish History*, http://www.clevelandjewish history.net/silver/titans.html, accessed August 27, 2014.
13. Wise, *Challenging Years*, 277.
14. Urofsky, *Voice*, 320.
15. Ibid., 322.
16. Robert W. Ross. *So It Was True: The American Protestant Press and the Nazi Persecution of the Jews* (Minneapolis: University of Minnesota Press, 1980), 174–75.
17. *New York Times*, November 5, 1943.
18. David Farneth, "Kurt Weill and We Will Never Die," United States Holocaust Memorial Museum, Holocaust Encyclopedia, http://www.ushmm.org/wlc/en/article.php ?ModuleId=10007047, last modified June 20, 2014.
19. *Encyclopedia Judaica*, 2nd ed., s.v. "Kook, Hillel."
20. *Palestine Post*, July 23, 1946; see also *New York Times*, March 10, 1992.
21. Michael Oren, "The Rescuer," *New Republic*, October 28, 2002, 29–33.
22. Ibid.
23. David Wyman, *The Abandonment of the Jews: America and the Holocaust, 1941–1945* (New York: Pantheon, 1984), 346.
24. Nahum Goldmann, "Attitude of Zionists toward Peter Bergson," Department of State Memorandum of Conversation, May 19, 1944, 867N.01/2347, National Archives of the United States.
25. Haskel Lookstein, *Were We Our Brothers' Keepers? The Public Response of American Jews to the Holocaust, 1938–1944* (Bridgeport, CT: Hartmore House, 1985), 164.
26. Oren, "The Rescuer."
27. *New York Times*, August 6, 2011.
28. Efraim Zuroff, *The Response of Orthodox Jewry in the United States to the Holocaust: The Activities of the Vaad-ha-Hatzala Rescue Committee, 1939–1945* (New York: Yeshiva University Press, 2000), 257–64.
29. Arthur Hertzberg, "Marching with the Bergson Group: A Memoir," *Journal of Ecumenical Studies* 40, no. 4 (Fall 2003): 390–92.
30. *New York Times*, October 7, 1943.
31. William Hassett, *Off the Record with FDR* (New Brunswick, NJ: Rutgers University Press, 1958), 209.
32. Lipstadt, *Beyond Belief*, 225n.
33. "Jewish Organizations Press the President to Act," Jewish Virtual Library, https://www .jewishvirtuallibrary.org/jsource/Holocaust/fdrmemo.html, accessed September 10, 2014.
34. Adolph Held, "Report on the Visit to the President," December 8, 1942, http://www .pbs.org/wgbh/amex/holocaust/filmmore/reference/primary/index.html#pres.
35. Wise, *Challenging Years*, 277.
36. Ibid., 278–79.
37. Urofsky, *Voice*, 329.

38. Alex Grobman, *Battling for Souls: The Vaad Hatzala Rescue Committee in Post-War Europe* (Jersey City, NJ: KTAV Publishing, 2004), 42.

39. Plater Robinson, "Deathly Silence Teaching Guide: Everyday People in the Holocaust: The Bermuda Conference," Southern Institute for Education and Research, Tulane University, http://www.southerninstitute.info/holocaust_education/ds7.html, accessed August 25, 2014.

40. Ibid.

41. Jewish Telegraphic Agency, May 30, 1943.

42. *Diaries of Henry Morgenthau, Jr.*, Book 694, 190–192, Franklin D. Roosevelt Library, Hyde Park, New York, http://research.archives.gov/description/589213.

43. Morse, *While Six Million Died*, 92–93.

44. John W. Pehle, "The Executive Order," *American Experience: America and the Holocaust*, http://www.pbs.org/wgbh/amex/holocaust/filmmore/reference/interview/pehle03.html, accessed August 27, 2014,

45. "War Refugee Board (WRB)," Shoah Resource Center, International School for Holocaust Studies, http://yad-vashem.org.il/odot_pdf/Microsoft%20Word%20-%206488.pdf, accessed August 25, 2014.

46. Gerhard Riegner, "Summary of the Auschwitz Escapees Report by Gerhard Riegner, World Jewish Congress, Geneva, Sent under Cover of R. E. Shoenfeld, US Chargé to Czech Government in London, to Cordell Hull, Secretary of State, July 5, 1944, Report on Conditions in the Concentration Camps of Oswieczin and Birkenau," *American Experience: America and the Holocaust*, http://www.pbs.org/wgbh/amex/holocaust/filmmore/reference/primary/bombsummary.html.

47. Goodwin, *No Ordinary Time*, 515–16.

48. A. Leon Kubowitzki and John J. McCloy, "The World Jewish Congress in New York Asks the War Department to Bomb the Crematoria at Auschwitz, August 9, 1944. The War Department Turns Down the Request (August 14, 1944)," *American Experience, America and the Holocaust*, http://www.pbs.org/wgbh/amex/holocaust/filmmore/reference/primary/bombworld.html.

49. Michael Berenbaum, "Why Wasn't Auschwitz Bombed?" *Encyclopedia Britannica*'s Reflections on the Holocaust, http://www.britannica.com/holocaust/article-9342910, accessed October 19, 2014.

50. "Extracts from the US Strategic Bombing Survey, Summarizing 15th Air Force Bombing Attacks in August and September 1944 on Oswiecim (Auschwitz), Synthetic Oil Plant of I. G. Farben at Oswiecim near Krakow, Poland," *American Experience: America and the Holocaust*, http://www.pbs.org/wgbh/amex/holocaust/filmmore/reference/primary/bombextracts.html.

51. Rafael Medoff, "George McGovern, a Pacifist Who Wanted to Bomb Auschwitz," Jewish Telegraphic Agency, October 21, 2012, http://www.jta.org/2012/10/21/news-opinion/politics/george-mcgovern-a-pacifist-who-wanted-to-bomb-auschwitz#ixzz3GWbjbWOl; see also Stuart G. Erdheim, "Could the Allies Have Bombed Auschwitz-Birkenau?" *Holocaust and Genocide Studies*, Fall 1997, 11, (2), 129–70.

52. Berenbaum, "Why Wasn't Auschwitz Bombed?"

53. Goodwin, *No Ordinary Time*, 516.

54. Ibid., 573–85.

55. Franklin D. Roosevelt, Address to Congress on Yalta, March 1, 1945, http://millercenter.org/president/speeches/detail/3338.

56. Urofsky, *Voice*, 347.

57. *New York Times*, March 17, 1945.

58. Wise, *Challenging Years*, 232.

59. *New York Times*, June 12, 1972.

442

Notes

60. Wise, *Challenging Years*, 232.
61. Geoffrey Ward, *Closest Companion: The Unknown Story of the Intimate Friendship between Franklin Roosevelt and Margaret Suckley* (New York: Simon and Schuster, 2009), 201.
62. Urofsky, *Voice*, 328.

CHAPTER 25

1. Keith Olson, "The G. I. Bill and Higher Education: Success and Surprise," *American Quarterly* 25, no. 5 (December 1973): 596–610.
2. Oren, *Power, Faith, and Fantasy*, 442–45.
3. Voss, *Servant of the People*, 248.
4. Libo and Shakun, "Clash of Titans."
5. Abba Hillel Silver, "Endnote: The Biltmore Program," http://www.clevelandjewish history.net/silver/endnotes.html#wise, accessed October 19, 2014.
6. *New York Times*, January 4, 1947.
7. Ibid.
8. Urofsky, *Voice*, 348.
9. *New York Times*, April 21, 1945.
10. Jewish Telegraphic Agency, May 10, 1962.
11. Merle Miller, *Plain Speaking: An Oral Biography of Harry S. Truman* (New York: Berkley/Putnam, 1973), 213–18.
12. Libo and Shakun, "Clash of Titans."
13. Urofsky, *Voice*, 348.
14. Jewish Telegraphic Agency, May 13, 1945.
15. Eliahu Elath, *Zionism at the U.N.* (Philadelphia: Jewish Publication Society of America, 1976), 45, 81–82, 113.
16. Urofsky, *Voice*, 354.
17. Richard Crossman, *A Nation Reborn* (New York: Atheneum, 1960), 69.
18. Wise, *Challenging Years*, 304.
19. *International Herald Tribune*, December 28, 2006.
20. Sachar, *History of Israel*, 296.
21. "Michael Ezer Weitzman [*sic*]," http://www.geni.com/people/Michael-Weizmann /386089165620010229, last modified July 25, 2013.
22. *New York Times*, April 25, 2005.
23. Samuel G. Freedman, "American Jews Who Reject Zionism Say Events Aid Cause," *New York Times*, June 25, 2010.
24. Arfa, *Reforming Reform Judaism*, 174–75.
25. Ibid., 176.
26. Thomas Kolsky, *Jews against Zionism: The American Council for Judaism, 1942–1948* (Philadelphia: Temple University Press, 1992), 85, 123–24, 140, 169–71, 191.
27. Voss, *Servant of the People*, 266.
28. Voss, *Rabbi and Minister*, 346.
29. Harold Marcuse, "Martin Niemöller's famous quotation: 'First They Came for the Communists . . .' What Did Niemoeller Himself Say? Which Groups Did He Name? In What Order?" http://www.history.ucsb.edu/faculty/marcuse/niem.htm, last modified September 20, 2014.
30. Voss, *Servant of the People*, 277–78.
31. *Free Synagogue Bulletin*, May 28, 1943.
32. Wise, *Challenging Years*, 320.
33. Ibid., 320–21.

34. Ibid., 320.
35. Michael A. Meyer, *Hebrew Union College: A Centennial History, 1875–1975* (Cincinnati: Hebrew Union College Press, 1992), 163–64.
36. Ibid., 168.
37. Wise, *Challenging Years*, 141.
38. *New York Times*, December 11; December 13, 1947.
39. Wise, *Legend of Louise*, 93–95.
40. *New York Times*, March 18, 1949.
41. *New York Times*, March 17, 1949.
42. Ibid.
43. Voss, *Rabbi and Minister*, 348.
44. Urofsky, *Voice*, 369–70.

CHAPTER 26

1. George Ritzer, *Sociological Theory* (New York: McGraw-Hill Higher Education, 2008), 372.
2. Voss, *Rabbi and Minister*, 348.
3. Jewish Telegraphic Agency, April 20, 1949.
4. Howard Thurman, *Deep Is the Hunger: Meditations for Apostles of Sensitiveness* (Richmond, IN: Friends United Press, 1990), 59–60.
5. Voss, *Rabbi and Minister*, 350–51.
6. Voss, *Servant of the People*, 296–97.
7. *New York Times*, January 23, 1951.
8. Rudin, *Cushing, Spellman, O'Connor*, 58–59.
9. *New York Times*, April 19, 1959.
10. Leonard Dinnerstein, "What Should American Jews Have Done to Rescue Their European Brethren?" Museum of Tolerance, A Simon Wiesenthal Center Museum Annual, 1997, http://www.museumoftolerance.com/site/c.tmL6KfNVLtH/b.8324731/.
11. Alexander M. Schindler, "Zionism and Judaism: The Path of Rabbi Abba Hillel Silver," in Mark A. Raider, Jonathan D. Sarna, and Ronald W. Zweig, eds., *Abba Hillel Silver and American Zionism* (New York: Frank Cass, 1997), 1, 5.
12. Rafael Medoff, *FDR and the Holocaust: A Breach of Faith* (Washington, DC: David S. Wyman Institute for Holocaust Studies, 2013), 40–41.
13. *Jerusalem Post*, September 25, 2008.
14. National Public Radio Staff, "'FDR and the Jews' Puts a President's Compromises in Context," March 18, 2013, http://www.npr.org/2013/03/18/174125891/fdr-and-the-jews-puts-roosevelts-compromises-in-context.
15. Urofsky, *Voice*, 372.
16. Ibid., 325, 331.

Bibliography

Abzug, Robert H. *America Views the Holocaust, 1933–1945: A Brief Documentary History*. Boston: Bedford/St. Martin's, 1999.

Adler, Cyrus. *I Have Considered the Days*. Philadelphia: Jewish Publication Society of America, 1941.

Adler, Selig, Moshe Davis, and Robert Handy, eds. *America and the Holy Land: A Colloquium*. 1st ed. Jerusalem: Institute of Contemporary Jewry and the Hebrew University of Jerusalem, 1972.

Albion, Michelle Wehrwein, ed. *The Quotable Henry Ford*. Gainesville: University of Florida Press, 2013.

Alperin, Aaron. "Jewish Delegations in Paris." *YIVO Annual of Jewish Social Science*, Vol. 2, Yiddish Scientific Institute. YIVO: New York, 1947.

Analyticus (pseud. for James Waterman Wise). *Jews Are Like That*. New York: Brentano's, 1928.

Arfa, Cyrus. *Reforming Reform Judaism: Zionism and the Reform Rabbinate, 1885–1948*. New York: University Publishing Projects, 1985.

Baker, Roy Stannard. *Woodrow Wilson and the World Settlement*. 3 vols. Garden City, NY: Doubleday, Page and Company 1922.

Barea, Ilsa. *Vienna: Legend and Reality*. New York: Alfred A. Knopf, 1966.

Baron, Salo W. *Modern Nationalism and Religion*. Philadelphia: Meridian Books and the Jewish Publication Society of America, 1960.

Benson, Michael T. *Harry S. Truman and the Founding of Israel*. Westport, CT: Praeger, 1997.

Ben-Zvi, Abraham. *John F. Kennedy and the Politics of Arms Sales to Israel*. New York: Frank Cass, 2002.

Bernays, Edward L. *Biography of an Idea: Memoirs of Public Relations Counsel Edward L. Bernays*. New York: Simon & Schuster, 1965.

Bishop, Joseph B. *The Chronicle of One Hundred and Fifty Years: The Chamber of Commerce of the State of New York*. New York: Charles Scribner's Sons, 1918.

Black, Conrad. *Franklin Delano Roosevelt: Champion of Freedom*. New York: Public Affairs, 2003.

Breitman, Richard. *Official Secrets: What the Nazis Planned, What the British and Americans Knew, 1933–1945*. New York: Hill & Wang, 1998.

Breitman, Richard, and Alan M. Kraut. *American Refugee Policy and European Jewry, 1933–1945*. Bloomington: Indiana University Press, 1988.

Breitman, Richard, and Alan J. Lichtman. *FDR and the Jews*. Cambridge, MA: Harvard University Press, 2013.

Breitman, Richard, Barbara McDonald Stewart, and Severin Hochberg, eds. *Advocate for the Doomed: The Diaries and Papers of James G. McDonald, 1932–1935*. Bloomington: Indiana University Press in Association with the United States Holocaust Memorial Museum, 2007.

Browning, Christopher R. *The Origins of the Final Solution*. Lincoln: University of Nebraska Press, 2009.

Burns, James Macgregor. *Roosevelt: The Lion and the Fox*, Vol. 1. Norwalk, CT: Easton Press, 1956.

———. *Roosevelt: The Soldier of Freedom*. New York: Harcourt Brace, 1970.

Burns, Michael. *Dreyfus: A Family Affair from the French Revolution to the Holocaust*. New York: Harper, 1992.

Cecil, Lamar. *Wilhelm II: Emperor and Exile, 1900–1941*. Chapel Hill: University of North Carolina Press, 1996.

Cohen, Naomi W. *Not Free to Desist: The American Jewish Committee, 1906–1966*. Philadelphia: Jewish Publication Society of America, 1957.

Cohen, Sadie Alta. *Engineer of the Soul: A Biography of Rabbi J. X. Cohen*. New York: Bloch, 1961.

Crossman, Richard. *A Nation Reborn*. New York: Atheneum, 1960.

Davis, Kenneth C. *Don't Know Much about History*. New York: Harper, 2012.

Davis, Moshe. *America and the Holy Land (with Eyes Toward Zion)*. Westport, CT: Praeger, 1995.

———. "The Human Record: Cyrus Adler at the Peace Conference, 1919." *Essays in American Jewish History*. Cincinnati: American Jewish Archives, 1958.

Dawidowicz, Lucy S. *The War against the Jews, 1933–1945*. New York: Holt, Rinehart, and Winston, 1975.

Denovo, John A. *American Interests and Policies in the Middle East: 1900–1939*. St. Paul: University of Minnesota Press, 1963.

Divre Yeme Emanuel, The Chronicles of Emanu-El: Being an Account of the Rise and Progress of the Congregation Emanu-El, Which Was Founded in July, 1850, and Will Celebrate Its Fiftieth Anniversary December 23, 1900. RareBooksClub.com, 2012.

Dreiser, Theodore. *Sister Carrie, Jennie Gerhardt, Twelve Men*. New York: Library of America, 1987.

Eastman, Max. *Reflections on the Failure of Socialism*. New York: Devin-Adair, 1955.

Elath, Eliahu. *Zionism at the U.N.* Philadelphia: Jewish Publication Society of America, 1976.

Encyclopedia Judaica, 2nd ed. 22 vols. Detroit: Macmillan Reference USA / Thomson Gale, 2006.

Evans, Richard J. *The Third Reich at War*. New York: Penguin Press, 2009.

Eyman, Scott. *Empire of Dreams: The Epic Life of Cecil B. DeMille*. New York: Simon and Schuster, 2010.

Feinberg, Nathan. *La Question des Minorites a la Conference de la Paix de 1919–1920 et L'action Juive en Faveur de la Protection International des Minorities*. Paris: Rousseau & Cie, 1929.

Feingold, Henry L. *Bearing Witness: How America and Its Jews Responded to the Holocaust.* Syracuse, NY: Syracuse University Press, 1995.

——. *The Politics of Rescue: The Roosevelt Administration and the Holocaust, 1938–1945.* New Brunswick, NJ: Rutgers University Press, 1970.

Feld, Marjorie N. *Lillian Wald: A Biography.* Chapel Hill: University of North Carolina Press, 2008.

Fisher, Eugene J. *Faith without Prejudice.* New York: Paulist Press, 1977.

Fishman, Hertzel. *American Protestantism and a Jewish State.* Detroit: Wayne State University Press, 1973.

Flavius Josephus. *The Complete Works, Antiquities,* book 18. William Whiston, trans. Nashville: Thomas Nelson, 1998.

Fleg, Edmund. *Land of Promise.* Louise Waterman Wise, trans. New York: Macaulay, 1933.

Foreign Relations of the United States: The Lansing Papers, 1914–1920. 2 vols. Washington, DC: Government Printing Office, 1939.

Free Synagogue Pulpit. Vol. 5. New York: Bloch, 1920.

Freidel, Frank. *Franklin D. Roosevelt: The Ordeal.* Boston: Little Brown, 1954.

——. *Franklin D. Roosevelt: A Rendezvous with Destiny.* Boston: Back Bay Books, 1991.

——. *Franklin D. Roosevelt: The Triumph.* Boston: Little Brown, 1956.

Friedman, Maurice. *Martin Buber's Life and Work, The Early Years.* Vol. 1. Detroit: Wayne State University Press, 1988.

Friedman, Saul S. *The Incident at Massena.* New York: Stein and Day, 1978.

——. *No Haven for the Oppressed.* Detroit: Wayne State University, 1973.

Friess, Horace Leland, *Felix Adler and Ethical Culture: Memories and Studies.* New York: Columbia University Press, 1981.

Gabler, Neil. *An Empire of Their Own: How the Jews Invented Hollywood.* New York: Anchor: New Edition, 1989.

Ganin, Zvi. *Truman, American Jewry, and Israel.* Teaneck, NJ: Holmes and Meier, 1978.

Geller, Lawrence D., ed., *The Papers of Denise Tourover Ezekiel.* New York: Hadassah, 1984.

Gellman, Irwin F. *Secret Affairs: Franklin Roosevelt, Cordell Hull, and Sumner Welles.* Baltimore: Johns Hopkins University Press, 1995.

Gilbert, Martin. *Auschwitz and the Allies.* New York: Holt, Rinehart and Winston, 1981.

——. *Kristallnacht: Prelude to Destruction.* New York: HarperCollins, 2006.

Goffman, Erving. *The Presentation of Self in Everyday Life.* New York: Doubleday, 1959.

Goldman, Alex J. *Giants of Faith, Great American Rabbis.* New York: Citadel Press, 1964.

Goldstein, Sidney E. *The Synagogue and Social Welfare: A Unique Experiment.* New York: Bloch, 1955.

Goodwin, Doris Kearns. *No Ordinary Time.* New York: Touchstone/Simon & Schuster, 1994.

Griffiths, William, ed. *Newer Roosevelt Messages.* New York: Current Literature Publishing Company, 1919.

Grobman, Alex. *Battling for Souls: The Vaad Hatzala Rescue Committee in Post-War Europe.* Jersey City, NJ: KTAV Publishing, 2004.

Grose, Peter. *Gentleman Spy: The Life of Allen Dulles.* Boston: Houghton Mifflin, 1994.

Halpern, Ben. *Clash of Heroes: Brandeis, Weizmann, and American Zionism.* New York: Oxford University Press, 1987.

Hand, Samuel B. *Counsel and Advise: A Political Biography of Samuel I. Rosenman,* New York: Garland, 1979.

Hassett, William. *Off the Record with FDR*. New Brunswick, NJ: Rutgers University Press, 1958.

Heller, James G. *Isaac Mayer Wise: His Life, Work, and Thought*. New York: Union of American Hebrew Congregations, 1965.

Herman, Floyd L. *Some Aspects of the Life of Stephen S. Wise to 1928*. Master's thesis, Hebrew Union College–Jewish Institute of Religion, Cincinnati, 1964.

Hersh, Seymour M. *The Dark Side of Camelot*. Boston: Little Brown, 1997.

Herzl, Theodor. *The Jewish State*. New York: Dover Publications, 1988.

Hichborn, Franklin. *The System: As Uncovered by the San Francisco Graft Prosecutors*. San Francisco: The Press of the James H. Barry Company, 1915.

Hirsch, Samson Raphael. *Horeb: A Philosophy of Jewish Laws and Observances*. 7th ed. Isidore Grunfeld, trans. Brooklyn: Soncino Press, 2002.

Hofstadter, Richard. *The American Political Tradition: And The Men Who Made It*. New York: Vintage, 1989.

Holmes, John Haynes. *I Speak for Myself: The Autobiography of John Haynes Holmes*. New York: Harper & Row, 1959.

House, E. M., and Charles Seymour, eds. *What Really Happened at Paris*. New York: C. Scribner's Sons, 1921.

Howe, Irving. *World of Our Fathers: The Journey of the East European Jews to America and the Life They Found and Made*. New York: Schocken, 1983.

Israel, Fred L., ed. *The War Diary of Breckinridge Long: Selections from the Years 1939–1944*. Lincoln: University of Nebraska Press, 1966.

Jacob, Walter, ed. *The Changing World of Reform Judaism: The Pittsburgh Platform in Retrospect*. Pittsburgh: Rodef Shalom Congregation, 1985.

Janowsky, Oscar I. *The Jews and Minority Rights*. New York: Columbia University Press, 1933.

The Jewish Encyclopedia. Isidore Singer, ed. 12 vols. New York: Funk & Wagnalls, 1906.

Johnson, Paul. *Modern Times: The World from the Twenties to the Eighties*. New York: Harper and Row, 1983.

Jones, Maldwyn Allen. *American Immigration*. Chicago: University of Chicago Press, 1960.

Kaplan, Dana, ed. *American Judaism*. Cambridge: Cambridge University Press, 2005.

———. *Conflicting Visions*. New York: Routledge, 2001.

Katz, Jacob. *A House Divided: Orthodoxy And Schism In Nineteenth-Century Central European Jewry*. Hanover, NH: University Press, 1998.

———, ed. *Toward Modernity: The European Jewish Model*. Piscataway, NJ: Transaction Books, 1987.

Katz, Steven T., ed. *The Shtetl: New Evaluations*. New York: New York University Press, 2007.

Kisch, Guido. *Two American Jewish Pioneers of New Haven: Sigmund and Leopold Waterman*. New York: Historica Judaica, 1942.

Klausner, Joseph. *Yeshu Ha-Notzri*. Jerusalem: Shtibel, 1922 (English ed.: *Jesus of Nazareth: His Life, Times, and Teaching*. Herbert Danby, trans. London: Allen and Unwin, 1925).

Kleber, John E., ed. *The Kentucky Encyclopedia*. Lexington: University of Kentucky Press, 1992.

Knight, William, ed. *Memoirs of Thomas Davidson*. Boston: Ginn and Co., 1907.

Kolsky, Thomas. *Jews against Zionism: The American Council for Judaism, 1942–1948*. Philadelphia: Temple University Press, 1992.

Korn, Bertram W. *Eventful Years and Experiences*. Cincinnati: American Jewish Archives, 1954.

Kranzler, David, and Isaac Lewin. *Thy Brother's Blood: The Orthodox Jewish Response during the Holocaust*. New York: Mesorah Publishing, 1987.

Kraut, Benny. *From Reform Judaism to Ethical Culture: The Religious Evolution of Felix Adler*. Cincinnati: Hebrew Union College Press, 1979.

Laqueur, Walter, and Richard Breitman, eds. *Breaking the Silence*. New York: Simon and Schuster, 1986.

Larson, Erik. *In the Garden of the Beast: Love, Terror, and an American Family in Hitler's Berlin*. New York: Crown, 2011.

Lawrenson, Helen. *Stranger at the Party*. New York: Random House, 1975.

Leff, Laurel. *Buried by the Times: The Holocaust and America's Most Important Newspaper*. Cambridge: Cambridge University Press, 2006.

Linn, James. *Jane Addams: A Biography*. Champaign-Urbana: University of Illinois Press, 2000.

Lipsky, Louis. *A Gallery of Zionist Profiles*. New York: Farrar, Strauss and Cudahy, 1956.

———. *Memoirs in Profile*. Philadelphia: Jewish Publication Society of America, 1975.

Lipstadt, Deborah E. *Beyond Belief: The American Press and the Coming of the Holocaust, 1933–1945*. Boston: Free Press, 1986.

———. "*The Protocols of the Elders of Zion* on the Contemporary American Scene: Historical Artifact or Current Threat?" In Richard Allen Landes and Steven T. Katz, eds., *The Paranoid Apocalypse: A Hundred-Year Retrospective on* The Protocols of the Elders of Zion. New York: New York University Press, 2011.

Litvinoff, Barnet, ed. *The Letters and Papers of Chaim Weizmann, 1898–1931*. Piscataway, NJ: Transaction Publishers, 1983.

Lookstein, Haskel. *Were We Our Brothers' Keepers? The Public Response of American Jews to the Holocaust, 1938–1944*. Bridgeport, CT: Hartmore House, 1985.

Luzzatti, Luigi. *God in Freedom: Studies in the Relations between Church and State*. New York: Macmillan, 1930.

Mack, Julian W. "Jewish Hopes at the Peace Table." *Menorah Journal* 5 (1919).

Mango, Andrew. *Ataturk: The Biography of the Founder of Modern Turkey*. New York: Overlook Press, 2002.

Manuel, Frank E. *The Realities of America-Palestine Relations*. Washington, DC: Public Affairs Press, 1949.

Marino, Andy. *Quiet American: The Secret War of Varian Fry*. New York: St. Martin's Press, 1999.

Marrus, Michael R., ed. *Bystanders to the Holocaust*. Westport, CT: Meckler, 1989.

Mazzenga, Maria, ed. *American Religious Responses to Kristallnacht*. New York: Palgrave Macmillan, 2009.

McCullough, David. *Truman*. New York: Simon and Schuster, 2003.

McJimsey, George, ed. "FDR's Protest of the Treatment of Jews in Germany, 1938." *Documentary History of the Franklin D. Roosevelt Presidency*, Vol. 12. Bethesda, MD: University Publications of America, 2001.

Medoff, Rafael. *FDR and the Holocaust: A Breach of Faith*. Washington, DC: David S. Wyman Institute for Holocaust Studies, 2013.

Mendelsohn, John, ed. "Relief and Rescue of Jews from Nazi Oppression, 1943–1945." *The Holocaust: Selected Documents in Eighteen Volumes*, Vol. 14. New York: Garland, 1982.

Merkley, Paul C. *The Politics of Christian Zionism: 1891–1948*. New York: Routledge, 1998.

Meyer, Michael A. *Hebrew Union College: A Centennial History, 1875–1975*. Cincinnati: Hebrew Union College Press, 1992.

Miller, Merle. *Plain Speaking: An Oral Biography of Harry S. Truman*. New York: Berkley/ Putnam, 1973.

Montefiore, Simon Sebag. *Jerusalem: The Biography*. New York: Vintage, 2012.

Morgenthau, Henry, Sr. *All in a Lifetime*. Garden City, NJ: Doubleday and Page, 1922.

Morse, Arthur D. *While Six Million Died*. London: Secker & Warburg, 1968.

Morton, Frederic. *A Nervous Splendor: Vienna, 1888–1889*. New York: Penguin Books, 1980.

Nasaw, David. *The Patriarch: Joseph P. Kennedy*. New York: Penguin Press, 2012.

Neufeld, Michael J., and Michael Berenbaum, eds. *The Bombing of Auschwitz: Should the Allies Have Attempted It?* New York: St. Martin's Press, 2000.

Neumann, Emanuel. *In the Arena*. New York: Herzl Press, 1976.

Newton, Verne W., ed. *FDR and the Holocaust*. New York: St. Martin's Press, 1996.

Nodel, Julius J. *The Ties Between: A Century of Judaism on America's Last Frontier*. Portland, OR: Congregation Beth Israel, 1959.

Olson, Keith. "The G.I. Bill and Higher Education: Success and Surprise." *American Quarterly* 25, no. 5 (December 1973): 596–610.

———. *The G.I. Bill, the Veterans, and the Colleges*. Lexington: University Press of Kentucky, 1974.

Oren, Michael. *Power, Faith, and Fantasy: America in the Middle East, 1776 to the Present*. New York: W. W. Norton, 2007.

Parkes, James. *The Emergence of the Jewish Problem*. London: Oxford University Press, 1946.

Pentkower, Monty Noam. *The Holocaust and Israel Reborn: From Catastrophe to Sovereignty*. Champaign-Urbana: University of Illinois Press, 1994.

Peterson, Merrill D. *Starving Armenians and the Armenian Genocide, 1915–1930 and After*. Charlottesville: University of Virginia Press, 2004.

Polier, Justine Wise, and James Waterman Wise, eds. *The Personal Letters of Stephen Wise*. Boston: Beacon Press, 1956.

Powe, Lucas. *The Supreme Court and the American Elite, 1789–2008*. Cambridge, MA: Harvard University Press, 2011.

Preston, Andrew. *Sword of the Spirit, Shield of Faith: Religion in American War and Diplomacy*. New York: Anchor, 2012.

Proceedings of the New York State Conference of Charities and Correction at the Sixth Annual Session. Albany, NY: J. Archibald Clark, 1906.

Prothero, Stephen. *American Jesus: How the Son of God Became a National Icon*. New York: Farrar, Straus & Giroux, 2001.

Raider, Mark A. "The Aristocrat and the Democrat: Louis Marshall, Stephen S. Wise, and the Challenge of American Jewish Leadership." *American Jewish History* 94, nos. 1–2 (March–June 2008): 91–113.

———. "Stephen S. Wise and the Urban Frontier." *Quest: Issues in Contemporary Jewish History, Journal of Fondazione CDEC*, no. 2 (October 2011).

Raider, Mark A., Jonathan D. Sarna, and Ronald W. Zweig, eds. *Abba Hillel Silver and American Zionism*. London: Frank Cass, 1997.

Reznikoff, Charles, ed. *Louis Marshall, Champion of Liberty: Selected Papers and Addresses*. Philadelphia: Jewish Publication Society of America, 1957.

Rischin, Moses. *The Promised City*. Cambridge, MA: Harvard University Press, 1962.

Ritterband, Paul. *Counting the Jews in New York, 1900–1991: An Essay in Substance and Method*. Jewish Population Studies. Papers in Jewish Demography, volume 228, no. 29. Jerusalem: Avraham Harman Institute of Contemporary Jewry, 1997.

Ritzer, George. *Sociological Theory*. New York: McGraw-Hill Higher Education, 2008.

Roosevelt, Elliott, ed. *FDR: His Personal Letters*, Vol. 3. New York: Duell, Sloan & Pearce, 1947–1950.

Roosevelt, Franklin D. *Public Papers of Franklin D. Roosevelt, Forty-Eighth Governor of the State of New York*, 4 vols. Albany: J. B. Lyon & Co., 1930–1939.

Rosenbaum, Fred. *Cosmopolitans: A Social and Cultural History of the Jews of the San Francisco Bay Area*. Berkeley: University of California Press, 2009.

Ross, Robert W. *So It Was True: The American Protestant Press and the Nazi Persecution of the Jews*. Minneapolis: University of Minnesota Press, 1980.

Roth, Phillip. *The Plot against America*. Boston: Houghton Mifflin, 2004.

Rudin, James. *Christians and Jews: Faith to Faith—Tragic History, Promising Present, Fragile Future*. Woodstock, VT: Jewish Lights, 2010.

———. *Cushing, Spellman, O'Connor: The Surprising Story of How Three American Cardinals Transformed Catholic-Jewish Relations*. Grand Rapids: William E. Eerdmans, 2012.

———. *Israel for Christians: Understanding Modern Israel*. Philadelphia: Fortress Press, 1983.

Rudy, Willis. *The College of the City of New York: A History, 1847–1947*. New York: City College Press, 1949.

Sachar, Howard M. *A History of Israel: From the Rise of Zionism to Our Time*. 2nd ed. New York: Alfred A. Knopf, 1996.

Samuel, Maurice. *Blood Accusation: The Strange History of the Beiliss Case*. New York: Alfred A. Knopf, 1966.

Sarna, Jonathan D. *American Judaism: A History*. New Haven, CT: Yale University Press, 2004.

———. *A Great Awakening: The Transformation That Shaped Twentieth-Century American Judaism and Its Implications for Today*. New York: Council for Initiatives in Jewish Education, 1995.

Schickel, Richard. *D. W. Griffith: An American Life*. Montclair, NJ: Limelight Editions, 2004.

Schlesinger, Arthur M., Jr. *The Coming of the New Deal*. Boston: Houghton Mifflin, 1959.

Schneer, Jonathan. *The Balfour Declaration: The Origins of the Arab-Israeli Conflict*. New York: Random House, 2010.

Schorske, Carl E. *Fin-De-Siècle Vienna: Politics and Culture*. New York: Vintage, 1981.

Schweitzer, Albert. *The Quest of the Historical Jesus: First Complete Edition*. John Bowden, ed., W. Montgomery et al., trans. Minneapolis: Fortress Press, 2001.

Segev, Tom. *One Palestine Complete*. New York: Henry Holt, 1999.

Seltzer, Robert M. *Jewish People, Jewish Thought: The Jewish Experience in History*. New York: Macmillan, 1980.

Shafir, Shlomo. *The Impact of the Jewish Crisis on American-German Relations, 1933–1939*. Ann Arbor: University Microfilms International, 1971.

Shapiro, Robert D. *A Reform Rabbi in the Progressive Era: The Early Career of Rabbi Stephen S. Wise*. New York: Garland, 1968.

Silver, Matthew M. *Louis Marshall and the Rise of Jewish Ethnicity in America: A Biography.* Syracuse. NY: Syracuse University Press, 2013.

Simon, James F. *FDR and Chief Justice Hughes: The President, the Supreme Court, and the Epic Battle over the New Deal.* New York: Simon and Schuster, 2012.

Sizer, Stephen. *Christian Zionism: Roadmap to Armageddon.* Leicester: InterVarsity Press, 2004.

Smith, Neil. *American Empire: Roosevelt's Geographer and the Prelude to Globalization.* Berkeley: University of California Press, 2002.

Snyder, Louis L. *Encyclopedia of the Third Reich.* 1st ed. New York: McGraw-Hill, 1976.

Sobel, Ronald B. *A History of New York's Temple Emanu-El: The Second Half Century.* New York: New York University, 1980.

Spiel, Hilde. *Vienna's Golden Autumn: From the Watershed Year 1866 to Hitler's Anschluss, 1938.* New York: Grove Press, 1987.

Stein, Leon. *The Triangle Fire.* New York: Lippincott, 1962.

Stephenson, George M. *A History of American Immigration: 1820–1924.* New York: Russell & Russell, 1964.

Strachan, Grace C. *Equal Pay for Equal Work.* New York: B. F. Buck & Co., 1910.

Strong, Sydney, ed., *What I Owe to My Father.* New York: Henry Holt and Company, 1931.

Strum, Phillipa. *Louis D. Brandeis: Justice for the People.* New York: Schocken: 1984.

Teller, Judd. *Strangers and Natives.* New York: Delacorte, 1968.

Temkin, Sefton D. "A Century of Reform Judaism in America," *American Jewish Yearbook.* New York: American Jewish Committee and the Jewish Publication Society of America, 1973.

Teveth, Shabtai. *Ben-Gurion and the Palestinian Arabs: From Peace to War.* New York: Oxford University Press, 1985.

Theoharis, Athan, and John Stuart Cox. *The Boss: J. Edgar Hoover and the Great American Inquisition.* Philadelphia: Temple University Press, 1988.

Thomas, Gordon, and Max Morgan Witts. *Voyage of the Damned.* New York: Stein and Day, 1974.

Thurman, Howard. *Deep Is the Hunger: Meditations for Apostles of Sensitiveness.* Richmond, IN: Friends United Press, 1990.

Urofsky, Melvin I. *American Zionism from Herzl to the Holocaust.* Lincoln: University of Nebraska Press, 1995.

———. *Louis D. Brandeis: A Life.* New York: Pantheon, 2009.

———. *A Voice That Spoke for Justice: The Life and Times of Stephen S. Wise.* Albany: State University of New York Press, 1982.

Vorspan, Albert. *Giants of Justice.* New York: Crowell, 1960.

Voss, Carl Hermann. *Rabbi and Minister: The Friendship of Stephen S. Wise and John Haynes Holmes.* Cleveland: World Publishing, 1964.

———, ed. *Stephen S. Wise: Servant of the People, Selected Letters.* Philadelphia: Jewish Publication Society of America, 1969.

Ward, Geoffrey. *Closest Companion: The Unknown Story of the Intimate Friendship between Franklin Roosevelt and Margaret Suckley.* New York: Simon and Schuster, 2009.

Wasserstein, Bernard. *On the Eve: The Jews of Europe before the Second World War.* New York: Simon and Schuster, 2012.

Weizmann, Chaim. *Trial and Error.* New York: Schocken, 1966.

Wepman, Dennis. *Immigration: From the Founding of Virginia to the Closing of Ellis Island.* New York: Facts on File, 2002.

Whelan, Richard J. *The Founding Father: The Story of Joseph P. Kennedy: A Study in Power, Wealth, and Family Ambition.* New York: New American Library, 1964.

Wilson, Edmund. *A Piece of My Mind: Reflections at Sixty.* Garden City, NY: Doubleday, 1958.

Wise, James Waterman. *Legend of Louise: The Life Story of Mrs. Stephen S. Wise.* New York: Jewish Opinion Publishing Corporation, 1949.

Wise, Stephen. S. *Challenging Years.* New York: Putnam, 1949.

———. *The Improvement of Moral Qualities.* New York: AMS Press, 1966.

Wise, Stephen S., and Jacob de Haas. *The Great Betrayal.* New York: Brentano's, 1930.

Woeste, Victoria Saker. *Henry Ford's War on Jews and the Legal Battle against Hate Speech.* Stanford, CA: Stanford University Press, 2013.

Wyman, David S. *The Abandonment of the Jews: America and the Holocaust, 1941–1945.* New York: Pantheon, 1984.

Wyman, David S., and Rafael Medoff. *A Race against Death: Peter Bergson, America, and the Holocaust.* New York: New Press, 2002.

Zola, Gary P. *The Americanization of the Jewish Prayer Book.* New York: Central Synagogue, 2008.

Zugay, Brian C. R. *The Interchurch World Movement and the Scientific Survey of American Religious Architecture, 1919–1924.* Sleepy Hollow, NY: Rockefeller Archives, 2010.

Zuroff, Efraim. *The Response of Orthodox Jewry in the United States to the Holocaust: The Activities of the Vaad-ha-Hatzala Rescue Committee, 1939–1945.* New York: Yeshiva University Press, 2000.

Index